Ian Fleming

ANDREW LYCETT

PHOENIX

A PHOENIX PAPERBACK

First published in Great Britain in 1995
by Weidenfeld & Nicolson
This paperback edition published in 1996
by Phoenix,
an imprint of Orion Books Ltd,
Orion House, 5 Upper St Martin's Lane,
London WC2H 9EA

An Hachette Livre UK company

Reissued 2002, 2008

3

A CIP catalogue record for this book
is available from the British Library.

ISBN 978-1-8579-9783-5

Printed and bound in Great Britain by
Clays Ltd, Elcograf S.p.A.

The Orion Publishing Group's policy is to use papers that
are natural, renewable and recyclable products and
made from wood grown in sustainable forests. The logging
and manufacturing processes are expected to conform to
the environmental regulations of the country of origin.

'Super... ...tifully written, ...fast-paced and extremely perceptive. Andrew Lycett has done a massive amount of research and shows himself very understanding of his tricky subject, seeing both the pathos and the comedy inherent in the Fleming paradox – the sharp contrast between the much-promoted image and the man'   Selina Hastings, *Sunday Telegraph*

'[Fleming's] life was a gift for a biographer and Lycett has done it sympathetically, thoroughly and straightforwardly, with an unobtrusive authorial presence'   Alan Judd, *Spectator*

'Thoroughly readable . . . a fascinating historical work'
Mark Porter, *Sunday Express*

'Truthful, substantial, eye-opening . . . considerable scoops . . . quietly explosive revelations'
Gerald Isaaman, *Hampstead & Highgate Express*

'The most complete biography of Fleming'
Philip Ziegler, *Daily Telegraph*

'Fascinating reading . . . a spellbinding exploration of a complex character'   *Northern Echo*

'Masterly biography . . . a timely exploration of the enigmatic man behind the myth'   *Eastern Daily Press*

'Andrew Lycett's book is far more than a biography, and it is indeed an exceptionally good biography. It is also a psychological case study of human relationships: of the bonding (the pun is inevitable) of incompatible partners; a social history of upper-class Britain over three decades from the thirties to the fifties; an informative glimpse of war-time intelligence work, and above all a compelling "read"'
John Gray, *Books in Scotland*

'With a cast just as good as a 007 movie, this is a book to savour slowly, wallowing in the glamourous, golden era long gone'   Sharon Davey, *Today*

Andrew Lycett read history at Oxford University. He worked for some years as a journalist, specialising in foreign reporting. He has been a full-time biographer since 1992, with highly praised lives of Rudyard Kipling, Dylan Thomas and Arthur Conan Doyle. He lives in north London.

By Andrew Lycett

Qaddafi and the Libyan Revolution
(with David Blundy)
Ian Fleming
Rudyard Kipling
Dylan Thomas: A New Life
Conan Doyle: The Man Who Created Sherlock Holmes

Contents

Illustrations   vi
Foreword   vii

1 Etonian rebel   1
2 Foreign initiation   29
3 "The world's worst stockbroker"   64
4 Chocolate sailor   101
5 Ian's Red Indians   127
6 Newspaper romance   159
7 Succumbing to marriage   186
8 Bond promotion   220
9 Escaping the 'gab-fests'   251
10 Jamaican attraction   279
11 Emotional turmoil   310
12 Film options   343
13 Heart problems   376
14 Kent and Wiltshire   403
15 Name in lights   430

Acknowledgements   454
Bibliography   458
Index   462

Illustrations

The young Etonian (Lord O'Neill)

Ian as caricatured by Amies Milner; and winning the steeplechase at Eton (Lord O'Neill)

Eve Fleming and her sons: Peter (left), Richard, Michael, Ian (Lord O'Neill)

Country house life: with Deirdre Hart-Davis at Aldwick, 1929; and with Nora Phipps, Joyce Phipps (later Grenfell) and Henry Tiarks at Furneux Pelham, 1928 (Deirdre Inman)

With Monique Panchaud de Bottomes beside Lake Geneva in 1932

With Muriel Wright in Austria (Captain Jeremy Elwes)

In Capri, 1938 (Weidenfeld & Nicolson archive); and golfing with Count Paul Munster and Robert Sweeny

Commander Fleming RNVR in Room 39 (Weidenfeld & Nicolson archive)

Demob happy at Eton, 4 June 1945, with members of the Pitman family (Jemima Pitman)

Early days at Goldeneye. Ann Rothermere's first visit in 1948 (Lord O'Neill); and with Ivar Bryce (Weidenfeld & Nicolson archive)

Messing about in Jamaica: with Barrington Roper and barracuda; with Noël Coward; and with Blanche Blackwell (Jemima Pitman)

With Ann in Capri, 1960 (Alan Ross); and outside High Court, London, 1963 (Camera Press)

On set: with Sean Connery (Weidenfeld & Nicolson archive); Ursula Andress (Weidenfeld & Nicolson archive); and James Bond producers Harry Saltzman and "Cubby" Broccoli

Mr and Mrs Ian Fleming in their drawing room, Victoria Square, London (Lilly Library, Indiana University, Bloomington, Indiana)

At Raymond and Georgina O'Neill's wedding: Caspar (left), Francis Grey, Joan Sillick, Ann and Ian (Joan Sillick)

At his Mitre Court desk (Camera Press)

With Blanche Blackwell (Jemima Pitman)

In the gazebo at Goldeneye (Hulton Deutsch); with Ann, Cecil Beaton, Noël Coward, and friends at Blue Harbour (Cecil Beaton photograph, courtesy of Sotheby's, London)

Cecil Beaton's portrait of Ian, bon viveur (Cecil Beaton photograph, courtesy of Sotheby's, London)

Foreword

I have been lucky to stumble across a twentieth-century icon whose turbulent and enthralling life was much more interesting than I, or the general public, ever envisaged. When I first encountered Ian Fleming's novels in the early to mid 1960s, they were, like Beatles' albums, part of a teenager's cultural rites of passage. Following the release of *Dr No*, the first James Bond film, in 1962, the suave secret agent portrayed on screen by Sean Connery became a worldwide popular hero. For a generation of schoolboys such as myself, Fleming's paperbacks, which proliferated in the films' wake, offered a potted guide to what we dimly perceived as sophisticated experience. Huddled under scratchy blankets in dormitories after lights-out, our torches flickered and our eyes wearied as we eagerly participated in underwater battles in the Caribbean or death-defying tangles with spies on the Orient Express, while our unfocused libidos were roused by steamy sexual couplings, the likes we could only dream of. The action was more traditionally exciting than Micky Spillane and the bedroom scenes more direct than Harold Robbins. Not for nothing did Fleming, in his frequently self-disparaging manner, call his books the product of an adolescent imagination (another of his descriptions was "fairy tales for grown-ups").

Returning to Ian Fleming's novels as an adult, I found them surprisingly enduring. They were a clever concoction all right: like a good salad dressing, they required the right ingredients, their author used to say. But what once had been sensational now seemed a natural part of the story, and what stayed in the mind was the ebullience of the writing: the freshness of the images, the thoroughness of the factual research and the scope of the imaginative vision. Fleming was a much more engaging wordsmith than "Sapper" and the purveyors of clubland heroes from a generation earlier, while few latter-day imitators have been able to match his innate style.

My interest in Fleming as a subject for a biography started from my supposition (only partly true, I later found out) that he was a prototype James Bond, a wartime spy whose various exploits could be charted from papers in the Public Record Office which had recently been released either under the normal thirty-year rule or, if more secret, as a result of the Major administration's "open government" initiative.

The existing literature did little to dispel this gung-ho impression. In 1966, only two years after Fleming's death, John Pearson wrote a lively biography which suffered, through no fault of his own, from being too close to its subject, both in time and in perspective (the book was initiated by the *Sunday Times* for which both he and Ian had worked). Pearson managed to flesh out Ian's wartime career, showing how certain incidents provided material for the later Bond books. But in doing so, he helped establish the myth of Ian as 007 template, while his need to work closely with Ian's widow Ann precluded serious examination of his subject's emotional life.

Since then, an interesting memoir by Ian's lifelong friend, Ivar Bryce, first published in 1975, made little impression on the world, partly because it was beset by legal problems, and partly because it was unjustly dismissed by reviewers as an essay in self-indulgence. Nevertheless it provided useful insight into the power of Ian's personality (as well as his gift for friendship). Otherwise most biographers and memoirists have tended to appropriate Ian as a trophy acquaintance, without adding much to an understanding of his character (an exception would be Peter Quennell), while studies of three members of his immediate family – his brother Peter, his sister-in-law Celia Johnson and his half-sister Amaryllis – have portrayed him as an amiable eccentric, operating at a tangent from the accepted Fleming norm.

Ian's inner self became clearer with the publication in 1985 of Ann Fleming's witty and perceptive correspondence (edited by Mark Amory). But while these letters, a boon to would-be biographers, were often painfully explicit about the Flemings' marital ups and downs, they did little (apart from detailing Ian's moodiness and love of golf) to put such matters in context. There was no reference, for example, to Blanche Blackwell, the Jamaica-based woman who enchanted Ian during the last few years of his life.

It did not take me long, once I had begun to talk to those who had known Ian, to understand that he was a much more intricate and elusive man than had been warranted. Winkling out the details was not always easy. Often, I had to weigh up the claims of two distinct camps devoted to the memory of either Ian or Ann. He himself was a chameleon-like showman who presented the side of his character he thought people wanted to see. Confused or even blinded as to the reality, many friends were therefore satisfied with the consensus view of Ian as a none-too-precisely-defined agent-entrepreneur. One or two more sceptical associates questioned my motives in attempting a new biography. Strangely, they could not accept that I found the man interesting, and wanted to write as truthful an account of his life as possible. ("But what is your angle?"

asked one, when she could discern no obvious hidden agenda. "If you're collecting material for a prurient account of Ian and his girlfriends, count me out.")

Attractive though it was, I had to resist the temptation to write Ian into all the most daring, unexplained wartime secret service exploits. According to various witnesses, it was he who personally arranged for Hess to fly to Scotland in May 1941, he who regularly liaised with Admiral Canaris, head of the German Abwehr, and, most fantastic of all, he who single-handedly was responsible for the operation which brought Hitler's deputy, Martin Bormann, to Britain in 1945.

As with many people, the truth was more interesting. Slowly a more rounded picture began to emerge of a charming chancer who, dogged by the memory of an upright father killed on the Western Front in May 1917 and pushed by an ambitious and headstrong mother, had, by the time he was thirty, tried his hand at various careers – army officer, diplomat, journalist, banker and stockbroker – without ever finding his *métier*. War, however, proved his making, satisfying a powerful need to conform while providing unexpected outlets for his imaginative genius.

Returning to civilian life, Ian was never quite the same. His existence was dominated by his enduring love for Ann Rothermere, whom he married in March 1952. She provided the inspiration for him to start writing his James Bond novels (the first, *Casino Royale*, was published in 1953). But when their relationship turned sour, and Ian found it difficult to reconcile his problems to his childishly precise view of emotional experience, he retreated into himself, reserving his energy for his novels and for a late-flowering love affair.

What for me had started as an examination of a leading figure in twentieth-century intelligence mythology became a much more personal quest – a complex character study, a double romance, and a tragedy. At one stage I used to tell questioners that I was writing four separate books – a social history of the 1930s, a biography of a wartime naval intelligence officer, a love story, and a literary criticism of the Bond novels.

Luckily, I was helped by an array of delightful people who introduced me to the world of Ian and "Annie" and made sure that three years of my life were both an education and an entertainment. Singling out anyone is, as they say, invidious. But there are four individuals without whom I could hardly have proceeded. Ian's step-daughter Fionn Morgan not only gave me access to all her mother's papers (over and above the selection already made by Mark Amory) but also provided regular advice and support. Without her material, Ian would have emerged as a much drier and less sympathetic individual.

Nichol Fleming, Ian's nephew (his brother Peter's son) gave initial encouragement, putting me in touch with family and friends (including his godmother, Lady Mary Clive, who proved a witness *sans pareil* about Ian in the 1930s: her ability to remember precise details of texture, environment, conversation and mood after more than half a century was truly remarkable). Sadly, Nichol did not see the end of this project since, at only fifty-six, he was struck down by a heart attack while playing tennis. (Unlike his uncle, who died at the same age, Nichol was in otherwise excellent health. When I saw him a week before his death, he was full of boyish energy. The only similarity, perhaps, was a poorly functioning Fleming heart.)

While Nichol and his two sisters, Kate and Lucy, were Ian's heirs and represented his family in Glidrose, the company (51 per cent owned by the multinational Booker) which holds the Bond literary rights, the day-to-day administration and exploitation of that property are carried out today, as in Ian's lifetime, by Peter Janson-Smith, a consummate professional, who opened Ian's working files to me and fielded my persistent questions with great patience and charm.

Finally, a late bonus in personal and biographical terms, there was my access to Blanche Blackwell, the woman who provided Ian with love and support towards the end of his life. When I first met Blanche she was courteous and informative, while maintaining that she did not want to feature in Ian's story. However, as mutual respect was established and she came to realize that I intended a serious study, she began to relax and talk freely about the more personal aspects of her relationship with Ian. Through her I came to understand the importance of Jamaica in Ian's life – part retreat from the world, part tangible representation for his own values of hardiness and adventure, part mere fantasy outlet. One of the highlights of my research was flying to the Cayman Islands to spend a few days with Blanche at her seaside house, where, as at Goldeneye in the old days, shoals of exotic fish still congregate in the water at the bottom of her property. These colourful creatures not only reminded me of the range of Ian's interests but also provided a fitting image for the sparkling luminescence and darting romanticism of his original mind.

1

Etonian rebel

1908–1927

His father was a Fleming, his mother a Rose – enough said, according to the sociobiologists who interpret Ian Fleming's tantalizingly short and ambivalent life as a continuous battle for supremacy between two radically different sets of genes: the dour Scots respectability of his paternal line and the raffish capriciousness of the maternal.

Ian's grandfather, Robert, was one of the pioneers of popular capitalism, a resourceful Dundee clerk who developed the concept of investment trusts (forerunners of unit trusts) so that small investors could participate in companies' growth. Like many successful financiers, he sprang from a modest, even underprivileged, background. The Flemings like to trace their antecedents to fourteenth-century immigrants from Flanders, who were attracted to England and later to Scotland by opportunities in the textile trade. By the early nineteenth century one branch had made its way up to the Highlands and was living off the land as farmers, just south of Braemar. With ambitions to better himself, Robert's father, John, pioneered a lint mill on the banks of the River Isla. But the venture failed, and he was forced to move to Dundee and find work in a jute factory. Robert was brought up in the Liff Road, one of the city's poorest slums. Conditions were so harsh that five of his brothers and sisters died in childhood of diphtheria: only he and his brother John (later knighted as Lord Provost of Aberdeen) survived.

Robert determined to succeed where his father had failed. Forced to leave the local high school at the age of just thirteen, he worked his way up to the post of bookkeeper in the dank offices of an eminent Dundee jute merchant. His employer, Edward Baxter, proved smart enough to recognize his young recruit's financial acumen, and, at the age of twenty-five, Robert was despatched to North America to look after the jute king's dollar securities. He returned convinced of the economic potential of the United States following the end of the Civil War. Equally important, he saw an opening for himself to make money. With Dundee's fifty-year-long dominance of the world jute trade under threat from competition from mills in Bengal, the local "jutocracy" and their dependants needed new outlets for their savings. The 1862 Companies Act, which introduced the concept of limited liability, provided the catalyst. Robert realized that he could use this legislation to establish an investors' club, or trust, which, when floated as a company, would enable shareholders to participate in a variety of ventures at little risk to themselves.

After securing the services of four well-known Dundee businessmen to act as trustees, he issued a prospectus for the First Issue of the Scottish American Investment Trust in 1873. The aim was to raise £150,000 in £100 certificates, giving investors a guaranteed return of 6 per cent per annum. But the launch proved so popular that his original prospectus had to be withdrawn and replaced with a new one raising £300,000. That too was oversubscribed, and was followed by two larger issues.

Following these successes, the industrious Robert found himself in demand to advise other companies on their northern American holdings. Inevitably he was drawn to London where he set up the Investment Trust Corporation in 1888 and, two decades later, Robert Fleming and Company, the merchant bank which still bears his name and operates out of its original premises in Crosby Square in the City of London.

Robert specialized in American railroad securities, which had an insatiable demand for capital wherever it came from and paid handsome returns, particularly given the going rate for the dollar. He was a regular visitor to North America, sailing the transatlantic liners like a present-day businessman might fly Concorde – seven crossings in 1894, during a period of economic depression when roughly a quarter of American track was in receivership. But Fleming's tenacity (that was the word most often used about his business skills) and his undoubted mastery with figures ensured that investors in his trusts were not affected. The Pennsylvania, Union Pacific and Atchison, Topeka and Santa Fe were among dozens of railroads which owed their existence to his financial backing. He helped raise funds for railroad projects in Cuba, Mexico and Guatemala. At one stage he was a director of the Matador Land and Cattle Company which owned one and a half million acres in Texas and forty thousand head of cattle roaming on them. Closer to home, he was involved with the formation of the Anglo-Persian Oil Company (now British Petroleum). In the process he became a respected international financier, rubbing shoulders, doing business, and, most important, establishing close personal relationships with leading bankers in the United States, including J. Pierpont Morgan, Jacob Schiff at Kuhn Loeb, and the New York Warburgs.

By the age of thirty-five, Robert felt rich enough to take a wife. When not poring over accounts, he had a reputation for being monosyllabic. Nevertheless he found the words to propose to Kate Hindmarsh, the strong-willed daughter of an Inland Revenue officer. A handsome girl who liked open-air pursuits, she was twelve years his junior when they met in the Lindsey Street Congregational Church in Dundee. After their marriage in February 1881, she produced four children for him at two-yearly intervals, starting with Ian's father, Valentine, in 1883, and then his aunts Dorothy in 1885 and Kathleen in 1887 and, finally, his uncle Philip in 1889.

By that time Robert, Kate and their young family had joined the steady trail of self-made Scots millionaires to England. That meant a radical change of lifestyle for the austere Flemings. The prevailing City ethos required Robert to behave like a moneyed English gentleman. Spurred by his socially ambitious wife, he bought a large house in Grosvenor Square in Mayfair (it was later demolished to make way for the present-day American Embassy). And then in 1903, when that was not enough, he acquired a run-down estate at Nettlebed in Oxfordshire. Later the same year he bought a nearby house, Joyce Grove, to go with his two thousand acres of beechwoods and farmland. But he and Kate were not content with this perfectly respectable, modestly sized William and Mary mansion, which supposedly took its name from the regicide Cornet Joyce, one of Oliver Cromwell's right-hand men during the Civil War. Despite their Scottish parsimony, they wanted a more obvious statement of their international plutocrat status. So the existing structure was pulled down to make way for a massive, red brick palazzo with vaguely Gothic pretensions. It came complete with forty-four bedrooms, a dozen bathrooms, and a plaque on the front wall affirming the family motto, "Let the deed shaw". The world in general declared the new Joyce Grove a monstrosity, though the architectural historian Nikolaus Pevsner was later prepared to hedge his bets.

To ease their passage into the Edwardian establishment, Robert and Kate committed their two sons to a conventional upper-middle-class English education. Since only the best would do, Val and Phil were sent to Eton and Oxford. Val emerged from Magdalen College, Oxford, in 1905 with a degree in history and the manners and bearing of a perfect English gentleman. As Ian was to learn, often to his cost, Val did everything in his school and university career right. At school, he was a member of the oligarchic Eton Society, or "Pop", and rowed in the eight. At Oxford, he continued to row, but still found time to act as field master of the New College and Magdalen beagles for two seasons, and also as president of the Undergraduates' Common Room. He subsequently read for the Bar, but never practised. There was never any doubt that his scholastic and sporting achievements were simply well-defined milestones on his effortless path towards joining the family firm.

There was the wilful air of a young professional in a hurry in the way Val got married less than a year after leaving Oxford. A man needs a wife with his line of business in prospect. But, to give Val his due, there was nothing dynastic about his choice. He might have opted for the quietly supportive, rank-enhancing daughter of one of the peers whom Robert frequently invited down to Joyce Grove to shoot. Instead he plumped for the lively, attractive daughter of a local solicitor who lived a dozen miles from Joyce Grove in the Thames-side village of Sonning.

With her big dark eyes, high cheek-bones and trim figure, Evelyn Beatrice Ste Croix Rose was the very antithesis of Fleming thrift and heartiness. She played the violin and was a good water-colourist for a start: none of the Flemings had any pretensions to music or art. She was frivolous, snobbish and vain. Money, as far as she was concerned, was for spending rather than saving. One of her extravagances was her wardrobe: she dressed with a theatrical originality which later often caused Ian and his brothers acute embarrassment. Gold, purple and green were her colours; exotic materials and outsize hats her style.

Eve, as she was known, came from a distinguished enough family. Her grandfathers on both sides had risen to the summits of their professions and been knighted for their services. Her father's father, Sir Philip Rose, had been legal adviser to the Prime Minister, Benjamin Disraeli. (A caricature by Spy in *Vanity Fair* depicted him as Lord Beaconsfield's Friend.) Her mother's father, Sir Richard Quain, went one better. As a leading London surgeon and editor of the renowned *Dictionary of Medicine*, he was frequently called upon to pronounce on the health of Queen Victoria. Sir Richard's stock in trade was a genial Irish manner and a quick way with intuitive diagnoses. He ended his life a hugely popular man though, like Robert Fleming, he had started it very humbly – in his case, in County Cork, where his first job was as a tanner's apprentice.

Somehow the mingling of Rose and Quain genes never quite worked. Although Eve's parents were contentedly married, her two brothers, Ivor and Harcourt, turned out to be notorious rakes. For all their Eton and (in Harcourt's case) Oxford educations, they both managed to be declared bankrupt and, by the end of their lives, they had both been married three times. On the Oxfordshire–Berkshire borders, around Henley, they were known as the "wild Roses", a dissolute couple whom Eve later forbad her children to see. Her sister, Kathleen, fared little better: a would-be actress, she married and separated young, tried unsuccessfully to write plays, and hung around for ever after, a forlorn figure on the fringes of Eve's society.

According to family legend, Val and Eve met at a ball, possibly an Oxford Commemoration ball, and fell for each other instantly. Brother Harcourt may have been the intermediary, since he knew Val at both Eton and Oxford. Eve's father, George Rose, was an enthusiastic rower who, for two decades, presided over the Sonning regatta. One can imagine that Eve first saw her future husband rowing in her father's regatta and was attracted by his physique and sporting prowess.

Despite reservations about his son's choice of wife, Robert settled a sizeable sum, a quarter of a million pounds, on Val when the couple married in February 1906. Val used some of this legacy to buy his own mock Gothic pile, Braziers Park, well-endowed with woodland and hedgerows for shooting, at Ipsden in Oxfordshire, just four miles down the road from his parents at Nettlebed. Shortly afterwards he and Eve took a short lease on a property in Mayfair, again just round the corner from the Robert Flemings. And it was here, at 27 Green Street, off Park Lane, that their first son, Peter, was born on 31 May 1907, to be followed, with almost indecent haste, by Ian on 28 May 1908.

Weighing in at just under nine pounds, Ian Lancaster Fleming, in contrast to his elder brother Peter, was a big, bouncing baby. He was given his second name because, in keeping with the petty snobbery which used to annoy her in-laws, Eve liked to claim descent from John of Gaunt, Duke of Lancaster and fourth son of Edward III. (Later, she would insist that her own family, the "wild Roses", were true Highlanders, unlike the parvenu Lowland Flemings, and would dress Ian and his brothers in Rose tartan kilts.)

Like her mother-in-law before her, Eve was philoprogenitive: Ian was followed in fairly quick succession by two more sons, Richard in 1911 and Michael in 1913. In many respects, the young Flemings could not have been born in happier circumstances. It was the Edwardian era, the Indian summer of genteel country-house living. The family commuted between two substantial homes. Braziers Park was a child's paradise with its dedicated nurseries and playrooms, its maze of passages and cupboards, its stables and kennels (for Val's pack of bassets), its hidden pathways and its rolling acres of woodland. And in London there was a smart new residence, a Georgian mansion on the edge of Hampstead Heath, which was renamed Pitt House, after the statesman, William Pitt, first Earl of Chatham, who had lived there nearly a century and a half earlier.

If this seemed the epitome of civilized living, it was something of an illusion. The established social order had received an unprecedented buffeting as a result of the prolonged agricultural depression in the last quarter of the nineteenth century. Confrontation loomed as the landed classes tried to keep the growing demand for social and political change at bay. The turning-point came when David Lloyd George, Chancellor of the Exchequer in a Liberal government, introduced his People's Budget in 1909, and called for increased land taxes, supertax and other duties to pay for his new concept of old-age pensions. The House of Lords, with its massive majority of Conservative peers, rejected the measure, whereupon the government resigned and called a general election in January 1910 on the twin issues of the budget and the power of the Lords. Although they were returned with only a reduced majority, political feelings were running so high that the Liberals determined to introduce a new Parliament Bill, curbing the powers of the Lords to vote on financial legislation. Since the

Conservative majority in the House of Lords still obtained, and it was unlikely to accede to its own emasculation, a second general election was called for December. The issue this time was solely the Parliament Bill. The position of the parties remained much the same as a result of the voting, and the Bill was passed the following year, after the government threatened to create up to five hundred new Liberal peers.

All this might have been the hazy historical backdrop to Ian's life if his father had not been elected as Conservative MP for the Henley Division of South Oxfordshire in the first election of 1910. The previous year Val had joined his father as a partner in the latter's newly created bank, Robert Fleming and Company. (The other partner was a Scottish accountant called Walter Whigham.) Now, demonstrating their skill in drafting the upwardly mobile to their ranks, the landed classes sent the young banker, not yet thirty, to fight their corner in crucial parliamentary battles to come.

Val had done his political legwork. Although a newcomer to the area, he had already been commissioned into the local yeomanry regiment, the Queen's Own Oxfordshire Hussars. He rode with the South Oxfordshire and South Berkshire hunts. These acts of geographical identification, together with his personal charm and level-headedness, inspired the countryfolk of the Henley Division to dump their incumbent Liberal MP, Philip Morrell, and vote for Fleming. An incident in the immediate aftermath of the polls suggested that Val had a useful electoral asset in his pretty young wife. For Lady Ottoline Morrell, the rich artistic patron who was married to his opponent, was so incensed by the result that she marched up to Eve and publicly shook her by the lapels.

The purchase and deliberate renaming of Pitt House signalled Val's ambitions to succeed in Conservative Party politics. Till then it had been known variously as Wildwood House and North End House or Place. But, in the century or so since his death, the elder Pitt had become a symbol of muscular Toryism. Lowe, Goldschmidt and Howland, the Hampstead estate agent which put his former ivy-clad mansion on the market in November 1908, advertised it as "the house in which Great Britain lost America" – a reference to the notion that, if Pitt had not hidden himself away there in the 1770s, the government would not have imposed its dreaded tea tax on North America and Britain would not have lost its most valuable colony. It did not matter that Pitt's stay in his now eponymous house had been devastatingly unhappy. The former Secretary of State was riddled with gout and refused to see anyone, not even his butler, who was forced to serve his master's meals through a hatchway with double doors. The outer door had to be closed before Pitt would open the inner to get his food. (Ironically, before the Flemings, Pitt House was owned by Harold Harmsworth, the first Lord Rothermere, and father of Esmond, the man whose wife Ian Fleming courted and later married.) Eve fell easily into the role of metropolitan hostess. Her striking looks proved as much of a draw as the general conversation for several of her husband's colleagues, including the young MP Winston Churchill, a fellow officer in the sociable Oxfordshire Hussars, who liked to call Val and his brother Phil the "flamingos".

In this political hothouse, in the rather more relaxed, rural setting of Braziers Park, and, no less importantly, in the strongly tribal atmosphere of Joyce Grove, Ian made his first tentative steps into the world. From the start he was fighting for attention with his elder brother Peter who, stricken by a debilitating form of colitis, went four times with his mother to Switzerland for special treatment. On at least one occasion, the whole family accompanied them. Staying in Lausanne, five-year-old Ian was so angry at the special favours shown to Peter that he had to be carried screaming from the dining-room of the Hotel Beau Rivage. Usually Ian was left alone with his nanny, under the supervision of his indomitable grandmother whom he greatly respected. He learned to cope with the twin pressures of sibling rivalry and familial conformity by becoming a childhood prankster. On one occasion he performed the unlikely feat of unscrewing a lavatory pan and moving it into the drawing-room. As the 'delicate' Peter got the attention and later the plaudits for his precocious intelligence, Ian became quietly resentful. The two brothers fought "like cats and dogs", Peter later admitted, though he also made out that their relationship was close, "like two fox cubs". Ian was not so sure: he called Peter "turnip" or "pudding", and when, thirty years later, a friend told him a story about his brother – how, as a child, Peter had so disliked his porridge that he had thrown great slabs of it out of the nursery window – Ian wailed, "Oh, I wish I'd known that at the time. He always seemed so perfect."

The Fleming boys found ready-made playmates in the extended clan which Robert insisted on building around him in Oxfordshire. Mabel Barry, Granny Kate's sister, had moved to Nettlebed, with her son Bill and her French foster-daughter Sybil Mayor. Then there were the Harley girls, Primrose and Dido, daughters of a friend of Eve's. Three summers in a row the Flemings and the Harleys travelled to Salcombe in Devon for their summer holidays. Ian quickly adopted a role as the naughty brother. When Peter came across him and Primrose dismembering a container of limpets for fishing bait, he was shocked. "You cruel brutes! How could you do such a thing?" he exclaimed, and waltzed out of the room, leaving the youthful culprits in tears at the sin of their misdemeanour.

Despite such incidents, Ian looked back fondly on these family holidays. In his books, he frequently translated his own experiences into those of his hero James Bond. He described Salcombe in *On Her Majesty's Secret*

Service, where Bond recalled his own childhood, and its memories of "the painful grit of wet sand between young toes when the time came for him to put his shoes and socks on, of the precious little pile of sea-shells and interesting wrack on the sill of his bedroom window ("No, we'll have to leave that behind, darling. It'll dirty up your trunk!"), of the small crabs scuttling away from the nervous fingers groping beneath the seaweed in the rock-pools ... What a long time ago they were, those bucket and spade days! How far he had come since the freckles and the Cadbury milk chocolate Flakes and the fizzy lemonade!"

On a West Country beach, Ivar Bryce, who became a lifelong friend of Ian's, first encountered "four strong, handsome, black-haired, blue-eyed boys" energetically building a fortress in the sand. "The fortress builders generously invited me to join them, and I discovered that their names were Peter, Ian, Richard and Michael, in that order. The leaders were Ian and Peter, and I gladly carried out their exact and exacting orders. They were natural leaders of men, both of them, as later history was to prove, and it speaks well for them all that there was room for both Peter and Ian in the platoon." The year was 1917, and Ian was still only nine.

The Flemings were staying on that occasion at the Tregenna Castle Hotel in St Ives, where Ian's favourite pastime was searching the local caves and beaches for treasure. Having read his Stevenson, Verne and Rider Haggard, he was particularly on the lookout for amethyst quartz. He also knew his Stacpoole and was fascinated by the idea of ambergris. One day he was convinced he had found some. Deep in a cave, he came across a football-sized lump of grey gooish paste which fitted his image precisely. He was thrilled: he would be rich and able to live on his favourite Cadbury's milk chocolate Flakes for ever. He wrapped his *objet trouvé* in his jersey and rushed back up to the hotel to show his mother who was seated in the Palm Court having tea with a handsome admirer. She feigned surprise and then horror. What had he done to his nice clean grey jersey? she shrieked. But Ian was not concerned: he had found his ambergris. When his mother called a waiter, Ian ordered him not to touch his prize. On being informed that this was not ambergris but a slab of butter from a New Zealand supply ship which had been torpedoed off the shore a few months earlier, Ian burst into tears and rushed out of the room.

For the boys in general, that particular family holiday was marred by the enforced absence of their father who, in August 1914, had ridden off to the war as a captain in the Queen's Own Oxfordshire Hussars. During his four years in the House of Commons Val had made his mark with a series of non-controversial interventions in various debates. His first speech, as might have been expected, addressed the Constitutional issue, where he defended the merits of the bicameral system. His friend Winston Churchill described it as "good and simple – but a trifle too long". As a well-meaning constituency MP, Val had raised the important issues of water supply in Garsington and postal facilities in Wallingford. His most passionate speech was in March 1912 when he argued forcibly in favour of National Service on the grounds that "improvement in the national physique and in the habits of order and discipline among the people of the country ... do real good to the working classes, and in the end very largely increase the efficiency of labour for the manufactories of this country". During this speech Val had referred to his experiences in the Oxfordshire Hussars, where he had enthusiastically signed up for all available instruction courses, including periods at the Cavalry school, Bathraven, and the School of Musketry, Hythe.

Captain Fleming was therefore one of the best trained volunteer officers in the British Expeditionary Force when he set off for France. The Hussars' job was to accompany the Royal Marines as reinforcements for the Dunkirk garrison. They drew some flak from the press for the favoured treatment they received from the Admiralty, where one of their own officers, Winston Churchill, was First Lord. Churchill, whose brother Jack was serving with Val, made sure the regiment had extra lorries and other equipment from Admiralty stores. But for the first few months of hostilities, Val's men were in reserve, and he enjoyed the sportsman's equivalent of a busman's holiday, running every day, playing polo and bringing some of his beloved bassets across the Channel for coursing with French hares. When he had a few days off in the autumn, Eve was able to visit him once at Malo-les-Bains.

In November 1914, however, the war took a more serious turn, and Val, newly promoted to major, found himself increasingly involved. Left to her own devices, Eve needed a boarding-school for her sons. Durnford, near Swanage in Dorset, was an expensive prep school with a reputation as a nursery for Eton, where there was never any question that the young Flemings would follow their father. Eve struck an immediate rapport with the rotund, ruddy-faced headmaster, Tom Pellatt. He remembered her as a "striking beauty", whose spirituality was not done justice to in her four later portraits by Augustus John.

Pellatt, or TP as he was known to parents and pupils alike, was one of those schoolmasters who, because they never grow up themselves, have the knack of talking to young boys at their own level. He was also a well-read man who was quick to identify the scholastic strengths and weaknesses of his pupils. TP's professed educational method was to allow his boys freedom to express themselves. He wrote, "Our policy was not to suppress anything in a child, i.e., if there was a kink in the boy's nature, let it appear, and then you could see what it was and possibly cope with it."

For all his classroom success and his communication skills with parents, TP presided over a harsh and often cruel establishment. Durnford retained much of the licensed anarchy found in early nineteenth-century schools. If it existed today, it would certainly be closed down. Conditions were primitive (no proper lavatories, only earth-closets, for example), the food was appalling (made worse by the privations of war) and bullying was widespread. One former pupil, who later served with distinction during the Second World War, remarked that, after Durnford, the Special Air Service (SAS) was a "piece of cake".

Ian first escaped the clutches of his French governess and came to this strange, character-forming place at the start of the autumn term of 1916. He was accompanied by Peter, who had been considered too fragile to attend earlier on his own. Ian initially hated it, finding friends hard to make because, as he wrote to his mother, "they are so dirty and unreverent". No doubt the brothers were arrogant and uncommunicative for Peter reported back in much the same vein: "Most of the chaps hate us, and there's one beast that always says something beastly to us when he passes us." But, like true Flemings confronted with a hostile world, the two boys stuck together and Ian confirmed to Eve that, whatever their differences at home, "Peter is a great help to me." To keep Ian's spirits up, Eve plied him with gifts, including a knife and a watch. But TP had clearly imposed himself as a looming and threatening presence. In thanking Eve for the watch, Ian noted, "My coff has grown the whoping coff now, please dont tell Mister Pellat, cause just this morning he said that nun of us had coffs." He did not spell out what punishment TP might inflict if he found Ian had contradicted him.

As Ian began to find his feet, there were at least compensations. Pellatt was supported in his enterprise by his wife Ellinor (known to the boys as Nell because that was what he would scream whenever he encountered a problem). On Sunday evenings all the boys would gather in the hall of Durnford's main building, a shabby eighteenth-century manor-house. Then, while her feet were tickled by some unfortunate child, Nell would read them an adventure story. The general favourites were *The Prisoner of Zenda*, *Moonfleet* and, towards the end of Ian's time, *Bulldog Drummond*. Laurence Irving, a pupil shortly before the Flemings, found that he "never read those books again without hearing [Nell's] tone and inflexion". The same went for Ian, though he preferred the populist works of Sax Rohmer, who opened up a more fantastic world with his "yellow devil" villain, Dr Fu Manchu.

The school's most unusual feature was Dancing Ledge, a freshwater bathing pool which TP had blasted out of the rocks at the edge of the sea. Any passably decent summer day the boys stopped their classroom work at noon. They then raced over the downs to the Ledge where they threw off their clothes and leapt into the pool for a dip *au naturel* with the masters. Irving recalled Pellatt wrestling with learners clad in nothing but a "battered panama hat with a puggree of I Zingari colours and shod with sodden once white buckskin shoes". TP was a different animal in this environment. He allowed himself to be ragged by the boys and, according to Irving, "his pursuit and chastising of his mockers was most endearing". Indeed, for all TP's robust eccentricity, the boys loved it. Irving described how "we plunged into the clear blue water fathoms deep and swam in shoals to nearby island rocks to dive like seals from their summits, and revel in the invigorating chill of the open sea". Ian's abiding love of the sea and its creatures was spawned on Dancing Ledge.

More conventionally, Ian played his first tentative rounds of golf, a sport which engrossed him later in life. As a games enthusiast (he had captained Oxford University at football and played Second XI county cricket), TP had seeded a course on a vacant plot near the woods. Nell provided Ian with clubs and balls, the cost of which was then added to the termly bill sent to his indulgent mother. Ian also gained a taste for another sport which occupied him as an adult. The Pellatts had a strapping daughter called Hester (later, the biographer Hester Chapman) for whom, Ian liked to boast, he experienced his first yearnings of heterosexual passion.

As expected, Ian did his best to keep in touch with his father at the Front. As a family, the Flemings had a penchant for nicknames: Val was Mokie and Eve Miewy, Mie or even M. In one card to Mokie (a child's attempt at 'Smokie' – because Val often had a pipe in his mouth), Ian stated manfully that he liked school "or at least some things are nice", adding the hope that "the war will soon be over". Val kept Johnny, as he called Ian, amused with tales of life in the trenches. "I saw a lot of aeroplanes today. The place where they live is near here. They send up rockets in the evening in case any of them lose their way in the dark."

For his friend Winston Churchill, Val provided a more realistic account of the Battle of Ypres in November 1914. "Day and night in this area are made hideous by the incessant crash and whistle and roar of every sort of projectile, by sinister columns of smoke and flame, by the cries of wounded men, by the piteous calls of animals of all sorts, abandoned, starved, perhaps wounded. Along this terrain of death stretch more or less parallel to each other lines of trenches, some 200, some 1,000 yards apart, hardly visible except to the aeroplanes which continually hover over them, menacing and uncanny harbingers of fresh showers of destruction ... It's going to be a long long war in spite of the fact that every single man in it wants it stopped at once." A few months later he took Churchill to task for failing to end the war. The situation had become so bad that his wife, Eve, was travelling in the tube to save the national petrol bill. "I do wonder what on earth you are really doing?" he pleaded.

While Jack Churchill managed to transfer on to the staff of Sir John French, the commander-in-chief, Val had no such easy let-out from life on the front line with the Oxfordshire Hussars. He soldiered on in this desolation for two and a half more years before his war was abruptly halted. In the middle of May 1917 Val's squadron was ordered to Guillemont Farm, an exposed post in the British Expeditionary Force's front line, opposite the Hindenburg Line, north of St-Quentin. In the early hours of Sunday 20 May, the Germans opened a heavy bombardment. Although his men bravely held their position, Val was hit by a shell and instantly killed, as he and another officer tried to wriggle their way between two trenches.

Brother officers, politicians and friends were quick to praise Val's qualities, both as a man and as a soldier. Winston Churchill wrote an appreciation in *The Times* which hailed Val's "lovable and charming personality". In 1904 Churchill had crossed the floor of the House of Commons from the Conservative to the Liberal benches, and at the time of Val's death he was Liberal MP in the one-time Fleming heartland of Dundee. So there was an element of special pleading in the turncoat Churchill's opinion that Val would be sorely missed in Parliament because he was "one of those younger Conservatives who easily and naturally combine loyalty to party ties with a broad liberal outlook upon affairs and a total absence of class prejudice ... He was a man of thoughtful and tolerant opinions, which were not the less strongly or clearly held because they were not loudly or frequently asserted. The violence of faction and the fierce tumults which swayed our political life up to the very threshold of the Great War, caused him a keen distress. He could not share the extravagant passions with which the rival parties confronted each other. He felt that neither was wholly right in policy and that both were wrong in mood."

Within the Fleming family the respectful eulogies soon gave way to hagiography. Val became the paragon of manly virtues. The boys learned to finish their nightly prayers with the words, "... and please, dear God, help me to grow up to be more like Mokie". In later years, in his various houses, Ian always displayed a copy of his father's *Times* obituary, duly signed by Winston Churchill. Peter went one better: he kept the good soldier Val's sword in his umbrella rack. Eve led the way, taking naturally to widowhood and revelling in the theatricality of it all. Her large eyes and slight figure were well set off by her weeds. Val's memory became a psychological weapon to beat her sons. Frequently she told them she had had a nocturnal message from their father forbidding them some course of action, such as smoking. Val's uncomplicated Lowland stoicism became the code by which she brought up her boys. As he had grown older, Val had rediscovered his Celtic roots – to the extent that, at the start of the war, he had sold Braziers Park and acquired Arnisdale, an estate in Argyllshire, which was ideal for stalking. Now Eve had all the rooms in the lodge at Arnisdale painted black. She managed to suppress any antipathy she felt towards the Flemings' origins: the boys were enjoined to celebrate their Scottishness.

Val left one bitter and enduring legacy, however. In his will, signed on 7 August 1914, just days before he departed for France, he had left Pitt House and most of his effects to his 32-year-old wife. But the bulk of his estate, valued at over £265,000, he committed to a trust fund for his children and their families. Eve was granted the income so long as she remained a widow. But if she ever remarried, her stipend was to be reduced to £3000 a year. Although this sum was generous enough in anyone's money (around £70,000 in 1995 prices), it would have meant a significant reduction in Eve's standard of living. She resented the implied restriction on her freedom of action and, years later, told Peter it had been a "bad will" which clearly had never been read by Val.

Because Peter was at home recovering from having his tonsils out (his usual pampered existence, his brother would have thought), Ian was on his own at Durnford when he heard the devastating news of his father's death. His grief at the loss of such a powerful role model proved enduring though, like most young boys, he soon learned to suppress his feelings, and, when Laurence Irving visited his old school towards the end of the summer term in 1917, he found the Flemings running the show. Ostensibly little had changed: boys still rushed over the fields to Spyway Farm and then slithered down the cliffside to Dancing Ledge. But "now the school appeared to be captained efficiently by the Fleming brothers; Peter, as I later might have guessed, had appropriated the transport, goading a donkey with its cartload of sandwiches, garibaldi biscuits and lemonade to the farm where it was off-loaded to boy-bearers for the last precipitous lap of the picnic path."

One immediate consequence of Val's death was that Ian and his brothers spent more time with their grandparents. A wing of Joyce Grove was put at their disposal as a weekend home, where Eve felt obliged to persevere with her show of Fleming heartiness. She put on a yellow skirt and taught her sons to fish. She took them for long walks in the Oxfordshire countryside. It all seemed rather hard work to Ian, and it was almost a relief when Granny Katie summoned her Rolls-Royce and took him to Huntercombe, the local golf course, where she liked to play one round in the morning and another after lunch. She always amused him with her individual form of tipping, presenting her caddies with toothbrushes.

Ian was unconvincing in his attempts to show interest in gentlemanly country pursuits. He enjoyed golf, particularly after learning to play properly at the age of fifteen, and he taught himself to shoot. But he had little time for animals. At the age of six he had been set upon by one of his father's bassets. Then, when he was twelve, he was despatched to a local

hunt meeting on a kicker of a horse. Young Ian initially kept away from
the rest of the hunt. But when the Master and hounds set off, his steed
careered backwards in their direction, lashing out with its hooves. "We
scythed our way through the hunt," Ian later recalled, "kicking the Master's mount and one or two hounds on the way, and were only brought
up by a clump of gorse. We waited, I pale and trembling, and my monster
sated – a dreadful Bateman cartoon – until ordered home 'until you can
learn to ride'." Further bad experiences with horses at Sandhurst left Ian
in profound agreement with whoever said that horses are dangerous at
both ends and uncomfortable in the middle.

When the time came for Ian to follow his father and older brother to
Eton in the Michaelmas half or autumn term of 1921, Eve introduced him
to the school uniform by requiring him to wear an Eton collar, as well as
boots and tweed knickerbockers, for two weeks of the previous summer
holidays. Showing a growing streak of wilfulness, Ian was infuriated at her
demands. Since Val's death, she had comforted herself by taking complete
charge of her sons' lives. But Ian was not a boy to respond to such a
regime: although he loved his mother dearly and wanted to please such
an obviously attractive woman, he resented her fussiness and over-
protectiveness, and the seeds of future conflict were sown.

If Ian showed any youthful rebelliousness, his Eton housemaster was
the sort of man designed to break it. Ian, like Peter, had been put down
for the Timbralls, a solid red-brick house on the road into the town from
Slough. E. V. (Sam) Slater had just taken charge there. He was a tough, no-
nonsense bachelor who enjoyed wielding the cane. In his official history
of Eton, Tim Card had no compunction about describing him as a sadist.

By now Peter was emerging as an outstanding scholar; the sort of pupil
schoolmasters dream about – able, with equal facility, to translate a piece
of Latin, compose witty and adult-sounding verse, and act the lead in
school plays. Ian, however, showed little aptitude for the classroom and,
in some desperation, he sought his salvation on the sports track. If athletics
were considered unimportant and infra dig at Eton in general, this was
doubly the case at Slater's. Possibly because of the lack of official encouragement, Ian took enthusiastically to running, jumping and hurling missiles. His height and well-developed physique gave him a boost, as he later
disarmingly admitted. (A friend recalled that Ian had another advantage:
he was the only boy who, as a junior, wore spiked running shoes.) But
here at last was a field where Ian could excel in his own terms, without
having to compete with, and suffer in the shadow of, his scholarly elder
brother.

Ian first made his mark as a sportsman by winning the junior (under
sixteen) long jump competition in his house sports in March 1922. His
athletics prowess received wider acclaim the following year when he won

the school junior hurdles title and, using his height to great advantage, returned some remarkable bowling figures for his house junior cricket team, including seven wickets for sixteen runs in one match against a College A side. That autumn, although still only fifteen, he was awarded his house colours for robust performances in the long position in the Field Game, Eton's idiosyncratic combination of soccer and rugby. Slater's house sports book noted of Fleming minor, "On some days he plays very badly indeed; but on others and these are – dieu merci – in the majority, he plays with a calmness, fortitude and even genius quite out of proportion to his years."

Team games held little fascination for Ian, however. The rugged individualism of the Flemings required him to star in dramas of his own making. Pounding round a sports track appealed to his solitariness and determination. Continuing his winning ways on the athletics track in the spring of 1924, his victory in the junior mile in February may have been a trifle lucky. His time of 4 minutes 54 seconds was creditable enough, but the *Eton College Chronicle* reported, "Bickersteth led all the way till just before the end when a cart unfortunately got in his way and he lost a good deal of ground and after getting untangled from the obstacle ran neck and neck with Fleming, who beat him by half a yard." Nevertheless Ian went on to win six more events (out of ten) in the junior section of the school sports – a feat never accomplished before or since. His achievement in 1925 and 1926 was equally remarkable: he became the first senior boy in living memory to become Victor Ludorum, or champion athlete, in two consecutive years. He was not even expected to carry off this coveted prize in 1926, his last year at the school, because the previous autumn he had broken his nose in a football game, following a collision with Henry Douglas-Home, brother of the future Prime Minister. A small copper plate was inserted in the bridge of his nose, adding a rakish imperfection to his otherwise flawless features. The plate was to cause him unending problems: he held it responsible for the blinding headaches which dogged him later in life, and which must have afflicted him even at this stage, because he was not allowed to compete in four events – the mile, half-mile, quarter-mile and steeplechase. In spite of this handicap, however, he was still more successful overall than anyone else.

In his introductory essay to *Gilt-Edged Bonds*, a compendium of three novels published in the United States in 1961, Paul Gallico makes significant play of a story Ian had told him about being severely caned just before running in an important steeplechase. According to Gallico, who befriended Ian during the war, the young Fleming had accumulated a series of bad marks for petty misdemeanours and unsatisfactory school work. The tradition at Eton was that boys were beaten at noon. But, since this was the time for the scheduled start of the race, Ian had his birching brought forward by a quarter of an hour. Gallico reported that Ian then ran the steeplechase with "his shanks and running shorts stained with his own gore". He interpreted this incident as the cause of Ian's later interest in torture and sadism in his writings. Several details in Gallico's account do not ring true, not least that Ian was competing in the steeplechase in an attempt to win the Victor Ludorum for a second time. But this was the year 1926, when Ian was prevented from running in that particular race. There must have been some truth, however, as Ian read Gallico's piece before publication. His large distinctive hand suggested various small changes to Gallico's manuscript, and the gist of that story was not among them. Rather, Ian objected to Gallico's attempt to link the experience to a lifelong interest in torture. Where Gallico wrote that it had left Fleming "with an implacable distaste for Eton which has lasted to this day", Ian changed the words "an implacable distaste" to "a mysterious affection", and added, at the end, the brief, dismissive sentence, "So much for torture."

For all his nostalgia towards his old school thirty-five years later, Ian did not like being at Eton. As he moved unhappily up through the school, he renewed his friendship with Ivar Bryce, the boy he had met on the beach in Cornwall a few years earlier. A couple of years older than Ian, Bryce was more exactly an Eton contemporary of Peter's. But he and Ian discovered they both enjoyed the kind of laddish escapades frowned upon by school authorities, like playing truant and meeting girls. Ivar brought a touch of exoticism to Ian's life. He was the scion of an Anglo-Peruvian family which had made a fortune trading guano, the phosphate-rich deposit of fish-eating seabirds which had been widely used as a natural fertilizer. With his thick, sensuous lips, Bryce was distinguished by satyr-like good looks which he owed to his part-Aztec Indian origins. His mother provided an artistic balance to his father's business background: she was a painter and a published author of detective stories (she had even produced a book on witchcraft).

This maternal influence inspired Ivar to try his hand, with a couple of friends, at publishing a magazine. There was an Etonian tradition that boys with literary ambitions could produce one-off publications, known as ephemerals. In a modish reference to D. H. Lawrence, Ivar's was called *Snapdragon* and it was produced for St Andrew's Day 1924, a school holiday, when parents and friends came to watch another tradition, the Wall Game. Bryce managed to secure a contribution – a typically scholarly ghost story – from the Eton Provost, M. R. James. Ian may have written some of the jokes and fillers, though there is no record of his authorship in the magazine. What distinguished *Snapdragon* was its great commercial success. Bryce succeeded in filling it with advertisements for – *inter alia* – Moss Bros, Thomas Cook, Turnbull & Asser, Kodak, van Heusen, Sunbeam

Motors, Lancia, the Public School Alpine Sports Club and the Hyde Park Hotel, venue of the Eton Dance (with tickets at thirty shillings a head, dancing to Vassie's Band). As a result of this entrepreneurial coup, Bryce and his two partners shared a profit of £90.

Bryce used his windfall to buy a Douglas motorbike which he had seen advertised "as new" in *Exchange & Mart*. He and Ian then used this vehicle for illegal forays around Windsor, where it was garaged. Ian later recalled some of these trips (to nearby towns such as Bray and Maidenhead) in his short novel *The Spy Who Loved Me*. In that book he also recorded in what several critics thought was rather too graphic detail the seduction of his heroine Vivienne Michel on the floor of a box at the Royalty Kinema in Windsor's Farquhar Street. As Ian later told his friend Robert Harling, this was where and how he first made love to a woman.

On the first available holiday Ian and Ivar rode the Douglas up to London where the British Empire Exhibition at Wembley promised all the excitement of the best type of funfair. Having feasted themselves on its various attractions, the two boys were making their way back to Eton at the slow pace the motorcycle allowed when they were overtaken by their German 'beak', a particularly severe and unpopular master called 'Satan' Ford who clearly recognized them. Ian feared the worst: expulsion was a distinct possibility. But when he next was 'up to' Mr Ford, the German teacher was most affable. "Very good, Fleming," he commented wryly on Ian's composition. "You must have put in some work during the holiday."

Ivar was not the only one with literary ambitions. His success with *Snapdragon* encouraged Ian to try his own hand at producing a similar publication for the Eton and Winchester match at Lords in June 1925. Selling at one shilling, *The Wyvern* did not enjoy the advertising cornucopia of its predecessor, though its thirty-two pages contained an inappropriate full page display for a fashion house, featuring the glamorous and sexy (certainly to Eton schoolboys) actress José Collins, otherwise Lady Innes-Ker and an intimate friend of the Canadian-born newspaper proprietor Lord Beaverbrook. *The Wyvern's* main selling point was its list of contributors whom Ian had prevailed upon to help. All were friends of his mother's. There were sketches by Augustus John ("specially drawn for *The Wyvern*") and Sir Edwin Lutyens, a poem by Vita Sackville-West, and a piece by Oliver St John Gogarty, who was also a friend of James Joyce. *The Wyvern* produced an editorial much the same as *Snapdragon's*, suggesting their consanguinity. Its instigators were portrayed as nitwits –

> Treble, treble, tosh and twaddle,
> That's the Editorial model.

Among the other articles by contemporary Etonians was a piece of propaganda in favour of British fascism ("a non-party organisation, whose primary intention is to counteract the present and ever-growing trend towards Revolution ... it is of the utmost importance that centres should be started in the universities and in our public schools") and a short story, 'The Ordeal of Caryl St George', by one signing himself I.L.F. This was Ian's first published piece: he later described it as "a shameless crib of Michael Arlen", the fashionable chronicler of London salon life, whose most famous novel *The Green Hat* had been published the previous year. Starting with some typically deft Fleming scene-setting, this was a sophisticated tale (with references even to drugs) of two lovers who are surprised by the sound of the woman's husband shooting himself downstairs. In a fit of confusion and cowardice, the male partner decides to flee, whereupon the husband appears, revealing that he has only faked his suicide to show up the shallowness of his wife's lover. He does not propose to hang around, however: she has had her fling, and now, clutching a handful of one-way railway tickets, he indicates that he is off to enjoy himself on permanent vacation in Venice. As he leaves the flat, she is beside herself with remorse. But there is a twist in the tail: "as she sank to the floor in a dead faint, she heard his steps across the landing". He was coming back and she knew that she was forgiven.

Ian later claimed that he made £90 out of this publishing venture, a figure which mirrors Ivar Bryce's so precisely that it suggests one of them was wrong. In retrospect, Bryce's *Snapdragon* was the more commercial product. Nevertheless *The Wyvern* drew plaudits in the subsequent issue of the *Eton College Chronicle*, which was edited at the time by Peter Fleming. Ian's brother welcomed "that *rara avis*, a really good ephemeral. Its editors have obviously aimed at something much higher than the conventional hotch-potch of abstruse personal allusions and mildly interesting articles, and they have succeeded in producing a very enjoyable and original literary cocktail". This was an early example of the skill Ian demonstrated throughout his subsequent career of orchestrating good reviews and public relations for himself.

For all their differences and occasional rivalry, Peter seldom stinted in his support for his younger brother. He took his obligations as head of the fatherless Fleming family seriously, and was also responsible for getting Ian into Pop. A member himself since January 1925, he first proposed his younger brother in September. But Ian received seven black balls and was not elected. He had more luck when he was put up again at the end of December: on this occasion Ian was proposed four more times and vetoed on three before being finally elected with just three black balls against his name. The president noted that the meeting finally adjourned after one hour and thirty-seven minutes "of extremely boring electioneering".

Ian's elevation to Pop indicated that he was generally liked. Because of the success of his brother, he tended to associate with older boys (like Bryce) rather than his immediate contemporaries. He shared a study – in Eton parlance, "messed with" – Robert Gladstone and Reginald Turnbull, who were both in the year above him. In his memoir *The Arms of Time* Peter's friend Rupert Hart-Davis recorded that on April Fool's Day 1926 he ate two enormous meals at the Red House, a restaurant by the River Thames. One was in the company of Peter, and the other with Ian: "they are a charming family".

While Ian did not lack social graces, he already showed signs of a pronounced and often antisocial moodiness. He made no secret of preferring his own company to that of his peers. Bryce recalled how his friend used to sit in his study on his own: Ian would say he required three-quarters of an hour's solitude each day. And although Ian had friends, he also had enemies. "He was that sort of person," said Bryce. "He aroused very positive reactions from people. No one could be indifferent to him."

Ian's brusqueness and lack of communication towards others reflected the adolescent identity crisis he was going through. The catalyst was the marked change in his mother's lifestyle. In 1923 Eve had decided to stop playing the grieving widow. Selling Pitt House, she moved to Chelsea, buying three small workers' cottages adjoining one another on the River Thames at the 'wrong' end of Cheyne Walk close to Lot's Road power station. The three houses were knocked into one, which she called Turner's House, after the painter J. M. W. Turner, who had lived there towards the end of his life. Eve had Turner's fifty-foot-long studio, at the back of the complex, extravagantly redecorated. It was hung with gold canvas wallpaper; brightly coloured sofas and cushions were festooned around the room; and a Bechstein grand was wheeled in. Then Eve proceeded to reinvent herself, no longer an aspiring political hostess, but a patron of the arts, a pillar (if such an oxymoronic position is possible) of Chelsea Bohemianism.

One of the few tangential benefits for Ian was being able to ask several of her new artistic friends to contribute to his ephemeral, *The Wyvern*. But he did not bargain for another consequence: that his mother would become romantically entangled with her near neighbour Augustus John, the leading painter of his day. It was a remarkable liaison: she not yet forty, still strikingly pretty, vivacious and, above all, rich; he charming, unkempt, lecherous and contemptuous of the well-heeled society ladies who sought his favours as portraitist and stud. Against all the odds, Eve fell deeply in love with him, and he enjoyed having a wealthy mistress and benefactor. Notwithstanding John's string of other girlfriends, Eve determined to trap him into marriage and, when this proved a vain hope, at least into siring a baby. Having had four sons, she craved a girl. The child did not even have to be hers; it simply had to be Augustus's. So, after Chiquita, one of his models-cum-mistresses, gave birth to a daughter called Zoë, Eve did her damnedest to adopt the infant. When the mother demurred, Eve persevered, first plying her with baby clothes, sewn with Fleming name-tapes, and then kidnapping Zoë and taking her to North Wales.

John put a halt to that nonsense, but Eve would not let him go. She introduced him to influential friends, including Winston Churchill and Lord D'Abernon, British Ambassador to Germany. John ruthlessly exploited them as patrons of his art. When D'Abernon invited him to Berlin in the spring of 1925, he tried to go alone, but Eve insisted on accompanying him. Both obtained what they wanted from the trip: he painted the German Chancellor Gustav Stresemann and she returned home pregnant. In the late summer, Eve summoned her staff and told them without a hint of remorse that they would have to find new employment as she was going on a lengthy cruise. She duly closed up her house and made off for the rest of the year. When she reappeared in December, she was holding a baby girl in a shawl and telling anyone who cared to listen that she had adopted a daughter, called Amaryllis. "It seems quite a humorous brat," Peter told Rupert Hart-Davis.

Ian resented the diversion of his mother's attention, the whole episode only adding to his adolescent insecurity. For four years he had toiled up the scholastic ladder at Eton, without significant success, and certainly without the plaudits which were regularly handed to Peter. Ian's best subject was languages, recalled Quintin Hogg, later the Conservative peer Lord Hailsham, who studied in the same French Division, taught by M. Larsonnier. Otherwise Ian's main interest was literature. His copy of *The City of Fear*, an evocative volume of First World War verse by the Old Etonian Gilbert Frankau survives, with the inscription "Ian L. Fleming Eton 1923". In poems like 'How Rifleman Brown Came to Valhalla', Ian discovered the awfulness of the trench warfare his father had suffered on the Western Front. Encouraged by his sybaritic friend Ivar Bryce, Ian began to withdraw slightly and see himself as a romantic Byronic figure. The early nineteenth-century poet-revolutionary was enjoying a post-war revival with two biographical studies in 1924 – one by Sir John Fox and another by Harold Nicolson, son-in-law of Eve's friend Lady Sackville – and a third in 1925 which Ian certainly bought, *The Pilgrim of Eternity: Byron – A Conflict* by John Drinkwater. (Five years later he also acquired a French biography of Byron by André Maurois.) In keeping with this dashing self-image, he became an enthusiastic supporter of the mildly avant-garde. After Leonard and Virginia Woolf's Hogarth Press had published the controversial novel *Turbott Wolfe* by the young South African William Plomer in autumn 1925, Ian was so impressed that he dashed off a fan letter which the author received in Japan and duly answered. On the surface, *Turbott Wolfe* was a steamy tale of love across the colour bar in his native South Africa. But there was another dimension to the book. In discussing interracial liaisons, the homosexual Plomer also tackled another sort of taboo relationship – between persons of the same sex, though it is not clear if Ian understood this. In a later encomium, Plomer could not remember what had so interested Fleming in the book. He felt young Ian "might have been guided by his sharp flair, like that of a mine-detector, for a new threat to dullness and complacency".

For all Ian's literary interests, they did not help him in his school results. By Michaelmas 1925, when Peter was effortlessly preparing for his Oxford entrance exams, seventeen-year-old Ian had only reached the Fifth Form's Upper Division B Second Remove. So the powerful Eve decided on drastic measures. One has to imagine the circumstances. She was in emotional turmoil over her pregnancy. Ian was suffering his own tribulations and, out of a sense of pique and bloody-mindedness, was performing poorly in the classroom. Eve resolved that, if the exceptional Peter was destined to emulate his father at Oxford, her more physical and difficult son, Ian, would surely benefit from following in Val's footsteps in the Army.

So she went to work on her royal connections. By then the Fleming reach extended directly into Buckingham Palace. Granny Katie had developed an endearing friendship with Queen Mary, who frequently descended on Joyce Grove and "admired" various attractive *objets d'art* which she expected to be sent to her. Through the Queen, Eve met George V's cousin, Princess Marie-Louise, who became a lifelong friend and who provided Amaryllis's second Christian name. Some deft string-pulling by Eve ensured that a commission would be available for Ian, if required, in the most fashionable infantry regiment, the 60th Rifles, or King's Royal Rifle Corps. Then, for the following term, the Lent quarter of 1926, she had her son pulled out of the academic mainstream and attached to Eton's Army Class Division – seven boys who were studying to enter one of the two training schools for army officers: Sandhurst, near Camberley in Surrey, for those joining infantry or cavalry regiments, or Woolwich, in south London, for potential gunners and sappers.

If not quite a repository for dunces, the Army Class was hardly designed to breed intellectuals. Ian took this message to heart, failing to understand quite why his mother had condemned him to this torment, and became rather more recalcitrant. So, with the Sandhurst exams looming in June, Eve decided to act unilaterally once again. At the end of the Lent term, just after regaining his Victor Ludorum title, he was unexpectedly removed from Eton and sent to a special tutorial college. There were respectable enough precedents: Val's friend, Winston Churchill, had attended a 'crammer' in London, and still only managed to get into Sandhurst at the third attempt.

Ian's school career had not quite finished. After reading a request for contestants in the *Eton College Chronicle*, he had entered the sprint hurdles race in the Public Schools Athletics Championship at Stamford Bridge in April and won. The *Chronicle* duly congratulated Fleming on his feat. But by that time Ian had decamped to his crammer, run by Colonel William Trevor, at Newport Pagnell in Bedfordshire.

Once again Ian was consigned to the B team. Colonel Trevor's was a traditional uncompromising establishment whose *raison d'être* was preparing stragglers and non-performers for their exams. Ian's contemporaries included Eddie and Geordie Ward, twin brothers of Lord Ednam, later the Earl of Dudley, and David Herbert, the effete son of the Earl of Pembroke. Herbert did not take to Ian: he found him amusing enough, but also "spiky" and "not at all kind about people". Ian only attended Colonel Trevor's between April and June but, during that short period, he demonstrated that he was his father's son by rallying to the established order at the time of the General Strike in May. Ian helped man the signals at Leighton Buzzard railway station, for which act of class solidarity he later received a medal from the president of the executive of the London Midland & Scottish Railway Company. The award was backed with an inscription hailing his "Generosity of Service to the Salvation of the Commonwealth", and an accompanying citation informed Ian that the medal had been struck to "commemorate the success of the loyal citizens of the country in their resistance to the menace to the constitution".

For the most part, however, Ian knuckled down to the results-orientated regime. When he sat for the Sandhurst entrance examination, he passed creditably, coming eleventh out of 120 candidates, and was given a prize cadetship. Colonel Trevor was impressed by his pupil's performance. He wrote to Eve that Ian "ought to make an excellent Soldier", though Trevor could not help adding the rider, "provided always that the Ladies don't ruin him".

Having qualified for Sandhurst, Ian returned to his other interests – literature and producing small magazines. After the success of *The Wyvern* the previous year, he planned to produce a successor, called *Medley*, for the Eton and Harrow match at Lords. He wrote a letter to potential advertisers, telling them he proposed to print 500 copies and suggesting: "It might be in your interest to advertise in it."

Medley was never published. Indeed the only evidence of its existence is a draft letter Ian composed on these lines in an old Eton exercise book. Interestingly, he signed the letter "R. Coranville", a name which had special connotations for him, because the same black-covered volume contained several of Ian's poems, philosophical jottings and even a frag-

ment of a short story, and some of the poems, though clearly in Ian's
hand, are signed with the curious, sexually ambiguous name, Cary Anan.

Ian may have done enough to please the Sandhurst examiners, but
his literary juvenilia only emphasized the extent of his adolescent soul-
searching, which can be interpreted as either intelligent introspection or
desperate *angst*. The spirit of the writing is world-weary and melancholic,
as if Ian is striving for a Byronic romantic effect. "What are words?" he
asked, rhetorically, in one of his scrapbooks. "At best a mirrored string of
thoughts." This was an idea he liked, because he followed it up with a
similar aphorism, the full effect of which can only be gained from repro-
ducing his setting and (lack of) punctuation:

> what is a book?
> a mirrored pool
> of thoughts, ideals
> so often better left unsaid
> so often better left
> with the soft outline of dream

His most promising material was his poetry. Ian wrote a chillingly spare
verse drama about a raven watching a kestrel drop from the sky and devour
a thrush. He also tried his hand at short stories. Eve's new friends in the
Chelsea arts crowd may have contributed to the cynical tone of a story
fragment, called 'Purple Domesticity', about a writer who asked an artist
to illustrate his book which he says is about "style, just style". The artist
nonchalantly "throw(s) paint at [his canvas] from a distance of two yards"
and knocks off his commission in four hours. But when the book is
published, the author is fêted (in 'Books and Bookies') for "the depth of
feeling in the script" and the artist for "the breadth of conception in the
illustrations". And in case anyone had not understood the message, Ian
parodies the critics, saying, "Deep, deep, stuff. Broad, broad, yet how high,
how high."

If Ian was disdainful of what passed for sophistication in London, he
cared little either for his hearty family's excursions across the border
into Scotland – "all those dripping evergreens", he used to describe the
landscape there. He did not seek to benefit from the codicil to his father's
will which stipulated extra monies to any of his sons who spent more
than two months a year at Arnisdale. While at Eton, he dutifully went
through the motions and joined the Flemings at their annual gatherings
on a succession of rented estates in the Highlands. Glen Borrodale, a
bizarre red sandstone castle in Caithness, at the furthest tip of Scotland,
was the most interesting. Grandfather Robert had rented it from a Paisley

mill-owner made good. The owner's son, Kenneth Clark, the art historian, remembered letting the castle to a "grim old Scottish financier called Fleming, who might have been the hero of Hatter's Castle". The tenant had a "a very pretty daughter-in-law" who interested young Clark. But he could not get near her "because she had four brilliantly equipped sons, three of whom, Peter, Ian and Michael, scared the wits out of me, and continued to do so when I met them in later life". Then there was Braemore in Caithness, Rannoch in Perthshire and, finally, Black Mount in Argyllshire, a magnificent 90,000-acre deer forest which Robert Fleming rented in 1924 and later bought outright from the impoverished Breadalbane family. At Black Mount, sixteen-year-old Ian shot his first stag on 9 September 1924, and then five more on the 11th, 17th, 18th, 19th and 22nd.

But his heart was not in it. At his mother's *haute bohémienne* salon in Cheyne Walk, his idea of artistic endeavour was playing the Hawaiian guitar (he took lessons from an Italian woman). He liked to put his feet up to a record of the Royal Hawaiian Serenaders when, as he put it, he "should have been out of doors killing something". Unlike Eve, an accomplished violinist, his musical tastes were moulded in Tin Pan Alley. At Eton, his favourite song – indicative of leisure pursuits, perhaps – was the popular 'Does Your Mother Know You're Out, Cecilia' by the baritone, Whispering Jack Smith.

Even at that stage Ian enjoyed doing things which were exotic and slightly unusual. In August 1924 he had spent a summer holiday in the mountains around Engadine in Switzerland. So, two years later, he was quite happy when his mother suggested that, before going to Sandhurst, he might like to spend a couple of months in Austria brushing up his languages. From a friend she had learned of the Tennerhof, a finishing school for young gentlemen in Kitzbühel, run in slightly cranky fashion by Ernan Forbes Dennis, a former British diplomat and spy, and his American-born wife who wrote novels under the name Phyllis Bottome. After the trials of the examination room, Ian resisted the couple's attempts to interest him in the French classics. The balmy Alpine summer offered other diversions, and Ian treated his two months in Kitzbühel as if he were at a glorified holiday camp. He climbed 2000 feet to the top of the Kitzbühler Horn before dawn. He swam in the Schwarzsee with middle-class holiday-makers from Munich and Vienna. And he sampled the joys of Austrian café life, where his aloof good looks were much appreciated by the local girls.

Ian was still mentally attuned to the easy freedoms of Austria when he arrived at the Royal Military College at Sandhurst on 3 September to start the regular eighteen-month training course for officers. Gentleman Cadet Fleming was attached to 20 Platoon of Number 5 Company, commanded by Major Lord Ailwyn. Few of that year's 5 Company intake went on to scale great heights militarily: the best known was a young Punjabi, Ayub Khan, who joined the Indian army and later became President of Pakistan.

Even after the exigencies of Eton, Sandhurst provided a rigorous regime. Ian spent his first six weeks 'square bashing', or drilling up and down the college's main parade-ground, the Old Building Square, being bawled at by a series of unsympathetic regimental sergeant-majors. Ian was kitted out for uniform: a khaki tunic, plus-fours, puttees and boots for military parades and exercises; red and white striped blazer, white flannels, brown shoes and red and white silk square for everyday wear, including lessons; and 'blue patrol' consisting of formal jacket and blue trousers with a red stripe down the side for dinners and other ceremonial occasions. He was tested for other skills such as riding, which he hated, and shooting, in which he took some enjoyment. Four afternoons a week were devoted to games, with inter-Company matches on Saturdays. There was little time for other activities: everything was done at the double or, if that was not quick enough, on bicycles.

In common with his fellow cadets, Ian always appeared to be parading somewhere or other. His day started with a pre-breakfast 'shaving parade' when everyone had his uniform inspected. The strict regimentation continued right through the day until after supper, when Ian had to stand outside his room, while another of the non-commissioned officers, whose business was to make life unpleasant for the well-heeled cadets, inspected his rifle, kit and living quarters.

After being 'broken in', Ian was introduced to military topics such as tactics, weapons training and map reading. An element of constitutional history was thrown in for good measure. At the end of his first term, his performance was judged to have been adequate, but unspectacular. He received 882 marks out of a possible 1350, coming 141st in the order of merit. Sporting achievement was considered important, and, as a hurdler, Ian gained some kudos by stepping straight into the Sandhurst athletics team. Major Lord Ailwyn was happy at what he saw and reported to Eve that her son should do well.

Already the budding officer was beginning to rail against college restrictions. More than ever in this environment, he needed his solitude. But free time was difficult to come by, and getting out of the place even harder. Cadets needed written permission to visit private houses and only in special circumstances were they allowed out after 10 p.m.

This proved especially galling when, as was bound to happen, Ian fell seriously in love for the first time. He was introduced to Peggy Barnard, the pretty daughter of a former Indian army colonel, by her best friend, Biddy Pellatt, the younger daughter of his former prep-school headmaster.

Peggy had a neat, attractive figure, fair curly hair and violet eyes with long lashes. Cyril Connolly who pursued her later said her face had "a look of alertness, intelligence, good sense and cupidity, all of which vanish into an occasional melting smile". Biddy suggested contacting Ian at Sandhurst because he owned a car, a battered two-seater khaki-coloured Standard tourer. Since Peggy came from a strict military background, Ian was at his most correct when he first came to her parents' house in nearby Fleet, accompanied by a fellow cadet. She found him "extremely attractive, delightful, irresistible" and he began to write to her daily. Soon he was allowed to take Peggy for drives in the commuter belt. Their favourite trysting-place was a respectable pub, the Hind's Head, not far from Eton, at Bray on the River Thames. They hired what she described as an electric punt for afternoons messing about on the river. Then they joined the *thé dansant* where Peggy was not the last woman to remark on his lack of skill as a dancer. In *The Spy Who Loved Me*, Ian had this place in mind when he (or, rather, his heroine Vivienne Michel) wrote, "That day he took me as far as Bray, to show off the car, and we tore through the lanes with Derek doing quite unnecessary racing changes on the flattest curves ... He took me to a fearfully smart place, the Hotel de Paris, and we had smoked salmon, which cost extra, and roast chicken and ice cream and then he hired an electric canoe from the boat-house next door and we chugged sedately up-river and under Maidenhead Bridge and found a little back-water, just this side of Cookham Lock, where Derek rammed the canoe far in under the branches. He had brought a portable gramophone with him and I scrambled down to his end of the canoe and we sat and later lay side by side and listened to the records and watched a small bird hopping about in the network of branches over our heads. It was a beautiful, drowsy afternoon and we kissed but didn't go any further ..."

At the same time Ian was taking his first tentative steps into London society. His combination of good looks, private income and military uniform was popular at debutantes' dances – at least as far as mothers, looking for eligible escorts for their daughters, were concerned. He himself never liked the big occasions, and it showed. He failed to impress Janet Aitken, Lord Beaverbrook's daughter and one of that year's crop of debutantes. She mixed in the most fashionable circles, including Londonderry House on Park Lane, where 'Circe' or Edith, the wife of the 7th Marquess of Londonderry, held court. Compared with her escorts, Ivor Guest, the son of Lord Wimborne, and Prince George, later Duke of Kent, she found Ian "rather boring", adding retrospectively that he was "ruminating too much perhaps on the future adventures of James Bond". More likely, he wished he was at the Kit Kat or Embassy, one of the fashionable nightclubs of the time. These places offered a moneyed English version of twenties America, with short skirts, the 'Charleston', and a mixture of ragtime and jazz music. Ian loved the energy and informality of it all.

Ian responded to the mixture of discipline and opportunity by ignoring the Sandhurst rules. He frequently stayed out late. One morning John Stephens, a fellow member of the athletics team, was preparing for the regular 'shaving parade' when he saw someone running down the passage towards him. It was Ian, looking bleary-eyed and hung-over, improbably attired in full evening dress, including tails. Stephens was senior under-officer, the top cadet rank, in 5 Company (also known as Champion Company because of its success in various competitions). Theoretically he could have disciplined Ian. Instead Ian implored his assistance to get to the parade in time. Stephens, later a brigadier in the Gurkhas, bundled Ian into his room and helped him off with his clothes. He then took him at the double to the shower room and "made him have a good soaking". He forced Ian to pull on his uniform and got him to the square just in time. "He had a lot to thank me for," recalled Stephens.

Ian still refused to take his future as an army officer seriously. When he was caught climbing over the wall yet again, he was severely reprimanded, and it seemed that he would be "gated" for most of his last or "senior" term. Major Lord Ailwyn once more seemed unperturbed. In his report for the "intermediate" term ending July 1927, he said Ian had "all the qualities to make an officer" but needed to "make the best of what is, to him, a bad job and settle down".

High jinks at Sandhurst have never been a bar to military preferment. Bernard Montgomery, later Field Marshal Montgomery of Alamein, was once carpeted for setting fire to a fellow cadet in a dormitory. Ian, too, might have made a good soldier one day, commanding in the Western Desert, perhaps, or leading a commando unit. That was not to be, however, for his army career came to an abrupt end, as Colonel Trevor had predicted, because of "the Ladies". He was still much in love with Peggy who, during the summer, was invited to meet his mother in Cheyne Walk. Eve seemed to take to Ian's pert young friend, who arrived in a state of considerable embarrassment because a child had been sick all over her legs in the train travelling up to Waterloo. Eve could not have been more solicitous, telling Peggy, as soon as she arrived at Turner's House, to remove her stockings and her maid would wash them immediately. Another time, when Peggy went to spend the weekend at Joyce Grove, Eve gave an unaccompanied recital on her violin after dinner. At the end Peggy blurted out, "Oh, that was lovely, it sounded just like the bagpipes" – a remark which received a frosty reception. Nevertheless, at the end of the summer term, she accompanied Eve to the Sandhurst annual sports day where they watched Ian winning the hurdles. Afterwards, a man arrived to take Peggy to an Oxford Commemoration ball. She had already told Ian about this long-standing arrangement. But he was still angry and, bursting with passionate first love, begged her to pull out and spend the evening with him. Otherwise, he threatened, he would go up to London and "find myself a tart". Being well-brought-up, Peggy felt unable to let her other suitor down. That evening Ian duly made his way to the 43 Club in Soho. He did not demur when a hostess arrived at his table and asked if he wanted to share a bottle of champagne. After a hasty coupling in a back room he returned to his mother's house where, a few days later, he found, to his horror, that he had contracted a dose of gonorrhoea.

Ian was no stranger to his mother's wrath. This time she tore into him mercilessly. He had let down the family, the regiment, her friends, all that she held dear. She had obtained royal patronage for him, and now her reputation at court would be in ruins. Apart from that, gonorrhoea was a dangerous and antisocial disease. Taking every opportunity to humiliate her son, she booked him into a nursing home in Beaumont Street for a residential course of treatment. Then she contacted Sandhurst informing the authorities that Ian had been taken ill, and requesting that, although he was due to be commissioned at the end of the year, he should be allowed a term away from his course to recover. A note was placed on Ian's official record: "Drop term – sickness." But within a short time Eve had reassessed her son's position. His behaviour was clearly symptomatic of some deeper malaise which needed sorting out. Although Ian too was convinced he was not cut out for a military career, it was with a heavy heart and sense of shame that he fell in with his domineering mother's wishes, and, some time in August, composed a letter of resignation to Major-General C. E. Corkran, the Commandant at Sandhurst. The record was changed to read curtly, "Resigned w.e.f. 1 Sep 1927."

In later years Ian put the whole incident out of his mind by lying about it profusely. In one of his last interviews before he died in 1964, he told the American journalist Ken Purdy, "I didn't become a soldier after passing out from Sandhurst because they suddenly decided to mechanize the Army and a lot of my friends and I decided that we did not want to be glorified garage hands – no more polo, no more pig-sticking and all that jazz." This was hilarious enough – Ian as a polo player! He even got the date wrong, continuing with a *non-sequitur*, "This would have been round about 1925, and disillusionment of that kind – and kinds more severe – was common then, as you know." Intriguingly, there was some kernel of truth in this elliptical statement. Ian was trying to say that he was an immature child of the jazz age, and military discipline was not for him.

2
Foreign initiation
1927–1933

Having encouraged Ian to become a soldier, and then forced him to pull back, Eve had not yet finished with her son. She felt his 'disgrace' personally, believing that she had done everything in her power to bring up her children in accordance with her husband's wishes. Yet Ian, the boy with whom she outwardly had most in common, continued to defy her. He, in turn, could not understand how he managed to incur her anger so unfailingly. He loved his beautiful mother, but she seemed for ever to be telling him he was no good, a disgrace to his father's memory. On a superficial level, two powerful egos were engaged, while deeper down Ian struggled to come to terms with the conflict between his conventional upbringing and his growing reputation as the black sheep of his family.

If Ian did not know how to deal with this perplexing situation, Eve did. She had decided to send him away, somewhere where he could resolve his adolescent anxieties and discover himself as a young man, without further embarrassing her and, she liked to think, the family. Initially she wanted to despatch him beyond the civilized pale to Australia, before wiser counsels prevailed, and she arranged for him to return to the Villa Tennerhof in Kitzbühel for further schooling.

She was encouraged in this latter course after Peter had spent a short time at the same establishment during the summer, his first long vacation from Christ Church, Oxford. Ostensibly her eldest son needed to brush up his German, but the burdens of single parenthood were weighing particularly heavily on Eve, and she was determined that he should escape the romantic attentions of Sybil Mayor, the French-born foster-child of Granny Katie's sister, with whom he had become besotted. Peter cut a swath through the Tennerhof. His effortless intelligence made an immediate impression on Ernan Forbes Dennis, who contrasted it favourably with Ian's temperamental intransigence the previous year. Curiously, Peter felt the same towards Austria as Ian did to Scotland, complaining to Rupert Hart-Davis, "It rains most of the time, and in the intervals one gloomily climbs a mountain."

Eve had charged Forbes Dennis with keeping her eldest son in Kitzbühel until 31 July 1927, when Peter was due to join Ian and the rest of his family for a holiday on the north-west coast of Ireland. She had taken a house in County Donegal, where the Fleming brothers were joined by their childhood friends, Primrose and Dido Harley, and by Rupert Hart-Davis and his beautiful, doe-eyed sister, Deirdre, who had just turned eighteen.

In the meantime, in an outrageously manipulative manner, Eve had prevailed on Ian to write to Peggy calling off their affair. The agreed "party line" was apparent in his unconvincing protestations that he had decided that they were too young; it might be better if they did not see each other any more; he was sure she would find someone else. The unfortunate Peggy was being made a scapegoat for Ian's troubles, and he played along.

Inviting the Hart-Davises to Ireland was a charitable act by the essentially warm-hearted Eve. Both teenagers were recovering from the early death of their once vivacious mother, another Sybil, in January. The daughter of a prominent surgeon, Sir Alfred Cooper, 'Sibbie' had been a leading light in literary and artistic circles just before the First World War. She had wanted to translate J. M. Synge's *Playboy of the Western World* into French, and was drawn by William Nicholson and by Augustus John, who had been her lover several years before Eve appeared on the scene. Her brother Duff Cooper was already forging a name for himself, having swapped a promising career at the Foreign Office for the greasy pole of politics in 1924. He made a fashionable marriage to Lady Diana Manners, daughter of the Duke of Rutland, who found fame as an actress, notably in the long-running play, *The Miracle*. But Sibbie herself had turned her back on her gilded existence, lapsing in her later years into a curious melancholy, before turning to Roman Catholicism and dying.

Deirdre was particularly devastated. She had been close to her mother who had introduced her to many of her writer and artist friends. Arthur Symons was so taken by Deirdre's innocent beauty (aged eight) that he composed a poem to her in the Café Royal. The last verse ran:

She had taken my hand, then turned
Her eyes on me, pure as the sky.
If ever a man's heart to her yearned,
Mine did, I know not why.

Ian could see what the poet meant when he first met Deirdre at Ards House, the villa Eve had rented on the windswept Atlantic shore on the border of the newly formed Irish Free State. With Eve's attention focused on the infant Amaryllis, the older boys and girls amused themselves, swimming, organizing picnics and fishing in an antiquated motor boat. In the evenings they stayed indoors, playing games and reading. A photograph shows all four Fleming brothers in the drawing-room with books in their hands. A haughty Peter is engrossed in his volume, oblivious to any intrusion; Richard (in a kilt) is confident, every inch the aspiring banker; Michael appears round, jovial and bored; while Ian wears a pleasant, rather supercilious expression, the only one making a conscious effort to project to camera.

During six weeks in Ireland, two discreet liaisons developed amongst the young people: Ian with Deirdre, and Rupert with Primrose Harley. Both Ian and Deirdre were in the same reflective mood, he because of the sorry consequences of the last few weeks, and she following the death of her mother. Ian needed someone intelligent and sympathetic to talk to, partly about his sense of dejection at having let his family down, and partly, with an adolescent's earnestness, about growing up and seeking to define his experiences in literature. Deirdre was very aware that the spectre of Eve weighed heavily on Ian. Over fifty years later she recalled, "He and his mother argued all the time. She didn't trust what he wanted to do, and he had a hopeless feeling that he could simply do no right in her eyes."

Unlike the extrovert Peggy, Deirdre was bookish and reserved; by her own admission, young for her age. His gentleman cadet's confidence partly dashed, Ian reverted to an earlier faltering romanticism, rediscovering an aptitude for verse as he struggled to express his feelings for Deirdre in couplets like: "How much I loved that way you had / of smiling most when very sad." In keeping with his mental state, he had a more agonized line: "If the wages of sin are Death / I am willing to pay" and "I am so weary of the curse of living / the endless, aimless torture, tumult, fears." But he could also show touches of humour:

> There once was a girl named Asoka
> Who played three young fellows at poker
> Having won all their money
> She thought it so funny
> They calmly decided to choke her.

Then, halfway through September, Ian was dragged away from this burgeoning romance. "Eve, you have no right to be sending as attractive a boy as that over to the Continent," grumbled kindly Granny Katie as she watched her uncomprehending grandson kitted out with warm sweaters and lederhosen at Joyce Grove, before being packed off into the care of the Forbes Dennises. Luckily for Ian, it turned out to be an inspired stroke and, before long, this unlikely couple would become the seminal influences on his life. Ernan was a handsome Scot whose slight prissiness was a legacy of severe wounds on the Western Front at the end of the First World War. Phyllis, his wife, was a successful writer, whose Quaker background gave her a strong sense of moral purpose. After the war they had lived in the devastated city of Vienna where Forbes Dennis worked as the British government's passport control officer with responsibility for Austria, Hungary and Yugoslavia. The post was more interesting than it sounded. According to convention, the office of passport control officer provided cover for members of the Secret Intelligence Service (SIS) or MI6.

Forbes Dennis was not a man to be tied down in a profession like espionage. He was an idealist with a deeper sense of vocation, and his wife encouraged him to develop that side of his character. Without initially having a precise idea, he wanted to work in education, which the horrors of war had convinced him held the key to a more tolerant world. In 1925 he took a diploma from London University to teach German. But that same year his wife was stricken with tuberculosis and, although she quickly recovered, this was the spur the Forbes Dennises needed to realize their dream of acquiring a house in an area with a good climate and good sports facilities, where they would set up a school for British and American boys wanting to learn German.

They found what they were looking for in the small Tyrolean town of Kitzbühel. Situated at 3000 feet in the Eastern Alps, Kitzbühel stood in a lush valley protected on three sides by snow-capped mountains. Winter sports were becoming fashionable after the war, and Kitzbühel, with a railway station on the route of the transcontinental Arlberg Express, was one of the first resorts to understand the long-term economic potential. Running water had only been introduced in the 1920s. By March 1928 the first moving cabin had been built to take skiers up the Hahnenkamm. The price for one trip, including insurance and the use of skis and a rucksack, was six Austrian schillings. At the time there were 72 schillings to the pound, which helped make it an attractive destination for English holiday-makers.

After one false start, the Forbes Dennises rented the Tennerhof, a substantial villa set in a sloping meadow of apple trees on the Kitzbühler Horn side of the valley. An important criterion was that the building was large enough to accommodate some twenty pupils. Even so, the Forbes Dennises did without a private apartment and lived almost communally with their young charges.

After Ian's crisis, Forbes Dennis had suggested to Eve that her son should return to Kitzbühel for the winter to "see what we can do". He convinced her that his own carefully developed educational philosophy had something to offer. Always intellectually curious, he was particularly interested in what makes boys tick. Dissatisfied with the uncompromising approaches of Freud and Jung, he had found what he wanted in the writings of the Austrian psychologist, Dr Alfred Adler. In examining human nature, Adler had evolved a post-Freudian synthesis which he called the science of individual psychology, several tenets of which seemed to apply to Ian. The good doctor was not alone in believing that the first five years of a child's life were very important. His unique contribution was to suggest that, during this formative period, a child adopts a member of his family as a 'Gegenspieler', with whom he then competes at all costs in a frenzied, neurotic manner. Sometimes the Gegenspieler is a parent but, more often, thought Adler, it is a living brother or sister, by whom the child feels usurped or bettered. The problem is that, unless treated, this unconscious neurosis is destined to repeat itself in subsequent close relationships, with the child, even as an adult, exhibiting the same antagonism towards anyone he loves.

Adler claimed that the neurotic individual in this situation cuts himself off from society "by a mechanism consisting of hypersensitiveness and intolerance". He falls back on a much smaller group which he tries to dominate in order to gain a feeling of superiority. "Thus estranged from reality, the neurotic man lives a life of imagination and fantasy, and employs a number of devices enabling him to side-step the demands of reality, and for reaching out towards an ideal situation which would free him of any service for the community and absolve him from responsibility." The cure, as posited by Adler, was to change the patient's environment entirely and "turn him definitely and unconditionally back into human society".

This indeed was what Villa Tennerhof attempted to do. It was not exactly an Adlerian forcing house, nor was Ian outstandingly neurotic. But these were the Forbes Dennises' broad principles as they set about their task of reconciling a still shattered Ian to himself and the world. Despite its prevailing culture, the school was unstuffy. The Forbes Dennises treated their pupils as guests. There were hardly any rules, only a timetable which dictated the course of their day. Lessons were always conducted between breakfast and lunchtime. (Phyllis Bottome used this period to write – scribbling furiously in bed.) Then the boys spent the afternoon outside engaged in "active sports". From teatime to supper, they prepared for the next day's work in their own rooms. After supper they rearranged the furniture in the big dining-room so that they could play table tennis and listen to the gramophone.

Forbes Dennis's first educational task was to encourage Ian to enjoy the process of learning – something the boy had spurned in the wake of his older brother – and then to harness his lively ambition to some realizable goal; in his case, this was to be the highly competitive examinations for the Foreign Office.

The syllabus for the examinations offered Forbes Dennis considerable scope in devising a tailor-made course which would give Ian the sort of broad-based education he had hitherto neglected. Languages, the *sine qua non* of diplomacy, were not a problem. Ian already spoke French and

German well. His skills were honed by Forbes Dennis's idiosyncratic but effective method, which was to have two teachers, one who spoke the pupil's own tongue, and the other the language he was trying to learn.

During his studies Ian translated the complete text of *Anja and Esther*, a play by Klaus Mann, from German into English. Quite why Ian bothered with this inconsequential work by Thomas Mann's brother is not clear. It is a dreamlike period piece set in an old monastery which has been transformed into a home for fallen children. But the finished product so delighted Ian's mother that she had it typed up and bound in handsome black card, with a printed sticker proclaiming: '*Anja and Esther*, A play in seven scenes by Klaus Mann, Translated from the German by Ian Fleming'. Ian's first publication had been completed.

Additional volumes – all proudly bound – show how Forbes Dennis worked to broaden his pupil's interests. He encouraged him to study modern history (in French) and to follow a London University degree course in English literature. One of the books contains Ian's neat notes on the Peninsular War, another a series of model answers, which can only have been supplied by Forbes Dennis himself, to questions on Byron, Shelley and Keats. Outside the classroom Forbes Dennis introduced Ian to the classics of European literature. Years later, in *Thrilling Cities*, Ian – with, perhaps, minor embellishment – recalled the wide range of his influences (unfortunately he had forgotten how to spell his teachers' name): "I remember in those days before the war, reading, thanks to the encouragement of the Forbes Denises, the works of Kafka, Musil, the Zweigs, Arthur Schnitzler, Werfel, Rilke, von Hofmannstal [sic], and of those bizarre psychologists Weininger and Groddeck – let alone the writings of Adler and Freud – and buying first editions (I used to collect them) illustrated by Kokoschka and Kubin."

As he immersed himself in books and words, Ian became conscious of the power of his imagination. His mentor in this field was Phyllis Bottome, building on foundations laid at Durnford by Nell Pellatt. As the evenings drew in that winter, the silver-haired novelist would gather her young men around her, either at the supper table or afterwards in her workroom, and she would begin to weave a tale. They were expected to contribute their own embellishments to the story. The competition to tell the most spell-binding saga was often palpable since two other pupils, apart from Ian, went on to become writers – Ralph Arnold, the novelist and publisher, and Nigel Dennis, Ernan's nephew and author of the successful play, *Cards of Identity*. All subsequently attested to the profound influence Phyllis Bottome had on their work and choice of career.

As later often happened with his books, Ian found some of his best material closest to hand. He was fascinated by the exploits of the local aristocrats, the von Lambergs. The Graf (or Count) Max von Lamberg had a formidable reputation for drinking and womanizing. While his wife and three children lived in the family castle, a sugary Gothic confection called the Schloss Kaps, Graf Max camped out in a nearby chalet with a blonde mistress who worked in the photographer's shop and who was consequently known as the Photo-Grafin. Count Max's exotic sister, Paula, was a close neighbour in the Schloss Lebenberg. She was an artist and sportswoman, who was widely known as the best female ski-jumper in the world. She married a Czech adventurer who adopted the name 'Count Schlick' and who started the first ski club in Kitzbühel. Schlick ran through her money, but not before introducing her to motor racing which led to her death. She was competing with her husband in a race at Salzburg, when she mysteriously fell out of the car and was killed. Local gossip had it that she was pushed by Schlick who, having inherited her castle and land, methodically sold it off piece by piece. Ian liked to concoct stories about the evils perpetrated by Schlick, including graphic details of tortures the villainous Count devised. Phyllis Bottome wrote a rather more sober account of this colourful set-up in her book *Devil's Due*, also known as *Wind in His Fists*, which she described as the first ever skiing novel. She took it to Hollywood where John Emerson, a producer married to the fashionable author Anita Loos, wanted to film it, until he discovered its potentially salacious subject matter.

Phyllis also encouraged Ian to set some of his tales down on paper. Only one, dated 1927, has survived in full. Titled "A Poor Man Escapes", it tells the story of a ragged old man who, following the death of his wife one freezing snowswept Christmas Day, pawns his belongings and uses the proceeds to buy himself coffee, cakes and vermouth in Vienna's smartest café. After paying for his treat, he falls asleep in a haze of contentment, only to be rudely woken by a waiter who, thinking he is a tramp, wants to throw him out. He protests: he has paid his bill and is entitled to stay, but the management is unconvinced and calls the police. As he waits, the old man remembers he has a bottle in his back pocket. He pulls it out and finds it is labelled POISON. As he hears the policeman arriving at the café, he takes a swig. By the time the law reaches his table, he has slumped down dead. The manager says, "There he is, asleep again. He has no money, arrest him. He can't pay his bill." The story ends, "But Henrik had paid and was rich for the first time in his life." It is a poignant piece of writing, marked by its imaginative leap (it must have been hard for an English banker's son to describe the feelings of a Viennese tramp) and by its evocative sense of place.

The Forbes Dennis regime was beginning to work. The couple's faith in his abilities inspired in Ian a new confidence, which manifested itself as much outside the classroom as inside. The girls he had met in the Café

Reisch the previous year now became regular companions. Chief among them was Lisl Jokl, a plain-looking Jewish girl who was eight years older than he. At the café one evening, she and her friends saw Ian come in, order a coffee and, true to form, start reading a book on his own. He was noticeable not just for his good looks – "with sleepy blue eyes and a romantic face" recalled Lisl – but also because he was wearing a navy blue knitted shirt, of a type never seen in Kitzbühel before, as well as a pair of dirty grey-flannel trousers.

The girls giggled among themselves trying to decide how they could meet him. Their solution was that Nini, the prettiest, would walk past his table and, in the process, accidentally on purpose, she would manage to trip over his legs. This she duly did, but when Ian stooped to see if she was all right, she fluffed her lines, and the whole incident became a big joke. So the introductions were made, and Ian soon became an honorary member of Lisl's sorority which – at the weekends and during the summer months – was boosted by several rich young bourgeois from Vienna.

Ian took immediately to their uncomplicated outdoor lifestyle, which revolved around skiing in winter and swimming and tennis in summer. In the fresh Alpine air, there was little attempt at sexual restraint. The girls found Ian amusing and fun. They did not have to worry about him hanging around as a husband or a neighbour for the next fifty years. So it was not long before Ian had resumed his interrupted sex life. He always remained an eager proponent of sexual liberation, though he did later affect to show some reservation about the manner in which Austrian girls threw themselves at his young English body. "Technique in bed is important," he wrote, somewhat bizarrely, in one of his notebooks, "but alone it is the scornful coupling that makes the affairs of Austrians with Anglo-Saxons so fragmentary and in the end so distasteful."

While he fooled around with the local girls, he had not forgotten his sweetheart at home. Throughout his first year in Kitzbühel, he kept up a regular correspondence with Deirdre, usually enclosing a poem with any letter he sent. Dating is difficult, but the following was certainly part of his output:

Were it not for vain imagining
I could let time for ever pass
Without a thought.
But now the tinsel mist that memory brings
Colours my loneliness.
Since I met you, I see you everywhere
The azure of your eyes, your red, red lips
The golden mystery of your hair.

Well, now I am content
To pass my life in dreams
Of when we meet again.

Until that time, until he was reunited with Deirdre, Ian often went hiking in the hills with his male friends from the Villa Tennerhof. Sometimes they spent a couple of nights in Alpine huts before descending to the Haus St Franziskus, a café on the run down from the Kitzbühler Horn, where he would order a 'brunch' of coffee and his favourite dish of scrambled eggs. He put this experience to good use in "Octopussy", his short story about an army major who tricks a local Kitzbühel mountain guide into taking him to a hut where he knows two bars of Nazi gold have been hidden. Then the Franziskaner Halt was "an uninhabited mountaineers' refuge on a saddle just below the highest of the easterly peaks of the Kaiser mountains, that awe-inspiring range of giant stone teeth that give Kitzbühel its threatening northern horizon".

At the end of six months, Forbes Dennis felt he had seen enough of young Fleming to pronounce on his future. Eve had given serious thought to this while her son was away. She still dreamed of his entering one of the manly, old-fashioned professions: if he could not emulate his father as an army officer, a career in the diplomatic service might be the next best thing. When she asked Forbes Dennis about this, he was delighted, as he had already begun to point Ian in that direction. Demonstrating a useful gift for flattering rich parents, he told Mrs Fleming reassuringly that, although Ian was still a trifle undisciplined, with a bit of application, the lad could could be a serious candidate for the Foreign Office examinations in 1931 or 1932.

"Ian's qualities are considerable," Forbes Dennis informed Mrs Fleming in a letter from the Tennerhof in February 1928. "His general intelligence is above the average; he has imagination and originality, with the power of self expression. He has excellent taste; a love of books, and a definite desire both for truth and knowledge. He is virile and ambitious; generous and kind-hearted." On the downside, Ian still had some growing-up to do. At nineteen, he had yet to discover how to handle the varying demands of his complex personality. He was "going through the most difficult period of his development. With unusual physical and intellectual maturity he has not yet acquired mental discipline or a working philosophy. He therefore lacks stability and direction. His ambitions are considerable but vague. He has not yet learnt to enjoy work or to subordinate his impulses to his permanent aims, nor has he yet grown out of the schoolboy's fear of authority and the mental dishonesty which such fear often produces. This, coupled with the strength of his desires, often makes him below his theoretically high standard of conduct. These facts should not cause dismay. He requires time, in order that he may learn to handle a complex nature." Personally, Forbes Dennis was amused to note that, as with many difficult youths, Ian was remarkably conformist. When he ordered a pair of flannels with a pinkish hue, Ian commented disdainfully, "But there's not a grocer's assistant in the country who would be seen buried in them."

Forbes Dennis's report only encouraged Eve in her long-term plans. When Ian was next in London in the late spring, she arranged for him to appear before a Foreign Office Selection Board. The procedure was simple enough: any time after attaining the age of nineteen, a prospective candidate could go before a Selection Board which would pronounce on his general suitability for the diplomatic service. Later, aged between twenty-two and twenty-five, he would be required to take a written examination. Prodded by his mother, Ian asked two carefully selected family friends to vouch for him: Lord D'Abernon, until recently British Ambassador in Berlin, and E. E. Holmes, the former vicar of Sonning, now Archdeacon of London. Holmes considered Ian "exactly the type of character needed in the diplomatic service today". He did not deny some of the problems associated with Ian's candidature, but felt they could be turned to his advantage. "His chief fault has been an independence of character which, while sometimes leading him into boyish scrapes, augers [sic] well for his stability and work as a man, & I believe that his defects as a boy will turn into asssets as a servant of his country." At 11.30 a.m on May Day 1928, a Tuesday, Ian duly made his way from Turner's House to 6 Burlington Gardens where his initial interview for the Foreign Office was chaired by the First Civil Service Commissioner, R. S. (later Sir Roderick) Meiklejohn. It was a daunting encounter: also present on the Board were Sir Hubert Montgomery, the Assistant Under-Secretary of State for Foreign Affairs, a Private Secretary to the Secretary of State, a General and three MPs.

Ian did not falter at this hurdle. His next task was to prepare himself adequately for the written examination in three or four years' time. Languages were his strong point, but there was always room for improvement. With this in mind, Forbes Dennis suggested Ian might benefit from spells at the universities of Munich (where he would be required to speak German) and Geneva (where the language of instruction was French).

At this stage Ian felt he had earned a decent holiday. Deirdre was visiting Venice for the summer season with her chaperone, Marie Ozanne. The plump and puritanical Miss Ozanne had been one of Sybil Hart-Davis's best friends. The eldest of three daughters of a French Protestant clergyman in Calais, she ran a well-known finishing-school in Paris which Sybil had attended two years previously. En route to Italy to see his love, Ian composed a poem, proudly entitled "On Crossing the Brenner Pass":

While everyone was feeling tired and hot
Alone I was in love with all the world
I felt how far apart I was from all the train,
I thought I was a part of some small stream
Just on from all the scrambling rivulets
Which hurried down towards the sunkissed south
Eager to greet the emerald sea which lay
Flawlessly still in amber gold setting.

A fragment of a short story described his arrival. "Venice station was at its hottest, dustiest, dirtiest. Tony stepped out of the frying pan of his train into its fire. His collar freed itself from his neck in a stream of perspiration." Deirdre was staying in a hotel with Wanda Holden, another of Marie Ozanne's charges. Sadly for Ian, she was being "fiercely chaperoned". After she was forbidden to join him in a gondola, Ian came round to visit. But Miss Ozanne "suspected all young men" (she had once counselled young Nancy Cunard, "Nancy, attention aux hommes"). So Ian's meetings with Deirdre amounted to little more than "whispered conversation, all very unsatisfactory".

With an eye perhaps to another publishing venture, on his return to London Ian collected his poems in a book called *The Black Daffodil*. Ian showed Ivar Bryce the slim, black volume but later became so embarrassed by its juvenile contents that he rounded up and burned every copy. Now, as he began to regain his self-assurance, he was less introspective and acted more overtly like a rich young man with money to spend. With Ivar Bryce, who was studying in Strasbourg, he explored the restaurants and night life of Paris. On one occasion they met at the Larue, a gourmets' paradise on the rue Royale, to "catch up on each other's affairs". As Bryce doodled on the menu, coming up with "Fine Lingam" as an appropriate anagram of "Ian Fleming", his friend spoke for the first time of his ambition to write thrillers.

Cars were now an abiding interest of Ian's. With delight he recorded his thrill when, driving a three-litre Bugatti along a long straight stretch outside Henley, close to Joyce Grove, he first exceeded 100 m.p.h. on the open road. His own car was his more modest Standard Tourer, which he drove at breakneck speeds around Kitzbühel. Once, returning to the Villa Tennerhof, he arrived at a level crossing at the same time as a train. The front of his car was hit, and the vehicle was dragged for fifty yards before Ian emerged, shaken but not badly hurt, from the wreckage.

Following Forbes Dennis's suggestion, Ian enrolled as an external student at Munich University in the autumn of 1928. He found a room as a paying guest with the Mirbachs, an aristocratic family from Roggenburg, near Ulm, who kept a house in the Habsburgerstrasse in Munich. Even now, Forbes Dennis was never far away, remaining in the background to advise on educational and other matters. Still keen for Ian to benefit from proper psychoanalysis, he arranged for him to see Dr Leonard Seif, one of Adler's leading followers, who worked in Munich. Ian did as he was bidden, but the consultation was not a success. Ian was not in the mood for discussing family politics and refused to say a word.

Otherwise Ian responded well to being on his own. The Countess Mirbach spoke glowingly to his mother of his progress: he was talking "German already exceptionally well and with a pronunciation one rarely finds with foreigners. He is going on studying very hard and is doing everything to make further progress." But Eve felt she needed to check up on her son's progress for herself. In November she descended on Munich, clutching a letter of encouragement for Ian from her friend Lady Sackville, the striking illegitimate daughter of Lionel Sackville-West, the second Lord Sackville, and a flamboyant Spanish dancer whom he had met in Paris. After marrying her cousin, also called Lionel, the artistic Lady Sackville became chatelaine of Knole, the Sackville family house in Kent. Their daughter, born in 1892, was the headstrong Victoria, or Vita, who, while married to the diplomat Harold Nicolson, shocked her mother and friends by conceiving a grand and uninhibited passion for Violet Trefusis. In late 1928 Lady Sackville was not her usual ebullient self, partly because she was temporarily estranged from her daughter over the latter's lesbian affair. Ian was told to put pen to paper to cheer her up.

Writing on 4 December, he spun an amusing tale about his mother's stately progress through Munich, flourishing her ten words of German, winning admirers and dealing out colossal tips wherever she went. (Having met Eve during her visit, the Adlerian Dr Seif told Forbes Dennis that, with a mother like that, there was little hope for Ian.) Ian had therapists closer to home. With her outgoing continental disposition, Lady Sackville acted as an emotional sounding board for her friend's young son. Ian admitted one of his problems was that he was "too apt to be affected by externals. They force themselves so much upon one that it is difficult to ignore them unless one is a hermit or a fanatic of some sort, in which case one is generally a large brain with a tiny little forgotten body attached. But when one is fairly equal parts brain and body – as I am – neither half is strong enough to exclude the other, and consequently at least half my life is made up of externals, which always try their best to intrude on my poor other half." However at least this was better than extremism in either direction, he observed.

If Ian had been in the slightest interested, his last few words might have related to the political situation in Germany. His year-long stay in Munich coincided with one of the most turbulent periods in the city's history. After a poor performance in the elections of May 1928, Hitler's Nazis threw themselves into frenzies of reorganization over the next couple of years. Huge Nazi rallies took place across the country. In an atmosphere of increased political polarization, made worse by the worldwide economic depression of 1929, Hitler's pronouncements became increasingly racist and extreme.

But Ian was curiously unaffected by his environment. Regarded as amusing and slightly eccentric, he turned up at a friend's house for a musical soirée wearing dinner jacket (as required) and, rather egregiously, one white sock. He had been playing tennis and had forgotten to change one foot. Ian returned to England for Deirdre's coming-out dance in May. Towards the end of the month, she borrowed her aunt Diana Cooper's cottage at Aldwick, near Bognor, where she invited friends for the weekend. Ian never liked house parties: "all that endless walking in crocodiles", he sneered. Nevertheless, he welcomed an opportunity to show off his Alpine-bronzed physique to fellow guests, including Joyce Phipps (soon to be Grenfell) and her friend Virginia Graham. While frolicking in the garden with Deirdre, he demonstrated his skills at archery and performed daring circus-like manoeuvres on "the Wheel", the latest craze among the Bright Young Things – a contraption of two outsize wheels joined together with a bar.

Although now officially attending university, Ian could not escape the annual ritual of the summer holiday with his mother and family. The destination in 1929 was Corsica. In late July Eve left her three-year-old daughter at home with a nanny and travelled with Ian to Nice where they were joined by Peter and Rupert Hart-Davis, who had motored through France together. The two young men shared the same tight circle of friends, many with aspirations in the theatre. Rupert had just rejected his girlfriend, the actress Celia Johnson, and taken up with her fellow professional, Peggy Ashcroft, who would briefly be his wife, while Celia went on to marry Peter. Despite a distinctly histrionic aspect to his character, Ian purported to disdain all forms of dramatics. Perhaps he felt he had enough in his own life. But, with Deirdre at his side, even he was drawn into the thespian circle. A camera recorded him in a clinch with Joyce Grenfell, performing a sketch on the lawn of Furneux Pelham Hall in Hertfordshire, while Henry Tiarks, an Old Etonian member of the banking family, entertained fellow guests with the marvels of science, inviting them to look at the sky through his powerful new telescope.

At noon on 28 July, the vacationing party set sail from Nice on the ferry, the *Emperor Bonaparte*. But by the time they reached Bastia, on the north-east coast of Corsica, it was dark and the boat was unable to get alongside the jetty. They were saved by local youths who swam out to the boat with ropes. These were used to let down the luggage, which was loaded on to a donkey-cart and transported to a waiting car.

After driving for three hours along a bumpy track to Algajola, sixty miles away, they had to wake the concierge at the Castle Inn, where they had booked to stay, in the middle of the night. Next morning the hardships of the journey were quickly forgotten. The inn was an old fortress, part Roman, part dating from the sixteenth century. Its food was good and its situation even better: on one side the sparkling blue Mediterranean, on the other, the giant Haute-Corse mountains, stretching up to Monte Cinto, 9000 feet high. Ian loved swimming, and took to the water five or six times a day. Otherwise, he played sentimental German songs on the gramophone he had insisted on bringing.

Before long this pleasant but mindless existence began to pall, and Peter loped off to hunt boar with the local mayor, while Ian made the acquaintance of a couple of homosexuals living in the hills with whom he passed the time in noisy rubbers of bridge. After Peter left on 4 August, so as to reach Scotland in time for the grouse season, Ian stayed for another week, arguing incessantly with his mother, usually on the topic of money, another glaring form of her control. Back on the mainland, Ian left the party and, with considerable relief, drove back to Austria, while Rupert accompanied Eve on the journey home by train, he travelling third class, she first. In London, she presented Rupert with an ungainly tea-basket which he had carried around for her throughout their holiday. As she boarded her taxi for Turner's House, she said it was his reward for "being so good with Ian".

Although slightly his junior, Ian got on well with Peter's friend, and was one of only four people who called him Rupe. After Rupert moved into a flat on the fourth floor at 213 Piccadilly the following year, he used to invite Ian to his literary soirées. In 1933 Rupert joined the publisher Jonathan Cape, where one of his first titles was *Brazilian Adventure*, Peter Fleming's celebrated account of his journey to South America. When, twenty years later, Ian needed a publisher, the family link was one of several factors that led him to Cape, though by then Rupert had moved on to found his own firm.

Another factor was Ian's friendship with William Plomer, who later became a reader for Cape. As a result of their earlier correspondence over *Turbott Wolfe*, Plomer contacted Ian when he first came to London in 1929. He was invited to a party at Cheyne Walk and, encouraged by Eve, the two men became firm friends. Despite their very different lifestyles, Plomer was one of the few people with whom Ian could always relax. Ian fired off witty, inconsequential *bons mots* (either by letter or in person), and Plomer always came back with an apposite reply – a literary reference or quotation – to entertain and stimulate him.

Ian's literary initiation had continued after his return from Corsica when, strolling down Bond Street, he saw a notice in the window of

Dulau, the bookseller, which caught his fancy. The notice said simply, "The new D. H. Lawrence", and was set beside a volume of poetry called *Pansies*, a self-conscious pun on the French word, *pensées*. On entering the shop, Ian met the manager, a dapper, schoolmasterly figure called Percy Muir. When Muir responded enthusiastically to Ian's enquiries about the book, the young Fleming asked him if this was out of salesmanship or idolatry. "Neither or both," said Muir in deadpan manner, adding that, although he thought Lawrence might well be the greatest living English writer, his characters and ideas were execrable. Ian liked the reply and began to look around the shop. Soon he had accumulated a pile of books which he proposed to take on the next phase of his educational odyssey – to the University of Geneva. After further discussion, the two men decided to have lunch together. Ian was so fascinated by what the older man had to say about collecting books seriously that, although he was tied up for dinner, he asked to meet Muir later in the evening. Again they talked incessantly, into the small hours of the morning. Ian was particularly interested in the economics of first editions. "Do you mean to say", he asked naively, "that, when that D. H. Lawrence book I bought this morning is reprinted, my copy will immediately and automatically be worth more than I gave for it?"

It was the beginning of another lifelong friendship. Ian stayed in touch with Muir when he moved fom Munich to Geneva that autumn to continue his studies. He asked Muir to send him copies of new books which he thought might interest him. He also wrote regularly asking for specific titles. One of his first requests was for a subscription to *Transition*, the surrealist-inclined magazine, which provided a platform in Paris for avant-garde writers and artists. One of its contributors was the sun-worshipping poet Harry Crosby, nephew of John Pierpont Morgan Jr, head of the J. P. Morgan banking business. Ian's request to Muir for a subscription to *Transition* came shortly after Crosby's premature death in December 1929. With his grandfather's link to the Morgans, and with Eve's various friendships in Paris, Ian would have heard of Crosby, if not actually met him. The iconoclastic literary-minded nephew of the great banker exerted a lasting influence. When two decades later, Ian helped his employer Lord Kemsley run two small publishing houses, the Dropmore Press and the Queen Anne Press, one of his models was the Black Sun Press, the small, non-commercial imprint set up by Crosby and his wife Caresse.

Forbes Dennis had done all he could to make life in Geneva easy for Ian, arranging for him to stay with Mme Claparaide, a professor's widow who took in lodgers at her apartment in the rue Lausanne. But Ian did not like her staid respectability: claiming he wanted to be closer to his studies, he moved to the rue Rudolphe Toepffer in the old city just round the corner from the university's Ecole des Beaux-Arts. Having signed Ian up for a number of courses, including social anthropology, psychology and, useful for a diplomat, Russian, Forbes Dennis continued to oversee his pupil's education from Kitzbühel. One project involved translating an obscure treatise on the sixteenth-century Swiss physician, Paracelsus, into English. Although this was about as recherché as his earlier rendering of Klaus Mann, Ian went to the trouble of writing to the work's author, the well-known Zurich psychiatrist Dr Carl Jung, and asking his permission.

In an article for his series on 'Thrilling Cities' in the *Sunday Times* three decades later, Ian admitted his ambivalence about Geneva. Part of him approved of the neatness and precision of the city. "With surroundings clean as the whistle of a Swiss train, soothed by the clonking of the cowbells, besieged by advertisements for dairy products and chocolate, and with cuckoo clocks tick-tocking in every other shop window, the visitor to Switzerland feels almost as if he had arrived in some gigantic nursery." Another part rebelled against Swiss smugness and reserve. It was all in sharp contrast to the naturalness and openness of the Tyrol. Even the yodelling was different. In Switzerland it was a melancholy moan – "an echoing plaint against the strait-jacket of Swiss morals, respectability and symmetry". Ian found himself wanting to take a tin-opener to see what went on behind the bland façades of the great houses and banks.

At least Ian now felt happier with himself, but there was still an unpredictable streak in his nature, and his 21-year-old's strategy for dealing with the solid burghers of Geneva was to accentuate this aspect of his character and present himself as a slightly wild expatriate Englishman. He drove carelessly around Geneva in his latest acquisition, a magnificent black two-seater Buick sports car. He hung around in cafés where he was regarded as rather flash; a practical joker in some people's eyes, he was feared for his caustic wit by others. During the winter months he skied competitively with the local *jeunesse dorée* at Megève and, closer to the capital, at St-Cergue. But, in keeping with his environment, his pastimes were generally more solitary and restrained. He found golf increasingly enjoyable, playing occasionally on the local Geneva course, rather more frequently at the scenic Divonne club, just across the French border. He went climbing around Chamonix, also in France. Like most places he visited it stuck in his mind. When he wrote James Bond's obituary in *You Only Live Twice*, he revealed that both his hero's parents had been killed in the Aiguilles Rouges above Chamonix. And there is more than a touch of Ian's own experience when he writes of Bond flying to Istanbul in *From Russia, With Love*. Crossing the Alps, Bond looks out of the window "at the dirty grey elephant's skin of the glaciers and saw himself again, a young man in his teens, with the leading end of the rope round his waist, bracing himself against the top of a rock-chimney on the Aiguilles Rouges as his two companions from the University of Geneva inched up the smooth rock towards him".

On a day-to-day basis, Ian mixed with a set of young diplomats at the League of Nations. As a Foreign Office candidate, imbued with a hazy globalist philosophy by the Forbes Dennises, Ian wanted to know more about the detail of international relations. Martin Hill, an Irish economist at the League and another recent arrival in the town, introduced him to Gisela von Stoltenberg, a plain, high-powered German woman who worked in the International Labour Organisation. Although their relationship was platonic, Ian found her a sparkling companion and used to sit with her discussing Goethe and Schiller in the Cozy Corner café, a favourite among his friends for its *thés dansants*. Through these connections Ian arranged a holiday job at the League of Nations. From 14 July to 13 September 1930 he was employed as a temporary civil servant in the League's International Bureau of Intellectual Cooperation, under Baron Beycha Votier, later Austrian Ambassador to the Lebanon. The experience served only to impress on Ian the uselessness of international bureaucracies: they "waste a great deal of money, turn out far too much expensively printed paper, and achieve very little indeed", he later wrote.

Soon after returning to his desultory studies in the autumn, Ian ran into Monique Panchaud de Bottones, a slim, dark-haired local beauty from Vich in the canton of Vaud, just inland from Lake Geneva, some fifteen miles outside the city. Her father was a respectable local landowner, whose eighteenth-century château produced passable Swiss Gamays and Pinot Noirs, while her mother came from a rich family of Lyon textile merchants called the Barbezats. Having met Ian at a ball given by one of her many cousins in Geneva, she was impressed by his intelligence, charm and sensitivity, though she cannot have failed to notice what everyone else saw: that he was also spoiled and self-centred, little more than a playboy. He found her chic, cultured and amusing, the very essence of a modern French-speaking girl. Before long they were inseparable.

The following spring Ian moved along the lake to be closer to Monique, initially taking a first-floor room in the Hotel du Lac at Coppet around four miles from the Domaine de Vich. Ian returned to "the hamlet made famous by Madame de Staël" – as he liked to emphasize – in his novel *Goldfinger*. Coppet provided the venue for his villain Auric Goldfinger's Swiss factory. Bond drove up into the woods behind the village to spy on Goldfinger stripping out the gold from the bodywork of his Rolls-Royce Silver Ghost. Ian's Swiss experiences played a formative role in his fictional world. James Bond's mother, killed in a climbing accident in the Aiguilles Rouges, was called Monique Delacroix, a Swiss woman from the canton of Vaud. (If one speculates a bit further, the "croix" suffix referred back to Eve Fleming's maiden name.)

During the summer of 1931 Ian found lodgings in the village of Mies, between Coppet and Geneva. Since he spent most weekends at the château, the young couple, in deference to the local Calvinism, were deemed to be unofficially engaged. As a de facto member of the Panchaud family, Ian liked to stretch out his lanky frame on their sofa, reading thrillers by the Belgian writer Georges Simenon. He chatted enthusiastically in French with Monique's father, and sat to have his bust sculpted by her mother.

For the first time since Sandhurst, he was able to relax with a girl he loved, away from the demands of his mother, and without the benevolent paternalism of Forbes Dennis, who knew all the details of his "disgrace". When not at the château, he and Monique spent most of their free time out of doors, swimming in the lake most mornings and meeting various friends. Her slim body glowing with the aphrodisiac effects of sunshine and love, she introduced him to a family acquaintance called Krebs, who owned a renowned library on medieval medicine in the nearby town of Nyon. Ian, who had kept in touch with his bookseller friend Percy Muir, was again inspired with the idea of building his own collection. As well as books, he discovered a taste for Picasso prints and managed to track down and purchase Mussolini's passport.

In September Ian tore himself away from this idyll and returned to London to sit the written part of his Foreign Office examination. The results, posted to Ian at Turner's House at the end of the month, showed that, although he had reached an adequate pass standard, coming twenty-fifth out of sixty-two candidates (the top twenty-seven all passed), he was not being offered a job. That honour was reserved for only the top three candidates in the examination. Ian was mortified, but even more so was his mother who, having been disappointed at her son's failure to make the grade as a soldier, had set her heart on his becoming a diplomat. Amid more recriminations, she convinced herself that the reason for his failure was Monique, who had distracted him from his studies in Geneva. From now on, Ian's "fiancée" was on the hate list.

Eve was not prepared to let her son stand still, however. Within a week, she had forced him to write to Sir Roderick Jones, head of Reuters, the international news agency, asking him for a job. Jones, a small, dapper man, was married to one of Eve's friends, Enid Bagnold, grand and statuesque and later the author of the twice-filmed novel, *National Velvet*, and of the play *The Chalk Garden*. In a letter from Turner's House on 1 October, Ian half-apologetically reminded Jones that they had met at his mother's. He explained that he had just taken the Foreign Office examination and, although he had passed "adequately, but not brilliantly", he was so keen on starting regular work that he had decided against trying to enter the diplomatic service again.

He ran through his various accomplishments, including "one book" (his Klaus Mann play) and several articles translated from the German, and stressing that, "above all else", his education had been international. Although Ian finished his letter with a declaration that he would be "gratefull" if Sir Roderick should decide to take him on, the Reuters chief was prepared to overlook this elementary spelling mistake. Jones had learned his journalism in South Africa, where he had seen the High Commissioner, Lord Milner, build up his kindergarten of brilliant young men. At Reuters, he sought to do much the same. As the son of a Lancashire hat salesman, he was inordinately impressed by social position. Ian came from the right background and had given a good account of himself in his introductory letter. So Jones was happy to put the wheels in motion for him to join the agency.

It all happened very quickly after that. On 7 October Ian travelled along the Thames to the Reuters office on the Embankment at the end of Carmelite Street, close to Blackfriars Bridge. There, on the first floor, he was interviewed again, first by Bernard Rickatson-Hatt, the editor-in-chief of the service, and then by Cecil Fleetwood May, a wireless technician who, following the introduction of the City ticker-tape three years earlier, was beginning to develop the business information side of the service. Both were impressed by the young man's qualities. Rickatson-Hatt, a former Coldstream Guards officer, with a clipped moustache and a monocle, had worked with Associated Press in the United States and was keen to introduce AP's speed and efficiency to European news-gathering operations. He reported to Jones that Ian was "quite the right type and seemed most intelligent". He added, "After leaving Eton, he went to Sandhurst. He will therefore know the value and importance of discipline." Rickatson-Hatt suggested that Ian should be hired initially on a trial basis for one month without pay.

The aspiring young journalist started work at Reuters on Monday, 19 October 1931. In the circumstances, Ian was particularly anxious to do well and within a couple of days Rickatson-Hatt was commending the new recruit to Sir Roderick. His only negative comment was that Ian suffered from a slight Foreign Office "bump". He promised, however, that "you can depend on us to put some pep into him before many days have gone by." The Reuters chief also had Ian's praises heaped on him from another source. Ever mindful of her maternal duties, Eve Fleming wrote to thank him for taking her son on, gushing, "He has great character and is supposed to be very intelligent, though I ought not to say so!" She dissembled slightly when she said that she was disappointed that Ian was not trying again for the Foreign Office since he had never been expected to get in first time round.

After his month's trial, Ian was judged a success and offered a permanent post at a salary of £150 a year. Two of his references were taken up. Neither knew Ian personally, but again his family name sufficed. Lord D'Abernon had become such a firm favourite of Eve's that she kept his photograph beside her bed. Their innocent relationship allowed the noble lord to write confidently, "I have known Mr Ian L. Fleming's family for many years, and regard them as people of exceptionally strong character and intelligence. I have no personal experience of Mr Ian L. Fleming's work, but I understand he has brilliant ability, with an unusual knowledge of foreign affairs."

Despite starting a new job, Ian had not forgotten Monique. To confirm his engagement, he invited her to stay with his family in England over Christmas. He asked Martin Hill to accompany her from Geneva to Dover where Ian was waiting at the quayside. Monique was so delighted to see him that she managed to leave her luggage on board the ship. Ian must have warned her what to expect at Turner's House, but even so it was a shock. Eve had made up her mind that a Swiss bourgeois was not good enough for her dear son. Already blaming Monique for distracting Ian from his Foreign Office exams, she was determined to make life as unpleasant as possible for her. Monique recalled, "She did her best to try to separate us. When I dared to go into Ian's room, she threw a fit. 'My dear,' she said haughtily, 'we don't do things like that in England.' She was simply jealous. The poor maid was not even allowed to light a fire in my room." Peter, who had just returned from his first trip to China, recognized what was happening and tried to intercede with his mother on Monique's (and Ian's) behalf, but without much luck. Although Eve did not ban her son's romance outright – she used to say he had "bought the usual diamond bracelet" to signify their engagement – she was at her manipulative worst when she interceded with his employer. Male staff at Reuters still needed the company's permission to marry. She simply asked Rickatson-Hatt to do all in his power to prevent her son proceeding with his idea of matrimony. As an additional form of psychological warfare, she used to ask Ian, "How would you feel if you were married to her?", and, such was the force of her personality, that he would shudder at the thought of spending all his time with the one woman.

Back at the agency, Ian immersed himself in the different aspects of his new profession. With around a dozen other young men, he sat at long tables on the first floor of the Reuters building. Ian's table was by the window, overlooking the River Thames. His main job was rewriting the stories sent in by correspondents. Because of his aptitude for languages, he escaped some of the tedium by monitoring the ticker-tapes carrying the latest news from rival foreign agencies, Havas in Paris and the Woolf

Bureau in Berlin. His job was to "taste" their copy, translate and rewrite it, and later send it out again as original Reuters material. He also had to answer mundane enquiries from the newspapers which subscribed to Reuters. Early on he won plaudits from Rickatson-Hatt for his courtesy and efficiency in helping the *Financial News* obtain statistics about French and German trade.

As part of his training, he dabbled in the commercial side of the agency, where his social connections proved useful in drumming up new business – a factor which Jones and Rickatson-Hatt doubtless had in mind when they hired him. In January 1932 Fleetwood May, the head of commercial services, thanked Ian for approaching Major C. E. Hoare of St Phalle, a small firm of stockbrokers. Reuters had been in negotiations to sell its service to St Phalle for some time and Fleetwood May felt sure that Ian's intervention would lead their talks to a successful conclusion. Ian confirmed his reputation as something of a social butterfly in May, when he asked the Reuters manager, W. Lints Smith, to arrange a visit for his friends, the Prince and Princess de Polignac, to *The Times*. This was not Winnaretta, the best known Princess de Polignac of the period – the Sapphic Singer heiress from the United States, who became one of Europe's most enlightened patrons of the arts, helping to introduce Stravinsky, Prokofiev and Diaghilev's Ballet Russe to Parisian audiences – but Prince Pierre de Polignac and his wife Princess Charlotte, daughter of Louis II, sovereign of Monaco. In the event, the de Polignacs were unable to keep their appointment. Ian had to apologize profusely on their behalf. He explained that they had been invited to St James's Palace by the Prince of Wales.

One of his early journalistic assignments was to freshen up five hundred obituaries in the Reuters files. One example was his memoir of "Boni", the Marquis of Castellane, ironically the only man whom Winnaretta was ever supposed to have found physically attractive. Subheaded:

> *"Boni" the Prince of extravagance*
> *Famous marriage and divorce*

Ian noted in the obituary that "for more than a decade, including the closing years of the nineteenth and the opening years of the twentieth centuries, the Marquis de Castellane was one of the most conspicuous figures in French society". The Fleming touch can be discerned in his attention to certain details in his description of this foppy French aristo-crat. Ian reported how, for his daily stroll down the Champs-Elysées, the Marquis was particularly careful in his choice of waistcoats, which ranged in colour from pale blue to vivid red, although heliotrope appeared to be his favourite shade.

The 'kindergarten' which Ian joined included several young men who went on to be successful journalists – among them, Alaric Jacob and Alexander Clifford, both respected war correspondents, Christopher Chancellor, who later headed Reuters, and Robin Sheepshanks, a brilliant young Etonian who was killed in the Spanish Civil War while his friend, Kim Philby, who had been turned down by Reuters, narrowly escaped death. Another of Ian's colleagues, James Robertson Justice, became better known as an actor.

Ever socially conscious, Sir Roderick used to invite his young men every year to a dance at his London house at Hyde Park Gate. The more favoured were also asked to stay with Jones and his wife at their weekend cottage, North End House (once owned by the artist Edward Burne-Jones) in Rottingdean, Sussex. When Ian attended one of these gatherings, the diplomat Harold Nicolson was so impressed by his reliability and *savoir faire* that he made him a character in *Public Faces*, one of his few attempts at fiction. The novel, published by Constable in 1932 and dedicated "without permission" to the society hostess and, later, interior designer Sibyl Colefax, shows Nicolson – at that time an active supporter of Sir Oswald Mosley's pre-fascist New Party – as an unreconstructed pacifist. His book is an informed indictment of the international arms trade, raising early concern about the dangers of atomic weapons. In order to forestall some fiendish French plot, British Foreign Office minister Arthur Ponsonby contrives to plant a story in foreign newspapers which tells of an experiment with an atomic bomb which goes tragically wrong, causing a tidal wave that inundates Charleston, South Carolina.

Ponsonby's chosen medium for disseminating this false information to the world is Reuters. He charges his private secretary to telephone the agency chief, Lord Rottingdean (no prizes for guessing who he is based on). The secretary tells Lord Rottingdean that he needs to put out an urgent and "very complicated" communiqué which must appear on the front pages of foreign newspapers next day, but not in the British newspapers.

"What I want you to do is to ring up your man in charge of the office," the Foreign Office man requests, "and warn him that I shall shortly arrive with a Government communiqué which has to be issued immediately. What is his name? Hemming? Oh yes, I know, young Fleming. Yes, I know him personally – that makes it easier. Well, I should be most obliged if you could ring him up and tell him to do exactly what I ask. Impress on him that the thing is vastly confidential and all that."

Throughout his life Ian had a knack of impressing older men. His Reuters colleagues were more difficult to win over. As far they could make out, Ian was a rich, aloof Old Etonian, who kept himself to himself and whose only obvious extravagance was his dashing Buick motor car. The *on dit* was that Ian was actually rather delicate, kept on a tight rein by his mother. When he did escape her influence, he went to the stuffy diplomats' club, the now defunct St James's in Piccadilly, where he played bridge with men twice his age. Only Alaric Jacob, his best friend at the agency, was permitted to see any other side to Ian's personality. He sometimes borrowed Ian's membership card at the International Sportsmen's Club, which he used to go swimming. In return he lent Ian his flat in Marylebone Lane for occasional uncomplicated romantic assignations.

Jacob was one of the few people with whom Ian could discuss books. He was impressed by young Fleming's comprehensive knowledge of European literature: Ian could recite great passages of his favourite novel, *The Magic Mountain* by Thomas Mann. Once, having invited Jacob back to Turner's House, Ian was embarrassed to find that his mother was taking her supper in bed. She told "the boys" to go into the drawing-room, with her portraits by John and others. But even then she refused to let go. "Ian," she shouted imperiously from upstairs, "you're not to give that friend of yours any cocktails. Sherry, but no hard liquor."

Jacob recalled these experiences nearly two decades later in his autobiography, *Scenes from a Bourgeois Life*. In it Jacob wrote of a suave opportunist who was an enigmatic hit on the London social scene. Anticipating a trick Ian himself used in subsequent Bond books, Jacob gave his creation a composite name, Hugo Dropmore, which concealed clues to the person's identity – Hugo, after the novelist Hugo Charteris, a friend of Jacob's journalistic colleague, Alexander Clifford, and later Ian's brother-in-law, and Dropmore, after the country house of Ian's post-war employer, Lord Kemsley. Hugo Dropmore was unmistakably Ian in the early 1930s, though Jacob took the liberty of incorporating elements of Ian's career in the intervening years as well.

Despite several good points, the ambitious Dropmore was not a lovable character. According to Jacob, he was a cross between Mr Darcy, Jane Austen's supercilious matinée idol in *Pride and Prejudice*, and the hero of a book by Stephen MacKenna. Jacob commented incisively on the unreal, almost fantastic element in Dropmore's make-up: in a novel he would have been incredible, but as a real person he was simply "a most satisfying piece of fiction". Once a member of Pop at Eton, Dropmore "had decided it would be a pleasant contrivance if one could remain in Pop for the rest of one's life". He had succeeded "by dint of shooting a line so high into the empyrean that no matter how much one subtracted from it, Hugo still found himself with rope enough to hang all his contemporaries and sufficient left over to ensure his own get-away".

Jacob built up a meticulous picture of a well-bred chancer. Hugo or Ian looked like a young actor who had never toured but who was starting his career right in the West End. He had impeccable taste – so good, in fact, that "you never observed what he was up to until it was too late". Despite knowing little Latin or Greek, he could speak all the languages that mattered. A Romanian baroness was his mistress, but otherwise he wasted little time over women: friendships were his main concern.

He came from a Palladian family, where the young men played all the right games and found jobs in all the right professions. Remarkably, however, the Dropmores were of very humble origin, a Tennant family *de nos jours*. Young Hugo's questionable antecedents were manifest in his curious snobbishness. He could never get it quite right who to be superior towards. Although he "knew all about Stein and Rilke, ... played bridge beautifully and skied like a ghost", he cultivated all the wrong people – unEnglish plutocrats and "the crudest and vulgarest of the newspaper Lords". It was a jaundiced assessment, born, clearly, out of jealousy and resentment, but its tenets ring true.

Luckily for Ian, his employers showed no falling-off in their estimation of his qualities. Rickatson-Hatt noted that he was "accurate, painstaking, and methodical" and, at the same time, had "a good business instinct – doubtless a family trait". As a result, the flinty editor-in-chief arranged for his protégé to make his first trip abroad as a Reuters special correspondent. Ian's destination was promising: the Bavarian city of Munich, which he knew well from his stay at the university three years earlier. But Ian was not being sent to chronicle the rise of Hitler. His first assignment was the rather more mundane task of reporting on the Alpine motor trials which were taking place in late July and early August 1932. In what might pass for a modern media trade-off, Ian was granted unique access to the event. He would navigate for the leading British rally driver, Donald Healey, in the latter's 4.5 litre Invicta and, in return, Healey and Invicta stood to benefit from any attendant publicity. In sending Ian on this jaunt, Rick-atson-Hatt was doing his young friend a personal favour and giving him an alibi, despite his mother's opposition, for visiting his Swiss fiancée.

The editor-in-chief's indulgence could almost be justified on journalistic grounds. In the run-up to the Second World War, cars were becoming symbols of national pride: their production and successful performance were important indicators of economic strength. The Alpine trials, which had started life as an Austrian domestic event, had now been extended over Germany, Italy, Switzerland and France, as well as Austria. Run over 1580 miles of steep mountain passes, they were one of the most gruelling tests of drivers' skills and cars' durability in the rallying calendar.

To reach Munich, Ian and Healey first had to negotiate 700 miles of roads through France and Germany. They crossed the English Channel on the Townsend Brothers car ferry, the SS *Forde*, and travelled down through Rheims, where they spent one night, and Freudenstadt in the Black Forest, night number two. In Munich, Healey parked his Invicta, registration PL 9682, with the other competitors in the square in front of the Motor Transport Corps barracks. While the cars were being checked, Ian visited old friends, including Kenneth Dickens, the recently arrived Reuters correspondent, who had worked with him in London. Dickens joined him for the torchlight procession before the start of the rally at 4 a.m. on the morning of Thursday 28 July.

It was raining at the time, and the roads out of Munich immediately degenerated into a skid patch. In such conditions, Healey excelled himself. For a week he led the field, carrying off a coveted Coupe des Glaciers – for drivers who completed the event without penalty points. On the third day, between Merano and St Moritz, he set a new record (23 minutes 44 seconds) for the speed of his ascent of the Stelvio Pass.

That night, in St Moritz, Healey and his young navigator stayed at the Grand Hotel, leaving their car parked with all the others on the hotel tennis court. Ian must have found the atmosphere intoxicating. He was back in his favourite Alps. In addition, he was participating in an event which combined all the leisured charm of amateur sportsmanship with the thrill of fierce international competition – from manufacturers such as Mercedes-Benz, Steyr, Lancia and Bugatti. He was experiencing the world of fast cars, flashing exhausts and international rivalry which he had only read about in Sapper's Bulldog Drummond novels.

On the last day, making their way down from Grenoble to the rally finishing point in San Remo on the Mediterranean coast, several of the smaller cars caught up with the leaders. Almost on cue, they were greeted, according to the report which appeared in the influential British motoring magazine, *The Autocar* "by Fleming, Healey's navigator, with 'What on earth are you doing among the grown-ups?'"

As soon as the rally was finished, Ian filed his report for Reuters. Four days later, Healey was back in the Alps taking second place in the Swiss Automobile Club's annual hill climb and Ian was ensconced with Monique in Vich. Rickatson-Hatt's thoughtfulness in posting Ian near his "fiancée" almost backfired when he received an angry letter from Arthur Watson, editor of the *Daily Telegraph*, complaining about the Reuters coverage of the trials. The paper had learned that, contrary to Ian's reports, the event had not been an overwhelming victory for British cars. If Reuters was indulging in an unsolicited promotion for British cars, the *Telegraph* would prefer to do that kind of thing its own way, Watson fulminated. Rickatson-Hatt immediately wrote to Ian at the Panchauds' house demanding an explanation. He received a five-page letter by return, arguing that Watson had got the wrong end of the stick. The trials had not been a race but a test of skills, Ian said, and the British victory had been overwhelming, as he had reported. Rickatson-Hatt accepted the young man's explanation, saying he had brought up the matter not in any spirit of retribution but simply as a piece of useful criticism.

On his return to London, Ian felt secure enough to write confidentially to Sir Roderick on 7 September, reminding him that, in three weeks' time, he would have been at Reuters for a year, and asking if it was not time for him to have an increase in salary. At the League of Nations, he claimed, he had been paid the equivalent of £800 a year. "This is a materialistic age, and the day is past when a career was merely a hobby."

Sir Roderick took five weeks to reply. Then he authorized his secretary to contact Ian discreetly and to agree to his request. But the letter was to emphasize that Jones was making an exception of Ian and would only give him an additional £75 immediately (to add to his then current salary of £150 per annum), with a further £75 to come on 1 January. (When in June 1937 Ian was being pursued by the Inland Revenue about his income tax, he wrote to Reuters to ask how much he had earned between 6 April 1932 and 5 April 1933. The answer was £206. 5s. 0d.) Jones ordered that Ian was not to reveal details of his salary rise to anyone, not even Rickatson-Hatt. "A definite exception" was being made for him "because of the special circumstances of the case". On receiving this information, Ian wrote from his club, the St James's, to thank Sir Roderick: "It is most encouraging to feel that you have not considered my application too ambitious," he fawned.

Ian's family connections again proved useful in February 1933 when Ian sent a memo, marked strictly private and confidential, to Rickatson-Hatt outlining a conversation he had had with Maurice Bridgeman, who ran the press section of the Anglo-Persian Oil Company. With its access to strategic crude oil in the Middle East, Anglo-Persian (A-P), the forerunner of British Petroleum, had developed into Britain's leading oil company. Because it was responsible for a vital economic resource, and because it was partly government-owned, Anglo-Persian's operations were still shrouded in an atmosphere of state secrecy. Ian had more access than most people, however, because his family bank, Robert Fleming and Company, had helped fund the fledgling oil giant. Ian tried to turn this connection to career advantage in a three-page memo about secret Anglo-Persian papers purporting to show how Reuters' Jerusalem correspondent had been filing false reports about the oil company's operations in the Middle East and how Anglo-Persian itself was beginning to turn its back on Reuters and look more favourably at the output of other news agencies. It was a legitimate matter to raise, though there was an undertone of corporate machiavellianism, even toadying, in Ian's memo: "I hope you will regard this as strictly confidential, as I am at the moment in a position to get certain favours from the Anglo-Persian which might be of use to us in the future, and I was shown these private files in the very strictest confidence."

Having investigated the charges, Rickatson-Hatt tended to play the matter down. As he informed Sir Roderick Jones, "On the whole, I am inclined to think that ILF's report is a little too 'windy'. The A-P are naturally not going to minimise any particular grouse, whether justified or unjustified, that they may have." Nevertheless, the same day he put out an editorial order for Reuters employees not only to take care when reporting the affairs of A-P but also to check anything "reflecting on the status of the company" with A-P's London office.

In early March 1933 Ian returned to Switzerland for a short skiing holiday at the Panchauds. Rickatson-Hatt again obligingly gave him some veneer of official cover: Ian was there to monitor German radio transmissions in the period around Hitler's notorious "Reichstag election" in Germany on 5 March. This was the election when the Führer consolidated power, having arrested communist deputies and suspended most aspects of the Constitution following the Reichstag fire on 27 February. The Nazi Party's private army, the SA, was given full rein to act as thugs, though in a broadcast aimed at foreign audiences on 10 March, Hitler duplicitously urged "restraint". On the personal front, however, there was no hiding the fact that Ian's relationship with Monique had reached an impasse. No wedding had yet been planned, and Monique and her very respectable parents were demanding an explanation.

Shortly after returning to London Ian met an Old Etonian friend, Gerald Coke, a relative of the Earl of Leicester. The cultivated Coke, who later became chairman of Rio Tinto Zinc and a trustee of Covent Garden Opera, was then employed by Industrial Steel, part of the Vickers armaments company. He told Ian that six senior engineers working for Metropolitan-Vickers, an affiliate of the group, on large-scale electrification projects in the Soviet Union had been arrested and charged with espionage. The next morning, Saturday 18 March, Ian went to his office and quietly wrote up this potentially explosive story. Only then did he show it to Rickatson-Hatt who was involved with other business. His editor-in-chief requested that he should clear it with the Foreign Office as it would be difficult to publish anything if delicate negotiations were still taking place.

Ian's colleague, Alaric Jacob, sped round to the Foreign Office, which had no objection to the story, though it could neither confirm nor deny anything about the specific charges. Rickatson-Hatt then had to make a decision on how to dateline the story. He decided that the story should come from the Latvian capital, Riga – a petty falsehood of the kind he affected not to like, but otherwise, as he explained to Sir Roderick Jones, it would be obvious that the story had been leaked by either Vickers or the Foreign Office, and Ian had given his word not to divulge his source.

What was to become a major international incident had started the previous weekend when a large detachment of the Soviet secret police, the OGPU, had descended on the Metro-Vick electrical company's dacha at Perlovka, a few miles outside Moscow, brandishing warrants for the arrest of Allan Monkhouse, the company's chief electrical engineer in the Soviet Union, and Leslie Thornton, who oversaw its construction staff. The OGPU took the two Britons away, along with four local employees. Four other British Metro-Vick engineers were subsequently arrested, and again several more Russians.

It was strange that the case blew up in this way. Metro-Vick was one of the oldest-established Western companies in the Soviet Union. Even when diplomatic relations between London and Moscow were severed in 1927, Metro-Vick maintained its presence in the Soviet Union. It carried on its business of supplying and installing heavy electrical machinery, including generators, transformers and switchgear. Metro-Vick's continued presence contributed significantly to the success (such as it was) of the Soviet Five-Year Plans.

But the Soviets have suggested that there was another side to the story. In his interrogation, Metro-Vick's Monkhouse admitted compiling reports on the general state of the economy and sending these back to his head office in London. To most disinterested observers, this would be sensible business practice in a highly competitive industry. But the Russians claimed it was spying. Recent evidence has lent them some support. Metro-Vick, Siemens of Germany and General Electric of the United States pooled their commercial intelligence (and possibly other kinds as well). More to the point, they operated a price-fixing cartel, which worked against the interests of the nascent communist state. The Russians also alleged that Metro-Vick had handed out bribes to obtain its contracts, and twenty-five of its turbines did not even work.

Vickers protested to Reuters about the way Ian had handled a delicate story. Once the popular press got hold of it, there was no holding back the sense of outrage in the British public. The British Ambassador in Moscow, Sir Esmond Ovey, also took a hard line, claiming that the engineering company's employees had been framed. But the wider diplomatic context was complicated. One month later, in April 1933, the existing trade agreement between the two countries was due to be renegotiated, and London had threatened not to renew the pact unless Moscow improved its balance of trade by letting more British imports into the country. In normal circumstances, the Soviets might have opted to placate Britain. But Stalin was consolidating his position and, if the Soviet Foreign Ministry was inclined to see reason, the OGPU took a different view. The affair coincided with the first reports of widespread famine throughout the country. British newspapers had taken the lead in exposing this disaster – another reason, so Stalin's hardliners thought, to take a severe line against foreign saboteurs who were either wrecking or deliberately talking down the Soviet economy.

The Moscow authorities reacted to the famine stories by banning foreign correspondents from travelling freely inside the country. This widened an obvious split in the foreign press corps. On one side were the appeasers, epitomized by Walter Duranty, the veteran one-legged correspondent of the *New York Times*, who was prepared to gloss over details not just of famine but of Soviet oppression in general. His rose-tinted reporting of developments under Stalin created the climate for the resumption of diplomatic relations between the Soviet Union and the United States in November 1933. On the other side was most of the remainder of the foreign press, including goatee-bearded A. T. Cholerton of the London *Daily Telegraph*, and the high-minded young Malcolm Muggeridge of the *Manchester Guardian*.

Such was the interest in the Metro-Vick affair in the United Kingdom that the British Embassy feared that Duranty, an Englishman by birth, might be asked to report the forthcoming trial for *The Times* of London. Britain's leading newspaper took the principled stand that, as long as press censorship existed in the Soviet Union, it was not prepared to maintain a correspondent there. At that time too, the *Manchester Guardian* was without a reporter, as Muggeridge had left the country, partly in protest against his paper's reluctance to give adequate space to his famine pieces. The scarcity of resident British correspondents only increased the competition between the news agencies. As a result Rickatson-Hatt decided to boost his on the spot team with Ian. "I AM SENDING YOU IAN FLEMING ONE OF OUR ABLEST YOUNG MEN TO HELP COVERAGE OF TRIAL", he cabled Robin Kinkead, the young American who was Reuters bureau chief.

Ian's itinerary took him to Moscow via Berlin and Warsaw. He left Croydon, then London's principal airport, on the morning of 6 April, on a five-hour Lufthansa flight to Tempelhof in Berlin. There a car was waiting to speed him to Berlin central railway station, where he boarded the six o'clock Nord Express to Moscow. At the Russian border, he changed carriages to the wider-gauge Russian train, with elaborate pre-war fittings. At around ten o'clock on 8 April, a clear late-spring morning, he pulled into Moscow's Belorussky station, and from the moment he stepped off the train, it was obvious he meant business. Not for him a discreet tailored businessman's suit: Ian had been to the high street chain, the Fifty Shilling Tailors, where he had acquired a loud hound's-tooth check outfit. "Wouldn't dare wear it at home," he breezily told Kinkead, who was there to meet him.

On his journey from the station in Kinkead's plush rented Lincoln, Ian got his first taste of the drabness of Moscow along Tverskaya Street (now Gorky Street). He noticed there was little on sale in the stores, apart from busts of Stalin and Lenin. His hotel, the National, was the most comfortable in a poorly served town, with the best restaurant and the least rude service. It also had one of just two American-style bars in Moscow, serving imported drinks, including gin, Scotch and vermouth, but at a steep price, which took even Ian by surprise. At the National, Ian met the rest of the press corps, including his immediate competitors, Eugene Lyons of United Press, Stan Richardson of Associated Press, and Linton Wells of the International News Service.

The hotel was blessedly close to the House of Trade Unions, formerly the Hall of Columns or Noblemen's Club, where the trial was due to begin at noon in four days' time. Ian had specific instructions to get to work as soon as he reached Moscow. A couple of good colour stories were required to signal that the Reuters staff man had arrived. Ian scored with an exclusive piece, written against the advice of the British Embassy, about preparations and pre-trial nerves in the Metro-Vick dacha. The day before the proceedings were due to start on 12 April, he filed a well-polished curtain-raiser, containing just the right mixture of cliché, atmosphere and polemic: "(Moscow, Wednesday) As the famous clock in the Kremlin Tower strikes twelve the six Metropolitan-Vickers employees will enter a room which has been daubed with blue in the Trades Union Hall and thronged with silent multitudes in order to hear an impassive Russian voice read for four or five hours the massive indictment which may mean death or exile. Within the packed room there will be a feeling of the implacable working of the soulless machinery of Soviet justice calling to account six Englishmen to decide whether the Metropolitan-Vickers raid was a vast bungle or a Machiavellian coup." Ian realized he was being treated to a sanitized version of a Stalinist show trial. The OGPU, which was orchestrating the proceedings, was keen for an exemplary sentence. It wheeled on a stern, unyielding judge, along with a hectoring, unscrupulous state prosecutor, and a specially chosen "audience" of around four hundred people who audibly expressed their satisfaction at any damning details. The alleged Russian accomplices had to grovel, confess and plead for their lives. In the event, the Foreign Ministry prevailed with its view that too harsh a verdict would result in a damaging trade embargo. Two of the six Britons were given short sentences, later suspended, and the rest were let off.

Because of the competition between the various news agencies, Ian worked hard to ensure that his reports reached London before any others. One technique was to drop his copy from a window of the upstairs courtroom. A young boy stood at the bottom to rush it to the censors for their red stamp and then on to the telegraph office. Ian is said to have ripped the wires out of the telephones in the Palace of Nobles to ensure that no one was able to report the verdict before him. But he was stymied because, by chance, the Central News correspondent was on the line exactly when the judge pronounced, and he was able to beat the Reuters report by a full twenty minutes. Ian remained in Moscow for a few days trying, without success, to obtain an interview with either Stalin or Litvinov, the Commissar for Foreign Affairs. He enjoyed the vodka and caviare, and was generally appreciated by his journalistic colleagues who – at his behest, one might imagine – cabled Sir Roderick Jones with praise for the "pukka chap" who "has given us all a run for our money."

The caviare took its toll. On his return he found he was infected with a huge tape worm which he attributed to bad Beluga. He was unable to work for three days because of what he called his "Loch Ness monster". Colleagues initially attributed his absence to another attack of his well-known hypochondria. Ian was frequently absent from the office with some form of a headache or a cold. They did not know that Ian's maladies had a mixture of physical and psychosomatic causes. He occasionally suffered blinding migraines, brought on by the plate which had been placed in his nose after his football accident at Eton, and he still had black moods of melancholia which made him want to get away from everybody. Then he preferred gentler pursuits than journalism. His bookseller friend Percy Muir remembered, on days off from Reuters, that Ian would ring him up and plead, like a spoiled child, "I'm bored, Percy; can you come round?"

His golden boy image was further sullied in June when he was fined three guineas at Oxford court, with £3 18s 6d costs, for driving an unlicensed car. His solicitor apologized for Ian's non-attendance, explaining that his client had been at the World Economic Conference. The Chief Constable was not amused by his excuse, telling the Bench, "That is a new one to me." Neither were his Reuters bosses particularly receptive. A pencil note in his personal file at the news agency carried a cutting reporting the incident and an anonymous pencilled comment, which read simply "Ugly".

In mitigation, as a probation officer might say of a delinquent charge, Ian was going through a difficult patch. On his return from Russia he had formally broken his engagement to Monique. Again his mother's hand can be discerned. According to a later girlfriend, Ian was presented with a stark ultimatum by Eve. He must choose either Monique or London and, if he decided on the former, he must be prepared to forgo further financial backing from her or his family. Once more, too, there were ugly and unforeseen consequences. For, furious at Ian's cavalier treatment of his daughter, Monsieur Panchaud threatened to sue for what in Switzerland was the serious offence of breach of personal contract. Ian had to utilize all his personal funds to ward off a court case. Shortly afterwards Ian told

Percy Muir, "In our house, money is an even worse subject than sex, and that's saying something."

Ian's decision was eased, perhaps even hastened, because he was running at least two other relationships at the same time. As was often the case, there was an older woman, for soul-searching meaningful discussion, and a flighty young thing to go to bed with. The older woman, who played an important role in his life, was Maud Russell, a banker's wife. Maud's German maternal grandfather, Augustus Conrad, had been Master of the Mint first in Frankfurt and then, after German unification in 1871, in Berlin. Her father, Paul Nelke, was a German Jew who came to Britain and established a successful stockbroking firm, Nelke Phillips, which numbered the high-living politician, Winston Churchill, among its clients. As a result of anti-German fervour during the First World War, Nelke was forced to sell the broking side of his business to its established rival, Vickers da Costa, whereupon he moved into personal banking. In 1917 his daughter Maud married Gilbert Russell, the witty and well-read cousin of the Duke of Bedford. Gilbert was sixteen years older than Maud, who was twenty-five and an intelligent connoisseur of the arts. After prospering in the post-war oil boom, Paul Nelke decided to set up his new son-in-law in his own merchant banking business. Russell, who had worked as the London agent for Salomon, the New York bankers, joined together with two jobbers who had also profited from the oil market – Hugh Micklem, an Old Etonian, and Anders Cull, an anglicized Swede. As the fourth partner in what was known as Cull and Company, they made room for Hermann Marx, a financial genius and relative of the founder of communism.

Cull and Company quickly established a niche for itself as a good merchant bank. Its main clients were Selection Trust, an aggressive multinational mining company run by Chester Beatty, whose son was at Eton with Ian, and British Celanese, the artificial fabric manufacturers headed by George Whigham, brother of Robert Fleming's original partner in London. It had good contacts in the oil business, bringing Ultramar to the market and working closely with Calouste Gulbenkian.

By the 1930s Gilbert and Maud enjoyed a comfortable and sociable existence in Prince's Gate in London. All they lacked was a substantial country house where they could entertain friends such as the Churchills and Duff Coopers at the weekend. In 1934 Gilbert bought Mottisfont Abbey, a dilapidated part-twelfth-century mansion on the banks of the River Test in Hampshire, and made it over to his wife to renovate and embellish. Over the previous few years, the Russells had rented several similar piles, including Heveningham Hall in Suffolk and Stanway on the edge of the Cotswolds in Gloucestershire, where they had lived for extended periods as a sort of trial run.

Knowing Eve from the extended bankers' wives' circuit, Maud first met

Ian at a cocktail party at Turner's House in November 1932. By this time, as a Cecil Beaton photograph records, she was an attractive, sensual woman in her early forties, with dark hair, a retroussé nose and large soulful eyes. Her husband was a kindly asthmatic, rising sixty, and it was clear, as a family member put it, she "found comfort in other places". Maud was much taken by Eve's handsome and amusing son, the successful Reuters journalist, seventeen years her junior. In early December and again in January she invited him down to Moor Farm, which the Russells were renting over the holiday period. Ian's name often cropped up in the visitors' book over subsequent months – at Stockton and Stanway and finally at Mottisfont. Quite when he and Maud first became lovers is not certain but, according to Alexie Mayor, Maud's niece, they made little secret of their affection for each other. Stanway, by coincidence, was the seat of the Charterises, one of the half-dozen families at the core of the Souls, the self-conscious group of high-minded but sociable aristocrats who flourished in the late nineteenth century. At Stanway, in November 1934, with the Russells in temporary residence, Ian first met the vivacious 21-year-old Lady O'Neill who as Ann Charteris had spent a happy childhood at Stanway and who had recently married Shane, the third Baron O'Neill. Eighteen years later, she was to become the first Mrs Ian Fleming. But that is running ahead of the story.

Ian did not confine his attentions to rich middle-aged women. For trysts in Alaric Jacob's borrowed flat in Marylebone Lane, there was Olivia Campbell, the fun-loving daughter of a younger son of the Earl of Cawdor. A vendeuse for Victor Stiebel, the Bond Street dressmaker, she was one of the tribe identified by Peter Quennell as 'Lost Girls', adventurous, deracinated women who flitted around London and who forty years later might have joined a commune. She once shocked a nanny by declaring she had always been prepared to sleep with any young man who gave her a decent meal. Ian was always happy to oblige. On one occasion, after returning from Moscow, he took her to a cocktail party at the Russian Embassy. When she went away, Ian apologized for not inundating her with postcards "as what I wanted to say was unprintable. Hurry up and come back, gorgeous."

Occasionally when he was bored, Ian enjoyed the company of nightclub dancers. He once boasted uncharacteristically about his romance with a "rather spiffing" bubble girl called Storm. He explained that a bubble girl was "someone who leaps around the stage with very little on". But the relationship was not satisfactory, he complained: "When the public performance was over, it was always the same old thing: 'I'm sorry, darling, but I'm too tired. I've got to appear at the Embassy tomorrow night'." Actresses and entertainers are boring women, he opined, because they are always thinking about their careers. "You could only conceivably think that they are sexy if you've no experience of them." But that was an old man's jaundiced reminiscence. Earlier, he had had happier memories of the affair. He told a friend that, after he and Storm had made love in the back of his mother's Daimler, Eve could not understand why the car's interior was littered with black boa feathers.

Back at Reuters after the holidays, Ian's contretemps with an Oxford magistrate had not been held against him. At the beginning of October, Sir Roderick Jones summoned him to his office and proposed he might like to take up an overseas posting in Shanghai. He made little effort to gild the lily. No money was mentioned and he stressed pompously that Ian would have to work very hard as assistant to the bureau chief, Christopher Chancellor. Sir Roderick urged Ian to take the long view: if he did well he would be appointed Chancellor's deputy. Almost as an afterthought, Ian informed his boss that his much mooted marriage was definitely off. As a result he requested a week to consider the job offer.

Ian's response took rather longer. Two weeks later he was posted temporarily to Berlin to reinforce the office run by the hard-pressed Victor Bodker. No sooner had Ian arrived than he was phoning through a story about the complicated background to the plebiscite which was due to take place on 12 November. Inside the country Hitler had tightened his grip harder than ever over the previous six months. Outside he was lobbying concertedly against any brake on his war machine. Two days before Ian flew to Berlin, the German dictator had pulled out of a multilateral disarmament conference in Geneva and withdrawn from the League of Nations altogether. The plebiscite was being held to approve, or rubber-stamp, his action. Bodker quickly concluded that his colleague's assistance was invaluable and asked his head office to let him stay, at least until after the elections. He arranged for Ian to meet Joseph Goebbels, the propaganda minister, and there was talk of his interviewing Hitler on a plane.

Since seeing Sir Roderick, Ian had learned that his remuneration in China would be £800 a year – "barely enough to cover my opium consumption", he later joked but in fact the same as he had been paid, pro rata, at the League of Nations two years earlier. A week after arriving in Berlin, Ian used a lull in the proceedings to compose his long-awaited reply to Sir Roderick. When his letter arrived in London two days later, it created considerable consternation. Having considered his position, Ian had decided to offer his resignation.

In a sorrowful tone, Ian explained that he had been ready to accept the Shanghai post until he met an acquaintance who offered him a much more lucrative deal. Although he did not spell out names, he told the Reuters chief that his contact worked for a merchant bank: the man was due to retire in two years' time, and he proposed to give up his partnership to Ian, who would have learned the business in the meantime. After discussing the matter with Robert Fleming and with a director of Barings, Ian said he had decided to take the job, and therefore reluctantly he asked permission to leave Reuters. As he explained in language Jones would understand, "A partnership would be quite remarkably lucrative and I would acquire before I was 30 a position which is unusual to obtain before the age of 50, if at all."

Ian was deeply apologetic about his decision. Realizing that Jones had given him "unique opportunities", he predicted that his time at Reuters would remain among the happiest memories of his life. And, indeed, throughout his subsequent career, Ian continued to look back on his short period at Reuters as a high point. In his last interview, published after his death, he described his three years there as "the most exciting time of my life". He compared news agency work in the 1930s to "a gigantic football match, and Reuters and the Associated Press of America were part of the Allied Agency group, and there were freebooters such as United Press and International News who were trying to break into our territories all around the world. We had some superb battles in Germany and Russia ... It was in Reuters that I learned to write fast and, above all, to be accurate."

To Rickatson-Hatt Ian was more forthcoming about the reasons for his resignation – family pressures and the lure of money. "It's a beastly idea giving up all the fun of life for money, but I hope to be able to make a packet and then get out and come back into journalism from the other end. Anyway the decision had to be made and I was pretty well pushed into it from all sides. I was assured it was the 'right thing to do' for the sake of the family – so there it is."

"The world's worst stockbroker"
1933–1939

The bank whose name Ian was reluctant to divulge in his letter to Sir Roderick was the up-and-coming Cull and Company, and his "acquaintance", due to retire in a couple of years' time, Gilbert Russell, one of its partners. But the driving force behind Ian's switch from journalism to the City was once again his mother, with a little help from the second most influential woman in his life, Gilbert's enigmatic wife, Maud.

Eve was responding in matriarchal fashion to important changes in her family's material circumstances. At the end of July 1933, soon after Ian's return from Moscow, his 88-year-old grandfather Robert had died after suffering a heart attack at Black Mount, his final and best-loved deer forest in Argyllshire. Eve, at least, had expected Robert to remember that her four boys were the children of his first-born son and to leave them the inheritance she considered their birthright. But Robert, his mind perhaps befuddled with age, believed that Ian and his brothers were already well provided for. He left his estate (worth nearly £3 million) in trust to his widow Katie, with the provision that, at her death, it should pass to his surviving children, Philip, Dorothy Wyfold and Kathleen Hannay. Robert's second son, Philip, had already been earmarked to take over the family bank. For Eve and her sons there was nothing.

Within three weeks of Robert's death, the redoubtable Eve had reassessed the situation and was pointing the way forward for her sons. "I think the time has come when I should tell you that my task as far as you all are concerned is practically finished," she wrote to them, in extravagant, emotional style. "I can do little more for you. You know what is right and what is wrong, and I have tried to instil in you the great truth (which is not preaching but simply common sense) that to do right is the only happy way of life ..." Begging their forgiveness for any mistakes she might have made in their upbringing, she told them, somewhat surprisingly, that after years of devotion to the memory of their father, she was finally thinking of marrying again. Entreating them not to breathe a word to anyone, she told the boys, "Someone is in love (genuinely in love) with me whom I might marry in a year or so's time. He has a fine mind and character and I could trust him to guard my body, my spirit and my honour in the ways I would have you guard your wives *and all women you meet.*"

There were two messages in this rousing valedictory. One was the unambiguous call that the time had come for the boys to stand on their own feet. The other, rather more coded, was that their ageing mother might sooner or later become a financial burden on them. As they all well knew, under the terms of their father Val's uncompromising will, if Eve married again, she stood to lose all but £3000 per annum of the sizeable income she enjoyed from the trust fund he had established. For this reason Eve had rejected all previous offers of marriage (of which, she claimed in this same letter, there had been many).

Of the four brothers, Peter was the least put out about the apparent oversight in his grandfather's will. He heard about Robert's death while on an expedition to China, from where he wrote to Celia Johnson, "It is funny how anxious I am that he has not left me anything to speak of: I really should hate it now, it would make me even more unreal." Having tried his hand in the City in the 1920s, he had realized he was not interested in money. Looking for a way to escape his banker's destiny, he had discovered his *métier* as a traveller and writer. *Brazilian Adventure*, his witty account of his hazardous expedition to find the missing explorer Colonel P. H. Fawcett, was an immediate success when it was published in August 1933, shortly after his grandfather's death. By then Peter was already out of the country again – on his way to the Far East, where his trans-Manchurian journey provided the basis for another book, *One's Company*, published to even greater acclaim in August 1934. Both Richard and Michael had already joined the family bank, and were on the inside track to make serious money if they wanted. Only the unfortunate, error-prone Ian was stuck in career limbo. He had done well at Reuters, everyone seemed to agree, but it was hard work and he had little prospect of accumulating the capital to keep himself in the style to which he had become accustomed.

The City being a more intimate place in those days, family connections still counted for a great deal. Robert Fleming's successor as chairman of his bank was his original London partner, Walter Whigham, one of six remarkable Scottish brothers. The youngest, George, will be remembered for his daughter, Margaret, who, having just married the American businessman Charles Sweeny, was immortalized in the song "You're the Tops", from Cole Porter's 1934 hit musical *Anything Goes*, and went on to achieve some notoriety as Duchess of Argyll. In his own right, George Whigham was the distinguished chairman of British Celanese, which was Cull and Company's most important corporate client. Another brother, Gilbert, was a director of Burmah Oil and British Petroleum. Yet another, Charles, was on the board of Morgan Grenfell, which had offices next door to Cull and Company, and had worked with John Pierpont Morgan Jr., son of Robert Fleming's old associate, on negotiating American loans which helped put Britain back on its feet after the First World War.

Calling on these powerful connections, Eve adopted a twin-track approach to her son's future – a mixture of behind the scenes female collusion with Maud Russell, and some traditional lobbying in the male preserves of family and City. Having proved his worth at Reuters, Ian is likely to have learned from Walter Whigham that if he served his apprenticeship at Cull and Company and absorbed a few tricks of merchant banking, he could expect in time to be welcomed along the road at the family firm.

For all his mother's planning, it was not long before Ian realized that, like his brother, he was not cut out for banking. Quite why he, or anyone, ever imagined he was is a mystery, but money talked and, at the end of the day, it seems he had little choice in the matter. Cull and Company had offices at 11 Throgmorton Avenue, behind the Stock Exchange, close to the Bank of England. The four principals sat facing each other at two large partners' desks in a hornets' nest of a main office. Ian was crammed into a smaller room next door, where the highlight of his first year was Cull's underwriting in August 1934 of the flotation of James and Shakespeare, an established trading company (and bank client) which was being developed as a vehicle for the interests of Garabed Bishirgian, a seemingly respectable Armenian-born commodities broker. But the company failed to mention in its prospectus that, in an attempt to corner the world's pepper and shellac markets, it had a contract to buy £2 million worth of pepper the following January. When the contract fell due, and James and Shakespeare was not able to meet its obligations, Cull and Company was left looking stupid, particularly after a public enquiry and a trial which led to Bishirgian being jailed. Cull's involvement in this City scandal may have caused Ian's more established banker relatives to voice their displeasure at his "fringe" financial activities and so hastened his decision to look for employment elsewhere. Normally he would have had little else to do but wait for Gilbert Russell to vacate his paper-strewn desk and retire to Mottisfont after his sixtieth birthday on 1 June 1935.

Ian was not particularly concerned as he was far too busy enjoying himself – one of his intentions when making his career move in the first place. As his Reuters colleague Alaric Jacob observed of him (as Hugo Dropmore), "He merely wanted a job which would give him leisure and money enough for an entertaining life." Banking added to his social cachet. No longer was he either a student following some indeterminate course at a foreign university or even an indentured journalist who hobnobbed with diplomats at the St James's Club. Now he was a serious young man about town, with a serious salary to match. As he told Forbes Dennis, "London has got its claws into me." His friends became more clannish and City-orientated – men like Charles Sweeny and Kenneth Wagg, Old Etonian scion of the family which owned the established issuing house, Helbert Wagg (which later merged with Schroders bank to form Schroder Wagg).

For relaxation, these young men liked playing competitive but very sociable golf. While Sweeny and his brother Bobby competed in the British Open amateur championship, Wagg and a solicitor friend organized the first of their private annual tournaments at the recently opened Scottish resort of Gleneagles in June 1934. They invited around fifty friends, plus assorted "wives and concubines", to travel from London on a specially chartered train, which came complete with one carriage for gambling and another for dancing. They took over the whole of Gleneagles which, to simplify matters, was owned by the railway company, the London Midland & Scottish. The total cost of the weekend to each participant was ten guineas. With his flat, ungainly swing, Ian was an enthusiastic participant in this and many other golf tournaments. A photograph shows him striding up the fairway at Gleneagles with Lord Haddington's son, the Conservative MP for Bath, Charlie Baillie-Hamilton, who had married Deirdre Hart-Davis's friend, Wanda Holden, in 1929.

Often this crowd ventured further afield. Their favourite destinations were the French resorts of Le Touquet and Deauville, where the casinos offered an opportunity to gamble as well as play golf. The young bloods crossed the Channel – some in their private planes – for regular weekends of gaming and carousing, interspersed with the odd round of golf to cure hangovers and give the impression they were doing something healthy and good for their constitutions. Ian was sometimes joined by Ivar Bryce who recalled his friend's growing fascination with the mechanics of gambling and, in particular, the game of baccarat, which had been introduced into fashionable society by the Prince of Wales, later Edward VII. The casino in Deauville was run by a group of wealthy East Mediterranean shipowners and financiers, known as the Greek Syndicate. Ian was not a natural gambler – most stories tell of him playing for lowish stakes – but he liked the excitement of the green-baize gaming room and he was fascinated by the precision and cool intelligence of Nicholas Zographos, the Syndicate's best-known dealer.

Ian's latest girlfriend was Daphne Finch Hatton, the lively young daughter of the Earl of Winchilsea (and niece of Denys Finch Hatton, the doomed lover of the Danish author, Baroness Karen Blixen, several thousand miles away in Kenya's Happy Valley). Daphne found him "very grown-up, sophisticated and attractive" after he had driven her back from a party in the country. Approving of this upwardly mobile friendship, Eve encouraged Lady Winchilsea to invite Ian to her house in Hampshire for weekends. On two occasions, Daphne paid return visits to Joyce Grove where she was not the first or last person to be puzzled by the complexity of Ian's personality. "He was a complete schizophrenic. He was tough and quite cruel, but at the same time he could be very sentimental. He was an emotional character who was good at suppressing his feelings." She could not help noticing, either, the bad blood which still existed between Ian and his mother. He used to wince in horror when she retired to the nursery wing to play her violin and was clearly embarrassed at her liaison with Augustus John. To add to the tension at Joyce Grove, Eve had taken against her mother-in-law. She resented the fact that Granny Katie had benefited from Robert's will and not she. And she resented it all the more because her own brothers, the "wild Roses", Ivor and Harcourt, could do nothing for her, while her sister Kathleen was dependant on her after her short and loveless marriage to Gerald Deane, the secretary of Tattersalls.

When, in August 1934, Daphne was invited to stay with her friend Caroline Paget in Anglesey, she asked if she could bring Ian. Caroline, one of five daughters of the Marquess and Marchioness of Anglesey, had already been introduced to the Flemings as a girlfriend of Peter (and a niece of Diana Cooper). Indeed, the ambitious Eve considered her a much more suitable long-term prospect for her eldest son than Celia Johnson. The 265-mile journey to Anglesey usually involved an overnight rest. But Ian's sporty, open-topped Buick completed it in one day. On the way Daphne asked him not to make their relationship "too obvious" at Plâs Newydd, the Marquess's family seat on the island. When Ian interpreted this as a rejection, perhaps even a social put-down, she was annoyed at his over-sensitive attitude. By the end of five days, playing tennis and messing around in boats with fellow guests such as Ivor Guest, the Wimborne heir with whom Janet Aitken had compared Ian unfavourably, and Arthur "Boofy" Gore, the Earl of Arran's son, Daphne had decided she was "completely turned off" by Ian and their romance was over.

Later that year he felt enough time had elapsed since his break-up with Monique for him to return to Geneva to visit old friends and ski. Martin Hill was back in town after a sabbatical of eighteen months in Vienna and Cambridge. With him was his slender new bride, Diana, known as Didy, the carefree daughter of a Master of Foxhounds from County Cork. Ian had been scheduled as best man at their wedding in Ireland but had not been able to attend. Didy quickly realized that, even after the passage of time, Ian still pined for Monique. He felt bitter and guilty, clearly blaming his mother for the ending of the relationship. "He often referred to it as some disaster," recalled Didy. That did not stop him establishing an instant rapport with his friend's young wife, who shared his taste for practical jokes. Once Ian briefed Georges Berthoud, a respectful Swiss bureaucrat at the League of Nations, on the protocol involved in meeting a visiting dignitary. Berthoud was told to bow deeply when he met the man, who turned out to be a London acquaintance. In the Cozy Corner Martin seemed not to notice Didy dancing rather too close to his best friend. Even fifty years later, she happily described Ian as the "most fascinating and attractive man" she ever met. "He had a sort of magic that just stood out. He was very tough, very hard and at the same time a very good friend."

By early 1935, it was clear that Ian had no future as a banker. Following its involvement in the Bishirgian affair, Cull and Company was due to change its status and become a limited liability (as opposed to purely private) bank in June 1935. The other partners asked Gilbert Russell to postpone his retirement and stay on, even on a half-time basis. So Ian, taking the initiative himself this time, did another trawl of his friends. With the help of Albert Wagg, his friend Kenneth's uncle, he landed a job at Rowe and Pitman, a leading firm of stockbrokers, with offices in Bishopsgate. In the short interlude between jobs, he returned to Geneva in May. Driving his Buick, he was taking one of the leisurely continental motoring holidays which gave him pleasure throughout his life. This time he intended touring round the South of France before returning to Le Touquet for some golf over Whitsun. The skiing season had just ended and spring was in the air. Finding that Martin was out of town, he asked Didy to join him for a day, which turned into a week. "You're bored, I'm bored," he told her. "Martin's away, and I love your company." They made for Tours in the Loire Valley, where he had a favourite hotel and restaurant he wanted to show her. "He had no compunction," she recalled. "If he saw someone, he thought he must have her. I don't flatter myself: he wanted somebody and it happened to be me." She found Ian a good lover, despite the fact that he was "very selfish and wanted his own pleasure when he wanted it". He enjoyed her company so much that he asked her to accompany him on the long journey north to Le Touquet. But he did not want her at the golf tournament. "I wish you could stay," he told her, "but I wouldn't want you hanging around." So he bought her a silver poison ring (a joke – in case she felt remorse) and put her on a train to Geneva. He told her to call him if Martin was not at the station to meet her. He even wrote to his friend telling him what a good girl his wife had been. "He was not the slightest bit humble," Didy said. "He thought he could get away with murder."

At Le Touquet Ian bumped into Hughie Vivian Smith, nephew of Alfred Wagg's friend, Lancelot (known as Lancy) Hugh Smith, the senior partner at his new employer, Rowe and Pitman. Soon to become good friends, they met on the golf course only because Ian was recognized by Hughie's young wife, Lady Helen, granddaughter of Lord Rosebery, the late Victorian Prime Minister. She had known Ian since the previous decade when he had visited her family's rococo pile at Mentmore with his mother, and

Lady Helen had subsequently stayed with the Flemings. After she had introduced her husband to Ian, the two men hit it off so well that she was ignored and forced to walk round the course "feeling frightfully bored".

Although Hughie later classed him "among the world's worst stockbrokers", lacking staying-power and bored by the minutiae of money making, and although he only worked there properly for four years, Ian's period at Rowe and Pitman had a lasting influence on his life. On joining the firm as a partner in June 1935, Ian came into the orbit of the distinguished City family, the Hugh Smiths, whose small town bank, originally based in Derby, had already grown into the National Provincial (later the National Westminster). His most important contact was the autocratic Lancy Hugh Smith, third son of Hugh Colin Smith, Governor of the Bank of England from 1897 to 1899. Lancy was one of six brothers who, like the Whighams, all rose to commanding positions in public life. Three others became grandees in the City – Vivian, later chairman of Morgan Grenfell with the title Lord Bicester, and father of Hughie; Owen, who ran the family firm, Hays Wharf; and John, a tough businessman who was managing director of Hambros Bank and chairman of the British Metal Corporation. (Rowe and Pitman had close links with Hambros, occupying the fourth and fifth floors of its main office in Bishopsgate.) Two more brothers achieved high rank in the Royal Navy – Aubrey, a rear-admiral who was Deputy Director of Naval Intelligence; and Humphrey, a vice-admiral who went down with his ship, the *Manchester Brigade*, in September 1940. Two sisters, Olive and Mildred, helped shore up the dynasty, Olive not least by marrying a Baring. (The Hugh Smiths also had matrimonial links with the two other leading City families, the Hambros and Rothschilds.)

The writer Nicholas Davenport who worked at Rowe and Pitman in the 1920s described a "clan which had brothers, nephews and cousins entrenched in merchant banks, investment trusts and other financial institutions throughout the City", and all doing their business through the family stockbrokers. The leftist-leaning Davenport wrote an uncomplimentary portrait of the senior partner, whom he described as standing for "the Establishment as I had imagined it to be – pompous, powerful, upright, unbending, alert to defend the pound sterling to the last million of the reserves, and to the last million of the wretched unemployed". As Prime Minister during the First World War, Herbert Asquith had described Lancy, slightly more charitably, as "precise, cheerful, businesslike and not very much more". Certainly the firm's senior partner was a martinet: he refused to speak to anyone lowlier than a department head and frequently reduced secretaries to tears with his rudeness.

But Lancy was a hard-working stockbroker who used his connections to good effect, seeking out new clients and new issues. He assiduously courted royalty – both domestic and foreign. (Jock Bowes-Lyon, brother of the Duchess of York, later Queen Elizabeth, was a partner until dying in 1930 of alcoholism brought on by old First World War wounds.) He also had an eye for a good deal. As a youngish man, he travelled to the United States where he developed a useful working relationship with the ubiquitous J. P. Morgan Jr., particularly on railway issues. He had good South African connections through his friends the Oppenheimers, who ran the De Beers diamond cartel. And his wartime jobs as principal delegate of the British Mission to Sweden and chairman of the Tobacco and Matches Control Board brought Rowe and Pitman two of its most successful issues – for Bryant & May and Swedish Match.

Lancy was also a romantic, which contributed to his rapport with Ian. He never married, but he enjoyed the company of several young women, including the tragic West Indian born novelist Jean Rhys. When they met in 1910, she was less than half his age, a young *ingénue* from the *demimonde*, working in a theatre chorus line, and he a rich middle-aged blade living in a large family mansion in Roehampton. Of course, there was an exploitative element in such a relationship. But she, who was extremely sensitive, came to love him dearly, and he treated her as well as circumstances permitted. After she had an abortion, he put her on a regular allowance, until her writing allowed her to be independent. Later, as he became more cantankerous, Lancy liked to surround himself with efficient young men. This was a moderately self-abasing role Ian found it easy to play. With his wit and social skills, he was good at buttering up older men, seeming to delight in and, for complicated psychological reasons, need their approval. One former colleague described him as "a hell of a tart", a facility which would enable Ian to get on well with men as diverse as his wartime boss, Admiral Godfrey, the newspaper proprietors Lord Kemsley and Lord Beaverbrook, and writers and artists like Noël Coward and Somerset Maugham.

Lancy helped introduce Ian to the trappings of the intelligence world. His own sensitive commercial postings during the First World War (for which he was awarded the CBE) had given him cover for clandestine operations. His brother Aubrey had been Deputy Director of Naval Intelligence at a time when Room 40, the Admiralty's incipient Naval Intelligence Divison (NID), was the most professional and effective of the secret services. In addition, Rowe and Pitman frequently provided a home for intelligence personnel, including the Old Etonian Claud Serocold, who was personal assistant to Room 40's chief, Admiral "Blinker" Hall, during the First World War (the role Ian played for Admiral Godfrey during the Second World War), and Sidney Russell Cooke, who died in mysterious circumstances, possibly murdered by the Russians. The best man at Cooke's wedding was Sir Campbell Stuart, the Canadian-born deputy director of propaganda in enemy countries during the First World War and head of Electra House, which Ian came to know as Department EH, responsible for propaganda at the start of the Second World War. Lancy held the ring between them all, to the extent that even the unpublished official history of Rowe and Pitman concedes, "It is interesting to speculate whether R&P's Lancelot Hugh Smith was, by his own involvement and through the medium of his brother, a long-term talent spotter for British Intelligence."

The practice at Rowe and Pitman was for new recruits to attach themselves to a senior partner as an apprentice. Ian was lucky to find himself working closely not with Lancy but with another older man, Hugo Pitman, nephew of the eponymous founder, Fred Pitman. Hugo was very different from the thrusting Lancy. An Old Etonian (like most Rowe and Pitman partners) and Oxford rowing blue, he was a charming gentleman of the old school. An accomplished painter and connoisseur of the arts, he may have helped bring Ian to the firm. For in the late 1920s he and his wife Reine, niece of the painter John Sargent, had lived round the corner from Ian's mother in Mulberry Walk, Chelsea. (Later they lived in the same road at Queen's House, one of the finest mansions in Cheyne Walk.) There were other connections: Hugo was a cousin of Christopher Chancellor, the Reuters correspondent in Shanghai whom Ian had declined to join and, more importantly, he was a serious collector of modern art, having befriended Augustus John in 1928. Reine frequently (and Hugo occasionally) sat for John but, according to Nicolette Devas, another member of their Chelsea artists' set, he never managed to capture Reine's frail sensitivity, turning her into an orthodox chocolate-box beauty.

In the City Hugo tried to introduce Ian to the delights of stockbroking, but without much success. The young Fleming liked the social side of the business, lunching his clients, either at White's or at the Savoy. (He had joined White's in July 1936, having been proposed by the Earl of Rosebery, Hugh Vivian Smith's father-in-law, and seconded by Lancy.) But Ian was bored by office paperwork and simply not very good at the nitty-gritty business of recommending decent investments. Bill Corney, who joined the firm as a clerk in 1937 and later became a partner (the first person to rise 'from the ranks' in this way), said that, while other partners "had a list of clients as long as your arm", Ian only had one regular customer. While Pitman was skilled in counselling high-grade equities, Ian preferred to suggest "very speculative securities", remembered Corney. This was the recollection at the family bank, Robert Fleming, which Ian used to visit in his search for new issue work and "usually managed to give the impression that he had received underground information about some very unorthodox investment – a silver mine in Bulgaria or something of that sort".

New issues were a grey area for Ian, as was apparent when he tried to promote a transatlantic cable service to his recent employer, Reuters. In

November 1936 Ian wrote to Sir Roderick Jones asking to see him on a matter which he described as strictly private and confidential. Ian turned up at Reuters with a mysterious companion called Mr Secretan "of the Foreign Office". He informed Cecil Fleetwood May, the company's chief of commercial services, that a company was being formed to carry telegrams between London and New York at a rate of 3.6 pence per word, compared with the existing rate of 5½ pence. It would do this by using a code which would allow it to "pack" telegrams and send different clients' cables to one central address. He felt that Reuters might be interested in knowing more about this service before the rest of the press found out.

Ian should have known that Reuters had already looked into but rejected such money-saving methods. Technology was moving fast and the agency was increasingly using wireless, rather than cable, to disseminate its news. Fleetwood May pointed out to Ian that customers might want to send one- or two-word messages, but the cable companies stipulated a five-word minimum. However his main caveat was more basic, as he demonstrated when he read Ian clause 51, paragraph 3, of the International Telegraph Regulations, clearly stating, "The office of delivery must stop telegrams addressed to a telegraphic reforwarding agency well known to be organized with the object of enabling the correspondence of third parties to evade the full payment of the charges due for transmission, without immediate reforwarding, between the office of origin and the office of ultimate destination." Dumbfounded, Ian hedged and said he did not know why this point had not been brought to his attention earlier. He apologized and promised to come back to Fleetwood May after making further enquiries. Unsurprisingly, nothing more was heard from him. But when Reuters asked the Foreign Office about Mr Secretan, who had been introduced as the inventor of the code, it could learn nothing. He was apparently unknown, the circumstances suggesting the involvement of the secret services.

Hugh Smith tried to interest Ian by putting him to work on the firm's monthly investment newsletter, printed on blue paper. Bill Corney remembered an amusing article entitled 'Pandora's Box', in which Ian reflected on his methodology of proving how the more risky investments – such as Chinese bonds and Argentinian railways – actually gave better returns than copper-bottomed certainties, such as war loans. Ian was also asked to write a short history of Rowe and Pitman. When, after leaving it on the senior partner's desk to read, he had no reaction, he plucked up courage to ask Lancy what was happening. Lancy told him his work was no good: it dwelt too much on the role of the Pitman family. So the future bestselling author's prose was consigned to the waste-paper basket, and Lancy rewrote the monograph himself. Ian's literary endeavours brought him into regular contact with the research department where Corney worked.

One of his first comments to Corney, just out of Imperial College, was, "So, what do you know about women?" "Well, nothing much," stammered the young graduate. "We'll soon alter that, you'll see," retorted Ian who was later scolded by Hugo Pitman for his familiarity with a junior. "We don't talk to clerks like that," he was told.

Hugo clearly liked his spirited charge, however, and, in an effort to boost the young man's flagging career, he agreed to take him on one of his regular meet-the-clients trips to the United States. Ian expected to be bored – as usual – for, before departing in October 1937, he contacted Jock McDougall, a director of the publisher Chatto & Windus. Shamelessly he asked McDougall, who was married to an American, for entrées into the Greenwich Village scene, which he seemed to equate with literary pre-cocity (Scott Fitzgerald was already a firm favourite), artistic bohemianism and, no doubt, attractive and available women.

McDougall had no difficulty understanding Ian's requirements. "I suppose by Greenwich Village you mean some milieu neither essentially social nor financial." Knowing, it seems, that Ian harboured nascent ambitions as a writer, he gave his friend a letter of introduction to Bennett Cerf, the proprietor of Random House, whom he described as "one of the liver wires in New York publishing with a wide acquaintance". As for women, McDougall suggested Ian look up his two sisters-in-law, whom he described as "personable wenches, one of them extremely intelligent, and they are much more in touch with the modern equivalent of Greenwich Village than might be supposed".

Ian was going through a period of renewed literary interest at the time. He knew McDougall partly through Peter and partly because Chatto & Windus had published the weekly magazine *Night and Day*, which flour-ished briefly from July to December 1937, when it was closed down after a film review by Graham Greene had precipitated a celebrated libel suit from the actress Shirley Temple. Demonstrating his continuing interest in publishing, Ian was a minor shareholder in Night and Day Magazines Ltd, and probably lost £100 as a result of his investment.

Once in New York, Hugo introduced Ian to the influential Morgan banking family who, knowing the Fleming bank well, became firm per-sonal friends. Whether Ian managed to penetrate Greenwich Village or meet the Manhattan literary mafia is not recorded, but his interests were clearly not on Wall Street. One night, before dinner with an important client, Hugo impressed on his young protégé that he had to be on his best behaviour. Halfway through the meal, however, Ian told the guests apologetically that he was feeling ill and asked permission to return to his hotel, the St Regis. Following later, Hugo went to Ian's room to enquire how he was. He found the aspiring stockbroker propped up in bed, glass of whisky in hand and an attractive blonde at his side.

In his efforts to escape further tedium, Ian travelled to Washington to see his old Reuters colleague, Alaric Jacob, who was now the agency's correspondent in the United States capital. Jacob was unable to put him up, so the two men met for drinks at Ian's hotel, the Mayflower. Jacob then took him for dinner at the National Press Club where Ian pumped him for information on the finer details of President Roosevelt's foreign policy. Jacob formed the impression that his friend had another agenda and was snooping in some capacity for the intelligence services.

Charming and amusing as he was, Ian's superciliousness often grated at Rowe and Pitman. According to Bill Corney, "A lot of partners did not like him. They said he did very little for the firm and attributed this to his having too many outside interests." Ian sinned against the cardinal City rule that one must at least appear to take the mechanics of making money seriously. His associates might all behave like prep school boys. A contemporary memoir by a stockbroker put their intellectual level at "about Form Four in the schools they had never really left. But they were doing their job efficiently, and were activating the capital market which is the key-stone of the whole capitalist system." Sometimes Ian tried to play the game, wearing an Old Etonian tie and, when Alaric Jacob asked him why, replying tartly, "Oh, the colours are really quite unobjectionable." He adopted some of Alaric's affectations which later became habits, like smoking custom-made Morland cigarettes blended from three choice Turkish tobaccos. But his heart was never in the City, and it showed.

As another diversion he began to take his book-collecting more seriously. His mentor, Percy Muir, was a very different character: a self-educated cockney, fourteen years older than Ian and with markedly left-wing leanings. Their relationship is a testament to Ian's talent for developing unusual and unstuffy friendships. Following their meeting in Dulau's bookshop in London in 1929, Ian invited Muir to Kitzbühel, where the scholarly bibliophile adapted easily to the Alpine air, becoming a good friend of Lisl Jokl. To pay for this and later trips Muir would proceed to Berlin where he had traded with the book dealer Paul Graupe since the early 1920s; so closely, in fact, that he married Graupe's Jewish assistant Toni Silverman. Gradually, through her, he learned how to use the purchase of books to help Jews withdraw money from Germany. His basic, simple technique was to underpay in German marks and allow his contacts to build up reserves of foreign currency in Britain. His book-collecting connection – in Britain, Germany and Austria – became part of an underground railway for Jews wanting to escape from Hitler. After coming to Britain in 1935, Lisl, who was also Jewish, assisted Muir in this enterprise, though another German-born author, Sybille Bedford, was not flattering in her portrayal of him as the cold Jamie in her novel, *Jigsaw*. After marrying a Manchester tailor called Popper, Lisl, who was good at design, found a job with Jaeger.

During his employment at Reuters, Ian had little time to think about books. But around 1934, when he was trying and failing to become a merchant banker, he began visiting Elkin Mathews, Muir's new firm of antiquarian booksellers in Mayfair. Elkin Mathews provided business amusement for two foppish brothers, Eddie and Robert Gathorne-Hardy, sons of the Earl of Cranbrook, who brought in fashionable customers like Lytton Strachey and Ottoline Morrell. Through mutual City connections, Ian befriended another director, Greville Worthington, scion of the Midlands brewing family. He encouraged the lanky Worthington to make a takeover bid for the company following a boardroom row in 1935. The Gathorne-Hardys duly bowed out and Worthington and Muir became partners, with Ian as a third non-executive director, holding the ring between the two.

By now Ian had made up his mind to specialize in a particular area of book-collecting. Having made £250 (about £6000 today) on a Stock Exchange deal, he asked Muir to spend it on acquisitions for a proposed library of books which had been responsible for technical or intellectual progress since the year 1800 – "books that made things happen". It was an opportunistic, mercenary move: a young man's attempt to develop an as yet untapped market. Muir had no illusions that Ian intended to do any research or hard graft: that would be left to him. Nevertheless, during the summer of 1935, Muir began sending the first books to Cheyne Walk – among them, *Married Love* by Marie Stopes (a snip at 15s 0d), the *Origin of Species* by Charles Darwin (£25), *Quantum Theory* by Nils Bohr (£1 1s 0d). The boundaries of what constituted progress were elastic: in June 1935 Muir provided – at no extra charge – a first edition of the official rules of the game of ping-pong. To house his collection, in September Ian purchased fifty-one black buckram boxes, each embossed with the Fleming crest and carrying a coloured label to denote its general category (red for science, yellow for philosophy, et cetera). As the black boxes increased in number, they formed a distinctive, sombre backdrop to Ian's various houses.

Ian was not an easy patron. Muir had to produce a mini-prospectus for any title he hoped to purchase, outlining why it was a seminal work. The older man was often annoyed that Ian spent money on accoutrements, such as boxes, rather than on actual books. He tried unsuccessfully to curb Ian's desire to extend his library to include first editions of modern works of literature, feeling this would reduce the amount of money available for core works. However, copies of the original publications Ian had in mind were generally cheap. As the Fleming collection grew, the two men congratulated themselves on their foresight in identifying a new area of book-collecting.

In a flush of bibliophile enthusiasm, Ian joined Percy as a member of the Left Book Club, which had been started by Victor Gollancz, the publisher, in February 1936. But in December that year both men decided to resign. They subsequently returned their February 1937 book choices, which caused some bureaucratic confusion because the club said it needed six weeks' notice. It seems that they had supported the original aim of the club – "to help in the struggle *for* World Peace and a better social and economic order and *against* Fascism" – but had become disillusioned by its increasingly Marxist fellow-travelling stance. Nevertheless Ian remained involved in a variety of anti-Nazi and refugee causes. He could hardly avoid being so, with friends such as Percy Muir, the Forbes Dennises and even Maud Russell – all, in their different ways, activists.

After moving into Mottisfont Abbey in 1935, Maud Russell's new house became a country retreat for liberal intelligentsia loosely opposed to appeasement. As a hostess, Maud mixed the old liberal establishment – grandees like Asquith's widow, Margot, and her nephew Christopher Tennant, Lord Glenconner – with men of influence such as the barrister St John Hutchinson and the MPs Sir Archibald Sinclair and Harcourt Johnstone. Both Johnstone and Sinclair were prominent members of the Focus, a semi-secret lobby group which assembled around the back-bencher Winston Churchill in the fight against Nazi aggression. In the background too was Maud's friend Sir Robert Vansittart, the Foreign Office Permanent Under-Secretary, whose "private detective agency" of businessmen in Europe worked closely with the secret services in charting the rise of German militarism. So influential was Vansittart that, on becoming Foreign Secretary in 1935, Anthony Eden set about sidelining his senior civil servant who was acting like "a sincere, almost fanatical crusader, and much more a Secretary of State in mentality than a permanent official".

Ian's membership of the Left Book Club was a homage to his schooling in Central Europe, and particularly to his literary luminary, Phyllis Bottome. As she later wrote in her autobiography *The Goal*, "We longed to develop an international spirit in the new generation that might place a brick in the invisible structure of World Peace." To this end she worked on two fronts, trying to educate an apathetic London public about both the dangers of Nazism and the merits of Alfred Adler as an educator. When Adler visited London in the spring of 1936, she prevailed on her friend Lillian Beit, wife of the wealthy randlord, Sir Otto Beit, to host a reception for him, attended by the Minister of Education, Oliver Stanley, another of Maud Russell's circle. And when Adler returned to tour Britain the following year, the committee which arranged his visit included Lillian Beit's son Alfred (at that time a young Conservative MP) as chairman, with Ian Fleming ("our old friend, one of our Kitzbühel boys", announced Phyllis proudly) as treasurer. Adler's tour ended in tragedy when he collapsed and died of a heart attack while delivering a lecture to the City Child Guidance

Society in Aberdeen. Ian's involvement, while insignificant in itself, indicated not only his wide range of commitments, but also his abiding sense of loyalty to his friends. Never personally interested in any way in Adler's philosophy, he was nevertheless happy to turn out for Phyllis Bottome who, with her husband, had contributed so significantly to his development.

There was something curious about a stockbroker in his late twenties still living at home, particularly when he enjoyed such a turbulent and ambivalent relationship with his mother. But Ian liked the creature comforts at Turner's House, and he had considerable independence from late 1934 when Eve decamped to the country. Tired of having to adapt to the Spartan ways of Granny Katie every weekend, she decided to buy her own house, Greys Court, just three miles down the road from Joyce Grove. The idea was that the boys could still visit their widowed grandmother as regularly as before, but she herself would no longer have to compete with her mother-in-law for attention. Eve was so delighted with her new purchase, an attractive gabled mansion dating from the seventeenth century, that she spent most of her time there, overseeing restoration work which included transforming a derelict stable block once used by Cromwell's soldiers into a library for Peter, the wandering author. During 1935 she hardly visited Turner's House, even putting it up for sale, so Ian was able to make full use of it as a quasi-bachelor residence. But in December that year Peter suddenly married Celia Johnson, who was beginning to enjoy success as an actress. Eve was incensed that her high-flying son, who had once courted the daughter of the Marquess of Anglesey, should settle for a woman who trod the boards, little better, she felt, than a chorus girl. She resorted to her well-honed skills of emotional blackmail, even threatening to cut Peter out of her will.

Springing faithfully to his brother's defence, Ian urged Eve, in a touching letter, to forgive Peter. "I feel disappointed myself [about Celia's middle class family] and yet glad at the same time that he is married. I should feel annoyed about not being told and not being best man and one thing and another, but I really don't mind him treating me as a minor criminal and as utterly untrustworthy because he does know best in so many other things that one can't expect him to be tolerant and humane in all others." Ian called upon his mother to put up with the "particularities which have made him without question one of the 2 or 3 most brilliant men of his generation". Without any sense of irony, he added, "We mustn't get in the way of having a perfection complex about him. The outstanding is always a little inhuman – and always must be, in order to be outstanding, and, darling Mama, we, and ultimately the whole of England, have a lot to be grateful for in Peter's existence. He really is setting a standard of sanity and truthfulness for a whole generation – he alone, a lot of people think – and if correction is necessary it should be done gently and in perspective."

Eve refused to budge, insisting that Greys Court had been bought specifically with Peter in mind. In his letter Ian had referred to his brother acting a little theatrically lately. Eve showed that anything her first-born could do, she could match a hundred times. In a fit of wounded pride, Greys Court, rather than Turner's House, was put on the market, and Eve moved back to Chelsea.

Ian's easy metropolitan existence was disturbed by the return not only of his overbearing mother, but also of his "adopted" sister Amaryllis, now a strapping eleven-year-old, and fast developing into an accomplished cellist. Spurred by Percy Muir's gasps of astonishment at the way Eve could still tell her 28-year-old son to put his napkin straight, Ian decided it was finally time to break free of her suffocating embrace and find somewhere of his own to live. As an antidote to City conformity, he continued to affect a mantle of mild eccentricity. So the place he alighted on was not a typical mansion flat in Chelsea but a converted nonconformist school on the edge of Belgravia in what is now bedsitterland adjoining Victoria Station. Built in Classical temple style by J. P. Gandy-Deering in 1830 and fronted by two large Doric columns and a portico, 22 Ebury Street sported under its pediment a large Latin inscription, which reads in translation, "The Right Honourable Viscount Milton laid the first stone of this building on 14th May 1830. May the Holy Spirit direct this task, undertaken for the instruction of boys in Christ's faith and moral and literary arts."

A century later, the Pimlico Literary Institution was divided into four flats, one of which had operated as a dressmaker's premises and another as a studio for Clough Williams-Ellis, the artist and architect of Portmeirion in Wales. Ian's flat, 22B, was leased for five years to Sir Oswald Mosley who, according to its owners, the Grosvenor Estate, used it for meetings of his British Union of Fascists. But after he married Diana Mitford, a family friend of Ian's, in a ceremony arranged by the German propaganda minister in October 1936, he needed something larger. When he found his ideal house in Grosvenor Road, close to the River Thames, he agreed to sell his lease on Ebury Street to Ian. Up till the last minute, Eve tried to deter her son, telling him he was "extremely stupid" to want to live in such accommodation.

Ian had what amounted to the top half of the chapel-like interior. Visitors entered by a steep set of stairs to the right of the entrance hall. In front was a large open-plan space, with an altar-like recess at the far end converted into a bathroom and lavatory. The nearside left-hand wall was completely taken up with shelves for Ian's growing collection of first editions. On the far right was a large fireplace with a rug in front. On the immediate right stairs led up to a narrow gallery, where Ian could just fit four guests round a dining table, and beyond that a tiny bedroom. In the centre of the parquet-floored living-room was a large wooden table surrounded by a plush sofa and two armchairs, both upholstered in a distinctive striped navy blue and white suiting material which Ian had acquired from his Uncle Phil.

Ostensibly Ian had had the place decorated by Rosie Reiss, a young German refugee who had come to London via Percy Muir's underground railway and was beginning to make a name for herself as an interior designer. But, as was the case later with his James Bond book covers, the concept was very much his own: a tall, dark, masculine bachelor's pad, loosely based on the vast downstairs studio at the back of his mother's Cheyne Walk house. The overall effect was daunting: "Renaissance Jewish", Lisl Popper described it. The walls were painted grey, and there were no windows: only a skylight and, otherwise, artificial lighting. Around the main room Ian placed various nick-nacks to flesh out his personality. Under the gallery hung a landscape of the Kitzbühler Horn and over the fireplace an execrable portrait by Ian Campbell-Grey, which Ian had won in a bet with the artist, a favourite of Maud Russell. The table in the middle of the room was dedicated to advancing the thesis that Ian was a follower and even a patron of the avant-garde. It was piled with recent novels, copies of the *Paris Review* and, prominently displayed, three photographs by the surrealist Man Ray. Other paraphernalia included the framed obituary of his father, an enamel miniature of Admiral Nelson, who had become a substitute hero, Mussolini's passport from Switzerland, and a shelf-full of silver cups he had won at Eton.

Ian was determined that his flat should make a personal statement. Taking his cue from his mother who had no problem living surrounded by portraits of herself by Augustus John, Ian toyed with the idea of running an autobiographical frieze along one of the walls. Peter later adopted this idea for Merrimoles, the house he built on the Flemings' Nettlebed estate. His frieze which, unlike Ian's, was actually executed, told the story of the Fleming family, including a portrait of Ian as Victor Ludorum at Eton. Ian's was rather more self-centred and theatrical. He drew up a plan for what he described as a diorama of his young life (he was not yet thirty), depicting it as a sort of psychological thriller. (A diorama, as he noted from Larousse, was a sort of glorified peepshow – a series of pictures, illuminated by shafts of light, with the spectator remaining in darkness.) Ian's span on earth was to be depicted in five "portrait souvenirs", each with a meaningful title. One would represent his childhood, with the significant rubric "The cause of the crime". This would be followed by representations of Durnford and Eton; Sandhurst; Kitzbühel and Munich; Tours, Geneva, and Exams. Underneath the diorama, Ian proposed to run a quotation from the late eighteenth-century German Romantic poet, Novalis: "Wir sind im Begriff zu erwachen / Wenn wir träumen, dass wir träumen." meaning "We are about to wake up when we dream that we dream."

Ian used his self-consciously personalized living space to entertain two different types of friends. One was a civilized group of clubmen who congregated for regular games of bridge. And the other was a steady stream of women, who never knew what to expect: Ian might try to shock them with his collection of (mainly French) pornography, he might seduce them, or he might simply ignore them.

Ian's male friends were now different from the brash, City types he had known earlier in the decade. They were educated, artistic, rather droll and essentially undemanding, an important criterion for Ian. In light-hearted vein, he devised a name for their special camaraderie, dubbing them 'the Cercle', short for *Le Cercle gastronomique et des jeux de hasard*. There was Gerald Coke, an Old Etonian who enjoyed Ian's hobby of collecting manuscripts, though his were harpsichord music of the eighteenth century – the basis for the world's finest private collection of original editions of Handel. A nephew of the Earl of Leicester and later son-in-law of Sir Alexander Cadogan, Vansittart's successor as Permanent Under-Secretary at the Foreign Office, Coke sauntered nonchalantly on to scale the heights of industry and public life. Sir George Duff-Sutherland-Dunbar was a witty barrister but, unlike Coke, he could not be bothered to strive for anything, least of all high office in the judiciary. Instead, when not playing bridge or relaxing on a golf course, he liked to collect Wedgwood china. In describing him, Ian provided a thumbnail sketch of his ideal male companion: Duff Dunbar, as he was known, was a "strange and vivid person ... an eccentric, an intellectual in the purest sense, a stoic and a solitary" who, although he had countless friends and a great sense of humour, "never fostered his friendships nor did he allow any of them, with either sex, to develop into serious attachments". Dunbar was a great exponent of the game of draughts, which he said was vastly superior to chess.

Other members of the Cercle came from the same school of solitary eccentrics. John Fox-Strangways, a younger son of the Earl of Ilchester, whose father still owned Holland House, is best remembered for kicking the socialist politician Aneurin Bevan on the steps of White's in 1951. In his books *Live and Let Die* and *Dr No*, Ian appropriated his friend's name for the SIS station chief in the Caribbean. Then there were Dr Jack Beal, who became Ian's GP; David Nichol, a brilliant engineer who went to work in the family firm of wine merchants, Hedges & Butler; Laurence

Strangman, whose involvement in the restaurant business added some authenticity to the Cercle's gastronomic ambitions; and Bobbie Gordon-Canning, a Fascist sympathizer who was imprisoned during the war under Regulation 18B.

On weekday nights the Cercle restricted its activities to bridge – a game at which Ian had the potential but not the patience to excel. At weekends its members swapped their pinstripes for plus-fours and piled into their cars (for Ian a red Graham Paige had taken the place of his Buick). They would race one another to their favourite golf courses on the coast – Cooden in Sussex, Royal St George's at Sandwich in Kent, and, occasionally, Le Touquet on the other side of the Channel. They stayed in nearby hotels: the Guilford Hotel, close to Royal St George's, remained a firm favourite of Ian's. From time to time Ian would invite his friends to Joyce Grove and they would play the local Huntercombe course.

Ian's other main pursuit at 22B Ebury Street was women. After the break-up of his affair with Monique, Ian boasted that he was "going to be quite bloody-minded about women from now on" and would take what he wanted "without any scruples at all". A myth has subsequently developed about Ian, the priapic Lothario, but this is too simplistic. His attitude to the opposite sex was a complex construction built not just from his experiences with Monique but also from his feelings of disgust and inadequacy at the consequences of catching gonorrhoea at Sandhurst, and from his powerful love–hate relationship with his mother. Consequently he often appeared arrogant and supercilious in the company of women, who, while appreciating his gaunt good looks, did not necessarily care for his vain and prima donna-ish manner. Lady Mary Pakenham, sister of Peter's fellow Oxford undergraduate Frank Pakenham (later the Earl of Longford), once told him he behaved just like his mother without her violin. At parties, his technique was to initiate a conversation with a put-down. With *ingénues*, this set up a frisson of sexual excitement but, according to Lady Mary, "the average girl simply did not like him". He made little effort to hide the fact that he found women inferior. "He looked on them as a schoolboy does," remarked Mary. "They were remote, mysterious beings who you will never hope to understand but, if you're clever, you can occasionally shoot one down." It was rare for him to make the running with anyone he fancied, and he kept clear of real entanglements.

The woman who suffered most from Ian's reluctance to commit himself was Muriel Wright. Twenty years later she would have stepped straight out of the pages of a Bond novel. Pretty and lively, with a pert figure, she had a distinctive shock of frizzy blonde hair that protruded like a halo. Her fresh face reflected her enthusiasm for the outdoor life. She skied like a dream, rode to hounds and was one of the leading female polo players in Britain. She came from a good county family: her Old Etonian father, Henry, had been an MP with Val Fleming and had also served as High Sheriff of Derbyshire. (A more contemporary point of reference: her niece, Susan Wright, married Major Ronald Ferguson and had a daughter who became the Duchess of York.) With plenty of money behind her, an attribute Ian appreciated, 'Moo' never had to work, though she had a lucrative sideline as a model – one of the first women of her class in this field. Her speciality was showing off sports clothes, particularly the latest ski fashions. She also did beachwear: photographs of her modelling a bikini on the promenade at Monte Carlo in August 1939 are so unself-consciously sexy that they might have been shot half a century later.

Not surprisingly, Moo inspired jealousy in other women. One female acquaintance described her disparagingly as "hearty" and another as "frightfully tiresome", for the not very good reason that Moo would insist on skiing on powder snow after her guide had advised against it. This same source said that Ian "picked her up skiing", which is not true. Moo and Ian first met in Kitzbühel in August 1935 during one of his regular summer jaunts. She was twenty-six. Over the next four years they returned often and also visited other Alpine resorts. Ian was beginning to prefer summer trips to winter. Mountains were more suitable for walks, he felt, than for madcap dashes through the snow, and he was not the sort of man who would have liked the fact that Moo was a much better skier. Also, as a chain smoker and drinker, he was no longer quite as energetic as he used to be. Mary Pakenham remembered that when they went for walks, he was for ever telling her to slow down.

Ian was dazzled by Moo's looks and vitality, but that was about as far as his feelings went. What held him back was her lack of intellectual ambition. In simple terms, she was not very bright. As long as she was in England, her great interests in life were her horses and her dogs. Ian visited her vast family house at Yeldersley Hall, near Derby, only reluctantly. He was unimpressed that it had its own squash court. Once he went up for the local Meynell hunt ball and came back appalled at the braying of the county hunting and shooting set.

Moo, however, adored Ian, a situation he clearly enjoyed and even exploited. He would invite her to Joyce Grove where, every weekend, he and his brothers were encouraged to bring their friends. Often (through no fault of her own) an impromptu guest, Moo was remembered as a scatterbrain and 'beatnik' who frequently arrived without a nightdress or toothbrush. At one stage, an embarrassed Granny Katie took Ian aside to tell him, "You are not to ask that girl again, unless I ask her." Moo made up for any minor social solecism by insisting on carrying her lover's clubs whenever they played Huntercombe golf course.

Another female friend noted unequivocally, "He loved having a cowering slave." The result was an unbalanced relationship, with, apparently, little long-term future. Moo's family saw what was happening and wrote Ian off as a cad. Her brother, Fitzherbert, who had been at Eton and Sandhurst only three years before Ian, took the matter into his own hands and arrived on Ian's doorstep with a horsewhip. But Ian had received advance intelligence of 'Fitz's' intentions, and had slipped off with Moo to Brighton for the weekend.

Mary Pakenham herself enjoyed a rather different type of relationship with Ian in 1938. For one thing, she was more literary and was already employed as a journalist on the *Evening Standard*. For another, she decided from the start that their friendship would be platonic. Nevertheless she provides a good account of the natural cycle of one of Ian's affairs. First, there was a long period of incubation when Ian was reluctant to commit himself. "I noticed for a long time that he had his eye on me. But he left it to me. For two years I heard him talking about this new flat. But when I finally got there, I realized I was as safe as houses. He was not at all bold and brassy and brave. Rather he was feminine and nervous. I'm sure he never assaulted anyone but just waited for them to assault him."

Not that Ian failed to take her through his full seduction routine. When she first came to supper, Mary was let into the flat by a giggly Irish maid, also called Mary. Ian was seated on the sofa in front of a blazing fire with his books around him. His visitor was immediately struck by his look of melancholy and loss, with an expression "like a fallen angel's". She attributed this to his puritan conscience – as if the upright Fleming part of him was vying with his baser instincts.

Mary found that Ian liked to talk, and she was an intelligent listener. He had two main topics of conversation – himself and sex. As for the former, it was often in the confessional mould. Ian had an uncompromising sense of his own failure. As a boy he had hated, more than he dared admit, having to play second fiddle to Peter, who was always more virtuous and more intelligent. His inability to stay the course at Sandhurst or to win a place at the Foreign Office still grated, perhaps because these flops were ultimately so self-inflicted. As for stockbroking, the very word annoyed him: he was deeply ashamed at having adopted such a profession.

So Ian took flight in realms of fantasy, talking of himself as a Renaissance man, with his vision of an ideal house, complete with details like gold taps and a fountain in front with a statue of Triton carrying off a nymph. But when Mary drew it for him, and added underneath the words – 'Stockbroker's Desirable Residence' – he was furious. He worked out his dream day: starting with a bathe in the sea, a fast drive up to London for breakfast at Brown's Hotel, and a good visit to the lavatory. And he talked for the first time of wanting to write a thriller. He even had an idea of his villain – a fat spider-like creature sitting in an armchair sniffing Benzedrine, the stimulant Ian himself sometimes affected to enjoy, particularly if he was trying to ham up the impression that his flat was vaguely sinister. In fact, it was Bond who sometimes resorted to Benzedrine, as a pick-me-up to help him "keep my wits about me tonight", as he put it in *Moonraker* in 1955.

Ian talked of writing in the Sapper mould. But he had recently discovered another, more sophisticated thriller writer, who impressed him greatly. In 1937 Geoffrey Household had published his first novel *The Third Hour*, which Ian thought tackled contemporary issues in an exciting and realistic manner. He gave it to his friends "in enormous quantities" that Christmas, though he complained to Jock McDougall, the book's publisher at Chatto & Windus, that each present cost him 8s 6d. His account at Elkin Matthews shows that at least six people received copies, including his lovers Mu Wright and Didy Hill.

Not a conventional thriller, like Household's second and better known novel, *Rogue Male*, published in 1939, *The Third Hour* told the story of Toby Manning, a liberal British businessman who went to Mexico to sell German-made toys. There he came across a couple of old friends, a Spanish bourgeois who had taken to the hills as a Marxist revolutionary, and the German Countess Irma von Reichensund who was visiting Mexico on a propaganda tour for the Nazis. The anarchism of Central American insurrection encouraged them to abandon their narrow political prejudices and to establish a fellowship dedicated to nobility and honour and opposed to nationalism and mass culture. Perhaps Ian saw this type of half-baked mystical internationalism as a way out of the imminent war with Germany. Or, as a putative novelist, he might have drawn inspiration from the explicit description of the scene where Manning raped the cold Nazi Countess, with her long hips and a mouth like "a firm gash from cheek to cheek".

Sex, inevitably, was one of Ian's fantasies. "He was always trying to show me obscene pictures of one sort or another," recalled Mary Pakenham. "No one I have known has had sex so much on the brain as Ian in those days." He pressed on her books from his collection of French pornography. He also gave her a copy of Elinor Glyn's risqué novel *Three Weeks*, which told the story of a torrid love affair between an exotic unnamed lady and a younger, typically self-confident Old Etonian. On its original publication in 1907, the book had a *succès de scandale*, largely because it depicted the woman as the seducer, making the running in the relationship from a recumbent position on her cushions and famous tiger-skin rug. It is likely that Ian met Glyn: in 1936 she had retired to a cottage near Taplow in

Buckinghamshire, where her closest admirer was Lord Ilchester, father of Ian's friend, John Fox-Strangways. By then she had published her novella, "It", which attempted to define the nature of sex appeal. "To have 'It'," she wrote, "the fortunate possessor must have that strange magnetism which attracts both sexes. He or she must be entirely unselfconscious and full of self-confidence, indifferent to the effect he or she is producing, and uninfluenced by others." As well as seeing something of himself in that description, Ian would have been pleased to note that Glyn's hero was called John Gaunt, an almost exact reference to the founder of the Lancastrian dynasty whom Eve liked to appropriate as an ancestor.

Another of Ian's female visitors recalled that often she had to wait for Ian to complete something. In those situations, he would point to a bookcase full of erotica and exclaim, "There you are, take a look at that." Most of the volumes were variations on a theme about flagellation – "books about women dressed up as schoolmistresses in lace collars, standing over manacled men with a whip". Since Ian's guest had never seen such material, she was fascinated. "After a while he would give me a casual glance and ask pointedly, 'I say, are you getting a kick out of that?'"

The first time Mary Pakenham visited Ian, he was so intent on talking about himself that he had to be reminded she had come for supper. The script then told him to put a Viennese waltz on the gramophone and light the candles on the balcony table. But that was as far as the special effects went. There was no attempt at *haute cuisine*. As she soon learned, Ian always served the same menu to his guests – kedgeree or sausages, washed down with champagne and whisky, and followed by coffee. From the supper table it was but a simple manoeuvre down to the bedroom at the end of the balcony. Mary had no intention of succumbing and, at the appropriate moment, made her excuses and left, though she did later notice that Ian kept a beautifully embossed silk counterpane on his bed.

As she got to know Ian, she became fascinated by his multifaceted character. She compared him to the layers of an onion: as fast as she peeled one layer away, there was always another. At the end she was not sure what was left. Ian remained an enigma. And that had its disturbing side. "You simply never could anticipate how Ian would behave. In a wreck I simply don't know whether he would go off in the first lifeboat, or go down with the ship. In the war, if the Germans had invaded and Ian had turned out to be a great Quisling, I would never have been surprised. He was totally unpredictable."

He did have one great quality which – for the most part – she found endearing: his boyish enthusiasms. If, for example, he decided to take her to the Chelsea Flower Show, his energies were totally focused on building up the excitement of that event. But he could overdo it. He once took Mary to what he described as a "special" restaurant behind St George's,

Hanover Square. In a fit of romantic fervour, he made her promise that she would never return there with anyone else. This struck her as odd since she had been before with her old governess, and she thought it was a very ordinary place indeed.

In another foray in June 1938 Ian took her to an international surrealist exhibition at a Mayfair gallery. While walking round the show, Ian suddenly doubled up with a pain in his stomach. After he was diagnosed as suffering from appendicitis, his mother paid for him to have his appendix removed in a nursing home. She then offered to send him away for a month to convalesce. Ivar Bryce was already bound for the fashionable island of Capri, off the Italian coast south of Naples. Since Ian had heard about the island from the Forbes Dennises who had frequently stayed there, he decided to join his friend and bring Mary as well.

The trip started inauspiciously. On the overnight railway journey through France Ian was happy for Mary to sit up in a second-class carriage, while he lorded it in a sleeper. After Turin Ian suddenly became annoyingly hearty, frequently exclaiming, "Isn't this all fun?" as they travelled down through Mussolini's Italy. If Ian's boyish exuberance had seemed attractive at home, it now became tiresome and repetitive. Before they had reached Naples, Mary was clear that her holiday with Ian was going to be a failure. "You might think that going to Capri with two fantastically good-looking men would be tremendously exciting, but in fact it was frightfully dull." One problem was that Ian had this idealized picture of life on Capri. He had worked himself up into a fever pitch of excitement about the place and what he expected to happen there – so much so, in fact, that "there was finally no chance for anything actually to happen".

Others, such as the writer Peter Quennell who came to know Ian later, have remarked on Ian's air of appearing to look for a lost piece of a jigsaw puzzle. They usually tended to see it in a romantic light, as if Ian were embarked on some great quest. But Mary saw it as an expression of Ian's egocentricity, or, as she put it, he was so obsessed with himself that he arranged his life round the most romantic or the most exciting prospect in sight. Again this was an important feature of his character that was noticed by others. After his death his widow Ann put it in much the same way, "You must realise that Ian was entirely egocentric. His aim as long as I knew him was to avoid the dull, the humdrum, the everyday demands of life that afflict ordinary people. He stood for working out a way of life that was not boring and he went where that led him. It ended with Bond."

Ian's self-centredness often came across as little more than rudeness. One example had already occurred on the train; another when the young travellers rented rooms in a cliffside pension overlooking the Bay of Naples. (Ivar had travelled separately.) Ian was completely unperturbed by the primitive facilities – the lack of hot water and the lavatory in a box on

the balcony. He even seemed to like that. He was, however, determined to
have the room with the best view at the top of the house. Ian made
straight for this room, without bothering to ask Mary.

He emerged on the hotel terrace wearing a black-and-white-striped
bathrobe with a red sash. He was sitting there one sunny morning, underneath the scented lemon trees, eating breakfast with his two friends, when
Bryce suddenly blurted out joyfully, "Think of all our school friends stuck
in offices now." Ian did not reciprocate but remained curiously silent.
Much as he liked an easy life, his puritanism was offended by Bryce's
sybaritism. Even when he might have forged out on his own – after the
war, for example – Ian preferred the regularity and order of office life. As
Mary put it, "He never wanted to be a playboy. He wanted to be a respected
citizen."

Ian was carrying a letter of introduction to a wealthy American socialite,
Mona Harrison Williams. One morning, after methodically grooming
himself, he called at her *fortino* at Marina Grande, overlooking the Bay of
Naples. He returned looking pleased. Not only had he won 25 shillings
playing backgammon with some of her cosmopolitan friends, he had also
been invited to stay with her. Ivar took note of this connection, and when
Ian and Mary left after a month, Bryce moved up to Mona's *fortino*, where
he enjoyed a brief fling with a Hungarian aristocrat, Margit, Countess
Hedervary.

Ian could amuse Mary by reciting the A. A. Milne poem "James James
Morrison Morrison", which he had learned at school, but his limitations
as a travelling companion were further exposed when the three holiday-
makers crossed to the mainland for a day-trip to Mount Vesuvius. Ian built
the journey up with a "frightful song and dance", recalled Mary, so that
it was as if they were visiting Mount Everest. Once again he spoiled the
experience for her because "his ego seemed to burn up everything in
sight".

It was no surprise that when they returned to London their relationship
petered out. But Ian still had to go through the final scene in his mating
ritual. Like other girls before her, Mary had to receive a literary memento
of what had passed. He gave her a copy of *Toi et Moi*, a series of vivid
lowbrow ditties which described the progress of a relationship and ended
with the girl leaving the man's flat for ever. As it was raining, he allowed
her in again, telling her to sit down as before – *"moi dans mon solitude, toi
dans ton ennui"*.

Although Ian valued his solitude, he still had plenty of time for other
girlfriends. He maintained contact with old loves, such as Didy Hill, who
used to see him when passing through London. As a reminder of Geneva
days, he invariably took her to the raucous Café Royal. "He preferred
brassy places to chi-chi nightclubs," she recalled. Ian also kept a predator's

eye peeled for pretty girls on the rebound from his friends. He had known Pamela Tiarks since, as a tongue-tied sixteen-year-old, she would attend dances at the Winchilseas'. In those days she was Pamela Silvertop, daughter of a naval officer. Later she married Peter Tiarks, brother of his friend, Henry, whose family bank, Schroders, was involved in important financial negotiations with Germany. But when this relationship failed, she often used to make her way round to Ebury Street to share Ian's sausages and champagne.

In the background, as always, was the sphinx-like Maud Russell, whom Ian used to describe as his *"maitresse en titre"*. In London they dined at the Savoy and in Hampshire Ian was still a regular guest at her weekend house parties. Under Maud's direction, Mottisfont Abbey was gradually transformed into a fine country house, an artistic as well as a political meeting-place. Geoffrey Jellicoe helped design the garden, while Rex Whistler painted a magnificent *trompe l'oeil* Gothic saloon, complete with stucco ceiling, trophy panels, urns and the Russell arms and motto: "Che Sara Sara". Maud collected Picasso among other modern artists and was herself either painted or drawn by Sargent, Nicholson, Orpen and Matisse.

Maud's attraction for Ian was never obvious. "Secretive" and "inscrutable" are two words frequently used of her. After visiting Mottisfont on an occasion when Ian was a fellow guest (along with the Duff Coopers and the Glenconners), Conrad Russell, Gilbert's brother, was annoyed to find no soap in his room. He contrasted Maud as a hostess with Diana Cooper, whom he adored. "Diana makes her guests a fulltime occupation," he said approvingly. But Maud had other qualities. Conrad noted that she was "just the oldest thing I know – it is the Orient does it, I'm sure. Her ancestors were sophisticated when Ecclesiastes' philosophy was *vieux jeu* and when our ancestors wore woad and ate beech mast. Her immense calm and tranquil epicurean Quietism is what we can't approach try as we may." Ian showed his appreciation by giving her an English translation of the *Breviary of Love* by Jeanne Aurélie Grivolin, published by Constable in 1938. It bore the subtitle 'Being the private journal written at Lyon and Cherbourg during the years 1802–3' and inscribed simply "Maud from I 1938". She responded by presenting him with the cigarette case he used for the rest of his life. It looked like ordinary gun-metal, but in fact was made of oxidized gold.

Maud was both his confidante and his archetypal fantasy figure. With her aloof continental *savoir faire*, she might have stepped from the pages of the Household novel Ian liked so much. She kept him *au fait* – as much as an intelligent stockbroker should be – with increasingly complicated machinations in the struggle against Hitler, which was a personal crusade for her. She not only arranged for eleven families to flee Germany, but she also bought them houses or flats when they reached England. On at least one occasion she flew to Frankfurt to arrange her relatives' departure from the country and, on her return, she went to see 'Van', Sir Robert Vansittart, at the Foreign Office. So Ian was introduced to the absorbing world of secret contacts and back channels. On one occasion in December 1938, he was at Mottisfont at the same time as Sir Joseph Ball, a former member of MI5 and founder of the Conservative Research Department. Ian had a heavy cold and, thankfully for him, was unable to take part in the weekend's shooting, so Sir Joseph was called into service as an extra gun. Like Vansittart, Ball was a seasoned behind-the-scenes manipulator though, unlike him, he was an ardent proponent of accommodation with Germany. At the time, as adviser to Prime Minister Neville Chamberlain, Ball was the middleman in secret talks between Downing Street and the Italian Embassy. Lord Blake, historian of the Conservative Party, called him "a quintessential *éminence grise*", a quality which attracted Maud.

With introductions and subtle encouragement not just from Maud but also from Forbes Dennis, who had returned to Vienna to work with refugees, and from Lancy and his partners at Rowe and Pitman, Ian was becoming increasingly aware of the world of clandestine services. As war with Germany loomed, he seems to have identifed intelligence as an area where he would like to work – to the extent that when he was in Germany or its neighbours he kept his eyes open for useful pieces of information. On one of his regular trips to Kitzbühel with Muriel in the mid-1930s, he met Conrad O'Brien-ffrench, who worked for another of the semi-autonomous intelligence networks which proliferated at the time. O'Brien-ffrench was a member of Claude Dansey's élite Z Organization, which recruited top businessmen as agents to work alongside the Secret Intelligence Service. He had been sent to Kitzbühel to keep an eye on the build-up of German forces in Bavaria. As cover he set up a travel firm called Tyrolese Tours which offered a two-week round trip from London to Kitzbühel, with full board, for fourteen guineas.

In early 1937 Ian was visiting the town with his brother Peter, newly married to Celia Johnson. They were sitting at a table in the Tiefenbrunner café with Arthur Waley, the Orientalist, and Ella Maillart, the Swiss explorer who had travelled in China with Peter a year earlier, when O'Brien-ffrench joined them with his attractive Swedish wife, another Maud. Ian was positioned slightly apart from the others reading, appropriately, a Buchan novel. At the arrival of the newcomers, Ian immediately sat up and began to take notice. When Maud wanted to go off on her own, Ian offered to accompany her. She said she would be delighted, adding, "I hope you will not accept too much." Ian pounced on her lack of familiarity with the English language and said, "I shall accept all that I am offered."

O'Brien-ffrench bumped into Ian again at Reisch's bar shortly afterwards. He had already noted how Ian's glamorous looks and nervous energy combined in a powerful sexual magnetism. Like many others, he attributed Ian's restlessness, cynicism and ambition to his unceasing competition with his older brother who had recently published yet another successful book about his trip to China and who seemed to do everything with such ease. As a result, O'Brien-ffrench thought Ian "was ruthless with his girl acquaintances as if, by taking it out on them, he could fulfil himself. A Casanova depends upon conquest after conquest to convince himself that he believes in his true manliness."

Nevertheless the two men became friendly, and Ian started opening up to this experienced spy, stating provocatively that he believed financial security was all that mattered in life. O'Brien-ffrench was a "little doubtful of his sincerity, coming from one who was a complete romantic about money. To Ian it was more a medium of freedom from the material grind. A very complicated, imaginative and subtle character was Ian, who lacked stability and staying power and yet was most intolerant of failure in others. The realities of business bored him. There had to be movement, excitement and glamour. And so it was that Ian never stayed long with any undertaking." The paradox was that, because he was still emotionally immature, Ian needed routine, preferably office routine, in order to achieve anything. Thus he felt at ease (if not necessarily happy) among his City stockbroker colleagues. As O'Brien-ffrench percipiently noted, "Latent in his character, deep in his subconscious, was the billycock hat and an umbrella of city life." O'Brien-ffrench introduced Ian to several friends, including Baron Rudolfo von Gerlach, his best local agent, and a German called Markwert who was believed to work for the Gestapo. When Ian found it hard to resist asking O'Brien-ffrench about his work and contacts, the older man told him more than he intended because, as he later noted, "in a way Ian was a more blatant and irascible me, and I was inclined to be more open with him than I should".

Ian returned to Austria and Germany periodically over the next couple of years. At some stage, he must have passed through Berlin and tried to interest the British Embassy in his reports on political and economic developments. For although Ian's accounts have not come to light, the energetic military attaché, Colonel Noel Mason-Macfarlane, who might have been sympathetic to Ian because he was married to a Pitman, indicated that he was unimpressed with them. Referring specifically to Ian's intelligence summaries, he described the young stockbroker as "gullible and of poor and unbalanced judgement".

Austria was again Ian's destination in the early summer of 1938 when he cabled his friend Ivar Bryce, then living in France, "MEET SELF GRAHAM PAIGE BOULOGNE MARITIME 1500 THURSDAY RESERVE FORTNIGHT ONWARD JOURNEY DO NOT FAIL IAN." Amazingly Bryce responded to this peremptory message. Ian came off the ferry arm in arm with a pretty, well-dressed American girl

whom he introduced as Phyllis. Bryce assumed that she would take the
train as Ian was driving a two-seater sports car. Instead Ian ordered his old
friend to perch between the gears and proclaimed, "We have to be in
Rheims for dinner." It emerged that Ian had met Phyllis at a party the
previous week and had invited her to join him for a mystery tour of the
Continent. After two days of the most uncomfortable journey in Bryce's
life, during which Ian kept up a non-stop and perfectly amiable conversation with Phyllis, the threesome arrived at the Hotel Vierjahreszeiten
in Munich, at which point Ian announced that their eventual destination
was Kitzbühel. However, his enthusiasm for Phyllis had by now rapidly
diminished; he began railing against her "Anglophobic American prejudices" and, next morning, refused to take her any further. When she began
to weep (having told Ivar earlier that she had fallen in love with Ian), he
cold-bloodedly advised her to return to Boston. Later he told Ivar, who
had witnessed this sort of behaviour before, that she would have made
their lives miserable.

While Ian was in Kitzbühel, the writer Cyril Connolly arrived in town
in pursuit of a woman. The surprise of encountering him – someone Ian
had barely known at Eton sixteen years earlier – was nothing to meeting
the woman Connolly was chasing, who turned out to be Ian's first girlfriend, Peggy. Having just left her Mosleyite husband, Emerson Bainbridge,
she turned white when she saw Ian, and later explained the background
to Connolly. He could not but fail to be dazzled by Ian and Ivar: "It would
be hard to imagine two more distinguished-looking young men; a Greco-
Roman Apollo and a Twelfth Dynasty Pharaoh". Although Connolly did
not share Ian's enthusiasm for climbing the Kitzbühler Horn, he found
him an agreeable companion, and the two men were soon whiling away
their time at marathon games of bridge.

During his time in Austria that summer, Ian was determined to follow
his own amatory instincts. Staying on the Wörthersee on the other side
of the country in Carinthia was Ann O'Neill, the spirited and stylish peer's
wife whom he had first met at Stanway in 1934. She was enjoying a short
holiday at the Karinder Hütte, a traditional wooden house on the water's
edge belonging to Jimmy Foster, an Old Etonian cousin of the composer
and novelist, Lord Berners. Foster, who had lost a leg in the First World
War, surrounded himself with a cosmopolitan crowd of patrons and practitioners of the arts. One of his guests, "Nin" Ryan, later a good friend of
both Ian and Ann, was the astute daughter of the German-born New York
financier, Otto Kahn, who had backed the acting career of Diana Cooper.
Another, Peggy Munster, was a talented interior decorator, who, as the
first partner of Sibyl Colefax, had launched fellow-designer John Fowler.
Fifty miles away towards Villach, her husband, Count Paul Munster, a
golfing friend of Ian's at White's, owned Schloss Wasserleonburg, which

had been lent to the Duke and Duchess of Windsor for part of their honeymoon the previous year. Nin Ryan was clear that Ian was there for only one reason – to see Ann – and she dated the start of her friends' affair from that lakeside summer holiday.

Ian had made no impression on the newly married Ann at their initial meeting at Stanway, and vice versa. As far as he was concerned, she was the bright, attractive, rather naïve daughter of the manor. If he had bothered to enquire further, he would have discovered that her predominantly Scottish family, the Charterises, had owned the house, with its Inigo Jones gatehouse and façade, since the seventeenth century. Stanway was usually inhabited by the eldest son of the Earl of Wemyss, but since the 10th Earl of Wemyss survived to the ripe old age of ninety-six, his cold, philandering son, Hugo, Viscount Elcho (Ann's grandfather), lived there through most of his adult life. During the late nineteenth century, largely through the influence of Hugo's long-suffering wife, Mary, the house had been imbued with the spirit of the Souls, the circle of gifted and cultured aristocrats. Born a Wyndham, one of the six core Souls families, she was famously painted as a society belle by Sargent (with her two sisters), but is better observed in languorous, contemplative pose in a portrait by Edward Poynter. When she tired of her husband's extra-marital affairs, she entered her own "tendresse" with a fellow Soul, the future Prime Minister, Arthur Balfour – one of the more intriguing "did they or didn't they?" relationships in modern history.

In 1912 Hugo Elcho's amiable but feckless second son, Guy Charteris, married Frances Tennant, a member of the wealthy Scottish chemical manufacturing family. Ann, their first child, was born the next year, followed by two daughters, Laura and Mary Rose, and a son, Hugo. In 1925 Ann's carefree childhood was blighted when her mother, not yet forty, was struck down by cancer. The Charterises became more peripatetic as they flitted between their comfortable London house, originally financed by Tennant money, and Stanway, where her grandparents, now the Earl and Countess of Wemyss, still lived for a large part of the year. The rest of the time the Wemysses were in Scotland which meant that Stanway could be rented to rich bankers such as the Russells. Generally, however, they lived separate lives, Grandfather Hugo with one of his mistresses, and Grandmother ("Grumps") Mary surrounded by members of a literary rump of the Souls, including L. P. Hartley, Angela Thirkell and Sir James Barrie, who wrote a special play, *The Wheel*, for Ann and her sisters and Tennant and Asquith cousins. (The Souls and their children, known as the Coterie, often intermarried: Ann's great-aunt Margot, née Tennant, was the second wife of the Liberal Prime Minister, Herbert Asquith, later Lord Oxford and Asquith, and, to complicate matters, her aunt Cynthia, married the Oxfords' son, Herbert Asquith.) As a result, Ann

had little formal education (lasting just one term at Cheltenham Ladies'
College), but she was striking, intelligent and well-read. (At Stanway
Dickens, Walter Scott and Jane Austen were declaimed aloud as part of
everyday life.) After losing her mother, she needed some stability in her
life and married one of her first serious suitors, the forceful Shane, Lord
O'Neill, in 1932, when she was still only nineteen.

Sometimes such marriages work. But Ann was flighty and immature.
Her more conventionally pretty sister, Laura, with whom she competed
throughout her life, recalled cattily how, when Ann received her first
chaste kiss on the cheek aged sixteen, she was terrified she was going to
have a baby, and when she returned from her honeymoon, she was still a
virgin because her sunburn had made lovemaking too uncomfortable. So
Ann had a lot of growing up to do, which she achieved with some
patronage from society hostesses such as Sibyl Colefax and Maud Russell.
Her path next crossed with Ian's at a golfing weekend in Le Touquet in
May 1936. She noticed him as a "handsome moody creature" sitting on
the other side of a swimming-pool. She saw more of him after he joined
White's the following month and came increasingly into contact with her
husband, Shane, an enthusiastic sportsman. Lord O'Neill began inviting
Ian back to his London house in Montagu Square for bridge evenings. By
now his marriage to Ann had broken down and she had embarked on an
affair with Esmond Harmsworth, son of the newspaper proprietor, Lord
Rothermere. But she could not help being attracted by her husband's
amusing companion, Ian Fleming, who was known to her girlfriends as
"Glamour Boy". So, as she expressed it candidly, when she could not see
Esmond, she found Ian "the best antidote" among her other admirers.

When Ian returned to London that summer of 1938, he tried to interest
Cyril Connolly in a project he was contemplating. After the recent demise
of *Night and Day*, he had ambitions to set up a new magazine on the lines
of the *New Yorker*. Ian came up with a detailed proposal for a weekly review
which, together with staple fare such as a books page by Graham Greene,
would include such modern reader-friendly features as share tips and
consumer advice. Although the paper was not party political, Ian declared
forthrightly, "Pretentiousness, dishonesty and bombast will be the chief
targets. In fact the paper will aim at 'cleaning up' and revitalising Democ-
racy so that it may be better able to make a stand against the inroads of
younger and more exciting creeds, such as Fascism and Communism. It
will be aimed at building up the '*amour-propre*' of this country to face the
national spirit and pride of, for instance, Germany."

The review never materialized but, in an effort to broaden his own
minimal understanding of politics, Ian paid his one and only visit to the
House of Commons in late 1938 when, as he put it, "we were unattractively
trying to cajole Mussolini away from Hitler". (His curiosity may well have

been stimulated by meeting Sir Joseph Ball at Mottisfont.) But Ian "found the hollowness and futility of the speeches degrading and infantile and the well-fed, deep-throated 'hear, hears' for each mendacious platitude verging on the obscene." If this was politics, he reflected, he "would much rather not see it happening". He swore never to re-enter the Chamber and never did. The secret world of clandestine activity, or what academics call parapolitics, beckoned.

In the meantime, the death of Ian's respected grandmother in March 1937 precipitated the same kind of family crisis as had occurred after her husband's death four years earlier. So untroubled had Granny Katie been by the prospect of her demise that she failed to make a will. Thus, any hopes that Ian and his brothers had of an adjustment to the apparent oversights in their grandfather's will were dashed. All Robert's estate, which had been held in trust for their grandmother, passed, as ordained, to their Uncle Phil and his two sisters Dorothy Wyfold and Kathleen Hannay. Phil generously sought to make amends by giving Peter the Joyce Grove estate, minus the house, which had been presented to St Mary's Hospital, Paddington, as a nurses' and then a convalescent home. In 1938 Peter began to build his own house, Merrimoles, on his 2000 acres of well-ordered land. It was designed by Joyce Grenfell's father, Paul Phipps, and later contained the frieze depicting the history of the Fleming family.

Eve brushed away any disappointment by holding a lavish fancy-dress party at Turner's House. Ian was now her only unwed son. Although her other three boys had all married perfectly respectably, their wives, in her eyes, were never quite right. "It only remains for Ian to marry a barmaid," she intoned, as she watched Ian, dressed as a Cossack, dancing with Muriel.

Even at this stage Eve lost no opportunity to promote her sons. Meeting her husband's old friend, Winston Churchill, in November 1938, she was amazed to learn that he had never been painted by Augustus John. In informing Churchill of her efforts to arrange a sitting with John, she hazarded the hope that he thought she had "done well by Val's boys". And just to make sure he knew what she was talking about, she enclosed brief curricula vitae for all four sons. Ian's were more or less correct, though she had him as Victor Ludorum at Eton three times and winning the Public Schools' hurdles for England. As for his latest venture into the City, Eve noted correctly, "This is not his métier really." Churchill's non-committal acknowledgement – "What a wonderful record your four boys have. You have indeed set them on the highway" – suggested that Ian's espionage exploits had so far been low-level and that Eve's second-born was not yet a member of any established intelligence network, certainly not of one which was supplying information to Churchill.

In "early 1939" Ann O'Neill first plucked up courage to dine alone with

Ian in Ebury Street. After Austria, she had seen him again with an unnamed mistress in Biarritz in November. With holidays in Kitzbühel, Capri and Biarritz, all in the course of a few months, it is clear why Ian is not remembered for his stockbroking. Ann found meeting him on his own turf a disconcerting experience. Ian was at his non-communicative worst. Claiming to have a migraine and to be unable to speak, he gave her a book and told her to keep quiet for an hour "till I am ready for you". Ann noted in her diary, "Considering the slightness of our acquaintance, very odd behaviour." But she was the type of woman who was attracted to Ian's mixture of arrogance and physicality. As far back as 1931, well before her marriage, she had asked her diary rhetorically, "Why do I like cads and bounders?" And Ian's blasé non-committal approach to relationships appealed. "I might marry you if you had a broken leg", was one of his throwaway expressions. Some time over the next few weeks, Ann first went to bed with Ian, probably – so is the consensus – at a golfing weekend in Sandwich. But it meant very little to either of them. As her friend Nancy Hare noted, "When young, she [Ann] couldn't understand why people took their emotions so seriously," and, given half a chance, Ian was happy to concur.

When, in March 1939, Ann was due to accompany another friend Lady Maureen Stanley, the wife of Oliver Stanley, the trade minister, on an official tour of the Balkans to promote British fashion, she invited Ian to join her. He declined because, undeterred by his failure to make headway in defence circles in Berlin, he had decided to revisit Moscow, the scene of his 1933 triumph as a journalist. His brother Peter was already working part-time in Military Intelligence. So to boost his own ambitions in this direction, Ian obtained temporary leave of absence from Rowe and Pitman, and with Peter's help was taken on by *The Times* as a special correspondent to report on a British trade mission to the Soviet Union.

The mission, headed by Robert Hudson, Secretary of State for Overseas Trade, was more important than it appeared. Economic relations between the two countries had yet to recover since Ian's earlier visit to Moscow for the Metro-Vick trial. Now, with Hitler threatening on the Polish border, the Soviet Union needed to be encouraged to keep up its natural combination of anti-Germanism and anti-Fascism.

Apart from Ian, one other journalist, Sefton Delmer of the *Daily Express*, was on the trip. With the benefit of hindsight, Delmer noted how Ian used to type whenever the Russians looked his way. He had no illusions that his tall suave newspaper colleague "with the profile of a Tarquinian piper" was involved in other business and was only "ostensibly representing *The Times*". Once across the Russian frontier, Hudson invited the two reporters to his sumptuous official Pullman car to sample the Crimean champagne and Georgian brandy which the Soviet Commissar for Foreign Affairs, Maxim Litvinov, had provided, while all the time they knew their conversation was being recorded by hidden microphones in the panelwork.

The talks were not a great success. The Soviet negotiators were manipulative and obstructive, angling for concessions from Britain only as a means of leverage to obtain more from Nazi Germany. Indeed, five months later the Soviet Union surprised the world by signing a formal non-aggression pact with Germany. Even Ian was unable to find much colour in the proceedings, producing three uninspired articles, including a description of a formal visit to the opera to see Glinka's reworked *A Life for the Tsar*, for which *The Times* paid him £2 18s 0d.

Ian stayed at the same hotel, the National, as six years earlier. But he found the Russian capital a depressing city – like the Gorbals in Glasgow, he later said. So he attempted to enjoy what he could in his own way. Peter had given him an introduction to Fitzroy Maclean, a junior diplomat in the British Embassy. When Hudson's American wife wanted to invite "that nice young Mr Fleming" to dinner, Maclean went to Ian's hotel room and found him in bed with a young lady from Odessa. The young diplomat returned to the minister's wife with the reply that Ian was sorry he could not accept her invitation as he was "very, very busy".

After five days of impasse, Ian and Delmer packed their bags for the long journey home on the Warsaw Express. As the train neared the Russian frontier, Delmer, who was no novice in intelligence matters, tore up his copious notes and threw them away. Ian mocked his friend: "Why don't you swallow them? All the best spies do." But the last laugh was on Ian. At the border, the Soviet customs went through his baggage with a fine-tooth comb. In the process they found a packet of Russian contraceptives made of artificial latex. As an amateur agent keen to impress some agency or other, Ian was carrying them to London where their rubber content would be examined to determine the success of recent Soviet industrialization. As the customs officer held each sample to the light and examined it, Ian fidgeted with embarrassment. Delmer could not resist telling his friend, "You should have swallowed them."

Back in London Ian completed another two turgid summaries for *The Times*, before turning his attention to a much longer essay on the strength and morale of the Soviet Union's armed forces. Ian concluded that, if the USSR's military might were directed towards limited objectives, it could provide "the very greatest strategic value to the Allies" in any future war against the Axis powers.

However, *The Times* was unimpressed by Ian's analysis and declined to publish it. So Ian added a few "cautionary notes" to his report, warning that, despite all he had written, "Russia would be an exceedingly treacherous ally" and would "not hesitate to stab us in the back the moment it

suited her", and sent it to on 19 April to Philip Nichols, a friend in the
Foreign Office, asking for his comments.

Two days later Nichols minuted his diplomat colleagues, noting that
Ian had recently returned from Moscow and seemed to "take a special
interest in foreign affairs". Over the next week Ian's memo found its way
round three experienced Soviet-watchers in the Foreign Office's Northern
Department. Having noted the ambivalence in Ian's attitude ("the Soviet
Union would be a useful ally but treacherous . . ."), they became embroiled
in an unproductive civil service debate about how they should reply to
him. They felt that, however reliable Ian might be, they could not be seen
to endorse his conclusions in anything so formal as a letter. They decided
they could invite Ian to visit them to give him their reactions verbally.
Nichols said his friend would be "delighted and flattered" at this suggestion. So on 2 May Ian called in to see Lawrence Collier of the Northern
Department. Collier later noted that Ian had struck him "as a man of
good judgement" who appeared to be in touch with a number of good
journalistic sources such as A. T. Cholerton of the *News Chronicle*.

Seeking to be still better informed about Europe and the wider world,
Ian began attending meetings of the Royal Geographical Society where
Peter was already a Fellow. Lady Butler of Saffron Walden remembered
seeing Ian "occasionally" at lectures, having been introduced by her first
husband, the Arctic explorer August Courtauld, whose family knew Ian
through Maud Russell.

Ian's diligent research took him back to Europe in the last few months
before the war (the exact date is not certain). On his trip he met Diana
Napier, the sexually adventurous actress wife of the operatic tenor, Richard
Tauber. Later he used to boast of his one-night stand with her in a wagon-
lit. Ian told how he bribed the attendant to allow him into her carriage.
Then he and Diana made love to the "hasty metal gallop of the wheels" –
a phrase he used to describe a similar encounter in his 1957 novel, *From
Russia, With Love*. According to Lady Mary Pakenham, "It was the sort of
incident Ian liked to think he was having all the time. He liked to make
believe he never got on a train without something like that happening.
He was very good at describing it. He had an excellent gift for narrative."
After his night of lust, so Ian's story went, he told Miss Napier he never
wanted to see her again.

Back in London, Ian's freelance intelligence-gathering at last received
some recognition. On 24 May he was invited to join Admiral John Godfrey
for lunch at the Carlton Grill at the bottom of the Haymarket. The donnish
Godfrey had been appointed Director of Naval Intelligence (DNI) three
months earlier. Having been plucked directly from his ship, HMS *Repulse*,
he had worked hard to acquaint himself with the secret world. He had
met insiders like Admiral "Quex" Sinclair, head of the Secret Intelligence

Service (known as "C"), and his deputy, soon to succeed him, Colonel Stewart Menzies. He was visited by his distinguished predecessor, Admiral 'Blinker' Hall, who told him that one of his most important assets would be a good and trustworthy personal assistant. During the First World War, Hall had enjoyed the services of the successful Old Etonian stockbroker Claud Serocold. With war now looming again, Godfrey put out the call for someone similar – a self-starter (as they say in the recruitment advertisements) who would act as his eyes and ears in the Naval Intelligence Division (NID) and Whitehall, who would liaise with the other secret services, and who would generally make life easier for him.

The answer came from the City, where Admiral Hall had recommended Godfrey to cultivate close relations. Hall had put him in touch with Sir Montagu Norman, the Governor of the Bank of England, Sir Edward Peacock, head of Barings Bank, and Olaf Hambro, chairman of Hambros Bank. One day Norman rang the new DNI to say he had found him his man. The Governor refused to let Godfrey come down to the City to discuss the matter. "On no account. You are much too busy to waste a morning in the City. I will come and see you at the Admiralty tomorrow morning at 10 a.m." At ten o'clock on the dot, Norman was there. He insisted on calling Godfrey 'Sir', and told him about Ian Fleming, another Old Etonian stockbroker, albeit less successful than Serocold. The Governor already knew Ian through his own friendship with two of Eve Fleming's suitors, Lord D'Abernon and Augustus John, and through his chief of staff, Bernard Rickatson-Hatt, Ian's old boss at Reuters.

The Carlton Grill was part of the Carlton Hotel which, for a while at the turn of the century, was run by the great hotelier César Ritz, with his protégé Escoffier as chef. By 1939 it had lost some of its cachet, but was ideally placed for anyone working in the Admiralty. Godfrey and Ian were joined there by another admiral, Aubrey Hugh Smith, Hall's former deputy and a member of the Rowe and Pitman establishment, and Angus McDonnell, a City businessman with close links to the intelligence services.

Godfrey did not let on much about the job he had in mind. More interested in "having a good look at the fellow", he suggested Ian might like to come into the NID at the Admiralty on a part-time basis and get the feel of the place. Ian began attending for three or four afternoons a week in June. Within a fortnight, Fleming had mastered his limited brief and was asking Godfrey for something more challenging. Godfrey had already seen enough: as he recorded in his unpublished memoirs, "I quickly made up my mind that here was the man for the job." In late July Ian was appointed to the newly formed Special Branch (dealing with intelligence and meteorology) of the Wavy Navy, the Royal Naval Volunteer Reserve (RNVR). He joined NID full-time the following month and was firmly installed, with enough inside information to advise Percy Muir to move his book collection to the countryside, and enough work on his desk to have to cancel his engagement as best man at Gerald Coke's wedding on 2 September, the day before war began.

4

Chocolate sailor

1939–1941

For thirty-one years Ian had progressed fitfully, with some help and cajoling from his mother, along a traditional career path – Eton, Sandhurst, the City – without ever (except for a few months at Reuters) fully engaging his personality. Now, as a result of a behind-the-scenes process that may have involved nothing more complicated than Eve writing one of her gushing promotional letters to Montagu Norman, Ian was following his father into the armed services in defence of his country. Since his death on the Western Front in May 1917, Val Fleming had been the ghost at Ian's feast, the blameless paragon of manly virtues, whom his son could never hope to match.

So, it was with some trepidation that Ian donned the blue doeskin uniform of the Royal Navy with two shimmering gold stripes on its sleeve signifying his rank as a lieutenant in the Voluntary Reserve. His discomfort was evident when he was invited to join the O'Neills for dinner on 4 September, the first full day of the war, and Shane O'Neill felt it necessary to telephone ahead to tell his wife that Ian was sensitive about his new dress order and she was not to laugh at it. Ian was joined at Montagu Square by Ann's guests, a rather harder, more caustic gaggle of aristocrats than his own usual bridge-playing friends. They included her confident sister Laura looking equally out of place in her newly acquired auxiliary nurse's outfit, Ed Stanley, a brandy-swilling buccaneer, and Anthony Winn, a current beau whose regiment was guarding a police station round the corner. Fired with adrenalin, uncertain what the future would hold, the party was filled with what Ann described as a "strange gaiety", joking about gas masks and what they would do during inevitable air raids to come. In the general badinage, Winn, not having had the benefit of his host's warning, described Ian as the 'Chocolate Sailor', a reference to the stripes on his coat, which made him look like the man in the Black Magic advertisements. Ian hated the phrase, which has been wrongly attributed to Lord Beaverbrook and others. It seemed to suggest sugariness and superciliousness, rather than the seriousness of purpose with which he was already imbued in Room 39 of the Admiralty. To his disgust the name was taken up by Ann and her friends, and stuck.

The atmosphere in the Admiralty, where Ian had come from, was very different from the nervous anticipation to be found in the O'Neills' drawing room in Montagu Square. The sense of industry in its Room 39, where Ian worked, has been likened to the newsroom of a great newspaper (by Donald McLachlan) or to an Arab bank in Tangier or Beirut (by Sefton Delmer). This was the bustling antechamber to the Director of Naval Intelligence's more sedate office looking out on Horse Guards Parade, with a view to Downing Street and the Foreign Office in the distance. It was also the ideas factory or, as Admiral Godfrey called it, coordinating section, for the most professional arm of British Intelligence at the start of the war.

The Naval Intelligence Division had attained this pre-eminence *faute de mieux*. The Secret Intelligence Service was a shadow of itself in the early months of the war, when its effectiveness was badly undermined by the death of its chief, Admiral Sir Hugh Sinclair and, more alarmingly, by the compromising of its whole European intelligence-gathering apparatus after two officers were enticed across the Dutch border at Venlo and captured inside Germany in November 1939. The Special Operations Executive (SOE) was yet to be established with its mission to "set Europe ablaze" with sabotage and covert activities. Instead its responsibilities were split between a number of competing organizations. As a result, during the tense 'phoney war', NID was required to operate way beyond its strict brief of collecting, collating and distributing information about the war at sea. It still derived considerable kudos from its First World War successes in tracking U-boats and deciphering coded messages. It enjoyed good sources of basic intelligence through its worldwide network of naval attachés and reporting officers. Since 1936 it also had a modern Operational Intelligence Centre (OIC) housed in the concrete bowels of the Citadel beside the Admiralty. Working in close cooperation with the Government Communications Headquarters (GCHQ) at Bletchley Park, the OIC digested every last signal about enemy ship movements, allowing British vessels to take evasive or, alternatively, offensive action as required. And, from the start of the year, running this sometimes rusty but generally stately and well-engineered machine was Rear Admiral John Godfrey, a steely, irascible taskmaster, whose high-handedness antagonized many, but who manifestly got things done.

Room 39 was the bridge of Godfrey's ship. Here, around a marble fireplace, with iron coal-scuttles at its side, sat the DNI's hand-picked think-tank of (at the height of the war) twenty men and women – some experienced naval officers; some, like Ian, neophytes from civilian life. Known collectively as Section 17, they handled the mountain of secret signals, reports and maps which poured into the office, not just from the OIC, but also from other geographical and technical departments within NID and from the wider Whitehall bureaucracy. They discussed the contents and formulated policies and ideas to put to the DNI and more senior service chiefs. Often they had to formulate quick replies to Winston Churchill's 'prayers', or requests for vital pieces of information. Pray, the recently appointed First Lord of the Admiralty, later the Prime Minister, would ask, what is being done to harass enemy shipping in the Yucatan Channel, and someone from NID 17 would try to ensure that Churchill had an instant briefing on his desk by the time he had finished his afternoon nap.

From his large wooden desk immediately outside Godfrey's green baize door, Ian quickly fell into his allotted role as the DNI's liaison with the outside world. His easy manners and wide range of contacts made him an ideal person to carry out delicate inter-Whitehall missions, particularly liaising with other clandestine services. Ian was equally adept at paying a formal call on a senior member of the SIS as he was casually chatting up an official of the newly formed Ministry of Economic Warfare at one of his clubs.

Having been taken on as a lieutenant, Ian was promoted to commander on 8 September, entitling him to wear three full stripes on his uniform. While rendering him liable to further ribbing from Ann and her friends, his new rank gave him the confidence in his official capacity to confront anyone from an admiral to a Cabinet minister. As his colleagues liked to point out, Ian never subsequently suffered from Senior Officer Veneration. He managed to cut through barriers of rank, nationality and even class. This facility brought additional benefits: from the beginning, Ian never felt any reticence in contributing his own bright, often fanciful, ideas for securing vital naval intelligence. And he was an excellent conduit for others wanting to bring similar schemes to the DNI's notice.

Godfrey soon recognized the young man's potential. "Not only did Ian carry out the multifarious duties of personal assistant, a job which has no defined frontiers, with outstanding success," the DNI noted, "but he represented me on various interdepartmental committees and later in the year took over the function of intelligence planning, for which he had a very marked flair." In a post-war memo about his job, Ian described himself as "a convenient channel for confidential matters connected with subversive organisations, and for undertaking confidential missions abroad, either alone or with DNI".

As Godfrey understood, his PA was more than just an effective public relations man. Underneath his personable exterior, behind the affected façade of the man around town, Ian possessed the essential toughness of character to convey unwelcome intelligence information convincingly. His wit and charm could always sugar a bitter pill and make it go down effectively. Crucially also, Ian had a flair for intelligence planning. Later, Godfrey, a man not given to hyperbole, declared, "Ian should have been DNI and I his naval adviser." Within a short period, the Director felt happy about giving Ian considerable licence to pursue his own initiatives. As Godfrey later explained, he had learned this technique of motivating subordinates from Captain Rudolph Burmester, under whom he had served on HMS *Charybdis* during the First World War, and he was convinced it "was the only method likely to achieve success under modern conditions".

Ian responded well to Godfrey's enlightened despotism. As his colleague Donald McLachlan realized, Ian "enjoyed power within limits, and with a bridle on him he was happy". For the first time in his life, he was prepared to work extremely long hours and was surprised to find that he enjoyed it. Robert Harling, a later recruit to NID, saw something masochistic in Ian's willingness to jump at the Director's beck and call, striving to please a tough father figure. Other team members gave Ian more credit for his skilful handling of the relationship. Peter Smithers felt that only Ian was capable of the wit and sophistication to handle the complex character of 'Uncle John' (as Godfrey was known to his inner circle). According to McLachlan, "No one ever jollied along an obstinate admiral more effectively than Fleming." McLachlan, who had previously worked on *The Times*, also understood an important psychological element in Ian's response to his new job. Secret service work appealed to Ian's romanticism. Here, he was experiencing the thrill and excitement which he had only previously read about in the novels of Buchan and Phillips Oppenheim. "Here in this intelligence world," wrote McLachlan perceptively, "where there was so much violence and evil and duplicity on paper, Fleming and others acquired an attitude towards the cloak-and-dagger profession rather like that of Cervantes to the obsolescent knighthood of his day. But they knew it was deadly serious as well as intellectually stimulating." At last, after flailing around unproductively in the City, Ian was finding an outlet for his disparate talents, which included sociability, organization and imagination.

Gradually, as official duties in Room 39 came to be shared around, Ian found himself, in addition to being Godfrey's personal assistant, responsible for NID's relations with the Secret Intelligence Service and, later, the Political Warfare Executive. He was also charged with the appointment of Royal Naval Volunteer Reserve (RNVR) officers to NID, with handling some of the "special" intelligence emanating from the GCHQ at Bletchley Park and with liaising with the Joint Intelligence Committee. The JIC, strictly the Joint Intelligence Sub-committee of the Chief of Staffs Committee, was established in 1936 and played an important role in coordinating the work of the various service intelligence organizations with that of the Foreign Office and the Ministry of Economic Warfare. Its chairman was Victor (known as Bill) Cavendish-Bentinck, later the Duke of Portland, who became a close friend of Ian.

In managing this heavy workload, Ian relied on another older man,

Captain Charles Drake, who was theoretically the senior officer in Room 39. A former career naval officer, 'Quacker', as he was known, had been invalided out of the service some years earlier, after a shell exploded in his face. Like Ian, he had worked in the City as a stockbroker. But his sharp mind and skilled training as a navigator were much valued in the Admiralty and, as war clouds gathered, he returned to lend his experience to NID and, as it turned out, to Ian. Drake was NID's representative on the Joint Intelligence Staff, the backroom boys who drafted position papers for the Joint Intelligence Committee. Ian often helped Drake with NID's input into the JIS, though Drake acknowledged the importance to the Division of Ian's independent channel into the decision-making JIC through his personal friendship with Cavendish-Bentinck.

Summoning hitherto hidden resolve, Ian endeavoured to arrive at the office at six o'clock in the morning, and to have sifted through the night's signals and prepared situation reports ("sit reps") by the time Godfrey arrived around 8.30. A small select staff meeting was held every morning at 9.30, with a wider heads of department conference on Mondays. Ian's main luxury was an extended lunch. He left the office sharply at one, bound for the Carlton Grill, if he had an important meeting, or the "Senior", as the United Services Club at the top of the Duke of York's steps was known, if he was with Godfrey. Sometimes he might range further afield to Frascati's in Soho or the White Tower in Fitzrovia. Then around the middle of the afternoon, he sauntered back to the Admiralty for an evening session which often lasted well into the night.

Apart from Ann, Ian had little time for other women or for his family in those first few months of the war. He occasionally also saw Muriel Wright, who was working as an air raid warden and lived round the corner in Belgravia. Once before the end of the year, he managed to drag himself down to Nettlebed where Peter was putting the finishing touches to his new house, Merrimoles. On 11 November, he uncharacteristically joined Peter on a shoot with Tim Nugent, and David Bowes-Lyon, the Queen's brother, who was later to work with him on propaganda. "Masses of birds, warm muggy day, v agreeable company", recorded Peter in his new game book.

Otherwise his social life largely centred around the game of bridge. Sometimes, at the Tufton Street house of Oliver Stanley, who briefly became Secretary of State for War in January 1940, he even managed to combine this pastime with seeing Ann O'Neill, who came along as a friend of Stanley's wife, Maureen. Perhaps because Ian was still embarrassed about his status when he was not actually fulfilling his service duties, he continued to provoke mixed reactions among the other guests. Henry Hopkinson, who worked for the War Cabinet, remembered Ian as "a little too big for his boots but also full of brilliant comment".

But these same qualities attracted another bridge player, the priggish and impressionable newspaper magnate, Lord Kemsley. Since censorship and liaison with the press were among NID's responsibilities. Godfrey did his best to court the various proprietors, but he left day-to-day liaison to Ian, who struck up an immediate rapport with Kemsley, the influential owner of the *Sunday Times*. Just before the war, in July 1939, Kemsley had blotted his copybook by personally travelling to Bayreuth to interview Hitler. He thought this would help prevent war, but all it did was give the German Chancellor a useful propaganda platform. Looking, perhaps, for a way into intelligence-gathering circles, and discovering that Ian shared his enthusiasm for bridge, Kemsley invited him to his houses in London and Farnham, Surrey, where his lively Mauritius-born wife, Edith, made it clear that she enjoyed the addition of the dashing young commander to her salon. On Saturday 18 November, Ian drove down to Farnham for the weekend with Kemsley's daughter, Pam, and 'Jock' Colville, the Assistant Private Secretary to Neville Chamberlain. Already the gossip was about the Prime Minister's inevitable resignation. But who was to succeed him? Kemsley demonstrated his lack of political nous by ill-advisedly fancying the chances of Samuel Hoare, a proponent of appeasement.

At White's Ian's golfing and City friends were still lobbying for decent niches in the war apparatus. He must have been surprised to be contacted by Evelyn Waugh, a fellow member he hardly knew, who came to the Admiralty on 17 October to ask about a job in Naval Intelligence. Ian could do little more than inform the successful novelist that his name was "on the list". Over the next few months his club provided a good base to meet new acquaintances from arcane branches of the secret services. But even at this stage Ian could not help occasionally betraying an ambivalence over his role. Henry Cavendish, a member of the crack 601 Squadron, used to tell the story of seeing Ian enter the lobby of White's in his uniform, looking rather deflated after mistakenly saluting a Marconi messenger outside.

Before long Ian was well pitched into NID's operational work. One of the Division's major concerns at the beginning of the war was monitoring the movement of German warships. The Royal Navy wanted to stop them breaking out of the North Sea into the North Atlantic where they could threaten the merchant shipping on which Britain's livelihood depended. Drake discussed this matter casually with Sydney Cotton, a maverick Australian pilot and technical innovator who had done valuable aerial photographic work for the SIS in Germany and France. In early September Cotton offered to fly over the North German ports and photograph what he could. The very next day he turned up at the Admiralty with clear pictures of the German fleet still at anchor in the Wilhelmshaven roads.

With the enthusiasm of youth, Ian was keen to inform the First Sea Lord and Chief of Naval Staff, Admiral Sir Dudley Pound, of this photographic coup as quickly as possible. Drake had to restrain him, saying he would telephone Pound's secretary, Paymaster Captain Shaw, to arrange a meeting. When Ian declared he would have rung Pound directly, Drake gently rebuked the new boy, "We don't do things like that in the Navy." But, as Drake himself acknowledged, Ian proved a notable exception to this hard-and-fast service rule. When, later that afternoon, Drake took the photographs to the First Sea Lord, the Director's personal assistant accompanied him. Ian remained in Paymaster Captain Shaw's office while Drake presented the photographs to Pound in person. On examining them, the First Sea Lord called next door for a magnifying glass. When his secretary was unable to find one, Ian picked up a glass bottle and suggested it would do the trick. At that stage Pound noticed Ian for the first time and asked who he was. After Ian had explained, Pound said, "Ah, I see, you're one of those chaps who can see in the dark." Young Fleming was beginning to impress the right people in high places.

Ian got on well with Cotton, who had the same commitment to cutting through red tape and getting things done as he did. More to the point, the Australian was a technical genius who obtained results. He had modified his planes so they could fly higher than conventional aircraft and solved the traditional problem of his equipment misting up by placing his sophisticated Leica cameras in the wings where they were heated by the aircraft's exhaust. Cotton became the first of a line of practical inventors befriended by Ian. Within a week – Cotton later recalled it was probably 10 or 11 September – Ian visited the Australian in his Mayfair flat for a brain-storming session on how technical innovation could help with intelligence gathering. As Cotton explained various gadgets, Ian would chime, "Amazing, Sydney, amazing." When Ian's "restless, fantastic mind" hit upon a possible weakness in Britain's defences – what if the Germans had established a series of submarine refuelling bays along the west coast of Ireland? – Cotton volunteered to photograph the area as an insurance measure. Any pipelines, barrels, beach installations or storage tanks would show up. (In the event, there were none.)

When Ian asked Cotton to undertake further assignments, he began to create interdepartmental waves. Cotton was nominally attached to the strength of Squadron Leader Frederick Winterbotham, head of the SIS's Air Intelligence branch, and paid through an Air Ministry budget. Winterbotham complained that Ian was courting Cotton and promising him all sorts of inducements – the rank of Captain and any backup he required – if he switched his allegiance to the Admiralty. He added, rather over-elaborating the story, "I naturally advised the Air Ministry, and as a result a violent row broke out between the Chief of Naval Staff and the Chief of Air Staff, not only because of the underhand way in which Ian Fleming had tried to entice Cotton, but also because there was a definite agreement between the services that the RAF alone was responsible for aerial photography."

Ian enjoyed raising the Air Ministry's hackles. When Cotton revealed that he had grave doubts about the effectiveness of the RAF's pre-radar aircraft detection devices, Ian took him in to see Pound. Together they devised an experiment. Cotton would fly from Heston to Portsmouth to Weymouth and then back to Heston. Ian later sent a message to the Air Ministry saying that NID had heard on good authority that an enemy aircraft had been sighted over Weymouth between eleven and twelve o'clock the previous morning. The Air Ministry replied that no plane had flown there, enemy or otherwise: one up to the Navy, and more fuel for those arguing in favour of the development of radar.

In those early days, with other secret services still in disarray, the battle of the Atlantic yet to be engaged, NID continued to be drawn into covert activities outside its normal province. Somehow this was expected of the heirs to Blinker Hall. As Godfrey himself acknowledged, he took it upon himself to initiate "a number of clandestine operations aimed at cutting off the supply of Swedish iron ore, blocking the Danube, crippling the Romanian oil refineries (on which the Germans were very dependent), sabotaging barges on the Danube and double agent chicken food. It was difficult to obtain official approval on a high plane for such operations." Godfrey noted that his opposite number, the Director of Military Intelligence, had set up a small dirty-tricks department called MI(R), where Ian's brother Peter worked, but otherwise the top brass were not interested in such matters, the Foreign Office hostile, and financial resources meagre. Even Churchill, as First Lord of the Admiralty, seemed apathetic.

Soon all sorts of agents and spymasters were beating their way to Room 39, where they could be sure of a sympathetic response, initially from Ian, who guarded Godfrey's time jealously and filtered out unnecessary enquiries. Sefton Delmer came to see Ian on his return from France at the start of the war. He found his recent Moscow colleague not only dressed in uniform but sporting long-shafted elastic-sided seaboots. Ian wheeled him in to see Godfrey, who was interested in Delmer's ideas about the use of different types of rumour, disinformation and propaganda.

This stimulated Ian's imagination and he began proposing possible projects – a light metal disc with the image of a five-mark piece on one side and a propaganda message on the other ("cheap to make", he noted), forged German banknotes ("a simple way of attacking the German currency and of enraging the Germans"), and one that took Godfrey's fancy – a radio-propaganda ship in the North Sea which, Ian suggested, would draw the Germans' fire and demonstrate conclusively that they did not control that particular stretch of water ("the tone of the broadcasts should be peremptory and occasionally scornful"). In February the signs of a novelist manqué could be discerned when Ian went to the trouble of labelling his 'Most Secret' message "A Plot". Since the Germans had recently enticed two SIS members across the border from Holland, why not try something similar on the German secret service? Ian suggested. "It occurs to me that the Italian–French frontier in the neighbourhood of Monte Carlo would be a likely *'mise en scène'*. It could be conveyed to the Germans that there was considerable disaffection among the French Generals of the Southern Command. With the help of the Deuxième Bureau, a nucleus of disaffection could be created, and it would be arranged for this nucleus to get in touch with the German SIS. The situation would then be allowed to develop according to taste." However, Ian's ideas, even when acted on, created few reverberations inside Germany. In a paper on "Rumour as a Weapon" in July, Ian argued that much wider media coverage had to be given to rumours in order "to get a really healthy whisper going in Germany". He added, "It is submitted that there is no lack of suitable 'rumour ammunition'; it is an effective 'rumour gun' which needs to be devised."

Ian quickly learned to take a strategic view of the war. As the Admiralty's intelligence arm, NID needed to inform itself about everything which might affect the movements of the Royal Navy's ships, now and in the future. As a result it took a special interest in developments in the Iberian peninsula, and in particular in Spain. Although nominally neutral, under its pro-German dictator, General Franco, Spain controlled a long Atlantic coastline and hovered threateningly over Gibraltar, the key to Britain's position in the Mediterranean and North Africa. Godfrey arranged for the post of naval attaché in Madrid to be upgraded and for his trusted confidant, Captain Alan Hillgarth, to be appointed. Hillgarth had come to the DNI's attention in 1938 when, as British consul in Majorca, at the height of the Spanish Civil War, he skilfully engineered the evacuation of British subjects by the battle-cruiser HMS *Repulse*, under Godfrey's command. Ian struck up an immediate rapport with this suave former diplomat with a penchant for writing thrillers. (One, *The Passionate Trail*, published in 1925, has a particularly modern theme: the consequences of the rise of Islamic fundamentalism in Egypt.) The First Lord, Winston Churchill, also appreciated Hillgarth, describing him as a "very good" man "equipped with a profound knowledge of Spanish affairs".

In September, the first month of the war, Hillgarth sent his top Spanish agent, Don Juan March, to London to discuss a plan to create problems for the Nazis. March was one of Spain's richest men, a Majorcan millionaire with interests in shipping, oil and property. His idea was to buy up fifty-five German ships which had been holed up in Spanish ports since the start of hostilities, and thus take them out of commission. The Foreign

Office hummed and ha-ed, saying such a move would run counter to the rules of neutrality in wartime. But the spirited Godfrey saw an opening. He asked his PA to liaise with friends in the City and the new Ministry of Economic Warfare. (One of the people Ian approached was Barings managing director, Sir Edward Peacock, who had been one of his sponsors.) They came up with a plan to set up a Spanish company which would buy the ships with British money. Sir Andrew Duncan at the Ministry of Transport was opposed to the idea because of March's dubious pro-Franco past, but Churchill was willing to give the wily Majorcan the benefit of the doubt. Duncan wrote a memorandum which survives with Churchill's red-inked minutes (in brackets): "Juan March was pro-German (why shd he not be?) and later pro-Nazi (why not?) and he is a clever self-seeking rogue (both adjectives are ticked). He would certainly double-cross us if he could (not certain). He has made a lot of money (why not?) and moneymaking is his main interest (quite untrue; he was ready to sacrifice everything for Franco)."

This bureaucratic toing and froing continued for some weeks until February 1940 when Ian, warming to his role as trouble-shooting, busy-body staff officer, decided it was time for action and wrote to Godfrey, "I think we should quickly get this matter out of the docket stage and see if it will walk. Otherwise let it die. It is already half-throttled with paper." Ian's decisive intervention did the trick. Secret funds to buy up the German ships were released.

Another area of special interest for NID was, surprisingly, the River Danube. It wanted to prevent Germany gaining control of the river and, with it, access to oilfields in Romania and to other valuable minerals and resources in the littoral states. One plan, only partially successful, was to set up a British shipping company to charter Danubian barges – and thus deny them to the Germans as transport. Another was to make the river unnavigable by scuttling cement-laden barges at its narrowest point, the Iron Gates, between Romania and Yugoslavia.

These covert operations required a high degree of organization. Godfrey entrusted his Personal Assistant not only with liaison with other interested bodies, such as MI(R) and Section D, the forerunner to SOE, but also with recruitment of crucial NID personnel, including Merlin Minshall, the ineffectual British vice-consul in Bucharest, and Michael Mason, who was despatched to the same city with cover as a chauffeur in the British Legation.

Thirty years later Minshall wrote an unreliable account of his wartime activities. Read in an appropriately sceptical frame of mind, it does however offer some insight into Ian's languid, club-orientated *modus operandi*. Minshall had arrived at the Admiralty with one big asset. After an Oxford education, he had sailed an antique Dutch boat through the waterways of Europe from Le Havre to the Black Sea. During his prolonged cruise he came to know Central Europe well. At the onset of war, he joined the Royal Naval Volunteer Reserve and tried to interest various agencies in his area of expertise. Only Ian, the RNVR point-man at NID, showed the slightest interest. When the two men met in October 1939, Minshall soon understood why NID needed help. On being handed an internal report on the Danube, Minshall was amused to read the town of Giurgiu, Romania's main oil-terminal port, described as a "small fishing village". When he expressed reservations about the document, Ian gently rebuked him, "My dear Minshall, you can't really tell me that our Balkan Division doesn't know its stuff." When Minshall started to speculate about how the Danube could be used to defeat Germany, Ian remained uncertain. "Some of the Top Brass won't like it at all," he said. "Why on earth not?" demanded Minshall. "Don't they want us to defeat Germany?" "Sometimes, old boy, I wonder if they do," replied Ian laconically.

Nevertheless Ian introduced Minshall to Admiral Godfrey and then invited him round to White's to meet another admiral, Roger Bellairs, who had been instructed by Pound to make an assessment of the development of the war from the German viewpoint. The upshot was that, after a spell at a spy school near Guildford, Minshall was sent to Bucharest in January 1940. The city was the spy capital of Central Europe, awash with German and Allied agents observing each other from the comfort of the celebrated Plaza-Athenée Hotel. Minshall was specifically told by Ian to book himself into a small hotel and keep a low profile. Once in situ, his job was to assist Michael Mason in chartering the six or so barges needed for sinking in the Iron Gates and in organizing the British and Australian crewmen who had been brought in to sail them. But far from avoiding attention, Minshall managed to get himself arrested. Worse, he tried to secure his release by saying he was a British naval officer.

The barges having gone ahead, Minshall followed them up the Danube in a high-speed Air Sea Rescue Launch which was to be used to off-load the crews and spirit them out of the country. He claimed Ian had arranged for the ASRL to be sent from naval headquarters in Alexandria. But one hundred miles short of the Iron Gates, Minshall's boat ran out of fuel (he blamed German agents). Clearly aware of what was happening, the Romanians turned up, with local Nazis in tow. Within ten minutes of boarding the barges, they had discovered the explosives which would be used to scuttle the vessels. At last showing the aplomb which had impressed Ian, Minshall asked for time to change into his naval uniform. This allowed him to make a dash for the ASRL and, having somehow secured extra fuel, to effect his escape. The Romanians chased for two hours, but the British boat was too fast. Minshall eventually escaped across the border and made his way to Trieste.

This botched operation caused a major furore, with Dr Goebbels railing in the German media about the British use of a neutral country to try to block the Danube. On 11 April Minshall was back in Ian's office. The DNI's personal assistant informed him that the Foreign Office was very angry. But, he added, "the Admiralty will take care of you and as far as you are concerned we'll tell the Foreign Office boys to take a running jump at themselves".

According to Minshall's account, Ian offered to find him a job as Night Duty Officer on a secret Admiralty project researching new applications for direction-finding equipment. Minshall did not like that, and soon asked for a transfer. Ian arranged for him to go to Portsmouth, where he joined a team involved in gathering radio intelligence which was used to pinpoint the exact whereabouts of German U-boats and other naval vessels. Minshall later presented himself as a prototype for Ian's fictional character James Bond. While that was far- fetched, Ian did indeed draw on this period of the war when he came to invent his famous secret agent. He did not have to look far for detail. Bond's code number 007 was based on Ian's knowledge of NID's great triumph in the First World War. 0070 was the German diplomatic code used to send the Zimmerman telegram from Berlin to Washington. It was cracked by Blinker Hall's cryptanalysts in Room 40, bringing the United States into the conflict. Bond's character incorporated a number of naval attachés and spies – a small part perhaps of the rugged Minshall, but much larger and more obvious elements of Michael Mason, a tough, landed gentleman, who had boxed at a high level and lived as a trapper in Canada, of Commander Wilfred "Biffy" Dunderdale, the SIS station chief in Paris who drove around town in his bullet proof Rolls-Royce and financed his espionage network out of his own considerable fortune, and of the personable Commander Alexander "Sandy" Glen, an Old Fettesian (like Bond), who, while assistant naval attache in Belgrade, had become romantically involved with the wife of a Belgian diplomat.

Ian's patronage of Minshall was typical. Throughout the war and after in civilian life, he identified, promoted and stuck by his protégés. Later, in July 1943, Ian arranged for Minshall to be sent to Yugoslavia as head of a British naval mission to Tito's Communist partisans. A promised military party was originally to have gone without naval input. Ian insisted on sending his man. And, an indication of interservice rivalry, he impressed on Minshall to report directly back to him personally in the Admiralty and not to attempt to communicate through the apparatus of the military mission.

By the time Minshall returned to London from his Balkan escapade in April, Ian's brother Peter had joined the war in Norway. Over the preceding months, Peter had stayed restlessly at home, attacking modish pacifists in the pages of the *Spectator* and dashing off his light novel *The Flying Visit*, which told of the strange problems caused by Hitler's unexpected arrival in England, after being shot down while gloatingly watching a bombing raid in action. When the Führer's deputy Rudolph Hess did fly to England in May 1941, Peter was credited with either great prescience or extra-ordinary inside knowledge.

In early April 1940, after Hitler outwitted British strategists by invading Norway, the War Office ill-advisedly dispatched an expeditionary force to retaliate. Because the extent of the Nazis' control over the country was unknown, it initially sent a small team, including Peter, to scout out the area around Namsos, one of the proposed landing sites. When the British counterattack started, it was mercilessly bombed by the Germans. At one stage it was feared that Peter had been killed, and a report to that effect appeared in the *Daily Sketch*, owned by Ian's friend, Lord Kemsley. Although Celia, Peter's wife, blamed her brother-in-law for not doing enough to check or halt a report which caused her much distress, Ian's mother saw it differently, telling Geoffrey Dawson, the editor of *The Times*, that her "second boy had a ghastly time" until he found out that the newspaper account was not true.

Eve had been trying to enlist Dawson's support to stop Peter being sent back to Norway. In fact, Peter survived another short spell with General Carton de Wiart's doomed expeditionary force in Norway before returning to London to take up a temporary post rather like Ian's, as an assistant to the Director of Military Intelligence, Major General Paddy Beaumont-Nesbitt. In their professional capacities the two brothers enjoyed an unusual Whitsun weekend together in the Essex seaside resort of Southend. The trip arose out of an anonymous letter to the Minister of Home Defence. Purporting to come from a German agent with a soft spot for the British people, it told of an imminent German attack on Southend on Whit Sunday. Since there was no such minister, the letter was forwarded to the Minister of Home Security and on to MI5, whence it was referred to the Joint Intelligence Committee. With the evacuation of British troops from Dunkirk already in motion and everyone feeling jittery, the JIC was inclined to take the letter seriously. Ian and Peter, however, impressed on their respective chiefs that, if such an attack were to take place, it would be exploited by the German propaganda machine. In order to be sure that a different point of view appeared on the BBC, they suggested that they should be present on the Essex coast to act as official observers. So on Whit Saturday afternoon they drove to Southend in a small camouflaged staff-car. Expecting the place to be deserted, they found, instead, a bank holiday weekend in full swing. At dusk they joined a naval observation post on the roof of a large hotel. But as the night wore on, and they received no reports of unusual enemy aircraft movements, they found it increasingly difficult to take the idea of an impending attack seriously. At around one o'clock they roused their driver, who was drunk, and asked to be taken back to London.

After this none-too-serious encounter with the phoney war, Ian joined the real thing in France the following month. His main point of contact was through Peter Smithers, another of his dashing RNVR recruits to NID. A young high-flying barrister, with an Oxford first in history, Smithers had been posted at the start of the war to an auxiliary yacht in the English Channel. But in January 1940 he had the misfortune to contact measles and was forbidden further on-board naval service. Luckily he knew a girlfriend of the NID's Commander Clive Loehnis (later head of GCHQ). Somehow the message that he was looking for a job filtered through her and Loehnis to Ian. Smithers was lying in Haslar Naval Hospital in Portsmouth in March when he was called to the telephone and informed that the Director of Naval Intelligence wanted to see him. And who was that speaking? Smithers enquired politely. "Commander Fleming here," said the clipped voice at the other end.

When Smithers duly presented himself at the Admiralty, he was never introduced to Admiral Godfrey. Instead he was given the usual perfunctory interview by Ian, and told to go to Broadway, the SIS headquarters close to St James's Park, where his contact, Jimmy Blyth, ordered him to Paris to report to 'Biffy' Dunderdale, the dashing Odessa-born station chief. Always immaculately dressed, with gold Cartier cuff-links, Biffy's greatest professional coup had come the previous year when, as a result of close links with eastern European emigrés in Paris, he had learned of the progress of Polish cryptanalysts in breaking the German Army's otherwise secure three-rotor Enigma encoding machine. In August 1939 he sent his superiors in London plans of the Polish 'bombe' which deciphered Enigma, plus two Polish copies of the actual German machine. These were vital in helping members of the British Government Communications Headquarters (GCHQ) break the most resilient German codes and produce top-secret Ultra intelligence from their wartime establishment at Bletchley Park.

Smithers was given a job in the SIS office in the rue Charles Flocquet debriefing Dutch tugboat captains. But when the Germans began to close in on Paris in early June, and it was clear that the SIS could not longer maintain its presence in Paris, he and his colleagues were ordered to move to the Château le Chêne, an SIS safe house in the Loire Valley.

Having monitored these developments closely from London, Ian flew to Paris on 13 June, and for the next two weeks was in his element, coordinating different British intelligence operations as France collapsed around him. First he needed some cash. Knowing that the SIS kept its funds at the Rolls-Royce office in Paris, Ian, who enjoyed close links with the French secret service as well as with Dunderdale, was able to gain access. The substantial amount of money he found in the safe proved invaluable in his operations over the following fortnight.

Making his way to Tours, the temporary home of the French Ministry of Marine, Ian found he had an important liaison job to do for Godfrey. The long-established naval attaché, Captain Cedric 'Hooky' Holland, had left France two months earlier, and his successor Captain Edmund Pleydell-Bouverie had not, as Godfrey's biographer Patrick Beesley discreetly put it, "yet had time to establish the same close relations with Darlan and his Staff as had his predecessor". In fact the two men were at loggerheads. Pleydell-Bouverie had made it clear that he did not think the French had the will to continue. As a result the French Ministry of Marine kept him at arm's length.

The war was entering a critical stage and Churchill, the new Prime Minister, needed up-to-date intelligence on French intentions. Of particular importance were the plans of the French navy. If France capitulated, what would happen to its battleships? Churchill favoured a plan to encourage them to sail to England. Godfrey initially wanted his assistant simply to find out what was happening. But Ian quickly gathered how serious the breakdown between Darlan and Pleydell-Bouverie had become. In a communication with Godfrey over the naval attaché's private teleprinter line to the Admiralty, Ian suggested that he should attach himself to Darlan's staff and act as the necessary link with the French Navy.

Meanwhile Smithers had gathered with his SIS colleagues, their wives and mistresses at the Château le Chêne. But after only five days' rest on the Loire, they were required to move on again. The Germans had overrun Paris on 14 June and were pushing south. The SIS team took to its heels again, making its way to Bordeaux and possible escape by ship to England. Smithers went on ahead to make arrangements, followed, for different reasons, by Darlan, the French Admiralty and Ian Fleming from Tours.

The bleakness of the situation in Bordeaux has been described by Geoffrey Cox in his book *Countdown to War*. There were no rooms to be had, and although the elected Cabinet of Paul Reynaud met to decide if France should carry on, no one was at all surprised when, on 16 June, it capitulated and what became known as the Vichy government under First World War veteran Marshal Pétain took over. Cox found the British consulate, close to the quayside by the wide River Garonne, besieged. Frenchmen, Poles, Belgians and Britons all packed the staircase leading to the consulate offices on the first floor, pleading for visas and passages. At the Chapon Fin, the best restaurant in town, a noisy group of expatriate Britons was carousing. They had just arrived from the Riviera where, Cox noted disdainfully, "they had been helping the war effort by eating French food rather than returning to eat rationised foods in Britain". Now, with Italy in the war and the odds against the good life lengthening, they were "making a bolt for home", armed with their gold and their diamonds. Their "arrogant raucous voices rang out across the room".

Having finally accomplished his task of ferrying his SIS charges on board the cruiser HMS *Arethusa* in the mouth of the Gironde estuary, Smithers was looking forward to his return journey to England when he was ordered to disembark and make his way back to Bordeaux where, he was told, Commander Fleming would give him his orders. The two men met at the British consulate where Ian was busy burning every paper in sight. When he had completed the job, he locked the office (the staff had been evacuated on HMS *Berkeley*) and wondered what to do with the key. His solution was to take it the American consulate for safe-keeping. When the resident US consul declined to accept it, saying he had no authority, Ian would brook no nonsense and placed the key firmly in the official's pocket. Smithers looked on admiringly: "Ian acted in such an authoritative manner that he never gave anyone any grounds for thinking there might be another solution to a problem."

From Ian, Smithers learned that the new First Lord of the Admiralty, A. V. Alexander, had arrived to negotiate with his French opposite number, Admiral Darlan, the Minister of the Marine in the new Pétain government, for the despatch of the French fleet to Allied ports. But he needed someone to act as his flag lieutenant and Ian proposed Smithers for the job. With the best part of a day to kill before dining with Alexander that evening, the two NID officers drove to the anchorage at Le Verdon, at the tip of the Gironde's southern peninsula, where several hundred refugees were congregating, hoping to board a ship to England.

Looking out into the roads, Ian saw seven merchant ships at anchor. Borrowing a motor boat, he travelled round them all, asking them to take the refugees to Britain. When some captains refused because they were going elsewhere, Ian was not prepared to let such trifling matters stand in his way. All the ships had suffered from bombing over the previous couple of nights. Ian told them firmly, "If you don't take these people on board and transport them to England, I can promise you that if the Germans don't sink you, the Royal Air Force will."

His threats having had the desired effect, Ian's next task was to convey the stragglers, many of them Jewish, to the ships. In Bordeaux there was a small car ferry which could carry one hundred people at a time. But the harbour-master refused to let Ian use it, claiming in a long speech, full of invocations to "*la patrie*" and "*l'honneur*", that this might not be what the Marshal wanted. After Ian fished in his pocket for some of the crisp French franc notes which had until recently lain in the SIS safe in Paris, the harbour-master swiftly capitulated. When the car ferry finally arrived at the quayside, Ian ordered that no one could take more than two suitcases, and what they were wearing. He and Smithers stood at the edge of the steps of the ferry, trying to maintain a sense of official decorum as they examined the passports of the ragtag army of refugees sweltering in jewels and fur coats on a hot summer's day.

That evening the British and French general staff dined together for the last time at the Chapon Fin. Alexander's talks with Darlan having failed, the atmosphere was maudlin and unworldly. The demoralized French were jealous of their British colleagues who at least would have one more opportunity to prove themselves. With the Germans apparently on the doorstep, the patron of the Chapon Fin uncorked the finest wines in his cellar. But no one, not even Ian at the conclusion of a particularly tiring day, was able to enjoy them.

Smithers returned to London with Alexander on a Sunderland flying boat while Ian made his way to Portugal and on to Madrid, where he needed to take stock of the situation with Hillgarth. With the fall of France, Hillgarth was the naval attaché in closest contact with the Vichy regime whose fleet, having declined all invitations to sail to Britain, would shortly be bombed in its North African port of Mers-el-Kebir, if only to prevent it falling into German hands. France's defeat already had important strategic implications for the progress of the war in Spain, North Africa and the Atlantic. For Germany had gained immediate access to the whole length of France's west coast from which to strike at British merchant shipping. It had also brought Germany to the threshold of Spain, later described by Churchill as "the key to all British enterprises in the Mediterranean". Hitler did not even need to occupy the country; if he could only break down Spain's resolve to remain neutral, then not only would his navy have more ports from which to operate, but also he would sound the death-knell for Gibraltar and, with it, Britain's prospects in North Africa and the Atlantic. Spain had many good reasons for falling for Nazi blandishments – not just the prize of Gibraltar and possibly French possessions in North Africa, but also German support to fight the Allied blockade of Europe, which was hurting her economy badly. Hillgarth and his Ambassador, Sir Samuel Hoare, had the delicate diplomatic task, in this unpromising situation, of trying to stiffen Spanish resolve against the Germans.

With the situation so finely balanced, the Spanish might be bought off if Britain turned a blind eye to their territorial ambitions in North Africa. But this would antagonize the Vichy French, whose support (once the ignominy of Mers-el-Kebir was forgotten) might be crucial at a future stage of the war in North Africa. Then the consequences of the possible loss of Gibraltar had to be considered. A provisional plan to capture the Portuguese islands of the Azores as an alternative centre of British naval operations in the Atlantic was drawn up. Alarm bells had sounded sharply on 13 June when Spain announced that it no longer considered itself neutral but simply "non-belligerent". But there was less concern the next day when Spanish troops decided to walk into Tangier – ostensibly to preserve the peace. The international city of Tangier seemed a safer prize for Spanish irredentists than anywhere in French Morocco. All in all, the fall of France had substantially increased the threat to Gibraltar and to British shipping in the Atlantic.

According to an NID colleague, when Ian arrived in Lisbon, only Germany's Lufthansa was flying to Madrid. Initially the enemy airline refused to transport him, but, showing the tenacity he had demonstrated in the mouth of the Gironde, Ian insisted that as a commercial carrier it had an obligation to take him where he wanted. So in late June 1940 Ian Fleming arrived in Madrid on a German aircraft for important consultations with Hillgarth. While this story sounds apocryphal, it gives an indication of the myth Ian was creating for himself.

By the time he returned to Room 39, the prognosis for the war at home had also deteriorated. Following the fall of France, the German Luftwaffe began to target England. The first shots of the aerial combat known as the Battle of Britain were fired in July, and regular bombing of London and other cities soon followed, leading to the full-scale Blitz in the winter. At sea, the German U-boat commander, Admiral Dönitz, had started to move his headquarters to Lorient on the west coast of France, from where he could more easily wreak havoc on British merchant shipping in the Atlantic.

At least NID no longer had to concern itself directly with dirty tricks in Europe. Godfrey breathed a sigh of relief when in July 1940 "the whole paraphernalia of subversion, sabotage and clandestine warfare was turned over to the 'Special Operations Executive'" and he "continued to keep in touch with their activities through liaison officers", including Ian. Nominally reporting to the Ministry of Economic Warfare, the SOE was a politically inspired hybrid which brought together two covert departments, the War Office's MI(R) and the SIS's Section D, with the Foreign Office's black propaganda unit, Elektra House.

Having notably proved himself in the field, Ian went back to his gadfly existence, representing the DNI's interests in committees and clubs and conclaves of spies. He was invited to a high-level brain-storming lunch by Robert Bruce Lockhart, the deputy Under-Secretary at the Foreign Office, who later headed the Political Warfare Executive which handled the vital anti-German propaganda effort. Also present were Ian's action-man hero, the SIS's Dunderdale, who was now working with the Free French in London, and the British diplomat Fitzroy Maclean, whom he had met in Moscow the previous year.

Ian kept up his contacts at the various edges of the war effort, visiting the Free French, dining at the Carlton Grill with Prince Bernhard of the Netherlands, and liaising with the Norwegians over the development of the "Shetland bus" service which carried agents across the North Sea into Scandinavia. Despite his lack of enthusiasm for shooting, Ian became fascinated with firearms and other gadgets of war. He spent long periods with Robert Churchill, the gunsmith, "working on gas pistols and God knows what", recalled Peter Smithers. "He gave me a gas pistol disguised as a fountain pen. It had two kinds of cartridges, lethal and non-lethal." Another haunt was the office of the bomb and dirty-tricks expert, Lord Suffolk, nephew of Lord Curzon through his mother, the American heiress, Daisy Leiter. Suffolk taught Ian how to kill a man by biting him in the back of the neck. Slightly later Ian linked up with Charles Fraser-Smith, nominally an obscure official in the Ministry of Supply but in reality the man who kitted up British agents with all sorts of gadgets from shaving brushes with secret cavities to shoelaces that acted as saws. Fraser-Smith remembered that Ian was particularly interested in his hollowed-out golf-balls, which were used to conceal messages to prisoners of war. He was amused to find a similar device used to transport uncut stones in Ian's book, *Diamonds Are Forever*. Fraser-Smith was the SIS's quartermaster, who enjoyed fleeting fictional appearances in Ian's novels as Boothroyd and was developed into the long-running character, 'Q', in the James Bond films.

Having completed his formative year as the DNI's personal assistant, Ian was in a position of considerable patronage. As well as recruiting RNVR and other officers, he managed to find jobs in and around NID for all sorts of personal friends. After dining one evening with Ian, Pamela Tiarks found herself at Bletchley Park on a three-month training course in secret Ultra signal work and then sent to join Rodger Winn's war-winning submarine-tracking room, part of the Operational Intelligence Centre, in the bowels of the Citadel. Since they worked closely together, Ian and Pamela often met for lunch in the National Gallery where they ate honey sandwiches and listened to Myra Hess's piano recitals. Ian's novelist friend William Plomer was brought into NID as a specialist writer, and other jobs were found within the organization for Maud Russell and for the explorer August Courtauld. When David Herbert, last observed at the crammer, Colonel Trevor's, was at a loose end, Ian arranged for him to join Captain Frank Slocum's secret navy ferrying agents to Norway and France in fishing boats and tugs. There was also an opening for Muriel Wright, who did not like being an air-raid warden because the uniform was so unflattering. At the Admiralty she was the most glamorous of a small team of despatch riders who roared around London on BSA motorcycles. Ian liked to tell a joke about the Wren despatch rider who swerved to avoid a child and fell off the sofa.

Within NID, mounting shipping losses in the Atlantic made improved cooperation with Washington imperative. But the United States was a neutral country and Joseph Kennedy, its Ambassador in London, was notoriously unsympathetic to Britain. Even routine intelligence contacts between the two countries were frustrated by the parochialism of the various US departments. Communication between the intelligence arms of the US Navy and US Army, the State Department and the Federal Bureau of Investigation was virtually non-existent. There was no overall American intelligence establishment to which people such as Godfrey and Ian could relate.

So began the interesting if time-consuming process of wooing the United States into taking intelligence seriously. The British wanted the Americans to follow their lead and develop an integrated intelligence service, and they already knew who they wanted to run it – William J. Donovan, the senior partner in a law firm which happened to include the pro-British banker J. P. Morgan among its clients. Indeed, after the First World War Donovan had worked for a couple of years as a private intelligence-gatherer for Morgan. He had already expressed firm ideas on the need to bring "unconventional" warfare within the orbit of intelligence, away from the prying eyes of Congress and the press – a very British point of view. But first the Americans needed to be convinced that Britain had not only a cause worth fighting for but also the will to succeed.

The softening-up process started with the arrival of another William – William S. Stephenson ('Little Bill' to Donovan's 'Big Bill') – in New York in June 1940 to take over as head of the British Passport Control office, later British Security Coordination (BSC), the blanket name for British intelligence operations there. Stephenson encouraged Donovan to visit Britain that July to study the situation at first hand. The British rolled out the red carpet: Donovan met everyone from the King and the Prime Minister downwards. He spent considerable time, including his last night in England, with Admiral Godfrey. When Donovan returned to Washington, he informed Frank Knox, the Secretary of State for War, that, contrary to what he was hearing from Ambassador Kennedy, the United States had little cause for concern: the British would not succumb. Donovan's clean bill of health encouraged Roosevelt to accede to Churchill's demands and to do what he had personally wanted all along – provide Britain with fifty destroyers and additional hardware, including a crucial hitherto secret bomb-sight, to aid her war effort. Although the United States extracted a hefty price – a 99-year lease on British bases in Canada and the Caribbean – the basis of a close working cooperation between London and Washington had been laid.

A more immediate quick fix against the U-boat threat to British convoys in the Atlantic was for cryptanalysts at GCHQ to read the German Navy's codes. They routinely read Enigma messages sent by both the German Army and the German Secret Service (Abwehr). But the Kriegsmarine had its own version of the three-rotor encoding machine. And hard as the boffins at Bletchley Park tried, they still had not managed to break naval Enigma.

NID thought of ways round this problem. One was to capture or sink a German vessel which would be certain to be carrying an Enigma codebook. This allowed Ian to come up with one of his bright ideas. The Germans had begun operating a new air–sea rescue boat out of Denmark. Ian was convinced this would carry the latest German code-books. If he and a few others could don some German uniforms and wait in a boat in the Channel, pretending to have ditched, the rescue boat would come to pick them up. The British could then overpower the Germans and capture the boat and its valuable contents.

In a note to Godfrey on 12 September, Ian suggested the following strategy to secure "the loot":

"1. Obtain from the Air Ministry an air-worthy German bomber.
2. Pick a tough crew of five, including a pilot, W/T (wireless/telegraph) operator and word-perfect German speaker. Dress them in German Air Force uniform, add blood and bandages to suit.
3. Crash plane in the Channel after making SOS to rescue service in P/L (plain language).
4. Once aboard rescue boat, shoot German crew, dump overboard, bring rescue boat back to English port.

In order to increase the chance of capturing an R. or M. [*Räumboot*, a small minesweeper; *Minensuchboot*, a large minesweeper] with its richer booty, the crash might be staged in mid-Channel. The Germans would presumably employ one of this type for the longer and more hazardous journey."

The head of the Operational Intelligence Centre, Rear Admiral Jock Clayton, lent his support, and Ian produced a more detailed plan. The bomber would take off just before dawn, at the tail-end of a German air raid. When it found a small minesweeper in the Channel, it would cut an engine and let out a screen of smoke, before dropping fast and pancaking into the water.

Ian anticipated aspects of his future fictional hero James Bond when he stipulated that the bomber's pilot should be a "tough bachelor, able to swim". He proposed an ingenious gloss on the story if the press got hold of it. Journalists would be told that the German minesweeper had been captured "for a lark by a group of young hot-heads who thought the war was too tame and wanted to have a go at the Germans. They had stolen plane and equipment and had expected to get into trouble when they got back."

Armed with a three-page memorandum on "Activities of German Naval Units in the Channel" compiled by Frank Birch, head of the Naval Section at GCHQ, Ian set about implementing his plan, which was given the code-name Operation RUTHLESS. Through Admiral Godfrey's good offices with Lord Beaverbrook, he acquired a twin-engine Heinkel 111 bomber, which had been shot down in a raid over the Firth of Forth and subsequently rehabilitated at the Royal Aircraft Establishment at Farnborough in Surrey. Smithers, who was working closely with Ian, was despatched to a store of captured enemy equipment at Cardington (near Bedford) to commandeer some German uniforms.

However, Group Captain H. J. Wilson, who was responsible for captured German aircraft, rather punctured the idea by stating that a crash landing in the Channel would collapse the Heinkel's Perspex nose, and that the crew would all drown. With some reluctance, he later backed off from this position. Ways were found to reinforce the Heinkel nose and to inject oil into the exhaust so as to give the impression of an engine fire.

Ian offered to accompany the special crew, but this was vetoed by Godfrey, who, according to Smithers, was adamant that "Ian was someone who simply could not fall into enemy hands because he was privy to everything." So in early October Ian made his way down to Dover to direct the operation from the shore but the plan ran into difficulties when no suitable ships appeared in the Channel. Eventually, on 16 October, the Dover command postponed RUTHLESS, recommending that it should be tried again from Portsmouth. Alan Turing, a leading Bletchley Park code-breaker, was furious that he had been denied his "pinch".

With German air raids now a daily occurrence, many Londoners moved to the country. While her husband was away at the war, Ann O'Neill rented a house in the Oxfordshire village of Buscot, where she settled with her two children, Raymond and Fionn, and various relatives. Unable to keep still, she shuttled between this rural retreat near Faringdon, her lover Esmond Harmsworth's house in Ascot, and the Dorchester Hotel in London, where many rich people took rooms under the misguided impression that its steel frame was built to withstand bombs. Cecil Beaton compared the scene in the hotel lobby to a luxury liner "with all the horrors of enforced jocularity and expensive squalor". Ann, ever observant, felt the whole place had "a strange feeling of synthetic safety", with "a mass of cabinet ministers, crooks and Mayfair remnants milling around". While Ann was staying with Esmond in Ascot in mid-October, his house was hit by a bomb. The following day she returned to the Dorchester where, by her own admission, she bored everyone rigid with her bomb saga. Hoping for some escape that evening over dinner in the hotel restaurant with Ian, she was eager to "hear the result of a secret trip to Dover, where he was doing a hush-hush job for the Admiralty". But Ian played dumb: "he was an oyster," she recorded, "so will seek information elsewhere." The Blitz had its advantages though. After another dinner with Ian, this time at the Lansdowne Club, she was too scared by the noise and the arc lights to make her way back to the Dorchester and had to stay with him. Ian enjoyed a more than usually peripatetic night-life around this time, because the skylights in Ebury Street could not be effectively blacked out in accordance with blitz procedures, and so had to move out of his flat and find temporary accommodation at the Lansdowne, the St James's Club or even the Carlton Hotel. "So the orchid has left the orchid house," quipped the writer Peter Quennell, a close friend of Ann's.

Ian himself had several narrow escapes during the bombardment. Three times in the autumn he survived while the building around him was destroyed. Once was in Dover when he was preparing for Operation RUTHLESS. A second time he was visiting Sefton Delmer in the latter's temporary accommodation in Lincoln's Inn. As Delmer later wrote, he and his wife Isabel were giving "a small and select dinner party when a small and select bomb dropped on my flat". Apart from Ian, the other guests were Leonard Ingrams, the influential Under-Secretary in the Ministry of Economic Warfare and his wife Victoria, Prince Bernhard of the Netherlands, with whom Ian occasionally lunched in the Carlton Hotel, and, to balance the numbers, two good-looking young women, Martha Huysmans, daughter of the Belgian Prime Minister, and Anna McLaren, whom the Delmers had met while escaping from France earlier in the year. The entrance hall to the flat was blown up and the 200-year-old staircase smashed to the street, but none of the distinguished guests was injured. Indeed, so convivial and interesting had the party been that no one bothered to go down to the air-raid shelter. After the bomb had fallen, Prince Bernhard got up from the dinner table, lowered himself twenty feet to the nearest bit of staircase still standing, and thanked his hosts for a "most enjoyable evening". Ian followed this perilous route to his dusty car parked below.

A third near-miss occurred in November. He was covered with plaster when a bomb destroyed his room on the third floor of the Carlton Hotel. After rescuing a waiter and a maid who had been pinned beneath debris, he went to sleep with everyone else in the Grill Room, only to be awoken by the sound of what seemed to be running water. He looked up to see an old man peeing on the carpet. The next morning he learned that his night-time neighbour with a bladder problem was an eminent bishop.

One dark cloud hanging over Ian's head throughout the latter half of the year was the knowledge that his lively brother Michael was missing in action in France after covering the retreat to Dunkirk with the Oxfordshire and Buckinghamshire Light Infantry. It was three months before Michael's wife Tish received a standard card informing her that he had been taken prisoner, though with a wound in his leg. Three months later, at the end of November, she was given the further, shattering news that he had died at the beginning of October.

Like most Londoners in the Blitz, Ian was forced to respond positively to all hardships and bad news, and delighting in his busy unpredictable existence. When, towards the end of November, Ian took Ann O'Neill to dinner at L'Ecu de France, he was in an "unusually human frame of mind", she confided in her occasional diary. This cheered her considerably, for the recent death of Esmond's father, Lord Rothermere, had presented her with a dilemma. Should she stick by her gentlemanly husband, who was fighting in Tunisia, or should she divorce and marry a man who, as a powerful young press lord, would give her regular access to the influential, clever people in whose company she delighted?

Ian might have resented Esmond's presence in Ann's life, but he didn't: indeed, like Shane O'Neill, Ian and Esmond were friends and bridge-playing partners. Both were guests at a small party Ann gave at the Dorchester to welcome in the New Year. She used some money she had won playing bridge to hire a suite normally reserved for Richard Tauber. Also present were members of her close circle of friends including Loelia, Duchess of Westminster, Oliver and Maureen Stanley and Duff and Diana Cooper. One of the band of pipers playing downstairs was inveigled to provide a feel of Hogmanay. At midnight, according to the Scottish custom, Ian, as the darkest man present, strode across the threshold and kissed everyone in sight. This proved generally popular, except with Duff Cooper who refused to start 1941 being kissed by a man.

Before long Ian was travelling again – to Lisbon and Madrid, and this time on to Gibraltar – on another important mission. Godfrey sent him to renew the contact he had made with Colonel William Donovan the previous summer. In the company of Churchill's personal representative, Colonel Vivian Dykes, and members of the SIS, Donovan was touring Britain's war installations in the Mediterranean and the Middle East. Uniquely, nothing was held back from the big American. British planners had decided to take him completely into their confidence and share their most prized military secrets in the hope that he would return home even more convinced of their resourcefulness and determination to win the war. With prodding from Stephenson, Godfrey cabled Admiral Cunningham, the Commander-in-Chief of the Mediterranean Fleet, about the importance of this American visitor: "THERE IS NO DOUBT THAT WE CAN ACHIEVE INFINITELY MORE THROUGH DONOVAN THAN THROUGH ANY OTHER INDIVIDUAL . . . HE IS VERY RECEPTIVE AND SHOULD BE MADE FULLY AWARE OF OUR REQUIREMENTS AND

DEFICIENCIES AND CAN BE TRUSTED TO REPRESENT OUR NEEDS IN THE RIGHT QUARTERS AND IN THE RIGHT WAY IN THE USA."

Ian's role in this latest act in the wooing of Donovan was to inculcate him into Operation GOLDEN EYE, a sophisticated NID plan to carry out limited sabotage and maintain essential communication with London if the Germans marched into Spain. Although GOLDEN EYE never had to be implemented, it involved Ian in detailed coordination with the SIS and with NID staff in Madrid, Gibraltar, Lisbon and Tangier. In Gibraltar, Ian set up a special GOLDEN EYE liaison office, with its own secure cipher link. If, however, Spain were to succumb to the Nazis, it was acknowledged that Gibraltar was unlikely to remain British for long. So, in order to protect vital Allied shipping interests in the Atlantic and the Mediterranean, a backup operation was set up in Tangier under H. L. Greenleaves, an agent who was given cover as assistant press attaché, later vice-consul.

GOLDEN EYE proved a cauldron for interservice rivalries, not only between NID and SIS, but also between the Foreign Office and the Admiralty (in his overcautious concern not to give pro-Nazi Spaniards an excuse to call in the Germans, Sir Samuel Hoare, the new British Ambassador in Madrid, was opposed to any suggestion of subversive activity on Spanish soil) and between NID and the new Special Operations Executive. Ian had to smooth over these differences and ensure that the logistics of the operation were in place. In Gibraltar, he presented GOLDEN EYE to Donovan, stressing that both the Allies and the neutral United States shared a mutual interest in preventing the Germans from winning unchallenged control of the sea. NID's contingency plans included the use of British colonies in the Caribbean. But their implementation was complicated by the agreement Donovan had helped negotiate the previous summer – swapping American destroyers for leases to British Atlantic bases. So this was a matter for further discussion with Donovan.

On his return to London, Ian was appropriately reticent about the reasons for the trip, only telling Maud Russell that he had enjoyed the spring almond blossom in Seville. He was even cagey with his friend Peter Smithers, whom he had arranged to be transferred to Washington as assistant naval attaché. He told Smithers he had been on "a slight excursion abroad, which was enormous fun, but about which I shall have to tell you later". But in a letter to Hillgarth, who shared responsibility for GOLDEN EYE with a colleague in Gibraltar, Ian noted how "greatly impressed" he had been with the naval attaché's organization: "it is lucky that we have such a team in our last European stronghold, and results have already shown the great contribution you are all making towards winning the war." He promised to send some fine long Henry Clay cigars, which he insisted his friend smoke himself "and not give them to your rascally friends".

Ian also maintained his contact with Donovan by providing him with some useful personal information. While in Bulgaria in January, Donovan had visited a Sofia nightclub where the Germans claimed he had got drunk and lost his passport. On his return to Washington in early March, he received a small package from Ian containing the BBC monitoring service's transcription of three reports of the incident carried by German language radio stations. Ian good-humouredly asked Donovan not to delay too long in America. Giving a clear indication of friendly rivalry over the fate of Britain's Caribbean colonies, he added, "Please don't forget my remedy for all our ills – namely that the man in the street should learn the names of our Dominion and Colonial Secretaries, and forget the name of our Foreign Minister. For the last twenty years the opposite has been the case."

While Ian played his important part in the developing intelligence relationship with the United States, his tripartite liaison with Ann and Esmond also flourished, albeit bizarrely. Some time in the spring, Ann persuaded Esmond that they needed to get married. Otherwise, she said, their relationship could not continue. But this necessitated a divorce and, before that, evidence of adultery. She and Esmond arranged to visit a hotel in Bournemouth where they would go through the rigmarole of being discovered in bed by a chamber-maid. At the last moment, however, the plan was aborted, Esmond balking at the seediness and scandal of it all. Since their trip to Bournemouth coincided with one of Ian's 48-hour leaves, they invited him to join them for a day's golf in Cornwall. On the long and seemingly unpleasant drive, Ann was sick at regular intervals from a mixture of nerves and guilt. "Ian told Esmond I was not to be indulged," she later explained. "We were to stop at no more inns and I could damn well be sick in the hedge. When we arrived I went to bed. Ian came to my room, told me I was behaving very badly and must return to Shane. I burst into tears. The rest of the forty-eight hours was spent quarrelling with Ian, and Esmond getting him back to the Admiralty on time – in fact we only went to Cornwall to please Ian. He had a very dominating personality." In their different ways, Godfrey, Donovan and other practitioners of the secret trade were beginning to learn much the same.

5
Ian's Red Indians
1941–1945

Ian and his boss, John Godfrey, tried looking inconspicuous as they stepped off Pan American Airways' Dixie Clipper NC 18605 at New York's La Guardia flying-boat dock on the afternoon of 25 May 1941. They wore civilian suits and described themselves as government officials on their immigration forms. But their arrival in the United States coincided with that of the elegant Italian-born couturier Elsa Schiaparelli who was starting a new life in Manhattan. They, and Arthur Smith, the assistant colonial secretary in the Bermuda government who accompanied them, were surrounded by press photographers fighting for access to Mme Schiaparelli, and found themselves pictured, looking slightly shifty, in the *New York Times* the following day.

Ostensibly Ian and Godfrey had come to examine security in American ports – a matter of vital importance to the British war effort (and indeed the official reason for the presence of British Security Coordination – BSC – as William Stephenson's conclave of spies, propagandists and economic warfarers in New York was now permitted to call itself). But they had also been authorized by the British chiefs of staff to assist Stephenson in developing collaboration between the two countries on security matters. As a leading advocate of a unified American intelligence service – under Donovan's command if possible – Godfrey needed no prompting and was determined to advance that case.

Ian and Godfrey took the usual roundabout air-route from Britain – KLM to Lisbon, and then Pan Am to New York via the Azores and Bermuda. They stayed a couple of nights in the big Palacio Hotel on the Tagus estuary at Estoril, where one of the more heavily embellished incidents in Ian's wartime career took place. After dinner the second night, Ian wanted to play at the casino, a favourite pre-war pursuit which he had recently been denied. It was a sombre and uneventful evening in a dim-lit building. His fellow gamblers were Portuguese businessmen in suits, the stakes were not particularly high, and Ian lost. As he was leaving the gaming tables, he turned to Godfrey and, with a touch of imaginative genius, tried to invest the drab proceedings with some spurious glamour: "What if those men had been German secret service agents, and suppose we had cleaned them out of their money; now that would have been exciting."

This event is supposed to have inspired the memorable scene in Ian's first book, *Casino Royale*, where his hero James Bond outwitted the sinister communist spy Le Chiffre at the baccarat table. But others have also claimed responsibility for this incident, or something like it. One was Dusko Popov, the Yugoslav double agent who worked for the British while pretending to spy for the Germans. He had arrived in Britain at just the time in December 1940 when MI5 was gearing itself up to begin a campaign of deception at the expense of the Germans. Popov gave the British secret services an opportunity to "play back" some of the false information it wanted the Nazis to hear. Another was Ralph Izzard, a fellow member of NID, who played roulette with a group of expatriate Nazis in Lisbon while he was en route to South America on a wartime mission. Izzard later recalled how Ian had been very interested in his story.

Ian and Godfrey also stayed a couple of nights in Hamilton, the capital of Bermuda, an important mid-Atlantic clearing-house for British intelligence and the centre of the censorship service which routinely opened letters between Europe and the Americas. After running the gauntlet of the photographers at La Guardia, they made their way to the St Regis Hotel overlooking Central Park. The St Regis was owned by Vincent Astor, head of the New York branch of the wealthy Anglo-American family, who worked closely with BSC as Roosevelt's specially chosen coordinator of intelligence in New York.

Ian immediately took to Stephenson, a neat, "tightly put together" Canadian of few words and panther-like energy, who mixed the strongest Martinis east of the Rockies. In its offices on the 38th floor of the Rockefeller Center, the British Security Coordination ran a curious state within a state. Its various branches covered secret intelligence, censorship, security (with a special emphasis on watching the docks for signs of subversion and sabotage) and propaganda. Little wonder it drew the attention and, sometimes, wrath of the FBI chief, J. Edgar Hoover. Stephenson, a keen amateur boxer, had to smooth his way with the irascible Hoover with the help of their mutual friend, Gene Tunney, the former heavyweight champion of the world.

As well as visiting the downtown offices of the British Purchasing Mission on Lower Broadway, Ian introduced Godfrey to the Morgan banking clan, and his boss reciprocated by taking Ian to visit some friends on Long Island, where he wasted little time in asking an American girl to accompany him to bed. On off-duty moments, with his regulation $40 currency allowance to burn, Ian reacquainted himself with the 21 Club, which he had visited with Hugo Pitman four years earlier. Like his boss, Ian was dismayed to hear, almost as soon as he arrived, that the battle cruiser HMS *Hood* had been sunk by the rampaging German battleship *Bismarck*. But Ian had a way of shrugging off disheartening news. "He said,

'You wait'," recalled Godfrey, "and sure enough within forty-eight hours *Bismarck* went to the bottom."

After a short period in New York, the two men travelled on to Washington for the serious business of their mission. Godfrey was determined to put his case directly to the President; but where to begin? Godfrey had links to the sclerotic US naval establishment through the naval attaché, Rear-Admiral Bertie Pott, but these were limited to formal service matters. However Ian had what amounted to his own private intelligence service in Peter Smithers who, deciding that NA stood for "no action", had used his position as Pott's assistant to gather secrets not available through more formal channels. According to Donald McLachlan's history of NID, Smithers even managed to infiltrate the Office of Naval Information's cipher room and copy intelligence about the Japanese which was passed back "in the strictest secrecy to London where not even the First Lord might see it".

Ian and Godfrey decided to start by paying their respects to Hoover. The FBI chief granted them an audience for all of sixteen minutes – from 12.31 to 12.47 p.m. on 6 June. Within that short period, the two Englishmen kept very much to basics. Hoover "received us graciously", Ian recalled, "listened with close attention (and a witness) to our exposé of certain security problems, and expressed himself firmly but politely as being uninterested in our mission." With an air of doing them a favour, Hoover dismissed the two Englishmen to be shown the FBI Laboratory and Record Department and taken to the basement shooting-range where FBI agents received their weapons training. Ian acknowledged that Hoover already had his contacts with Stephenson and did not want to complicate matters by affording too much help to the visiting British DNI and his assistant.

Godfrey had to fall back on Stephenson to make the right connections. "Little Bill" (in contrast to "Big Bill" Donovan) contacted Sir William Wiseman, his predecessor as head of British Intelligence in the United States. With the help of Arthur Hays Sulzberger, publisher of the *New York Times*, Wiseman arranged for Mrs Roosevelt to invite Godfrey to a private dinner in the White House where the President was bound to be present. Roosevelt gave Godfrey a difficult time, but he listened attentively to the DNI, who was able to put his various points across, not least his enthusiasm for a unified American intelligence service, under Donovan.

Just over a week later, on 18 June, the President followed Godfrey's advice and nominated Donovan to head a new department of government, the Office of Co-ordinator of Information (COI), later the Office of Strategic Services (OSS). The consensus today is that much of the groundwork had already been done by others, including Stephenson. An important contribution to the overall effort was made by David Eccles, a young high-flyer in the Ministry of Economic Warfare, who briefed Donovan on the

British blockade of continental Europe and its effects on the delicate balance of power in the western Mediterranean, where the British were still successfully keeping General Franco out of the war by allowing him just enough of the raw materials he needed.

Having achieved his main goal, Godfrey left Ian in Washington to assist Donovan in drawing up his proposals for the new agency. He had noted how Ian mixed well with Americans, who liked the breezy but informative manner in which he briefed them about the U-boat war in the Atlantic. On 24 June, Eccles reported to Roger Makins at the Foreign Office, that, "in order not to break the continuity of collaboration between us and Bill [Donovan]" on this drafting, he had "installed Ian Fleming in my bed at Bill's house. He knows much more about the details of intelligence work than I do." Ian flitted between Donovan's Georgetown residence (later owned by Katharine Graham, the proprietor of the *Washington Post*), the nearby invitingly bachelor accommodation of Peter Smithers, and a house rented by Denny Marris, a former Lazards banker who headed the Ministry of Economic Warfare mission in Washington. Ian quickly made his mark in an ebulliently unwarlike town. He joined some Embassy friends for a relaxed picnic in Maryland, where he chatted politely to Isaiah Berlin, who had been seconded as a diplomat, about his book collection and made some casual comments on Russia's need for warm weather ports. Shelagh Morrison-Bell, another member of the Embassy, remembered him "looking simply smashing in naval uniform, standing waiting in the entrance of the War Trade Department".

In the middle of much socializing, Ian wrote at least two memoranda for Donovan. They were clear and practical – the very qualities which made him so valuable to Godfrey. One concentrated on how a new US intelligence service might cooperate with the British. Ian recommended the appointment of intelligence officers to US embassies in sensitive foreign capitals, where they should come under the command of the local SIS (i.e. British intelligence) representative until they were fully trained. He suggested that an American intelligence service "should be under the protection of a strong government department and it should be insured by every means possible against political interference or control". A typical Fleming touch was his no-nonsense prescription for the ideal intelligence officer who, he said, "must have trained powers of observation, analysis and evaluation; absolute discretion, sobriety, devotion to duty; language and wide experience, and be aged about 40 to 50".

Another Fleming memo, dated 27 June, addressed more immediate issues. It urged Donovan to establish at least some sections of his organization as soon as possible "if they are to put up any kind of a show, should America come into the war in a month's time". It named possible candidates for leading jobs in the Office of the COI, such as Henry Luce, the president and editor-in-chief of *Time* magazine, as head of "foreign propaganda".

On 18 July Fleming cabled Godfrey to tell him of his progress. Donovan had obtained an initial grant of $10 million and should be starting operations with a skeleton staff by the middle of August. However the Office of the COI was little more than a glorified think-tank. Its development into a proper intelligence service would depend heavily on Stephenson and his BSC, Ian suggested. But already the rumour that "Donovan is a British nominee and a hireling of British SIS is spreading and should be carefully watched." Berlin radio identified this new department of US government as "fifty professors, twenty monkeys, twelve guinea pigs and a staff of Jewish scribblers" bent on a plan for Judaeo-Christian plutocracy. Donovan clearly valued Ian's contributions. He gave him a .38 Police Positive Colt revolver and inscribed it, "For Special Services". This was later a prized possession of Ian's, one which led him with some exaggeration to claim to the American writer Cornelius Ryan that he had written the blueprint for the Central Intelligence Agency (which succeeded the OSS in 1947).

On his way home, via Lisbon, in late July 1941, Ian embarked on a quick tour of his GOLDEN EYE installations to explain developments in Washington. His letter to Godfrey from the British Embassy on his return to Lisbon underlined his extraordinary autonomy and initiative. In Madrid his recommendations for the coordination of vital escape routes from France had been acted on by the Ambassador. But the usual problems about responsibility for sabotage and subversion remained. Hillgarth was having difficulty distancing himself from this work, partly because the new SOE representative was his son-in-law, David Muirhead, of whom Ian had a poor opinion. In Gibraltar a Joint Anglo-American Intelligence Committee had been established at his suggestion to coordinate intelligence from North Africa and the Iberian peninsula. In Tangier Ian was full of praise for H. L. Greenleaves, the GOLDEN EYE representative, who, through his contacts with the Americans, was producing good intelligence about French North Africa. But Ian had little time for the indolent SIS resident, Toby Ellis, whom he described as "in many respects an undesirable individual". His stay in the Spanish-occupied international city was enlivened by a night on the town with Greenleaves. After getting uproariously drunk, both men broke into the bullring where they marked a twenty-foot-wide "V" sign across the sand. Greenleaves was temporarily imprisoned, which hardly improved his standing with Ellis. Ian later apologized to Commander G. H. Birley on the GOLDEN EYE team in Gibraltar. "I am afraid you will have received something of a shock on hearing of my escapade with Greenleaves, of which I admit I was thoroughly ashamed, but it appears to have created nothing but the most ribald mirth in London and so perhaps it was not as shameful an affair as I thought it was."

In the wake of what he otherwise described as "Operation Catastrophe" and "my game of Red Indians", Ian decided he needed a new challenge. He told Smithers he was now "straining at the leash to go and catch a few sturgeon in the North." What he meant in as informative a way as was possible in a transatlantic letter was that he was hoping to be posted to the familiar territory of the Soviet Union, which had come into the war on the Allied side in June 1941 and was demanding regular supplies and intelligence. Ian applied to go to Moscow as naval representative in the British Military Mission. However Major-General Noel Mason-Macfarlane, leader of the Military Mission, was not one of his supporters. As defence attaché at the British Embassy in Berlin from 1937 to 1939, he had witnessed young Ian's attempts to involve himself in amateur intelligence-gathering and he had not been impressed. More recently, as Governor in Gibraltar, he had seen Ian's handling of GOLDEN EYE. Now he begged the Director of Military Intelligence, Major General Francis Davidson, to do all he could to stop Ian being "foisted" on the Naval Mission. Ian was not needed, said "Mason-Mac", and it was generally felt he was coming to Moscow to snoop. "I know Fleming," he added, "and from my experience of his activities in Germany before the war and of the reports he used to write I know him to be gullible and of poor and unbalanced judgement. PLEASE if it comes your way do all you can to stop his being forced on us. This place makes for frayed nerves and cooped up as we are we don't want any discordant possibilities added to our already large and so far very cooperative and matey family." The General was not the only person with a poor opinion of Ian. Many others, who were not part of his charmed circle, felt he was arrogant, supercilious and too obviously used to enjoying the good life from the comfort of his office in the Admiralty.

Godfrey, however, still valued his personal assistant and considered him too useful a staff officer to lose on operational matters. When Ian next wrote to Smithers, he explained that "for various black-hearted reasons" he had not been to Moscow. He admitted this was a disappointment, though he couched it as a joke – "I had hoped to lose myself there for protracted winter sports, but I daresay skiing with a Panzer Division behind is less fun than the old-fashioned kind."

Instead Ian had turned his attentions more directly to the subjects of propaganda and deception which had fascinated him since his meetings with Delmer and Bruce Lockhart the previous year. The Special Operations Executive, with its emphasis on covert operations, had never been the right organization to run Britain's state proselytism. So in August 1941 a new Political Warfare Executive (PWE) was set up, with branches devoted to both white and black propaganda. (The distinction between the two –

officially demarcated but in practice blurred – was that white propaganda was put out normally by the BBC, while black referred to special clandestine media designed to confound and confuse the enemy.)

Before long Ian was making his own personal contributions to the PWE's output. As a German speaker, his commentaries were broadcast on the BBC German Service's special programme for the German Navy. "I hope you are listening in to our naval broadcast at 6.45 BST every day on the wavelengths we signalled you," he informed Smithers in Washington towards the end of the year. "You may have heard my austere tones on November 1st and 2nd telling the Germans that all their U-boats leak." He urged Smithers to impress upon his contacts, particularly the Swedes, the veracity of this output.

Leonard Miall, who ran the BBC German Service, recalled Ian arriving at the broadcasting centre, Bush House, to record a talk in December 1941. Two days earlier the Japanese had bombed the American fleet at Pearl Harbor, and Hitler had just declared war on the United States. "Ian bounded in. He was practically euphoric. His mood, reflected in his script, was, 'The war is practically over, now this bloody fool Hitler's gone and brought the Americans in'. I said to him, 'I'm sure you are right in the long run, Ian, but we've got a lot of fighting still to do.' 'Oh! you defeatist lot in the BBC,' he replied. We argued a bit, and he agreed to tone down what he'd written. The next day the *Repulse* and the *Prince of Wales* were sunk off Malaya. The Navy realised there was still work to be done."

Meanwhile, Sefton Delmer had moved to Woburn Abbey on the Duke of Bedford's estate to set up the PWE's black propaganda operation. To do his job properly, he required a regular supply of reliable up-to-date information about German activities. He quickly found his best source was NID which had an efficient organization for interrogating captured German crewmen, particularly those from U-boats. Consequently, details about sailors' morale or their reactions to new pieces of equipment could be slipped quickly and seamlessly into Delmer's broadcasts. Godfrey, with Ian egging him on, was the first intelligence chief to understand the advantages of cooperating with Delmer. As the war in the Atlantic continued to take its toll well into 1942, and with still no success in breaking the crucial naval Enigma ciphers, NID needed to use every trick at its disposal to disorientate and destabilize German U-boat crews and throw them off the scent of Allied convoys. Delmer's black radio stations had the added bonus of allowing the Admiralty to put out totally erroneous claims about the sinking of German ships.

Day-to-day liaison between NID and the propaganda teams was conducted by a new unit, designated 17Z by Ian and headed by Donald McLachlan, who worked in Room 39. In close cooperation with Delmer, McLachlan set up two successful counterfeit radio stations, Deutscher

Kurzwellensender Atlantik and Soldatensender Calais, which broadcast carefully crafted lies to Atlantic U-boat crews and helped break their remaining resolution from late 1942. But Ian was the impresario behind the scenes, calling on his wide range of contacts to ensure that propaganda output was integrated with operational needs. To ensure that 17Z was firmly under his control, he arranged for Robert Harling, whom he had met in publishing circles before the war, to be plucked from convoy duty in mid-Atlantic and sent to join McLachlan. At the same time he maintained contact with several other friends in the broad field of deception including Ellic Howe, who had worked for the printer James Shand and now specialized in counterfeit German documents; Dennis Wheatley, an occasional dinner guest who worked for the London Controlling Section masterminding deception projects; and Louis de Wohl, an astrologer who was used by NID to chart the exact moments when Hitler might be open to ruses and feints.

Delmer's extravagant untruths appealed to the fantasist and prankster in Ian. His personal interest was heightened after his brother Peter was posted to India as adviser on deception to General Wavell, the Commander-in-Chief of the Allied Forces in the South-West Pacific. At one of his regular lunches with Delmer, Ian suggested that, in the name of the Wehrmacht authorities, one of the PWE's black radio stations should order the German public to pick up the stray pieces of shell discarded by ack-ack batteries after air raids and place them in the nearest letter-box. The authorities, the radio was bidden to say, needed them to check on fragmentation. Somehow Ian's idea was never used, which must have been galling, given Peter's prominence in this type of operation.

Ian's boyish love for precise information encouraged him to provide his own input into Delmer's broadcasts. At least twice, having arranged for captured German naval officers to be given *laissez passer*, he took them for meals at fashionable London restaurants. On one occasion, he wanted the captain and navigator of a captured U-boat to tell him how they had managed to avoid British mines in the Skaggerak. He plied them with drink in the downstairs grill-room at Scott's in Coventry Street and they became quite boisterous. So much so that the waiter serving this table of German speakers was alarmed enough to call the police. "It was only when we got back to the Admiralty," Ian later recalled, "befuddled and no wiser about the Skaggerak, that a furious Director of Naval Intelligence told us that the only result of our secret mission was to mobilize half the narks of the Special Branch of Scotland Yard." On another occasion, he took officers from the sunken German battleship *Bismarck* to L'Ecu de France in Jermyn Street. Again he tried to get them tight so that they would reveal operational secrets. But, according to Delmer, the DNI's assistant, who never had a great head for liquor, was the first to become drunk. After the meal,

Ian took his party to an MI5 safe house, wired for sound, where his apparent tipsiness only encouraged them to continue their indiscreet ramblings into the small hours.

By the end of 1941 Ian had moved from his succession of clubs and hotels into a small flat in Athenaeum Court, just off Piccadilly, close to Godfrey's house at 36 Curzon Street and conveniently round the corner from Ann O'Neill's suite at the Dorchester. He saw her regularly, with or without Esmond Rothermere, who was often occupied with his responsibilities as a newspaper owner. Sometimes they dined out: once returning from the White Tower by tube – for them an unusual form of transport – they were surprised to discover thousands of people sleeping underground, sheltering from the Blitz. More often they stayed indoors and played bridge with Ann's friend, Loelia Westminster, making up the numbers. Her marriage to Bendor, the overbearing Duke of Westminster, now irretrievably broken down, she had developed an unseemly crush on Ian, whom she described as "the most attractive man I've ever seen". Ian liked to tease her mercilessly, calling her "Lil". Ann recorded how one cold, autumnal evening in late September, Loelia was persuaded to remain overnight by Ian "making advances and a general show of lecherous affection such as he is master of". Usually Ian preferred to keep his friends separate, but on one occasion he introduced Ann to Sefton Delmer who dropped by after broadcasting, in his persona as 'Der Chef' on the clandestine radio station Gustav Siegfried Eins, an instant rejoinder to a talk by the Nazi propagandist Hans Fritzsche. Ann was fascinated, not only by Delmer, but by the response he stimulated in Ian. "He is a clever, interesting man and rouses all Ian's brain mania, plus his sublimated homosexuality. Still, despite Ian's possessiveness, it was an amusing evening."

Another woman who occupied Ian's time was Joan Bright, an assistant to General Ismay, Winston Churchill's chief of staff in the War Cabinet offices. During the course of earlier work for MI(R) and SIS, she had met Peter Fleming, who introduced her to his family. Since Peter was married, Ian took on the none too arduous task of squiring a brisk and attractive young woman who was highly influential in the wartime bureaucracy. In the course of a few short weeks at the turn of the year he and Joan dined at the Ritz, the White Tower and Quaglino's, and visited the cinema – a passion of Ian's – to see *Blood and Sand*, *The Thin Man* and the latest (and last) Garbo, *Two-Faced Woman*. In January 1942, Joan attended a Fleming family luncheon party at the Queen's Restaurant off Sloane Square. Peter and Celia were also present, along with Mrs Val and Augustus John, who, around this time, made a quick sketch of the uniformed Ian, looking thin-faced and rather apprehensive.

Joan Bright lived off Eaton Place, round the corner from 'Honeytop', as Ian called Muriel – to distinguish her from 'Silvertop', her fellow Admiralty worker, Pamela Tiarks. Joan noticed that whenever Muriel passed on her despatch rider's motorcycle, she increased her speed and looked studiously the other way. Although Ian still saw as much as he could of Moo, she had to put up with his going out with other women, including Ann, Joan and Pamela, not to mention his visits to his stern mistress, Maud Russell, in her flat in Upper Grosvenor Street.

While Ian enjoyed the adrenalin rush and heightened intimacy of the Blitz, when no one knew what the next night would bring, he tired of the material hardships of wartime London. Although access to friends and colleagues were better than in Ebury Street, Ian disliked his "ratlike existence" in Athenaeum Court, "a large block of concrete monstrosities" in which he had discovered, by attaching a bottle to the end of a tie, that it was "literally impossible to swing a cat". He described his privations: "When I tell you that the Savoy Hotel are now mixing Martinis out of bath-tub gin and sherry you will know that we are rapidly progressing back to swamp life and the transitional period is distasteful." As for other elements in his lifestyle, he flitted "uneasily from one to another of the Soho restaurants in the evening". Josef, patron of the Hungaria was "still able to make bricks out of straw" but was "correspondingly expensive and crowded". Ian's new car was run on "a mixture of pool petrol, water and moth-balls which make the petrol last longer". His only real luxury was his Morland Specials. To mark his rank as Commander, each cigarette was now emblazoned with three gold bands. His special order increased to 400 a week, at 32s 0d a hundred. And to help him withstand the general rigours, he plied Smithers with requests – for Kolynos toothpaste, Chesterfield cigarettes and a "'service-PAK' canvas zip bag which will take one suit and various oddments". As Ann once remarked, Ian could suffer anything but discomfort.

Ian entered 1942 on a high note at Ann O'Neill's New Year's Eve party, where fellow guests included the Prime Minister's flighty daughter-in-law Pamela Churchill, Cecil Beaton, Frank Pakenham and the Home Secretary, Herbert Morrison – as Ann put it, "a strange assortment of old, young, good and bad". Ian's confidence reflected his pride in his Division. In a revealing note to Smithers, he enthused, "We are all full of blitz here and the division is now the finest I [intelligence] organisation in the world. We *know* this!!" He attributed this to NID's director: "a real war-winner", with "the mind and character of a Bohemian mathematician". And as he had intimated to Leonard Miall, he really did think the Americans' entry into the war after Pearl Harbor was a turning-point. However, Ian's good spirits were dashed the following month when the Royal Navy allowed the German warships *Scharnhorst* and *Gneisenau* to slip out of the French port of Brest and make their spectacular dash up the Channel to Wilhelmshaven, and a few days later the Japanese completed a miserable week for the British by capturing Singapore. At the same time, any temporary advantage GCHQ had gained for Britain in the war in the Atlantic by breaking the German's three-rotor Enigma machine was negated by the introduction of a new four-rotor device which remained secure for the best part of a year, causing a dramatic increase in Allied shipping losses.

Over dinner of lobster and beer at Wilton's, Ian informed Ann of his strong feelings about the loss of Singapore. The reason for the disaster was that "we no longer shoot deserters from the army", he said, demonstrating the less liberal side of his character. As for the break-out from Brest, Ann's view – that it was "the blackest day of the war and perhaps in the history of the British Empire" – may have been hyperbolic, but surely reflected Ian's own opinion.

During the spring the number of Americans in London increased dramatically. Apart from the U-boat war in the Atlantic, the main item on the joint agenda was the forthcoming invasion of Europe. With public opinion to consider at home, Roosevelt wanted cross-Channel action before the end of the year. Churchill told the United States President that this was not possible, and counselled an alternative policy – a series of Allied landings against Germany's soft underbelly in the Mediterranean.

Ian had little time for the proliferating intelligence bureaucracy. He found Bill Whitney, Donovan's representative in the British capital, "completely useless except on the propaganda side". He was having second thoughts about Donovan himself who "seems to continue to thrash around in Washington with as much energy as ever, but very little comes from his activities except a moderate amount of smoke". As a result, Donovan's minions had "that unfortunate partiality which we knew at the beginning of the war, for endeavouring to do everything by tortuous and subterranean means where a simple direct approach through official channels would be much more effective and less confusing to the united nations". Even Stephenson's office in New York came in for criticism: "an English camarilla in the United States whose functions should normally be carried out by the Embassy".

A British Joint Staff Mission, headed by Admiral Cunningham, the former Commander-in-Chief of the Mediterranean Fleet, had recently arrived in Washington. Ian found Captain Eddie Hastings, one of its naval members, a braying ass; "I have no patience with him or his inanities." He preferred still to work through Smithers, whom he trusted with a new programme of disinformation known as 'Justice'. Smithers used the Washington cocktail party circuit to start various rumours Ian wanted people discussing. "I daresay there is quite a stream of traffic going to Stockholm and Moscow prefixed 'A.1 Naval Source'," Ian congratulated him. "It would be valuable for you to let your Swedes know that 'the Straits of Gibraltar are now minded by an ingenious new method and that you think this has something to do with atomic mines invented by the Americans. This is a useful line in connection with the German U-boats in the Mediterranean against which we have had notable successes lately, and we would like to put the wind up them still further." Ian maintained a similar relationship with Commander Paul Furse, an Iberian specialist (and GOLDEN EYE backstop), with a peripatetic role within NID as Assistant Naval Attaché Europe and the Americas.

The prospect of an invasion of Europe or North Africa encouraged Godfrey to pile more work on Ian. In February he put his bibliophile PA in charge of equipping a modern library. This meant working with the Inter-Services Topographical Department in Oxford, to build up what would now be called a resource base of maps, information and personal contacts relating to countries and situations likely to be encountered when the operation started. At Godfrey's behest, Ian started a project to think about the shape NID should take after the war. He also kept in close touch with GOLDEN EYE and other developments in Spain, where the Germans had stepped up their intelligence activity. In February, the SIS learned that the Germans had established a sophisticated infra-red device to count the number of Allied ships passing through the Straits of Gibraltar. Although the British Ambassador lodged a series of strong protests in Madrid, the Foreign Office took its usual stand against any act of provocation, such as sabotaging the actual facilities. When Colonel Stewart Menzies, the head of SIS, followed the Foreign Office line, someone in NID, possibly Ian, wrote "appeasement" on his cable. Certainly Ian was opposed to mere diplomacy. As Donald McLachlan related, "In pressing for action to stop the Germans Ian Fleming played a leading part ... It was vital that what he called 'the detailed and deadly watch' of the enemy on the Straits of Gibraltar should be frustrated by one means or another." SOE took some of the immediate pressure out of the situation by blowing up a reciprocal installation on the North African side of the water.

In Room 39, Ian responded with one of his bright ideas. He had noticed during the German attack on Crete how the Germans had sent a special commando force into action with the forward troops in order to capture Allied documents, equipment and ciphers before they could be destroyed by their defenders. In a paper to Godfrey on 20 March 1942, Ian described this as "one of the most outstanding innovations in German intelligence" and suggested that NID should adopt the concept "when we reassume the offensive on the Continent, in Norway or elsewhere". Godfrey agreed that this was an excellent suggestion, but wanted any such unit kept within NID's ambit and not, as Ian had suggested, shared with Lord Louis Mountbatten's Combined Operations. Various divisional directors in the

Admiralty were canvassed over what German materials they might like to acquire. As the answers flooded back – hydrophones, ciphers, handbooks, RDF valves, anti-aircraft ammunition – the matter was raised at the Joint Intelligence Committee, where military intelligence argued that such responsibilities could be handled by the existing Field Security Police. But Ian had done his homework with the SIS, which agreed that a permanent force might be useful.

By late spring a compromise of sorts had been reached between the British and Americans about where the first offensive should take place. It was agreed that a full-scale invasion was not feasible, but a small landing in north-west France, code-named SLEDGEHAMMER, would go ahead in the autumn. On 29 April Ian proposed that this would provide a good opportunity to try out his idea of an intelligence-gathering unit. In the event SLEDGEHAMMER was cancelled. But since regular commando raids were already being made on German installations in France, it was decided – partly to appease the Americans in advance of TORCH, the invasion of North Africa, scheduled for November – to upgrade one of these into a substantial cross-Channel attack to test German defences in the French port of Dieppe in August.

Ian's small raiding party received its baptism of fire at Dieppe. Initially he had opposed Operation JUBILEE, as this dry run for an invasion was officially known. He had frequently visited Dieppe in the 1930s and considered the coastline unsuitable. (According to Captain Drake, Ian canvassed an invasion in the even more unlikely Bay of Biscay.) But he changed his mind and, although he was not allowed ashore (once again Godfrey said he was too valuable to be captured), Ian was able to accompany his prototype unit on its first operation as an observer. Without revealing anything about his specific mission, he later wrote an account of the raid for the NID's Weekly Intelligence Report. Since it provided an early indication of his ability to evoke atmosphere and action, it is worth quoting in some detail. Ian sailed out of Newhaven on a Hunt-class destroyer in the early evening of 18 August. Contrary to expectations, the weather was fine. At about three in the morning, Ian was snoozing in an armchair in the wardroom when he heard the thud of gunfire. He went up on deck and saw tracers and 4-inch shells being fired about twenty miles to the north. 'The night was warm and still, and the red, green and white tracer in the distance seemed undangerous and even friendly.'

Lord Lovat's commando had been drafted in to lead the attack on the German defences high on the cliffs to the north of the town. As day broke, they came alongside Fleming's 'Hunt' to transfer their wounded. So confident were they about the success of the operation that it seemed the raid was all over bar the shouting. But from that moment on, the news from the front grew steadily worse, and the Canadian troops, which were leading the attack on the port, suffered hideous losses.

Ian observed everything from his ship which was tacking at ten knots about seven hundred yards away from the beach, making smoke to protect landing craft as they went in. If he failed to do justice to the full surrealism of the scene, little cameos caught Ian's eye. As the battle intensified during the morning, and fighters and bombers joined the fray on both sides, he saw a member of his ship's spare gunnery crew sitting on a crate of ammunition, engrossed in a book and oblivious to everything around him. Ian looked over the man's shoulder and saw the title of the book, *A Fortnight's Folly*.

In a style that was to become familiar, Ian commented on the extraordinary medley of sounds during the battle. "The volume of the naval 4-inch predominated with their usual whiplash crack; then there was the continual undertone of machine-gun fire with the heavier punctuation of Oerlikon-type guns, the hasty bark of pom-poms, and the soft stutter of fighter cannon far above. Above all one heard the varying hum of the RAF cover, occasionally overshadowed by the deep whine of a Junkers going into a steep dive to let go his bombs. But the noise which I remember best was the deliberate, wooden, knock, knock, knock of (I think) German anti-tank guns. This noise seemed so unhurried and deliberate that it cut through the permanent welter of sounds with a disturbing authority. It was the sort of noise one hoped we were making rather than the enemy." Charmingly, Ian referred to a Landing Craft Tank (LCT) as a TLC, which was a commodity in short supply that day.

Already the battle was slipping away from the Allies, and around 11 a.m. a withdrawal was ordered. At this stage Ian's destroyer was hit at the base of the funnel, killing one man and wounding four or five others. The large gunboat adjacent to the Hunt started pumping out 4-inch shells into the enemy gun emplacements in the cliff-face. This boat contained Ian's secret raiding party. As he coyly put it, "I had been instructed to return to England independently directly a certain mission had been accomplished and when it was clear that the gunboat was not going to able to carry out her original instructions, the Government exhortation, 'Is Your Journey Really Necessary?' came to my mind, heavily underlined by the shells from the shore batteries which came zipping through our rigging."

Other irreverent thoughts came to Ian's mind as his boat moved away from the shore. The main front at Dieppe, which he knew well, had been flattened. He confessed to "an unholy delight (remembering painful pre-war visits to French tables)" at seeing the casino destroyed. Ian's Hunt proceeded home at a leisurely five or six knots. At about 7 p.m. she left her convoy and was shepherded into Newhaven by light escort vessels, berthing around 3 a.m., whereupon Ian, a visiting American general and the Colonel of Marines disembarked in search of beds in the best hotel in town. Ian may have initially opposed the raid, which proved exceedingly controversial, but in his report he gave it the positive write-up required at the time. "It had been a long and nerve-racking day and it was difficult to add up the pros and cons of what was a bloody, gallant affair. But one thing was clear: intelligence, planning and execution had been nearly faultless. The machinery for producing further raids is there, tried and found good. Dieppe was an essential preliminary for operations ahead."

Three days later on 22 August, switching back effortlessly to the social scene, Ian lunched with his sister-in-law Celia and David Eccles, who was back from Washington. Celia sent her husband Peter in Delhi a favourable update on Ian. "Ian was in very good form indeed," she wrote, "and most nice and friendly. He disclosed halfway through lunch that he had been at Dieppe and told me lots of queer and frightening things about it. He said that, when all hell broke loose and everything was whizzing around everywhere, he began to think 'Is my journey really necessary?' (I forget if that depressing slogan was stuck up on all booking halls when you left but it is now.)"

Celia asked Peter not to worry his mother with the news that Ian had been at Dieppe. Ian did not want that, and "there is no point in her knowing after all". "It must have been hair-raising and awful and wonderful and as fearful as anything could be. Even Ian, who in Fleming fashion understates nicely, seemed not exactly staggered but as if he had had his breath taken away once or twice." Eve herself had joined the general exodus to the country, taking a cottage in Nettlebed and then a haunted house, known as The Abbey, in the Oxfordshire village of Sutton Courtenay, where Muriel Wright, on her motor bike, was a much more regular visitor than Ian. She had befriended young Amaryllis whom she used to take riding in Richmond Park. It was as if, frustrated in her efforts to see Ian with any regularity, she was determined to attach herself to the nearest available thing, his relatives.

As more detailed plans for Allied landings in North Africa were hatched, NID's relations with the American intelligence apparatus in London improved. Ian was appointed the Division's liaison officer with Colonel Whitney H. Shephardson, acting head of the London branch of the Office of Strategic Services, as the American COI had been renamed in June 1942. Initially Ian fielded mundane requests, such as for back copies of the NID's Weekly Intelligence Reports. But the OSS clearly valued his help for in the autumn it appointed a special officer, Commander Junius Morgan, to London to deal specifically with NID.

This was welcome news for Ian, for Morgan was not only a leading member of the famous banking family he knew well but also the secret treasurer of clandestine OSS operations in Europe. In September, shortly before his second trip to the United States with Godfrey, Ian wrote to Shephardson, expressing appreciation at Morgan's hard work and asking, "Please let me know if there are any matters which you think may be assisted by DNI's intervention in Washington or which I could take up on a lower level, and if there are any private wars in which you are engaged I shall be delighted to fire a salvo on your behalf in any direction you require."

However, on the eve of their departure, to Ian's considerable shock, Godfrey was unceremoniously sacked. He had just been promoted to Vice Admiral when he was told that he was being relieved of his duties at the end of the year and sent to Bombay as Flag Officer Commanding Royal Indian Navy (FOCRIN). No official reason was given for this devastating move. Godfrey's prickliness, so well managed by Ian, had certainly antagonized others in the wider intelligence community. With offensive action starting in earnest, a more emollient, team-playing personality was perhaps called for. However, one NID veteran believed that the DNI took the blame for lapses in cipher security which, when taken together with the four-rotor Enigma, had given Germany such an advantage in the U-boat war in the Atlantic during 1942.

In the circumstances the two men's trip to the United States was something of an anticlimax. In New York Ian liaised with various NID departments teaching the Americans techniques which Britain had learned earlier in the war, such as interrogation and propaganda. On 11 October Leonard Miall, on secondment from the BBC, noted in his diary, "Must take up these points with Ian Fleming", after learning of a young US ensign who was being told by his superior officer that the Royal Navy was outmoded and ineffective.

Ian made a point of seeing Hugo Pitman's daughters, Rose and Jemima, who had been evacuated to the United States in June 1940. Much as he liked the young girls, his visit had an official dimension. For the two Pitmans were staying at Salutation, the Long Island estate of Junius Morgan, the man who had recently been appointed OSS liaison officer to NID. Morgan had already proved his worth as an important point of contact for Ian with the American intelligence establishment. Ian's Room 39 colleague, Captain Drake, recalled that the link was of "immense value: whenever Ian wanted anything, he sent a signal to Junius Morgan". (Rose and Jemima were not the only children with important City of London connections staying with members of the Morgan family. Hugh Vivian Smith's son and daughter, and their cousin Neil Primrose, Lord Rosebery's heir, were lodged with Junius's father, J. P. Morgan Jr., while several Hambro offspring were with his brother, Harry Morgan.)

On a personal level, Ian's stay in New York was interesting for his introduction to a man who was to remain a close friend throughout his life. Ernie Cuneo was a large, rumbustious lawyer, a leading member of the Roosevelt political machine, who had been seconded to liaise between Donovan and the BSC. As with Stephenson the previous year, Ian took to him immediately, or almost immediately. The two men met in the drawing-room of William Stephenson's apartment in the Hotel Dorset, a cosy penthouse he rented from William Hearst's widow, Marion Davies. The "quiet Canadian" and others were debriefing a British cruiser captain who had just returned from a convoy on the murderous Murmansk run, transporting weaponry and raw materials into the Soviet Union. When the captain had finished, Cuneo remarked tritely that it would continue to be tough going. Clearly annoyed, Ian jumped in to say that he thought Admiral Ernest King, Chief of US naval operations, was driving "too hard a bargain" and was not supporting the Russian convoys forcefully enough. Cuneo sprang to the American admiral's defence: King was giving all possible cooperation, he said, and noticing Ian was a mere commander, he added that junior British officers would be unlikely to know about that. "Do you question my bona fides?" Ian asked angrily. "No, only your patently limited judgement," Cuneo replied, and both men laughed, for this sort of mock-aggressive banter was typical among the British and Americans working together.

Cuneo observed that Ian looked more American than British. It was not just his broken nose, which gave him the appearance of a lightweight boxer. It was the way he carried himself, like an American athlete. "He did not rest his weight on his left leg; he distributed it, his left foot and his shoulders slightly forward." Cuneo saw that Stephenson considered Ian one of his special "boys". "Obviously Fleming had privileges far and above his rank of the Commander in the Wavy Navy." Cuneo shared Ian's enjoyment of the 21 Club. He introduced him to his circle of friends, who included several important opinion-makers, such as Walter Winchell, the king of the gossip writers, whose columns had done much to stir up Americans against the Nazis.

Ian's friendship with Ernie Cuneo was based on a shared whimsical, Runyonesque view of the world. Although they seldom discussed operational matters, Cuneo could not help noticing Ian's steely patriotism. Once, when the tide of the war had improved, Ernie teased him that it was proving the Royal Navy's most magnificent performance since Trafalgar. "And", he added provocatively, "with such dirty, lousy ships too." Ian leapt to the bait: "Why, God damn it, I messed aboard the [USS] Wisconsin and the Goddamned ship looked as if it hadn't been washed down for a month." "It hasn't," replied Ernie, "It has been at sea for months – out protecting the Royal Navy." At this stage Cuneo realized that he had gone

far enough "and that the Royal Navy was too close to [Ian's] heart for
thrusting, even by banter". He later told Donovan that, as far as he could
ascertain, England was not a country but a religion, and that where
England was concerned, every Englishman was a Jesuit who believed the
end justified the means. "I further added that there wasn't a game British
Intelligence couldn't play, from archbishops to safe crackers, and they
could deliver either in 24 hours."

The articles of this religion meant that Ian no longer had Smithers to
entertain him in Washington. In the flurry of activity prior to TORCH, when
the security of Atlantic sea routes was paramount, the assistant naval
attaché had been posted to Mexico, where he was needed to investigate
the possibility that the Germans were communicating with their sub-
marines from the shore. Ian did not stay long in the US capital for his
presence was required at an Anglo-American naval conference in the
wartime backwater of Jamaica. In his lame-duck period, Godfrey felt he
was better occupied paying a long-postponed visit to Canada.

Without his director, Ian arranged for his friend Ivar Bryce to accompany
him. As an SIS agent attached to Stephenson in New York, Bryce had been
running dangerous missions into Latin America. Since he – or, rather, his
wife, Sheila – also owned Bellevue, one of Jamaica's most beautiful 'great
houses', where Ian's hero, Horatio Nelson, had once stayed as a young
man, Ivar might prove useful. The conference took place in the old colonial
Myrtle Bank (popularly known as the Turtle Tank) Hotel in Kingston. But
Ian and Ivar decided to forgo the unbearable humidity of the capital and
spend their nights at Bellevue, up in the relative cool of the Blue Mountains
above the city. When they arrived at the house the first evening, no one
was expecting them. The rainy season had just started and it poured
continually. A Jamaican servant, Elizabeth, rushed around and found them
some chicken for dinner. As they sat on the balcony, drinking grenadine,
the only bottle in the house, Ian was enthralled by the potent combination
of Bellevue's magnificent situation, high in the hills overlooking the ocean,
the memory of Nelson, and the sad sound of the torrential rain, dripping
incessantly through the tropical trees. Each day the two men drove down
to the Myrtle Bank for the conference. Each night they returned to the
hills for peace, solitude and rain. Ivar thought his friend had loathed the
whole experience. But on the flight back to Washington, Ian turned to
him and said, "You know, Ivar, I have made a great decision." Ian waited
a moment for effect and added, "When we have won this blasted war, I
am going to live in Jamaica. Just live in Jamaica and lap it up, and swim
in the sea and write books." Ian had made a dramatic mental commitment
to realizing the dream he had toyed with four or five years earlier.

On his return to London, Ian concentrated on two particular aspects of
the forthcoming invasion of North Africa. One was Spain where GOLDEN

EYE was put on a state of alert after the Axis powers, suspecting that something was about to happen, stepped up their snooping and sabotage in the peninsula. When, in November, the Italian crews of three miniature human torpedoes were captured trying to blow up two aircraft carriers and two battleships in Gibraltar harbour, they claimed they had slipped out from a submarine. But, after a similar incident, it transpired that they had exited from a trapdoor in the bottom of the *Olterra*, a 5000-ton Italian tanker which had been holed up in Algeciras Bay, opposite the Rock, since the start of the war. Hillgarth took the lead in exposing this subterfuge, which provided the inspiration for the underwater trapdoor to Emilio Largo's yacht, the *Disco Volante*, in Ian's novel *Thunderball*.

Even in this fraught theatre of the war, Ian remembered his friends. On one of his trips to Lisbon, he met an outstandingly pretty secretary at the Embassy called Mary Grepe. When she wanted a job in London, Ian recommended her to Joan Bright who pushed her to work for Commander Christopher Arnold-Forster in SIS. When, later, Air Marshal Medhurst required a secretary to accompany a delegation he was taking to Portugal to discuss the vexed issue of Allied landing rights in the Azores, Ian suggested he should take Mary. When Mary entered the meeting in Lisbon, the whole Portuguese delegation rose to welcome her and the Foreign Minister kissed her hand. Medhurst found to his delight that negotiations which were proving sticky were quickly wound up.

The second area which occupied Ian's attention was his intelligence assault unit. Although the JIC had entrusted the project to the Chief of Combined Operations, Lord Louis Mountbatten, and he had chosen Commander Robert 'Red' Ryder VC, the hero of the commando raid on the German-held port of St Nazaire on the French Atlantic coast earlier in the year, as leader of what was temporarily called the Special Engineering Unit, Ian kept a careful watch on developments in the run-up to TORCH. Ryder set up three troops – from the Royal Marines, the Army and the Royal Navy. But the naval Number 36 Troop was different from the other two. It initially had only five officers, compared with two officers and twenty men in the two troops which were regular fighting forces. No. 36 Troop's responsibilities were described as "technical", which meant exactly the kind of sensitive equipment-grabbing Ian had first suggested. And the Admiralty insisted that it remained under naval command, which gave Ian ample reason to involve himself at the unit's new training school in a requisitioned farmhouse near Amersham.

As at Dieppe, the full unit was not ready for action by the time of TORCH in November. So a special ad hoc No. 33 Section of seven men was established, under the Navy's (or No. 36 Troop's) Lieutenant Dunstan Curtis RNVR, who had taken part in the raids at both St Nazaire and Dieppe. Curtis's rudimentary force acquitted itself well in the landing at

Algiers, beating the Field Security Police to the headquarters of the Italian Armistice Commission by a clear two hours.

Even at Christmas Ian could not escape what was happening in North Africa. He had gone to spend a few days at Himley Hall, near Birmingham, the seat of Lord Dudley, the government's powerful Regional Commissioner for the Midlands, who was preparing to marry Ann O'Neill's sister Laura in the New Year. Among the other guests were Ann with Esmond Rothermere, and Duff and Diana Cooper with their teenage son John Julius. TORCH was much discussed because Cooper was shortly to move to Algiers to take up his appointment as British Minister. On Christmas Eve the house party was shocked to hear that Darlan, the French admiral whom Ian had tried to convince to bring his ships over to the Allied side in June 1940, had been assassinated in Algiers. His killers were two French patriots who were later executed. It subsequently emerged that they had been set up by the SIS. Whether or not Ian was in the know, he would have dismissed all requests for information about the incident with an impenetrable sardonic smile.

The start of the new year, and the arrival of Captain (later Rear-Admiral) Edmund Rushbrooke as the new DNI, marked a change of pace for Ian. He remained the Director's personal assistant. But the job had altered. Room 39 was no longer the buzzing ideas factory it had once been. Although Rushbrooke had served as head of Operational Intelligence in the Far East, his style was steady and bureaucratic, in keeping with his specific brief to cooperate with other service intelligence chiefs more closely than his wayward predecessor. Ian quickly impressed his new director with his command of his intelligence material. As the Division's official history noted, on 5 January 1943, Ian, in his traditional role as purveyor of special intelligence from the diplomatic sphere, "produced a gem at a daily meeting. In an answer to a question (which we had not intercepted) and depending for his reply on a source which was given but the decyphering of which was corrupt, the Japanese Ambassador in Berlin provided his Foreign Minister and ourselves with a detailed summary of German losses and accretions in merchant shipping since the outbreak of war." Ian held Rushbrooke's hand and piloted him around the Whitehall establishment. In mid-February, they visited Air Marshal Sir Arthur Harris, the ordnance-friendly head of Bomber Command. "Harris was in great form," Ian recalled, "with the saliva dribbling down his chin as he described the squelching of large large portions of the German population in complete disregard for the military value of this particular target."

Soon Ian was telling Smithers that "everything is going as it should, though creeping paralysis is noticeable in certain quarters". This did not stop Ian from keeping up his broad range of service interests. In March, he introduced his friends Robert Harling and Alexander Glen, who had been assistant naval attaché in Belgrade, to Vladimir Wolfson, the naval attaché and SIS resident in Istanbul. Like Dunderdale, Wolfson was much admired by Ian as a stylish secret agent of the old school. Strangely, like Dunderdale, he was also Odessa-born. Ian wanted the three men to cooperate on a survey of beaches in Albania, northern Greece and parts of Yugoslavia – part of an elaborate gambit to convince the Germans that, after TORCH, the next Allied advance was likely to come in the Balkans rather than in Sicily. In a related ruse later in the year, Ian assisted in one of the Navy's most elaborate hoaxes ever, The Man Who Never Was. Brilliantly executed by Ian's Room 39 colleague Commander Ewen Montagu, this exploit, which was later filmed, required the Germans to believe that the body of a sailor washed up on the Spanish shore carried valuable operational information about an impending Allied invasion in the eastern Mediterranean.

With the pressure slightly off, Ian had time to attend to business interests. At Hugo Pitman's insistence, he was still paid his salary as a partner at Rowe and Pitman. So, as often as he could, he dropped in to see his old colleagues in Bishopsgate. In February 1943 Lord Bicester, the banking Hugh Smith brother, who was chairman of Morgan Grenfell, called on Ian's advice over a deal he was contemplating. Ian's former employer, Cull and Company, had again run into financial difficulties and Morgan Grenfell was considering bailing them out. Bicester wanted to know what to do with Hermann Marx, the acknowledged financial brains of the firm. Ian had no doubt that Marx would be an asset to Morgan Grenfell: "You would not find his personality disturbing so long as you regarded and treated him as a technician, which he is first and foremost ... It is the name of his *firm* rather than his *name* which is ill regarded in the City."

As an example of the chance, inconsequential meetings which happen in wartime, Ian was walking home to Athenaeum Court one night when he found himself in the middle of an air raid. To wait for the all-clear, he stepped into a pub off Piccadilly, where the only other person at the bar was the homosexual poet James Kirkup, nursing a glass of Algerian wine. As a conscientious objector, Kirkup had been working on a farm in Essex and had come up to London for some weekend amusement. But after cruising Piccadilly without success, he had stopped for a drink. Kirkup could tell immediately that his new companion was not gay – more like a raffish businessman, he thought. Kirkup's hands were shaking with fear from the air raid. Ian looked at him quizzically, and asked, "What's that muck you're drinking?" When Kirkup told him, Ian introduced himself, took a silver flask from his Burberry coat pocket and poured the young poet a stiff brandy. "Here, have a proper drink on me," he said.

As the two men began to talk, they discovered a mutual interest in literature. Ian asked to hear one of his new acquaintance's poems. So with the bombs still falling, Kirkup slowly recited one of his more laboured and inscrutable works. When he came to the end, the air raid suddenly ceased. "You've stopped the Luftwaffe," shouted the Irish barman. "That's really quite sinister," announced Ian after some reflection. "I suppose the word 'cottage' has more than one meaning?" "If you like," replied Kirkup. "And I expect the 'inspector' is both a ticket inspector and a police inspector?" continued Ian. The poet agreed that his words were not to be taken literally: "The 'inspector' could be anyone in authority, come to take me away to jail or the loony bin." Ian sighed, "Your poor parents," – a veiled remark which Kirkup thought perceptive. Suddenly Kirkup threw out an idea. His "impenetrably hermetic" poetry could be used in wartime as an uncrackable secret code, its meaning understood only by sender and recipient. Ian thought about this for a moment and, as the all-clear sounded, turned to Kirkup and said, "That's very interesting. Let me have your address, and I'll get in touch."

Twice during the year Ian travelled across the Atlantic to participate in formal encounters between Churchill and Roosevelt – the Trident Conference in Washington in May (which fixed the date for the invasion of France the following year) and the follow-up Quadrant Conference in Quebec in August. In the American capital, he was roped into playing cricket on a baked earth baseball pitch in Georgetown, where his cynical comments from the slips were later recalled.

Running the administrative side of both conferences for the British was Joan Bright, taking time off from her new job distributing the latest secret intelligence to commanders-in-chief in the field. Starting with a visit to the topical film *Casablanca* in January, Ian had continued to see her regularly throughout the year. She was delighted to find that, attending the Washington conference as well as Ian, was his brother Peter, over from India, making an unsuccessful pitch for his unit to be allowed to run all strategic deception in the Pacific. So, when her day was done, Joan was able to spend the evening with both Flemings whom she described as "an attractive pair, amusing, good looking, sure of themselves and devoted to each other". She also noted, "Ian was more persuasive, had more apparent and vocal concern towards the people he liked, wanting them to do what he thought would be to their advantage; but he could also detach himself from them and temporarily but summarily dismiss them from his thought."

Joan's presence in Washington gave an added significance to Ian's remark to Peter Smithers who, by happy coincidence, was also in town. Walking along the banks of the Georgetown Canal, Smithers told Ian of his plans to marry an American woman in St Louis the following month.

Ian turned to his friend and addressed him intensely, "Well, old boy, I wish you all the luck in the world, but I can't see anything in it for me." It was one of Ian's clearest statements that he had weighed up the pros and cons of matrimony, and found it wanting.

Ian's attendance at the Quebec conference was unmemorable except for the fact that it was his only recorded visit to Canada. Stephenson, in his dotage, made much of his claim that Fleming was a graduate of Camp X, the tough establishment at Oshawa, near Toronto, where SOE and OSS jointly trained their agents for clandestine work in Europe and elsewhere. Ian, according to his mentor, was supposed to have been the camp's star pupil. He passed the key agent's initiative test – placing a bomb in the main Toronto power station – by bluffing his way into the complex and disarming everyone with his plummiest Old Etonian accent. He did the self-defence and unarmed combat courses, and performed an arduous underwater swim at night from the camp to an old tanker moored offshore, where – shades of James Bond in *Live and Let Die* – he fixed a limpet mine against the hull. But the historian David Stafford, who examined these claims, found no evidence that Ian had ever completed a course at the camp. Ian may have taken a day-trip to view an important establishment and may even have participated in some training. But, try as Ian might to inveigle himself some further action, the DNI was determined to keep him on a tight rein as a staff officer. According to Smithers, "Ian constantly longed to be personally engaged in the excitement. He was of an essentially aggressive nature. It was the repression of all these desires by authority, quite rightly, which in my opinion fired the imagination engaged in his books."

So three months later, in November 1943, Ian was off to another Churchill–Roosevelt conference, dubbed 'Sextant' and held in Cairo, to prepare the way for the big summit meeting between the two Western leaders and Marshal Joseph Stalin of the Soviet Union in Tehran at the end of the month. Once again Joan Bright was managing the British arrangements. Luckily for Ian he was given a seat in the heated Dakota in which Joan was flying with the Minister for War Transport, Lord Leathers, and two female colleagues. Otherwise he would have bumped uncomfortably across two continents in one of the two accompanying transport aircraft which had unpressurized cabins and bucket seats. Ian was an easy travelling companion, Joan found. Like the off-duty gunner on his Hunt destroyer at Dieppe in May 1941, he had the capacity to switch himself off. If any problems arose, he simply took a book from his pocket and started reading, oblivious to all around him.

After a couple of nights' delay in a hotel in St Ives because of bad weather, the flight took off from Portreath in Cornwall on the evening of 19 November, proceeding via Rabat to Biskra in Algeria where they spent the night in a run-down, once comfortable French hotel. Ian amused Joan by urging her to visit a soothsayer who, he said, lived in the 'Garden of Allah'. When they reached the designated spot, no sage was to be found. Adopting his 'best Goon French', Ian asked a passer-by where the great man was hiding. The Arab went away promising to find him, but no one ever materialized. "I am sure it was an Ian Fleming 'spoof'," recalled Joan, "but he made it all sound so real and true that it was worth being fooled."

The Sextant Conference was held in the pleasant surroundings of the Mena House Hotel beside the Pyramids. But the atmosphere at what should have been routine and amicable preparation for the forthcoming Tehran summit was somewhat strained by the presence of a Chinese delegation under Generalissimo Chiang Kai-shek, who undermined the prevailing Anglo-American solidarity and encouraged US delegates to play up the idea that Britain was interested only in pursuing her colonial interests after the war.

Ian contracted bronchitis in Cairo and did not go on to Tehran. Convalescing in Egypt, he delighted in the luxury of fried eggs and fresh orange juice. He and Joan returned to England on HMS *London* in the second week of December. Each evening after supper they joined General Ismay in his cabin for a game of bridge. After reaching Gibraltar on 13 December, they had to wait five days for the escort they were sharing with HMS *King George V.* Some of the party were dismayed at this enforced delay. But Ian jumped at the opportunity to read and to eat more bacon and eggs. They set sail from Gibraltar again on 18 December, reaching England two days before Christmas. Ian described himself as having "been away for six weeks on a millionaire's Mediterranean cruise". Two days later, he was bouncing with enthusiasm and bonhomie at a Christmas Day gathering at Send Grove, the house Loelia Westminster had rented near Guildford in Surrey. He surprised the female guests by giving each of them an identical edition of Verlaine's poems, with suitable romantic passages marked at random. Ann was put out to find that her gobbet referred to the passion between two lesbians and convinced herself that Ian must have made a mistake.

She herself had been assisting the war effort by holding a series of "brains trusts" designed to introduce American servicemen to the British way of life. At the Dorchester, she never rivalled Nancy Cunard or even Sibyl Colefax as a wartime hostess. But, maturing quickly into a role as a newspaper baron's *de facto* consort, she began to surround herself with clever young men who performed at these events; men such as Peter Quennell, editor of the conservative *Cornhill Magazine*, and Alastair Forbes, a confidant of Churchill who combined a Boston brahmin background with a Winchester education.

With the Allied invasion of Europe imminent, the US presence in London intensified. At the joint intelligence headquarters at Norfolk House in St James's Square, Ian frequently met his 'opposite number', Lieutenant Alan Schneider, personal assistant to the US Navy's District Intelligence Officer, Commodore Tully Shelley. Schneider used to invite him to the American Officers Club in Park Lane, where Ian "ate everything at the buffets, and went back for seconds, or even thirds". At one Norfolk House meeting, they were joined by an attractive woman, who was a US Army captain. Schneider thought nothing about it until, around nine o'clock that evening, he received a telephone call from Ian asking him tersely to be down in front of his flat in North Audley Street in ten minutes. Before Schneider had time to ask why, Ian had rung off. Shortly afterwards, Ian arrived in a taxi. He ordered Schneider in, and there, sprawled across the seat, obviously very drunk, was the unfortunate Army captain. Ian directed the driver to nearby Claridge's Hotel, where he told Schneider to help her out. Again, before the American had had time to ask what was going on, Ian had given the driver another address and sped off. Schneider was left to take the woman to her room. "After tipping the hall porter, I walked back to my flat, which wasn't far, and called Ian. I told him what we had done. 'Thank you,' he said. 'Very decent of you,' and hung up before I could say another word. He never mentioned it again – not the next morning, not the next day, not ever."

Schneider attributed this eccentric behaviour to Ian's ruthlessness towards women. Whether they were well-born Englishwomen or US Army officers, "he treated them all the same way. He got bored with them fast and could be brutal about it. He had absolutely no jealousy. He explained to me that women were not worth that much emotion. But with it all, he had an abiding and continual interest in sex without any sense of shame or guilt." Ian told Schneider crudely that "women were like pets, like dogs, men were the only real human beings, the only ones he could be friends with".

The unreality of this pose was brought home to Ian rather brutally in mid-March 1944 when his faithful Muriel was killed in an air raid. All such casualties are, by definition, unlucky, but she was particularly so, because the structure of her new flat at 9 Eaton Terrace Mews was left intact. She died instantly when a piece of masonry flew in through a window and struck her full on the head. Because there was no obvious damage, no one thought to look for the injured or dead; it was only after her chow, Pushkin, was seen whimpering outside that a search was made. As her only known contact, Ian was called to identify her body, still in a nightdress. Afterwards he walked round to the Dorchester and made his way to Esmond and Ann's room. Without saying a word he poured himself a large glass of whisky, and remained silent. He was immediately consumed with grief and guilt at the cavalier way he had treated her. It only made matters worse to know that she had just been out on her motor bike to collect two hundred of his special order cigarettes from Morlands. He immediately became very sentimental about Muriel, refusing to return to restaurants they had once visited together. Dunstan Curtis, an Old Etonian in his intelligence assault unit, commented cynically, "The trouble with Ian is that you have to get yourself killed before he feels anything."

For some time, Ian wore Muriel's bracelet on his key-ring. One day, on a visit to Buscot, he temporarily lost his keys. Finding them, the precocious young Fionn O'Neill teased her mother's lover, "Who's got a girlfriend then?" Ian angrily snatched the keys from the child. The next day Ann explained the circumstances to her children's nanny, Joan Sillick, adding, lugubriously, that the bracelet was "all that was left" of Muriel as a result of the blast. When Celia Johnson noted that, on a visit to Merrimoles, "even the old clubman Ian was moved to tears (almost) by the prettiness" of the mild spring, she must have understood the pain her brother-in-law was suffering. Towards the end of April, Ian took a short holiday in Scotland with Ann, Esmond and the Dudleys. "Ann complained loudly and continuously that Esmond hadn't come up to scratch since Christmas Eve," Eric Dudley wrote to Duff Cooper in Algiers, "but whether this was intended to put him to shame or incite Ian Fleming, I couldn't make out." Ann later noted that Ian was taking all his leaves with her. "I never showed Ian I was in love with him. I knew instinctively it would be fatal, but I did know he was becoming more dependent on me."

Within Room 39, the main item on the agenda was the forthcoming invasion of Normandy. From March 1944 Ian had been running the secret BP Committee within NID. Its task was to ensure the flow of Special Intelligence from Bletchley Park to the naval side of the expeditionary force preparing for Operation OVERLORD. While 30 Assault Unit, as his intelligence-gathering commando was now called, had been rummaging in North Africa and Italy, he had engaged in only sporadic communication with it. (However, one friend, Andrew Mouravieff, a liaison officer at the French Army headquarters in Algiers, remembered Ian visiting the town and joining him and the British Minister Duff Cooper on a shooting expedition in the Atlas Mountains in early 1944.)

The run-up to OVERLORD allowed Ian to regain control of his "Red Indians". The strength of 30 AU had grown to over three hundred men – a core of naval experts rooting out essential intelligence material, and a larger unit of Royal Marines, who provided their colleagues with cover. Ian spent long hours compiling lists of German equipment to be captured. Although one of his charges found him "somewhat cold and austere, very 'Pusser' and on his dignity as far as the Unit was concerned", they generally appreciated Ian's interventions on their behalf, battling against local commanders who resented the presence of a freelance group in their midst.

A week before D-Day Ian held a dinner at the Gargoyle Club for 30 AU's naval officers, their wives and girlfriends. He came with Pamela Tiarks who commented on her escort's elusiveness to Robert Harling, the unit's topographical expert. Ian was "like a handful of seawater: he slips through your fingers, even while you're watching". On 6 June one section of 30 AU landed with Canadians at Arromanches in Normandy. It captured valuable documents, but was prevented by heavy fire from reaching its main objective – the radar station at Douvres. The remainder accompanied the Americans in the attack on Cherbourg. But again there was disappointment: the Germans had burned the most valuable codes and documents at their naval headquarters, the Villa Maurice.

Waiting for the next stage of the advance, 30 AU assembled in a camp at Carteret, opposite the Channel Islands, where, towards the end of July, Ian flew over to visit his men. He took them to task for their growing notoriety for rowdiness and indiscipline. They were "fairly piratical, particularly with the women", recalled one member; Admiral Cunningham dubbed them 30 Indecent Assault Unit. But they had fought hard and proved their worth. As a result, several members now resented their well-tailored superior crossing the Channel to tell them to behave. "He was one of those very superior type RNVRs who got their claws into their lordships early in the war and have kept them there ever since," wrote Tony Hugill in a lightly fictionalized account. "As our proprietary deity he felt himself entitled to demand offerings of Camembert and libations of captured Cognac of the better sort – 'But, my dear fellow, the stuff is undrinkable!' – from time to time. He also interfered with us on a high level." According to Charles Wheeler, a young Marine temporarily seconded to 30 AU, "Fleming was palpably envious of his highly independent charges in the field, living it up in the brilliant summer weather and obviously enjoying their war." Members of 30 AU like Dunstan Curtis thought their boss was "a bit of a fraud back there in the Admiralty", recalled Wheeler. They took a malicious delight in exposing Ian to positions where he would experience German fire. The American Lieutenant-General George S. Patton, to whose Third Army they were attached, also made his feelings felt. He disliked sailors in general, but if they had to be around, he made it abundantly clear that he preferred the US Navy to the Royal Navy.

For a couple of days at the end of July, shortly after COBRA, the operation to break out of Normandy, had started, the DNI, Admiral Rushbrooke, joined Ian and 30 AU at Carteret. He and Ian toured the battlefield, inspecting vast V-2 rocket installations. When Rushbrooke was invited to lunch with Patton, Ian ducked out. Commandeering a jeep he drove off for a picnic with Robert Harling. Halfway through the meal he asked his friend what he intended to do after the war. Harling almost choked on his Spam rations when Ian informed him he was "going to write the spy story to end all spy stories".

After acquitting itself well in the liberation of Paris, the bulk of 30 AU returned to England in September for further training in preparation for the invasion of Germany. Ian seized the opportunity to take some time off. But it was not an enjoyable holiday. He was visiting Ann O'Neill at Esmond Rothermere's house in Ascot in October when she received a telegram informing her that Shane had been killed in action in Italy. Like Ian a few months earlier, Ann was extremely distressed and guilty about her adulterous behaviour. "Death is the best revenge," she said melodramatically about her husband's motives for getting himself killed. Ian was the first person she turned to and he responded with practical emotional support. At Ann's request, he informed Rothermere and arranged for her children Raymond, the new Lord O'Neill, and Fionn to join their mother.

However welcome Ian's thoughtfulness was at the time, it sowed the seeds of further confusion in Ann's mind. Although she was practically living with Rothermere, she realized she did not love him – all the less so because, while O'Neill lived, her influential lover was unwilling to countenance the public notoriety of a divorce. As long as Ian kept surprising her with his compelling mixture of consideration and disdain, she remained in a desperate quandary about her future.

At this stage in the war, Ian had little inclination to sit still in the Admiralty. As the focus of hostilities shifted to the Far East, the DNI wanted a review of the intelligence infrastructure for the newly created British Pacific Fleet, and Ian volunteered to make the arrangements. Just before Christmas his old Reuters colleague Alaric Jacob saw him strolling down the steps of Shepheard's Hotel in Cairo. Ian was "flying around the world 'making contacts' with an impressive air of smooth secrecy", recorded Jacob, who was on leave from reporting for the *Daily Express* in Moscow.

Ian's next stop was the Indian Ocean island of Ceylon where his friend Alan Hillgarth had been appointed Chief British Naval Intelligence Eastern Theatre (CBNIET). As well as his official NID role, Hillgarth was Prime Minister Churchill's personal intelligence representative in Colombo, the capital of the British colony. Hillgarth did his own signals, with the help of his trusted Wren assistant, Clare Blanshard, an attractive and amusing woman in her late twenties, who joked that CBNIET stood for Chief Bloody Nuisance in the Eastern Theatre.

As soon as he arrived on 23 December, Ian struck up a close friendship with Clare who was swept off her feet by the handsome, educated naval officer in his tropical uniform. In a letter to her brother Paul a month later, "Since I last wrote (and continuously, every day, but about to be lopped off at a moment's notice like Marlowe's Faustus), a beauteous being has swum into my ken – on an official visit – and I like him very very very much indeed . . . As the Wrens say, whose letters I censor so monotonously, he's absolutely It. It doesn't make any difference that I don't mean anything to him as he's so awfully nice . . . so that is why I haven't written. Next time I write he'll have gone for ever and ever and practically won't have existed. But, believe me, he's the right shape, size, height, has the right sort of hair, the right sort of laugh, is 36 and beautiful. I wish I were more glamorous . . ."

Ian had arrived at the height of the Christmas party season in Colombo. He invited Clare to a dance at the Septic Prawn, the nightclub in the Galleface Hotel where he was staying. She was impressed that he was "a plodder dancer: I dislike men who dance well". She wore a stunning long white silk dress, plugged with little pieces of real silver. Ian was fascinated with the garment and, seventeen years later, sent her a postcard of the ballroom of a Sussex hotel where he was recuperating from an illness. He marked the front with an X and wrote, "I'm behind the palm tree on the right, watching you in the white dress clearing the floor in the centre." Clare recalled, "He couldn't get over that dress. He really minded about materials and such things."

He also expressed interest in exploring the Ceylon countryside. When Clare had told him about the jungle which straddled the railway on the way up to the hill-station of Kandy, he jumped at the opportunity to investigate. Enjoying the heat and mild humidity of the tropical island, he told Clare, "I'm never going to spend the winter in England again." He did not mention Jamaica, but his fantasy of his post-war existence was beginning to take shape.

After the festivities, he went to Delhi to see his brother, Peter. On his return to Colombo, he chided Clare and her friends for not telling him it was cold in the Indian capital during winter. He had travelled with only his tropical suit. Some time during his four weeks in Ceylon and India he found time to write two reports about local intelligence-gathering. Having typed them up herself, Clare was surprised to find Ian correcting them. When asked why, he gave her an insight into Fleming office gamesmanship. "You must always make one or two corrections on a report," he said, "otherwise no one will know you've read it." She loved having him around. In contrast to some of the other officers, Ian "had a wonderful laugh, and treated one with great social politeness. He would never belittle anyone."

Ian was accompanied by both Hillgarth and Clare on the next stage of his journey, across the Indian Ocean to Australia, on 22 January 1945. When their Catalina flying boat was forced to turn back to Colombo because of fuel problems, Ian was so annoyed that he said he would return to England the way he had come if they did not get back in the air the very next morning. According to Clare, he frequently made such vague threats. Nevertheless, she wrote to her brother, "I shall just die if F. decides he can't spare the time to come with us, and we go alone tomorrow." The gods were with her, and they managed to complete the journey to Perth the following day. During the flight in an unheated aircraft, Ian told Clare about the saturation air raids which were about to start on Japan, using B-29 Superfortress bombers from the Mariana Islands in the Pacific. These attacks culminated in the dropping of the atomic-bomb on Hiroshima in August that year.

It was high summer in Sydney, the trio's destination, and everyone was having a good time. The war seemed hardly to exist. Ian and Clare stayed at Petty's Hotel, eating cheap oysters and going to "slick" nightclubs. One weekend they travelled out to Whale Beach, which had been donated by the Australians for the use of British officers. On the sea front, they met a young lieutenant-commander who was desperate to return home as he was engaged to be married. Ian promised to fix it and, despite his apparent coolness to the idea of matrimony, he duly did so.

Ian completed his round-the-world trip through Pearl Harbor, returning to the Admiralty in early February to oversee the final crucial operations of his Red Indians. Under its new commander Colonel Humphrey Quill, a Royal Marine, 30 AU had moved into quarters in Guildford in mid-January. Six weeks later it followed the Allied troops into Germany where its immediate geographical targets were the industrial towns of Krefeld and Neuss. It also had specific scientific objectives, principally to discover evidence of the production of fast U-boats fuelled by hydrogen peroxide. 30 AU became the first British force to enter the important naval town of Kiel where, amidst the maelstrom (Admiral Dönitz and his colleagues had fled to Flensburg, close to the Danish border) Colonel Quill demanded safe conduct for his men. Kept busy with endless lists of targets from Ian, 30 AU uncovered a cornucopia of new German inventions, ranging from jet-driven hydrofoils to "Cleopatra", an amphibian device which exploded beach defences. Ian insisted that his men should find a German one-man submarine, but Admiral Ramsay, who had taken overall command of 30 AU, did not believe such a vessel existed. When Ralph Izzard found one washed up on the shore west of Ostend, Ramsay was still sceptical that anyone could use it. Asked by Izzard to look down the periscope, the doubting Admiral peered straight into the open eye of a dead German whose inflated, decomposed body could not be removed. Ian liked to tell that story.

Meanwhile a detachment under Lieutenant T. J. Glanville RNVR made its way south to the Bavarian Alps where it hoped to capture the German Navy's Warfare Science Department. At the entrance to the romantic Alpine Tambach castle, Glanville met Kontradmiral Gladisch (one of the authors of the German official naval history of the First World War), and two rear-admiral colleagues who explained that they comprised the War Science Department of the German Admiralty. Their job was to classify and store the archives of the German Navy, to prepare historical records, and to submit papers on naval policy to the High Command. Their library contained all the Admiralty's logs, reports and minutes from 1870. Dönitz had ordered them to surrender the archives intact (to prove that the German Navy had acted humanely), but Hitler loyalists were intent on destroying this vital historical record.

There were also differences of opinion among the Allies about what to do with such historical material. The Americans tended to look upon 30 AU as an arm of big business in Britain. It therefore took longer than expected for the archives to be moved. Eventually in May Ian himself travelled to Bavaria to hurry things along. Concerned that the records should fall into Russian hands, he ordered 30 AU to expedite the transfer of everything to London as soon as possible. But there was still the problem of what to do with the admirals. According to Cecil Hampshire in his book *The Secret Navies*, Ian considered them a menace. Taking a historical perspective and quoting what happened after the signing of the Versailles Treaty, Ian claimed that they were only interested in plotting the next war. He therefore charged Glanville with eliminating them. When the young lieutenant protested that he had not stooped so low as to murder prisoners of war, Ian backtracked. He admitted that plans were afoot to bring the admirals over to work for the Allies, but said that he personally did not feel happy with the idea.

Some commentators have suggested that Ian played an important part in coordinating the hunt for the Nazi deputy leader Martin Bormann in this period. A letter to Clare Blanshard gave the lie to any such idea. "Apart from stealing the archives of the German navy on the Czechoslovak border and flogging a few German WRNS I have had no devilry for too long," he complained on 30 May. Although he admitted his workload had increased since the defeat of Germany, it was "mostly worrying the carrion off the German navy and squabbling for the wish-bones". He therefore called on her to help him provide an interesting diversion. "You must create a good shambles and persuade Bueno [Hillgarth] to get me out to clear it up."

Still clearly smitten, Ian thanked Clare for sending him a cake (from ration-free Australia). It "was gobbled till the saliva ran down my chin". Keeping up the sensual tone, he hoped that her trip to Kashmir "has made you brown and swollen your curves". He pleaded with her not to "get thin or there will be nothing for your paramours to hold on to on the black satin divan with the orange cushions". To her comments on the DNI's recent visit to Colombo, Ian had nothing to add, except that his boss was known, hardly complimentarily, as Rush-Admiral Rearbrooke. Instead he reported that Hillgarth had come through London on "a triumphal passage", addressing the Joint Planning Staff and the War Cabinet, and seemed to be "in fine heart". Ian added that his friend was "a useful petard and a good war-winner" – a favourite phrase.

Ian was winding down from the hostilities now. By late spring Delmer's black propaganda stations were no longer needed and on 14 April, when Soldatensender West ceased broadcasting, Ian attended a party to celebrate the conclusion of a successful operation. Visitors to Room 39 found him doodling on Admiralty blotting-paper. Asked what he was doing, he said he was designing the house where he intended to live in Jamaica after the war. The book was also coming into focus. He told Pamela Tiarks it would be like making a salad dressing: you just needed the right ingredients in the right quantities. On hearing from Ian that he was writing a book, C. H. Forster of the Ministry of Aircraft Production asked how he would choose the names. "Oh, that's easy," said Ian. "I think of the first couple of names in my house at school and change their Christian names." "In my case," Forster told him, "the first names were James Aitken and Harry Bond. So you could have Harry Aitken and James Bond." The latter sounded better to Ian.

While maintaining a watchful eye on events in the Far East and overseeing a series of mopping-up operations by his 'Red Indians' in Norway, Ian was free to take a stroll with Ann O'Neill in Hyde Park on 27 June. She told him that, tired of waiting for him to make a move, she had decided to marry Esmond Rothermere. She was later adamant that if Ian had stopped her there and then and offered his hand, she would have called a halt to her wedding the following day. But he was not yet ready to commit himself. As Ann's friend Ed Stanley told Hugo Charteris, "It makes absolute sense. She's marrying Rothermere and Ian's round the corner in a flat." Ian needed a certain distance for his relationships to work, and it was only after seven more years of emotional turmoil that the circumstances were to change.

6
Newspaper romance
1945–1948

By the end of 1945 Ian was back at the Dorchester Hotel and wearing civilian clothes. The occasion was a sumptuous 'business as usual' dinner for over one hundred staff at his friend Lord Kemsley's eponymous newspaper group. The menu was stuffed with dishes such as *la crêpe Newburg* and *la volaille du Surrey rotie à la broche*, which it would have been impossible to find only a few months earlier. At the main table, sitting next to Lady Kemsley, was Ian, making a good show of enjoying himself in his new role as a charming, thrusting, not-quite-so-young newspaper executive.

Settling for the right post-war career had not been easy. Six years in Naval Intelligence had certainly matured Ian, but they had been exhausting, both physically and emotionally, and it was not yet clear how much they had taken out of him. In Room 39 the charming dilettante who had floated vaguely through the City in the late 1930s had at last found an outlet for his disparate talents. But although he had proved himself in uniform, he had yet to do so in civilian life (and his concern about his future helps to explain his lack of urgency towards Ann O'Neill.) One bonus which had arisen from his war service was that it had brought him closer to his older brother. No longer was Peter the unreachable Corinthian: having served together, the two men had developed a healthy respect for each other's qualities. Indeed, after weighing the options, Ian now realized that, in the long term, he would like to follow in Peter's footsteps and write books. But he was level-headed enough to understand some of the drawbacks. Not only was he partial to expensive living (and authorship was notoriously uneconomic for most practitioners), but also he needed regular discipline in his life. So some sort of office appointment seemed necessary; the question was which?

Hugo Pitman had generously kept his stockbroking job open and even paid him his partner's salary throughout the war. At one stage Ian was ready to return to the City and continue his efforts to make mountains of money. At another he considered staying in the Navy. But Kemsley offered him a deal he could not refuse – a salary of £4500 a year, plus £500 in expenses, two months' guaranteed holiday, and the none too onerous job of foreign manager of Kemsley Newspapers. The money was extraordinary (particularly when Peter's annual retainer for writing fourth leaders for

The Times was a mere £250), the leave would give him time to write, and the curious-sounding job – not foreign editor but manager – would ensure that he carried on doing what he was good at: acting as a superior's eyes and ears, while running a worldwide information-gathering organization.

In return Ian invested the Kemsley group with glamour, social cachet and credibility. He was already earning his money at the right hand of Lady Kemsley that evening. For Kemsley Newspapers had not come out of the war with their reputation enhanced. The group had been established in 1937, after the recently ennobled Gomer Berry and his brother William (Lord Camrose) fell out and divided their newspaper and magazine interests. Camrose obtained what he wanted, the influential *Daily Telegraph*, Kemsley was left with the *Sunday Times*, a lacklustre newspaper limping along with a circulation of 270,000, plus a handful of loss-making national titles, such as the *Sunday Empire News* and the *Daily Graphic*, and some disparate provincial papers. But he found it difficult to turn his business around or give it an authoritative voice. Having shown bad judgement with his hare-brained scheme to interview Hitler in July 1939, six weeks before the start of war, Kemsley again incurred official displeasure by inadvertently publishing a story based on Ultra intelligence. His source was never revealed, but it could well have been Ian and, speculating further, this incident may have strengthened the bond between the two men. Somehow, while other newspaper proprietors, notably Lord Rothermere, flirted with fascism and recovered, Kemsley had yet to find his feet. Although its circulation had risen appreciably during the war, the *Sunday Times* was but a muted clarion.

All the more reason why Kemsley was determined to make a good start after the war. Apart from Ian, he had recruited two other men who stood apart from his regular staff at the Dorchester. Harry Hodson was a brilliant, if austere, academic, a Fellow of All Souls, who had been drafted to give a sharper intellectual edge to the *Sunday Times*. Within five years he had moved into the editorial chair of the mild-mannered W. W. Hadley, who by then was in his late seventies. More bohemian and happy-go-lucky, Robert Harling was Ian's old colleague from NID. Knowing and admiring Harling's bold pre-war work as a designer and typographer, one of the tasks Ian had given him at the Admiralty was sharpening the bland look of the weekly intelligence reports. The two men were both still in naval uniform when Ian first recommended his colleague to Kemsley to redesign the *Daily Graphic*. On seeing Harling's proposed front page, based on an American afternoon newspaper, the unadventurous Kemsley looked at him witheringly and said, "I run a newspaper for profit, not experiment." It was a measure of Ian's influence that he was able to talk Kemsley into persevering with Harling as the group's design consultant, with a special brief to make the *Sunday Times* more presentable.

Meanwhile, somewhere in the same hotel building, another newspaper's future was being mapped out. Married to the proprietor of the *Daily Mail* only since June, Ann Rothermere had already made her mark on the paper. Still nominally residents, she and her new husband had got in first with their own party at the Dorchester, an election night gathering on 26 July 1945, when the Labour Party victory had been gloomily celebrated. By 6 August, less than six weeks after the Rothermeres' marriage, the American magazine *Time*, which in those days took an inordinate interest in the British upper classes, was already trumpeting that Ann had taken the reins at the middle-market *Mail*. It reported how, in a beautiful red straw hat brought by her friend the Duchess of Westminster from Paris, the vituperative Ann, 32, was forcing her "gloomy" new husband, 47, to pay more attention to his newspaper interests. As for him, his daily trips to the office were "becoming more and more irksome. He is longing to get away from the job, to travel, study, read." But Ann's ambitions for the *Daily Mail* were preventing him.

The *Mail* had emerged from the war in rather better shape than the *Sunday Times*. After taking control in 1940, Esmond Rothermere had steadied a newspaper which was tainted by his father's pro-German sympathies. He swung the *Mail* solidly behind Churchill and, if neither he nor the paper had quite the *succès d'éstime* of their rivals Lord Beaverbrook and the *Daily Express*, the *Daily Mail* in 1945 was still a lively, respectable and powerful newspaper.

Even before she was married, it was clear that this might not be quite enough for Ann's ambitions. Gerald Sanger, editor of British Movietone News, which produced newsreels as part of the Rothermere group, had been Esmond's private secretary. A fair-minded and unassuming man, who became a director of the *Daily Mail*, he kept a regular private diary. In June, shortly before the Rothermeres' marriage, Sanger had had a taste of Ann's imperiousness. On a visit to Bailiff's Court, Esmond's rented seaside retreat at Climping, near Littlehampton in Sussex, he sat next to Ann at dinner. The room where they ate chicken may have looked like an Elizabethan hall but in fact it had been built only twenty years earlier for the Guinness heir, Lord Moyne. Suddenly Ann began quizzing Sanger about news theatres. Why had Movietone not capitalized on its position as a purveyor of newsreels by setting up its own nationwide string of news theatres? she asked in "one of those top of the throat voices – eager and intent". Sanger replied that they had thought of it, but this would have led to a clash of interests with their main customers, the cinema chains. But there was no reason, he suggested, why the *Daily Mail* could not attempt it.

"Ah! the *Daily Mail*," she said. "That's what I've been telling Esmond. He ought to start a news theatre in every town of the country." Sanger recorded, "Astonished by the fervour of the lady, I leaned across the refectory table at Esmond and noted his amusement. She said, 'It's all very well for you to laugh, but the *Daily Mail* has got to get on and do things.'"

By October Stanley Horniblow, the editor of the *Daily Mail*, was complaining to Sanger about the new Lady Rothermere's interference in the paper. Over the next few months this theme recurred repeatedly, with Horniblow ruminating about "Milady's protégés" – such as Peter Quennell, whom he described as "one of her precious boyfriends", and who had been foisted upon him as book critic at a salary £1000 more than the incumbent. And then there was the vexed question of Frank Owen, the brilliant iconoclast Welshman who had been hired by the *Daily Mail* after editing the successful forces newspaper in Burma. Rothermere had promised Horniblow that there was no question of Owen taking over his job. But within months, in March 1947, Horniblow was out and Owen, one of "Annie's boys", was editing the paper.

William McWhirter, managing director of the *Daily Mail*, told Sanger, "Esmond will come to the office in the morning and announce something with a tone of finality, and you know perfectly well where it has come from. Then you have to set to work to argue against it, all the more forcibly because you know that his pride is involved and that he will have to go home and explain to Ann why it can't be done."

Esmond's pride would have been rather more piqued if he had realized that his wife was carrying on an affair under his nose. For, in seeking new professional challenges, Ian had not been able to turn his back on his liaison with Ann. Their curious uncommitted relationship had worked well enough in similar circumstances during the war, so why hurry to end it now? Indeed its very lack of structure appealed to Ian, enabling him to devote his energies to other engagements. It gave him a measure of emotional stability at a time of significant change, and besides, Ann was different from his other girlfriends, the jolly social "muckers" or the pretty flibbertigibbets, of whom he so quickly tired. With her flashing grey-green eyes and thick dark hair, Ann was not only striking but formidable, often frighteningly so. Ian was riveted by her sophistication – a natural combination of wit, vitality and breeding. Her dinner parties effortlessly brought together Cabinet ministers and authors, a different crowd from the acquaintances he lazily accumulated at his club or on the golf course, and very much the sort of people an aspiring newspaper executive should be meeting.

She for her part may have enjoyed dabbling in newspaper politics but she quickly tired of the monotony of her public obligations as a newspaper owner's wife. On a personal level, she appreciated Esmond's decency and intelligence, and later said that he had been the most satisfying lover in her life. But he could not offer her the excitement of the handsome, ruthless, former naval commander who, by refusing to marry her, remained so tantalizingly unobtainable.

Gerald Sanger enjoyed a front-row seat at the unfolding of an extraordinary marital drama which began so innocuously. For while cuckolding the unsuspecting Esmond, Ian remained a regular visitor to his houses, often dining or playing tennis with his "friend". One day in the autumn, after Esmond had been on a gruelling trip to Paris, Ann suddenly announced at lunch-time that she and Ian were driving to see Loelia Westminster at Send Grove. Sanger, by chance, lived in the same village as Loelia, and Ian quickly picked up on the fact that they were neighbours. "Tell me what the village says about Loelia," he asked mischievously. Searching for a reply, Sanger said that the people of Send were shocked that she had given up attending church. "That's good," enthused Ian, sensing some gossip with which to regale his friends. "I can make a story out of that. Does she take part in village life?"

Again Sanger had to rack his brain before answering that she presented prizes at the annual sports day, but she did not belong to the local Women's Institute. "The Women's Institute – I must make a note of that," remarked Ian, warming to his new role in journalism. "And what does the village say about all the comings and goings at her house?" Ian probed, in a cryptic reference to his frequent use of Send Grove for trysts with Ann. "There are a lot of rumours," Sanger replied enigmatically.

Apart from teasing Loelia, a favourite sport, Ian used to rib Ann that they were deadly rivals, working for two ruthlessly competing press combines. Their experiences of the same business provided considerable amusement and, as her lover, Ian was quick to offer advice about her role as newspaper proprietor's wife. Passing through New York at the end of the year, en route to Jamaica to start building his new house, he had lunch with Don Iddon, the *Daily Mail*'s star reporter in the United States, who confided that he wanted to write the sort of column that "makes the chancelries tremble". Thinking such journalism was an anachronism, Ian suggested that Iddon should write a world diary instead, later informing Ann, "If the idea comes home, you will know that I never cease to cosset my competitors particularly when I love their wives."

Picking up the threads of his wartime friendships in New York, Ian was moved to write to Ann, "I am very pleased we won when I think of this time last year when we didn't know where Germany was with the atom." But his enjoyment was muted by visiting the Morgans, the banking family who had known the Flemings for over half a century. Their Long Island pile reminded him too graphically of unhappy childhood holidays at Glen Borrodale in Caithness. And he despaired at the general ignorance of the Americans. Aspects of their culture enthralled him – the service, the speed, the practicality and (for a post-war Briton) the restaurants. But he could not help remarking on the deep gulf between the two English-speaking peoples. "I am submerged beneath a deep gloomth [*sic*]," he told Ann, "at the fabulous limitations of these people and their total unpreparedness to rule the world which is now theirs" – adding, "with the exception of you and Peter [Quennell] and Cyril [Connolly] and Ed [Stanley] and a few more prickly ones – on a list of whom you and I would disagree..."

Despite his strictures about Americans, Ian fell for the charms of Millicent Huddleston Rogers, a rich socialite who was heiress to the Standard Oil fortune. Millicent was zany and outgoing, even by affluent East Coast standards. A beautiful brunette in her mid-forties, she was famed for her collection of Fabergé eggs, which were said to be second only to Queen Mary's. She enjoyed appearing in public in extravagant costumes: she could be an Indian squaw one day, an Egyptian princess another. Her insatiable sexual appetite was common knowledge: a regular visitor to Jamaica, she once arrived there with two Navajo Indians, and informed anyone who asked, "I'm fucking them both."

In an odd attempt to excite Ann's curiosity, even jealousy, Ian told her he was having a "botched affair", though he did not say with whom. He described it – another example of the transatlantic gulf – as something out of Eric Linklater's novel *Juan in America* "where everything starts wrong and goes on wrong and getting wronger – and God knows what she thinks it's all about and it really isn't all one person's fault but just that both our sets of rules are wrong – like baseball and rounders, which is really what happens between most English and American people." The effect, he confessed, was to strengthen his love for her – "a damned inconvenient moment" to start admitting that, Ann later remarked.

Such letters were part of the regular flow of communications between Ann in England and Ian in New York and Jamaica that winter. They are delightful, often explicit, testimony to their growing passion. In his selection of Ann's letters, published in 1985, four years after her death, Mark Amory printed part of this correspondence, averring that "a few of Fleming's letters convey the style of them all". Even Amory's well-chosen letters were too much for Auberon Waugh, son of Ann's friend and relative, Evelyn Waugh. In a review in the *Sunday Telegraph*, "Bron" Waugh noted that, in justifying their inclusion, Amory had argued that Ann always believed in frankness. Waugh, however, felt they should have been excluded "on literary rather than on moral or compassionate grounds. They are banal and indifferent. They detract from the main point of Ann [Rothermere], which was her extraordinarily cheerful disposition and warm nature."

He was being over-censorious, for the various communications convey the playful intimacy and intense sexual longing of two otherwise tough and uncomprising characters. Ian seldom let his carefully cultivated, debonair façade drop, but in these letters one can hear his true voice. "But listen, listen, listen," he pleaded with Ann from his room in the Hotel Dorset, "have you got something to lock up? Please fix it. I know how you leave things around like a jackdaw and I expect every day that it will be the end. I do wish you'd take trouble and not leave my letters among your brassières and pants. *Do* please try. I know perfectly well that you are going to come along one day with a tragic face and say that all is discovered, fly – and all that is going to be for the sake of taking a tiny bit of trouble."

In Jamaica Ian concentrated on his accommodation. From his house at Bellevue, where they had stayed three years earlier, Ivar Bryce had already found his friend a seaside site on which to build. Working with a local agent, Reggie Acquart, he acquired two contiguous parcels of land – one twelve acres, the other two – on a former donkey racetrack just outside Oracabessa, a sleepy town on the north coast, best known for its banana trade. At night-time the air was filled with the chants of dockers loading the boats of the United Fruit Company less than a mile away. When Bryce first alighted on the larger property, known locally as Rock Edge (and before that Rotten Egg Bay) and owned by an Irish Jamaican called "Busha" Christie Cousins, it was covered with the green weed, *Mimosa pudica*, otherwise known as "shame lady" from its habit of folding up and shrinking at the slightest touch. Looking down thirty feet over the cliff edge, he saw a small strip of white sand, not much bigger than a cricket square, and, about ten feet out to sea, a rock covered with a single white Portlandia. Bryce rightly judged that this was the place for Ian. He even came up with a new name for it: Shame Lady. When he cabled his friend in London with the news, he received a Churchillian reply the very same day, "PRAY PAUSE NOT IAN". Ian arranged to transfer £2000 into the account of Cousins, who lived next door.

Now Ian drew out the plans he had originally sketched on his Admiralty blotter. His concept was a large living-room, and not much else. "Who wants a big bedroom?" he liked to say, and this frugality about space extended to his kitchen as well. His other main design feature was that he did not want glass in his windows. Preferring the tropical breezes to waft through the house, he built traditional slatted louvres, or jalousies, which could be folded back into the side of the window case.

The name Shame Lady was rejected, and also Alastair Forbes's punning Rum Cove. Instead Ian wanted his house called Goldeneye, after his wartime operation to frustrate the Germans in Spain. Ian saw a nice symmetry between Goldeneye and Oracabessa, literally Golden Head in Spanish. When he informed Reggie Acquart of the name, the old Jamaican shook his head and said, "Commander, it does not matter what you call the house. Everyone will always call it Rock Edge."

However, it was not the overgrown patch of land but the sea which excited and drew Ian to the place. Situated like a half-opened treasure-trove in the warm, translucent water some twenty yards out from the beach, was a thick, dark coral reef, which lifted the waves of the Caribbean Sea into the ripples of white foam stretching across the bay. On and around the reef swam a kaleidoscopic range of fish, from delicate golden angel fish to thickset rainbow parrot fish, and, just once in a while, something more dangerous in the fast, darting shape of a barracuda, with its razor-sharp teeth which can tear off a man's limb. In the pools and around the rocks at the side of the bay Ian discovered the less gainly creatures of the deep, the lobsters and octopuses, whose lumbering habits caught his imagination. He was immediately captivated by this vibrant and colourful natural world which existed, as if in a different time and space, at the bottom of his property. Wearing nothing but a mask, he spent long hours communing with his new neighbours, sometimes wielding a spear which he used to kill a lobster for dinner.

Ian was not the only person attracted to Jamaica after the war. Along the coast, the newly knighted Sir William Stephenson had acquired what he called "the finest house in the island" at Hillowtown, overlooking Montego Bay. Stephenson had turned his back on day-to-day espionage work, but still maintained his contacts with the world of secret intelligence. Feeling he needed "to do something for some of the talented fellows" in his British Security Coordination, he teamed up with former colleagues Sir Rex Benson and Olaf Hambro in London, and General William Donovan in Washington to set up the well-capitalized British-American-Canadian-Corporation (later the World Commerce Corporation), a classic 'spook' front company which specialized in the barter of goods with developing countries. A Jamaican affiliate, the Caribbean Cement Company, became one of the most successful businesses on the island.

Stephenson enjoyed the trappings of his wealth. Displayed on his walls at Hillowtown was his superb collection of J. B. Kidd's prints, *Views in the Island of Jamaica*. In addition, he owned a large Cadillac which General Motors built for General de Gaulle but which somehow found its way to the Canadian spymaster in Jamaica. Once, being driven by Stephenson's chauffeur along the north coast around Oracabessa, Ian was riveted by the speedometer. "It's amazing how this car rides at high speeds," he commented to Stephenson. "But don't you think Crawford's driving much too fast? He's up over eighty." The old man declined to let on that, because of its original destination, the Cadillac's speedometer was calibrated in kilometres.

Another war veteran with a house in Montego Bay was Lord Beaverbrook, the former Minister of Aircraft Production. Ian had had occasional dealings with him, but they had never been friends. Indeed the last time they had met – at Beaverbrook's house at Cherkley Court in Surrey only a few weeks earlier – Ian had been rash enough to attack the *Daily Express* over dinner for its bad taste in publishing an article about a businessman who had died of a heart attack in a brothel. Beaverbrook had been annoyed at this young man purporting to tell him how to run his newspapers. Stephenson claimed the credit for bringing the two together in Jamaica, and thenceforward Ian maintained a curiously deferential relationship to the newspaper tycoon, who was a close friend of Ann Rothermere.

More relaxing was the company of the Leiters, two of Ivar's wartime friends from Washington. Tommy Leiter was the scion of the Chicago family which had started the Marshall Field department store: his aunt Mary Leiter had been one of the procession of wealthy American women who had crossed the Atlantic to marry relatively impoverished English aristocrats earlier in the century (in her case, she had ensnared the very superior person, George, later Lord, Curzon). Tommy had an acknowledged drink problem, but his wife Marion, known as Oatsie, was a spirited Southern lady who struck up a close and lasting friendship with Ian. The Leiters had a house at Reading, in the hills overlooking Montego Bay, near Sir William Stephenson. The first time Oatsie met Ian she took him to task for his cavalier treatment of Millicent Rogers, who had joined the winter exodus to the sun. "Mr Fleming," she said, when they were introduced, "I consider you are a cad." "You're quite right, Mrs Leiter," Ian replied. "Shall we have a drink on it?"

Sailing back to London on the *Queen Mary* in March, Ian met Joan Bright who was returning from a series of post-war conferences in Bermuda. Also on board were Winston Churchill, who had just made his famous "Iron Curtain" speech in Fulton, Missouri, and Loelia Westminster. After the excitement of her wartime service, Joan dreaded returning to Britain and, since she had been close to Ian, she entertained vague hopes that he might marry her. But the voyage proved disappointing: Ian spent most of the time playing bridge with Loelia, and when Joan introduced Ian to Churchill, the old man made it clear that he would rather it had been Peter Fleming. Her main recollection was of Ian's single-mindedness about his future. "He said he had joined Kemsley and would wear nothing but a blue suit from then on. He was emphatic that he did not want to see his wartime colleagues again. He was starting a new life."

Although this was the sort of sweeping statement Ian often made, it was hardly true. His recent experiences were too important a memory for him and, although he might remove himself gradually from the machinery of war, he would never cut himself off from friends such as Stephenson and Cuneo. He attended the regular dinners of Admiral Godfrey's 36 Club of former NID colleagues. (Called after the DNI's official residence at 36 Curzon Street, the club's job was to keep the best NID talent together as a resource to tap in the event of any future war, in much the same way as Godfrey had been able to call upon his predecessor.) He maintained his training for the Royal Naval Voluntary Reserve. And when Clare Blanshard, the lively Wren from Colombo, returned to her mother's house in London in March 1946, she was greeted with a message that "a Mr Fleming has called". Ian invited her to lunch, the first of many such invitations, usually on Saturdays, after his working week was finished, and often at the Athenaeum Hotel, just around the corner from the wartime apartment he still inhabited. Knowing she needed a job, he helped her join the BBC where her former boss, General Sir Ian Jacob, was about to take charge of overseas broadcasting. Two years later, he recommended her as a personal assistant to Robert Harling, who juggled various freelance activities with a full-time career as director of an advertising agency.

Each working day Ian drove to the *Sunday Times* offices in Gray's Inn Road, halfway between the West End and the City. At Number 200, he parked his unflashy Morris Oxford in the car park close to Lord Kemsley's gleaming Rolls-Royce, and proceeded by the main entrance (his proprietor had one to himself) to his wood-panelled office on the second floor. On Tuesday mornings at ten o'clock he took his seat at the editorial conference, chaired by Lord Kemsley, who guarded his role as editor-in-chief jealously. As they mulled over the previous Sunday's efforts, Ian acted as the licensed gadfly and ideas man. "He might come up with half a dozen suggestions for articles, features or whatever," recalled Harry Hodson, "of which two would be nonsense, two quite impractical, two worth consideration; maybe one would come to fruition."

On a day-to-day basis, Ian did not write leaders or determine the paper's response to world events such as the partition of India. He did not want the responsibility or the grind. His job as foreign manager was to direct the Kemsley group's overseas coverage. He appointed its correspondents in the field, and kept in touch with them in the same personal manner in which he had communicated with favoured naval attachés during the war. In London he made sure their articles were circulated through the group's thirty national and provincial papers. Providing local angles on international stories for the *Evening Chronicle* in Newcastle or the *Press and Journal* in Aberdeen was just as important as servicing the *Sunday Times*.

As an aspiring foreign correspondent, Frank Giles visited Ian at Kemsley House to ask for a job. Like Ian before him, he had just failed his Foreign Office exams. Before he could be offered work, he was hired by *The Times*, then a rival, as its correspondent in Paris. Giles returned to the *Sunday Times* in the early 1960s, later becoming its editor. In the summer of 1946, he found Ian sitting at a desk and behind him was a map of the world full of flashing lights. These pinpointed the eighty or so correspondents of the

Kemsley Imperial and Foreign Service, better known by its cable address, Mercury, the Roman messenger of the Gods. The young Giles found Ian's show of gadgetry more than faintly ludicrous: "a fair old load of bullshit". Ian, he realized, was stuck with his network of agents in a strange limbo halfway between Admiral Godfrey of NID and his fictional 'M' of the Secret Service.

Ian liked to imagine Mercury (with its motto "Get it first, but get it right") as an adjunct to the secret services. If Godfrey's 36 Club had a role as a think-tank for intelligence-honed brains, his Mercury could provide operational experience for rank-and-file agents. Inevitably – given the war and his own role in it – many journalists with intelligence connections gravitated towards him. Antony Terry, an army intelligence officer who had been captured in the commando raid on St Nazaire in 1942, was a typical example. After the war he doubled as Ian's correspondent and an agent of the Secret Intelligence Service in Vienna and later Berlin. Before going to Vienna in June 1947, the German-speaking Terry married his girlfriend, Rachel Stainer, because, she recalled, the SIS would not employ a single man there. She was informed that her new husband was a spy, and Ian "arranged the cover" for them both to go to Vienna.

Mercury's regular use of spies as journalists was noted by Anthony Cavendish, himself a former SIS or MI6 agent, in his book *Inside Intelligence*: "At the end of the war a number of MI6 agents were sent abroad under the cover of newspaper men. Indeed the Kemsley Press allowed many of their foreign correspondents to cooperate with MI6 and even took on MI6 operatives as foreign correspondents."

Certainly several Mercury correspondents came from an intelligence background. Ian sent Cedric Salter of SOE to Barcelona, Ian Colvin who was closely linked to the SIS to Berlin, and the British intelligence asset Henry Brandon, né Brandeis in Czechoslovakia, to Washington. Several NID colleagues were also brought on board, among them Donald McCormick, Mercury's stringer in Tangier, and Lieutenant Commander William Todd who, appropriately for the former manager of Thomas Cook's Mayfair office, took charge of the service's travel arrangements.

Liaison was largely informal, the result of Ian's friendship with "Fanny" vanden Heuvel, the engaging Papal Count who oversaw the SIS's European operations. Before the war vanden Heuvel had travelled round Europe as managing director of Eno's Fruit Salts – a position which led to his engagement by Colonel Dansey's Z Organization. Ian probably met him through William Stephenson who also started his intelligence career as one of Dansey's men. According to Nicholas Elliott, who later succeeded vanden Heuvel in a similar role in London, "In those days SIS kept in touch with useful persons. And Ian was quite useful: he had important contacts in certain places, and every now and then he got hold of a useful piece of information. I would ask him if I needed someone in the City and, very occasionally, if someone out in the field."

Not all Ian's initiatives as a fellow-traveller of the intelligence services came to much. Retaining a romantic image of Tangier as a centre of espionage and skulduggery, he dreamed up a plan with Alan Hillgarth to purchase the small *Tangier Gazette* and turn it into an English-language newspaper serving the Mediterranean. He gained the backing of Lord Kemsley, who sent his son Dennis Berry to Tangier to investigate. McCormick, the Mercury man on the spot, ferried Berry around, but the project never materialized. More generally, Ian required his correspondents to produce regular situation reports, or Sitreps, giving background information, expressly not for publication, about developments in their parts of the world. According to McCormick, material from these Sitreps was "passed on to branches of Intelligence as and when this seemed justified."

Ian was aware that he needed other types of writers working for Mercury. In austerity Britain, he was determined to inject some flair and sophistication into his pages. So he asked several well-connected friends to contribute. From her *castello* in Florence, the artist Lina Waterfield kept him in touch with the complicated post-war Italian political scene. Having known her brother, Gordon Waterfield, at Reuters, Ian would cable her asking for reports on topics like "What the Italians do on a Bender". In Paris he hired Nancy Mitford to write a regular column. She immediately informed Lady Pamela Berry in delighted and gushing terms that, following lunch with "the fascinating Ian Fleming whom I had never met & he fascinated me", she had been asked to contribute to what she described as "Lady Kemsley's mag". A couple of weeks later she was wondering to Evelyn Waugh whether Ian had really been serious in his offer (her errant husband Peter Rodd had sown doubts in her mind). Although Waugh reassured her that she had been billed as "the most brilliant of the younger writers", she remained uncertain, particularly about the financial side of the deal. She felt she had allowed herself to be "mesmerized by handsome Mr Fleming" when she should have negotiated with the *Sunday Times* through her new agent (and Waugh's), A. D. Peters. She need not have worried: her work appeared regularly in the newspaper and won her many plaudits.

Ian also took Ann's epicurean cousin, the artist and adventurer Dick Wyndham, on board as a special correspondent. A model for Evelyn Waugh's hero Charles Ryder in *Brideshead Revisited*, the intrepid Wyndham flew his own tiny Moth plane around the trouble spots of the Middle East. His daughter, the writer Joan Wyndham, caught up with him at London's Hyde Park Hotel, on one of his trips back home from Cairo. "Just a minute, Joanie," he told her. "Got to finish my swindle sheet for the *Sunday Times*." She supposed him to mean "his expenses – mostly phoney – which seemed to cover several sheets of paper". In 1947 he narrowly escaped death when his plane crashed in Afghanistan. The following year he was not so lucky. While covering the first Arab–Israel war, incautiously wearing Arab dress, he was shot by a Jewish sniper and killed.

In his regular flow of bulletins, Ian instructed his correspondents as to what he wanted and how to write it. His main requirement was sharp, concise prose. "English journalism has much to learn from the contents of *Time*," he noted in the *Kemsley Manual of Journalism*, a worthy guide for those seeking a career in newspapers. He also wanted entertaining copy: as he told Antony Terry, "Try to cultivate a light touch ... We are trying to get a little more brightness and champagne into the foreign news at the *Sunday Times*, and with your intelligence and sense of humour, it should be possible for you to be both well-informed and readable." Through his newspaper position – and, later, in his books – Ian's promotion of a pithy, page-turning, adman's prose style had an important influence on post-war letters.

In the *Manual* he described his ideal foreign correspondent. "He must be a credit to his country and his newspaper abroad; he should be either a bachelor or a solidly married man who is happy to have his children brought up abroad; his personality must be such that our Ambassador will be pleased to see him when the occasion demands. He must know something of protocol and yet enjoy having a drink with the meanest spy or the most wastrelly spiv. He must be completely at home in one foreign language and have another one to fall back on. He must be grounded in the history and culture of the territory in which he is serving; he must be intellectually inquisitive and have some knowledge of most sports. He must be able to keep a secret; he must be physically strong and not addicted to drink. He must have pride in his work and in the paper he serves, and finally he must be a good reporter with a wide vocabulary, fast with his typewriter, with a knowledge of shorthand and able to drive a car." The overall job description differed only slightly from that of Ian's ideal American secret service agent, as described for Donovan in 1941.

Across town, Ann was also redefining her wartime role. Once the Rothermeres moved back into a refurbished Warwick House, on the edge of Green Park, she set about making it the leading politico-literary salon in London. With little compromise towards the socialist spirit of the age, her guests included "a large array of English Guermantes, distinguished both by their intricate family relationships and curious nicknames", Peter Quennell noted. But she had the knack of mixing her aristocrats with a broad range of interesting writers, artists and politicians. They were attracted by the company, by her wit and striking good looks (set off to maximum effect by daring off-the-shoulder evening dresses), and by the endless bottles of champagne effortlessly dispensed by Wright, the butler. Occasionally the combinations proved unsuccessful: Quennell remembered Ann's querulous brother-in-law, Eric Dudley, expressing disgust at the sight of the painter Lucian Freud absent-mindedly munching a bouquet of expensive purple orchids. But Ann's parties were fun, and the capital needed her slightly anarchic, quasi-bohemian influence to get things going in the dank days after the war. Her liveliness and popularity were signalled by a name-change. Gradually at first, but then taken up and promoted by Ian, the reserved schoolgirlish "Anne" became the more familiar, good time "Annie", designated and written as "Ann".

In late September 1946 Ann herself was off to New York, sailing with her husband on the *Queen Elizabeth*. Now it was Ian's turn to be jealous. When he learned that Esmond was proceeding to Canada on business, he told Ann that he would "get old Gomer to send me over". He duly flew across on the day the Rothermeres arrived. When Esmond went to Montreal, Ian presented himself at Anne's suite at the Plaza Hotel with a small suitcase and told her he was moving in. Ann, on her first visit to the United States, was terrified she would be found out. She told him that, as one of the trappings of her new position, she had a lady's maid who attended her every morning. "Get rid of the bitch!" demanded Ian, and she meekly did as he ordered. As she later recalled, "In the end I *nearly* always gave in to the Ian. So we enjoyed four unforgettable days and nights in New York." The only unsatisfactory note was the severe pain Ian experienced in his chest. On consulting a Manhattan specialist, he was given a simple explanation. He was smoking seventy cigarettes and, contrary to his dictates for foreign correspondents, drinking a bottle of gin each day. It was too much, even for a man of his relatively tender age (now thirty-eight).

When Ian passed through New York again in December en route for Jamaica, he was amused to find that Ann was still the talk of the town: she had "charmed New York to death", according to their friend, Nin Ryan. He himself was thinner and sadder than the previous year, Millicent Rogers informed him. This time, however, he did not try to torment Ann with tales of his gallivanting in Manhattan. If he looked thinner, he told Ann, it was only because she herself had kept him awake all night in London. "You have made bruises on my arms and shoulders. All this damage will have to paid for some time," he warned, indicating that physical punishment added some excitement and an element of compulsion to what was often a sado-masochistic relationship. And if he seemed sadder to Millicent, this was because he simply wanted to go to bed – his own bed, without her. "My eyes had gone dead on me," he wrote to Ann, "and I kept on smelling your small ghost which had its arms around my neck most of the time." Following this rebuff, Millicent packed her bags for Hollywood where she waged a determined but unsuccessful campaign to wed Clark Gable.

From Manhattan Ian provided Ann with her regular dose of newspaper gossip. By starting a new Scottish edition, the *Daily Mail* had hired some of the Kemsley group's best journalists north of the border. In the United States Ian learned that, as a consequence, the *Mail* had been forced to reduce its New York bureau and close its Washington office entirely. "So yah boo for having stolen so much of our Glasgow staff and for thinking the *Mail* can invade the Kemsley preserves SUCKSSUCKSSUCKS." If that sounded childish, Ian did not mind. "You have filled my life full of coloured lights and sweet sweet things which make me feel warm and weak inside and I don't care a bit if Peter Quennell does think it old-fashioned or that we are a pair of boobies. You are like a piece of barley-sugar in my pocket which I can lick at without it getting any smaller and I simply want to hug you until you squeak every time."

Ian travelled on to Jamaica where Goldeneye was at last taking shape. Initially, without the later benefit of vegetation, his concrete house looked barren and forbidding, like an itinerant district commissioner's lodge in some distant colonial land. Noël Coward once directed someone to the nearest "Golden eye, nose and throat clinic". On the seaward side, Ian hollowed out an area, some twenty yards long and a dozen feet in width, stretching from the doors of the main room to the cliff top, where he built a firm timber rail. A few petunias and 'sailor's hats' took root around this area which, once chairs and a table topped with a sunshade were laid out, used to be described as the sunken or, some wags would have it, the sinking garden. Next a steep set of steps was built out of concrete and rock, running down from the house to the sea. Ian used to dash up and down, laden with spears, fins and masks.

On this trip, Ian made his most important acquisition: a housekeeper called Violet Cummings. For the next seventeen years this selfless north-shore Jamaican cared for her beloved "Commander". To visitors, she became synonymous with Goldeneye. At first, Ian employed several additional members of staff: Daisy the cook, Holmes the factor, Hall the houseboy, Stewart the fisherman and an old lady, Ann, who used to clean out the lavatories. (The latter's name and occupation were a joke between Ian and his lover.) When Ivar Bryce and John Fox-Strangways came to stay, Goldeneye was a bachelors' paradise. The three of them swam naked in the warm sea before breakfast. Then, although it rained a lot that month, they humped earth as they tried to bring order to what would be the garden. Ivar gave Ian a dog called Fox – the prototype of the many mongrels which lazed around in the sun and became part of the property. First drinks of the day were served at eleven in the morning. Only one thing was lacking, Ian assured Ann: female company. "You might have given me a femme coloniale for us all to have. Your red wig would have looked very nice on it." Whether he was quite as celibate as he made out is debatable. One visitor remembered a "beautiful married blonde from Bermuda" as part of the general ensemble.

Ian stayed at Goldeneye for five weeks, but said he wished it could have been six months. With years of shared experience, Ivar understood his friend's intense attraction to the place. Ian had found a new adventure playground in the ocean. "Every exploration and every dive results in some fresh incident worth the telling: and even when you don't come back with any booty for the kitchen, you have a fascinating story to recount. There are as many stories of the reef as there are fish in the sea."

With rich Britons and Americans once more visiting the Caribbean for their winter holidays, entrepreneurial Jamaicans were beginning to turn stretches of the north coast into up-market resorts. One of the first off the mark was Carmen Pringle, a colourful *grande dame* whose sons John Pringle and Morris Cargill both became friends of Ian. She started the Sunset Lodge Club close to the airport in Montego Bay. With Ivar and John, Ian attended the opening night on 24 January 1947. He was surprised to find Lily Ernst, Beaverbrook's svelte Hungarian Jewish mistress, cracking a joke at his expense and that of his lover. She sidled up to him at the beach party and declared disingenuously, "We were talking about you the other night and I was trying to remember which paper you were mixed up with. I was certain your boss was a woman, but the only woman who seemed possible was Lady Rothermere which was impossible of course. Silly, wasn't it?" In a letter to Ann, Ian wondered if the woman was drunk or – more likely, he thought – she had been put up to it by Pamela Berry, the wife of Michael Berry, son of Lord Kemsley's brother, Lord Camrose. As a newspaper wife, Pam Berry competed fiercely with Ann for the acclaim of being London's most influential hostess. After working in the all-male preserves of the City and the Admiralty, Ian was discovering the informed bitchiness of the newspaper world, where everyone seemed to know about his relationship with Ann.

Observing with a canny journalist's eye, that Jamaica was becoming rather fashionable, he determined to write something about it when he returned to London. His chosen medium was Cyril Connolly's literary magazine *Horizon*. For five years, Connolly had been running an escapist travel series, *Where Shall John Go?* in which, in the form of advice to a young man wanting to emigrate, assorted literary figures told the world where they had been on their summer holidays.

Ian's article, published in December 1947, portrayed Jamaica as attractive and civilized – neither Croydon with jacarandas, nor Conradian tropical nightmare where moral disintegration was inevitable. Noting Jamaica's literary connections with Beckford of Fonthill and Smollett, he revealed how the *Horizon* editor had spent part of his "'blue' or post-graduate period" there as tutor to the young Charles D'Costa, a leading local businessman who became a friend of Ian's. He provided a lucid summary of various touristic sights, fauna and flora, and geographical phenomena, including one of his favourite pieces of physical trivia – referred to in several of his books – that Jamaica enjoyed its pleasant climate because every day at nine in the morning a light Doctor's Wind blew in from the sea until, at six in the evening, the Undertaker's Wind came on duty and reversed the process, blowing the stale air out from the land to the sea again.

Then as now, Kingston, the capital, was "a tough town", and Ian advised his young correspondent to avoid its "stews ... although they would provide you with every known amorous constellation and permutation" – one reason, he suggested, why the Royal Navy's Atlantic Squadron was based in Bermuda, not Jamaica. He admitted to one or two other drawbacks, such as sandflies and local politics, but he believed these compared "quite favourably with the more civilized risks – spivs, road-death, flu and vitamin deficiency – which infest your English life". And there were plenty of other compensations in Jamaica, including delicious food, exotic drinks and music, which he described as a variation of Trinidadian calypso.

Back in London in early 1947 Ian decided it was time to put down roots. After giving up his wartime flat in Athenaeum Court, he had taken a house in Montagu Place, north of Oxford Street. By chance or, more likely, design, the Rothermeres lived round the corner in Montagu Square. When Ann took her two growing children for walks in the park, Ian would appear, as if from nowhere, to accompany them. But Montagu Square had only been a temporary abode for the Rothermeres until Warwick House was fixed up. When they moved back, Ian followed in a southerly direction, taking a three-room mews cottage at the back of his mother's new house in Charles Street, Mayfair. But for the slight change of venue, he could have been living once more in Ebury Street. Number 21 Hays Mews was decked out in his favourite 'masculine' navy colours. Some of his books were displayed along the walls. (The main body of his collection was still stored in the Pantechnicon where it had been since the beginning of the war.) And, according to Amaryllis, a succession of pretty au pairs was despatched round the corner to Eve's to learn how to make Ian's favourite salmon kedgeree. "They all became devoted to him. He only had to ring for them to run his bath or pick up a cigarette lighter off the shelf and they would rush off and do it with alacrity."

Ann welcomed Ian's move: "I hope your darling foreign service is scooping everything, and you are pleased with your new house and that you think about me all day and night and I hope Boodle's Club is open again and keeping you away from all the other harpies who desire your black curls and blue eyes." From Boodle's Ian would saunter down St James's to Warwick House, where Rothermere, always the gracious host, was happy to welcome him as the spare man at a dinner table or a partner who knew the rules in a bridge rubber. Ian became an honorary member of an extended family that included Loelia Westminster, Ann's brother, Hugo, who lived at Warwick House briefly after he married Virginia Forbes Adam in 1948, and Ann's sister, Laura, who was in situ during the latter stages of her troubled marriage to Eric Dudley. But it was a curious schizophrenic existence. Whenever Esmond was away or simply at the office, Ian found his way up the stairs to milady's bedroom, and that caused all manner of tensions and confusions. Virginia Charteris recalled inadvertently surprising the two lovers during the "cinq à sept" period. "There was an atmosphere you could cut with a knife. Ian said apologetically, 'I'm just going.' They'd just had the mother and father of all rows. Clearly they thrived on it. They liked hurting each other."

For form's sake Ian did his best to construct a social life not too obviously centred on the wife of the *Daily Mail* proprietor. Tired of the relentless socializing and gossiping at White's, he had taken Duff Dunbar's advice in 1944 and joined the more leisurely Boodle's, where occasionally he played bridge with old friends such as Dunbar and Jack Beal, but more often was to be seen dining alone in a seat in the window. For more cerebral pursuits Ian followed his brother as a Fellow of the Royal Geographical Society. Otherwise, he fell back on what Robert Harling called his network of octagons. Ian's friends were grouped in bunches of eight, according to Harling, and, in true conspiratorial fashion, never did a member of one octagon – the golfers, bridge-players, bibliophiles, intelligence agents and newspapermen – meet someone from another. When Harling asked him why he did this, Ian drawled laconically. "Then they'd become friends, better friends with each other than they are with me." This would have given an answer to Ivar Bryce who remarked on the same phenomenon: "The male friends were kept, whether by chance or design I could never decide, in compartments: geographical compartments, chronological compartments or just compartments of interest and aptitude. He and I were very close, I knew, and there was very little in my life he did not know or share. But many of his dear pals and cronies were quite strange to me, even unknown by name or sight."

A few friends, such as Harling, Bryce and Duff Dunbar, were in a category of their own. Harling was Ian's favourite companion when his Scottish melancholy played up and he needed a lift after a difficult morning at the *Sunday Times*. Ian would ring and demand "a superficial lunch" at Scott's. Once seated at a table, he would open the menu and declare, "Let's see what's the cheapest meal we can have today." Harling talked to him amusingly about women and writers and architecture, and Ian returned to the office spiritually and intellectually refreshed. His other great friend was Hugo Pitman, whose mixture of Etonian confidence, schoolboy humour and guileless sophistication brought out the best in him. Hugo gave Ian licence to laugh and enjoy himself. His daughters, by now strapping teenagers, had very different reactions to their father's friend. Rose, the more practical of the two, never felt at ease with Ian, while Jemima, the more fanciful, followed her father in developing a teasing relationship with him. On the whole, Ian did not like the paraphernalia of children. But once on their wavelength, he put himself out. When, in the middle of rationing in Britain, Jemima asked him to bring back some bananas from Jamaica, he did so. On another occasion he enquired what sort of person she wanted to marry, and when she threw back the same question, he answered, off the top of his head, "A Dresden shepherdess". Through Hugo Ian met Hilary Bray, the ex-jobber who had taken over his former position, buying his partnership shares in Rowe and Pitman in 1945. A former army intelligence officer and golf blue, Bray was not a type one immediately associates with Ian. He was quiet and assuming, a keen bird-watcher, who retired early because he was not happy with the ungentlemanly direction the City was taking. But his low-key style appealed to Ian, and the two men were often to be found on the golf course.

Ian also found time for all sorts outside his immediate circle. Always happy to reciprocate with the obligations of friendship he valued so highly, he arranged for Andrew Mouravieff, who was dabbling on the fringes of journalism on the *Evening Standard* Diary, to meet with the hotelier Conrad Hilton when the latter was looking for a London-based public relations man. And he provided useful companionship to Alan Miller, an Anglicized Canadian who had pioneered wireless technology in his company Broadcast Relay, a forerunner of the worldwide Rediffusion group. Ian had originally known Miller as a client of the Robert Fleming bank and a friend of Archie Jamieson who went on to chair Vickers, the armaments manufacturer. During the war Ian and Miller had started playing "fierce and high stake" bridge at the Portland Club. In 1946 Miller brought his young American bride Nancy to England for the first time. At twenty-two, she was less than half his age and sensitive to the barbed comments of her husband's female acquaintances. Ian went to considerable lengths to put Nancy at ease, taking her and a friend on a cruise up the River Thames to Hampton Court where he pulled out a bottle of champagne to drink on the bankside. "He was not flirty," recalls Nancy Miller. "He simply wanted to make me feel at home."

In the background there were old girlfriends, particularly Lisl Popper and Maud Russell. When Ann learned of these two ladies' continuing role in Ian's life, she confronted him in a sensible, measured manner,

"Sometimes I am shaken by your total acceptance on all matters, both material and philosophical, of the edicts of Maud and Leisel [sic]. It is dangerous to live in an ivory tower to which only two elderly extremely intelligent Jewesses possess the key (to be discussed at leisure)." Later, when she was married to Ian, she told Ivar Bryce not to tell her what her husband was up to unless he was "near a middle-aged Jewess". Ian later admitted that his ideal woman was not a pert-bottomed nymphette but someone who was "thirtyish, Jewish, a companion who wouldn't need education in the arts of love. She would aim to please, have firm flesh and kind eyes."

Ian's octagons kept him occupied while Ann's frenzied life took her from Warwick Hut, as she coined it, to Bailiff's Court on the Sussex coast, and over to her sister Laura's house, South Wraxhall Manor, in Wiltshire. She now had two excuses for accompanying Esmond on business trips to Paris. She had taken over from Maureen Stanley as director of the British Fashion Council and she had been appointed to the board of the *Continental Daily Mail*. In the French capital she would breeze through the *haute couture* houses before alighting on the doorstep of her friend Lady Diana Cooper at the British Embassy. To her dismay, Esmond often insisted on travelling on to Monte Carlo, where he had inherited his father's love-nest, the comfortable Villa Roche Fleuri, and where he liked to relax on a tennis court – the sort of sporty existence she loathed.

Before one of her trips to France in May 1947, Ian gave his lover an 1816 first edition of Lord Byron's poems about Napoleon and Waterloo. He was not accompanying her, and his sense of the unpredictability of their relationship is evident in his inscription, "Quelques pensées sur la France et – page 21 – un paratonnerre contre l'avenir". On the prescribed page was Byron's poem, "Fare Thee Well":

Fare thee well! and if for ever –
Still for ever, fare thee well –
Even though unforgiving, never
'Gainst thee shall my heart rebel.

In the midst of her toing and froing, Ann did her best to keep in touch with Ian. But petty acts of deceit were tiring: it seemed that whenever she was on the telephone, Esmond or one of the children would wander into the room. She sought excuses to travel to places where she could meet her lover. But she could not afford to be too obvious. Staying at Wraxhall in August 1947, she excused herself from meeting Ian because she could find no pressing reason to spend a night at the Lygon Arms, Broadway. She might have been able to drive to Oxford for lunch on a Saturday, but that would have eaten into her petrol coupon: she joked that a kiss in Oxford

High Street would cost her half the population's basic ration for a year.

During the late summer Ann made a point of visiting the O'Neill estate at Shane's Castle in Northern Ireland. She argued it was important to bring up her two children with the sense that this was home. When Esmond departed on one of his regular business trips to Canada, Ann arranged to travel to Shane's via Dublin where she fitted in a short holiday with Ian. This brought unexpected domestic pleasures, along with the physical abuse which they both enjoyed. "I am afraid I loved cooking for you and sleeping beside you and being whipped by you and I don't think I have ever loved like this before," she wrote, half-apologetically, when she reached Shane's. "I hope you are safe at home and missing your black bitch and I long for you even if you whip me because I love being hurt by you and kissed afterwards." The only cloud on the horizon was that, once again, Ian had been unwell – a reminder of the corporeal weaknesses which beset this seemingly most robust of men.

Five months later, in January 1948, came the trip that both Ian and Ann had been dreaming about – her first visit to Jamaica. They both saw in the new year with Esmond at a typically eclectic party at the Chelsea Arts Club. Also present were Ann's friends Diana and Duff Cooper, her brother Hugo and his fiancée Virginia Forbes Adam, her cousin, the Mercury correspondent Dick Wyndham and his girlfriend of the time, and Frederick Ashton and Margot Fonteyn. The next day the Lady Rothermere closed the lid on her London life and decamped with Ian to Jamaica. For propriety's sake, Loelia Westminster came too. Arriving at Goldeneye one evening, Ann was immediately depressed by the animal tropicality of the place, with its noisy frogs and dark, impenetrable nights. But, within hours, she brightened up and grew accustomed to the dull lazy routine Ian had devised: early-morning bathe; breakfast of pawpaw, Blue Mountain coffee, scrambled eggs and bacon; then some reading in the sunken garden which was beginning to flower with roses (Ann noted, however, that each rose had a large black beetle eating its heart out), then more serious swimming, with masks and spears to catch lobsters. Ian made no concessions to his metropolitan guests at mealtimes. He had told Violet that he did not come to Jamaica to eat beef roll. So Ann and Loelia were introduced to the culinary delights of the national dish, ackee and saltfish, to curried goat and to grilled snapper.

Ian was thrilled to have Ann with him, though she noticed something she had not fully realized before: her chocolate sailor was prone to fits of moodiness and introspection. After dinner, they would lean over the railing at the bottom of the garden and watch the sea, the waves and the stars. "The air is so clear of dirt or dust, there is an illusion of vast universe and the sea horizon is very round," she wrote. Long after she had gone in, Ian remained out there "smoking and wallowing in the melancholy".

This was fine for two lovers, but Loelia found it unbearably tedious. She realized that she had only been invited, as she put it, "to spread a thin aura of respectability as chaperone" for her friend. In later years she frequently complained that she had been used. "Ian and Ann used to leave in a small boat to fish or study the reef and not return until dusk, while I was left alone with no one to talk to and nowhere to go. I became drugged with boredom and lethargy."

To amuse his two guests Ian had bought the 1947 Macmillan edition of the *Field Guide to Birds of the West Indies* by an unknown academic called James Bond. Loelia was unimpressed though Ann, a naturalist manqué, was delighted to have use of this work of reference. As a diversion, Ian also sought their advice on décor. The furnishings were still rudimentary: a desk fashioned out of local green mahoe wood, a couple of planters' chairs provided by an admiring sugar estate-owner's daughter, and a card table from the Governor's wife, Molly Huggins, a vivacious blonde who turned heads wherever she went. Hot water had yet to be connected and, for some reason, the concrete floor had been covered with a layer of black boot polish, which created a condition known as "Goldeneye foot" as it wore off on people's bare soles. Indeed, when Ian's mother and sister had visited the previous month (Amaryllis had been invited to play her cello at the Institute of Jamaica), they had been so dismayed by the lack of creature comforts that they had moved to a hotel along the coast.

Now, with fanciful ideas in mind of renting his house to rich Americans, Ian realized he needed to make the place more comfortable. But when Ann and Loelia hinted that, for example, his cherished Vienna riding-school prints might be placed in such and such a place, their suggestions were studiously ignored. Instead, when the carpenter arrived, the two women were banished to the garden. As for their idea that he should put up sensible curtains instead of his masculine slatted wooden louvres, he was outraged. Loelia had to endure huge insects fluttering around her room, which she abhorred. She could not have been more delighted one evening when Ivar Bryce turned up with his wife Sheila and insisted they all went out to dinner.

Ann never liked Ivar: she considered him a bad influence on Ian, though this feeling manifested itself fully only later. Indeed, the social life generally was dire, she complained. Ian told her it would be better if she and Loelia did not go around babbling Mayfair gossip. When they went to dinner with a neighbour, a military man, Ian's two guests were enjoined to keep quiet. As a result, the conversation was stilted and boring, but Ian insisted to Ann that he had "learned of local matters" and playfully hoped she and the Duchess would "continue to be silent". Thus was established a pattern which, again, became more pronounced later in their relationship: she needed people, frivolity and informed gossip; he liked the company of males from whom he learned facts and "how things work".

Ann enjoyed a brief respite when the sparkling author Paddy Leigh Fermor came for the day with his bride-to-be Joan Rayner. Leigh Fermor was swanning round the Caribbean collecting material for a travel book to be called *The Traveller's Tree*. As was often the case in the tropics, he hardly knew either Ian or Ann, having met her only briefly towards the end of the war at Emerald Cunard's table at the Dorchester Hotel. Leigh Fermor made his mark by breaking an underwater spear gun, but Ian did not seem to mind, and within days a replacement had been ordered from Paris.

In early February Ann left with Loelia to resume her other life. First stop was Miami where she joined her husband. Ian recorded how he watched her plane disappear into the sky. Next day he could not stand being alone. The house was "too full of a small black ghost with a spot on its chin and all the answers". So he got into his car and drove around the Blue Mountain, not returning home till five in the afternoon. In Florida, the Rothermeres, with Loelia in tow, plunged into the social whirl, which included cocktails with the Duke and Duchess of Windsor in Palm Beach. As they travelled northwards to New York, a deliriously happy Ann heard only a single tocsin – Ian-Ian-Ian – being beaten out by the train.

While Esmond went about his business, Ann amused herself in a city which did not labour under the austerity she experienced at home. From the Plaza, she kept Ian informed of her movements by letter. Loelia was proving "a great vampire", needing to be accompanied around the place. But there were compensations, like lunch with Martha Gellhorn, Ernest Hemingway's former wife who had been introduced to Ann by Virginia Cowles, a fellow American war correspondent in London. Ann prevailed on Gellhorn to tell her friend, Leland Hayward, that Ian's house in Jamaica was available for rent. "In case, repeat IN CASE, you do not know who he is," Ann wrote to Ian, "he is a well known producer who has just produced Henry Fonda in *Mister Roberts*, a drama on a supply ship in the Pacific. It has had rave notices in the provinces and opens here on Wednesday. Need I add Lady R. will be there and supper with Leland and Fonda after? That she would sooner catch lobsters with you is just a sign of insanity."

Ann implored Ian to let his house for dollars and come home soon. She felt the need for Ian's lash. "It's very lonely not to be beaten and shouted at every five minutes. I have no bruises and I am basking in flattery. [I] must be perverse and masochistic to want you to whip me and contradict me, particularly as you are always wrong about everything and I shall go on saying so for ever and ever."

While doing the social rounds in New York, Ann continued to pine for Ian and what she now saw as their shared existence at Goldeneye. In a letter from the Plaza she mentioned matrimony for the first time. Ian had jokingly told her about problems in his friend Ivar Bryce's marriage: it would have been better if Ivar had given his quarrelsome wife Sheila "a bit of roughage", he opined. Ann noted that "there seems to be some mental comparison going on in your nasty mind between a possible marriage of ours and their sad relationship". She forecast that if they were wed, she would play the restrained Ivar's role and he would be the angry Sheila.

Ann could not resist having some fun at her lover's expense. In an effort to rouse his jealousy, she told him about a man who had tried to pick her up and invite her to the Pierre Hotel. And when she met Cholly Knickerbocker, the widely read society columnist on the New York *Journal-American*, she informed him conspiratorially that Loelia had been staying with Ian in Jamaica. An oily article duly appeared, referring to "Captain Fleming" as "a sort of Beau Brummell of the islands". At one time he had been rumoured to be close to Millicent Huddleston Rogers, the Standard Oil heiress, it stated. But she had gone to Hollywood and Ian was left with Loelia. "How serious this flirtation might be is hard to tell. Only future history will record the happenings."

The Knickerbocker article caused Ian some consternation. He learned of it from the *Sunday Times* office in New York before knowing of Ann's involvement. "I hope it isn't as bad as I fear," he wrote to her at the Plaza. Dealing with the rival in New York was more easy. He promised her twenty strokes of the lash – "10 on each buttock! – because I am the chosen instrument of the Holy Man to whip some of the devil out of you and I must do my duty however much pain it causes me. So be prepared to drink your cocktails standing for a few days after my return."

Although she joked about it, Ann was worried about Ian's reputation as a womanizer. In a letter from the Plaza, she begged him to keep his promise to be good. "It would be an interesting feat to be faithful to someone for three weeks, you have never done it before and it might make you feel very happy." She swore that she could never be unfaithful to him. She said she had done what she had to since she left (presumably she meant she had slept with Rothermere): "luckily it called for no effort on my part because it has been the most difficult thing since I left you, and I don't feel very happy about it."

With the best part of a month to kill on his own in Jamaica, Ian tried to reassure Ann about his priapic tendencies. "I have been steadfast as a rock but I confess there has been little temptation to stick my umbrella into anything except the sea." Before she sailed back to England with Esmond on the *Queen Mary*, he wrote to her in New York expressing his boyish excitement at his participation in a shark hunt – the "most thrilling" thing he had done in his life, he said. He and Aubyn Cousins, his neighbour's brother, had dragged two animal corpses – a cow and a donkey – out to sea off Goldeneye. The smell had been so bad that Ian's friend, Tommy Lowther, had refused to accompany them. Two enormous sharks appeared almost immediately. The first bit the cow's head off completely before it was captured in Cousins's lasso. Rather to Ian's disappointment, the other shark was also taken in by Cousins. The local community was fascinated, however, when the two creatures were tied by the tail and brought ashore, still alive.

Not that Ian lacked for female company. The usual cast of sun-seeking sycophants and socialites passed through Goldeneye. Ian reassured Ann by telling her that one female guest, whose intentions clearly concerned her, was impossibly dull and he was more likely to rape a yam. Another visitor was the strikingly attractive novelist Rosamond Lehmann, but again Ian professed any relationship to be "strictly spiritual". And when the over-talkative and over-scented society writer Elsa Maxwell turned up for a bed, Ian put her to work clearing seaweed in the bay with a billhook. He appreciated the poem she wrote in his visitors' book when she left: "Serenely happy and overfed – at Goldeneye in Goldenhead – which I saw first as a shiny pup – It gleams still more when all grown up."

Before returning home Ian spent a weekend with the Stephensons and a night with the Governor of Jamaica, Sir John Huggins, and his bubbly wife Molly. Then it was one day in New York and back to London via Prestwick, from where Ian promised to ring Ann at "about 9 in the morning and I shall be very excited and I don't mind in the least if you know it". He asked her to keep that evening free for him: he had been amusing himself thinking "of all the things I shall do to you one by one when you come through the door of Hays Mews".

Ian's first tenant at Goldeneye came as a result of Loelia's, rather than Ann's, efforts. While Ann was ensconced at the Plaza with her husband, the "elephant-hided" Loelia was staying at the Stephensons' apartment at 450 East 52nd Street on the Upper East side. Released from her chaperone duties, she was invited by Broadway producer Gilbert Miller and his wife Kitty to a cocktail party where she faithfully told Noël Coward, another guest, about Ian's Jamaican hideaway. Noël was immediately excited, and he made special arrangements to see Ian during his 24-hour stay in New York on 6 March.

Two weeks later, Coward became Ian's first independent tenant at Goldeneye. He paid £50 a week to stay there till the end of May. Coward later complained about the hardships (particularly the beds), the food (he remembered a nasty dish of curried goat, followed by stewed guavas with coconut cream, which all tasted of armpits), the price (Ian told him, truthfully enough, that he was expecting American guests, but would be happy to let him have the house in preference; Coward, who had his parsimonious side, considered this was simply a ruse to get more money) and the situation: "If [Ian] had built it on the angle to the right, he would have had a full view of all the sunsets. But he built it flat, facing the sea, and therefore didn't get the sunsets. And the windowsills were too high, so that you sat in that lovely big room with the windowsill just about to your eye-level and you got an admirable view of the sky, and nothing else." (Ian's recent guest, Paddy Leigh Fermor, had rather enjoyed this effect. For him the dark wooden frames of the louvres "enclose a prospect of sea and cloud and sky, and tame the elements, as it were, into an overhanging fresco of which one could never tire". The main room was well-positioned to benefit from the breezes, he said; indeed, Ian's design might well become a model for new houses in the tropics.)

When Coward arrived on 22 March, his reaction was anything but jaundiced. "It is quite perfect," he wrote of Goldeneye in his diary; "a large sitting-room sparsely furnished, comfortable beds and showers, an agreeable staff, a small private coral beach with lint-white sand and warm clear water. The beach is unbelievable." And his comment in Fleming's visitors' book was equally positive. "The happiest two months I have ever spent," he wrote unambiguously. When Ian was back the following year, Coward had composed a song, which epitomized the friendly ribbing and banter between these two unlikely friends:

Alas! I cannot adequately praise
The dignity, the virtue and the grace
Of this most virile and imposing place
Wherein I passed so many airless days.

Alas! Were I to write 'till crack of doom
No typewriter, no pencil, nib, nor quill
Could ever recapitulate the chill
And arid vastness of the living-room.

Alas! I cannot accurately find
Words to express the hardness of the seat
Which, when I cheerfully sat down to eat,
Seared with such cunning into my behind.

Alas! However much I raved and roared
No rhetoric, no witty diatribe
Could ever, even partially, describe
The impact of the spare-room bed – and board.

Alas! I am not someone who exclaims
With rapture over ancient equine prints.
Ah no dear Ian I can only wince
At *all* those horses framed in *all* those frames.

Alas! my sensitivity rebels,
Not at loose shutters; not at the plague of ants,
Nor other 'sub-let' bludgeonings of chance,
But at those hordes of ageing faded shells.

Alas! If only common-sense could teach
The stubborn heart to heed the crafty brain
You would, before you let your house again,
Remove the barracudas from the beach.

But still my dear commander I admit,
No matter how I criticize and grouse,
That I was strangely happy in your house
In fact I'm very fond of it.

7

Succumbing to marriage
1948–1952

The couple of years since the war had gone better than Ian could have hoped. His new job was interesting, financially rewarding, and not over-demanding; he had successfully established the house of his dreams in Jamaica; and he was involved in a passionate if semi-detached relationship with one of the most imperiously attractive creatures on the London social scene.

He was brought back to reality when he returned to London at the end of March 1948 and discovered that Ann was pregnant with his child. Her reaction was predictably exuberant. With Esmond about to set off on a prearranged business trip to New York the following month, Ann contacted Ian, urging him to make the most of her husband's absence. "Let's have fun then, because after that I shall not be 'sortable' for a long time." But he was less sanguine about the future, wondering how the responsibilities of fatherhood (even though they were unlikely to be admitted publicly) would impact on his carefully regulated life.

With a heavy dose of irony, Ann enquired of her sister-in-law Virginia, who was also pregnant, "I hope your condition is as interesting as mine." During the early summer, she duly cut back on her usual punishing programme of social events. But, since her child was not expected for another few weeks, it was no surprise when the affable Esmond – in an effort, no doubt, to keep his highly-strung wife entertained – invited their friends Ian and Loelia Westminster to join them for a quiet golfing holiday in Scotland in August. They were all ensconced in a self-catering lodge at Gleneagles Hotel and embarked on an interminable game of bridge, when Ann suddenly began having contractions. She was rushed to 11 Randolph Crescent, the Edinburgh clinic frequented by her Wemyss relations, where, a month prematurely, she gave birth to a daughter, Mary, by Caesarean section.

The infant only survived eight hours, leaving Ann "very bruised and bewildered". The surgical and psychological scars lingered for what he believed was the rest of her life, while the two men closest to her were plunged into helpless guilt-ridden grief. Esmond stayed glumly by her bed, mourning for his lost daughter, while Ian struggled round the golf-course, trying to maintain his composure but feeling, if anything, even more devastated. Playing a round with his friend Roland Cubitt (later Lord Ashcombe) was hell: he could think of nothing but Ann's condition.

In her bossy head-girl's manner, Loelia insisted that, to keep their spirits up, they must continue to entertain. A long list of guests was expected and one day Rodney Berry, the nephew of Ian's employer, Lord Kemsley, turned up and had to be humoured. After dealing with these unwelcome diversions, Ian would sit down at the end of each day and pour his heart out to Ann on paper. He sent flowers and newspapers cuttings to cheer her up. She wrote to her brother Hugo that Ian was the only person she wanted to see.

Ian's letters to the unhappy Ann were thoughtful and sincere. Ann later said that his kindness at this stage led her truly to love him. Ian drew on his own periods of *angst* to compose sophomoric lines like, "I know how lonely one is where you are and that no one can keep you company in the shadows", or, another time, "I have nothing to say to comfort you. After all this travail and pain and all these adventures it is bitter. I can only send you my arms and my love and all my prayers. I can't be there to wipe up your eyes and kiss you and you must just lie through these days in your bed and think of all your blessings and try not to count your griefs." When she was better, he wrote calling on her to "kick the snakes in the teeth. Don't ask for double sixes too much and accept with a shrug the twos and threes and wear your comfortable shoes and not the high heels and feel your feet good and flat on the ground."

Through her morphine-induced haze, Ann loved this mixture of soppiness and worldly wisdom. She assured Ian that, after him, any other man would be a "frightful bore". Masochistically, given her current condition, she longed for his "pointless bullying, so harsh and then so gentle if I cry". With the incisiveness that made her such an entertaining correspondent, she enumerated his qualities: "Wonderful ideas and wrong-headed arguments, tremendous charm and occasional shocking manners; a very good mind which I fear will never expand to capacity owing to an unfortunate adroitness at short cuts and an unusual gift for well-organised leisure." The notion that Ian would never reach or even strive for his potential was accurate, though, in his esoteric way, he reserved his tremendous talent and application for his later Bond books.

As she slowly began to regain her strength, Ann touched on two other issues which were to assume great importance in Ian's life. From her Edinburgh hospital bed, she urged him to knuckle down and write the book (subject undefined) he had been talking about, even if, like Mrs Galsworthy and *The Forsyte Saga*, she had to sit in an upright chair knitting beside him. And, once again, she suggested that Ian's health might not be all it should, by wishing away the persistent pains in his neck and chest.

Rothermere could not compete with Ian's easy unctuousness. He mournfully told Virginia Charteris in London that Mary had been "a sweet baby, very like Ann". But he indicated his sterner side when he told her he was sending his chauffeur to meet his wife off the night train from Edinburgh. He insisted Ann needed to convalesce and, even though she described it as "a waste of time", he whisked her off in September, first to Paris and the *haute couture* shows (at Balenciaga she was dismayed to have to sit next to a baronet's wife with whom she knew Ian had had "carnal relations"), and then down to Italy where their friends Alexander and Jenny Clifford had just set up house in the picturesque fishing village of Portofino, east of Genoa. Clifford had been recommended by Ann to work for the *Daily Mail* in Paris, and still wrote for the paper as a special correspondent.

Clifford's best friend was Alan Moorehead, a fellow war correspondent, who, after visiting him and Jenny in Portofino earlier that summer, had written a piece about the attractions of the Ligurian coast in the *New Yorker*. Scanning the papers in his role as foreign manager, Ian came across this item and posted it to Ann, with a plea that she should start looking after her physical condition: "Please say No a bit from now on. Ian's theory of the imperative negative is still the best cure for stomach ulcers and galloping fatigue." This manoeuvre annoyed Ann who felt Ian should be writing her proper letters rather than filling envelopes with other people's clippings. The article itself infuriated her hosts and threatened a friendship because they said it had been plagiarized from the book that Jenny Clifford, daughter of Robert Graves, was herself writing about Portofino.

By the shores of the Mediterranean Esmond finally steeled himself to ask Ann about the exact nature of her relationship with Ian. Whether he understood that the baby Mary had been Ian's is not certain. But he must have suspected it, and soon afterwards he began demanding that she stop seeing the good-looking newspaper executive who was such a fixture at Warwick House. "I knew it would come and I know our weekends are going to be difficult," Ian conceded, without much fight. "Don't force an ultimatum, or I shall get too embarrassed ever to see [Esmond]."

While Ann was away, Ian made a special effort to keep himself occupied. At the end of September he paid a flying visit to Jamaica. (In return for a salary cut of £1000 per annum, he was allowed to "take leave of absence to see to his private affairs abroad". However, the reduction in his take-home pay was made up at the end of the year by the satisfying expedient of a bonus of £1000.) On his return to England, he renewed his new friendship with the eccentric essayist Edith Sitwell, whom he had met the previous December at a *Sunday Times* luncheon for her brother Osbert. She had originally treated Ian with patrician coolness because she had thought, from his obsequious manner, that he was the social secretary to another guest, Lady Cunard. To break the ice, Ian informed Miss Sitwell that they had a mutual friend in William Plomer, and that he was "very amused" to see that Plomer had listed her poem "Shadow of Cain," among his favourites in an article in *Horizon*. Sitwell purported to be outraged by his use of the word "amused". But as she subsequently wrote to Plomer, "He ran no immediate risk in saying this, as we were both guests at a luncheon party given in honour of Osbert."

Plomer promised to reproach Ian, but Miss Sitwell was not easily mollified. As she told Plomer menacingly, Ian "was very lucky to have been rude to me under those particular circumstances". Ian obliged with a suitably grovelling letter of apology, whereupon she invited him to lunch on 10 June at her London club, the Sesame Imperial and Pioneer Club, where the other guests were Plomer, the poet T. S. Eliot, the novelist Rosamond Lehmann and the academic Maurice Bowra. In accepting her invitation, Ian wrote a typically light and self-deprecating reply that he was horrified at the "array of talent" she had asked. "Please let me sit in the shadow of William," he begged, "so that I am not drawn into any discussion on your use of the semi-colon or the degree of emphasis inherent in italics. I just don't carry the guns for such abstrocities."

Knowing of Sitwell's interest in mysticism, Ian offered to bring her a copy of the "ham-fisted translation from the German" he had made nearly twenty years earlier of a speech by the psychologist Jung at Paracelsus's birthplace in Switzerland. "My English translation is almost as Germanic as Jung's original German, but there are one or two original points in the speech and it has never been published over here."

Sitwell was delighted at this generous gesture. On 17 June she wrote saying that Jung was one of her "principal manias, so you can imagine my excitement at having his pronouncements on Paracelsus, another mania". Ian replied that her favourable comments had encouraged him to write to Jung to see if his rights of publication to the translation were still alive in Britain (though there was no evidence that he actually did this). When he asked her deferentially if she might consider writing a small monograph on Jung to accompany this work, she suggested a better subject might be a book outlining the inspiration which Mystic and Hermetic philosophers such as Paracelsus had provided to poets in general.

An unusual literary friendship was developing. Knowing that she was touring the United States later in the year, Ian invited her to submit a piece to the *Sunday Times* about intellectual life in North America. With a talent for self-promotion, she accepted with alacrity and, having enlisted a new member of her literary cabal, proceeded to bombard him not only with poems for publication (Ian usually tried to oblige) but also with the names of obscure poets she wanted either praised or damned.

Before going to Portofino, Ann had teased Ian about his meetings with "his secret lover". By the time Ian met Miss Sitwell again, on 1 October, he was thoroughly bored with this birdlike intellectual twenty years his senior. He told Ann in Portofino that he was "exhausted after 2 hours of Edith Sitwell with no William P[lomer] or Rosamond L[ehmann] to help and only some miscellaneous frousts". He only wanted to see his lover again.

It was a feeling Ann reciprocated. Ignoring her husband's pronouncements, she arranged to meet Ian at the Ritz Hotel in Paris on her journey home. She reserved a suite with a sitting-room where she wanted to recreate the romantic atmosphere they had enjoyed at the Plaza in New York two years earlier. Ian was in charge of the homeward travel arrangements. But he found that securing sleeper berths for himself and a married woman presented problems. The train from Paris to London had few single compartments. So, as he told Ann, a double proved the "only answer". He pretended to the booking clerk that his travelling companion was his sister Amaryllis.

Ann used her enforced leisure to put her own pen to paper. Two interesting fragments of writing survive. One is the outline of a story, based rather too obviously on her life and Ian's. The second is a more finished study of the press lords of the day. She must have written her lightly fictionalized account of her relationship with Ian on a day she was feeling annoyed with him, for it is merciless in its dissection of his character and her feelings about him. A useful recapitulation of Ian's life, it is nominally the story of Gervase, "the bewildered product of a union between a beautiful egocentric woman ... and a Scottish banker". The father had been killed at the Somme leaving his fortune to his wife Sybilla, who, it did not take much imagination to discern, was based on Ian's mother, Eve.

In Ann's story, Sybilla's beauty was combined with "ferocious energy and manic vanity, sitting to great painters or royal academicians, playing spinets and clavichords, redecorating the London house or changing the country home, selling an Elizabethan mansion in Essex because she had found a Queen Anne gem in Sussex". These familiar-sounding activities hardly dented her energy, however, and she found ample time to write hectoring letters to her three sons at school. "The mildest moral relapse, a failure to retain a high place in the form, would reap a harvest of reproachful voluminous correspondence, pointing [to] the miseries of representing both parents, the work involved, and the ingratitude of the recipients. She was unaware they contained no message of love."

'Gervase' went to Germany and then France to study for the Foreign Office. With his mother's temperament and looks, he enjoyed great success with women in both countries. But when he returned to London he failed his exam for the diplomatic service. This was a shock to Gervase, who was a sullen, conceited and lonely young man, particularly as his brothers

were both successes in their fields – the older one at the Bar and the
younger in the family business.

He retreated into a comfortable existence in a London house, with a
regimental coat of arms forming the knocker on the front door and
with a pretty Austrian maid in attendance. His knowledge of human
relationships was limited to his circle of male friends and to a select band
of mistresses who "were only permitted the intimacies of the flesh, with
the exception of two ageing foreigners, who by undemanding flattery and
tact, combined with intelligence, had maintained a foothold for many
years". Ann was referring again to Lisl and Maud.

Happily Gervase's "length of limb, breadth of shoulder, abrupt manner
and cameo features" were appreciated by men as well as women. His
services were solicited by "middle-aged men of medium eminence" who
ensured that, not only did he get a good executive job in a large multinational firm but also when war came he was spirited immediately into
a comfortable intelligence job.

Gervase waits in his house for Geraldine, whose exact status is not
spelled out, though significantly she has Ann's second Christian name,
the same as both Esmond's aunt and grandmother. Gervase washes his
hands carefully with a bar of soap he spent a long time choosing in a New
York drugstore. His profile is still "Graeco-aggressive" but there are touches
of grey around his temples and "the first symptoms of an indulgent
stomach". When Big Ben strikes six o'clock, he hurriedly applies some
lipsalve and, knowing Geraldine is due, wants to finish reading the City
pages of the *Evening Standard*. In a revealing note, Ann wrote that "his
formalism demanded that the bell should not ring until he had read the
newspaper".

In her second literary offering, Ann was characteristically forthright
in her views about the men who owned the British press. The Labour
government had set up a Royal Commission to investigate the power of
the press, and Ian was helping Lord Kemsley marshal his evidence. She
made little effort to defend her husband and his fellow newspaper mag-
nates against accusations that they exerted undue influence. Unknown
before the First World War, press barons were "a new form of power and
an intensely exciting one", Ann opined; more exciting, indeed, than the
divine right of kings or feudal barons and "a far more corrupting and
intoxicating power than being a soap magnate or tobacco king".

Ann's comments on the newspaper owners themselves were pithy but
banal. Esmond was described as not having the drive or conviction of his
father – the result of a complicated childhood, she suggested. In his
defence, he had "the same qualities as the reed in the fable for weathering
storms". Beaverbrook admired John Fox and Calvin and was afraid of Hell.
Ian's boss Lord Kemsley was "more philanthropic but less intelligent"

than his elder brother, Lord Camrose. He stood for "Empire, family life and the Conservative party" and, while his approach to these principles might be ponderous, it was "unquestionably sincere".

Back in the real world in London, Esmond tried to invoke the Newspaper Proprietors' Union to take action against the hairy-heeled Ian. He complained to Lord Kemsley about his foreign manager's ungentlemanly behaviour. The priggish Kemsley summoned Ian and read him the riot act. But the reprimand was half-hearted: he still relied on his foreign manager to bring social respectability to his group. Anyway the two lovers were in little mood for compromise. Although they both felt constraints on their relationship, their minds were focused on the coming winter and another visit to Jamaica. Ann felt she would enjoy it even better second time round "because I shall have my tiny roots there and I always like that". As the time approached, she gushed, "It would be such anguish not to come with you, and how HOW can I do it without wrecking you with Gomer – I started fussing about it all ten days ago and I can't stop."

The solution was a measure of discretion. Since Ian had been good enough to rent him his house in Jamaica, Noël Coward invited him and Ann to use White Cliffs, his seaside cottage on St Margaret's Bay, near Dover in Kent. Another refuge of a sort was South Wraxhall Manor, the Wiltshire house which had originally belonged to David Long, her sister Laura's first husband, who had been killed in action in Normandy in 1944. In order to boost the shaky Long family finances, Ann often rented Wraxhall for short periods and, before long, like Buscot during the war, it became her country home from home. At Christmas 1948 she mixed family, lovers and friends with reckless abandon. Ian was there, of course, and the oddly compliant Esmond. Others in the house party included Count John de Bendern, his wife Patricia, and Alastair Forbes, who was working as a political commentator on Rothermere's *Sunday Dispatch*. Tensions were running high, which was not unusual when Ann was around. One morning, Forbes appeared at breakfast in a dashing new seersucker dressing-gown. When to his dismay, Ian managed to spill fruit juice on his cherished garment, he sprang at the foreign manager of Kemsley Newspapers, kneeing him in the chest. Ian retired, aggrieved, to his room, whereupon Esmond relaxed and began to enjoy himself, thinking that Forbes had attacked his wife's lover out of a misplaced sense of loyalty to him.

Ian and Forbes quickly patched up their differences and resumed their bantering friendship. Returning to London from Wraxhall, Forbes smelled what he thought was an electrical fault in the engine of his Citroën. He pulled up and looked inside the bonnet. There were twelve lobster shells which Ian had tied to his cylinder head. After such weekends, Ian often drove Peter Quennell back to London in his Morris Oxford. Their journey took them through the Kennett Valley, past Avebury Ring and Silbury Hill. When Quennell wanted to stop and look at the prehistoric burial mounds, Ian kept on driving. He had no need for such diversions. Quennell – about whom the young Fionn used to pray, "Oh please God don't let Mummy marry him!" – reflected that Ian was "a modern man, an addict of mechanical speed, who kept his eye on the road and his hands upon the wheel, though – a somewhat alarming practice – he occasionally drove with one hand while he lit an American cigarette or used a silver stick of lipsalve".

Ann's periodic urgings to Ian to take up his pen were having some effect for, on one of these trips, Ian informed Quennell that he was going to write a thriller. He provided a brief outline of his proposed fictional crime. It centred on a leg of lamb which, when frozen and straight from the fridge, served as a lethal murder weapon, which, when cooked and eaten, was nowhere to be found. Ian later presented this plot to Roald Dahl who adapted it for use in his successful story "Lamb to the Slaughter" published in 1952. A conventional detective story seemed to be gestating in Ian's mind at this stage. After reading a *Horizon* essay in which Christopher Hollis deliberated on the nature of death, Ian conscientiously marked several passages about the psychology of hanging and murder confessions.

In the event Ann refused to let anything stand in the way of her returning to Jamaica. She could not have been less guarded when she stepped off the Pan Am Clipper from New York on 6 January 1949. The *Daily Gleaner* reported her arrival with Commander Ian Fleming and their friends Mr and Mrs Henry Robert Harling. At Palisadoes Airport the Lady Rothermere announced she was very pleased to be back. She had visited the island the previous January and had had a very enjoyable holiday. The foursome then motored to the Bryces' house at Bellevue, readers were informed, before making their way to Goldeneye.

It seems odd that Ann should have been so brazen. As a newspaper owner, her husband was not without sources of information. She had told him that she was returning to the island to stay with her friend Noël Coward, whom everyone knew was no sexual threat. (Whether she really cared is a moot point: Esmond was never as celibate as he liked to make out. In a letter to her brother Hugo the following year, Ann referred to her husband's dalliance with an American blonde, "but I don't think it is serious".)

Coward did his bit to keep up pretences on Ann's behalf. When a photographer from *Life* arrived to take pictures of him in his new house, Blue Harbour, at Port Maria, the Master sent hurriedly to Goldeneye to fetch Ann. He later told his friend and biographer Cole Lesley, "There then began a very natty high comedy scene in which she kept forgetting that she was a house guest and asking us what we had been doing all the morning etc."

Ian's public relations exercise in *Horizon* had clearly been read. The gloom of war had finally lifted and people with money were flocking to the island, which had the added advantage of being in the sterling area. One expected the Americans – millionaires such as Henry Luce, boss of *Time* magazine, and his wife Clare, who went to stay with Lord Beaverbrook at Cromarty. But a remarkable number of British aristocrats also managed to escape domestic austerity and make the transatlantic trek. Like Ann's friend Judy Montagu, daughter of H. H. Asquith's muse, Venetia Stanley, they usually stayed at Carmen Pringle's Sunset Lodge, ostensibly the leading hotel on the north coast. Even it was not perfect: after Mrs Vincent Astor complained that she had found a rat in her room, Carmen refused to be taken aback, asking her guest acerbically, "What do you expect for $100? Lions and tigers?"

When at the end of February Ian, Ann, Coward and Graham Payn motored over to Sunset Lodge to see some of these friends, Ian contrived to have himself photographed by the *Daily Gleaner*, lolling languorously on the beach in the company of Diana Huggins, the Governor's daughter, Babe Paley, the glamorous wife of CBS chief Bill Paley, and Graham Payn. Ann stayed out of that picture. But Noël was avuncularly amused at the way, as he put it, "Elle et Lui discreetly (i.e. indiscreetly) had breakfast together on the balcony of his room! After this I descended upon them both and gave them a very stern lecture indeed. I must say they are very sweet but ... I have grave fears for the avenir."

Taking a leaf out of his friend Bill Stephenson's book, Ian helped patch up relations between Coward and the querulous Lord Beaverbrook. A low-level feud had existed for over twenty years. Coward suspected Beaverbrook of masterminding the poor notices he tended to receive in *Express* newspapers. He also had a specific grievance: he believed the Canadian peer had prevented him from taking up a wartime job working for Stephenson's British Security Coordination in New York. After Ian took him to lunch with Beaverbrook, Coward's anger abated: the old rascal "couldn't have been nicer", he said.

By the end of their holiday, Ian and Ann realized they needed to take some adult decisions about their relationship. "We will be brave one way or another before the end of the year," she promised. "I think it is you who must determine it because you have had a comfortable life and to share a few pennies with a snarky girl accustomed to money is a frightening undertaking. I can only promise to try to make you happy and if we had enough money for gin and cigarettes I think it might be very happy."

Even Ian, who had reached the age of forty studiously avoiding any commitment, was at last preparing to contemplate matrimony seriously. "Having never been married I cannot weigh the odds with any certainty and you must realize that," he declared, adding prophetically, "My difficulties may seem all right while you are in love with me, but it would be quite different if the love turned to the usual married friendship and you might get too irritated. I don't know ... Anyway, my dearest love, I am completely devoted to you and would like to look after you for ever and make a nest with you in the way we both like and you should know this when talking to Esmond."

These declarations of love were harshly interrupted when Ann arrived home in England after a short time in New York. She was met at Southampton docks by an emissary from her husband, who handed her a sealed envelope. Inside were curt orders that she should desist from seeing Ian forthwith, or he would divorce her. Ann's friends used to say there were three ways of imparting news: they could use "the telephone, the telegraph and the tell-Annie". So it was hardly surprising that, after she had informed her newspaper favourite, Frank Owen, about Esmond's ultimatum, it became common Fleet Street knowledge. Esmond's scrupulous former secretary, Gerald Sanger, noted that, when Owen asked Ann what she intended to do, she was not sure. But she thought Esmond was being "perfectly absurd ... He knows Ian Fleming has been my lover for fourteen years." She even accused her husband of hiring detectives to spy on her. When Owen enquired if she was fond enough of Ian to refuse Esmond's ultimatum, she replied defiantly that she thought she was.

The lovers coped by keeping a low profile and leasing one of the cottages adjoining Noël Coward's at St Margaret's Bay. The master entertainer had first alighted on this pebbly stretch of coast in October 1945, when his regular Kent house, Goldenhurst, was still occupied by the Army. His own White Cliffs was the best-preserved of a cluster of five unpretentious whitewashed cottages perched precariously under a crumbling chalk face. Until recently a large hotel had stood at the opposite side of the bay but, during the war, it had taken a direct hit and been razed to the ground. The area between its remains and the cottages was still covered with debris and barbed wire. But Coward liked the position, looking out over the English Channel, and negotiated a lease from the owner, local businessman John Guest. He wanted to rent all five cottages, but that was against the regulations at a time of housing shortages. So he arranged for his friends and relatives to move in around him. He took the largest, eponymous house at the end of the bay, his secretary Lorn Loraine most of the second, Cole Lesley the third, the author Eric Ambler the fourth, and Coward's mother and Aunt Vida the fifth.

In the early summer of 1949, Eric Ambler tired of his seaside property (he claimed he could not afford the rent) and Noël arranged for Ian and Ann to take over the lease. Now their visits became more regular. Ian was happy, for Summer's Lease, as their new cottage was appropriately named, was close to Royal St George's, one of his favourite golf clubs which he had joined the previous November. (Ian had originally been put up for membership in May 1939, but since his proposer, his 'Cercle' friend, Bobby Gordon-Canning, was subsequently interned as a fascist sympathizer, it was deemed appropriate to start the process again, this time with the pleasant-mannered stockbroker Hilary Bray as proposer.) As Lady Rothermere, Ann could still not afford too public a profile. So she settled back into the joys of domesticity. Her letters to Ian around this time were peppered with unfamiliar remarks about how much she liked cooking for him and how she was missing "our nest". She also showed signs of trying to develop a separate group of friends, such as the writer Cyril Connolly, whom she could share with Ian. To the recently divorced Connolly, she admitted another agenda: her child's death had made her "a tigerish Lady Pakenham with a feverish furious desire to have children annually until nature puts an end to it, which fortunately for everybody is not far off".

For reasons of enforced anonymity the couple's social life in Kent was largely confined to Coward and his friends. That meant a diet of amateur theatricals, cards and parlour games. When, in an effort to emulate Noël's success, two of his closest friends, Graham Payn and Cole Lesley, wrote the score for *Ghost of a Chance*, a musical which was never produced, Ian proved their most appreciative audience, rolling about with laughter at the jokes and assuring Lesley that he would do everything in his power to promote the project. When Noël's circle discovered the popular card game canasta, Ian and Ann were roped in to make up foursomes. Winifred Ashton, otherwise the author and playwright Clemence Dane and a regular visitor to White Cliffs, painted an evocative oil of Ian, Ann, Noël and Joyce Carey, the actress, carefully deliberating over a hand. Ann looks pretty and pert, toying with a cigarette. Ian is cool and fiercely determined to win even in this smoked-filled domestic environment. And when they had finished cards, there was always 'The Game', or charades, the then fashionable practice of miming the name of a book or a play to the assembled company's merriment and derision.

St Margaret's Bay, with Noël's quaint rituals like his cups of Horlicks and Bournvita, gave Ian and Ann a tantalizing glimpse of the settled life they both seemed to want. They discussed the possibility of establishing a base along the coast in Brighton. "What about starting the Brighton home?" he asked, half yearningly, half tongue-in- cheek, "and then I could commute and you could put out my slippers in front of the fire and ask me about my day at the office." However, once again he signalled his continuing ambivalence by listing the problems she might encounter. "Both your other husbands have been more lethargic and also more self-disciplined than I am and I'm afraid I shall never settle down until I settle into the earth!" On another occasion he coolly outlined the difference in their characters: she liked company, he preferred to spend his evenings alone; she had a position and dependants, notably her children, he had nothing except his "cherished freedom"; she was "natural", he was "unnatural" – a suggestion that Ian understood the extent to which he was a self-invention.

Ann was not going to be easily put off. She sent Ian in Hays Mews fresh eggs from the country and made sure he was supplied with still scarce consumer goods, like a Hoover from the Daily Mail Ideal Home Exhibition which it was one of her duties as Lady Rothermere to open each year. Although herself far from fully fit, she worried incessantly about his health: under his façade of bonhomie, he was showing undisguisable symptoms of stress. Ian's most persistent problem was his headaches. Ann attributed them to the plate which had been inserted in his broken nose at Eton. When they refused to go away, he took what he described as his first step towards the grave by acquiring a pair of spectacles. "I look very portentous," he boasted, "and shall be in a better position to keep you in order and influence the policy of the *Sunday Times*." More seriously, he continued to be plagued with pains around his neck and chest. "Listen my darling," Ann pleaded in late 1948, "please be honest with me about your chest pains. I am glad you are going to a specialist next week and I hope you will be sensible about what he says. I am sure you got very overtired at Sandwich, the reaction on Tuesday night showed that it had been a nervous and physical strain."

Ian booked an appointment to see Sir John Parkinson, an eminent Harley Street physician. His chest pains were the same complaint which had forced him to consult a doctor in New York two years earlier. This time Sir John gave him a cardiogram, which yielded no evidence of heart disease, though, like Dr Franz Groedel in New York, he advised Ian to ease back on his alcohol intake and, specifically, to forgo brandy, port and liqueurs after dinner.

But Ian still had periods of excruciating pain which, on being called to his bedside, Jack Beal, his doctor cum bridge partner, diagnosed as kidney stones. Dr Beal gave him intravenous morphia and advised him to drink at least three glasses of water each morning to wash out the acid that had collected in his kidneys overnight. On another occasion, Ian experienced rapid heart palpitations during an Old Etonian golfing weekend at Rye. This time Dr Beal could find nothing overtly wrong with him, but later admitted that Ian was probably showing the first symptoms of coronary heart disease.

With signs of uncertainty and stress in their relationship, Ian travelled alone to Jamaica at Christmas 1949. His way of forgetting his cares was to immerse himself in the secret world of his fishes in the waters off Goldeneye. This year, he was determined to make a proper study of it all. Demonstrating his innate combination of propriety and theatricality, he bought a naturalist's notebook and had it bound it black leather by Sangorski and Sutcliffe of London. Not wanting to imbue the venture with too much *gravitas*, he could not resist having the title "Sea Fauna or the Finny Tribe of Goldeneye" picked out in gold on the front cover. And, before setting out to record his encounters with the local marine life, he noted, with his talent for self-parody, a delightful quotation from *The Aquarium*, an 1854 study by the eminent zoologist Philip Gosse, father of the essayist and critic, Sir Edmund Gosse, who had worked on the *Sunday Times*: "A paragraph went the round of the papers some months ago, to the effect that an eminent French zoologist, in order to prosecute his studies on the manic animals of the Mediterranean, had provided himself with a water-tight dress, suitable spectacles, and a breathing tube; so that he might walk on the bottom of a considerable depth of water, and mark the habits of the various creatures pursuing their avocations. Whether a scheme so elaborate was really attempted I know not, but I should anticipate feeble results from it."

An example of Ian's industry was his observations during his first few days on two "Hunt-class barracudas" whom he christens Bicester and Beaufort. On 23 December he "declare[s] war" on them because they are "getting too big and frighten the customers", or other fish. The following day he takes a Champion spear gun and goes after Beaufort. "As usual he examines me with wary curiosity and a pronounced but possibly forced sneer. He allows me, moving very slowly and softly, to come within six ft, at which range I shoot and miss, probably low. Beaufort travels twelve ft like a bullet then stops dead, broadside on." But when Ian moves closer, the fish "merges silently away into the grey mists of deeper water". Chagrined, Ian takes it "out on a ½lb lobster, shot through the head."

On Christmas Day Ian reflects that "hunting fish under water is very similar to hunting game on land, but silence is even more necessary since water is a far better conductor of sound and other vibrations than air". The following day he sees Beaufort again, and congratulates himself that the fish is doomed. "The trident did not miss but gashed him forward of the dorsal fin. On my way out I see him with two inches of white flesh protruding behind his head. The parasites will have him within a day or so."

While Ian was recreating himself in the warm waters of Jamaica, Ann was beset with confusion in the social whirl in Europe. After attending a fancy-dress ball in Paris in March 1950, she admitted to Ian, "I don't even know if I am happy or sad." She wished "a fairy would arrive with a wand and make everything all right: give Esmond a perfect wife and put me in your bed with a raw cowhide whip in my hand so as I can keep you well behaved for forty years." With her unfailing acuity, she jotted down a poem which encapsulated both her love for Ian and her frustration at their situation:

Your philosophy is splendid in a selfish kind of way,
When your hair was black and curly but not now it is grey,
For you're well over forty and I fear you're getting fat,
You're apt to be forgotten and just an old bad hat.

This dear familiar face is not accustomed to neglect,
And still has the capacity to make other men erect,
So if by chance you meet a pretty Biarritz slut,
Just pause for thought and hesitate before you stuff her up.

And if you need adventure it'll be [as] much as you can do,
To cope with the variety of your ever loving Shrew.

Boiled samphire to you.

Although she could still joke about Ian's louche habits, she worried
incessantly about what to do. In August 1950 she confided in Hugo that
she was living in an emotional limbo because she lacked the "courage to
leap from the merry-go-round. I should not miss the fleshpots but I must
confess that I enjoy the excitement." She realized she would have to give
up a stimulating public life if she left Esmond. For the time being she was
not sure if she could discipline herself to being led (by Ian), rather than
leading. So she channelled her energies once more into the *Daily Mail*:
"The real boss wears a petticoat", trumpeted *Time* in a feature on the
paper, returning to the theme it had introduced five years earlier. Noël
Coward chimed in with "Up! Lady Rothermere's Organ, or Annie Get Your
Slug", a risqué ditty satirizing her influence at the *Daily Mail*. It begins:

Sweet Continental Daily Female
Hard at work upon the stone
Black curls tangled up in the lino
Type gummed up with acetone

Pencil red with "Fatal Apple"
"Falsies" heaving with the strain
See her rush the first edition
Off to catch the midnight train!

At least Ann's influence had helped her brother land a job on the *Daily
Mail*, which soon posted him abroad as Paris correspondent. This suited
her well: she had an excuse for extended stays at the Charterises' flat in
the Boulevard Suchet, close to the Bois de Boulogne. By chance, Ian often
happened to be in town at the same time, when she would join him in
the Hotel Continental where they were not to be disturbed. On one of

these trips Ian amused John Julius Cooper (and rather punctured his image of sophistication) by announcing that he had had a most unusual dish at lunch-time, a plate of raw mince called steak tartare. Virginia noted that her sister-in-law seemed more relaxed in Paris. "Ann enjoyed the clandestine aspect of the thing. It made their romance that much more romantic, which was what she wanted."

At the *Sunday Times*, Ian's position as Lord Kemsley's strategic planner was passing to Denis Hamilton, a dynamic Normandy veteran who was appointed group editorial director in 1950. Ian was happy to forgo this responsibility and act more as a general impresario. As he told Robert Harling, every great organization needs a lightning conductor on its staff. His demeanour emphasized his "minister without portfolio" status. While everyone else at the regular Tuesday morning editorial meetings followed Lord Kemsley's lead and wore stiff collars and subfusc suits, Ian was his own man in a personal uniform of a dark blue suit, short-sleeved blue shirt, and, more often than not, black polka dot bow-tie. (In a later interview, a journalist noted that his bow was knotted "loosely". When Ian vetted the text, one of his few requests was to change this adverb to "with Churchillian looseness".)

With this sartorial informality came a talent for humouring Lord Kemsley. Ian was the only person to call the chairman "Gomer" in the office – or his wife "Edith" outside. His ability to fly in the face of Kemsley convention earned him respect in the corridors of 200 Gray's Inn Road. He was clearly a man with influence with the proprietor. But the other side of his showmanship was an arrogance and aloofness which meant that he was not universally popular. Ian never accompanied his colleagues to the pub: at lunch-time he stalked out of the building on his own – en route for lunch with a male friend at Boodle's or Scott's. "It seemed that he belonged with the bosses," confirmed Dilys Powell, the *Sunday Times*'s film critic.

Ian's increasingly generalist role meant that, at one moment (in April 1948) he might represent his employer at a United Nations conference on Freedom of Information in his old stamping ground of Geneva; at another, a few months later, he wheeled into action and hired a family friend to oversee the group's features. This was a typical Fleming coup. Philip Brownrigg was a 36-year-old Old Etonian journalist who lived near Peter Fleming's estate at Nettlebed. Both he and Peter commanded local territorial regiments. But one day, Peter being indisposed, Brownrigg found himself playing golf with his younger brother at Huntercombe, Granny Katie's old stamping ground. Before they had finished a round, Ian asked him if he would be interested in joining Kemsley Newspapers. Brownrigg, whose career was stalled, jumped at the offer. He became the Kemsley group's features editor, reporting to Ian, and later, briefly, editor of the *Sunday Graphic*.

At Kemsley House, Brownrigg was able to observe his boss at work. He appreciated the way Ian shielded his subordinates from the wrath of other senior executives. He saw how Ian developed the hitherto neglected area of features. "Ian really changed the whole way of eating in this country," claimed Brownrigg, with some hyperbole. The main evidence was that Ian, with his appetite for American magazines, picked up on the quirky food columns of Gaylord Hauser, and insisted that Brownrigg introduce him to the readers of the *Sunday Graphic*. Hauser proved successful with a British public beginning to come off rationing. Ian also pushed for a strip cartoon featuring a leading astrologer, known as Lindo. He had a curious respect for the occult: when, just before the Festival of Britain in May 1951, Lindo saw the King's lifeline fading, Ian took the trouble of calling the police to warn them of possible physical danger.

As a general 'contact man' on the paper, Ian enjoyed considerable influence in the publishing world. Usually, as an accomplished networker, he tried to accommodate the suggestions of friends. But he was no push-over. The humorist Stephen Potter might have expected a friendly response. Like Brownrigg, his family lived near the Flemings in Berkshire, he had worked with Joyce Grenfell, and he played golf at Huntercombe. But when, after leaving Cape, Rupert Hart-Davis set up his own publishing house, Ian was unimpressed by his friend's first book, Potter's *Gamesmanship*, later a classic. "Who is this Potter?" he asked sniffily. "He's just a jumped-up journalist." Nevertheless he felt duty-bound to ask Leonard Russell, the literary editor of the *Sunday Times*, if he could review it. Russell's reply indicated the tone in which Ian must have approached him: "Here is Stephen Potter's *Gamesmanship*: a very good idea but somehow, as you said the other day, one grows a bit weary of it. 350 words by 29 October?"

Similarly, when, in May 1949, Jonathan Cape sent him a copy of *Eastern Approaches* by Fitzroy Maclean, hoping he would recommend it for serialization, Ian proved difficult to please. He disliked Maclean's "patronizing" tone and thought that the author had claimed too much personal credit for his wartime exploits. The book was not in "the tradition of such books by Englishmen", Ian told Cape portentously. He hoped the publisher – and perhaps even Maclean – would be satisfied if he arranged for the book to be reviewed by his brother, which was a generous gesture since Peter had suggested it to Cape in the first place.

When Ian was not liaising with publishers, he dabbled in their trade himself. Kemsley owned the Dropmore Press, a small imprint named after his new house near Taplow in Buckinghamshire. He made Ian a director and tried to involve him in commissioning a series of limited editions, including *Translations and Verses*, a small volume by Duff Cooper, in 1949, and *The London Bookbinders 1780–1806* by Ellic Howe, one of Sefton

Delmer's wartime black propagandists, in 1950. As a book collector, Ian had good contacts in the trade and enjoyed looking for promising material. Under its original name, the Corvinus Press, Dropmore had published a short run of T. E. Lawrence's diary of his period in northern Syria in 1911. When it wanted to do a further edition of 1000 copies, Ian sought permission from Lawrence's copyright holder, Jonathan Cape. Attached to the Dropmore Press, and printed by it, Kemsley owned the *Book Handbook*, an occasional publication for bibliophiles, which he bought for £250 from its founder, Reginald Horrox, the resident book expert at Sotheby's. Again Ian played a peripheral role, requesting the odd article from friends like Percy Muir and the scholarly John Hayward. But, despite Ian's efforts to convince him of the kudos which might accrue to his name, Kemsley never took the Dropmore Press seriously. Instead, he virtually bankrupted it by insisting it published an elaborate and unsaleable edition of *King George V Stamp Book*.

Despite his literary endeavours, Ian retained overall responsibility for the Kemsley group's foreign coverage. But no witty exchange of letters with publishers could disguise the fact that Ian's beloved Mercury, his *raison d'être* at Kemsley House, was not functioning as well as it should. The bald figures seemed to suggest a successful enough operation. From 2.5 million words in Kemsley newspapers in 1946, Mercury's contribution grew to 4 million words three years later. But little of this gross wordage actually appeared in the *Sunday Times*. Most foreign reports were passed on to Kemsley's provincial newspapers, which snapped up items like Donald McCormick's report on the activities of the 2nd Battalion of the Cheshire Regiment in Tripoli, Libya, which was used as a spread in the *Macclesfield Times*.

Ian was well aware of the situation. In a bitter letter of complaint to his chairman in the summer of 1949, he vented his disappointment about the way the group as a whole was functioning. The Foreign Department, he admitted, "hardly ever gets a request from an editor and is so out of touch with our papers that it scarcely ever receives praise or blame and works, so to speak, in a vacuum". More generally, he complained that, when he joined the group, Kemsley had promised to improve the calibre of his recruits to journalism. But four years later Ian saw no sign of this. Despite initiatives like the Kemsley Empire Journalists' Scheme, which brought promising young reporters from Commonwealth countries to Gray's Inn Road, Ian felt at least half the paper was "not pulling" and sales were clearly lagging. As a result, he confessed, "this summer I feel stale and disheartened".

Still the brickbats rained in on Mercury. Ian's intelligence service was proving a "fantastically expensive toy", it was said. The clamour against it increased after the devaluation of the pound in the autumn of 1949. An internal Kemsley committee attacked Ian personally for maintaining too large an administrative staff in London and for appearing to duplicate the news agencies with too many wire-type stories.

In a letter to Kemsley correspondent Antony Terry, who had moved from Vienna to Berlin, Ian admitted in June 1950 that "the economics of Mercury are causing grave concern to the Chairman". Ian's unorthodox solution was to hire Iain Lang, the editor of the *Sunday Graphic*, as his deputy, with special responsibility for improving the quality of foreign coverage. But this caused additional problems in the office, because Lang was a tough no-nonsense Scot who disapproved of Ian's cavalier approach to his job. As even the official history of the *Sunday Times* saw fit to note, Ian's idea of foreign news came from the pages of *Life* or *Paris Match*, not the *New York Times* or *Le Monde*.

The object of the exercise was to allow Ian to concentrate on running the service more efficiently. Post-war Germany may have emerged as a particularly important news centre, but it was also Mercury's most expensive bureau. So Ian approached Sir Ivone Kirkpatrick, the Assistant Under-Secretary at the Foreign Office, with a proposal to allow accredited newspapermen there to use the diplomatic mark, which enjoyed a favourable exchange rate. Paradoxically, given the need to save money, Ian also worked hard to obtain a visa for a permanent *Sunday Times* correspondent in the Soviet Union. Eventually after four years of effort (his visit to the "Freedom of Information" conference in Geneva in April 1948 was part of the lobbying process), he was successful. On 12 November 1950, in one of his irregular forays into print, Ian proudly announced that the *Sunday Times* had become the only newspaper in the British Commonwealth with a Moscow correspondent. The journalist appointed to this difficult position at the height of the Cold War was Cyril Ray, later better known as a wine writer and connoisseur. Ian was unperturbed that this prestige posting was to cost £12,000 a year, even more than the Berlin bureau. Strangely, while Antony Terry's wife, Rachel, found Ian friendly and supportive, Ray's spouse, Elizabeth, experienced the opposite. When Ian invited the Rays to lunch, she was struck by his cruelty. "It was extraordinary. I've only ever taken an instant dislike to two people in my life, and Ian Fleming was one of them."

Ian was performing true to type: if he wanted something out of a relationship – if he needed to impress a newspaper proprietor or entice a pretty girl to bed – he could be utterly charming. But if he saw no mileage in a transaction, no return for himself, he was often cold and rude. His correspondents were lucky not to experience this latter side of him. As in NID, he kept up his regular communications, encouraging them to feel part of a team. It was often a fairly cynical act. As Ian told Robert Harling, "The greatest way of building up friends is sending letters and making occasional phone calls." According to Harling, Kemsley had once wanted to make Ian foreign editor. But Ian did not want the responsibility. "As foreign editor I'd be expected to write a regular think piece," he told his friend. "As foreign manager I can always call my secretary and tell her to send a letter of condolence to a wife. It's amazing what a reputation for care and welfare you can build up by telling someone else to do it."

Outside Kemsley House, Ian needed plenty of dilettante projects to amuse him, which, in his case, more than most people, meant keeping him and his overweening ego from getting bored. When Harling started *Alphabet and Image* (or, as Ian called it with typical verbal dexterity, "Frottage and Allage"), a quarterly magazine devoted to typography and design, Ian set its first competition in September 1947. He asked readers to devise a 27th letter for the alphabet. He promised to study the entries, which had to be in by November, and to award a prize of five guineas to the winner. But when judgement day arrived, Ian was nowhere to be found. He had absconded to Jamaica with Ann Rothermere. So the competition had to be held open until the following issue. In the meantime it was mentioned by the journalist MP Tom Driberg in a column in *Reynold's News*. This plug attracted several more entries, until the winner was finally announced – the inventor of a new representation of the "th" sound, or the Greek letter, theta.

Three years later, in August 1950, Ian ran into rather different problems when he tried to set a competition in the *Spectator*. This time he was swanking about his literary knowledge. Quoting two verses of a poem by Alfred de Musset:

> La vie est brève
> Un peu d'amour
> un peu de rêve
> et puis, Bonjour.
>
> La vie est vaine,
> Un peu d'espoir
> Un peu d'haine
> et puis, Bonsoir

he asked for a third verse on the subject of death and ending "Et puis, Bonne nuit." Only later did he remember that the accepted French pronunciation of his putative last line required five syllables (the "e" at the end of "bonne" is aspirated). He was forced to cancel the competition, but not before he had admonished one unfortunate reader for rhyming "tasse" with "extase" and related another self-promotional story about how the second verse of de Musset's little poem had been added to the minutes of the first meeting of the First General Assembly of the League of Nations at the printer's. (A curious sequel was that Evelyn Waugh later intended to use the phrase "A Little Hope" as the title for the second unpublished volume of his autobiography. But he could not remember where it came from until Ann recalled that Ian had used it in this competition.)

Similar lack of success surrounded another more unusual extracurricular exercise. Ann's cousin, Martin Charteris, was private secretary to King George VI's daughter, Princess Elizabeth, at Clarence House. When the young Princess was due to visit the United States in October 1951, Charteris, knowing that Ian was familiar with the workings of the American press, asked him to write a speech for her. Ian proudly reproduced what he thought were the appropriately solemn regal tones. He wanted the Princess, in talking to American journalists, to tackle the issue of responsibility in the age of mass communications. "We have faith," Ian's text ran, "that, in your profession, it will never be a greater sin to be slow than wrong, for if the Truth should ever come second to efficiency, then the great Trust you hold for us will have been broken." He added a note for Ann's cousin that he felt it was important for a member of the royal family, speaking in public, to leave "a grain of one of the verities" in listeners' minds. He had chosen his form of words because they were "eminently quotable" and would "touch the tiny soul of the journalist, who knows that the battle between speed and truth is the one he shirks every day of his life". Charteris was unimpressed with Ian's line, however. He felt the Princess's words needed to be addressed more directly to the American people rather than to the media. So he politely thanked Ian for his assistance, and Ian lost an opportunity for royal preferment.

Although Martin Charteris was willing to promote him, Ian was not generally popular with Ann's family. Her brother, Hugo, never hid his dislike of what he had identified as Ian's crude mixture of nihilism and opportunism. Several years later, he vented his spleen in a novel called *The Explorers* which provided a hostile if unmistakable portrait of Ian and Ann at this difficult stage in their relationship. The book was never published because Ann objected to its vituperative tone. At the time he wrote it, Hugo had recently returned from a trip to Africa, feeling particularly aggrieved because he thought, wrongly, that Ian had stolen his idea about illicit diamond-buying in West Africa to form the basis of his non-fiction book, *The Diamond Smugglers*, published in 1957.

The plot of *The Explorers* (originally titled *My Will Be Done*) hinged on the unlikely story of an expedition by a group of magazine journalists to report on an elaborate animist ceremony in the heart of Africa. As a

follower of the Swiss psychologist Carl Jung and a passionate advocate of
the spiritual dimension in life, Hugo was interested in the dynamics of a
clash between Western rationalism and African shamanism. His fictional
magazine, *Yours*, is owned by a media tycoon called George Graham. It is
common knowledge that Graham's business affairs are controlled by his
wife, Cynthia, known as the Bossess, whose lover, Ludovic Nutting, a
former army colonel, is director of a company called Euroflick Films.

In Hugo's novel Cynthia accompanied the *Yours* expedition to Africa,
together with her lover and others. This foreign odyssey provided the
backdrop for an examination of her turbulent relationship with "Ludo"
and the eventual breakdown of her marriage. The parallels with the lives
of Ann, Esmond and Ian are inescapable. And so is the author's antipathy
towards Ludo.

In London, before the journey, Ludo (or Ian) is presented as an insecure
and egocentric social climber, wavering between sadism and masochism.
"There was no limit, no limit at all, to his capacity for feeling inferior. So
you had to handle him like a bomb. In the past he had been attracted to
her atmosphere of caste as he had been by Bentleys. On another level she
had seemed the most delectable and legitimate candidate for destruction.
With tongue and hand he gave her pain – and her dark eyes went softer
still, and dumb – asking for more, morbid more; sometimes she provoked
more. He had been her first, last and only physical love affair, spanning
three husbands; always in the background."

The Explorers highlights the furious rows which permeated Ludo and
Cynthia's relationship. On one occasion, Ludo tells Cynthia (or Ann) that
he loathes her. The reason, she suggests, is "because I'm the only one of
your many mistresses who has even *ruffled* your love affair with yourself".
The correspondences between the fictional and the real are extraordinary.
Cynthia, "dark and pretty in a sharp hard way", flaunts her lover, and her
husband is initially forbearing. But when George Graham tires of being
cuckolded, he hires a private detective to spy on his wife. He orders her to
abandon Ludo and accompany him to New York. When that tactic fails,
he relents and offers her £100,000 as a divorce settlement. The lovers have
often discussed marriage and Ludo appears ready to take the plunge.
Echoing one of Ian's favourite catch-phrases, Ludo used to reply, "Barkis
is willing." But when, secure in the knowledge of her alimony, Cynthia
propositions him outright, "If I leave George tomorrow, will you marry
me?" he demurs. To lighten the moment she preserves, "Is Barkis still
willing?" In the face of his silence, "her short, uneasy laugh dies flat".

When Cynthia and Ludo go to Africa, they are accompanied by a pretty
young reporter, Lady Caroline Clifford, for whom Cynthia had secured a
job on the magazine, and John Nelson, a sensitive photographer – surely
an alter ego of the author – who weeps at the sound of Handel and is the

opposite of the strutting Ludo. In the bush Ludo strikes a ludicrous figure, in blue 'yachting' jacket and Brigade of Guards buttons. "The dyspeptic and choleric impression which even in his good moods could so easily be given by the one eye whose lower lid hung out slack and red like a bloodhound's and by his sulky mouth now melted into his extremely formal yet personal smile." The Africans, "whose sense of the ridiculous is poetic and immediate", name Ludo the Red Banana – "on account of his height, forward curve, nervous face and because of a conspicuously phallic atmosphere which emanated from his person".

In novelistic fashion, the lushness and unpredictability of Africa plays havoc with the travellers' consciousness – all except Ludo's. His "manner kept everything light, light as nothing – so he could retreat from anywhere that became untenable". Indeed, after two days of discomfort, he decides to return to the capital. But not before Cynthia, in a haze of brandy and aspirins, realizes that "she was at the mercy of one whose secret lack of mercy had been his chief attraction".

Now, with a new decade bearing down on him and with his real-life relationship with Ann still unresolved, Ian decided to move house again. Perhaps the prospect of some closer liaison with Ann had encouraged him to look for somewhere larger. With Hugo Pitman's help, he found a flat in Carlyle Mansions, a solid Victorian block overlooking the River Thames in Cheyne Walk, half a mile from his mother's former house. John Hayward, the lugubrious bibliophile with whom he was associated on the *Book Handbook*, lived two floors below in a curious ménage with T. S. Eliot. Ian took a five-year lease at £410 a year, a sum he considered cheap. He told his mother that he was looking forward to getting plenty of air and sunshine and not having "all the chauffeurs whistling me awake at 7 o'clock in the morning".

Eve was now living in tax exile in Cannes from where, in June 1950, she offered to help her son with the expenses of his move. Ian was pathetically grateful for her offer (and later asked for a further £1000). He said that, otherwise, he would have had to sell some of his "very meagre" portfolio of stocks and shares. Soon, with the help of Lisl Popper and visits to Peter Jones, he had once again recreated the distinctive Fleming décor – part gentleman's club, part ship's cabin. The old photographs of Ian at Eton, the hero of the school sports, went up in the drawing-room, and his pretty Austrian housekeeper agreed to accompany him to his new flat. Robert Harling, knowing Ian's innocent craving for roots, chipped in playfully with an enormous coat of arms which Ian placed at the end of a corridor with a spotlight trained on it. The rest of his family rallied round with offers of furniture (his brother Richard, who had just returned from a visit to Goldeneye, provided a useful corner table and covered stool) and recommendations of reliable tradesmen (the three Flemings in the bank had recently refurbished a town house in Hyde Park Square, where they each took a separate floor and ate communally. Ian employed one of the builders who had worked on the dormitory, as he called it).

Ian's feet hardly touched the ground that summer. For someone basically lazy and not blooming with health, he could set himself a punishing schedule at times. Every July he undertook two weeks' naval training which enabled him to retain his rank as a commander in the Royal Naval Volunteer Reserve. This year the venue was Scotland where his two weeks were spent in a submarine off Invergordon. He returned to London to move into his new flat at the beginning of August, and then went back to Scotland to join the rest of the Flemings at Black Mount. This proved no more enjoyable than in previous years. After an unproductive time as one of six guns on the 'Glorious Twelfth', his Uncle Phil asked him if, the following day, he would prefer to go out fishing or shooting again. Ian replied that he would rather catch no salmon than shoot no grouse, his best-remembered *obiter dictum* within the bosom of a famously sporting family. Ian was proud of it himself: he caused it to be published in the *Sunday Times* Atticus column, under the headline 'The Pessimist', and with himself described as "a distinguished Londoner of my acquaintance".

From Scotland he travelled to North America where Ivar Bryce had recently married for the third time. He had met his bride Marie-Josephine ('Jo') Hartford, a *jolie laide* American blonde, on the *Queen Elizabeth*. The fact that she was the granddaughter of George Huntingdon Hartford, founder of the A&P supermarket chain (originally the Great Atlantic and Pacific Food Company) in the United States, only made her doubly attractive to Ivar, who had an unfailing eye for well-heeled women. (Seeing him on the *Queen Elizabeth*, and primed no doubt by Ann, Lord Beaverbrook managed to stimulate his granddaughter Lady Jeanne Campbell's curiosity by pointing at Ivar and saying, "There's the wickedest man in Europe.") Within months, Ivar and Jo were married at the Tommy Leiters' house in Acorn, South Carolina. Part of Jo's wealth included properties in Manhattan, Vermont and the Bahamas. That August Ian paid the first of many visits to Black Hole Hollow Farm, her cherished pre-Revolution retreat, in the foothills of the Green Mountains, on the borders of Vermont and New York. Ivar maintained the fond illusion that the farm, set beside a river in five hundred acres of forest and rolling hills, "answered some atavistic call" in Ian's Scots soul. While there was a grain of truth in this, Ian fell for Jo's Vermont bolt-hole because it was everything that the Flemings' spartan retreat at Black Mount was not. It gave Ian a comfortable New England version of country living, mixing a certain formality (everyone dressed for dinner), with Jo's love of luxury and Ivar's sense of fun. As an added bonus, there were always plenty of pretty young girls, including Jo's lively secretary-companion, Sarah Boissevain, to whom Ian was particularly attracted.

Black Hole Hollow Farm was all the more interesting because Ian's wartime friend Ernie Cuneo had a summer house a mile and a quarter away at Cambridge just inside New York State. Often Ian would call on Ernie when he took a pre-breakfast stroll. "I thought you might like to walk to the top of Goose Egg," he would nonchalantly announce. Ernie could think of nothing worse than climbing the hill which rose steeply from the fields at the bottom of his garden. But he could not help being carried away by Ian's boyish enthusiasm. Ian yomped ahead like a paratrooper breasting the heights of Mount Stanley. Every so often he stopped and pointed out a fine view of the road or of some local beauty spot. Several points in the hills now have names first given to them by Ian. For example, Bumble Bee Peak is the resting-place where Ian used to stop and point out the best view of Spruce Peak, the highest of the Green Mountains. Ian returned to these favourite hills several times in his novels. Echo Park, the venue for the action in the title story of his collection *For Your Eyes Only*, is based on Black Hole Hollow Farm. "Now he could see everything – the endless vista of the Green Mountains stretching in every direction as far as he could see, away to the east the golden ball of the sun just coming up in glory, and below, two thousand feet down a long easy slope of treetops broken once by a wide band of meadow, through a thin veil of mist, the lake, the lawns and the house." And Ian returned to the area again, less successfully, in *The Spy Who Loved Me*.

Having reached the top of Goose Egg, Ian asked Ernie if he realized that it took more effort to go down a mountain than to climb it – the theory being that one's muscles had to fight the force of gravity. Ernie replied that this was rubbish: in New England one threw oneself down the mountain, braking one's speed by grabbing a pine bough as one hurtled by. Ian could not wait to start. "We came down the mountain like two whirling dervishes," recalled Cuneo. "Sweated and happy, we pulled up on the upper field, laughing like mad." Suddenly Ian affected seriousness. "Let me tell you, Ernie, I was worried," he said. And when his friend enquired why, he replied, "About how the hell I'd ever get a mule like you down the mountain if you had broken a leg." After a plunge in an icy pond, Ian then walked back to the Bryces for scrambled eggs and coffee.

From now on, Ian returned to Vermont nearly every summer, a conscious act of escape which, as with most things connected with Ivar, Ann quickly perceived as a threat. During the holidays, she took her children to Shane's Castle, where she was surprised to receive a call from Ian at Black Hole Hollow Farm telling her that he had been bitten by a snake. Ian's voice upset Ann because, despite his mishap, she could tell he was enjoying himself "surrounded with golden orioles and sunshine". To Hugo she confided that his holiday certainly sounded "gayer than mine".

Encouraged by her sons' tales of the Caribbean, Eve was also on the move. Her sons were in the plural because a couple of years earlier Peter had visited Barbados, from which he returned with good reports. Eve now talked of setting up home in Barbados, but after Ian took soundings from friends, including Jo Bryce, she agreed that the Bahamas might be preferable for someone of her age. When Ian next travelled to Jamaica in January 1951, he passed through Nassau, the capital of the Bahamas, where Eve was already ensconced in Emerald Wave, her new house on Cable Beach. She had startled her son by asking him to bring ammunition for her Browning automatic pistol. The gun had been inspected by the local CID, she said, but as her only cartridges dated back to 1914, she had been told she should have more. "The thing is to let the blacks know that I have a pistol," she added. More alarmingly, Eve revealed that she had formed an attachment to the Marquess of Winchester, a fellow expatriate in Nassau. No matter that he was nearly twenty years older than she, or that he had left England following a financial scandal in 1929. With the prospect of ending her days as Britain's premier marchioness firmly in mind, Eve became engaged to the old aristocrat and was set to marry him.

At Goldeneye, Ian was joined by Ann and later, to her displeasure, by the Bryces. In early February the newlyweds from Vermont embarked on a belated honeymoon – a cruise in the Caribbean, accompanied by their friends the Leiters, along with Jo's daughter Nuala and her husband, Claiborne Pell, a State Department official who later became the Democratic Senator for Rhode Island. Setting off from Miami, their only pre-arranged destination was Oracabessa, where they intended to dock at the United Fruit Company terminal and spend some time with Ian.

Having reached the north coast of Jamaica, the Bryces disembarked to take a short drive before dining with Ian and Ann at Goldeneye. Suddenly a tropical storm blew up. With the captain of their yacht, the *Vagrant*, also ashore (on a date with Jo Bryce's maid) the crew got their hands on the liquor store. As a result they were in no fit state to prevent the ship slipping its anchor and smashing against the reef. The Leiters and the Pells, who remained on board, were hurled around their cabins. The crew belatedly tried to launch a motor boat but that got stuck on the reef. Eventually the passengers were rowed to safety in a small boat manned by a brave and enterprising young Jamaican. Assisted by the Bryces who had returned from shopping in Ocho Rios, they made their way to Goldeneye where Ann showed little sympathy for their bedraggled state. "Don't bleed on the floor," she barked brusquely at Pell, whose forehead was badly gashed. In a letter to Lady Diana Cooper she painted a ghoulishly amusing picture of "four of the USA's richest citizens [falling] into the room snow white and dripping water, they had the black marks of lifejackets round their necks and purple bruises from diamonds crushed between skin and jacket". Ann reported that Noël Coward, a guest at dinner, and Ian helped rescue the crew, though Nuala Pell remembered it differently. She said that Ian was "conspicuous by his absence" from any of the rescue operations. "He was not exactly James Bond." (Ian was smarting from the fact that he had declined an invitation to dine with Lord Beaverbrook that very evening. The press lord had asked him to bring Ann and Noël Coward, but Ian cabled back grandly, "ALAS WE ALL INVOLVED IN BANQUET I'M GIVING TO VISITING YACHT STOP.") Coward enjoyed an unexpected bonus, however. He took the prettiest sailors to a nearby hotel for recuperation. The following day he and Ian sauntered down to the wreck to see what they could find. Noël found a small piano which worked, and Ian was content with what was left of the ship's supply of gin.

Problems of a different kind occurred with the appearance of Rosamond Lehmann. One of Edith Sitwell's literary circle, she had been visiting Jamaica since the 1930s and had stayed at Goldeneye before. This time, however, she had just finished a nine-year-long romance with the poet Cecil Day-Lewis and was feeling sorry for herself. Seeing an opportunity for a sexual conquest, Ian invited her to Goldeneye where he told her gallantly that she could sit and write poetry at his desk. It was a classic case of crossed signals. According to Noël Coward, she arrived on the island consumed with a grand passion for Ian, who she was positive would soon take the place of Day-Lewis in her life. Ian only wanted to go to bed with "one of the most beautiful women of her generation", as she was described by Stephen Spender. Somehow he seemed to think that Rosamond would come when he was alone in the house. But she arrived on his doorstep when Ann was still there, which created all manner of complications. Resorting to low tricks to hasten Rosamond's departure, he threw a live squid into her room, telling her that this was lunch. She calmly insisted that he put it back in the sea, while he mouthed platitudes about the ineffectualness of her pseudo-liberalism in the face of the cruelty of nature.

In a panic the next day, Ian rushed along the coast to Blue Harbour where he implored Coward to help him by taking Rosamond off his hands. Coward said he would do so at a price. When he went to collect her, he pointed to Ian's new camera, which he said he would like. Ian readily agreed. And when Coward added, "And I think I'll need the tripod as well," Ian did not demur. Later, Coward took him to task: "You, my dear, are just an old cunt-teaser." As Peter Quennell noted, Noël "treated Ian as he might have treated a difficult social beauty or a wayward prima donna, and often criticized the extremely unfeeling use to which he put his great attractions". Quennell, who observed this intriguing relationship closely, added that Noël's attitude to "Ian's dark moods and passionate prejudices was always subtly understanding. He humoured, scolded, occasionally derided, yet somehow never did the smallest damage to Ian's *amour propre*." By the same token, Ian was one of the few people who could confidently talk back to Noël. In one memorable exchange, Ian told Coward, "Don't be a silly old bugger", to which Noël replied, "We don't talk shop here, dear boy." Two paintings owned by Raymond O'Neill are testament to the two men's friendship. Both show the same Goldeneye beach scene: one, by Coward, is lush and colourful; the other, scratchy and childlike, is perhaps the only surviving picture by Ian.

Back in London, Ian reluctantly resigned his RNVR commission during the summer, realizing that he no longer had the time for the required two weeks' annual training. As an alternative, he lobbied for a NID-run course which would prepare naval intelligence officers for future hostilities. When this failed to meet with Admiralty approval, he pleaded with his former NID colleague Captain Vladimir Wolfson, "As foreign manager of the *Sunday Times* and Kemsley Newspapers, I am engaged throughout the year in running a world-wide intelligence organization and there could be no better training for the duties I would have to carry out for the DNI in the event of war." And he added portentously, "As you know, I also carry out a number of tasks on behalf of a department of the Foreign Office and this department would, I believe, be happy to give details of these activities to the DNI." This department provided him with "rigorous intelligence training" but not naval training as required by the RNVR. "Department of the Foreign Office" in this context could only have been a euphemism for the SIS, and Ian was referring obliquely to his connivance at the use of *Sunday Times* correspondents for spying purposes.

He had reason to stress this point because Richard Hughes, the *Sunday Times*'s correspondent in the Far East, had recently been approached to work for the Russian secret service. Hughes, a hard-drinking Australian who did not appear to fit the identikit profile of a KGB agent, made his name reporting the Korean War. He reported this approach to Ian as his boss. Ian consulted the SIS and wrote back to Hughes in the jocular pseudo-spymaster's tone he had perfected in Room 39 a decade earlier: "Demand that they double whatever pay they offer you. They will be impressed by this professional, if avaricious, approach and it will establish your bona fides." Ian arranged that the SIS man in Bangkok should provide Hughes with false information to feed to Russian diplomats and military advisers in Tokyo. Hughes never made anything out of it: his earnings as a double agent were all channelled back to fill the SIS's coffers in Britain.

Ian's main contact at SIS was now Nicholas Elliott, a sociable Old Etonian who used to hold regular dinners at White's for a few selected people to meet the SIS chief, Sir Stewart Menzies. Elliott recalled Ian attending one such gathering in 1951 – possibly the occasion Ian mentioned in a letter to William Stephenson in October 1951 when he said he had just dined with Menzies, who had revealed his intention to retire before long. "Charmingly indiscreet as ever", the spy chief had suggested he would be "succeeded by his deputy – Sinbad", as Sir John Sinclair, a former Royal Navy officer, was known. Ian added that Menzies "told me that his own choice would have been his Number 3, Jack E. [Jack Easton] Personally, I don't think either will set the Thames on fire, but E. has certainly got a better brain than Sinbad and is tougher."

Ian used to call these regular communications with Stephenson his "crystal-gazers" – part insider gossip about intelligence, part speculation about politics, the stock market and the world. They confirmed Ian's continuing contacts with the security services, while leaving no doubt about the *naïveté* of his political thinking, a sort of proto-Thatcherite or anarcho-Tory populism. With a general election looming in October 1951, Ian amused Stephenson with a lightweight commentary on what might happen after the polls. He hoped that "Winston" would put the accent on youth, but was afraid "we are bound to get Anthony Eden at the Foreign Office". The key remained the unions, Ian felt, and there were promising "signs that they are prepared to put the country first". Stephenson replied laconically that it did not matter which party was elected: Britain's economic position was worse than it appeared and the future would be difficult whatever happened. As compensation, he offered Ian one of his periodic share tips. "Years ago I talked with you about Brazilian Traction, Light and Power Co. Have another look at it. They are shortly going to split the stock." Stephenson advised that this stock had vast potential in an area larger than the United States, and stood to gain "from large expenditures on rearmament by other western countries".

After Churchill's narrow election victory, Ian gave Stephenson the latest news. He did not think the result would affect Menzies' decision to retire. But Sinclair's tenure in office was likely to be short-lived because he was not well. Showing all his old facility for flattery, Ian added, "It is being freely said that the former Lord of the Manor of Reading, Jamaica [i.e., Stephenson himself] should not be far away." Curiously, Ian did not mention the intelligence-related matter which obsessed the chattering classes of the time – the disappearance in May of two senior Foreign Office officials, Guy Burgess and Donald Maclean, who were suspected of being communist spies. When Ian and Ann had entertained Cyril Connolly and Noël Coward in September, they had spoken of little else. How could such pillars of the Establishment have nurtured an ideological commitment for Marxism? It was a betrayal which cut to the quick of the post-war political consensus. As for the recent election, it seemed small beer. The new government was full of "round pegs in square holes", Ian reported. The

Conservative Party's problem, he suggested, was that it was inextricably connected with the rich. It would fare much better if it changed its name to the People's Party as soon as possible.

Ian's view may have been coloured by the traditional election-night party at the Rothermeres. It was a notably raucous occasion, with Ann – to Harold Nicolson's dismay – leading the triumphalist cheering every time a Conservative was returned to Parliament. It was also the last big social event she held at Warwick House. For that same month, after more than six years of stressful marriage, Esmond and Ann finally agreed to divorce. As Ann put it, "I knew I must desert not a marriage but a job and seek humanity." She had few illusions about the support she had given her husband in her "job". After taking advice, she asked for £100,000 by way of a financial settlement. Esmond told his friend Ali Forbes lugubriously he thought that was "the going rate".

The immediate upshot was that Ian and Ann were free to marry if they wanted. Her pay-off would provide a useful financial platform; indeed they would live off the capital for the best part of a decade. But even at this stage it was not as clear-cut as that. Initially she told very few people. Her son and daughter only learned what was happening when the three of them were travelling back to London by train after spending Christmas at Shane's Castle. Somewhat apprehensively, Raymond tapped the tips of his fingers together and said, "Do you think that's a wise move?" But Fionn was delighted because it meant her mother would marry Ian: Esmond had been a "bland figure downstairs who we seldom saw", while she had been devoted to Ian since the age of four.

Ann did not tell her children anything about being pregnant. But when Ian informed his sister Amaryllis that he had finally made up his mind to marry his lover, and she answered, "How ghastly! How could you?", he said quietly, "It's no use making a fuss. She's going to have a baby." Amaryllis, who disliked Ann intensely, let fly at Ian, who was nearly twenty years older, "I thought the Flemings had enough guts not to let that sort of thing influence them." And she was not the only person who felt this way: Hugo Pitman also expressed horror at Ian's decision. He did not feel that Ian was the marrying type.

The important question is what motivated Ian. The relevant date to bear in mind is 12 August the following year, when Ann gave birth to their son, Caspar. This confirms that she must have realized she was pregnant before travelling to Jamaica with Ian in mid-January 1952. But she cannot have known much before, and certainly not at the time when she decided to leave Esmond. So what happened in between? Did Ian prevaricate, and did she become pregnant in order to ensnare him? Several people believe so, suggesting that once Ian knew she was carrying his child, he understood he had been presented with a *fait accompli*. However much of a cad Hugo

Charteris and others might consider him, not even Ian could deny a woman who had suffered so much from the death of their daughter her wish for another child. At the same time, Ian had a very conventional side and, as Ann certainly knew, he could be relied on to "do the right thing", albeit reluctantly.

By the time they both reached Goldeneye they had definitely decided to marry, and as soon as possible, in Jamaica. Given her previous medical history, once she was at Goldeneye, Ann nursed her pregnancy carefully, sitting under a large straw hat in the sunken garden and painting fish and flowers, while Ian did his best to take his new circumstances in good humour, joking, perhaps a trifle grimly, that he was looking forward to dining every night with Lucian Freud and the rest of Ann's cronies. In the isolation of Jamaica, Ian was touched when Hugo and his wife Virginia sent a letter of support. He wrote back saying he looked forward to having them to stay in Carlyle Mansions. Although the day-to-day domesticity of marriage still attracted him, he had few illusions about the problems which lay ahead. "We are of course totally unsuited – both Gemini," he told Hugo and Virginia. "I'm a non-communicator, a symmetrist, of a bilious and melancholic temperament, only interested in tomorrow. Ann is a sanguine anarchist/traditionalist. So china will fly and there will be rage and tears. But I think we will survive as there is no bitterness in either of us and we are both optimists – and I shall never hurt her except with a slipper."

Arriving in Jamaica on 16 February, Noël Coward went round that same evening to dine with the betrothed couple. As usual, they had an uproarious time, complete with several rounds of canasta. But, Coward noted in his diary, he "sensed that Annie was not entirely happy". This may have been because, as she informed Cecil Beaton, she was beginning to find the Master overbearing – or, as she put it, "the deserts of pomposity between the oases of wit are too vast". Nevertheless Noël rose to the occasion to compose an uplifting prenuptial ditty, which first set the scene:

> The quivering days of waiting
> Of wondering and suspense
> Without regret
> Can at last be set
> In the Past Imperfect tense.

and then went on to offer some friendly advice:

> Don't Ian, if Annie should cook you
> A dish that you haven't enjoyed

> Use that as excuse
> For a storm of abuse
> At Cecil and Lucian Freud.
>
> Don't Ian, when friends are arriving
> By aeroplane motor and train
> Retire to bed
> With a cold in the head
> And that famous redundant "migraine".

In a diary fragment around this time, Ann noted, "This morning Ian started to type a book. Very good thing." Ian had finally decided to launch into the novel which had been rattling around in his head for so long. He was not a man to tackle such projects half-heartedly. Every morning after a swim on the reef, he breakfasted with Ann in the garden. When he had finished his scrambled eggs and Blue Mountain coffee, he kissed her and made his way across the small veranda into the main living-room. He shut the big doors, closed the jalousies, and opened his big roll-top desk. For three hours he pounded the keys of his twenty-year-old Imperial portable typewriter. At noon he emerged from the cool of his retreat and stood blinking in the heat of the day. After lunch he slept for an hour or so, and then, around five, he returned to his desk to look over what he had typed earlier in the day. When he had made his corrections he placed his manuscript in the bottom left-hand drawer of his desk. Ian was a man of routine, and that writing regime, now established, continued for the next dozen years, whenever he was at Goldeneye.

Later, when Ian was trying to encourage Ivar Bryce to write his memoirs, he warned his friend about the necessary drudgery of the process. "You will be constantly depressed by the progress of the opus and feel it is all nonsense and that nobody will be interested. Those are the moments when you must all the more obstinately stick to your schedule and do your daily stint ... Never mind about the brilliant phrase or the golden word, once the typescript is there you can fiddle, correct and embellish as much as you please. So don't be depressed if the first draft seems a bit raw, all first drafts do. Try and remember the weather and smells and sensations and pile in every kind of contemporary detail. Don't let anyone see the manuscript until you are very well on with it and above all don't allow anything to interfere with your routine. Don't worry about what you put in, it can always be cut out on re-reading; it's the total recall that matters."

John Pearson has dated the birth of James Bond to the morning of 15 January 1952. He added that Ian's book, *Casino Royale*, was finished on 18 March. Writing a 62,000 word manuscript in eight weeks would have been an achievement. But other evidence suggests that Ian may have completed the job in an even shorter time. Ann's reference to his starting the book followed a visit by Noël Coward to dinner. Since Coward did not reach the island until 16 February, that indicated that Ian completed his first novel in just four weeks, an average of just over 2000 words a day.

Ian used to say he wrote *Casino Royale* in order to take his mind off the horrific prospect of matrimony. He peddled this line so consistently that Ann became infuriated (because, in the process, it belittled her). While it is true that he was in a state of considerable nervous tension, the reality was more complicated. On one level, Ian's old family tensions pushed him towards the typewriter. For the previous summer Peter had written *The Sixth Column*, a light-hearted satire on the bureaucratization and stupidity of the security services. Touched as Ian was that his brother had seen fit to dedicate the book to him, *The Sixth Column* was a stern reminder that he, not Peter, wanted to write serious spy novels and he was determined not to let his brother steal a march on him again.

Closer to present-day home, it was not so much his forthcoming marriage that spurred Ian as the *fait accompli* of Ann's pregnancy, which created a new set of circumstances, partly physical – with her need to take her pregnancy carefully, she was *hors de combat* sexually, so Ian had time and energy on his hands – and partly psychological – Ian realized that, at the age of forty-three, the imminent arrival of his first-born child would change his life more radically than anything he had done before. With no great financial resources behind him, he needed to provide for his offspring, whatever sex it turned out to be. *Casino Royale* was to be his child's birthright.

More subtly, Ann herself could now provide the support he needed to tackle his long-mooted work. No longer was she always about to disappear, her attentions invariably focused elsewhere. At last Ian had the psychological stability to attempt what was to be his life's task of writing novels. He could begin to settle into his necessary routines, firm in the knowledge that her strength and ebullience would lift him from any "moods". But that still did not explain why he put pen to paper. In a compelling sense, he needed to write for her, to show her that she had been correct in leaving Rothermere and the comforts of Warwick House for him. The combination of her haughtiness, intellectual sharpness and unassailable social position inspired him to perform for her, to create some literary manifestation of their sado-masochistic relationship. His book was both a present to her, and his entrée, however modest, into her grown-up world of letters and ideas.

Their wedding took place in the Town Hall in nearby Port Maria on Monday 24 March. Noël Coward noted, it was "a very simple affair, rather nicely done". He and Cole Lesley were the only witnesses. They wore ties and formal white suits for the occasion. By the time Ian and Ann arrived, a small crowd had gathered, among them an old woman singing an impromptu calypso. Ian was wearing his usual tropical uniform – belted blue-linen shirt, blue trousers. Ann looked pretty and unusually nervous in an eau-de-nil silk dress, a Dior copy, which had been run up by a local seamstress.

The ceremony was marred by the bad breath of the Registrar, forcing Ian to whisper to his bride, "Try to keep upwind of him." Ann was beginning to look pregnant and Coward could not help wondering who would get to the altar first – Ann or the baby? Afterwards the foursome repaired to Coward's Blue Harbour for what Ian called the *"vin d'honneur"* – a potent dry Martini mix, which Ian, mindful of his recent literary endeavours, insisted was made "without bruising the gin". The party – with Niki de Gunzberg, a Polish-Russian balletomane, now in tow – was merry by the time it made its way round the headland to Goldeneye where Violet had prepared a wedding dinner. Ian had carefully drawn up the menu which was then mercilessly pilloried by Coward. It included self-caught turtle (compared to "chewing an old tyre" by Noël), black crab served in its shell ("like eating cigarette ash out of an ashtray"), and a cake with green icing (evocative of "bird-lime").

Soon everyone was smashed. Noël produced yet another song, a calypso, which he had composed for the occasion. And so they crooned:

> Mongoose listen to white folks wailin'
> Mongoose giggle, say "Me no deaf!
> No more waffle and Daily Mailin'
> Annee Rothermere's Madame F."

At the end of the evening Ian pronounced that it was time for Old Man's Thing. To fits of giggles from Noël, he called for a bowl, and for an orange and a lime. Ceremoniously he cut the peel of each fruit, making sure it did not break. He placed it in the bowl, followed by the contents of a bottle of white rum. Ian then turned off the lights, took a match and set fire to the concoction, which was used for a variety of ribald toasts.

> Hey for the Alka-Seltzer,
> Ho for the aspirin,
> Hey for the saltfish, ackee canja, booby's eggs, Gordon's Gin

ran an appropriate refrain from the calypso.

Alka-Seltzer or not, Ian and Annie both showed remarkable constitutions in managing to catch their plane the next morning. They flew to Nassau, where they were met at the airport by Jo and Ivar Bryce, a calypso band and garlands of hibiscus and frangipani, and on to New York for four more days of partying. Ann had half expected that the New York Social Register would reject her as a divorcee. But she found instead that Ian and she were fêted like Tristan and Isolde. When Ian returned to London, not only was he a married man, but also he carried a typescript of *Casino Royale* in his suitcase.

8

Bond promotion
1952–1953

Ian's first try was reasonable enough: "Scent and smoke and sweat hit the taste buds with an acid thwack at three o'clock in the morning." Second time round it came out rather lamely: "Scent and smoke and sweat can suddenly combine together and hit the taste buds with an acid shock at three o'clock in the morning." Finally he got it right: "The scent and smoke and sweat of a casino are nauseating at three in the morning." Thus Ian dragged his readers into the fast, racy world of James Bond at the start of *Casino Royale*. His hero had decided to take a break from his own gambling exploits and observe his quarry, the Russian agent Le Chiffre, at the roulette table in the *salle privée* of the refurbished Baroque Casino in the fictional town of Royale-les-Eaux – a sort of Trouville to Le Touquet's Deauville.

Within the first few pages Ian had introduced most of Bond's idiosyncrasies and trademarks. Agent 007 looks like Hoagy Carmichael, with something cold and ruthless in his eyes. He drives a 1933 4½-litre Bentley, one of the last with the supercharger developed by Ian's friend Amherst Villiers. He drinks champagne and dry Martinis, shaken, not stirred: "three measures of Gordon's, one of vodka, half a measure of Kina Lillet. Shake it very well until it's ice-cold, then add a large thin slice of lemon peel." He carries his Morland cigarettes (a special Balkan and Turkish blend with their triple gold band) in a flat, light gun-metal box. Underneath his dinner-jacket he sports a flat .25 Beretta automatic. And on his arm is the enticing Vesper Lynd, his dark, blue-eyed assistant seconded from the Deuxième Bureau, wearing a black velvet dress – "simple and yet with the touch of splendour that only half a dozen couturiers in the world could achieve" – a thin necklace of diamonds at her throat, and "a diamond clip in the low vee which just exposed the jutting swell of her breasts".

In later years, after a combination of material success and intense self-criticism had taken their toll, Ian liked to make out that his books were nothing more than entertainments. "James Bond is the author's pillow fantasy," he told an interviewer in July 1963. "And fantasy isn't real life by definition. It's very much the Walter Mitty syndrome – the feverish dreams of the author of what he might have been – bang, bang, bang, kiss, kiss, that sort of stuff. It's what you would expect of an adolescent mind – which I happen to possess."

But there was ample evidence that at the start, at least, Ian attempted something more ambitious than simply updating the swashbuckling secret service adventure stories of his childhood. At first reading, the plot did not amount to much. Le Chiffre, the undercover paymaster of a communist-controlled trade union in Alsace, has blotted his copybook with the Russians by diverting official funds into a disastrous private venture running brothels. After getting wind of his plan to recoup his losses at the casino in Royale-les-Eaux, the British Secret Service calls on the best gambler on its books to thwart Le Chiffre's personal ambitions and undermine a dangerous Soviet initiative in Europe. Drawing on Ian's own experience in Estoril in 1942, Bond duly accomplishes this in a high-stake baccarat game at the casino, though at one stage it looks as if he has lost all his money, and is able to continue his contest with Le Chiffre only as a result of some subtle refinancing by his CIA sidekick Felix Leiter.

Subsequently Bond is kidnapped and tortured by an angry Le Chiffre. He is saved by the intervention of an unlikely *deus ex machina* – the Russians' SMYERT SHPIONAM, meaning "Death to Spies", and dedicated to assassinating their own traitors and double agents. Having caught up with Le Chiffre, SMERSH, as this agency was known, assassinate him as the penalty for double-crossing them. Bond subsequently enjoys a torrid romance with Vesper Lynd, but at the end of the book she admits that she also was not what she seems. In a note she informs Bond that she had been blackmailed into becoming an unwilling double agent for the Russians and that her love for him has temporarily encouraged her to reject her controllers. But now, realizing that SMERSH had tumbled her, she has decided to commit suicide rather than submit to her certain liquidation. The short novel ends with Bond vowing to stop "playing Red Indians" – Ian's description of his wartime exploits in 30 AU was now used for the mundane work of the SIS – and concentrate on the serious business of hunting down the ruthless murderers from SMERSH.

What raised *Casino Royale* out of the usual run of thrillers was Ian's attempt to reflect the disturbing moral ambiguity of a post-war world that could produce traitors like Burgess and Maclean. Although Bond is presented like Bulldog Drummond with all the trappings of a traditional British fictional secret agent (such as his Bentley), in fact he needs "Marshall Aid" from Leiter to enable him to continue his baccarat game with Le Chiffre. Bond is rescued from his kidnapper not by the British or the Americans but by the Russians, who complete the job he should have done of eliminating Le Chiffre. Bond does not even get the girl: she has been duplicitous throughout, betraying not only him personally but all Western intelligence's anti-Soviet operations. No wonder, feeling let down and abandoned, he fails to conceal his bitterness at the end and spits out, "The bitch is dead now."

Ian skilfully matched this hard-edged delineation of contemporary reality with a more mythical interpretation of events. Bond is taking on the forces of evil, a heroic St George-figure fighting on the side of virtue (and the free world), saving and bedding the girl, and attempting to slay the dragon (here called Le Chiffre, later known by other names such as Mr Big, Sir Hugo Drax, Dr No and Goldfinger). Only through such an epic battle, Ian was saying, can the function of good be understood. In a discussion with a fellow agent in *Casino Royale*, Bond spells this out. "Le Chiffre was serving a wonderful purpose, a really vital purpose, perhaps the best and highest purpose of all. By his evil existence, which foolishly I have helped destroy, he was creating a norm of badness by which, and by which alone, an opposite norm of goodness could exist."

With his gimlet journalist's eye, Ian added telling details to his ambitious story outline. References to leading brand-names and stylish living create a sophisticated world which, in the age of mass communications, his readers can begin to aspire to. He juiced his narrative with worldly and entertaining discursions about subjects which interested him, like gambling ("Bond had always been a gambler. He loved the dry riffle of the cards and the constant unemphatic drama of the quiet figures round the green tables ... Above all, he liked it that everything was one's own fault. There was only oneself to praise or blame. Luck was a servant not a master. Luck had to be accepted with a shrug or taken advantage of up to the hilt") and women ("The lengthy approaches to a seduction bored him almost as much as the subsequent mess of disentanglement. He found something grisly in the inevitability of the pattern of each affair. The conventional parabola – sentiment, the touch of the hand, the kiss, the passionate kiss, the feel of the body, the climax in the bed, then more bed, then less bed, then the boredom, the tears and the final bitterness – was to him shameful and hypocritical.")

For Ian, part of the fun of writing was to pepper his prose with references to his friends and relations. In *Casino Royale*, he introduced his CIA agent, Felix Leiter – Felix, as in Bryce's second Christian name, and Leiter, as in their mutual American friend. 'M', Bond's boss as the head of the secret service, was based on Admiral Godfrey. His secretary was called Miss Pettavel (known as Petty) until Ian changed her name to the more memorable Miss Moneypenny, a character in *The Sett*, an unfinished novel by his brother Peter. Bond's original Secret Service control in Jamaica, Charles de Costa of Lascelles de Mercado, also experienced a name-change during the course of the manuscripts. He became Charles da Silva of Chaffrey's to avoid any embarrassing problems for the real life D'Costa in his business in Kingston.

Vesper Lynd's name came from an incident Ian had experienced with Ivar on Jamaica's north coast. One afternoon they had visited a large, isolated mansion tucked away at the end of a long drive. They were surprised to be met by an old butler who informed them, "The Colonel will be delighted to receive you." They were ushered into a dimly lit drawing-room where an old grey-haired gentleman sat. After chatting amiably for a while, they were interrupted by the butler carrying a tray with three glasses. "Vespers are served," he announced stiffly. This turned out to be a mixture of iced rum, fruit and herbs which the Colonel habitually drank at six o'clock every evening. After a relaxing hour's conversation Ian and Ivar rose to leave. They promised they would return to see their elderly host. They never did, but, in their boyish manner, the name Vesper took on its own aura of romance. They invented their own gin-based cocktail, the one ordered by Bond in Royale-les-Eaux, and called it Vesper. When Ian came to write his novel he appropriated the name, with its fiery connotation, for his heroine.

Bond himself was a composite, both in character and name. Having taken Dunderdale, Mason, Smithers and others as his models and produced, as he put it, a "fictional mixture" of commandos and secret agents he had met during the war, Ian still had to come up with the right name. In keeping with his desire to reflect contemporary reality, Ian used to say he had consciously decided on "James Bond", rather than, say, the more old-fashioned Sapperish Peregrine Maltravers, because he wanted him to be "unobtrusive. Exotic things would happen to and around him but he would be a neutral figure – an anonymous blunt instrument wielded by a Government Department." He had first noted the surname Bond in Rodney Bond, a commando colleague of Peter's. His own wartime acquaintance C. H. Forster claims to have alerted him to the combination "James Bond", on which the seal was set when Ian looked up from his desk at Goldeneye and noted the author of his Macmillan's *Field Guide to Birds of the West Indies*.

Of course, as a perennial fantasist, Ian could not help introducing a strong element of wish-fulfilment into his creation. James Bond was the man of action he would have liked to have been, if his nature had not been more passive, reflective and chameleon-like. Again Bond was a projection of the heroic image of his father, which he spent his life measuring up to and not quite emulating. More prosaically, Bond gave at least fictional form to Ian's frustrated urge to have been out in the field during the war, a full-time secret agent, rather than a competent staff officer sitting, office-politicking and dreaming in Room 39 of the Admiralty.

After sticking to his writer's task with such discipline and intensity, that last line – "The bitch is dead now" – with all its ambiguous connotations, expressed Ian's feelings exactly. "I had killed the job," he later said. But when he returned to London, he had no time for thinking about his manuscript. His instant family was crammed into his medium-sized flat overlooking the River Thames. It was a novel and sometimes alarming experience. Ian had never lived in close proximity with anyone, not a woman, and certainly not a couple of spirited teenagers. Generally quiet and serious, eighteen-year-old Raymond's favourite relaxation was playing jazz music as loudly as possible on his gramophone. Ian refused to be put out by his stepson, who was about to embark on a short service commission in the 11th Hussars. When he travelled to the United States, he made a point of searching out the latest records, including the elusive sounds of Errol Garner. A couple of years younger than her brother, Fionn was prodigiously intelligent but less in evidence because, having already passed her A-levels, she was studying in Paris. Her place in the ménage was taken by another new arrival at Carlyle Mansions, a talking parrot called Jackie. Ann had acquired the bird as an amusement during the last year of her marriage. It used to infuriate Esmond by addressing him as "Old Buzzard". Now it arrived on Ian's doorstep as part of Ann's trousseau, in a brass Regency cage.

Ann was not sure how she would be accepted by her friends. Somerset Maugham told her grudgingly that, in his young days, her behaviour "would have shut all the doors of Mayfair against you, but I daresay in these degenerate times you may get away with it". Even the staunchly Roman Catholic Evelyn Waugh found a way to accept her. While holding no truck with divorce, he told her he had never approved of her earlier marriage to Esmond Rothermere, a divorcé. Thus, with Jesuitical logic, he was able to consider it annulled. As he told Diana Cooper, "Only recent good news Ann's liberation from lout Rothermere. I live so out of world Times announcement knocked me arse over tip as if with feather."

To escape from the constricting domesticity of Carlyle Mansions, Ian still had St Margaret's Bay as a bolt-hole. At the end of 1951 Noël Coward decided to leave White Cliffs and move back to Goldenhurst, his larger house nearby. Ian and Ann, who had been renting Eric Ambler's Summer's Lease a couple of doors away, took over the Coward establishment, which soon became their regular weekend retreat. Among their first visitors were Cyril Connolly and his vampish new wife, Barbara Skelton, who owned her own Kentish cottage at Elmstead near Ashford. Ian had grown to like Connolly – one of his few journalistic colleagues of whom that could be said – and had played a part in confirming his appointment to the *Sunday Times*'s panel of regular book reviewers the previous year. The observant Barbara remarked how happy the two newly-weds seemed – Ian "tanned, fretful and thinner" and Ann "greyer, older, happier and obviously pregnant". They were "more lovebirdy than ever and kept putting their heads together to inspect holes in the carpet, and then nesting chirrupy noises would follow as to whether it should be sent to be repaired now or when they were next in Jamaica". The upbeat effect was accentuated when Ann got rid of Coward's two bulky pianos and redecorated the house from top to bottom. Even so, the contrast with Ann's previous grand residences was marked. When Duff Cooper first visited, he could not believe she could be living in such an unprepossessing seaside bungalow. "This, I suppose, is how the poor live," he was heard to say.

This *outré* domesticity suited Ian. When his old girlfriend, Lady Mary Pakenham, now Lady Mary Clive and a war widow, came to visit the Flemings at Carlyle Mansions, she found an unusually ebullient Ian, brimming with funny stories about their quirky Caribbean marriage ceremony and showing mock concern about the imminent birth of a child. Lady Mary noted that he "bubbl[ed] over with talk about the situation, and we all three had a good laugh about the various complications" including finance: how could he ever live and keep his extravagant wife on his newspaper executive's income? Ian seemed "really grateful" to Ann for marrying him, recorded Lady Mary, but she could not help adding the caveat, born out of experience,that he "has more characteristics than anyone I know, and the opposite of each too. None of the ordinary rules of 'men's likes' or 'men's dislikes' apply. The only way to treat him is as a child."

As a wedding present for himself -- a reward for completing his book -- Ian splashed out on a custom-made typewriter from New York. He placed an order with the Royal Typewriter Company for a special gold-plated version of its Quiet de Luxe model, priced at $174. Astutely, he had arranged for his old girlfriend Clare Blanshard to take over as the Kemsley group's office manager, and act as his eyes, ears and legs in New York. Even she, his greatest supporter, considered this bauble juvenile, not to say vulgar. Nevertheless, she agreed to handle the on-site negotiations, while Ivar Bryce provided the dollars for its actual purchase. And because other options fell through, Ivar gamely transported the machine across the Atlantic as part of his personal baggage on the *Queen Elizabeth*. (His impedimenta included three bottles of whisky for the newly-weds and a mantle and hat of Ann's.)

For Ian the typewriter was a magnificent joke. He told a colleague that he was arranging for his "personal goatherds in Morocco" to provide a thousand sheets of vellum for use in the machine. These would then be sent to Cartier to be studded with diamonds. And if people were still not convinced that he was a "writer of distinction", he would complete the picture by writing with his own blood as ink. His high spirits led him to ask Clare to perform another little task. Would she please arrange for another wedding present, "Robert's mug", the classic seventeenth-century silver tankard given by Robert Harling, to be auctioned at Christie's with a provenance "from the collection of Loelia, Duchess of Westminster"?

Again, Clare was outraged, but this time he was pulling her leg: "That mention of Christie's was a joke – JOKE – one of those things you used to hear when you lived in England."

It was not until 12 May that Ian got round to inviting his friend William Plomer to lunch at the Ivy restaurant. They were well into their main course when suddenly he asked his friend, "William, how do you get cigarette smoke out of a woman once you've got it in?" Plomer thought he was going to be treated to some intimate bedroom secret. But Ian persevered with the prosaic observation that he could not use a word like "exhales", while "puffs it out" sounded silly. At this stage Plomer sat up with a jerk. "You've written a book!" he exclaimed. Ian admitted sheepishly that indeed he had, but he had been "too ashamed" to do anything with it. He agreed to send his friend the manuscript. But again he stalled. Only two months later, after Plomer had sent a postcard to remind him, did he do as promised. Even then he was exceedingly diffident about *Casino Royale*. He wanted to know if any of the work was worth saving so he could revise it when next in Jamaica the following spring. He told Plomer that he had tossed the novel off, using only half his brainpower. He had not read it through until recently and he was appalled to discover the vulgarity of his writing and "so far as I can see the element of suspense is completely absent". Plomer was enjoined not to mention "this dreadful oafish opus" to anyone.

Plomer refused to be put off by Ian's childish protestations. He liked the manuscript and sent it to Daniel George, his fellow reader at Cape. George was equally enthusiastic. He admitted he did not quite understand the scene where Fleming's villain Le Chiffre tortured his hero James Bond with a carpet beater, but, overall, the book had given him "very great pleasure".

Next the manuscript had to be submitted to Plomer's and George's employer, the eponymous Jonathan Cape. Initially the old man was not enthusiastic. Not for the first time, Ian's brother Peter put in a good word, which was enough to sway Cape. He told Frank Pakenham, who had just delivered the first volume of his memoirs, that "Peter's little brother" had written a book. It was "not up to scratch" but Cape intended to publish it "because he's Peter's brother". He added, "He's got to do much better if he's going to get anywhere near Peter's standard."

As a belated wedding present in June Lord Beaverbrook sent the Flemings a consignment of fine wines which he took pleasure listing in full:

from Cherkley
48 bottles of Oestricher Doosberg 1934
12 bottles Louis Roederer 1942

from Justerini & Brooks
10 bottles Veuve Cliquot 1928 Old Landed
18 halves of the same
15 bottles Pommery and Greno Old Landed

from Fortnum & Mason
28 bottles Cockburn's 1912.

But when the Flemings opened two bottles of the Oestricher Doosberg for their dinner guest, Lord Kemsley, they were dismayed to find them corked. Ann apologized and told Ian's employer they were a magnificent wedding present from Beaverbrook – as she reported to the donor, "hoping to encourage him to give his foreign manager a small token of his regard".

Kemsley paid no attention. Thinking that the Flemings must be rich from the proceeds of Ann's divorce settlement and knowing that she enjoyed the power which came with running newspapers, he offered to sell them one of his ailing newspapers, the *Sunday Chronicle*, for £1 million. When that sum was clearly beyond their means, Kemsley suggested they might think about buying his recently reconstituted book publishing companies, a project in which Ian was already involved. Nominally the Dropmore Press still existed as a commercial printer, but it had fallen into abeyance as a small publisher – the victim of general editorial indifference and one huge failure, its expensively produced *King George V Stamp Book*.

Instead, towards the end of the previous year, Kemsley had decided to set up a new imprint, the Queen Anne Press, covering much the same ground as the Dropmore, but this time giving Ian editorial control and having his friends, Percy Muir and John Hayward, much more involved as directors. Kemsley also relaunched the *Book Handbook* as the *Book Collector*, a scholarly quarterly, with the same three men in charge, and with Robert Harling in the background as design consultant.

Ian enjoyed having what amounted to his own publishing house. It gave him additional cachet in the eyes of his new wife and her intellectual friends. Even before departing for Jamaica he had established the convivial, gentlemanly tone of the proceedings by holding his first editorial meeting in a private room at Frascati's and negotiating his first book, *A Time to Keep Silence*, a tasteful repackaging of an essay on monasticism which Paddy Leigh Fermor had written for the *Cornhill Magazine*. An approach to Gallimard in Paris about an unpublished novel by Proust proved unfruitful. But Evelyn Waugh seemed happy to dust down some of his old material. Initially he planned to collect a few robust reviews under the title *Offensive Matter*. Ian suggested that "if you would then consider embellishing the whole with a short introduction on the virtue of being offensive and the decline of invective, a book could be put together

which would give pleasure to yourself as well as to your public". Waugh
subsequently felt this would be "altogether too testy", and settled for an
illustrated edition of *The Holy Places*, based on an article which he had
originally written for *Life* magazine. "It would make a particularly appropriate Christmas present," noted the commercially-minded Waugh in
May. At the same time Ian contacted Cyril Connolly about publishing a
novella of not less than 10,000 words. The edition would run to 500
copies, and Connolly would be paid 150 guineas.

By mid-July Ann had reached "the stage of permanent discomfort" in
her pregnancy. She told her brother and sister-in-law that she expected to
be released by Caesarean section around the opening of the grouse-shoot-
ing season, or three weeks before the end of her natural term. Her pre-
diction could not have been more precise. Right on cue, on 12 August
1952, the "Glorious Twelfth", when the Fleming clan was gathered at
Black Mount, Ann gave birth to Ian's first and only son, Caspar, after a
difficult and painful Caesarean operation.

If Ann had to grit her teeth and bear it, Ian found the perinatal tension
too much. In the room next to his wife in the private Lindo Wing of St
Mary's Hospital in Paddington, Mrs Ludovic Kennedy – better known as
Moira Shearer, the dancer – had just delivered her daughter Ailsa. At about
ten o'clock that evening, she was lying in bed reading a book, when a tall,
gaunt man she did not recognize entered the room. Her first reaction was
to raise the alarm but, when she realized he was crying uncontrollably,
she tried her best to comfort him. He knelt beside her bed, buried his face
in her lap and continued to sob. After some time he looked up and said,
"Please forgive me, but my wife is having a terrible time next door." It was
true that Ann was in labour next door, and James Bond's creator was
having difficulty coping with her pain. But his weeping came from the
intense anguish he personally was feeling. After the death of their first
child, and the concerted rearguard action he had waged against getting
married, he realized he had reached the defining moment in his relationship with Ann.

Miss Shearer took some time to realize that her nocturnal visitor was
Ian Fleming, whom she had never met personally but whom she knew
was married to the woman in the next room, someone she had once
known as Ann Rothermere. As principal dancer in the Royal Ballet, she had
occasionally accompanied Frederick Ashton to Ann's parties at Warwick
House. But Ann had always been standoffish towards this younger, attractive woman. "Who's that red-headed woman over there?" she asked in
Moira's hearing on more than one occasion.

So Moira had taken little interest in Ian, who nevertheless seemed to
recognize her, possibly because a couple of nights earlier, looking very
pregnant, she had accompanied her husband to dinner at the St James's

Club, and Ian had also been there. After a while beside her bed, he recovered his composure. "We talked very mildly about this and that," remembered Miss Shearer. "Suddenly he got up, took my hand, kissed it and said, 'You've been such a help.' I never saw him again."

Later that night Caspar was born. Ian's attraction to this unusual name is a mystery. It did not run in the family. "It's a good Biblical name," Ian told his Washington friend, 'Oatsie' Leiter. If so, it was a biblical name with a lighter side. Only a few months earlier Ian had been visiting his friends the Harlings, in Suffolk. At the time Phoebe, Robert Harling's wife, was expecting her third child. Her husband told Ian that, if they had a son, they intended to call him Caspar. Ian put his head back and roared with laughter. "You can't call him that!" he exclaimed. "There's only one test for a name: can you shout it out along a beach?" The inference was that he felt that "Caspar" did not fit that bill. Nevertheless the appellation stuck in Ian's mind. Another incentive was his admiration for Caspar John, the son of his mother's former lover, Augustus John. Caspar John had overcome his bohemian background and become naval air attaché in Washington during the war and later Admiral of the Fleet.

Then there was the matter of Ian's bet with Ernie Cuneo. Ernie had married a quiet Canadian woman, Margaret Watson, one of Bill Stephenson's girls at British Security Coordination in New York. A well-read man, he knew Southey's poem "The Battle of Blenheim," in which old Kaspar relates the action to his grandson Peterkin. And he was also aware of the wimpy James Thurber character, Casper Milquetoast. The name became such a running joke between Ian and Ernie that they embarked on a reckless wager: whichever of them first sired a son promised to call him Caspar. In the event Ian beat Ernie by a few months. Ernie's son Jonathan, now a lawyer in Washington, was born a few months later and is thankful not to be burdened with the name. The Harlings' baby was not called Caspar either. They had a girl, named Amanda.

Out of a sense of obligation towards Ernie, Ian stuck to the name Caspar. The spelling took some time to evolve. When Ann wrote to her friend Clarissa Eden (née Churchill) asking her to become a godmother, she called him Kasper (and he was also known as Kaspar and Kasbah). At his christening at Chelsea Old Church at the end of October, he was named Caspar Robert Fleming. 'Robert' was a tribute to his great-grandfather, the founder of the Fleming dynasty whose good name he was now to carry on. Clarissa's fellow godparents were Noël Coward and Cecil Beaton – both Ann's choices – and Peter Fleming and Sir George Duff-Sutherland-Dunbar – described by Ann to Clarissa as "some stout golf player (Ian's choices)". As wife of the new Foreign Secretary, Lady Eden was unable to attend the ceremony which, Ian insisted, had to be held in the evening. Peter's wife, Celia, stood in for her. "I wonder what the child will grow up

to be?" Beaton wrote to his friend Greta Garbo. Caspar's birth had proved
so traumatic that Ann was detained in the Lindo Wing for a further two
weeks. She hated it. For five days she was on an intravenous drip and, as
she remarked, all her bodily functions were performed by tubes. She
affected annoyance at finding that her fellow patients were rich Jewesses,
fifteen to twenty years younger than she. To take her mind off her ordeal,
Ian brought her a review copy of Hemingway's latest book, *The Old Man
and the Sea*. He praised her courage and made appreciative noises about
his "most heavenly child".

While Ann was still doped up in hospital, he travelled down the Great
West Road to The Aviary in Osterley on the outskirts of London, where
his old girlfriend Lady Daphne Finch-Hatton was living in some style with
her husband, Whitney Straight, the rich American-born deputy chairman
of BOAC. The bluff businesslike Straight never bothered to hide his
irritation at Ian's supercilious manner. But this time his visitor wanted to
discuss a matter of mutual interest. The *Sunday Times* had commissioned
Cyril Connolly to write about the diplomats, Guy Burgess and Donald
Maclean, who had defected to Moscow the previous year, and Ian, who
was fascinated by the subject, suggested that Connolly should drop the
idea of writing a novella and expand his pieces into a publication for his
Queen Anne Press instead. Both Whitney Straight and his brother Michael
were personal friends of Burgess's. While an undergraduate at Trinity
College, Cambridge, in the mid-1930s, Michael had been recruited by
Anthony Blunt in collaboration with Guy Burgess to work as a Soviet
agent of influence in the United States. Intriguingly, the Straight brothers'
late father had been a partner in the J. P. Morgan bank. Blunt and Burgess
had wanted Michael Straight to act as a pro-communist "sleeper" at the
highest levels of American society. Ian needed to discuss this background
with Whitney. But not even this "man's talk" could stop Lady Daphne
noting Ian's happiness, an impression which was reinforced when he
spontaneously picked some flowers for Ann from the garden.

Mary Clive had much the same impression when she saw him briefly at
the end of September. Ian had used the period of Ann's hospitalization to
tap away on his "golden" typewriter, revising the manuscript of *Casino
Royale*. (Afterwards, he packed away this ornate new machine and reverted
to his trusty Imperial portable.) By the time of Caspar's birth "already the
corpses of split infinitives and a host of other grammatical solecisms are
lying bloody on the floor". A month later he was satisfied with his labours,
and Lady Mary recalled that he was "very excited over getting his book
taken, charmingly naïve. 'Heady' was the word he used." But, ever conscious of the paradoxes in Ian's character, she observed, "However, he is
such a box of tricks and so fond of playing at this and that, that one can't
say."

When not working on his book and his publishing interests, Ian occupied himself with literary trivia, like the warmed-up travel piece on Jamaica which he produced for the *Spectator* in June. Another article burning a hole in his drawer concerned road safety. During his late-summer visit to the Bryces in the United States in 1950 he had become fascinated with the apocalyptic vision portrayed in the road signs. Americans were not afraid to suggest that car accidents led to deaths, he noted, while the most strident warning to be found on the roads in Britain was 'Major Road Ahead.' On his return to Gray's Inn Road, he asked Rodney Campbell, the New York correspondent of the *Sunday Times*, to do some further research which Ian used to write an article, 'Death is so Permanent'. But the *Sunday Times* editor, Harry Hodson, was not impressed by Ian's efforts. "I don't think it quite makes the grade," he told Ian stiffly. Nearly two years later Ian rediscovered the text and decided that the most certain way of having it published was to enlist the support of his chairman. On 17 September he submitted it to Lord Kemsley with a polite covering note. The very next day, it was printed as a full-page spread in the Kemsley group's tabloid, the *Daily Graphic*. His article had become "An Open Letter to the Transport Minister". It listed some of the crassest of Campbell's American road-safety signs – for example, 'The Smaller the Child, the Bigger the Accident' – and suggested they should be copied in Britain. Although he provided no evidence that the American way of doing things led to fewer road accidents, Ian claimed he "really believe[d] they'll make the road-hog in his juggernaut and the motor-cyclist trying to break the sound barrier remember that he is aiming a loaded gun from the moment he leaves the garage." Although Ian had signed his original letter with his own name, in the *Daily Graphic* he became Frank Gray, an unaccustomed pseudonym.

At this stage Ian had no literary agent. He conducted his own negotiations with Cape, showing a toughness which suggested that if the City had been able to engage his interest he would have been a consummate deal-maker. As in NID, Ian showed no sign of "senior officer veneration". The respected Jonathan Cape himself was treated as little more than a tradesman – to be bested at every opportunity. At one meeting in September the two sides had agreed that he would receive royalties of 10 per cent on all sales up to 10,000 copies, 15 per cent from 10,000 to 15,000, $17\frac{1}{2}$ per cent from 15,000 to 20,000 and 20 per cent thereafter. But when Ian examined these figures again in the cold light of the following morning, he felt "for symmetry's sake" Cape might like to pay him $12\frac{1}{2}$ per cent for sales of between 5000 and 10,000 copies. "NO" was Cape's pithy response, marked in red pencil on Ian's letter making this request.

Ian then wanted to know how many copies would be published. He demanded a first print run of 10,000 books. "I hope this figure will not give you sleepless nights," he told Cape, adding the cheeky incidental information that his publisher "might be interested to know" that Nicolas Bentley's first thriller *The Tongue-Tied Canary* had sold 13,000 copies since it was first published in 1949 and was still selling. Again Cape refused to be impressed by this neophyte. He coldly dismissed Ian's request as a "pointless and an entirely unnecessary imposition upon a publisher in present circumstances" – given the falling paper market and quick facilities for reprint.

Undeterred by these rebuffs, Ian took it upon himself to provide his own artwork for the book cover. He informed his publishers that he had "designed a jacket of exquisite symmetry and absolute chastity", based on a central motif of the nine of hearts, which figured strongly in his story. He also tried to involve himself in the production timetable, suggesting 15 April as a possible publication date, and informing Cape that the word 'Royale' in the title might help pick up some extra sales over the Coronation period. "I do hope you won't find any of these suggestions unreasonable," he added with mock affability, "since I am only activated by the motives of a) making as much money for myself and my publishers as possible b) getting as much fun as I personally can out of the project."

By 10 October Ian agreed – "since this is my first book" – to accept Cape's terms "with a good grace". Clearly indicating he was in for the long haul, he added the hope that "at least in the case of the second book, you will temper the wind to the shorn author". For the first time he mentioned that he had sold the rights in *Casino Royale* to a company he called Glydrose Productions Ltd. with whom he asked Cape to draw up a contract. This complicated matters slightly, particularly as Ian had misspelt the name of the company. On the advice of his accountant Vallance Lodge, Ian was in the process of buying a small theatrical agency called Glidrose Productions (after its two principals John Gliddon and Norman Rose). The idea was that he would assign all rights, other than film and serial rights, to this company. By the end of November Ian had completed his takeover of Glidrose, and installed himself and his wife as directors. In time-honoured fashion, he owned 999 shares, and Ann (the company secretary) one.

Throughout the autumn Ian continued on his business plan for his book. With his talent for promotion, he was conscious of the need to create pre-publication interest. Paul Gallico had written some features for the *Sunday Times*, and the two men had established a warm relationship. Now Ian felt Gallico could help him with some literary contacts in the United States. He sent him the manuscript of *Casino Royale* and was delighted to hear back from Gallico in Rome. "The book is a knockout. I thought I had written a couple of pretty fair torture scenes in my day, but yours beats anything I ever read. Wow!" More to the point, Gallico offered to inform his Hollywood agent, 'Swanee' Swanson, about it. "I can tell him from earnest conviction that here is a rib-snorter which would make a marvellous movie. No one has EVER had the bright idea to couple gambling with espionage and economic sabotage and this gimmick of yours would film marvellously." Ian was so delighted that he copied the letter verbatim to Jonathan Cape.

Other friends were called in to find a publisher for the book in the United States. Ivar Bryce offered to tell a friend at Harcourt Brace about it. But Ian felt this house was a little too stuffy for the kind of book he had written. "What I want is not a publisher, but a 'factory' which will shift this opus of mine like 'Gone with the Naked and the Dead'." So Bryce asked a mutual friend, Iva Patcevitch, the Condé Nast boss, to put in a good word for *Casino Royale* at Doubleday, which also happened to be Gallico's publisher. (Ironically, Ian's employer, Lord Kemsley, had run a campaign to ban Norman Mailer's novel *The Naked and the Dead* when it had been published in May 1949. Ian noted that his proprietor's pious strictures had had the opposite effect and had helped boost Mailer's sales.) All in all, Ian felt happy with his efforts: "There is a merry buzz in the market place and my signature is beginning to look more and more like Shakespeare's."

Having achieved that much, Ian concentrated his energies on ensuring a favourable response from the reviewers. Even before *Casino Royale* went to the printer, Ian boasted to Plomer that he could count on the patronage of Lords Beaverbrook and Kemsley, and that the latter had specifically asked him who he would like to review the book in the *Sunday Times*. (Lord Rothermere was another matter. Although not a vindictive man, he never forgave Ian for running off with his wife. For the next decade, the James Bond novels could expect nothing more than politely cool notices in the *Daily Mail*.) Ian also claimed he could count on the support of W. H. Smith, the leading chain of booksellers, which was owned by family friends.

Ann remained at White Cliffs for most of this period. Initially she was worn out from the exertions of birth. But help was at hand. For years she had told Joan Sillick, the sensible nanny who had tended Raymond and Fionn, that she expected to call upon her services again. She had only "loaned" Nanny Sillick to the Labour MP Aidan Crawley and his American wife Virginia, she said. Every time she visited the Crawleys at Steeple Claydon in Buckinghamshire, she had whispered to Nanny, "I'm going to get you out of here soon." Miss Sillick had been all set to return to Ann four years earlier when Mary was born. Now she was asked to join Ann in St Margaret's Bay where she quickly took charge of Caspar.

As Ann's strength slowly returned, so did some of the frenetic social life she had left behind at Warwick House. Her near neighbours, the

Connollys, often came to visit, as did London friends such as Peter Quennell and Lucian Freud. Curiously, however, with Ann's mending came
Ian's first almost imperceptible signs of frustration with his marriage. One
place was in bed with his wife. Ann made noises to some correspondents
about how, during her hospitalization, Ian had been revolted at the various
drips and tubes she had had attached to her. When she returned home,
his horror of physical abnormality became focused on the great scars
which Anne's second Caesarean operation had left on her stomach. Ann
used to say that for this reason lovemaking ceased almost immediately
after Caspar's birth. While this seems unlikely, it certainly cast a heavy
damper over proceedings. Robert Harling used to observe that there was
little intimacy between the Flemings. But when he asked his friend how
many times Ann had sat on his knee, Ian looked at him as if he was mad.
More obviously, Ian did not like the domestic consequences of his wife's
recovery. For it meant her energies were again turned towards her "fuddy-
duddies", or "boobies", as Evelyn Waugh called them, and he was no
longer the contented recipient of her love and affection. So Ian retreated
into his private world, making himself scarce whenever Ann's friends
appeared. Even the Connollys, whose company he enjoyed, were not
exempt from this treatment. When they came for lunch one Sunday ("the
usual mediocre Fleming meal" said Barbara), Ian excused himself after the
first course and disappeared to play golf.

With his fine understanding of Ian's moods, Noël Coward saw what was
happening and how it affected his friend, and his regard for Ann, once
considerable, waned abruptly. On her own she was sweet, he remarked
after dinner with the Flemings the following year, but in the company of
her "set" she became "shrill and strident, like one of those doomed
Michael Arlen characters of the twenties, I am really surprised that Ian
doesn't sock her in the chops and tell her to shut up".

Perhaps to preserve a sense of mutual activity, Ian encouraged Ann to
take an interest in the Queen Anne Press. In November she invited a first
division of contributors to St Margaret's for the weekend. Waugh was
there, along with Paddy and Joan Leigh Fermor, and Duff and Diana
Cooper. Ann hoped Cooper might write a suitable essay for the Press
after he had finished his autobiography. In the event, it was "a difficult
weekend", remembered Leigh Fermor, with Ann showing her less attractive, manipulative side. Waugh did not like mixing, even in this stimulating
company. Before coming he asked Ann petulantly why she had to invite
anyone else. "It is you and Ian I come to see." In fact Waugh hated having
the husbands of his women friends around. He only accepted Ian on
sufferance and heartily disliked Duff Cooper. Waugh's demeanour was not
improved by the poor job he felt Ian had done in producing *The Holy
Places*. In later letters to Diana Cooper, he referred to "Ian Fleming's idiot

printing firm" making "a great balls-up of a little book of mine" and to his "horrible arts-and-crafts misprinted book". Ian reeled with the punches, trying to bluster his way through the proceedings, with often hilarious results. When, in the middle of a discussion, Ian asked Waugh casually, "And what would the Holy Man think of that?" Waugh affected not to understand what he meant. "Well, you know, God," said Ian. His guest was not amused. With great solemnity, he proceeded to lecture Ian on the theological implications of his question. "First of all, He's not a man, and then ..." Ian looked amazed at his guest's pedantry.

Waugh was justified in attacking the poor production of the Queen Anne Press books. Percy Muir was furious when the Leigh Fermor book appeared soon afterwards. It had "several rather severe shortcomings", he told Ian, "and does not do us the credit that it ought to". Without accusing Ian in person (though the implication was there), Muir added, "I cannot help thinking that the rather light-hearted atmosphere of our monthly meetings has been misconstrued in some quarters and several of our affairs are not being tackled with the businesslike promptitude and energy that is needed." Muir subsequently identified another problem which clearly weighed on his mind: the Queen Anne Press was publishing scraps "fished out of writers' waste-paper baskets".

The Connollys returned to St Margaret's for Christmas lunch – traditional turkey and soggy Brussels sprouts – with Peter Quennell and Loelia Westminster making up the numbers. Ian had just been in the United States for ten days canvassing publishers and researching his next book. After the meal, he distributed some nick-nacks of dubious taste which he had picked up in New York, including a fake carton of Lucky Strike cigarettes which, when one put it up to the light and turned a small handle, displayed an exotic gallery of naked girls. After listening to the Queen's speech on the wireless, the party indulged in the snobbish pastime of poking fun at the royals. Wasn't the Queen Mother the most middleclass of the lot? someone asked. Barbara Skelton was not impressed. Taking a leaf out of Hugo Charteris's book, she found everyone "smug, confident and spiritless".

For the next few days these same people were in and out of each other's houses. The day after Boxing Day they all travelled over to see Noël Coward at Goldenhurst for a further distribution of presents, followed by the inevitable game of charades. (On another occasion, a guest recalled Ian making a good imitation of a moorhen and becoming angry when Coward said he had done it all wrong.) On 4 January 1953 the Flemings were invited back to the Connollys. By this time Christmas overindulgence was playing havoc with Ian's liver. On arriving at Elmstead in the snow, he asked Barbara Skelton aggressively, "Had any good rows lately?" "Not since yesterday," she answered sweetly, and confided to her diary that Ian did little for her: his eyes were "too close together and I don't fancy his raw beef complexion". (Ian was aware of this feature of his eyes and used to say it meant he could not be trusted.) Similarly she found Ann Fleming lacking in sex appeal. Ian's wife was very handsome and well-bred, she felt, "but why does she always rouge her cheeks like a painted doll?"

By now it was clear that Ann was not going to settle in Ian's flat in Carlyle Mansions. Whenever possible, she stayed at St Margaret's Bay, lobbying for a comfortable town house where she could spread herself and entertain properly. As Ian steeled himself for a move, Robert Harling came up with a suggestion: he knew a clothes manufacturer called David Blairman who was selling an attractive property in Victoria Square, boxed between Buckingham Palace and Victoria Station. Number 16 was no mansion: it had no garden or even back yard, and looked more like a doll's house than a proper residence for an important newspaper executive. Fionn, who was sensitive to Ian's feelings, called it his "gilded cage". But Ann liked the urbanity of Matthew Wyatt's early-Victorian design, with its cream stucco façade and impressive bow which rose the full length of one side of the building. So the Flemings decided to buy it, and while they were away that winter the contractors moved in to make the necessary renovations. Ian, who could manage a wry joke about most things when he was in the right mood, observed that, if he were ever given a peerage, he would trump his wife's previous husbands by taking the title Lord SW1.

Before leaving for Jamaica – domestic responsibilities disrupted the usual timetable – the Flemings lunched with Malcolm Muggeridge and his wife Kitty. Having recently been appointed editor of *Punch*, Muggeridge talked enthusiastically about his plans to develop the magazine into an English *New Yorker*. Having had similar ideas in the late 1930s, Ian enjoyed being privy to discussions about *Punch*'s future, describing the lunch to Cyril Connolly as "most inspiring". But if Ian saw a role for himself on a relaunched publication, he was mistaken. Muggeridge considered Ian "definitely a slob" and confided in his diary that he could not understand why Ann had fallen for him.

By that time Ian was longing for the freedom of Jamaica. He complained playfully to Connolly that he was suffering from *Abschiedschmerz* and *Ankunftsangst* (the pain of saying goodbye and the fear of arriving), "but the Doctor Birds are waiting in the Crown of Thorns bushes and the Butterfly fish on the reef". Arrangements still had to be made to park Caspar and Nanny at Carlyle Mansions. (A non-driver, Miss Sillick refused to be left alone battling the elements at St Margaret's Bay.) So it was mid-January before the Flemings boarded the BOAC Stratocruiser for the overnight flight to New York, en route for Jamaica. Ian had made a point of asking Clare Blanshard to arrange for the Bryces' Rolls-Royce to meet them at Idlewild Airport. But she considered it vulgar to specify the type of car. Ian was disgruntled to find the Bryces' chauffeur at the wheel of a Lincoln rather than a Rolls. In his next book, the vehicle became a black Buick with Dynaflow gears. "The driver chose the Triborough Bridge," Ian wrote, "and they soared across the breath-taking span into the heart of up-town Manhattan, the beautiful prospect of New York hastening towards them until they were down amongst the hooting, teeming, petrol-smelling roots of the stressed-concrete jungle." (It was later pointed out that the Triborough Bridge does not lead into up-town Manhattan.)

The Flemings stayed only one night in New York because Ian had further research to do in Florida. *Casino Royale* had highlighted the sophisticated malevolence of his old gambling haunts in Europe. His new book, tentatively titled 'The Undertaker's Wind', was to be a study of organized crime in his new domain of the Caribbean and North America. Ian was too sophisticated to have a traditional Italian mobster as his villain. He invented a sinister black hoodlum called Mr Big who practised voodoo and financed the Soviet espionage operation in the region. As well as racketeering in Harlem, Mr Big ran a fish business in Florida, which was a cover for smuggling pirate treasure into the country from Jamaica in the bottom of its boats. The colourful locations allowed Ian to combine his sense of the excitement of the United States with his intimate knowledge of the history, folklore, topography and marine life of Jamaica. (The title, which acted as a metaphor, referred to one of Jamaica's two prevailing winds, which, as a character in the book noted, "blows all the bad air out of the island at night".)

During his brief stay in New York in December, Ian had – with William Stephenson's and Ernie Cuneo's help – spent a night out on the Upper West Side with a couple of detectives from the local precinct. On previous trips he had enjoyed visiting Harlem dance clubs, where he delighted in their energy as much as their music. Now his eyes had been opened to a seedier reality. He met a local crime boss and witnessed with alarm the hold that drug traffickers were gaining in the neighbourhood. From his friends, with their local intelligence connections, he would have learned of the latest conspiracy theory which suggested that the National Association for the Advancement of Colored People was a dangerous communist front.

Now, a month later, Ian's research took him by train to St Petersburg in Florida to investigate the site he intended for Mr Big's fish factory. In his book, Ian recreated the journey in lively style. At New York's Pennsylvania Station, he and Ann boarded one of the great old Pullman trains, the *Silver Phantom*. "It lay, a quarter of a mile of silver carriages, quietly in the dusk of the underground station." As the train rumbled through sidings full of empty freight cars, he noted the romantic-sounding names of railroad companies from all over the United States, including "the lilting

'Acheson, Topeka and Santa Fe' " – a company once rescued from oblivion by his grandfather. In his story, however, James Bond, travelled not with his wife but with an exotic Haitian girl whom he had snatched from the evil hands of Mr Big. To escape detection by Mr Big's ubiquitous intelligence service, the two lovers travelled as Mr and Mrs Bryce, Ian's laconic acknowledgement of his hosts in New York.

After establishing a suitably banal waterfront location in St Petersburg for 'Ourobouros Inc. Live Worm and Bait Merchants. Coral, Shells, Tropical Fish', Ian flew with Ann to Jamaica. He did not have to look far for a model for Surprise Island, Mr Big's local hideaway. Situated off Port Maria was Cabritta Island, where the seventeenth-century privateer Sir Henry 'Bloody' Morgan careened his ships and supposedly left his treasure. Soon Ian was tapping away at his old Imperial typewriter, dropping his friends' names into his story (the Secret Service chief in the Caribbean was called Commander John Strangways), recycling odd scraps of information (his article about road signs in the United States was good for a paragraph), casually demonstrating an understanding of the growing communist threat in the Caribbean, and given a massive plug for Paddy Leigh Fermor's *The Traveller's Tree* (partly written at Goldeneye) as his source about Haitian voodoo.

The finished product was so full of pace, incident and colour that it overwhelmed Ian's attempts to remind his readers that he was writing a serious novel. Nevertheless 'The Undertaker's Wind', later known as *Live and Let Die*, was interesting for its development of Ian's theory of the banality of evil. This time the vehicle was the character of Mr Big, in whose ramblings one can hear echoes of religious-tinged conversations with Evelyn Waugh at White Cliffs: "Mister Bond, I suffer from boredom. I am prey to what the early Christians called 'accidie', the deadly lethargy that envelops those who are sated, those who have no more desires ... I take pleasure now only in artistry, in the polish and finesse which I can bring to my operations." Surprisingly for a non-religious man, Ian often returned to this concept of spiritual sloth as one of the causes of criminality. It allowed him to build up Bond as a decisive antidote to accidie, providing another expression of the Manichaean suggestion in *Casino Royale* that Bond was acting on the side of the angels, or, more specifically, that the evil manifest in Le Chiffre was required in order for good to exist. Ian was also making a personal statement: the side of his own character that he (and his puritanical Scottish genes) most feared was his capacity for indolence. That is why he populated his life with so many diversions, that is why he revered but could never emulate the saturnine Ivar Bryce, and that, at least in part, is why he created James Bond.

Ann's children tried to keep the newly married couple *au fait* with what was happening at home. On 9 February, Fionn enthusiastically revealed the arrival of six-month-old Caspar's first tooth. "Tell Ian," she urged her mother. "Don't flap; it's in his mouth – bottom right hand as you face him, of werewolvian appearance." More urbanely, Raymond wrote that he had not yet been able to find a Lancia for Ian. Instead he had bought an antique Rolls-Royce station-wagon as a general vehicle for use on the O'Neill estate in Northern Ireland.

Goldeneye would not have been the same without its endless stream of guests. That winter the Flemings were joined by Ann's charming, otherworldly father, Guy, and his spirited second wife, Violet, who had sailed from England in the unlikely company of Lucian Freud. Vi, as she was known, had married Guy in 1945, twenty years after the death of Ann's mother, Frances. Ian and Ann travelled across the island from Goldeneye to welcome their visitors on their arrival in Kingston. But they had to stand by the quayside for the best part of a day waiting for a storm to subside. When the ship finally docked, Ian was surprised to be summoned on board where he learned that Freud was down to his last ten shillings in cash. Ian had to promise to be responsible for the artist's finances before he was allowed ashore.

The naturalist's diary kept by Guy Charteris cast a pleasingly unaffected eye on the day-to-day routine at Goldeneye. Within a day of arriving at Goldeneye, he was commenting on the moths, the fireflies and the choir of tree frogs: everything was "wonderful and bewildering", he thought. He was particularly struck by the local solitaire bird. Ian had already noted the name and adopted it for the Haitian heroine of the novel in his typewriter. When Guy came across a praying mantis, he was asked to keep it for Lucian Freud to paint.

The Charterises' visit was accompanied by the usual round of north coast drinks and dinner parties. One day the assembled company (minus Ian who was writing) went to lunch with Angus Wilson, an orchid enthusiast who lived in Ocho Rios with his companion Odo Cross, a former Guards officer who liked to wear his mother's pearls. The following week Wilson and Cross were invited back to dinner – a special from Violet (the housekeeper) consisting of land crabs and stuffed sucking pig. Ian's combination of Martinis, rum and the killer 'Old Man's Thing' was too much for Cross, who became paralytically drunk and had to be carried off by Lucian Freud to recuperate on Ian's bed.

Returning from Blue Harbour, Noël Coward's house at Port Maria, one night, Ian and his party were attracted by the sounds of insistent drumming and singing. They got out of their car and found they had chanced upon the local variation of a voodoo funeral. Ian was riveted, as voodoo was an important theme in his book. He wanted to stay and watch. From behind a tree they looked on in amazement as women in white dresses and turbans flailed around and foamed at the mouth. When they returned to their car, the local spirits had had their revenge for this voyeurism. The engine would not start. As the local bus was passing, Ian flagged it down for the remaining three miles' journey to Goldeneye. When Coward's house-guest, the actress Katharine Hepburn, paid a return visit to the Flemings, she managed to antagonize Ian by sitting in his special wheel-back chair. As Vi Charteris put it, Ian was "what we Scots like to call pernickety".

The same adjective might have described another author staying in the vicinity. For the first time in her carefree life, Ann had become interested in the concept of sin and, in this context, she had been riveted by Evelyn Waugh's reports about his fellow Roman Catholic writer Graham Greene. When she discovered that Greene was staying with his mistress Lady Catherine Walston at the Tower Isle Hotel in Ocho Rios, she was determined to meet him. When he ignored her sirenian cries to visit Goldeneye, she enlisted Ian's support and travelled along the coast to track the errant novelist down at his hotel. Greene continued to be elusive. She noted that he was difficult to pin down in any conversation and the evening was ruined by the arrival of several other visitors, including King Edward VIII's former Lord-in-Waiting, Lord Brownlow, and the wartime spy, Rex Benson. On returning to Goldeneye, she told Vi Charteris that Catherine Walston was very beautiful, despite having had six children, all by Caesarean section. Although this was physically impossible, it indicated Ann's particular sensitivity on this topic.

After lunch the following day, 14 March, Ian and Ann left Goldeneye for Montego Bay, from where they were due to fly out to Nassau, and then home to London, via New York. Guy Charteris was amused at the way the members of the staff were formally lined up to bid their master and mistress goodbye. He, his wife and Lucian Freud stayed a bit longer, during which time an incident occurred which became part of the Goldeneye folklore. At dinner one evening, Violet, the housekeeper, served some vegetables in a Pyrex dish. When Freud tried to help himself to what he thought were sausages, he discovered they were actually Violet's fingers on the other side of the dish.

In London Caspar and Nanny Sillick had already moved to Victoria Square – along with the builders – because, while Ian and Ann were still in Jamaica, the lease on Carlyle Mansions ran out. On his return Ian tried, rather clumsily but with great affection, to show an interest in his son's upbringing. With his enthusiasm for new artefacts and ideas, he had picked up on the cult of the American paediatrician Dr Benjamin Spock. He duly presented Nanny Sillick with a copy of Spock's seminal *Baby and Child Care*. Unimpressed, she told her employer she had been dealing with babies for long enough not to have to study a book. When he persisted, she got up, placed a towel across his knees, and said, "Well, if you think one can learn from this book, perhaps you should give it a try." Ann entered the room at this stage, and looked on in great amusement. "Oh! Nanny, what have you done to Mr Fleming now?" Of Ian's ability as a father, Nanny had few illusions. "He couldn't cope at all," she recalled.

The geography of the new house was cramped but functional. The Dickensian basement served as a flat for Ann's new cook, a powerful Welshwoman called Mary Crickmere, whose husband Edgar acted as Ian's valet, drove occasionally and waited in the evenings. She had gained a reputation working for Lady Sysonby, Loelia Westminster's mother, and was equally at home preparing elaborate dinners for Ann's friends as she was rustling up scrambled eggs for Ian to eat beside the fire. On the ground floor, making full use of the bow-window feature, was the dining-room, with a round oak table which seated eight comfortably but was often filled to overcapacity with as many as a dozen guests. On the other side of the entrance was the kitchen. Climbing the stairs one came to the drawing-room, which was light and relaxing, with carefully arranged Regency furniture and a panoply of pictures, ranging from an impressive Freud portrait of Ann, which captured the strength of her Charteris features, to a couple of Ian's favourite inlaid-brass drawings. The second floor was reserved for Ann and, occasionally, the baby, while on the top were two smaller bedrooms used by Ian and Fionn. Ian's bed was dominated by an old family quilt of Queen Victoria's head, which set off the five classical bas-reliefs above the bed and the small busts on a nearby shelf. There was also a small collection of bedtime reading matter, including a volume of Swift, some French pornography, and Michael Arlen's *Hell! said the Duchess*. Across a corridor, Ian and teenaged Fionn shared a bathroom, where he meticulously set out his carefully selected Fleur des Alpes soap from Guerlain, his Pinaud hair tonic and his special silver-handled toothbrush bought in New York. Since Ian liked to sit on the lavatory and smoke, Fionn always associated him with the smell of that bathroom, a heady mixture of perfumes and Morland cigarettes.

Once again, to escape builders, office and the emotional turmoil of moving, Ian arranged, almost as soon as he was home, to disappear on one of his walkabouts for the *Sunday Times*. At a party given by the publisher Hamish Hamilton, he had met Jacques Cousteau, the dapper French underwater explorer. When Cousteau invited him to visit his next project – raising the remains of an ancient Greek trading vessel in the South of France – Ian jumped at the chance, even though it meant being out of England on *Casino Royale*'s actual publication date of 13 April.

Ann went too, welcoming the opportunity to call on Somerset Maugham at the Villa Mauresque in Antibes. So she was beside her husband when he manoeuvred his car on to the air ferry at Lydd and flew the short distance to Le Touquet. The Morris Oxford had given way to a much racier two-and-a-half-litre black Riley, capable of 100 m.p.h. They drove down through France to Antibes, and then Ian continued on to Marseilles where Cousteau had assembled his team of divers on a 300-ton research vessel, the *Calypso*, an exotic name that might have come from one of Ian's own books. The ship they were exploring had sunk around 250 BC off Grand Congloué, a small island just outside the Bay of Marseilles. Ian was happy to observe and pick up further details about the mysteries of the deep for his new book. His articles in the *Sunday Times* conveyed his usual enthusiasm and sense of wonder. Diving is "a lonely and queer business", he wrote in the third of his reports to the paper. "The visibility has that annoying degree of opaqueness you meet motoring at dusk. You can't quite see and yet you would see still less with your lights on." Understanding the significance of Ian's personal quest, Cousteau presented his guest with a copy of his own book, *The Silent World*. As a keepsake of their earlier meeting in London, the intrepid explorer signed it, "En souvenir d'une soirée à Londres, où il y a beaucoup été question de poissons ... et d'illusions menacées."

After two weeks surveying the ocean floor, Ian hurried along the Côte d'Azur to rejoin his wife at the Villa Mauresque. Through Ann, he had grown to like Maugham: they frequently met for bridge at the Portland Club when the old boy was passing through London. He had sent the curmudgeonly author a copy of his new novel and, when Maugham had replied in favourable terms, praising Ian's ability "to get the tension to the highest possible pitch", the young pretender fired off another letter discreetly asking permission to quote from this unexpected encomium. Maugham clearly thought this impertinent: he would not do this even for the author of the Book of Genesis, he replied.

In this case Ian's precocity got the better of his natural awe of published writers. He might have had little "senior officer veneration" when dealing with admirals and field marshals but, when it came to respected authors, Ian found it difficult to hide his "schoolboyish idolisation". John Russell, his *Sunday Times* colleague (whose phrase this was), noticed this trait a couple of years earlier when Ian asked to be introduced to Angus Wilson, the novelist. "He was goggle-eyed, just as if he were meeting Vivien Leigh."

As Ann's friend, Maugham was rather different. In his company, Ian adopted the teasing, fawning role which served him well in dealings with other older men. Ann was intrigued and possibly alarmed at the similarities between the two writers. They both needed order in their domestic lives. They both liked much the same material objects, such as exotic-smelling soaps in their bathrooms. And she also had "a curious feeling that they both regarded 'women' with mistrust". On the Flemings' departure, the famously mean Maugham took his secretary-companion, Alan Searle, to task for the number of towels that had been used. Anthony Powell uncharitably recorded in his *Journals*, "It then appeared that the towels so prodigiously sent to the laundry were used to alleviate the smart where Ian Fleming whipped his wife during the sexual encounters taking place during their visit."

The reviews of *Casino Royale* were waiting back in London. As Ian had striven to make sure, they were generally enthusiastic. In the *Sunday Times*, the notice was signed Christopher Pym, in fact a pseudonym for Cyril Ray, who had recently returned from a stint as the paper's correspondent in Moscow. In his short notice, Pym/Ray managed to plug the author's "startlingly vivid turn of phrase", compare him to Le Queux and Oppenheim, and conclude, "If Mr Fleming's next story has half the swiftness of this, as astringent an accent, and a shade more probability, we can be certain that he is the best new thriller-writer since Ambler." (The last six words were inevitably pulled, slightly out of context, to provide the blurb for the paperback edition of *Casino Royale*.) Strangely enough 'Christopher Pym' also reviewed the book in similar terms in another Kemsley newspaper, the *Daily Dispatch*.

In the rival Sunday newspaper, the *Observer*, Maurice Richardson made positive noises: "Don't miss this. A sort of Peter Cheyney de luxe, with everything of the very best and most expensive." The *Daily Telegraph* gave *Casino Royale* to John Betjeman, a friend, to review with a clutch of other books. He concluded, "Ian Fleming has discovered the secret of narrative art which is to work up to a climax unrevealed at the end of each chapter." Simon Raven, who did not know Fleming, was less appreciative in *The Listener*. He praised a "good story with strength and distinction" but, referring to subjects on which he was an authority, criticized the "clumsy ending and also the torture scene, which is really too monstrous to be excused even by its ingenuity". In the provinces, Julian Symons in the *Manchester Evening News* thought the plot "staggeringly implausible" but still managed to find the book "thoroughly exciting and absorbingly readable". Ian's own favourite review was in *The Times Literary Supplement* which pronounced, "Mr Fleming has produced a book that is both exciting and extremely civilized." Although anonymous, this was written by Alan Ross, a former naval officer who, as a literary friend of Ann, counted as "family". Ian bought a copy of the paper and retained it, intact, for the rest of his life.

Although she had declined to have the book dedicated to her, Ann did her bit for the cause. She wrote an elegant and amusing letter to Lord Beaverbrook, asking if she could count on him to "give Ian's book the reviews it deserves". She joked that, having sent a copy to Peter Quennell at the *Daily Mail*, she proposed to telephone him on April Fool's Day and ask him how many paragraphs he intended to devote to it. "He will wriggle on the hook, and I eagerly anticipate those elegant literary phrases, begging for mercy and making fulsome excuses."

After publication, Ian reverted to his mixture of flattery and cajolery in his dealings with his publisher. One moment he was berating Michael Howard, a Cape director, that his friends could not find the book in the shops, the next he was demanding advertisements: the thriller business was "a fly-by-night affair", he said, and he needed some expenditure on promotion if he were ever to lift his sales above 10,000 copies, or into the same class as Peter Cheyney, with whom he was frequently compared.

To push his case, Ian devised his own advertising flyer. This noted that Fleming had scored "a grand slam with the critics" and, to prove it, he copied the choice reviews, including those from *The Times Literary Supplement* and the *Sunday Times*. When Cape claimed they had already spent £200 on advertising, Ian said he could not see how this was possible and asked to see their advertising budget. And how about some promotion in the gambling resorts of Monte Carlo, Deauville and Le Touquet? he demanded.

Ian's perseverance paid off, for, by the end of May, *Casino Royale*'s first print run of 4,750 copies (priced at 10s 6d each) had sold out. A second printing followed that month, and a third a year later in May 1954. Only Ian's brother-in-law, who had returned from Paris to begin a career as a novelist, did not join the general acclaim. "Ian's thriller starts well," Hugo told his sister Mary Rose, "but ends as the most disgusting thing I've ever seen in print – torture such as Japs and Huns eschewed as not cricket, I always knew he was neurotic and tangled. But it's been reprinted already – which won't happen to my book."

By midsummer Cape was happily trumpeting the unverifiable fact that "since April the thirteenth a copy of *Casino Royale* by Ian Fleming has been sold every six and a half minutes that the bookshops were open". The publisher was also preparing to offer him a contract for three future books. But Ian was still far from satisfied. He told Jonathan Cape that he was being tempted by two other offers, one of which came from his friend Mark Bonham Carter at Collins. He claimed he had talked to "a Cape author rather younger than myself" who had been granted a flat 20 per cent royalty on his book. "This was a severe blow to my *amour propre*, which could only be healed by somebody acting with equal generosity towards my own productions." (This was his friend Fitzroy Maclean with his book *Eastern Approaches*.) Ian could have done with his brother's more emollient qualities in his own dealings with Cape. He was not in the business of writing for vanity reasons, he told his publisher. If he was ever to free himself to write more books, he needed to earn more money. His profits from *Casino Royale* would "just about keep Ann in asparagus over

Coronation week". Cape initially demurred, noting that a 20 per cent royalty was "simply not possible", except after sales of 20,000.

But Ian refused to go away quietly, claiming that 20 per cent was being dangled in front of his eyes from another quarter which had not even read his manuscript. As a compromise he said he would settle for 15 per cent to 5,000, and 20 per cent thereafter. Cape tried to negotiate an intermediate category which would allow them to pay $17\frac{1}{2}$ per cent between 5,000 and 10,000 and 20 per cent after that. But Ian would have none of this. "I shall quite understand if you feel that these terms are not acceptable to your firm, and I can assure you that there will be no hard feelings on my side if you turn them down." In early June Cape duly backed down and agreed to Ian's original terms.

Whatever the future might hold for his books, Ian was still at that stage employed by the *Sunday Times*. But if Harry Hodson expected his foreign manager to knuckle down to some serious work on the paper on his return to London in May, he was mistaken. Somehow Ian arranged himself another couple of weeks out of the office to travel to the United States to sign his eagerly sought North American publishing deal. Three publishers – Doubleday, Norton and Knopf – had turned him down, but Macmillan finally agreed to take *Casino Royale*. Ian needed to discuss this and other matters with Curtis Brown, the New York literary agency which, on the basis of his dealings on behalf of Kemsley Newspapers, he had taken on to represent his interests in the United States. His excuse, if he needed one, was that he had some sorting-out to do in the Kemsley office in New York. He was determined that this should be a strong, working outpost of his personal empire. When his chosen agent, Clare Blanshard, was having difficulty easing out a local correspondent, Ian chided her, "The point is that I want an adult machine in New York as soon as possible, and it is up to you to create one, even though you may dislike having to use the surgeon's knife."

Crossing the Atlantic on the *Queen Elizabeth* allowed him to correct proofs of *Live and Let Die*. William Plomer had given the work an unqualified vote of approval. "The new book held this reader like a limpet mine & the denouement was shattering ... If I'm any judge, this is just the stuff – sexy, violent, ingenious, & full of well-collected detail of all kinds." The five-day voyage also allowed Ian to reflect on the first year or so of his marriage, and he professed himself pleased. In a letter to Ann, he described it extravagantly as "a far greater success than we could possibly have dreamt", though he also noted her concern about his "moods", excusing himself by saying that he could not be expected to give these up, as he had had them all his life.

New York was sweltering and Ian's discomfort was not alleviated by the lack of air-conditioning in Curtis Brown's offices. The main topic of conversation was the antics of the right-wing Senator Joseph McCarthy. Usually when Ian went to the United States, he tried to justify his generous Kemsley expenses by penning a journalistic 'notebook', often an inconsequential puff for the American book trade masquerading as an article about the best-selling American books of the day. But this time when he returned to London at the end of June, he wrote a very different type of piece, an incisive analysis of Senator McCarthy's growing influence in American politics. McCarthy had been appointed chairman of the Senate's Permanent Subcommittee on Investigations in January that year and was using his position as a base from which to attack and root out communist influence in the United States. Ian conceded that McCarthy had the knack of articulating the American people's grouses against their government. In this respect, Ian felt, he was similar to the influential and iconoclastic gossip columnist Walter Winchell who ironically, in his declining years, was a supporter of the Senator. Ian made it quite clear that he believed McCarthy's role in events was pernicious. He suspected the sinister hand of J. Edgar Hoover, the FBI chief who had dismissed him so promptly in 1941 or, as Ian uncompromisingly described him in the *Sunday Times*, "the Washington Fouché who has controlled the American secret police for the amazing span of twenty seven years".

Usually, if he wrote about politics, Ian presented a blimpish face. But this time his liberal instincts rose up. In describing these three men as "the overt and covert crusaders against un-Americanism", he added, "The sun would indeed be darkened if history were to bring them together, or any closer together, before this giant country has found itself."

Unsurprisingly Ian found office life no more attractive on his return than it had been a few weeks earlier. It was summer, his house seemed to be full of perambulators and, while Mercury still existed, his executive role at the *Sunday Times* was steadily being marginalized. Not that it mattered too much: he was a writer now, and wanted to be recognized as such. So he lobbied for further journalistic assignments which would give him not only welcome exposure but also an opportunity to research subjects relevant to his books.

A psycho-analyst might have something to say about Ian's fascination with submarine and now subterranean subject matter. After diving with Cousteau in April, Ian turned his attention to treasure-hunting and caving. He ascribed his interest to nothing more than boyish enthusiasm. Recalling his thrill when he discovered what he thought was valuable ambergris on the beach in Cornwall, he quoted Mark Twain: "There comes a time in every rightly constructed boy's life when he has a raging desire to go somewhere and dig for buried treasure."

He devised a typical journalistic stunt to indulge this urge. In May he had asked readers of the *Sunday Times* to write in with stories of buried treasure which they would like the paper to investigate. From their replies, he chose Creake Abbey, the ruin of a medieval Augustine foundation in Norfolk, largely because it was near Burnham Thorpe, the birthplace of his hero, Admiral Nelson. One hot July day he walked round the grounds of the abbey with a team of bomb disposal experts from the Royal Engineers, armed with the latest mine-detecting equipment. For two days they excavated areas where the detector suggested there was metal, or even treasure. The result was an anticlimax, Ian turning up thirty nails, one frying-pan, a mole-trap, an oil drum and some miscellaneous scrap-iron metal, but no treasure. Nevertheless, the search had been exciting and, if readers of the *Sunday Times* were disappointed, he personally had been enthralled.

The following month he and Ann piled into the Riley and made again for the Continent. Ann later marvelled at the ritual her husband went through to make a hotel bedroom into a home in ten minutes. "He would first unpack what he called 'traveller's joy', which was a large bottle of bourbon. Then he would put out his typewriter and the books he had chosen to read. He would ring the bell for some ice, and he would be as happy and relaxed as other people feel in their homes." This time their destination was the Pyrenees where, maintaining his interest in the bowels of the earth, Ian had a date to accompany the great French speleologist Norbert Casteret in his descent into the prehistoric caves at Pierre Saint Martin. But, unlike his time with Cousteau earlier in the year, this was not a 'hands-on' experience. A caver had been killed the previous year after his safety harness snapped a thousand feet underground. Ian found he had to report Casteret's exploits from the top of a deep hole. By that time he had rather gone off the project. To reach the mouth of the cave, he had to climb for four hours in the heat. Ann remarked that Martinis and champagne trickled from his pores and, as a result of his exertions, for a week he could not "walk downstairs without falling flat on his face". Ian duly filed two articles about the discovery of "a new wonder of the world" on the borders of France and Spain. But not even he could make such a non-event fly off the page. In a subsequent review Ian admitted that speleologists have a tendency to take themselves rather seriously. He hazarded the thought that their profession had "something to do with a return to the womb".

Before returning, Ian took Ann to Biarritz for a short holiday by the sea. They met a few vague friends – "international flotsam and jetsam", Ann described them – including Randolph Churchill's former wife Pamela, who as Mrs Averell Harriman later became United States Ambassador to France. Ian must have realized his caving articles were unlikely to set pulses racing back in London because he decided to write an unsolicited piece about

casinos, a subject he not only knew about personally but understood
would provide good copy. He would observe the rich at gaming tables in
Biarritz and spice up his observations with a practical guide to his readers
on "How to Win at Roulette with only £10". Ironically, at the first casino
he and Ann visited in Biarritz, they were refused entry because she was
wearing a pair of espadrilles. So they were forced inland to the more down-
market municipal casino in the Pyrenean town of Pau, where, annoyingly,
Ann proved more successful than Ian. Placing 400 francs on zero, she
closed her eyes and won.

Ian did his best to capture the moment. " 'Neuf. Rouge. Impair et
Manque.' The moment's silence and then the rattle of the losing chips
being raked across the baize, the buzz of comment and then the sharp
French voices firing the next bets at the cold, patient, croupiers." This was
not vintage writing, but it was identifiably Fleming. However, once more,
Hodson was unimpressed. He considered the article too racy for his pages –
or, as Ian put it, for "the non-conformist consciences" of the paper's
readers. So Ian recycled the piece for the American market and sent it to
Naomi Burton, his new agent at Curtis Brown New York. She sent "Roulette
without Tears", as it was retitled, to several American magazines, but it
failed to win approbation. Ian eventually published it, with added Bond
references, as a postscript to his book *Thrilling Cities* in 1960.

Ian's lacklustre accounts of his caving expedition did attract one fan,
however. They were read by Rosamond Lehmann who wrote to say that
they had churned her inside. She suggested that the experience must have
reminded him of "caverns measureless to man – down to a sunless sea"
and that Coleridge had clearly been taken to that particular cave in his
opium dream. When Ian read out her letter to Ann and Fionn at the
breakfast table, he could not understand when they both howled with
laughter. Ann had already made it clear that she thought the articles
"revealed only too clearly that there was no story to write". Now the
shock-haired novelist who had caused her such fits of jealousy only a
couple of years earlier revealed herself to be stupid and no longer a credible
rival.

Within a short time Ann had, as might have been expected, established
Victoria Square on the London social scene. If Ian tended to solitariness
and even melancholy, she was the opposite and, inevitably, the more he
showed that side of him, the more she needed to have people around her.
In early October she offered to hold a fiftieth-birthday dinner for Cyril
Connolly, but in reality it was an event for her 'boobies' to welcome her
back to the capital. Eight guests, plus herself and Ian, were joined after
the meal by a dozen friends, including Alan Pryce-Jones, Cecil Beaton,
Lucian Freud, Francis Bacon and Stephen Spender. Beaton rose to the
occasion with a paean of praise for the "style and apparent ease" with

which Ann had managed the change her situation from Rothermere's to Ian Fleming's wife. Already her parties in Victoria Square were considered more amusing than her grand soirées in Warwick House, he said. Connolly's was particularly convivial – "the talk was on target: no one wasting time in banalities". Beaton remarked that "Anne was enjoying the success of the party so much that she wanted her beloved husband, Ian, to savour every nuance of it". But Ian had other priorities, and she was disappointed to find that, by two in the morning, he had taken himself upstairs to his bed.

In New York, Al Hart, Ian's editor at Macmillan, was wielding the blue pencil on *Casino Royale*. Ian was unconcerned about possible mutilation of his masterwork. Indeed he specifically asked Naomi Burton at Curtis Brown, "Would Al Hart like to take a bit of the edge off the torture scene? He can certainly do so if he wants to." The incident, where Bond's genitals were whipped with a carpet beater, remained intact, but Hart did suggest some alterations to spare the blushes of American readers. Where Ian had written, "He slipped his hands down to her swelling buttocks and gripped them fiercely, pressing the centres of their bodies together. Panting, she slipped her mouth away from his and they clung together while he rubbed his cheek against hers and felt her hard breasts pressing into him" Hart's bowdlerized version did not quite have the same urgency: "His hand slipped down her back and pressed her body fiercely to his. Panting, she slipped her mouth away and they clung together; he brushed her ear with his lips and felt the firm warmth of her breasts against him." Hart asked plaintively, "That's not too emasculated, do you think?"

Ian could not care less. He told Hart that he had been kinder than Naomi Burton who had argued about "the relative impropriety attached to the front and back of a woman". However, at this stage, Ian was more interested in sales promotion than textual exegesis. With this in mind, he sent his editor a series of letters to dispatch to what he called "members of my 'apparatus'" with a copy of *Casino Royale* when the book was published. These were opinion-formers such as Bennett Cerf who, as well as being editor-in-chief at Random House, had an influential column in the *Saturday Evening Post*. With his eye for the tactical marketing detail, Ian begged Hart to "ensure that the machine doesn't start working until there are sufficient copies on the bookstalls".

By then *Casino Royale* had begun to attract the kind of interest Gallico had predicted from the movie business. This initially created bureaucratic problems because, although Cape ostensibly dealt with the film rights, Curtis Brown obtained the first nibble of interest from the studios. Associated British Pictures had contacted Curtis Brown's London office with an offer. But disinclined to film only *Casino Royale* (the cinematic pickings were too few), they wanted a synthesis of this novel and the next. There was also an approach from MCA in Hollywood. But this raised the delicate question – would Cape share its agent's commission with Curtis Brown? In the event Cape was happy to go halves, but Curtis Brown was not, so neither deal proceeded any further.

The most encouraging news on the film front came in early January, just before Ian and Ann departed for Jamaica. The producer, Sir Alexander Korda, a former associate of Bill Stephenson, wrote saying he had read a proof of *Live and Let Die*, and it was one of the most exciting books he had ever come across. "I really could not put it down until I had finished it. Then I gave it to my wife to read about midnight and she could not go to sleep before she had finished the whole book." Although Korda admitted he did not think it would make the ultimate secret service film Ian clearly wanted, he said he would show it to Carol Reed and David Lean for their opinions. He felt that "the best stories for films are always the stories that are written specially for films". In thanking Korda for his "exhilarating letter", Ian suggested that his third, yet to be written, novel might fit the bill more exactly. "It is an expansion of a film story I've had in my mind since the war – a straight thriller with particularly English but also general appeal, set in London and on the White Cliffs of Dover, and involving the destruction of London by a super V-2, allowing for some wonderful film settings in the old Metropolis idiom." After his impressive debut as a novelist, Ian's adoption by Pinewood, if not Hollywood, seemed imminent. In career, as much as in personal terms, it had been a remarkable twelve months.

9

Escaping the "gab-fests"
1953–1956

A neat front-page box in the *Sunday Times* proudly announced the appointment of a new Atticus, the paper's leading columnist. "Many distinguished men – politicians, authors, journalists – have worn the secret mantle of Atticus", it trumpeted in November 1953. This one was making his debut "under a title of his own choosing" – 'People & Things'. It was an appropriate, if uninspired, designation for a man stepping into the shoes of John Buchan and Sir Robert Bruce Lockhart. For while "people" have always been the staple of columns, "things" marked this one out as the work of Ian Fleming. Ian had a real journalist's love of facts. One reason he disliked Ann's smart friends was that they gossiped and spoke in riddles. He later told Nicholas Henderson, who became British Ambassador to France and the United States, that he was only interested in people with technical knowledge. He gave another friend an example of a really fascinating afternoon: it would be spent discussing silage. And he once railed against a dinner table of 'fuddy-duddies' that the craftsmen responsible for the cherished brass pictures on his walls would provide much better company than "all you lot".

Ian had manoeuvred skilfully for the Atticus job. Two years earlier he had annoyed Harry Hodson by going above his head to Lord Kemsley to bring about the dismissal of the then incumbent, Sacheverell Sitwell, whom he considered too whimsical and literary. Now, with his own Mercury service running down, he needed a new platform, and his lines of communication to the proprietor were still strong enough to secure it.

Having recently visited the United States, Ian devoted the lead item in his first Atticus column on 22 November to the theme of militant anti-communism he had tackled earlier in the summer. This time he reported how Senator Joe McCarthy's hordes had attacked the United Nations as an annexe of Moscow. Ian thought this "current prairie fire of fear, intolerance and hatred" was ridiculous, and said so. In Atticus the following week he returned to this topic. If people wanted to know the truth about any anti-American activities, they should ask J. Edgar Hoover, the head of the FBI. The fact that Hoover was not being asked, inferred Ian, suggested that he was part of the Red-bashing conspiracy.

Before long he had let slip one of the secrets of being a columnist – "the ability to write something out of nothing across the maximum space in the minimum time". Often willing to laugh at himself, he admitted he had done as much in his acerbic reply to an attack on pseudonymous columnists in Strix's Notebook in the *Spectator*. Few readers realized he was indulging in light-hearted banter with his brother, Peter, who wrote Strix. Ian managed to pull Peter up for "illiterately" describing such pseudonyms as "noms de plume" and revealing that this same Strix "has a fixation about pseudonyms dating from the cradle, in which he was known as 'Pudding'."

Ian's Atticus columns, which ran regularly from late 1953 to late 1955, and more sporadically for a year or so afterwards, were amusing testament to his wide range of friends and interests. He was unfailingly generous in plugs for people he knew – from Joan Bright who had started a literary research agency, through Ivar Bryce and his wife Jo to his contemporary hero Commander Jacques Cousteau, who featured regularly. "Things" tended to reflect long-standing enthusiasms, like Nelsonian memorabilia and cars, or adjuncts to books he was writing, like coins and diamonds.

Occasionally Ian used his prerogative as a columnist to launch a low-level crusade as when, after visiting Jamaica in March 1954, he took Jamaican hoteliers to task for charging outrageously high prices and thus driving their custom away. He had a productive line in espionage tittle-tattle – writing about the footballing passion of Vladimir Petrov, a Soviet intelligence officer who defected to the West in Australia in April that year. Another time Ian approvingly quoted Richard Sorge, the German Marxist who ran a leading spy-ring on behalf of the Soviet Union in the Far East during the Second World War. He called Sorge "the man whom I regard as the most formidable spy in history". (Ian's views were coloured by conversations with his friend Richard Hughes, the *Sunday Times's* correspondent and officially sanctioned double agent in Tokyo, who had known Sorge.) The actual quotation had the communist master-spy pontificating on why it is impossible for a woman to be a good agent: "espionage operations must be performed by a man with a good education and a clear mind," he said.

One person unimpressed by Ian's efforts at playing Atticus was Barbara Skelton. When she and Cyril Connolly assembled at White Cliffs for their annual Christmas get-together with the Flemings and, of course, Peter Quennell ("I can't imagine a Christmas without Peter," trilled Ann), Barbara noted specifically that, since starting as Atticus, Ian had "become a very dried-up and red-veined plain family man". He had "lost any semblance of glamour or good looks, a bottle-necked figure with a large bum". Her husband Cyril had another take on his friend's efforts: he proposed that the column should be renamed Attila to describe its generally philistine view of the world.

The Flemings' early 1954 sojourn in Jamaica began badly. Ian arrived with flu which he took some time to throw off. They were visited for twelve days – "twelve interminable days", noted Ann – by the pre-war socialite Tanis Guinness and her current beau Teddy Phillips, a relative of Ivar Bryce, whom she was later to marry. The visitors' endless mutual endearments grated. At one stage Ian was driven to announce at the luncheon table that he and Ann were going away for a short while, and that their visitors could, of course, continue to use the house. Since Ann had not been informed of this ploy, it caused some embarrassment. Ann had to produce some clever social footwork, which only resulted in Ian accusing her of being a traitor.

While the guests occupied themselves at cards, Ian tapped away at his typewriter. Recognizing that *Live and Let Die* had been more of an entertainment than intended, he wanted to make *Moonraker* his most ambitious and personal novel yet. Having already informed Korda of his expressionist cinematic subject matter, he deliberately focused on his home turf – the greensward of Kent and the green baize of clubland bridge tables – for another examination of the theme of duplicity which so fascinated him. Ostensibly Sir Hugo Drax was one of Britain's leading tycoons, a bit brash perhaps but part of the Establishment as a member of Blade's, London's most elegant club. Little was known about his origins because he had been found, badly injured, without papers and suffering from amnesia, on the Ardennes battlefield in the winter of 1944. Somehow he related to the name, Hugo Drax, an orphan from Liverpool, so that was what he remained as he climbed the social ladder, cornered various commodity markets and, finally, was rich enough to finance and build a new nuclear rocket for Britain's defence. But behind his impeccable façade, Sir Hugo was not quite the gentleman he seemed. He had been found cheating at Blade's, the unmistakable mark of a cad. Bond was brought in to play him and – in a vivid scene – beat him at his own game. Bond suspected that Drax was one of the German commandos, known as the Werewolves, who were infiltrated behind Allied lines as saboteurs at the time of the Ardennes offensive. This idea proved correct when he visited Drax's plant in Kent, where he discovered a corps of British-hating Nazi scientists, working for the Russians and bent on destroying London with their rocket.

Moonraker gave Ian an opportunity to wax lyrical about the England he loved – the "panorama full of colour and excitement and romance" that Bond saw from a Kentish cliff-top, the cooking (at its best "the best in the world"), and the atmosphere at Blade's where there might be cheats and perverts among the members "but the elegance of the room invested each one with a kind of aristocracy". Ian had his usual fun with names. Ann had suggested calling his villain Connolly Drax (after Cyril), but that would not have worked in German. Still Hugo Drax had resonances of Ian's brother-in-law, of Drax Hall, one of the "great houses" on Jamaica's north coast, and of Admiral Sir Reginald Plunkett-Ernle-Erle-Drax, who led the last pre-war mission to Moscow in August 1939. Duff Sutherland, "a scruffy looking chap", featured as one of the most successful bridge-players at Blade's. And Ian could not resist poking mild fun at Loelia Westminster, whom he introduced as Bond's secretary, Loelia Ponsonby, known inevitably as 'Lil' – "tall and dark with a reserved, unbroken beauty ... Unless she married soon, Bond thought for the hundredth time, or had a lover, her cool air of authority might easily become spinsterish."

Although overzealous in recording the trademarks of up-market con-sumer goods, such as Taittinger champagne and Henry Cotton golf clubs (he once explained this by saying he liked to acknowledge good craftsmanship), Ian skilfully reintroduced notes of ambiguity and realism into the life of his globe-trotting hero who for all his on-the-job pro-fessionalism failed to get the girl he wanted at the end of the book. Even his mission was beset with ambiguity. The Moonraker project which had started as a means of giving Britain "an independent say in the world", was subverted by a traitor and ended as "a giant hypodermic needle plunged into the heart of England". In acknowledging "the pain of failure that is so much greater than the pleasure of success", Bond was forced to a realization of himself as "the tough man of the world. The Secret Agent. The man who was only a silhouette." Ian carried this off with panache, while retaining his underlying sense of mythic archetypes (Drax was originally Graf Hugo von der Drache, and *Drache* is German for dragon).

Moonraker involved Ian in considerable homework. Having already asked Antony Terry for information about German V-2 rockets, he pleaded for "one more request. Has a book or a series of articles been published on the 'Werewolves' who were organized to harass us at the end of the war? Would you please let me have anything that there may be available? Incidentally, did they ever achieve anything? and what happened to them all?" Before coming to Jamaica, he talked to Phoebe Harling's employer, the Wimpole Street psychiatrist Dr E. B. Strauss, about the character traits of megalomaniacs. Strauss, a Roman Catholic who treated both Graham Greene and Evelyn Waugh, lent Ian a book, *Men of Genius*, which alerted him to consequences of childhood thumb-sucking. Ian told Strauss that Drax's "diabolical schemes for the destruction of this country stem, I have maintained, directly from a pronounced diastema of the centrals" – otherwise, the gap between his two front teeth.

The hard work continued in Jamaica. In a note to Clare Blanshard on

24 February he reported that he had written 30,000 words of *Moonraker*; there was no sex in it yet, and it "may be all right, may not". In admitting to Cape in early March that his first doubts about his creation were beginning to occur, he had "a horrible feeling" that he was beginning to parody himself. True, the logistics of writing thrillers were becoming clearer: "Readers don't mind how fantastic one is, but they must feel that the author believes in his fantasy." However, Ian could see that "the future of James Bond is going to require far more thought than I have so far devoted to him." In front of him was "nothing but a vista of fantastic adventures on more or less the same pattern, but losing freshness with each volume".

On 23 March *Casino Royale* was published by Macmillan in the United States. Ian's old ally Elsa Maxwell did her best to puff it by referring to his (and Ann's) passage through New York ten days earlier and describing his forthcoming novel as "one of the most breathtaking books I have ever read". But the reaction from reviewers was underwhelming. Anthony Boucher, the man who counted in the *New York Times Book Review*, complained that Ian had "[padded] the book out to novel length, leading to an ending which surprises no one but Bond himself". The *Cleveland Plain Dealer* found it all "rather passé" and the *Houston Chronicle* simply "disappointing".

Ian's "apparatus" reacted more favourably. Bennett Cerf, at Random House, called Naomi Burton to see if Ian was under option to Macmillan for his next book. He told Ian he had been disappointed to be given a positive response. "But in the unlikely event that you and Macmillan sever publishing relations in this country, we would consider it a great privilege to be allowed to negotiate with you." However, Cerf's interest was not sustained, nor did Korda return with any film offer. Despite Ian's efforts, the lucrative markets of both the United States and the movies were proving extraordinarily hard to penetrate.

Shortly afterwards *Live and Let Die* was launched in Britain, where the local literary mafia was primed to be more polite. Philip Day in the *Sunday Times* commented, "How wincingly well Mr Fleming writes" while George Malcolm Thomson in the *Evening Standard* found the book "tense, ice-cold, sophisticated; Peter Cheyney for the carriage trade", a phrase Ian could certainly run with. (Ann's overtures to Beaverbrook were taking effect, and Ian later wrote to thank him, adding that Thomson was "by far the best fiction reviewer and I wish we could steal him from you for the *Sunday Times*". Anthony Berry, one of Lord Kemsley's sons, who was temporarily editor of the *Sunday Chronicle*, played his part in the promotion of Ian's work by attributing a front page story from Colombo, the capital of Ceylon, on 11 April to "James Bond". The banning of *Live and Let Die* in Ireland in May helped the general publicity. But *The Times* sounded a sceptical note with its anonymous opinion that the book "works often on the edge of flippancy, rather in the spirit of a highbrow having immense fun in writing a parody of 'Sapper'". This was exactly the sort of reaction Ian did not want. And, shades of personal tensions to come, Ann's nomenclature was lukewarm: there was a note of deflating irony in Evelyn Waugh's remark to her that he had been "moved" to see how fully her husband shared her marine interests.

Two years into his marriage, Ian was adjusting to an annual rhythm. He wrote a book in Jamaica in the first three months of the year. He then returned to London to participate (or not, as the case might be) in the British publication of the novel he had written the previous winter. At roughly the same time, his American publisher put out the book he had started two years earlier. (This lead time became shorter towards the end of his career.) Ian's private agenda then called for him to escape the monotony of office life and travel to some exotic location on *Sunday Times* business. He would spend part of the summer brushing up the current book (this usually involved a trip to the Bryces' estate in Vermont), before starting to think about the next one, which would be written in Jamaica in the New Year.

Ian's post-Jamaica jaunt this year took him to the South of France. His release from Gray's Inn Road came after a chance perusal of a letter from Somerset Maugham to Ann. Maugham told her that he was unlikely to be in London for the foreseeable future because he was working on a long-mooted project – his interpretation of the ten best novels in the world and their authors. Ian recognized that this would make an excellent extended feature for the *Sunday Times*. Lord Kemsley agreed, and before long Ian was flying to Nice to discuss terms with Maugham. At first the wizened imp played hard to get. Perhaps we could buy you a Renoir, suggested Ian, but it would have to be a small one. Not interested, replied Maugham, as he invited Ian to join him for luncheon of fish soufflé, washed down by a dry vin du pays. When Ian later retired to his room for a siesta, his peace was disturbed by a knock on the door. Alan Searle, Maugham's secretary and companion, came in carrying a bulky typescript. "Willie says you'd better have a look at this," he told an astonished Ian. "He says if you don't like it he won't be offended." After further negotiations, the *Sunday Times* agreed to serialize the book for the none too exorbitant fee of £3000.

Ian had notably achieved what he had set out to do. The articles which ran in June were extremely successful. Maugham generously allowed the serialization to stretch out for fifteen weeks, during which time the paper put an extra 50,000 on its circulation of around half a million. The success of the Maugham articles encouraged Kemsley, Hodson and Hamilton to pursue the idea of starting up a separate magazine section, often with a major serialization at the front. In this way Ian influenced a major development in British newspaper journalism.

Moonraker's smartening-up continued through the summer. For the first time, however, William Plomer, Ian's sounding-board, had misgivings. Considerable restraint must have gone into his observation that Ian had "a tendency as the climax approaches to increase the strain on the reader's credulity". Plomer thought the introduction of Loelia Ponsonby as Bond's secretary did not work, and he did not like the title *Moonraker*, suggesting 'Hell is Here' would be better. (This was plucked from a good cinematic moment early in the book, when Bond noticed a flashing petrol sign which, instead of reading 'SUMMER SHELL IS HERE' said 'HELL IS HERE'.)

To cover his disappointment, Ian concentrated on basic fact-checking. Much of *Moonraker* was set in Kent, which meant that he did not have to stray too far from his cottage at St Margaret's. Raymond O'Neill timed his step-father's Riley to determine how long Bond's Bentley would take for various journeys. One of the incidents in the book had a lorry shedding its load of newsprint in front of the speeding Bond. Ian had conceived a Foden diesel truck delivering five tons of newsprint to a Ramsgate newspaper. But, before committing that to paper, he wrote to Bowater, the paper firm, asking if the details were correct and if, indeed, Bowater had a customer in the Ramsgate area. The company replied that the paper – fourteen tons of it – would generally be transported on a huge eight-wheeled AEC carrier. And while they had a customer in the nearby Isle of Thanet, they would not deliver, as Ian had suggested, at night.

To check technical details of rocketry, Ian called on Writers' and Speakers' Research, the small agency set up by Joan Bright and Joan Saunders, wife of another of his wartime NID colleagues. They proposed he should get in touch with Arthur C. Clarke. But, since Clarke was away in the United States, the British Interplanetary Society suggested another scientist to cast his eye over the manuscript.

Before long, the book was ready to be delivered into the hands of Wren Howard at Cape. The title was uncertain even at the beginning of July. It had been called *The Moonraker* until, shortly before Ian left Jamaica, Noël Coward reminded him that a much earlier author, Tennyson Jesse, had used the same title. Ian then played with calling it *The Moonraker Secret* or *The Moonraker Plot*. When those titles met with an unenthusiastic response, he proposed *The Infernal Machine*, *Wide of the Mark* or *The Inhuman Element*. The first was his favourite of these last three: "it is an expression everyone knows but has been long out of fashion". In fact, Coward was wrong: Tennyson Jesse's book, published in 1927, was, like Ian's, simply called *Moonraker*.

With Atticus established, Ian was able to turn his attention to his next book, a tale, set largely in the United States, of international intrigue in the diamond business. After gambling, American gangsters and Nazi infiltrators into English society, diamonds were an obvious topic for Ian. In his pre-war career at Rowe and Pitman, he had worked closely with Ernest Oppenheimer's Anglo-American Corporation, which operated a virtual monopoly of the world diamond market through its De Beers associate. After the war his friend Hugh Vivian Smith had left Rowe and Pitman and gone to South Africa as managing director of Anglo-American. At Ian's behest and with Vivian Smith's encouragement, Philip Brownrigg had also joined Anglo-American, quitting journalism to become the company's director of public relations. As a result of these connections Ian had little difficulty arranging a visit to the securely guarded headquarter of De Beers' Diamond Selling Organization in London, to view one of its regular diamond 'sights'. He was briefed by Sir Percy Sillitoe, a tough, uncompromising Scotsman who had recently retired as head of MI5 and was working for De Beers investigating illegal diamond buying.

In August 1954 Ian flew to the United States for further research on the book that was to be called *Diamonds Are Forever*. Conveniently, he had decided to set part of his book in Saratoga Springs, the spa town in upstate New York, close to Black Hole Hollow Farm. William Stephenson had sent him a magazine article about the place, which provided useful background detail for the guided tour Bond was given by Felix Leiter in the novel. (Leiter was now working for Pinkerton's, the detective agency, having lost an arm and a leg in a near fatal encounter with a shark in *Live and Let Die*.) "Eleven months of the year," explained Leiter, "the place is just dead. People drift up to take the waters and the mud baths for their troubles, rheumatism and such like ... And then for one month – August – the place goes hog-wild. It's probably the smartest race-meeting in America, and the place crawls with Vanderbilts and Whitneys." Ian/Bond fell in love with the green and peaceful town, "a mixture of Newmarket and Vichy, and it suddenly occurred to Bond that although he wasn't in the least interested in horses, he rather liked the life that went with them." Ian even wrote to inform Lord Rosebery, Hugh Vivian Smith's father-in-law and a great lover of horses, that he might at last be acquiring a taste for racing. On one occasion he and Ernie set out to visit Saratoga's famous mud-baths, but took the wrong turning and ended up in a peeling, inferior establishment on the outskirts of town. That provided Ian with the first-hand material to invent a seedy subculture of gangsters and hucksters who, from their base at the Acme Mud and Sulphur Baths, preyed on wealthy patrons of the racetrack.

For the first time a young man called William Woodward Jr was staying at the farm. His father, the majority owner of New York's Hanover Bank, had died the previous year leaving Billy a fortune, including a stake in the sumptuous Belair stud. Initially Billy was disinclined to follow his father into racing. But slowly, with prodding from his social-climbing wife Ann, he began to show interest. His colt Nashua had won the Florida Derby earlier that year, and was to go on to even greater things. Ian and Billy struck up a cool, sardonic friendship. Having spent several years in London, cutting a dash in Mayfair society, Billy had some style. Ian laughed at his insistence on cocktails before lunch, and pronounced him one of the best Americans he had ever met. Billy's problem was his wife. A poor white girl from the Midwest, who had worked as a showgirl, her social *faux pas* were beginning to grate in Billy's snobbish circles. When asked for advice on what to do, Ian drawled laconically, "Divorce her, old boy. Divorce her."

Ian was more interested in Woodward's car, an unusual Studebaker with a powerful Cadillac engine, known as a Studillac. While he might be bored by certain Americans, he was still fascinated by American things, and particularly American gadgets and engineering. He unhesitatingly appropriated the Studillac for *Diamonds Are Forever*. "There was a straight stretch of empty road in front of them. Leiter gave a brief glance in his driving mirror and suddenly banged the gear lever into second and thrust his foot into the floor. Bond's head jerked back on his shoulders and he felt his spine being rammed into the back of the bucket seat. Incredulously, he glanced at the hooded speedometer. Eighty. With a clang Leiter's hook hit the gear lever into top. The car went on gathering speed. Ninety, ninety-five, six, seven – and then there was a bridge and a converging road and Leiter's foot was on the brake and the deep roar of the engine gave way to a steady thrumming as they settled down into the seventies and swept easily through the graded curves."

When, on a later trip, Ian took out a real Studillac and put it through its paces, he was hauled up by the local sheriff for driving at over eighty miles an hour. But he avoided a speeding ticket – largely because the sheriff could not understand his well-rounded English vowels. Later, he might have said he was the creator of James Bond, but at that stage the name still meant nothing in the United States.

Ian's loving evocation of the Studillac's capabilities reflected not only his passion for American cars but also the extent to which his sojourns in Vermont allowed him to let his hair down and live out part of the fantasy life he hinted at in his books. In one of his dreams he was a successful newspaper tycoon. When, three years earlier, Ivar had suggested his friend might like to join him in a little business venture, reviving the fortunes of the ailing North American Newspaper Alliance (NANA), Ian flew at the chance. NANA was a features agency which had operated for three decades as a cooperative venture between several leading American newspaper groups, including the *New York Times* and the *Los Angeles Times*. In its early days it had been very successful. In 1930 it paid a record $270,000 to serialize the memoirs of General Pershing – a figure that was not bettered until after the Second World War. It hired Ernest Hemingway to report on the Spanish Civil War. But by the early 1950s, with the arrival of television, its star had begun to wane. Advised by Ernie Cuneo, who told him it was a sure way to meet anyone he wanted, Ivar stepped in and bought control. He appointed the shrewd Cuneo to oversee the American end of things from NANA's comfortable office in the *New York Times* building on West 41st Street. And Ian was brought on board to offer a professional news-paperman's advice.

It was not long before NANA was benefiting from some of the tricks Ian had learned at the Mercury Service. Everyone seemed to benefit. As European vice-president, with a salary of £1,500 a year, Ian negotiated for Paul Gallico to write regular pieces, including coverage of the Coronation. Another friend, Noel Barber, editor of the *Continental Daily Mail*, was hired to do a Paris column under the name Noel Anthony. Several of Mercury's stringers found that, at a difficult time for the Kemsley group, they had a welcome new source of income.

Demonstrating his skill at twisting Lord Kemsley round his finger, Ian convinced his boss that the *Sunday Times* might benefit from a formal relationship with NANA and within a short time Mercury correspondents were supplying a third of NANA's material. Kemsley gave NANA a London office in the *Sunday Times* building, where the agency installed a European editor, Sylvia Short, and a secretary, just down the corridor from Ian. In a letter to Cuneo in June 1953, Ian gave a cheerfully embellished picture of the first European NANA meeting "with the Vice-President [him] sitting on the Vice-Chairman's [Bryce's] knee, the London Editor and Manager [Miss Short] on the Vice-President's and a pretty secretary on the London Manager and Editor's. This is known in some circles as a 'Turkish sand-wich'." In business, as in everyday life, Ian, Ivar and Ernie saw no reason not to enjoy themselves.

Later that year, writing on smart blue notepaper with a new NANA logo designed by Robert Harling, Ian gave the clearest possible indication of looming problems at Mercury. He told Ernie of his fears that Mercury's demise would have a catastrophic effect on their own business. (Mercury was now providing half NANA's output.) Therefore Ian had "opened up negotiations" for "a cheap filler service" with Bill Aitken, Lord Beaver-brook's nephew, who ran the syndication side of Express Newspapers. Aitken liked what he saw, and within twelve months he was asking Ian what it would cost to buy NANA outright. Aitken admitted he was more interested in NANA's North American outlets (for the *Express*'s syndicated material) than in its product. When Ian quoted a price of $1 million, Aitken "very nearly swallowed his pipe" and asked if a partnership might be arranged. In relating this incident to Ernie, Ian admitted the agency was probably worth more like $500,000. But he urged careful consideration of the partnership idea. If that materialized, he believed that NANA could "become an entirely new business and perhaps really get into the Big League". This was one of the things Ian needed to discuss with Ivar and Ernie in Vermont.

While her husband was in America that summer, Ann took Fionn to the Greek island of Hydra to stay with Paddy and Joan Leigh Fermor, whose other guests included the Oxford don Maurice Bowra and the inveterate traveller Freya Stark. Separate holidays reflected the gap which was developing between the Flemings, with Ian opting for the easy modern-day luxury of the Bryce set and Ann for the rigours of classicism and intellectualism. Such a statement was not unexpected for it reflected a similar divide in England between Ian's preferred company (if any at all) of clubmen and golfers, and Ann's coterie of loquacious highbrows.

The plain fact was that, after two and a bit years, Ian was tiring of the effort and compromise of matrimony. In his first few months of living with Ann, he had been genuinely happy. But then the gap between the reality and his expectations began to intrude. He joked to Robert Harling, his safety-valve on such occasions, "in the old days I demanded or perhaps pleaded for three things in a wife. She should have enough money to buy her own clothes, she should be able to make incomparable Sauce Béarnaise, and she should be double-jointed. In the event I got none of these things." Ian's solution, whenever he was in London, was to spend more and more time on his own. In a letter to Alan Ross, he provided an interesting account of the sort of evening he enjoyed at Boodle's. In Ann's bedroom in Victoria Square, he had come across a copy of *Something of the Sea*, Ross's 1954 volume of poems about his wartime naval experiences. Normally, Ian suggested, he would not have seen it, but she had caught a cold and stayed in the country. "I use her lavatory – examine *her* books – find S.O.T.S. Stump off to Boodle's with S. – & New Yorker & latest U.S. thriller. Read S. through 4 gulls eggs, fried fillets of sole & $\frac{1}{2}$ bot Chablis. Quite enchanted ... Forgive telegraphese but must now play bridge with affronted members."

After such undemanding evenings at Boodle's, he looked forward to letting himself quietly into Victoria Square and padding his way up to the top floor without disturbing his wife's "gab-fests", as he called her regular gatherings, and without being caught in the crossfire of repartee between guests such as James Pope-Hennessy and Cecil Beaton. Since *Live and Let Die* had failed to attract the critical response he wanted, Ian was beginning to feel that Ann's friends looked down on him and his literary efforts. There is a widely reported story, though no one is prepared to admit being present, of Ian returning home to find a "booby" reading from one of his novels, while the rest of the party laughed at Ian's breathy rendering of some sexual encounter.

With the excitement (but not the underlying affection) in the relationship beginning to fail, the Flemings' domestic life began to take on something of a routine. From Monday to Friday they stayed at Victoria Square, where Ann (with the help of the Crickmeres) entertained at least twice a week. On Fridays they drove down to Kent where Nanny Sillick and a housekeeper remained all the time with Caspar. One could set a watch by Ian's timekeeping. As he told a bibliophile friend, Dr Alan Barnsley, he flashed through Barnsley's home town of Maidstone in his Riley, "every Friday evening ten minutes either side of 7 p.m. and back again every Monday morning ten minutes either side of 11 a.m."

One inevitable consequence of this lifestyle was that Ian had little to do with Caspar's upbringing. Even at St Margaret's Bay, Caspar stayed with Mrs Sillick in the servants' quarters until the early evening. Then he was brought along the connecting passage to spend some time with his parents. But often it was too much for him, and he would rush back crying to Nanny.

Ian tried to make up for this by being fussy and overprotective. One baking day the previous summer, Miss Sillick found Ian sitting with his son on the veranda outside the house. Caspar was in his pram, with the hood up and the storm-cover buttoned up to his chin. In her forthright manner, she rushed up and enquired, "Are you trying to suffocate the child?" Ian replied that he was afraid that the seagulls might get at Caspar. A couple of years later, when Ian learned that Nanny had taken Caspar into Dover on the bus, he rebuked her, "You do not take a child of mine on a public bus."

As winter drew on, the annual safari to Jamaica loomed. This time Ann's maternal instincts were to bring Caspar to Jamaica. But Ian refused to countenance it, claiming that a child of his son's age could not endure the dangers of the tropical sun and a shark-infested sea. Ann joked that Ian was frightened of letting Nanny see him swim naked.

But, first, Ian had another date in America. Ostensibly as a piece of field research for his next book, he had arranged to travel across the continent with Ernie Cuneo by train. His journey would enable him to meet some contacts in the movie business in Los Angeles and visit the gambling paradise of Las Vegas for the first time.

After crossing the Atlantic with Ivar Bryce on the *Queen Elizabeth* in early November 1954, Ian joined up with Cuneo in Manhattan. The first leg of their journey took them on one of America's classic railroads, the *Twentieth Century*, from New York to Chicago. In this company and these circumstances, Ian played his role as a crusty middle-aged English clubman

he young Etonian

Ian as caricatured by Amies Milner; and winning the steeplechase at Eton.

Eve Fleming and her sons: Peter (left), Richard, Michael, Ian.

Country house life: with Deirdre Hart-Davis at Aldwick, 1929; and with
Nora Phipps, Joyce Phipps (later Grenfell) and Henry Tiarks at Furneux
Pelham, 1928.

With Monique Panchaud de Bottones beside Lake Geneva in 1932.

With Muriel Wright in Austria.

In Capri, 1938; and golfing with
Count Paul Munster and Robert
Sweeny.

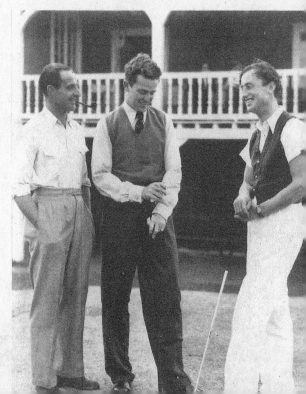

Commander Fleming RNVR in Room 39.

Demob happy at Eton, 4 June 1945, with members of the Pitman family.

Early days at Goldeneye. Ann Rothermere's first visit in 1948; and with Ivar Bryce.

Messing about in Jamaica: with Barrington Roper and barracuda; with Noël Coward; and with Blanche Blackwell.

With Ann in Capri, 1960; and outside High Court, London, 1963.

On set: with Sean
Connery; Ursula
Andress; and James
Bond producers
Harry Saltzman
and 'Cubby'
Broccoli.

Mr and Mrs Ian Fleming in their drawing room, Victoria Square, London.

At Raymond and Georgina O'Neill's wedding: Caspar (left), Francis Grey, Joan Sillick, Ann and Ian.

At his Mitre Court desk.

With Blanche Blackwell.

In the gazebo at Goldeneye; with Ann, Cecil Beaton, Noël Coward and friends at Blue Harbour.

Cecil Beaton's portrait of Ian, bon viveur.

to perfection. Ernie joked that it was not until they had reached the upstate capital of Albany that Ian had finished telling the steward how to mix his martinis. When Ian pronounced that his oysters and steak were excellent, Ernie noted that "he managed to inflect that slight touch of surprise that made it patronising". When he teased his friend that he could imagine an Englishman's delight in travelling on such a magnificent train, Ian barked back that Ernie should take a journey on the *Flying Scotsman* some time.

In Chicago Ian annoyed Ernie by demanding to see what he described as "America's greatest shrine" – the scene of the St Valentine's Day massacre. Ernie insisted that, before this, Ian should accompany him somewhere rather different, the Chicago Institute of Fine Arts. Contrary to expectations, Ian was enthralled by the masterpieces on show. "He commented in subdued tones," remembered Ernie. "It was as near as I ever saw him come to reverence." At the time, Ernie ribbed his friend, "Rather nice to find something like this out on the great American prairie, don't you think?" Ian was not amused. "Those pictures have no goddamned right to be in Chicago," he replied, before skulking off to his version of America, a place where Al Capone had wielded his machine-guns. On his return to his hotel, with his attention to detail, he scribbled what he had seen in a notebook.

A couple of days later the two men climbed aboard another great train, the *Super Chief*, for the next stage of their journey to Los Angeles. As usual, women and sex featured high among their topics of conversation. When Ernie opined that sex was a sport in New York, a profession in Hollywood, an art in Paris and a heavy industry in London, Ian shot back with the contrary view, "And a damned nuisance in Washington." As they crossed the Great Plains, the prevailing mood was contemplative rather than boisterous. Both men were in their mid-forties, both had recently started young families, and often the talk was about taking stock of their lives. They discussed war and fate and death. Ernie was surprised to hear Ian say that he expected eventually to return to Scotland to die. When Ernie ruminated that he could never go back to his childhood haunts in New Jersey because it depressed him so, Ian agreed. "Nobody can," he said, with a touch of Scots melancholy. "You can't go back to anything. But something calls you to the neighbourhood of your people's place. It's a mystique."

Ernie was not the first person to notice an intriguing feature of his enigmatic friend. Ian was never fully in touch with what was happening around him; he seemed to be searching, as Peter Quennell had remarked, for a lost piece in a jigsaw puzzle. In Ernie's romantic view, Ian was "a knight errant searching for the lost Round Table and possibly the Holy Grail, and unable to reconcile himself that Camelot was gone and still less that it had probably never existed". In another context Ernie likened Ian to a nineteenth-century Paris boulevardier who would lapse into melancholy pensiveness because he could not reconcile himself to the death of Henry of Navarre, more than three centuries earlier. Ernie felt this had not embittered Ian. "Much worse, it disappointed him, for bitterness is a form of life, and disappointment of heart is the hopelessness of accepted death." Others, Ann perhaps, might have said that Ian had an infuriating facility for disengaging from a situation when it did not suit him and seeking stimulation, sustenance or, increasingly, silence elsewhere.

In more upbeat mode, Ian talked to Ernie about his favourite author who at that moment was Somerset Maugham, and his favourite character, Jacques Cousteau. He was candid about his need for approval. "Know what I would consider the ideal existence?" he asked Ernie as the train rolled through the Midwest. (One might assume that it was late at night and Ian had drunk a fair amount.) "Know what I'd like if I could have anything I wanted? I'd like to be the absolute ruler of a country where everybody was crazy about me. Imagine yourself waking up in the White House. Instantly, the radio would announce to a breathless country, 'He's awake.' Bulletins would follow. 'He's shaving.' 'He's dressing.' 'He's breakfasting.' 'He's reading the papers in the garden.' Finally, at ten-thirty: 'He's ordered the car!' And at eleven o'clock I'd pass out through the gates, tossing medals to deliriously happy hundreds of thousands. I'd like that. And so would they." Ian was only half-joking; part of him really did crave that form of adulation.

When they tired of talking, Ernie arranged for Ian to ride in the cab with the driver and engineers. "He was all over the engine, went back into the inferno of noise in the diesel room – alone – and interrogated the engineer and his assistant on everything from the block signal system to the 'dead man control'." Ian was thrilled to see the care with which they took the *Super Chief* through the Raton Pass. He got off at every stop in New Mexico and Arizona, "talking to the men serving the train, walking briskly around the desert architecture stations, taking mental photographs by the score".

Once in Los Angeles Ian had film business to attend to. Over the course of the year his ad hoc team of agents had had some modest success selling his film and television rights. In May, in a deal engineered by John Shepbridge of Famous Players, the Hollywood producer Gregory Ratoff agreed to pay $600 for a six months' option on *Casino Royale*, plus a further $6,000 if the project went into production. Not to be outdone, a week later, Curtis Brown managed to sell the television rights to CBS for $750, a sum which was quickly increased to $1,000 when Ian asked. On 21 October CBS became the first company to portray James Bond on screen when it broadcast an hour-long live version of *Casino Royale* as part of its Chrysler Climax Mystery Theater series. The production took several additional liberties with Ian's story-line. Bond became an American agent, while Leiter was British. And because of technical problems, the coast-to-coast audience saw Peter Lorre, the actor playing Le Chiffre, get up off the floor after his "death" and begin to walk to his dressing-room.

Trading on his television debut, Ian paid a courtesy call on his West Coast agent "Swanee" Swanson, who told him that Stanley Meyer, the producer of *Dragnet* at Warner Brothers, had expressed an interest in *Live and Let Die* and *Moonraker*. Ian said he wanted $1,000 for an option, against $25,000 if the movie was made. Meyer offered $500 against $5,000 for these and subsequent books, but Ian did not consider this enough. Swanson subsequently informed Curtis Brown that "Fleming is a very nice guy and I would like to make a sale for him." However their mutual dealings had been frustrated because the author was "a very vague man" – not a charge often levelled against Ian. Clearly the pace of the movie world was unfamiliar.

Ernie tried to keep Ian amused by taking him to an American football game and to the races at Santa Anita. But Ian made it clear that the only place he really wanted to visit was the Los Angeles Police Department (LAPD). Ernie arranged for him to meet Captain James Hamilton, the sharp-minded chief of the LAPD's intelligence service. Ian was still totally unknown in the United States, but he and the policeman hit it off immediately. By way of introduction Ernie said, "Captain, Mr Fleming here has the usual distorted view of Englishmen. They believe, you know, our country is laced by organized gangs of racketeers, of tremendous wealth and of enormous influence." Hamilton answered simply, "Well, don't you?" When Ernie spluttered a denial, saying he did not think it would be possible to run a big business on a basis of corruption, the Captain asked casually. "Ever been to Las Vegas?"

Ian and the policeman sprang into an animated conversation about the criminal underworld. Hamilton took down charts and lectured his guest about the Mafia – its discipline, its territories, its members. He talked about murders that his department had solved but could not prove in court. He discussed criminal profiling and surveillance techniques, like the airport "tourist" with a shaving kit which contained a movie camera to film visiting mobsters. Ian's ears perked up when Hamilton complained that his greatest headache was the increasing use of drugs. Hamilton called in the local narcotics chief, who lectured Ian on various drugs, and how they were carried and concealed. Ian and Ernie were taken to a nearby precinct to see a small exhibition on the subject. Ernie was appalled, but Ian could not stop asking questions and noting down the answers.

Later at dinner at Chasen's, they bumped into Milt Wertheimer, a leading casino operator in Detroit and Miami. Ian pounced on him and pummelled him with questions. Did he ever come across people who ran "systems" to beat his casinos? "All the time," Wertheimer answered. "So how do you handle them?" "We send a car to the airport to meet them." Ian also wanted to know how casinos made their "real money". He whipped out his notebook as Wertheimer laughed in reply, "On the loser who's just going to stay until he breaks even. He's our boy."

From Los Angeles the two men flew to Las Vegas to investigate further. Ian had just stepped from the airplane when he whooped with delight. Among the various slot-machines in the arrivals hall was one which, for the price of a quarter, provided two minutes of pure, undiluted oxygen. Ian felt this told him everything he wanted to know about Las Vegas. They took a taxi to Sands where Ernie knew Jack Entratta, the manager. Before going to their rooms, they decided to try their luck at the blackjack tables in the hotel entrance, where Entratta noticed Ernie and insisted on moving him and his friend to his most luxurious suite and – the highest accolade in the house – allowing them access to the private barber shop.

Entratta enthused about the stars he had signed for his lavish shows. But when he claimed he was really only in the entertainment industry, Ian became visibly annoyed. Casinos as a branch of show business did not interest him. He wanted to know how they worked and how they dealt with crime. His eyes lit up when, on entering the gaming-room, he observed the psychological warfare when a gambler begins to win. First the pit boss comes over to watch the dealer. If the winning streak continues, he changes the deck, and then the dealer. If that still does not work, he calls a couple of deputy sheriffs over to sit beside the lucky punter – to "lean on him", as Ian learned to his amusement.

Ernie eventually became bored with his friend's ceaseless research. He proposed a casino crawl and promised they would beat the house in every joint in Las Vegas. Starting in Sands, Ernie bet one dollar on a game of blackjack. When he had won his stake back, he got up from the table, called a waitress, ordered a couple of glasses of champagne for Ian and himself, and moved on to the next casino. The two men worked down the strip through the Sahara and the Old Frontier until they had visited all the casinos in Las Vegas. As Ernie told the story, he stuck rigidly to his method. When they were one dollar ahead, they stopped playing, took a swig of champagne and walked on to the next joint. Eventually at four o'clock in the morning they found themselves out of town at Steamboat Springs, telling anyone who cared to listen that they had beaten all the houses in Las Vegas. How they got back to their hotel is not recorded. The two men slept most of the remainder of the morning. When they reached the airport to take the night plane to Denver and the East Coast, they were glad of a lungful of oxygen from the slot-machine.

Back in England a "tiring" family Christmas at St Margaret's Bay was enlivened by a fire in the next-door cottage which the Flemings had hired to house a visiting cook. Again it was mid-January before they departed for New York en route for Jamaica. A Boxing Day air disaster had only served to heighten Ann's fear of flying. One of her nightmares was that, if she and Ian were killed in an air crash, Caspar would be left without parents. So she insisted they travel separately.

Her reluctance to fly with Ian stemmed partly from a growing coolness towards Jamaica. She loved aspects of her Caribbean existence. She enjoyed painting under an umbrella in the sunken garden while Ian tapped away at his typewriter behind the jalousies in the drawing-room. But she had little genuine passion for tropical life. Whenever she was now at Goldeneye, she could not hide her disappointment that she was missing the splendour of an English winter turning into spring. Her letters from Jamaica in 1955 expressed a sadness and longing for her imminent return to Britain.

As a companion during the long periods when Ian was writing, Ann invited Peter Quennell to stay in February. Quennell was amused to find himself incurring 'the Commander's' displeasure by passing in front of his host's bedroom window on his way for an early-morning swim. It transpired that Ian liked to stare out to sea, thinking about what he was going to write after breakfast. Quennell disturbed his concentration and had to be asked by Ann to find another way down to the little beach. He later reflected that this was an example of Ian's perfectionism, some might call it childishness: Ian could not stand any jarring detail to disturb his overall imaginative composition. The highlight of Quennell's visit was his encounter with Evelyn Waugh, who came from the Brownlows' along the coast. Quennell had held Waugh in high esteem bordering on veneration, but Waugh had reciprocated by bullying and demeaning the man. Now, in the heat of the Caribbean sun, the two authors were forced to put their clubland differences aside. Ian booted them out of the house for a couple of days. He sent them with Ann to enjoy one of the highlights of the Jamaican tourist circuit, rafting down the Rio Grande in the company of one of the island's characters, a boatman-entrepreneur called Red Grant, whom Ian described as "a cheerful, voluble giant of villainous aspect" and whose name he appropriated for a SMERSH killer in *From Russia, With Love*. Waugh, who negotiated the Rio Grande in blue silk pyjamas and panama hat with a pink ribbon, enjoyed himself at the Flemings. After visiting Kingston, he wanted to return for a night. He told Ann, "Goldeneye was delightful, I should not have believed that a modern house could be so congenial. What an ideal life you have made for yourselves there."

Ian had completed most of the background research for *Diamonds Are Forever* before he came – the diamond sights at De Beers in London, Saratoga, Las Vegas. He even incorporated the oxygen machine at Las

Vegas airport, while Ernie Cuneo (with his name changed to Cureo) was called into service as a Nevada taxi-driver. He pulled some excellent description passages and one-liners out of his carefully kept notebooks (such as his description of the architecture in Las Vegas as from the Gilded Mousetrap School). But he had difficulty rendering Bond's love scenes. Waugh forced him to work at them until he was satisfied. "An author must be in a state of lustful excitement when writing of love," he said.

Lustful or not, Ian was experiencing renewed doubts about his creation. By the end of his stay he had completed four books, but as he wrote to Ann (she had returned home before him) the final product seemed "terribly silly". He told Hilary Bray that he thought he had exhausted his inventiveness "as it contains every single method of escape and every variety of suspenseful action". So, almost as an afterthought, he appended four extra chapters, recording what happens when Bond and Tiffany sail back to England on the *Queen Elizabeth*. These chapters form a coda to the main action, their only function being to allow Ian to deliberate, through the mouths of his characters, on the nature of marriage. Bond seems to be speaking for Ian when he tells Tiffany, "Most marriages don't add two people together. They subtract one from the other."

Ian's negativity reflected in part his failure either to interest the American book-buying public or to break into the film market. With a few changes for the local market, *Live and Let Die* was published in the United States in January to an unenthusiastic response. Only 5,000 copies were sold, and Al Hart at Macmillan was uncharacteristically blunt when he said, "Mr Bond will have to do better than this." Shortly afterwards, while Ian was in Jamaica, the Warner deal to film the book fell through, though there was better news in March when the producer Gregory Ratoff decided to convert his option and purchase the full rights to *Casino Royale*. But the sum involved was so paltry – $6,000 – that Ian decided to bank it immediately and buy himself a keepsake in the form of a big, powerful American car. However, it was not a Studillac of the type that had thrilled him in Vermont. For he had seen a Ford Thunderbird in the street and fallen in love with its hooded headlights, chrome grille and sleek chassis. So after a nervous test drive around Battersea Park he ordered a black T-bird with conventional gear-change, overdrive and interchangeable hard and soft top. For some reason, he stipulated that it should have as little power assistance as possible.

Ian considered the car the acme of American engineering. As he wrote in an article in the *Spectator* a couple of years later, "True, it isn't a precision instrument like English sports cars, but that I count a virtue. The mechanical margin of error in its construction is wider. Everything has a solid feel. The engine, a huge, adapted low-revving Mercury V-8 of 5 litre capacity, never gives the impression of stress or strain. When, on occasion, you can do a hundred without danger of going off the edge of this small island, you have not only the knowledge that you have an extra 20 m.p.h. in reserve, but the feel of it. As for acceleration, when the two extra barrels of the 4-barrel carburettor come in, at around 3,000 revs, it is a real thump in the back." Ann was less enamoured of Ian's new toy. She complained that sitting in the front seat with the roof invariably down brought on a condition she called "Thunderbird neck". "Thunderbird" also became a nickname by which Ann referred to her husband (particularly in letters to Evelyn Waugh).

The British critics gave *Moonraker* their usual civilized response when it was published in London in April 1955. In the *Observer* Maurice Richardson wrote that Ian continued "to be irresistibly readable, however incredible; seldom has an expensive education been turned more cunningly to account", while in the Roman Catholic weekly *The Tablet* John Biggs-Davison used that flattering comparison again: he thought *Moonraker* "establishes its author as Mr Eric Ambler's rival or successor". Once more, the only dissenting voice was *The Times* which said that Ian's tendency to parody himself, which had been apparent in *Live and Let Die*, had "taken charge" in the second half of this story.

Ian took heart from the comments of his older and more worldly critics. Noël Coward had read *Moonraker* in proof in Jamaica and pronounced, "It is the best thing he has done yet, very exciting and, although as usual too far-fetched, not quite so much so as the last two and there are fewer purple sex passages. His observation is extraordinary and his talent for description vivid. I wish he would try a non-thriller for a change; I would so love him to triumph over the sneers of Annie's intellectual friends."

Lord Beaverbrook may have been more her friend than his, but he was no intellectual. After publication, a cable arrived from him in the South of France, "SPLENDID BOOK MAKING UP FOR NO NEWSPAPERS INCLUDING SUNDAY EXPRESS AND SUNDAY TIMES". (The English papers had not been delivered in Cap d'Ail that day.) When Ian thanked Beaverbrook for this unsolicited praise, he was treated to a letter of appreciation about the "thrilling story about the good secret service bloke and the bad bastard. I promise you I enjoyed it immensely. And I am not a detective story fiend."

Now that Beaverbrook had bitten, Ian was determined to keep him sweet. He wrote a gratuitously sycophantic mini-profile of Beaverbrook in *Atticus*, saying, amongst much flummery, that when history came to decide between him and Northcliffe as to the greatest newspaperman of the twentieth century, the verdict would go to him. Again Beaverbrook rushed round his thanks. Ian's words had been "like the permanent effect of a bottle or two of Roederer 1947", he said. Ian had not completed his charm offensive. "For thirty years you have daily contributed to my pleasure," he wrote back, "and the least I could do, when I got the chance, was to hack out a stumbling tribute in my stuffy column. My greatest relief was to get it past [Lord Kemsley] without qualification and past Ann without a snort of contempt for my superlatives!"

But the criticism which meant most to Ian personally came from Raymond Chandler, whom Ian met at a luncheon party at the St John's Wood house of the poet Stephen Spender and his wife, the pianist Natasha Litvin. Never outgoing, Chandler was in a particularly morose and introverted mood following the deaths of both his wife and favourite cat. Ian was interested to meet the English-educated author who had stamped his fictional mark so authoritatively on the Los Angeles underworld. He liked to think that he might soon carve out a similar niche in British letters. He warmed to Chandler even more when the respected author praised *Casino Royale* and added that, if Ian wanted, he would say so for the benefit of his publisher. Never one to refuse a public relations opportunity, Ian sent him a copy of *Live and Let Die* and invited him to lunch at a favourite restaurant, Overton's, which he claimed had the best *pâté maison* in town. Ian managed to convey that he would indeed appreciate Chandler's written endorsement which would help him "make the fortune which has so far eluded me". Although Chandler normally resisted such overtures, he agreed to comply for a number of reasons. He was interested in the way English public-school boys (like himself) tackled writing about American gangsters, he saw Ian as a powerful manipulator and therefore useful ally on the London literary scene, and, besides, he genuinely liked the younger man's work. On 4 June he sent Ian a few lines which managed to praise him as "probably the most forceful and driving writer of what I suppose still must be called thrillers in England" while denigrating some of his predecessors in the field. (Of James Hadley Chase, he opined, the less said the better.) Chandler praised Ian for tackling the American scene. "Some of your stuff on Harlem in *Live and Let Die* and everything on St Petersburg, Florida, seems to me quite amazing for a foreigner to accomplish." In conclusion, he enquired tartly, "If this is any good to you, would you like me to have it engraved on a gold slab?" Ian wrote back understandably delighted. He was going to send this encomium to his publishers in Britain and the United States. He admitted, however, that it made him a trifle ashamed about his latest book, *Diamonds Are Forever*, which had "more fantasy" than *Live and Let Die* (and therefore was less realistic and potentially less interesting to Chandler).

As a thank-you Ian prevailed on Ann to invite the visiting author to one of her luncheon parties. Normally Ian steered clear of such events, but this time he returned specially from the office to welcome Chandler and his fellow guests, the Spenders, and an old friend, Rupert Hart-Davis, whom Ian described quixotically as "the best young publisher in Britain".

He promised a lightweight affair: "No one will say 'How do you think up those wonderful plots, Mr Chandler?'" The party was not a success, however, largely because of Chandler's evident discomfiture in this company. Nevertheless it helped Ian cement his friendship with Chandler, who later used to tease Ian about the ordeal of this luncheon gathering – the kind of event which Chandler made quite clear had led him to leave England thirty years earlier.

Another boost to Ian's morale came when Daniel George, the fiction reader at Cape, who worked closely with William Plomer in preparing Bond for the reading public, produced the world's first 007 parody. This amusing literary morsel had Bond "pitched from Cy Nide's supercharged, gravity-resisting helicopter" into a herd of elephants, looking for valuable radioactive mud. It is full of schoolboyish humour: " 'Well,' he uttered, 'I may have bitten the dust but I'm no stick-in-the-mud.' But the flash of his famous wit was too much for him. A dagger of pain transfixed him." Bond has an exotic maiden called Topazia, whom he calls "my double-breasted dusky beauty". He remembers that Plomer has warned him not to expect much of the Kikup tribe. Their females, Plomer had said, were unipapillate, steatopygous and retromingent. He has no idea what those words meant, but the development of the story shows them all to be true. Eventually Bond has to be rescued by "a lank, lean, hard-bitten figure", who comes crashing through the undergrowth with a profile like an Antonine emperor. "In his long prehensile arms he gathered Bond as tenderly as ever mother gathered babe, and plunged again into the jungle. 'Thanks, Ian,' said Bond laconically. 'Don't go too fast for Topazia.' When at length, over their ammoniated stengahs, Bond recounted his adventures, Ian smiled wryly. 'It's no good, I'm afraid,' he said. 'Cape's would never stand for it.' " Ian was delighted with this pastiche. He promised to distribute it among aficionados. "You only need 70,000 words of this thrilling material," he told Daniel George, "and your fortune is made." The next day, Ian informed his friend, he was off to Saratoga races "and another mud bath". Bond was now fair game for satire. Later that year the first printed spoof was published in the *Spectator*'s Christmas issue – an inside job by John Russell, Ian's friend and Atticus colleague, who poked fun at his penchant for proprietary names and meticulous detail.

Ian's reference to Saratoga indicated that, once more, at the end of July, he said goodbye to Ann and Caspar, and crossed the Atlantic to stay with the Bryces in Vermont. Again Ann felt Ivar was acting as an *éminence grise* to her husband and she expressed her dislike of him in a letter to Max Beaverbrook: "It's a pity [Ian's] so fond of crooks, particularly as [Bryce] is an unsuccessful one." Ann had been thinking of accepting an invitation to join an up-market Aegean cruise arranged by Elsa Maxwell as a publicity exercise on behalf of Stavros Niarchos, but she eventually thought better of it. Instead she stayed at St Margaret's, where over the August bank holiday she entertained Evelyn Waugh and Diana Cooper. Waugh's visit was notable for his bizarre encounter with the three-year-old Caspar, whom he described as "very obstreperous" and "grossly over-pampered". Having already decided he did not like the unfortunate, temporarily fatherless child, Waugh was palpably annoyed when Ann brought Caspar to tea at the Grand Hotel, Folkestone, and perched him on her knee. His reaction was to "put his face close to the child's dragging down the corners of eyes and mouth with forefingers and thumb, producing an effect of such unbelievable malignity that the child shrieked with terror and fell to the floor". Waugh thought this very amusing and later wrote to Ann, "I do hope that old Kaspar has nightmares about his visit to Folkestone. I shall, for many years." He invited her to stay, but pointedly noted that Caspar would not be welcome. To Diana Cooper, he commented uncharitably, "What a rotten housewife Ann turns out to be."

In Vermont the high point of Ian's three weeks at Black Hole Hollow Farm was his renewed acquaintance with Billy Woodward. Billy was there with his wife Ann keeping an eye on his champion colt Nashua, which was undergoing a special training programme in Saratoga in preparation for what had been billed (not least in Atticus) as one of the races of the century – a needle match with Swaps, his closest rival, in Chicago later that month. By now the Woodwards' marriage had deteriorated further. Ann had shocked Palm Beach society earlier in the year by appearing at a charity polo match with a bruised lower lip – the result of a slugging match with Billy the evening before. Although Ian did not stay for the race, he soon learned about Nashua's famous five lengths' victory and wrote about it in Atticus the following week. But a couple of months later came further devastating news that, following a Long Island party where they both openly quarrelled, Ann had shot her husband dead, apparently mistaking Billy for a prowler. Ann was later acquitted of murder, but few people agreed with the verdict. The Woodward killing, and its murky class-ridden background, became a *cause célèbre*, which was turned into fiction, first by Truman Capote in his novella *Answered Prayer* and later by Dominick Dunne in *The Two Mrs Grenvilles*. Ian paid his tribute by dedicating *Diamonds Are Forever* to Bryce, Cuneo and to "the memory of W. W. Jr., at Saratoga, 1954 and '55".

Soon after returning from the United States, Ian wrote to Denis Hamilton, the Kemsley group editorial director, who was convalescing after an illness. In a typically worldly homily, he advised his friend not to return home each night "with a briefcase loaded with bumf". This "ruins your health and private life", he said, "leading to the dread disability known as Barristers Impotence". Ian suggested it was better for Hamilton to conserve his energies, for affairs at the office were likely to get worse before they got better. His intelligence resulted from dining alone with Lord Kemsley and his son Lionel Berry the previous evening. This sad experience had convinced him that, under the Kemsleys' stewardship, the future of the *Sunday Times* was bleak or, as Ian put it to Hamilton, "there is absolutely no hope of our revitalising the machine at the present time or altering its inevitable progress towards the edge of the abyss."

Ian's overseas jaunts on behalf of the *Sunday Times* that year were low-key – a reflection of his jaundiced view of the world in general, and the paper's prospects in particular. In June he travelled to Cannes for the world's first Underwater Archaeology Conference. He was excited by the quality of films about life beneath the surface of the waves. But his participation was really only an opportunity to renew his friendship with Commander Cousteau. In September Ian joined Sir Ronald Howe, the Assistant Commissioner of Scotland Yard, for a trip to Istanbul for the International Police (Interpol) Conference. A friend of Lord Kemsley, Howe had appeared in *Moonraker* as Superintendent Ronnie Vallance (the surname came from Ian's accountants, Vallance Lodge). He had helped sort out some problems after Ian forgot to license the old Browning .25 rifle which he took to Jamaica every year. When Howe first mentioned the Interpol conference, Ian agreed to accompany him, thinking it might provide not only some interesting insights into international crime but also an exotic new location for his next Bond adventure. In the event the proceedings were drier than he could ever have imagined, and when, on his return, he was approached by Sidgwick & Jackson to write a book on Interpol, he turned them down flat.

There were compensations in Istanbul, nevertheless. He experienced some unscheduled excitement when he found himself caught up in serious anti-government rioting. And through a chance introduction he met Nazim Kalkavan, an extrovert Turk who saw the world as a place to be enjoyed with gusto. An Oxford-educated shipowner, Kalkavan proved a better guide to Istanbul than *The Mask of Dimitrios*, the pre-war Ambler thriller in Ian's hotel bedroom. Ian loved his fatalistic Orientalist attitude to life: when Kalkavan said he had smoked and drunk and loved too much, he added "One day the Iron Crab will get me. Then I shall have died of living too much." Kalkavan became the model for Darko Kerim, the ebullient SIS agent who assisted Bond in his fictional adventures in the city. *From Russia, With Love* was falling into place, and the plot became clearer when Ian returned on the Simplon-Orient Express, which, although unspeakably drab in his experience, became the exciting backdrop for Bond's fight to the death with Red Grant in his next book.

Because of his undemanding workload at the *Sunday Times*, Ian finally agreed to take on one of Lord Kemsley's ailing literary properties. For some time his employer had been trying to interest him and Ann in purchasing the Queen Anne Press and the *Book Collector*. At one stage in November 1954 Ann was convinced that they had bought the Press. She redoubled her efforts to corral her friends into providing suitable books. Evelyn Waugh was asked to write ten thousand words "on some saint with interesting habits, St Francis of Goa or Saint Cunegonde".

Six months later, however, Ian was still quibbling about the price and terms for the two businesses. At the beginning of July he offered £250 for the Queen Anne Press but, having run over the figures with his accountant, Vallance Lodge, he told Kemsley he regretted he could see no future for the *Book Collector*, which cost around £1000 an issue to produce. He appears to have been bluffing, for when a week later Lord Kemsley moved to close the quarterly down, Ian feigned surprise, even shock. He told his employer that the survival of the *Book Collector* "would bring much credit to your name amongst the scholars and librarians of the world". Only a hurried appeal to rich bibliophiles by Percy Muir and John Hayward secured the funds to underwrite the *Book Collector*'s continued existence. The largest contribution – £500 – came from the oil tycoon Paul Mellon who had worked with the American OSS in London during the war. As a result Ian offered to pay £50 for the privilege of taking the magazine off Kemsley's hands. The deal duly went through and for the first time in his life Ian found himself an owner-publisher, a role he was to play in an enthusiastic if – to his partners – infuriatingly detached style. As Percy Muir later pointedly remarked, "From Ian's point of view the *Book Collector* became more and more a pleasant toy to dine out on and to astonish people with the fact that the creator of James Bond was at the head of a board of an erudite publication of this kind." The role meant much to Ian, however: in *Who's Who*, he described himself as author and publisher. His purchase of the Queen Anne Press never proceeded: although Ian remained a director until his death, this arm of the Kemsley group was later bought by the rogue politician and businessman Robert Maxwell, a real-life Bond villain if there ever was one.

Ann was just starting her winter season in London when Ian returned from Turkey. The highlight was a dance she arranged at the Royal College of Art for a charity for East End children supported by her cousin by marriage, the journalist and broadcaster, Arthur "Boofy" Gore, later the Earl of Arran. Through her artist friends, Ann was familiar with several of the tutors at the college, including Robin Ironside and John Minton, the painters. But Ian had known the principal, Robin Darwin, since Eton. As a tribute to Ian's desultory career as an aesthete, to his dilettante collection of brasses and prints, and to his effortless patronage of typography and books (or, perhaps, more realistically, for reasons which do not extend much beyond old-fashioned patronage), Darwin arranged for Ian to be elected a member of the college's Council, or governing body.

At the end of September Ian and Ann visited the Edens at Chequers. The Prime Minister was unwell, largely as a result of the anguish he was experiencing about the enduring subject of the "Missing Diplomats". A White Paper on Burgess and Maclean's defection to Moscow had just been published and the government was being forced to lie about the case, falsely denying that the two traitors' colleague Kim Philby was the "Third Man". Clarissa Eden begged her guests not to mention any of these names in front of her husband. When they were alone, Ian and Ann asked her for more details. But she kept her counsel, admitting that although her husband had told her "interesting things", she was unable to repeat them – "very annoying", Ann informed Lord Beaverbrook.

By then Ian had departed on a fleeting autumn visit to North America, partly to discuss the future of NANA. The deal with Express Newspapers had fallen through and, with the gradual demise of Kemsley's Mercury Service, NANA's output was looking thin and its financial position insecure. In October Ian travelled to Montreal with Ernie to discuss selling a controlling interest in their agency to a Canadian syndicate. A deal was struck, and Ian emerged with a welcome profit.

Bond provided the other main reason for Ian's transatlantic jaunt. There were signs that the American reading public was beginning to take notice of him. In April a paperback version of *Casino Royale* had been published by Pocket Books, with a new title, *You Asked For It*, and a suggestive dime-store cover showing a girl in erotic *déshabillé*. By mid-May Naomi Burton was asking for a copy of Ian's new manuscript, *Diamonds Are Forever*. Realizing that he had his editing routine in London, she said, nevertheless, in the tongue-in-cheek manner which endeared her to Ian, "It makes me very humble to think my opinion is of less importance than that of G. Wren Howard." Ian promised to bring a copy when he came to New York in August. But "you won't like it", he said in one of his self-effacing moods.

By now his American publication dates were beginning to catch up with his British. *Moonraker* was set to hit the bookstores of the United States in mid-September, but it was delayed by a week when its Pennsylvania printer was badly hit by floods. The *New York Times*'s Anthony Boucher, who had given Ian's first two books the thumbs down, was more charitable towards his third. "I don't know anyone who writes about gambling more vividly than Fleming," he enthused, though there was a sting in his tail, "I only wish the other parts of his books lived up to their gambling sequences."

Film producers were not so chary, as Ian's Hollywood agent, 'Swanee' Swanson, had predicted. Although he himself was disappointed with the book, his professional nose smelled, "There's a picture in it." By mid-November his office had put Curtis Brown in touch with the actor John Payne who, after some brinkmanship, had offered $1,000 for a nine-month option on *Moonraker*, plus a further $10,000 if it went into production. At the same time, on the other side of the Atlantic, Cape was discussing a contract with the Rank Organisation, a leading player in the British film industry, and also the owner of Pinewood Studios, which later became the base for James Bond movie-making. Towards the end of November, Ian sent Curtis Brown an urgent telegram: "RANKS MAKES FIRM OFFER FIVE THOUSAND FOR MOONRAKER IF YOU FEEL POSSIBLE UNDO HOLLYWOOD DEAL STOP HAVE AGREED NOT USE THIS FIGURE FOR AUCTION STOP CAN ANYTHING BE DONE QUERY CAPES AGREE SPLIT COMMISSION WITH YOU STOP FINANCIAL CONSIDERATIONS APART WOULD BE SPLENDID IF RANKS COULD MAKE FILM."

He received a cable by return that it would be impossible to kill the Payne deal without facing legal action. So began an interminable round of arguments about rights and commissions. When Payne seemed to claim film and television rights not only in this book but also in all future James Bond books, Cape objected vehemently, saying that, come what may, it always retained the television rights. Ian tended to favour Cape and the Rank deal. On 11 February, as negotiations with Payne were reaching an impasse, Ian removed chapter 16 of *From Russia, With Love* from his typewriter at Goldeneye and tapped out a defiant note to Naomi Burton, "I don't mind in the least getting in bad with Hollywood. If they ever want one of my books, you can bet they'll buy it even if I'm Jack the Ripper." He told her these were his thoughts "without the usual silver coating of polite commerce".

The following month Payne tired of the wrangling and pulled out, leaving Rank in pole position. But the small print continued to present problems. Curtis Brown was still not happy to share its 10 per cent commission on the film deal with Cape. Also Macmillan was asked to assign its copyright to Rank, but this had to be done through the trust which Ian had established for his son Caspar and which actually owned the film rights.

As for Rank, Britain's foremost film company may have been good at promoting its stable of busty home-grown starlets, such as the young Joan Collins. But it was unable to decide what it wanted to do with James Bond. Several months later Ian was so frustrated by his dealings with Rank's script department that he wrote his own screenplay. As he explained to Joyce Briggs, Rank's script editor at Pinewood, he had originally conceived *Moonraker* as a film, and "the reason why it breaks so badly in half as a book is because I had to more or less graft the first half of the book onto my film idea in order to bring it up to the necessary length." But Rank still shilly-shallied and nothing came of Ian's efforts. The company's failure to sign up James Bond was similar to the Decca record company turning down the Beatles.

Not satisfied with journalism, books and now films, Ian was thinking of extending his repertoire into non-fiction. While in New York in the autumn of 1955, he had discussed an idea with Edith Haggard at Curtis Brown. On his return he knocked out a long proposal for a book about the French poacher turned gamekeeper Marthe Richard. As Minister of Social Welfare in the first post-war government in France, she had introduced an eponymous law which clamped down hard on brothels. Although this hardly seemed promising material, Ian, who was intrigued by the story, briefly mentioned in *Casino Royale* that this same Mme Richard had been a prostitute in her youth and had run a well-known bordello. She had been recruited as a spy during the First World War, and had used her privileged position to inveigle secrets out of German officers. She had repeated this during the German occupation of Paris from 1940 to 1945. Her post-war career as a politician had been cut short after she became involved in a succession of scandals involving bribery and corruption. When a writer suggested that she had been useless as a spy and had never obtained any worthwhile information, she sued for libel and was awarded one (old) franc. Ian claimed he had been offered full cooperation by the French Sûreté. He proposed to keep his book short, in the manner of *New Yorker* profiles. Curtis Brown played with the proposal, but decided it was not commercial. Ian took their decision with good grace and said he would keep the idea for an article which he never got round to writing.

The spurt of interest in James Bond, together with the ambiguities about rights and commissions, encouraged Ian to think for the first time about hiring an agent in Britain. For nearly four years he had muddled along, with Cape acting, in a traditional gentlemanly way, as both his publisher and his agent, and Curtis Brown representing him in the United States. The issue which caused him to begin to change this set-up was foreign rights. As part of his preparation for his next book, Ian invited Eric Ambler to lunch at Scott's in the autumn of 1955. In his quiet way, Ambler had helped Ian with details of the business side of authorship. He was able to do this because his parents had both been music-hall artistes and, as a result, he had excellent connections with show-business accountants and lawyers, whose expertise in creating trusts and sheltering royalties was far in advance of anyone in the publishing industry or even on the high street. (This was the basis of his friendship with Noël Coward.) When, three years earlier, Ian had asked about a decent accountant, Ambler put him in touch with Vallance Lodge, whose practice, in Lincoln's Inn and Tottenham, specialized in actors. Lodge, who drank only champagne, steered Ian towards Wedlake Saint, a firm of lawyers, which helped him devise an efficient system of reducing his tax burden. His literary rights were assigned to Glidrose, while his film, serial and, later, television rights were settled in trusts for Caspar. Although it was some time before any significant income accrued to the trusts, Ian was adopting a long-term, strategic approach to Bond from the start.

Since their days at St Margaret's, Ian had often lunched with Ambler. On this occasion, he invited him to Scott's to pick his brains about Istanbul. Not only had his friend written about the city in *The Mask of Dimitrios*, he was also an expert in matters Byzantine. During the course of lunch, Ambler revealed that he was setting up Peter Janson-Smith, the young man who dealt with his foreign sales at Curtis Brown, as an agent in his own right. This sparked a flood of complaints from Ian about the way that Cape was handling his own foreign sales. While Al Hart at Macmillan in the United States had sold rights for Chinese, Urdu and Thai translations, Cape had managed one small deal with the Swedish publisher Bonnier.

When Ambler offered to put him in touch with Janson-Smith, Ian jumped at the chance, although he claimed to Michael Howard he had done so reluctantly – because Ambler was "a very good man to have on one's side". (Ian showed this by giving Ambler's latest book *The Night Comes* a glowing review in the *Sunday Times*.) The new agency was established the following September. Within a month, Janson-Smith had sold his first four Bond books to the Dutch publisher, A. W. Bruna, and since then, the Bond books have never been out of print in Holland. A significant step had been taken towards introducing 007 to the wider world.

10
Jamaican attraction
1956–1957

The first time Blanche Blackwell met Ian Fleming she thought he was the rudest man in the world. They had both been invited to dinner at Long Lane, the luxury house belonging to Charles and Mildred D'Costa on the outskirts of Kingston. When the conversation turned to the north coast's burgeoning homosexual community, and Blanche, an attractive divorcee in her early forties, mentioned that her family owned estates on that part of the island, Ian blurted out crudely, "Don't tell me you're a lesbian then." He alienated himself further by informing another guest she was a stupid bitch. Blanche, who had been warned about Ian, considered him well-nigh insufferable.

She and Charles D'Costa were members of Jamaica's old plantocracy. Like the D'Costas, her family, the Lindos, were anglicized Sephardic Jews, originally from Europe. The Lindos had come to Jamaica in the seventeenth century, prospering as owners of banana and sugar-cane plantations. Essentially traders rather than landowners, the basis of their wealth was their ability to market their produce. Blanche's great-grandfather Abraham Lindo helped introduce the idea of the bonded warehouse, where goods are held pending the payment of duty. Over the years the Lindos' fortunes ebbed and flowed, none the less. They were revived by Blanche's uncle, Cecil, who decamped to Costa Rica, where he summoned his seven brothers, including her father, Percival, and where she was born in 1912. With a new injection of capital, the family trading firm, Lindo Brothers, prospered again, acquiring J. Wray and Nephew, Jamaica's leading rum producer, in 1916. While most of the brothers' agricultural interests were sold out to the New Jersey-based United Fruit Company in 1928, the family continued to own J. Wray and Nephew until 1957, when it was bought by another local Jewish family, the Henriques.

Trained as a solicitor, Charles D'Costa's father, Alfred, had been knighted for his role in developing the Jamaican economy and, in particular, for bringing the bauxite industry to the island. Charles himself merited a footnote in the annals of English literature. At Marlborough in the 1920s, he enjoyed the dubious distinction of being beaten by John Betjeman for not blacking the future Poet Laureate's boots correctly. He later received private tuition in Jamaica from the young Cyril Connolly, who described him as "quite humorous and quite affectionate" but also "incredibly selfish, greedy and conceited". Ian probably knew this background, though he pretended not to bother himself with the intricacies of family relationships. He once admitted to the journalist Susan Barnes that Ann got annoyed with him for never remembering who anyone's father was. "It's only people's jobs that I have the slightest interest in. I'm totally uninterested in their love affairs or gossip of any kind."

It was surprising that Ian and Blanche had not met before. She had known Ivar Bryce since the 1930s, when she married Joe Blackwell, a former Guards officer of Anglo-Irish extraction and a member of the family which gave its name to Crosse & Blackwell food products. With Joe, Blanche had once owned the finest string of racehorses in Jamaica, often participating (as on the first day of the war) in meetings on the old course now covered by Goldeneye. Then there was a possible City connection: Joe's father, Gordon, had been a member of the London Stock Exchange, and unknown to Blanche, one of his first cousins, David Blackwell, had handled part of Ian's investment portfolio after the war. Another, second, cousin, John Blackwell was known to Ian as a prominent member of Royal St George's. In addition, Roy Lindo, Blanche's older brother, had introduced Ian to Reginald Acquart, the family agent, whom Ian had employed in his early days at Goldeneye. Roy himself had a personal tie to Goldeneye. As a young man, he used to visit a cave beneath the property where he indulged in illicit cock-fighting (and gaming) with Chinese friends. Ian had had the cave blown in with dynamite.

Following the breakup of her marriage in 1945, Blanche moved to England, where she led a sociable life among the Berkshire hunting set, while she supervised her son Christopher's education. She frequently travelled back to Jamaica, but it was not until 1955, when Christopher had finished at Harrow, that she decided to return for good. At one stage, she met Ian's friend, Duff Dunbar, at David Blackwell's house. Dunbar told Ian about Blanche and even suggested they should get together. But Ian was lazy and failed to take the initiative. When she later challenged him on this, he said, "I thought you were a great big black Jamaican mammy."

When they finally met at the D'Costas' dinner table, Ian found that Blanche was petite, with shapely legs and the dramatic, dark features of a Velazquez beauty. Although strictly brought up by her mother, who remained a powerful influence, she had none of the self-importance and stodginess which Ian associated with frustrated colonial wives. Blanche managed to be both reserved and ladylike on the one hand, and lively and spontaneous on the other. Her discreet sensuality and *joie de vivre* had already won two very different admirers – Errol Flynn, the actor, who had wanted to marry her, and Noël Coward, a close friend and neighbour on the north coast.

If no longer Jamaica's most dynamic business family, the Lindos were still extremely wealthy and very much part of the Establishment, with three substantial properties on the north coast. Coward had bought a hillside plot on their 750-acre Wentworth estate at Galina, near Port Maria, where he had recently built a new villa, Firefly, a couple of miles inland from Blue Harbour, his ersatz boarding-house by the sea. Largely to get away from her domineering mother, Blanche also had plans to construct a house on the estate at Bolt, just down the road from Coward, and four miles from Goldeneye.

Ian had been on his own in Jamaica that winter, working on what was to become his most successful book, *From Russia, With Love*. Ann had initially wanted to accompany him, admitting to Evelyn Waugh, "I love scratching away with my paintbrush while Ian hammers out pornography next door." But Ian was again unhappy at the prospect of Caspar coming. She told Max Beaverbrook that her husband was being obstinate and neurotic over it. So, in a spirit of protest, she insisted on staying in England, partly to be with Caspar and partly because she had booked a week's treatment at Enton Hall, a large Victorian-built health "hydro" in Surrey – ostensibly for her fibrositis but also to wean her off the cocktail of pills, particularly barbiturates, to which she was becoming addicted.

Ian left London on 14 January and flew to Jamaica via New York. On the transatlantic flight he sat on the forward side of the first class, wearing a light Burberry coat which made him look like a secret agent from a Graham Greene novel, noted the Conservative MP, J. J. Astor, who was on the same flight. New York no longer held quite the same attraction for Ian. He stayed with the Bryces, who raised their eyebrows at the absence of his wife, although Jo Bryce was astute and reassuring enough to note that Ann was the only woman Ian had loved or would ever love. The sale of NANA was still going through, but Ian managed to withdraw some money from the company. On the plane down to Jamaica he chatted to the up-and-coming writer Truman Capote, who amused him with topical stories about his recent trip to Russia.

Once established at Goldeneye, Ian missed Ann badly. This was the first time he had been alone in the house since they were married. Writing shortly after his arrival, he recalled emotionally how, before leaving Victoria Square, he had said goodbye three times to her room and stolen a photograph of her and Caspar. This now stood behind a bottle of Aqua Velva in what he pointedly called *our* room at Goldeneye. He was drinking gin and tonics and, as he refilled his glass, his thoughts rambled and his syntax became more staccato. "What do you think I do when I'm abroad? Well I don't. I sit alone. In fact, I believe you'd rather I didn't. Any person rather than no person." He chatted inconsequentially about his new powder-blue Austin and new gardener called Felix. By the time he had finished his fifth drink, he was pleading with her, "Come if you possibly can. I love you only in the world."

Ann replied in much the same vein. Any suggestion of marital disharmony was forgotten as she fondly recalled her times at Goldeneye. She said she often thought about the bean soup, the clucking bird outside the window and Ian banging away at his typewriter. "I hope you won't learn to be happy there without me." As a token of her affection, she told him she had paid £8 for two brass horse pictures – the kind Ian loved.

A succession of guests helped Ian recover his sense of identity and purpose. The first was most unexpected: tiring of the rich, braying crowd at his hotel, Truman Capote asked if he could stay at Goldeneye because he needed some peace and quiet to write an article for the *New Yorker*. Any caveats Ian might have had that they were incompatible were quickly removed: Capote proved a "fascinating companion", regaling Ian with "wonderful stories all day long when we weren't working". Ian took his new friend to Firefly to see Noël Coward. Nearly a decade earlier Coward had been dismissive of Ian's house. Now Ian returned the compliment. Firefly was "a near-disaster" with the rain pouring into it from every angle and "even through the stone walls so that the rooms are running with damp".

Other visitors to Goldeneye included Micky Renshaw, the fey *Sunday Times* advertising director, whom Ian described as the least satisfactory of any guests who had ever stayed – "psychologically unable to say anything but to old foreign Duchesses", Sir Alfred Beit, his old Adlerian fellow-traveller from the 1930s and his wife Clementine – "like being slowly crushed with a steam roller" – and Al and Nancy Hart, his New York publisher and his wife. (Ian liked him, but found her unbearably garrulous. He was prepared to admit now that he was more averse to Americans than Ann "because I have seen more of them and ask less of people". He felt that "all foreigners are pestilential" and could not imagine what he had ever seen in them.) As Ian began to relax and feel happier with himself, there was added poignancy, even pathos, in his comment on the progress of their marriage, "I wish I could start again and wipe out the black patches in these four years but you can never know how desperately difficult I found it all."

Ann enjoyed the idea of Ian and Capote messing together. "Goldeneye was the last heterosexual household" in a growing gay enclave. "What will its reputation be now!" she exclaimed. In the meantime she had been in France, attending one of the events of the Parisian social season, Mme de Noailles's fancy-dress ball. The theme of the party was writers and painters from one's own country. Ann interpreted this rather loosely. Wearing a fetching high-waisted Directoire outfit, she went as the Regency courtesan Harriette Wilson, best known for her frank memoirs. But, as

Ann precociously pointed out to Ian, she was feeling and looking better than for ten years.

Ian received a welcome professional boost in late February when he learned that Dick Hughes, one of his Mercury team, had secured the first-ever interview with the British traitors Guy Burgess and Donald Maclean. This worldwide scoop resulted from a plan that had been hatched in December when Hughes was sent on a temporary assignment to Moscow, before returning to his regular post in Hong Kong. Ian, with his recent first-hand experience of the Prime Minister's discomfiture on the subject, had told Hughes, "I think Khrushchev is ready for an exclusive interview. Try to get it and of course home in on the Burgess–Maclean thing." After covering the Communist Party Congress, Hughes set about finding the two traitors. A tough hard-drinking Australian, he was uncharacteristically forced to visit the ballet not once but ten times in his quest. Having enjoyed no success, he was eventually ordered to return to London. But on Saturday 11 February, the day before he was due to leave, the Soviet authorities relented. Burgess and Maclean were brought to Room 101 at the National Hotel, where Ian had stayed over twenty years earlier. They handed Hughes a statement admitting to being communists at Cambridge but denying they had ever been secret agents. After distributing this document, which was also given to correspondents from Reuters, Tass and *Pravda*, the two men retreated, refusing to answer any questions. It was not much of an interview. But the encounter fell just right for Hughes's deadline. With the *Sunday Times*'s assistance, the old Australian pro was able to build it into an important news event. On his return to London, he was presented with a cheque for £1000 by Lord Kemsley.

Although Ian was happy at the successful outcome, it did little to halt his own growing disillusion with the paper. He felt Hughes should have made more of the story, in which he claimed to have played an important role. "I had such a fight getting him to Moscow," he told Ann, "and the saboteurs were after me until the day I left. I told [Hughes] to hell with Bulganin and to keep after the diplos and nothing else, I gather he has been received back in London like royalty. I don't think he made enough out of his scoop. A good observer should have been able to pick up a lot more facts and impressions." He complained that he was no longer satisfied with getting stomach ulcers in order to make his proprietor more rich. Gossiping with his guest Micky Renshaw probably led him to conclude that the *Sunday Times*'s future was now "more hopeless than ever". Ian's solution was to give it one more "bash ... or get out". He told Ann that he was glad he had not sold his book collection: "I can see us living on it yet."

Such ruminations about the future made the success of his latest novel all the more important. Before leaving London he had told Wren Howard confidently that he intended to "keep Bond spinning through his paces as long as possible". But he added darkly, "The trouble is that I take great pains with the factual background to these stories and my source material is running rather dry." It was also "very difficult to find new ways of killing and chasing people and new shapes and names for the heroines".

Ian's recent experience of Cold War machinations, albeit at a distance, provided useful background for his new book which showed no let-up in either his imagination or his ability to handle information in an exciting and entertaining manner. *From Russia, With Love* told of SMERSH's efforts to take revenge on the British Secret Service, and on James Bond in particular, by luring him to Istanbul to meet the beautiful Tatiana Romanova who apparently wanted to defect. Having been briefed by Grigori A. Tokaev (later known as Tokaty), a former member of Soviet Military Intelligence who had defected to the West in 1948 with valuable first-hand information about Russian rocket technology, Ian emphasized his familiarity with the internal workings of the Soviet intelligence services. For reasons, no doubt, of continuity, he persisted in giving SMERSH, the organization charged with assassinating traitors, a central role in his story, when in fact it had been disbanded in 1946. SMERSH's fictional head of operations was identified as the fiendish Colonel Rosa Klebb, Ian's first attempt to portray a woman as his villain.

More than its predecessors, the book was full of incidental detail about the international game of intelligence. Through the eyes of Lieutenant-General Vozdvishensky of RUMID, the Intelligence Department of the Ministry of Foreign Affairs, Ian provided an entertaining overview of Western secret services. The general, whose fictional career included training the Soviet master-spy Richard Sorge and helping run the Burgess and Maclean operation, found the Italian and Spanish intelligence services harmless, the French clever and dangerous, the American big and rich, and the British worthy of respect because of the quality of their agents. In a reference to his own experience, Ian noted, through his RUMID general, that British spies hardly ever receive decorations. They play the game well, but their real strength lies in their myth, like the myth of Sherlock Holmes, or, as he might later have said, the myth of James Bond.

Ian mixed insider gossip about intelligence with precise details about Bond's domestic environment. It was as if he were consciously trying to flesh his hero out and escape the charge of portraying him as an international cardboard cutout dummy. So in *From Russia, With Love* we learn about Bond's comfortable flat off the King's Road, his homely Scottish housekeeper, May, his Minton china and his three squat glass jars containing Tiptree 'Little Scarlet' strawberry jam, Cooper's Vintage Oxford marmalade and Norwegian heather honey from Fortnum's.

It was towards the end of his stay, with the book almost finished, that

Ian met Blanche Blackwell. His initial gaucheness was only an elaborate cover for the immediate attraction he felt towards her, and she, overcoming her own distaste, soon warmed to a fine physical specimen – "six foot two inches tall, with blue eyes and coal black hair, and so rugged and full of vitality". (With the eyes of what later became an enduring love, she managed to overstate his height by two inches.) Although still in awe of his strutting manner and even worse reputation, she invited him, in the spirit of good neighbourliness, for drinks when she was next on the north coast at Wentworth. However her house-guests, who had accompanied her to the D'Costas, showed no inclination to be charitable towards Ian, and informed Blanche they would be offended if he came. So she was forced to send him a telegram at Goldeneye, cancelling her invitation and telling him she had been detained at her mother's house in Kingston. Undeterred, Ian wired her back, saying that he would soon be visiting the capital, and would like to stay. When he informed Ann about his subsequent visit, he self-consciously played down his hostess's charms. He said it was just like staying with Blanche's brother Roy Lindo, "and do you remember the horror of that?" He only admitted that Blanche had helped him with his shopping. As a result he bought a scooter and a big Japanese train for Caspar to play with at Goldeneye the next year. (Ian had finally decided to allow his son to visit. And as a token of his intent, he arranged to have a small octagonal gazebo built on the north-western edge of his property, overlooking the channel where the banana boats entered Oracabessa. This would be his retreat for writing when his family arrived.) To Ann, he now hazarded a guess that, once Blanche's great new house at Bolt was completed, she was likely to be "quite a pleasant neighbour".

Since returning to Jamaica, Blanche had abandoned riding, her usual form of exercise, and taken enthusiastically to swimming. As Ian still had a few days left on the island, he invited her over to his beach at Goldeneye where, like many before and since, she was immediately attracted to snorkelling on the reef. "A complete fish", according to a friend, she introduced Ian to Barrington Roper, the powerful Jamaican swimming champion from nearby Port Maria, who acted as her boatman and guide to the offshore waters.

A shared love of the sea and its 'fishy fauna' created an immediate comradeship between Ian and Blanche, a bond which was strengthened by their mutual friendship with Noël Coward, who was settling into his new house on her land. As a result, Coward featured prominently in Ian's reports from Jamaica that year, though there was less reference to the lively woman who so clearly enjoyed acting as their local cheer-leader. Coward and his circle were happy to see Ian with Blanche, whom they genuinely liked, rather than with Ann, whose occasional off-handedness was beginning to grate.

Coward's move to Firefly coincided with his decision to leave Britain, sell his two houses there, and become a tax exile, living part of the time in Jamaica and part in Bermuda, where he became a resident. To celebrate this change of circumstances, he bought himself a vast sky-blue Chevrolet Belair convertible. When he took Ian and Cole Lesley for a drive along the coast, a local Jamaican, observing the extravagant vehicle and its high-spirited occupants, exclaimed, "Cheesus-Kerist", whereupon Coward asked, "How did he know?" Their stately progress was almost halted when they reached a petrol station. The car seemed to take an inordinately long time to fill up. When Coward asked the problem, Lesley informed him, "They can't find the hole." "We've all had that trouble at one time or another," replied Coward who refused to get out and look himself, thinking it would demean him in front of the natives. With the help of the instruction book from the glove compartment, Ian finally solved the problem: the petrol-tank cap was behind the stop light. "Anyone could have told you that," Coward pronounced airily. "It's interesting," Ian shot back, and he was the only person in the world who could have said this, "when you sweat with embarrassment the sweat runs down your face and drops off your first chin on to your second." "Don't be childish," blustered Coward.

Ian may have been winding down, but he refused to relax. He had left a week or so at the end of his stay so he could prepare a series of long articles for the *Sunday Times* on the natural history of the Caribbean. Rather too close to the truth for comfort, he joked to Ann that he was going to be treacherous three times. His first sortie was to the Negril beach, the other side of Montego Bay, where Coward and Graham Payn joined him – "nothing but buggers all around me," he complained to Ann. They rented a crumbling villa with iron bedsteads for a long weekend. Enjoying the rudimentary, Boy Scout existence, Ian cooked a twelve-egg omelette for the boys on an old wood-burning stove. They washed their meal down with cheap beer and, Coward recalled, never stopped laughing. "I think I've laughed more with Ian than with anyone," he later said. Today, as Ian predicted, Negril is a busy holiday resort. In 1956 it was an idyllic "five-mile crescent of unbroken, soft, white-gold sand, fringed for all its dazzling length with leaning palm trees in whose shade an occasional canoe is drawn up between a thatched hut and a pile of discarded conch shells as tall as the hut itself". The only white man in the vicinity was the splendid-sounding Dr Drew who, having moved to the bay after giving up his medical practice in Oxford forty years earlier, had built a fives court next to his modest dwelling, and was still living there at the age of ninety-three. Ian made no reference to any human companions in his piece for the paper, recording only the sensual pleasures of swimming in warm waters, wearing nothing but a Pirelli mask, observing and being caressed by colourful shoals of fish.

His second trip had him being dragged "out of the *luxe, calme et volupte*" of his beachcombing existence and taken climbing in the Blue Mountains in search of the sweet sad-singing solitaire bird. This time he was accompanied by Graham Payn and Cole Lesley, which allowed him to inform Ann, "More buggers". If Ian was trying to emphasize the asexual tenor of his escapades, he was no doubt giving the right impression, but he was not wholly truthful for another member of this expedition was Barbara Cargill, the energetic and intelligent wife of Carmen Pringle's son, Morris, a leading Jamaican writer and politician.

For his third piece, Ian flew to Nassau, where he transferred to a light Cessna aircraft for a further four-hundred-mile flight to Inagua, the southernmost island in the Bahamas group, within sight of the north-east coast of Cuba. This trip had come up at short notice. With just one week of his holiday remaining, he received a cable from Ivar Bryce in the Bahamas: "ESSENTIAL YOU ACCOMPANY FIRST SCIENTIFIC VISIT SINCE 1916 TO FLAMINGO COLONY MARCH FIFTEEN STOP PARTY CONSISTS ARTHUR VERNAY PRESI-DENT BAHAMAS FLAMINGO PROTECTION SOCIETY COMMA ROBERT MURPHY OF AMERICAN NATURAL HISTORY MUSEUM AND SELF STOP FAIL NOT BRYCE." Ian was excited by the prospect. He was beginning to feel his age and this sort of opportunity did not come often. "After the age of forty, time begins to be important and one is inclined to say 'Yes' to every experience," he wrote on his return, reiterating a favourite theme. "One should, of course, be taught to say 'yes' from childhood, but Wet Feet, Catching Cold, Getting a Temperature and Breaking Something add up to a traumatic 'No' that is apt to become a permanent ball-and-chain."

To Ann he wrote, "Can you imagine such an adventure and how ghastly it will be seeing all this without you?", in an unconvincing attempt to persuade her that another small diversion was necessary before he came home. Apart from Matthew Town, a small village whose one thousand inhabitants worked on the nearby salt-pans, Inagua comprised one hundred square miles of mangrove swamp. But this tropical wasteland was the enclosed and secure habitat for hundreds of thousands of birds – flamingo, Louisiana herons, American egrets, roseate spoonbills, stilts and a score of other species. Inagua became the model for Crab Key in Ian's next novel *Dr No* (dedicated, again, "To Ivar, who, as usual, provided the background, Ian"). Ian filled his notebook with descriptions of this infernal environment. Against the background of a "shocking pink horizon", the fetid mangrove swamp on Inagua gave off "a sulphur dioxide marsh gas". The naturalist Dr Murphy briefed him about the guanay or green cormorant bird, whose dung, a potent natural fertilizer known as guano, also contributed to the Crab Key economy. The party progressed through the swamp either by wading through the lagoon pushing a shallow-draught boat, or riding on a salt producer's swamp-buggy, described by Bryce as "a kind of Land-Rover mounted with huge wheels, giant tyres that supported the strange vehicle on the surface". This too became an important prop in *Dr No*. The purpose of the four-day safari, which remained a cherished memory for Ian, was to count the flamingos in the breeding season. The tally of 15,000 gave the Audubon Society enough evidence that this prehistoric bird was still resilient.

Ian returned to London with a personalized prescription from Noël Coward, who seemed to recognize he had lost some of his earlier interest in Ann:

> Squirt a little Seltzer in my Berncastel
> Dip my carnation in green ink
> I'm going to drop golf and learn pastel
> (Even Eton Ramblers shouldn't spurn pastel
> And – anyway – those playing fields are pink!)

For a while Coward's marriage-counselling seemed to work. In thanking Somerset Maugham for his kind words about *Diamonds Are Forever*, Ian joked that Ann's character had been greatly improved by her visit to Enton Hall. Her diet of orange juice had flushed out much of her Charteris bile. Ian confessed that there had even been moments since his return from Jamaica when she had shown signs of cosiness – "a terrifying manifestation which I must at all costs keep secret from her smart friends".

In his perennial search for influential male patronage, Ian offered to act as Maugham's *homme de confiance* ("and I mean confiance"), running any delicate errands he might have in England or abroad. If the grand old man of letters sent him instructions, Ian promised they "would be executed faithfully and naturally without a word to anyone – least of all to the daily newspaper I have married".

Ann's new-found cosiness did not extend to praising her husband's new book, or even taking it particularly seriously. Ian explained to Maugham that this was partly because it was set in the United States, whose existence she did not admit, and partly because he had used words like mirror instead of looking-glass. Ian observed that his wife did not "realise how terribly vulgar it has become to talk about looking glasses ever since Nancy Mitford wrote about them". (This particular social convention obsessed him. In an article for the *Spectator* the following year, he could not make up his mind whether a car had a wing mirror or looking-glass. Both descriptions were included in his manuscript.)

Ann was game enough to jump to her husband's defence and help defuse a potentially tricky legal problem when, on Easter Day, she received an apopleptic call from her relative by marriage, "Boofy" Gore, later the Earl of Arran. Gore had been alerted by Lord Lambton to a passage in *Diamonds Are Forever* which ran, "Kidd's a pretty boy. His friends call him 'Boofy'. Probably shacks up with Wint. Some of these homos make the worst killers. Kidd's got white hair though he's only thirty. That's why he works in a hood." Ian had done his usual trick of assigning the names of friends and acquaintances to his characters. But Kidd was a particularly unpleasant character. Gore railed against Ann: Ian was his best friend, how could she have allowed him to do this? Ann replied that she was only married to Ian: she had neither written nor even read the book in question. Still fuming, Gore contacted Ann's sister, Laura, who telephoned Ann, by then out at church for Easter Sunday matins. Fionn fielded her aunt's abuse: "Your mother may like pansies but other people don't. Don't forget Boofy has a million friends and Ian has none."

The book was received favourably when it was published on 26 March 1956. The Beaverbrook connection continued to work in his favour: "The author has proved his staying power," enthused George Malcolm Thomson in the *Evening Standard*. (Thomson was the reviewer whom Ian had told Beaverbrook he would like to have at the *Sunday Times*.) In *The Tablet*, Anthony Lejeune heralded an "adult and entertaining thriller". But the notice which meant most to Ian appeared in his own newspaper and was written by Raymond Chandler. Leonard Russell, the *Sunday Times* literary editor, had seized the opportunity to ask Chandler to write apparently his first-ever book review. Russell cut out a couple of sarcastic opening sentences in which Chandler, still smarting from the previous year's luncheon party, poked fun at Ian's pampered existence at Victoria Square. The tone of the rest of the review was quizzical and ambivalent. Adopting one of Ian's own lines, Chandler criticized the author for trying to make his descriptions of Las Vegas more fantastic than the real thing. He questioned if there was any point in presenting Bond as a thinking person. As far as Chandler was concerned, any cerebral activity from Bond was superfluous. He preferred 007 when he was "exposing himself unarmed to half a dozen thin-lipped killers, and neatly dumping them into a heap of fractured bones".

Whether this was quite what Ian wanted to hear, he was flattered at the literary attentions of the great man. He thanked Chandler profusely for the review and again asked him to lunch. The invitation was declined, but a lively correspondence ensued. Chandler's message was blunt: Ian needed to make up his mind what kind of a writer he was; he had great potential, but on the evidence so far it was only clear that he was a bit of a sadist. These criticisms touched a raw nerve in Ian. His wife's friends had been getting at him again, and in a letter of 27 April he could only reply with almost brutal frankness, "Probably the fault about my books is that

I don't take them seriously enough and meekly accept having my head ragged off about them in the family circle." But while Ian's upper lip remained stiff, and he could still joke about the fuddy-duddies and their reaction, there was a touch of hopelessness in his next sentence, which was cut from the version of his correspondence with Chandler which Ian published in the *London Magazine* in December 1959, shortly after his friend's death: "If one has a grain of intelligence it is difficult to go on being serious about a character like James Bond. You after all write 'novels of suspense' – if not sociological studies – whereas my books are straight pillow fantasies of the bang-bang, kiss-kiss variety." *From Russia, With Love*, the book Ian had just completed in Jamaica, was a worthy attempt to lift his work out of the latter category, but it was as if Ian were slowly and painfully realizing that his ambition of writing the definitive espionage novel was starting to elude him.

Ian's health did not contribute to his general good humour. Since returning from Jamaica, he had been in considerable discomfort from his recurring sciatica. Taking his cue from his wife, he booked a short stay in a garden chalet at Enton Hall. But he refused to take the naturopathic medical regime seriously. Discovering that a fellow guest, Guy Welby, kept a Rolls-Royce on site, he demanded to be taken for drives in the afternoons. His physical rehabilitation hardly prospered (his GP, Dr Beal, was subsequently forced to put him on a fresh course of drugs), but it proved a useful and entertaining diversion. Ian enjoyed his first taste of the antiseptic world of the health farm (which bore fruit in *Thunderball*, his next book but one), while Welby became a friend who employed Clare Blanshard in his family firm of jewellers when she returned to London later in the year, keeping Ian informed about different aspects of the gem trade as and when required. Ian later used to joke that he met some of his most entertaining and enduring friends in Enton Hall's gilded prison-cage.

Chandler could not care less about Ian's pain. "You know what you can do with your sciatica, don't you?" he told him dismissively. He simply wanted to convince Ian that he was not doing himself justice in his books. He claimed to have noticed a decline in Ian's standards since *Casino Royale*. His friend needed to raise his sights again, he said.

Before Ian could do that, he needed to placate his wife who, having spent the winter in England without him, was demanding a holiday abroad. Ian's unsatisfactory compromise solution was to invite Ann to accompany him to Vienna to cover the latest annual Interpol conference in June. Travelling in the Thunderbird, they stopped in Bonn to visit the Terrys and introduce Ann to what Ian called the "mythos of Teutonia", which seemed to translate as the delights of hock. In the Schaumburger Hof where the Flemings, to great amusement all round, took the room where Queen Victoria once stayed, Ian was fascinated to hear Rachel

Terry's account of Emma Wolff, a large, ugly NKVD agent with red-dyed hair, operating in Vienna, and added the details to his portrayal of Rosa Klebb, with her "thinning orange hair scraped back to the tight, obscene bun".

On his return to London Ian's strange illnesses took a new turn. This time he was again struck down by kidney-stones – so excruciating that only morphine – and a weekend in the London Clinic – blunted his pain and prevented him, as he put it, biting the dust. By now Ian's condition – part physical, part psychological – was making him increasingly sullen and introspective. This was reflected in the phrases and quotations he began to extract from his notebooks and other sources and to collect in a loose-leaf folder. Taken together, they indicated that, having reached the age of forty-eight in May, Ian was feeling his age. Although dating is difficult, Ian jotted down the remark "too old to cut the mustard" while he was writing *From Russia, With Love*. From this time too, he noted Scott Fitzgerald's remark, "It grows harder to write because there is much less weather than when I was a boy and practically no men and women at all." A year later he wrote, "One of the great periodic [crises] in one's life occurs in early middle age when you realize that the top people – the politicians, the generals, the managing director – who had seemed supreme, invaluable, are not so. You yourself are perhaps approaching the seat of power, or at least you can see it more clearly, and you suddenly realise that those who occupy it possess no more qualities than you do, except age."

One of Ian's favourite inspirational sources was a decade-old copy of *The Crack-Up*, Scott Fitzgerald's frank account (edited by his friend Edmund Wilson) of his nervous breakdown – "ten years this side of forty-nine, I suddenly realized I had prematurely cracked". Ian used it both as a barometer of his run-down state and (since it too adopted a largely epigrammatic style) as a sounding-board for ideas. For example, where Fitzgerald had written, "Remember this – if you shut your mouth you have your choice," Ian added in the margin of the book, "Once you've opened it you've either said yes or no." In his loose-leaf folder this became, "If you keep your mouth shut you still have your choice. Once you open it you're committed. You've either said yes or no." Ian was fascinated by Fitzgerald's experimentation with names, descriptions and phrases. Lifting the American's "passing within the radius of a girl's perfume", he rendered it in more socially acceptable form, "He came up close to her and into the radius of her scent."

Ian's maudlin mood surfaced in an unfocused complaint to Chandler in the United States, "My own muse is in a bad way," he confessed. "Despite your doubts I really rather liked *Diamonds Are Forever* but I am getting very fed up with Bond and it has been very difficult to make him go through his tawdry tricks" in *From Russia, With Love*. Chandler simply stuck to his line in a further letter: Ian could produce much better work. But Ian also refused to budge, claiming that Chandler laboured under a grave misapprehension. "My talents are extended to their absolute limits in writing books like *Diamonds Are Forever*. I am not short weighting anybody and I have absolutely nothing more up my sleeve. The way you talk anybody would think I was a lazy Shakespeare or Raymond Chandler. Not so."

His literary skills were hardly stretched by his contributions to Atticus in the *Sunday Times* that summer. The pieces emphasized his wide-ranging contacts, but little else. In May, for example, he fêted Lord Beaverbrook, on his seventy-seventh birthday, as "one of England's greatest bridge players". He was atoning for the misunderstanding which had occurred a few days earlier when both Ian and Ann received their usual invitation to Beaverbrook's annual birthday party at Claridge's. Ann had been ill and had cried off; Ian assumed that ruled him out and, to the embarrassment of all, did not attend.

Ian also knocked out short pieces about clubland (the annual White's Club golf tournament at Royal St George's, and how his friend Osbert Lancaster had done up the St James's Club), the book trade (the birth of the new Lion and Unicorn Press, the brainchild of his friend Professor Robin Darwin, principal of the Royal College of Art) and the world of the secret services (a puff for the work of the Joint Intelligence Committee, a pat on the back for Ian Henderson, the top policeman who broke the Mau Mau in Kenya, and a notice of the arrival of a new head of what he called the Secret Service). This last piece did not name Sir Dick White, only mentioning that he was a brilliant and dedicated man with a record of secret wartime service second to none. Ian surmised that White would be unmoved by the outcry against the 'Secret Service' (in fact, the Secret Intelligence Service, SIS) following what he admitted was "the shambles" of the Commander Crabb affair (which he said he had heard was the responsibility of an operational body over which the "Secret Service" had no control). Rather White and his staff would be concerned with getting on with the job, "whose only reward is a modest Civil Servant's salary and pension and an occasional secret victory of which the country will never learn" – similar words and sentiments to a passage he had written earlier in the year in *From Russia, With Love*.

By July Ian's advance guard at Cape had read his new manuscript. Daniel George pronounced it his best book so far, and William Plomer also gave a positive response. Their only criticism was that Ian's Russians appeared dull and two-dimensional. Ian countered that this was because "Russians are dull people and I intended to paint a picture of rather drab grimes. SMERSH is after all a machine whereas Drax was an individual." Doubts were also expressed about Bond's naïveté in accepting Tatiana's invitation to Istanbul. Ian seemed careless in his reply: "The point about Bond is that he makes a fool of himself and falls headlong into the trap. This is a change from making him the cardboard hero and I cannot help thinking this is a healthy change." Late in the day, it is clear from the manuscript, he also changed the book's ending. Instead of allowing Bond to enjoy a romance with Tatiana, as he had originally written, he left him crumpled on the floor, having just received a potentially lethal blow in his shins from a knife in Rosa Klebb's boot. The inference was that Ian was keeping his options open: he was again undecided whether to continue his hero's exploits in the future.

Ian's insouciance about Bond's fate suggested not only renewed doubts about his long-term prospects as a novelist but also a deeper boredom which was reflected in his middle-aged efforts to recapture some of the excitement of his youth. In his notebook folder, he had copied, "J'aime les sensations fortes", a phrase which Bond quoted approvingly when invited to attend a violent women's wrestling match in Istanbul in *From Russia, With Love*. In reality, Ian's sensations were considerably tamer. His need for comradeship was easily satisfied by playing more golf with his friends at St George's and Huntercombe. Since bridge in the sedate surroundings of Boodle's no longer set his pulse racing, he joined the Portland Club, where they played a more competitive game for higher stakes, but the ambience was not very different. (Previously he had always gone as someone else's guest.) And his sense of fantasy was stimulated by his loose association with Ivar Bryce, whose easy, cosmopolitan existence might have come from another age, perhaps chronicled by Scott Fitzgerald.

That summer Ian found a new haunt at Moyns, Ivar's childhood home in Essex, which Jo had acquired for her husband a couple of years earlier. Not long after moving in, Ivar told Robert Harling that he had advised his wife against purchasing the house: "I said to her, 'Jo, if you buy it for me, I'll come to love it more than you.' And you know what, Robert? It's happening already." Ivar imbued Moyns with a particular atmosphere, described by one young female visitor as "the sort of place where you felt that generation's sense of the rules of the club was being broken". On the surface it was the peaceful, well-ordered estate of a respectable English gentleman – a few hundred acres of park and woodland, where Ivar and Jo could indulge their passion for breeding horses and entertaining their friends. But, for all Ivar's love of the place, the Bryces never managed to put down roots. Their regular weekend house parties were sophisticated and fun, if a trifle ostentatious, with four butlers and a valet vying to wait upon a high-spirited mixture of card-playing aristocrats, eager Americans over for the 'season', and pretty girls invited to make things go with a swing.

Ian's stays were "brief but enthusiastic", Ivar remarked. Although not attuned to the diurnal rhythms of the countryside, "he was a fountain of ideas for improving or embellishing the property". He enjoyed the opportunity to escape from the competitiveness of Ann's drawing-room and relax and even shine among the Bryces' coterie of bright but not overly intellectual friends.

The Bryces had a couple of other places where they used to stay when not in the United States, and Ian was always welcome at these establishments as well. In the Bahamas, where Ian had recently played truant on his flamingo research trip with Ivar, Jo had long owned a house in Market Street in the centre of Nassau. After their wedding, as a thank-you present for Moyns, Ivar built her a 'love-nest' in a secluded spot beside the sea on the main island of New Providence. Xanadu, as it was called after Coleridge's pleasure palace, had all mod cons, yet it was exotically finished in shell, ivory and mother of pearl. Its crescent beach of golden sand was protected at either end by a sculpted sphinx.

With gambling still banned in Britain, Ian welcomed any opportunity to visit the casino in Nassau. The Bahamian capital itself was unexciting: his feelings about the place mirrored Bond's in his short story, "Quantum of Solace". "The winter visitors and the residents who had houses on the island talked of nothing but their money, their diseases and their servant problems. They didn't even gossip well. There was nothing to gossip about. The winter crowd were all too old to have love affairs and, like most rich people, too cautious to say anything malicious about their neighbours." But the Bryces always managed to surround themselves with colourful characters, the most engaging of whom was a former Harvard football star called John Sims Kelly, known as Shipwreck, or even Ship, who had married often and well, before finding his vocation in the Bahamas as a glorified beach-bum and unofficial jester to Jo Bryce. 'Ship' knew everybody, from Ernest Hemingway to the Duke of Windsor. One of his best friends was the Greek shipowner Aristotle Onassis, whom he later introduced to Ian.

The Bryces' other home-from-home outside the United States was Schloss Mittersill, a residential sporting club for the jet-setting super-rich in the Austrian Alps not far from Ian's old stamping-ground of Kitzbühel. American millionaires mixed there with the more outgoing members of European aristocracy – the same Hohenlohes, Bismarcks and Bourbon Parmas who might later be found at the Marbella Club. The Schloss Mittersill International Sport and Shooting Club had been founded in 1936 by three expatriate Austrians living in Paris, after some prodding from the society columnist, Elsa Maxwell. It was closed during the war when the Nazis used it as the centre for pseudo-scientific studies into Asiatic races. On their return the owners found thousands of skulls from

Tibet, India and China eerily stored on newly constructed shelves in all the rooms. This provided Ian with the model for Piz Gloria, Ernst Blofeld's scientific research station in the Alps, in *On Her Majesty's Secret Service*.

The club did not open again until 1953 with Prince Alex Hohenlohe as the new resident partner. Prince Alex, who lost most of his money when the communists took over in East Germany, had recently married an American, Patricia Wilder. Known universally as Honeychile (sometimes shortened to Honey), she was a lively former showgirl who had once danced in Bob Hope's troupe. She proved an articulate and amusing hostess at Mittersill. Ian was enchanted by her and appropriated her nickname for his flirtatious nature girl in his next novel, *Dr No*. After Baron Hubert von Pantz, one of the original founders, married an American heiress two years later, he was able to pump large sums into improving the property. By the middle of the decade, the club was again established on the European social circuit. "It was very grown-up, very sophisticated and rather debauched," remembered Ivar's cousin, Janet Milford Haven, who first went there before she married David, the 3rd Marquess of Milford Haven in 1960. "I couldn't believe people behaved like that." An intriguing photograph shows an inebriated-looking Ian at Mittersill with three women, one of whom has appended it, as if writing to a friend, "You know the two to my left, the one on my right is an Englishman named Ian Fleming. Writes terrible books. Handsome in an 'old shoe' kind of way. Very forward with the ladies. Loves black lingerie."

After four years of marriage, forwardness with the ladies was again part of Ian's repertoire, and seemed to be tied in with his restlessness and uncertainty about his future. Exactly when he began to stray from Ann is not certain: as might be expected, the recriminations only came later. But over the summer it grew clear that, while Ian had his amusements, Ann was leading a more independent and indeed sociable existence than for some time. To help her recover from the illness which prevented her attending his seventy-seventh birthday party, Beaverbrook sent her a case of claret and, by way of thanks, she invited him to dinner to meet her new friends, the Gaitskells. Hugh Gaitskell had been leader of the opposition Labour Party since December 1955. Although educated at Winchester College, he was a lifelong, rather dry and intellectual Socialist. Only the previous month, Gaitskell and his wife Dora had attended one of Ann's dinners, along with several other politicians including Robert Boothby and Randolph Churchill. She had struck up an immediate rapport with the Labour leader. He saw her as a spirited and amusing antidote to his dour professional life; she liked his brains and political clout, and considered it a challenge to wean him from his puritanical socialist principles to an enjoyment of the more overt pleasures in life.

Within a short time, he had helped Ann forget any marital tensions and encouraged her to live out the latter-day Souls existence – part cerebral, part social – which suited her. By early July Gaitskell and Ann had discovered a mutual delight in dancing. A Fred Astaire on his toes, he used to love twirling her around the Café Royal dance floor. Their relationship did not end there: the couple used to meet for trysts at the house of Anthony Crosland, a rising Labour politician, and Ann used to joke that when she went to bed with Gaitskell, she liked to imagine she was with the more debonair Crosland. Much as she enjoyed her unexpected romance, she could only cope with it by being slightly disparaging. As she told Beaverbrook, prior to one of her dancing dates, "I suppose I shall have to go dancing next Friday with Hugh Gaitskell to explode his pathetic belief in equality, but it will be a great sacrifice to my country." Six months later, after taking Gaitskell to a nightclub with Lucian Freud and Francis Bacon, and then to Chantilly to stay with Lady Diana Cooper, she reported to Beaverbrook that Gaitskell was a "changed man – all he wants is wine, women and song". On one level, she promoted Gaitskell with Beaverbrook and ensured that his policies received favourable Express group newspaper coverage in any internal Labour Party dispute with his left wing. On another, she subverted the Labour leader's pretensions to seriousness. Ann Fleming, the political hostess who split the Labour Party and kept the Labour right wing in business: it is an interesting and not implausible thesis.

While Ann kept Beaverbrook amused with Gaitskell's antics in London, Ian was seeing the aged press baron's favourite granddaughter, Lady Jeanne Campbell. Having got to know Jeanne in Jamaica, Ian took to visiting her whenever he was in New York, where she was trying to forge a career in the arts. Still in her twenties, she found Ian anything but boring, which was her mother Janet Aitken's description of him in the late 1920s. As he took her to the cinema and encouraged her to write, she formed the distinct impression that he viewed life like a movie. While Peter Quennell had portrayed him as looking forlornly for a lost piece of a jigsaw, she noticed the same characteristics and gave them a more positive gloss – Ian was determined that his personal filmset should not only be interesting but look good. When he left for the airport on one occasion, she remembered, he instinctively pulled up the collar of his overcoat to give himself a more Bond-like image.

In return for his avuncular advice, she put Ian in touch with her friend Henry Morgenthau III, whose father Henry Morgenthau II had been the highly influential US Treasury Secretary during the Second World War and had dealt closely with Beaverbrook. A budding film producer, Henry III had made contact with a Jamaican government minister about developing a local movie industry. His idea was to make a series of films for American television. But to start the ball rolling, he needed a good script with a credible fictional character.

More than four years after writing his first Bond novel, Ian was still striving for the elusive film deal. That summer movie papers on both sides of the Atlantic reported that Gregory Ratoff, the producer who had made the television film of *Casino Royale* for CBS in America in 1954, was coming to England under contract to Fox to shoot the same work for the big screen. But nothing came of this industry rumour. The deal with Rank over *Moonraker* was proving as elusive as ever. Thus Ian was delighted when Morgenthau approached him and Ivar Bryce and suggested they collaborate. Ian wrote a sample treatment for a half-hour television series starring an American secret agent based on Bond and called Commander James Gunn. (An idea to call him Commander Jamaica was swiftly dropped.)

The treatment showed Ian at his simplest and most inventive. His spring visit to Goldeneye had, if nothing else, rekindled his love affair with Jamaica, and his new story-line told of an ongoing battle of wits between the Commander and Dr No, an "international freelance spy of Chinese-German extraction", who was attracted to the Caribbean by the existence of the main Anglo-American missile test station on Turks Island, a dependency of Jamaica. Dr No's accomplice was a beautiful half-caste Chinese girl, Pearl, who was a champion underwater swimmer. In some accompanying notes, Ian suggested that the area around Goldeneye might be used as the backdrop for the series. He even suggested roles for his local friends. Cousins, his next-door neighbour, "would be an excellent labour boss and general fixer" while "Roper, the Caribbean overarm swimming champion" had "a slightly Chinese cast of countenance and a good deadpan face". And for a signature tune he recommended his favourite 'Mary Ann', "a little known Calypso with good words and a haunting melody suitable for playing at varying tempos".

Ian took this document on his annual visit to the Bryces in Vermont in August. Since Morgenthau lived nearby in upstate New York, Ian flitted between the houses, discussing the next steps. He polished up the proofs of *From Russia, With Love* and, as he had now got into the habit of juggling at least three literary works at the same time, he dealt with last-minute queries from Macmillan about his next US novel, *Diamonds Are Forever*.

Ian's much-needed holiday in Vermont was interrupted, however, by a recurrence of his kidney-stone problem. He was rushed in considerable agony to New York's Presbyterian Hospital where he told Ann he thought his $21-a-day suite would prove a "mighty spur" to recovery. For the time being, he assured her with his epigrammatic turn of phrase, "the Stone

Age at least is passed and now to strangle Dame Sciatica". The Morgenthau project was "interesting but no gold mine", he informed her. He intended doing a few film treatments, but their future really depended on whether Morgenthau and his colleagues could sell a pilot to "a fat sponsor". Ian would have options, and said he would continue with them if they were successful. They are "nice youngish people", he said, and they might even have an opening in Jamaica for someone with her "inspired pictorial ideas".

In hospital he was visited by Clare Blanshard. Always aware of the contradictions in his character, she had been touched by his courtesy and respect towards her religion. While in the old days Robert Harling teased her about her Roman Catholicism, Ian tended to treat her beliefs as hallowed ground. As she knew he was not a churchgoer, she once asked him what Christianity meant to him. He replied, "You can't grow up in the English school system without it having an effect on you." Now, while he was lying in bed, he surprised her by asking to have a candle lit for him in St Patrick's Cathedral. When she queried this, he said, "No, that's really what I want." Since Naomi Burton's office was nearer the cathedral, Clare asked her to see to Ian's request which, in true New York ecumenical spirit, was performed by Naomi's Jewish secretary. When Ian heard what had happened, he was delighted. But he still wanted to know when the candle had been lit. Learning that it was at four o'clock in the afternoon, he said that this was exactly the time when his pain had lifted.

As soon as he returned to London at the end of August, Ian wrote, as promised, a 28-page pilot script for *James Gunn – Secret Agent*. Ian did not ask much for his work – just $1000 for the outline, plus a further $2000 on acceptance of the pilot, in advance of royalties. But he did want to regain ownership of his scripts after six months if they did not take off. When the fruit of Ian's labours landed on her desk in early September, Jo Stewart, head of the TV department at Curtis Brown, suggested that the pilot might be more saleable if he played up a couple of the more intriguing characters from his treatment such as the "menacing Dr No" and the "desirable Pearl". She liked Ian's idea of using a calypso as the series' signature tune.

Although Morgenthau took the project off to Hollywood. Ian had few illusions that he would be successful, and he told Jo Stewart as much. Sure enough, in December, Morgenthau reported that he had failed. He blamed his lack of success on the tightening money market and the fact that Jamaica is far removed from the motion-picture capitals of the world.

At the end of May Ian received a "fan" letter with a difference. Geoffrey Boothroyd, a gun enthusiast in Glasgow, had been reading the Bond books. But, "like the aircraft buff who sees the hero leave the ground in a Spitfire, only to find it miraculously transformed in mid-air into a Hurricane", he had been distressed by 007's "rather deplorable taste in firearms". Until then, Ian's hero had employed a .25 Beretta pistol. But, as Boothroyd explained, this was a ladies' gun, not the type of weapon a hardened agent would use in the field. If he had to carry a light gun, Bond would be better off with a .22 rim fire, whose lead bullet would cause more destruction than the jacketed type in the .25.

Preferably, Boothroyd suggested, Bond should abandon his lightweight pistol and arm himself with a revolver. With a Centennial Model .38 Smith & Wesson Airweight, he would have a "real man stopper weighing only 13 oz", a hammerless gun that could be drawn without catching the clothing. And, while the .38 was a good personal gun, Bond clearly needed something heavier to carry in his car. For this role, Boothroyd recommended a .357 S & W Magnum. With the two, Bond "would be able to cope with really quick draw work and long range effective shooting". Finally, shoulder-holster causes problems: much better, Boothroyd felt, if Bond carried his gun in a Berns Martin Triple draw holster, which holds the weapon in by a spring and can be worn on the belt.

Ian was both delighted and overwhelmed. Although he knew something about guns, he was always happy to take advice from an expert in any field. He fired back a letter, arguing that Bond felt his accuracy was more important than any particular type of weapon, particularly as he was now so used to his Beretta. But he promised that he would introduce Boothroyd's suggested modifications in his next book but one (*From Russia, With Love* was more or less complete), adding, "As Bond's biographer I am most anxious to see that he lives as long as possible and I shall be most grateful for any further technical advice you might like me to pass on to him." He asked for further information about the mysterious Boothroyd and confessed that Bond was keen to know more about the guns his Russian opponents might use.

Boothroyd introduced himself as a 31-year-old Englishman working in Scotland as technical representative for the giant chemicals group ICI. He was a member of several gun clubs and owned a collection of forty-five weapons. His particular interest was drawing and shooting or, as he put it, the gun lore of close-combat weapons. In response to another query, he said Ian would probably have to go to the United States to acquire or even look at an S & W Airweight Centennial. The Berns Martin could be purchased by post, also from the United States. As for the kind of weapon a member of SMERSH might carry, Boothroyd suggested he might go for either a short-barrel 9-mm Luger (alternatively a Polish Radon P.35 or a Russian Tokarev) and, for medium-distance assassination work, a Mauser 7.63 Automatic.

Shortly before departing for the United States in August, Ian informed
Boothroyd he would try to purchase an S & W Airweight Centennial there.
He subsequently looked at several splendid examples in Abercrombies in
New York, but could not obtain a licence to export one. Ian also wanted
to know about silencers. In *From Russia, With Love*, Bond had got into
difficulties when, at the Ritz Hotel in Paris, he needed to draw his Beretta,
with silencer, from his waistband. Boothroyd replied that he had little
time for silencers. So few people knew the sound of a gun that he would
have no hesitation in firing one in any well-constructed building. Not to
be outdone, Ian countered that secret agents like 007 often needed to use
silencers. During the war, he said, British Intelligence had developed some
very good silencers. He himself had used one on a Sten gun and "all one
could hear was the click of the machinery".

On returning to England at the end of August, Ian had another request.
For fifty guineas, he had commissioned Richard Chopping, whom he
described as "the only English master" in the art of *trompe l'oeil*, to paint
him a picture of a revolver crossed with a rose for the cover of *From Russia,
With Love*. Over the course of the next decade Chopping, who had been
introduced to Ann through Francis Bacon, was to become widely known
for the meticulous detail of his distinctive Bond novel covers. On this
occasion Ian wanted to provide the artist with a real .25 Beretta from
which to work, but he had difficulty locating one. Knowing, however, that
Boothroyd owned a handsome Smith & Wesson .38 with a trigger guard
modified for quicker firing, he asked if Chopping could borrow the weapon
which, Ian promised, would become "forever famous". Boothroyd was
happy to lend the gun, so long as he received it back by 26 September,
when he needed it for a demonstration.

A week before its expected date of return, Ian received word that
Boothroyd had been visited by his local Glasgow constabulary. A murder
had been committed in the city, probably with a .38, and the police were
checking anyone who owned such a pistol. Having explained to them
that the gun had been sent to London, Boothroyd was concerned that the
police might now call on Ian who, they could insist, technically needed a
firearms certificate. Luckily Ian did have a valid certificate, number 109950,
covering various guns including the .38 Colt Police Positive awarded him
by General Donovan. Ian was indeed contacted, but was able to convince
a Scotland Yard detective that the gun could not have been used in
Glasgow on the date of the murder. Details of the weapon and its owner
were included on the dust-jacket when *From Russia, With Love* was published the following spring. Ian had told Michael Howard on 5 November,
"Boothroyd says that his note on the gun (which is very professional and
should not be altered) will prove irresistible to anyone in the slightest bit
interested in these things", and, as he correctly intimated, the lore of

Bond's guns became an essential part of his myth, and Boothroyd a regular performer on the 007 lecture circuit.

During Ian's summer visit to the United States, he convinced his American publishers to devote more energy to promoting him. In October Macmillan placed an advertisement in the *New Yorker*, heralding the publication of *Diamonds Are Forever* and emphasizing its local content: "Lady with diamond on garter $3,750 at your jeweler. Gentlemen may prefer blondes, but blondes prefer Bond, who is back with his trusty Beretta on a new assignment for M, mixing it with mobsters at Saratoga and Las Vegas. A new lethal package by Ian Fleming $2.75 at your bookstore." But America's most influential critic was still not wholly convinced. Fleming "writes excellently about gambling, contrives picturesque incidents but the narrative is loose-jointed and weakly resolved", opined Anthony Boucher in the *New York Times*.

Ian had a more sympathetic reaction from Al Hart who, having already received good reports from Cape, was delighted when he read Ian's latest manuscript. "You have surpassed yourself!" he told Ian. "The new one is far and away your best, from the very first page right through to that altogether admirable cliff-hanger of an ending. Pearl White was never more effective. Seriously, I mean it: *From Russia, With Love* is a real wowser, a lulu, a dilly and a smasheroo. It is all a clever and above all sustained piece of legitimate craftsmanship. My chapeau is not only off to you, it is over the windmill."

For all Hart's encouragement, Ian was dreading his next stint at his Jamaican writing-table. On 27 November he warned Michael Howard categorically that he would not be able to complete a book by the following April. He would be "very relieved" to be able to write one at all, because he felt once again and only half-jokingly, "the fountain of my genius is running dry". He used almost exactly the same words to Howard's father the following month, "When you talk airily of future books, I do beg you to believe that the vein of my inventiveness is running extremely dry and I seriously doubt if I shall be able to complete a book in Jamaica this year. There are many reasons for this, which I need not go into, but I am finding it increasingly difficult to work up enthusiasm for Bond and his unlikely adventures."

Ian's coolness stemmed, as he intimated, from a number of causes. What troubled him, and that only semi-consciously, was his premonition of the consequences of his family's forthcoming visit to Jamaica. Not only was he likely to be distracted by his son, but his finely tuned antennae told him that any forthcoming meeting between Ann and Blanche Blackwell was likely to be fraught.

Ian had reckoned without the power of what might be described as the

Bond imperative. He only dimly realized that, having worked so hard to establish himself, he was no longer in a position to turn back. James Bond was beginning to take on a momentum of his own which even Ian was unable to control. Both author and character received another unsolicited boost towards fame when the ailing Prime Minister, Sir Anthony Eden, asked if he could use Goldeneye as a tropical retreat after the stresses and strains of the Suez débâcle in November. Ann was the initial point of contact. Even before Anglo-French forces had withdrawn from Egypt she received a discreet telephone call from Alan Lennox-Boyd, Secretary of State for the Colonies, enquiring if the house was free. He pleaded with her to keep his interest secret and, thinking that he was planning an impromptu vacation with his wife, she thought nothing more of it until four days later Ian also heard from Lennox-Boyd. This time the minister came clean that it was the Edens who wanted to use Goldeneye. Sir Anthony had been advised by his doctor to take a complete rest. Ian was flattered and agreed to do anything he could to help. Although Lennox-Boyd specifically asked him not to tell Ann, he could hardly avoid it. So she was primed when a couple of days later Clarissa Eden chose to "confide" in her and asked for a woman's guide to Goldeneye. By then it was too late for Ann to dwell much on the disadvantages of the place. Lady Eden was not amused to learn that she would have to give two days' notice to have a bath. Ann decided to spare her such details as the persistent noises of the plumbing. But, even so, Ian was annoyed to learn, when he went to see the Edens the day before they left for Jamaica, that Ann had dared to say anything even slightly derogatory about his house. He was already counting the commercial advantages of the Edens' visit: it would greatly enhance the value of his property on the rental market.

Although his health was his overriding concern, Eden could not have chosen a worse time to be away from London. Britain was under pressure from the United States to start its withdrawal from Egypt. The actual announcement was made while the Prime Minister was in Jamaica. Eden asked to be kept in touch but his detractors were already talking about possible successors. Even his largely sympathetic biographer, Robert Rhodes James, called Eden's visit to Jamaica a fatal mistake.

In these circumstances, one of the Prime Minister's reasons for choosing Goldeneye was that, with Britain's standing in the world diminished and his own *amour propre* in shreds, Ian could be relied upon to show the utmost discretion. Nor did he let Lennox-Boyd or Eden down. Although he never particularly liked the Prime Minister, either as a man or a politician, Ian fired off a non-committal telegram to his new "attorney", Anthony Lahoud, in Oracabessa: "THREE IMPORTANT FRIENDS ARRIVE NOVEMBER TWENTY-SECOND FOR THREE WEEKS VISIT STOP PLEASE TELL VIOLET GET EXTRA STAFF PREPARE HOUSE STOP CLEAN YARD AND DRIVE STOP CABLE CON-

FIRMATION REGARDS FLEMING." The Martinique-born attorney cabled back
an appropriately languid message on 18 November: "EVERYTHING IS OK
LAHOUD". Goldeneye had had many visitors before: it was simply a matter
of opening up the house and making sure everything was in place. He can
hardly have expected the subsequent upheavals. The date of the mystery
visitors' arrival chopped and changed. It was put back to 26 November
and then brought forward to the 24th. Lahoud began to understand these
must be important people because the Commander cabled him to fix a
uniform for the cook and an extra maid and to be prepared for considerable
publicity.

The staff already knew Blanche Blackwell who, since meeting Ian earlier
in the year, had regularly used the Goldeneye beach for swimming. These
visits gave her an opportunity to keep an eye on her friend's house, and
no one thought that intrusive or peculiar. When Lahoud informed her
about his cable, she said she had no idea what it was about, "but knowing
Commander and Mrs Fleming it was probably something to do with either
the theatre or politics". Noël Coward was also in the dark. It was only
when she went to the other side of the island to see her mother in
Kingston, and was asked to call on the Governor, Sir Hugh Foot, that she
was let in on the secret.

The next time Blanche turned up at Goldeneye, she had Lady Foot, the
Governor's wife, and Cora St Aubyn, his private secretary, in tow. They
told the staff what was happening and tried, without ruffling too many
feathers, to make the place look less austere and more like a prime minister's holiday home. A team of six gardeners was hired to help the
incumbent Felix Bariffe tidy up the property. Two telephone lines were
installed in the drawing-room, and the new gazebo was commandeered
as a communications centre. Lahoud hired two additional maids and a
valet called Harry who would look after the Prime Minister and could also
cook. But when Lady Foot suggested that Violet, the housekeeper, might
like to make way for members of her own staff from Government House,
she was met with a blank refusal, "No, Lady, I obey my Commander."
When Lady Foot tried to convince her that the Queen would like this,
Violet remained adamant: "I still don't care, Lady. I respect the Queen but
I obey the Commander."

Back in England, the press were showing considerable interest in Eden's
winter sojourn at what they saw as the dashing Fleming's mysterious
hideaway home among the tax-exile crowd in Jamaica. Ann played her
role admirably, giving journalists the kind of copy they wanted: "There is
no telephone at the house. But there is a watchdog Alsatian called Max.
It's no luxury place. The Edens will have to rough it. But it's perfect to
get away from things." She further jeopardized her shaky friendship
with Noël Coward by telling David Wynne-Morgan of the *Daily Express*

on 23 November that she and Ian had lent the house to the Maestro seven years previously after he had "a fantastic flop [*Tonight at Eight-Thirty*] in New York. He went there for a few months to lick his wounds." As she confessed to Evelyn Waugh next day, she had ignored Ian's advice to "keep my trap shut" and "yesterday's *Daily Express* will mean a permanent breach with Noël Coward".

BOAC put on a special "crew familiarization" flight for the Edens, who arrived in Montego Bay on the morning of 24 November, after a fifteen-hour journey, via Bermuda. Violet and her expanded staff were waiting to meet them at Goldeneye. Clearly some confusion still remained about the housekeeping arrangements. No sooner had the Edens arrived than Blanche Blackwell received a telephone call from Violet, informing her that she had "forgot dair lunch". This was news to Blanche, who had arranged to eat with Noël Coward at Firefly. She was forced to grab their intended meal and send it down to Goldeneye. Not that the Edens were put out. They were already smitten by the place. That very evening they cabled their absent hosts: "EVERYTHING HERE MORE WONDERFUL THAN WE EXPECTED STOP A THOUSAND THANKS ANTHONY AND CLARISSA."

From the perspective of King's House, the Governor's seat, the visit was progressing well. Two days later Sir Hugh Foot contacted London with a message to pass on to Ian that Goldeneye was looking extremely smart. He explained that both his wife and Blanche Blackwell had been there, lending a hand with the domestic arrangements. Ian replied that he was delighted that the Prime Minister had chosen Jamaica – "my adopted island for which I have always the warmest affection" – for his vacation and that his own "modest" house had been singled out to receive such an important guest. He realized this must have been a surprise for the Governor, but "for real privacy and peace, they could hardly have chosen better". Ian admitted that he had "chuckled hugely" at the idea of Lady Foot and Blanche trying to turn Goldeneye into "a gracious home". He painted a picture of "them tut-tutting over rudimentary china and cutlery, and shipping over bales of comfort and necessities from the resources of King's House and Kingston". He promised to "rag Blanche unmercifully" when he saw her again in January. "I can just see her punching out the garish cushions and putting dainty vases of flowers beside the detectives' beds." Ian was only concerned that, as a result of all the publicity, the good-natured Violet would be enticed to oversee the housekeeping at some big hotel.

While the domestic arrangements continued almost unnoticed around them, the Edens began to enjoy their holiday. Their sense of amazement and gratitude never waned. Goldeneye was just what the mythical doctor ordered: a place where they could forget the cares of office and indulge in a restorative dose of sun-soaked lethargy. No matter that every white-coated policeman on the island seemed to be guarding the place. No matter that a posse of motor-cycle dispatch riders brought Cabinet boxes over from Kingston several times a day. No matter that the area outside the house was crawling with journalists who, in true rat-pack style, hired boats to spy on and photograph the Edens from the sea. It was all immaterial. Lady Eden indicated what was really happening, or not happening, when she wrote to Ann after a week: "A complete inertia has overcome us. We are blissfully happy and it is everything we had hoped for but far more beautiful. We haven't been outside the gates so far. Letters have been flowing in from Coward, Brownlow and Bryce urging us to use their beaches – but we think yours is as nice as one could find." Noël Coward, at his patriotic best, arrived at the gates of Goldeneye with buckets of caviare and Earl Grey tea, procured with difficulty in Kingston. But even he was not allowed in. The Edens had closed the shutters and were not coming out to play.

The big white Cadillac lent by Jamaican Prime Minister Norman Manley remained in the drive, barely used. The Edens put a stop to the practice of bringing lamb chops and other provisions from Kingston. They insisted on eating the local seafood. As Clarissa told Ann proudly, "We have finally got a line on langouste from Oracabessa." When, on one occasion, they did venture out, they "bought heavily" from Mr Antonio, owner of Ian's favourite general store in Falmouth. The Prime Minister purchased a pair of willow-pattern shorts and she had "some fancy pants run up by a local lady".

The Edens' timetable was so relaxed that Clarissa admitted they were missing the dawn bathe their hosts had recommended. The trouble was that they never woke up before 9 a.m. Then, after breakfast, they climbed gingerly down the thirty-six steps to the little cove. "After one claustrophobic splash, Anthony has absolutely refused to put his head under water, so he swims up and down in the deep bit, occasionally crashing himself into a reef of coral. I am obsessed by the fishes, and now swim about with a wet towel tied to my back on account of bad sunburn. I haven't found a way through the left-hand part of the reef yet, but will no doubt come upon it one day."

The only minor problem Lady Eden admitted was "all those squeaks and whizzings" at night. A week later, it became clear what she was referring to. On 12 December the *Evening Standard* reported that Sir Anthony was being pestered and kept awake by rats. He had organized a rat hunt and seven of the little beasts had been killed. Suddenly Goldeneye's image changed from exclusive millionaire's paradise to seedy Caribbean beach-hut. Mindful of the effect on his property's rental value, Ian countered that there were no "really bad rats". Anyway, they were field rather than house rats. And they had never given trouble before. All they did was "wake one up in the night, knocking coral and crockery off the shelves". Ian was sure they could never seriously frighten anyone.

One other problem was that Lahoud resented the intrusion of Lady Foot and Blanche Blackwell on his patch. For reasons best known to himself, he was particularly annoyed about Blanche's role there. Partly out of bloody-mindedness, he hit back, during the Edens' visit, by becoming the main disseminator to the press of news snippets about happenings at Goldeneye. According to Sir Hugh Foot, to obtain his information, the attorney used to go up to the house every day and cross-question the servants. But one day he seemed to have overreached himself. A report had flashed round the world saying that the Prime Minister had been sick and that a doctor had been sent for during the night. The Governor himself was off the island for a couple of days in New York. So Lady Eden and the formidable Cora St Aubyn took the matter on themselves and ordered that Lahoud's pass to Goldeneye be cancelled. The published story had not been true, Foot later told Ian. The local GP, Dr Lenworth Jacobs, had been to the house once, but this was "primarily" to see Lady Eden who had a temperature. Noël Coward heard another story: that Eden was having nightmares and would wail during the night. Whatever the circumstances, it was deemed the appropriate moment to discipline Lahoud. Ian's attorney did not take it lying down. He threatened all sorts of retribution, particularly against Blanche.

Ian clearly thought that Lady Eden had overreacted. While apologizing for Lahoud's behaviour, he showed the better side of his nature in pleading with Foot to ensure that his attorney was quickly rehabilitated. "In a small community like Oracabessa if he is stood in the corner it will do his standing in the community irreparable harm. He is a modest and almost illiterate little man and I am sure if he gossiped, it was the gossip of a child." Foot took note of Ian's paternalistic request and, despite the Edens' reluctance, he arranged that Lahoud's pass should be returned and that the attorney should be there in the parade of staff to shake the Prime Minister's hand when the Edens left the house. Honour seemed satisfied, though Foot was still not certain whether Lahoud had abandoned his threat to launch a press campaign against Blanche. Ian promised to put his attorney "in his place" when he came to Jamaica in January.

Shortly after returning to England, Eden wrote to Ian to thank him for the use of his house: "I do not think that there is any other place anywhere that could have given me the rest I had to have. The bathing, the beach, the seclusion, the size of the grounds were all just perfect to enjoy and be concealed." The Prime Minister could still "feel those warm seas now". But the main object of the exercise – the improvement of his health – had not been achieved. Within two weeks, Eden reluctantly was forced to step down as Premier. The memory of those warm seas remained with him, however. Two years later, the Edens bought their own seaside property on the West Indian island of Barbados.

As a footnote, just before the Edens' visit, Richard Helms, the CIA's Deputy Director for Operations, first learned of Ian's name. Helms, who later headed the agency, was a fan of spy fiction. In the autumn he picked up a copy of *Live and Let Die*, and was impressed enough to ask Roger Hollis, the new head of the British Security Service (MI5), about Fleming. Hollis claimed never to have heard of him. However, when a short while later Helms read that the British Prime Minister was going to stay at Ian's house in Jamaica, he concluded that Hollis, who would have had responsibility for the visit, had lied to him.

With four-year-old Caspar visiting Goldeneye for the first time in January 1957, Ian had preparations to make. Realizing his inquisitive son would want to investigate the reef, Ian wrote in some desperation to Al Hart in New York, asking him to order a rubber dinghy from Abercrombies, to deduct the $217.50 catalogue price from any royalties he might have accumulated in the United States, and to have the floating package shipped down to Jamaica. Hart compared Ian's calls on his publisher's time to Arthur Koestler's, though the latter's requests had been more menial and less fun.

Just before Christmas Ian had a date to play bridge at the Portland with Somerset Maugham, who was on one of his regular visits to London. Ian's new club was poorly patronized, and he worried that the old man might have lost too much. But when Maugham said he had enjoyed himself, Ian relaxed and gave an update on his marriage. After a brief honeymoon period earlier in the year, he reported, Ann was "now back in the coils of the telephone and the arms of Diana, Lucian, Evelyn, Randolph and the rest of her harem".

As had become customary, Ian and his wife travelled separately to Jamaica. He enjoyed the luxury of a transatlantic flight, with a welcome stopover in New York, while she took Caspar and Nanny, and her other son, Raymond O'Neill, on the liner, the *Caronia*. After a storm-tossed voyage, they were met at Kingston harbour by the Governor's aide-de-camp. Ian had arrived in Montego Bay by air the previous day, but claimed he did not have time to drive to the capital to pick up his family.

Ian arranged for Roper, the local champion, to teach Caspar to swim in the pool of the Tower Island Hotel. Every morning for a week, Ann took her son there, while Ian settled down in the gazebo to write his new book. Since he claimed his own muse had deserted him, he appropriated the story and background of the film treatment he had prepared for Morgenthau the previous summer. Dr No now lived and operated from Crab Key, an island very similar to Inagua. As cover for his mission to deflect US test missiles launched from nearby Turks Island, he exported guano and made life difficult for nature-lovers concerned about the bird sanctuary on Crab Key. The taut first chapter, in which three Chinese Negroes (wrongly described as Chigroes) posed as blind men to murder Commander John Strangways, the local representative of the British Secret Service, harked back to long hours Ian had enjoyed with Ira Patcevitch, the chairman of Condé Nast, discussing fictional espionage escapades. Ian's plot was more mythical than ever with a flame-throwing vehicle like a dragon (based on the buggy he had travelled in on Inagua) protecting Dr No's sanctuary, and a naked maiden named after his Mittersill friend, Honeychile Wilder, for Bond to save. There was even a walk-on part for Blanche Blackwell, whose first name was adopted for an aged guano tanker on Dr No's island.

When Blanche herself came over to report on the Edens' visit, she found Ian methodically instructing his four-year-old son in the correct Latin names of tropical fish. Ian was concerned that his son had adopted the habit of wearing a hibiscus flower in his ear and was calling himself Mary. (Caspar may simply have picked up the refrain from the calypso his father had not only recommended for his television series but also quoted in his new book as one of Bond's favourites.) Ann's letters were curiously silent about her initial reaction to Blanche, but it was significant that she did not stay long in Jamaica. Within a month she returned home to make arrangements for Fionn's twenty-first birthday on 9 March.

In retrospect, Ann had come to Jamaica with a predisposition to dislike Blanche, and Ian must have known it. Although there is no evidence of any intimacy between him and Blanche at this stage, Ann's female intuition would have picked up on Ian's obtuse signals about his dealings with an attractive and friendly neighbour. Her antipathy towards Blanche took root when she saw Clarissa Eden at Downing Street shortly before leaving for Jamaica. Ann asked innocently enough if she and her husband had met any interesting people during their holiday. "Only one," answered Clarissa, and she mentioned "someone called Blanche Blackwell" who had gone out of her way to ensure that their stay was as comfortable and interesting as possible. Ann's hackles were raised when she came to Jamaica and discovered the cosmetic improvements Blanche had made to Golden-eye. She immediately jumped to the conclusion that Ian was having an affair, and when he stupidly, perhaps boastingly, passed on the details of his wife's jealousy, Blanche was so angry at Ann's assumption of infidelity that she felt justified in retaliating. The best way of doing this was to give in to Ian's persistent and hitherto firmly rebuffed amatory advances. Or, as Blanche herself put it, she no longer needed to resist.

When Noël Coward heard about this female caterwauling, he seized on it as background material for *Volcano*, one of his lesser plays, an examination of the failing marriage of a volatile English couple, the Littletons, on the tropical island of Samolo. The action centres on what happens when Melissa Littleton arrives unexpectedly on the island, having been alerted by a friend to the very close relationship between her congenitally charming husband Guy and a local widow, a plantation owner called Adela Shelley. The rumblings of a volcano in the background provide suitable atmospherics, as Melissa develops a canny respect for her rival Adela, as they are united in their understanding of Guy's need for self-gratification. Coward realized that the play was not up to his usual standards, and no performance of *Volcano* has ever been given.

Ian stayed on alone at Goldeneye for an extra couple of weeks, ostensibly putting the final touches to his book. But he managed a trip to Kingston to see Blanche, and then, "Treachery!", as he brazenly informed Ann, echoing his line from the previous year, he agreed to accompany her and her friend Anne Carr for a weekend in the neighbouring Cayman Islands. (In Quarrel, a Cayman Islander, Ian had conceived in his manuscript as near a sympathetic portrayal of a West Indian as he was able, and he wanted to see the tiny islands that had spawned such intrepid seafaring folk.) Since they had neglected to book in advance, all three had to share a room in the Bay View Hotel on their first night in the Caymans. Unromantically Ian stuffed himself with sleeping pills and snored loudly, forcing Blanche to retreat halfway through the night to the porch, where she was badly bitten by mosquitoes. In an effort to play down events, Ian described it all to his wife as "very chaste and proper ... Blanche jabbers and the other is v dull and cold". But he is unlikely to have struck the right note with his heartfelt but nevertheless inappropriate comment, "Wished you didn't mind aeroplanes. We miss so many adventures."

Evidence of a new, more acrimonious phase in the Flemings' marriage soon followed. For Fionn's party, Ann asked a few friends to look in and amuse her while the youngsters – Waughs, Chancellors, Lytteltons, Rothschilds and Pryce-Joneses – danced to "rock and roll". Malcolm Muggeridge declined the invitation, saying he was too old. But around this time he did meet both the Flemings together, and he was struck by their petty quarrelling. Ian "complained that she was packing her daughter's party with oldsters like Rose Macaulay (this did seem a bit hard), and her gang – Paddy Leigh Fermor, Lucian Freud, etc. She in turn complained that Ian had been bitten by one of his girlfriends." Although Muggeridge would not have known the background, he added, with some foresight, "All a kind of elaborate show, legendary, set for a long run."

11
Emotional turmoil
1957–1958

The North African city of Tangier was unseasonably cold when Ian flew in on an Air France Caravelle in early April 1957. The Levanter whistled in over the mud-flats as he ordered a taxi to take him to the El Minzah Hotel, a gracious old Arab building with tiled forecourt, arched windows and hanging gardens, near the centre of town. He booked into room 52 and sat down to await the arrival of his 'Zulu'.

Ian's Mediterranean adventure had begun with a conversation at the *Sunday Times*. He was sitting in his office on the second floor at Gray's Inn Road, attending to the duties of his growing international fame – "I had just answered a letter from an expert in unarmed combat writing from a cover address in Mexico City, and I was thanking a fan in Chile" – when Denis Hamilton suggested he might be interested in a story about the international diamond trade. Hamilton recalled how, when Ian was writing his novel *Diamonds Are Forever*, he had been curious about the undercover operation mounted by the former head of MI5, Sir Percy Sillitoe, against diamond smugglers in Africa. That particular job having ended, Sillitoe was seeking some publicity and wanted to send his deputy, another retired MI5 agent called John Collard, to discuss it. If Ian were to meet him, Hamilton suggested, he might find material for some articles, even a book.

Such a rendezvous needed to be hush-hush, however, for Sillitoe's employer, De Beers, was not backing his moves to go public. Indeed the one-time MI5 chief was taking the unusual step of revealing what had happened because he had fallen out with the world's biggest diamond traders. He had been led to believe he had been hired to investigate a communist-run smuggling ring which was stealing diamonds for dangerous use in the international arms trade. But Sillitoe had subsequently discovered that diamonds were not used in the manufacture of the atomic bomb; besides which, the Soviet Union had its own plentiful resources of the stone. As he had painfully come to understand, the object of the exercise was much more simple, much more commercial. His job was to expose the mainly Lebanese merchants whose activities in West Africa were threatening to break De Beers monopoly control of the world diamond market. For, by paying more than De Beers, Lebanese dealers in

Liberia and Ghana had encouraged a spate of illicit digging for diamonds in neighbouring Sierra Leone. As expected, Sillitoe's investigations were used to encourage the newly independent Sierra Leone government to license and therefore legalize the entrepreneurial local diggers who, as a result, were more or less forced to sell their output to the De Beers-dominated Sierra Leone Selection Trust, and thus on to the De Beers central selling house in London.

To Ian the story seemed to offer an excellent opportunity to revive his journalistic career which had been rather overshadowed by the recent success of his novels. His own research among friends at De Beers convinced him that although the company was lukewarm towards the project, it had no overriding security objections to the story being told. The only potential difficulty was that his contact, John Collard, was still in South Africa, out in the bush in Zululand (thus Ian's cryptic reference to his 'Zulu'). But Ian did not intend to be put off by logistics. Domestic tensions made him particularly anxious to get out of London in that dull, cold period just after his return from Jamaica. Looking at the map, he alighted on Tangier as a suitable place to rendezvous, roughly halfway between Johannesburg and London.

At the El Minzah, Ian had a couple of days to kill before Collard arrived. Although he had visited Tangier briefly during the war, he liked neither the city – "the paint is peeling off the town and the streets are running with spit and pee and worse" – nor its inhabitants – "the Arabs are filthy people and hate all Europeans". Since the weather was appalling, Ian had little to do in the early evenings but walk down the hill from the hotel to Dean's Bar, a cosy hole in the wall which he somehow envisaged as a "sort of mixture between Wilton's and the porters lodge at White's". Morocco had only won its independence the previous year, and Tangier retained much of its wartime atmosphere as a free city. At Dean's Bar Ian downed tumblerfuls of vodka and seemed happy to talk to members of the local expatriate community, many of whom were homosexuals. But in a letter to Ann, he complained that around him was "nothing but pansies, and I have been fresh meat for them". He admitted that his old friend David Herbert – "a sort of Queen Mum" – had been "very sweet", inviting him to work in his garden. But Fleming had refused this offer, complaining that he was "fed up with buggers" who "do absolutely nothing all day long but complain about each other and arrange flowers".

There was some heterosexual interest for Ian, however. Patricia Ellis was a young local beauty who was well-known in Tangier as the daughter of Toby Ellis, the local wartime SIS agent. According to a fellow guest, Ian began "to make a play for her" at dinner one night. Embarrassingly, this was not a gentle or subtle seduction. He delighted in telling Patricia exactly what he wanted to do with her. In front of several others, he said he would

throw her down on his bed, grab hold of her beautiful long hair, and pull
her head behind the bedstead. Then, he promised, she would be screaming
for mercy. Luckily she was able to defuse the situation with impeccable
good taste: "Ian, you know, I don't think I'd like that. It all sounds terribly
uncomfortable."

Ian put the inclement conditions to good use. He had been introduced
to Gavin Young, a 28-year-old Arabophile who was working for the English
service of Radio Morocco and was afraid that, if some other job did not
crop up soon, he might have to return to London to work in the City.
Perhaps in order to save an adventurer from a fate he himself had loathed,
Ian befriended the young man, inviting him for long pre-prandial walks
along the blustery beach. Young told him about the Marsh Arabs he loved
and later wrote movingly about in his books and in the *Observer*, while
Ian collected seashells in a battered briefcase and pointed to promising
bits of greenery: "Now there would be a good place to read a book or make
love to a girl, don't you think?" Ian said little about himself, but Young
remembered him as "not only fun, but interesting: he had been places,
done things, and he was interested in people."

When Collard arrived on 13 April, Ian quickly sized him up as a typical
English "reluctant hero". A former lawyer who had worked in Military
Intelligence during the war, he had operated clandestinely with MI5
tracking down communist subversives. As one of the team which provided
the evidence to arrest the atomic spy Klaus Fuchs in 1950, Collard was
plucked from the Security Service by his former boss, Sir Percy Sillitoe. For
three years he had gone to ground in Africa, working to flush out the
diamond smugglers. Even now he preferred to maintain a pseudonym,
John Blaize, and was nervous about being spotted in a well-known
centre of espionage and intrigue. Ian made a great joke of this, inventing
a story that Collard was an expert in the coelacanth, a primitive fish,
and that they were there to write a story together. He even prevailed
on Collard to carry a tin canister into which he could occasionally drop
worms. If the ex-MI5 man wanted cover, James Bond's creator could
provide it.

In the sitting-room attached to room 52, Collard, as Ian put it, would
"unburden himself of his story", verifying dates and facts from untidy
scraps of paper. Sometimes they strolled down to the Café de Paris in the
main square. It was so chilly that they sat inside sipping their espressos.
With the cine camera he had used to film security arrangements at
diamond mines, Collard was able to shoot grainy pictures of Ian loping
through the gardens of the El Minzah. Discovering that his new colleague
was a golfer with a handicap of nine, like himself, Ian challenged him to
a game at the Diplomatic Country Club, but failed to win a hole. While
Collard stuck to the fairway, Ian found himself "too often in the rough,

ablaze with irises and asphodel, which lines the dry watercourses around and over which the course has been constructed".

As long as they talked, Ian became increasingly impressed by his friend's unassuming but well-grounded expertise. Although he seldom wrote about the profession of espionage, he was prompted to reflect on the different types of secret agents. There are drab private eyes, top professionals and "colourful spies like Sorge, the brilliant luxury-loving German who worked for Russia in Tokyo . . . But Blaize [i.e., Collard], like all Britain's best secret agents, belonged to none of these categories. He had common sense, a passion for accuracy and a knowledge of men and how to use them which would have brought him to the top of, for instance, the Civil Service. But he also had a taste for adventure and a romantic streak which in the Civil Service would have been sublimated into mountain climbing and amateur theatricals."

Each day Collard assembled his notes and related what had happened in South Africa and Sierra Leone. Then Ian would dictate his version of events verbatim to a secretary who had once worked in the Foreign Office. This way they kept up a prodigious output of 5000 words a day, and in a letter to Ann he had to excuse himself for not contacting her earlier: his brains had been "boiling" with his literary exertions. He was happy with the consequences – indeed, he called them "sensational" – but he begged her to keep his mission quiet. Otherwise, he said, the whole project could still be aborted.

By then Ian's new novel *From Russia, With Love* had been published – to the accompaniment of a major promotional campaign seeking to cash in on the publicity generated by the Prime Minister's visit to Goldeneye. Cape claimed that Ian had sold over a million copies of his books in the English language. If Ian had been concerned about his foreign sales eighteen months earlier, he must have welcomed the news that his books had now been translated into a dozen languages.

Once again *The Times* was the only obvious dissenter in the chorus of praise for the new novel, its anonymous reviewer observing that, unlike Peter Cheyney in the Second World War, Ian's output was irrelevant to the conduct of the Cold War. Predictably, there was no such carping in the *Sunday Times*, where one of his "apparatus" was wheeled in to review the book. Sir Ronald Howe, the former Deputy Commissioner of Scotland Yard, who had accompanied him to Istanbul in the early stages of his research, pronounced him "the most readable and highly polished writer of adventure stories to have appeared since the war". Howe noted astutely that if a psychiatrist and a top copywriter had got together to produce a fictional character who epitomized twentieth-century subconscious male ambition, the result would be James Bond. Only a handful of people knew that although Howe's name was on this piece, it was even more of an inside job, having been penned by John Pearson, a young Cambridge graduate who had recently joined the paper.

One or two reviewers picked up the clue that Bond might not have survived his clash with Rosa Klebb at the end of the book. But by now Ian had regained his confidence and no longer needed such an obvious ruse to lay down his pen. To readers who cared to ask he sent a polite letter saying that a bulletin had recently been posted on the canteen noticeboard at the Secret Service headquarters. After a period of anxiety, it read, 007 was showing signs of definite improvement. He had been suffering from severe Fugu poisoning, caused by a virulent member of the curare group obtained from the sex glands of Japanese globe fish. However, he was responding to treatment; no further bulletins would be issued.

Returning to London from Tangier, Ian found that his interest in diamond smuggling had plunged him into a heated argument with his brother-in-law. It was a row which had been waiting to happen for years. Hugo had never hidden his antipathy towards Ian who he thought was an unfeeling cad. There was no doubt some professional jealousy in his attitude. Hugo had laboured hard as a novelist for little reward, while Ian had enjoyed conspicuous success with his rather slighter offerings. Hugo's ill-feeling erupted now because he felt Ian had stolen an idea of his. He also had been in West Africa earlier in the year, on an expedition to Sierra Leone with his Eton friend and fellow writer, Nicholas Mosley, son of the pre-war Fascist leader, Sir Oswald Mosley. Hugo's previous novel, *The Tide is Right*, had had to be withdrawn because he had disparagingly, if warm-heartedly, chronicled the antics of a decaying Scottish clan which bore a remarkable resemblance to his wife Virginia's family, the Forbes Adams, and they had threatened to sue for libel. He was therefore all the more determined to succeed with a new book about his African experiences (*Picnic at Porokorro* was published the following year). But Ian seemed to be about to steal his thunder.

The flare-up between the two men started in Victoria Square at the beginning of June. Hugo was already angry because Ian had vetoed a generous offer by Ann to buy her brother a house. (At the time Hugo, his wife and three children – with another on the way – were living in some penury in Scotland.) Against her husband's wishes, Ann invited her brother, who had been suffering from a heavy cold, down to St Margaret's Bay for some rest. But that was hardly how he would have described the tempestuous time both Flemings subsequently gave him. As Hugo told his other sister Mary Rose, who was struggling with an alcohol problem, "I can't go into the details of their beastliness – but Ian is a subtle bitch and in fact married to no one but himself. He has always disliked me (Ann has told me this) but what I never guessed was that he must also have feared me – to a certain extent – for he never before attacked me – but only when

I was too low almost to move." In a letter to Evelyn Waugh, Ann down-played the row, attributing Hugo's venom to the fact that, after one request, she had forgotten to ask him to show his slides of Africa and "his swollen sensitive ego did not permit him to suggest it a second time". But Hugo clearly had other slights in mind when he informed Mary Rose that their sister was kind but stupid and self-destructive. "Esmond was a come down from Chain [sic] – but Ian was really falling through the floor. And I believe she has really suffered with him – as one must being married to a person who really exists only for themselves – and who is neurotic and verbally violent into the bargain. But she has been secretive and dignified about all that has happened and taken her medicine very privately." As a result the strain was showing rather obviously. Ann had given up a lot to be with Ian, Hugo felt, but he had made not one sacrifice for her. Ian even refused to let her travel with him from London to St Margaret's Bay "so little does he wish for company". So she was forced to fling herself more and more into entertaining – "promiscuous lion hunting most of it".

As a diversion, Ian was childishly gratified to be asked to participate as a celebrity in a charity golf tournament at the Berkshire club towards the end of June. He took the opportunity to repair his rather ancient clubs. The head of Excalibur, his driver for over thirty years (and one of the first with a steel shaft) was loose, and his double-faced chipper (Tom Morris, circa 1935) needed rebinding. He also re-read the relevant chapters in Tommy Armour's How to Play Your Best Golf All the Time, his favourite golfing manual which he had mentioned in Diamonds Are Forever. In the competition, he was drawn to play against Peter Thomson, who had won the Open Championship three times. Given a generous stroke's advantage at each hole, he found he was easily able to match Thomson's relaxed 72. His bemused account of the experience – "Nightmare Among the Mighty" – was published in the Sunday Times the following week and later became a minor golfing classic, an archetypal tale of the rookie making good on the green. Pleased with his efforts, Ian advised Collard to read his piece, noting, "It seems to have stirred the bowels of most amateur golfers."

There were plaudits too for his latest manuscript, Dr No, which, to Ian's delight, Daniel George pronounced his "best yet". As usual Ian was determined to involve himself in planning the cover. Since the fictional Honeychile had reminded Bond of Botticelli's Venus, he suggested a picture showing her standing on a Venus elegans shell and, with typical thoroughness, sent along a reproduction. "I would like to No what you think of the Doctor!" he asked Michael Howard. Borrowing an idea from Somerset Maugham, he added "Personally I think From Russia, With Love was, in many respects, my best book, but the great thing is that each one of the books seems to have been a favourite with one or another section of the public and none has yet been completely damned."

Ian's opinion of *From Russia, With Love* was shared by Edward Pickering, managing editor of the *Daily Express*, who wanted to turn James Bond into a cartoon strip. Taking his cue from William Plomer, Ian at first was cautious. He feared, irrationally, that Bond in comic form would lead to a falling-off in the standard of his books – that "inflation would not only spoil the readership, but also become something of a death-watch beetle inside the author. A tendency to write still further down might result. The author would see this happening and disgust with the operation might creep in." But by the time the first James Bond strip appeared in the *Daily Express* the following July Ian had managed to overcome his misgivings. As he told his publisher, the *Express* were paying through their teeth for the privilege and he expected it would have a useful effect on sales.

For most of the summer, however, Ian's mind was focused on completing his diamond smugglers book, which was causing him more problems than he had imagined. Not being a practitioner of the modern, confrontational school of journalism, he had shown the proofs to his friends, Harry Oppenheimer, chairman of De Beers, and Chester Beatty, chairman of Selection Trust and owner of West African diamond companies which were important suppliers to the Diamond Corporation, telling them it would be a useful publicity exercise.

Three weeks later, he contacted Sir Percy Sillitoe again, congratulating himself on the success of his ploy. His "friends at the Diamond Corporation" had proposed a few minor changes but were generally happy: "altogether my 'old boy' network seems to have operated a hundred per cent". But while Ian may have felt in the clear, the Diamond Corporation was not averse to putting some subtle pressure on its former employee, Sir Percy, who rang Ian "in a flap" a few days later. Ian told him "to stand firm, put his trust in God, keep his bowels open and leave everything to me". In the event, even Ian, with his charm and his contacts, could not steamroll his way through the numbing bureaucracy of a multinational. Within a week Ian was writing to Collard about "sharp snags" at the Diamond Corporation and Selection Trust. "At first they were entertained by the series but then they got more and more worried and they are all now having various kinds of kittens." So Ian was forced to make further adjustments before joining the Bryces in Vermont in August. Even on the train down to Southampton, from where he had booked a passage on the *Ile de France*, he sat poring over the text with Philip Brownrigg, his friend who worked in the De Beers organization. Most of his time on the water was taken up in the laborious task of rewriting.

At Black Hollow Farm Ian was able to relax for the first time that year. The American outdoors had a special appeal for him. On 12 August he wrote to Ann telling her about two greater horned owls which were living on the lake. They were huge – "nearly as big as Caspar," he noted, with a touch of parental nostalgia – and very majestic. The mountains where he frequently walked were full of deer. He particularly enjoyed the strange chill – "like October, with a brilliant sun". It was all "immensely peaceful" and Ann would love everything about it, he suggested. Strangely, Ian left a rather less tranquil impression on a fellow guest. As his marriage continued to founder, Ian was getting into a bad habit of lunging suggestively at young women. On one occasion he lumbered into the drawing-room, clutching a glass of whisky, and told Mary Chewning, an attractive friend of Nuala Pell, that he wanted to beat her. Not knowing how to deal with this approach, she ran into the next room, where Bill Walton, an artist, told her casually not to worry. Ian was known for his little predilection: "that's why Annie's always black and blue". Mary recalled that Ian was "the most attractive fun man, until he had had a couple of drinks".

Before leaving for the United States Ian had started the publicity ball rolling for *The Diamond Smugglers*. On 17 August, his favoured outlet for publishing gossip, the diarist Whitefriar in *Smith's Trade News*, was speculating about the *Sunday Times*'s "blanket of secrecy" over its forthcoming autumn serialization. Then, on 1 September, Atticus came out with an unashamed puff reporting that his colleague Ian Fleming had written about the international diamond trade, making "even his fiction plots seem almost dull by comparison".

After publication in the newspaper later that month, Ian's articles were compiled in book form by Cape in November when they received mixed reviews. Anthony Sampson in the *Observer* thought Ian "(caught) the sparkle" of illicit diamond smuggling, but Dan Jacobson in the *Spectator* felt that Ian had failed to make the most of a journalistic opportunity. The topic of cross-border smuggling was, he felt, "the stuff for a large-scale farce ... or for some serious political reflection; but Mr Fleming's book seems to indicate that there really isn't much in it for a writer of thrillers".

At least Ian was beginning to succeed in his efforts to attract critical attention for writing other than Bond. And there were other compensations. Rank, which was still stalling over *Moonraker*, stepped in with an offer of £13,500 for the film rights to *The Diamond Smugglers*. Ian told them he would provide them with a full story outline for a further £1000, but was unable to bind himself to "do the master scene script or to be available in England for all those consultations".

Now that he had tasted the fruits of non-fiction success, he was determined to enjoy more. When he contacted Cape on 26 November, enclosing the corrected proof of *Dr No*, he informed Michael Howard, "Apart from whatever opusculum I am able to produce in Jamaica, it looks as if you will have another bonus Fleming on your hands next year if you want." He was referring to a *Sunday Times* proposal, tentatively called 'Round the World in Eight Adventures'. The idea was for him to report on a series of real-life escapades, and Ian had them "more or less mapped out – a real treasure hunt that is going on in the Seychelles, the Great Cave of Niah in North Borneo, gold smuggling in Macao, and so forth, and I shall take a Leica." The objective was the sort of thing that appealed to Ian: to show "that the world is still a very exciting place in spite of aeroplanes and Sputniks and that just because some types of adventure are old fashioned doesn't make them less exciting". His paper had suggested that Ian should depart at the end of the following April for two or three months.

Soon after the Edens had returned from Goldeneye the previous December, Ian had been in touch with Alan Lennox-Boyd, the Colonial Secretary who had arranged the trip, saying, "Let's work together again. We seem to be quite an efficient team." Now Ian reminded the Secretary of State that his predecessor Oliver Chandos had once asked him to visit the Seychelles and write about them for the *Sunday Times*. Ian told Lennox-Boyd he was embarking on a world tour: was the Colonial Office still interested in 'publicity' for the Seychelles and could it help him get there from India some time towards the end of April? Lennox-Boyd replied that this sounded an excellent idea and suggested a local adventure story which Ian might like to investigate. Ian already knew the background: eight years earlier, a group of bounty hunters from Kenya had become very excited about £120,000-worth of treasure which they said had been buried on the island of Mahé by Olivier Le Vasseur, an eighteenth-century French pirate. On the gallows, so the story went, Le Vasseur had thrown his treasure chart to the crowd, shouting, "Find it who can." In 1949 Reginald Wilkins, a Kenyan-based prospector, acquired a copy of this chart and raised money from investors to make further enquiries. But after identifying a likely site on a hill at Bel Ombre, he was unable to proceed because of lethal underground gases.

Ian had heard the tale a year or so earlier from one of his correspondents in Kenya, who had told him that the local police considered it a fraud. This being the period of the Mau Mau rebellion, he added, to whet Ian's appetite, "Nairobi is a real spy's paradise. Every other person I meet is doing some sort of special job and a number of chums from Palestine have wandered down into Special Branch and Field Intelligence."

The Kenyan prospectors had offered to give the government 20 per cent of the proceeds of anything they found. "If you could find the treasure," Lennox-Boyd told Ian, "and give 20 per cent of it to the Seychelles Government that would solve a number of problems for all of us!" On a more practical note, the Colonial Secretary advised that it was easier to get to the Seychelles from Mombasa than from Bombay. The government was trying to develop a tourist trade between East Africa and the islands. But it was not being helped by the marked lack of interest shown by the shipping companies. Looking further afield, Lennox-Boyd promised to arrange for Ian letters of introduction in Hong Kong and Singapore. But, a sign of the times, he warned that "arranging 'adventures' might be rather tricky in both places particularly in a colony so delicately situated as Hong Kong. Neither you nor I would want your adventures to give the Chinese People's Government any excuse for propaganda!" In the meantime, to fill in the details about the Seychelles, he suggested a January meeting between Ian and John Thorp, who was shortly to take up his post as the new British Governor there.

Ian replied to Lennox-Boyd that he knew about the treasure and intended using it as an excuse for writing up the attractions of the Seychelles. "Having visited Jamaica for twelve years for my holidays," he laid it on with a treacly trowel, "it is very much a bee in my bonnet that English people should become empire-minded for their holidays, and I shall encourage this idea in all my articles." However, Ian was unable to meet Thorp in January since he would be in Jamaica and he asked Donald McCormick, his assistant in the diminished Foreign Department at the *Sunday Times* to deputize.

Before departing for Goldeneye, Ian had embarrassing family business to attend to. Six years earlier, shortly after her move to the Bahamas, his mother, then in her late sixties, had become engaged to Britain's premier Marquess, Lord Winchester. The Marquess lived close to Eve on Cable Beach, where he had lain low following his involvement in a City scandal of the 1920s. But the expected nuptials never materialized and, instead, the following year, he married the austere Bapsy Pavry, daughter of a Parsee high priest. This hardly solved matters, for the newly married couple were soon living apart. The new Marchioness blamed the lure of Eve and sued her rival in a Bahamian court for alleged libel and enticement of her husband. Her action ended in an apparently amicable settlement. But when Eve moved to Monte Carlo (latterly to the Hotel Metropole) with the elderly Marquess, Lady Winchester claimed that the Bahamas accord had been breached and brought a new action against Eve in the British High Court.

This unusual case was heard in early November 1957. Ian stuck by his mother dutifully, if reluctantly, through the ordeal. He and his brothers, Peter and Richard, accompanied her to court every day, sitting stiffly by her side as they listened to the Marchioness in her crimson-and-gold sari claiming that Mrs Fleming had conducted a campaign of hatred, jealousy and venom against her and had wanted to murder her. Lady Winchester's counsel, Neville Faulks, accused Ian's mother of being "evasive, opinion-ated, worldly, snobbish and untruthful". Looking in excellent shape for her seventy-three years, Eve admitted that, when she heard about the Marquess's marriage, she told him that he "was letting down the House of Lords". But she failed to convince Mr Justice Devlin that she had not financed Lord Winchester's successful attempt to annul his marriage. However, the judge's finding was overturned in the Court of Appeal the following year, and Lady Winchester had to pay costs. As was often the case Ann captured the comedy of the substantive 1957 action: Mama sticking to her usual dress sense, the spitting image of Lady Ottoline Morrell or the Marchesa Casati, and her sons pleading with her, for the sake of appearances in court, to look less like the Jezebel she had been painted, and more like a hospital matron. "On Friday", she wrote to Evelyn Waugh on 9 November, "the poor old thing wished to wear a yellow satin picture hat with grey pearl hatpins the size of tennis balls – they had her out of that in a trice."

Around this time Ian met Norman Lewis, a fellow Cape author who seemed to share his interest in adventure. When Cape sent him a copy of Lewis's new novel, The Volcanoes Above Us, in July, Ian did not know the author. But he read the book on holiday in Vermont and was enthralled. He described it to Wren Howard as "one of the best novels I've read for years" and asked him to congratulate the author warmly though, following his initiation by Boothroyd, he also asked his publisher to tell Lewis to use a better weapon than a Beretta next time. "As you know, I'm killing the bloody gun in my next book – and on sound grounds."

During the autumn Ian chanced upon Lewis at a Cape party. As often happened at literary gatherings, he himself stood diffidently on the sidelines, scowling and uncertain how to relate to a group of chattering writers. Not recognizing the author he had recently heaped with praise, Ian asked if Lewis wrote poetry and seemed annoyed to discover that he did not. Learning of Lewis's knowledge of Central America, however, he invited him to his office to discuss the area, showing an interest which Lewis felt was more than a mere newspaperman's – more like an intelligence officer's. Ian wanted particularly to know if Castro's revolt stood a chance of success. He had heard from Edward Scott, the Sunday Times's occasional correspondent in Havana, that the revolutionaries would soon be finished. Ian did not believe it, and wanted more detail.

Scott was an intelligence insider, who after working with William Stephenson in the British Security Coordination in New York, had holed up as editor of the English-language Havana Post. Ian, for some reason unknown to Lewis, believed that Ernest Hemingway, a writer he idolized, was in touch with the rebels and really knew what was happening. He asked Lewis to fly to Cuba on behalf of the Sunday Times, make contact with the Big Man, as he called Hemingway, and file a report. But despite an introduction from Jonathan Cape who was Hemingway's British publisher and friend, the assignment failed to reveal anything new. Overall, Lewis was left with the distinct impression that Ian was something of a sadist. Bond's creator wore a habitual expression "of controlled fury relieved occasionally by a stark smile", seeming "to wish to inspire fear in others, and on several occasions said of someone under discussion, 'he is afraid of me' – a conclusion which seemed to give him pleasure." What Lewis did not understand was the stress Ian had been operating under – a raw, wearying, gut-wrenching pressure which was beginning to undermine him.

When Ian finally reached Goldeneye in the first week of January, he was physically exhausted, emotionally battered and alone. Not only had he been working extremely hard – performing his usual duties at the *Sunday Times*, while finishing two different books, and preparing for his next novel – but he had also suffered badly under the nervous strain of his mother's court action and his battered relationship with Ann.

In the manner of his puritanical Scottish ancestors, burying himself in his work over the previous few months had been a displacement activity, a way of keeping himself occupied so he could ignore, if not forget, the personal matter causing him most anxiety – the breakdown of his marriage. Blanche Blackwell was only the catalyst in a process that had been waiting to happen. It had not taken Ian and Ann long to realize that, for all their amusing and even happy moments in Victoria Square and St Margaret's Bay, they were not temperamentally suited to living together. The root of their problem was that they were both too selfish, refusing to make the necessary compromises that come more easily to other couples. Ian's own difficulties stemmed partly from an arrested emotional development, wanting to remain the attractive prima donna who had courted his way so effortlessly through the 1930s. Although his years in Naval Intelligence had hardened and matured him, they also took a lot out of him. After the war, he abjured real responsibility, preferring the company of clubland cronies and devoting his leisure to undemanding pursuits such as golf and bridge (he could never quite lend himself to the total sybaritism of Ivar Bryce), while channelling what energies remained into the Bond books. This did not leave much for Ann who, sensibly, remained fiercely committed to her wide circle of witty friends. But this in turn created its own problems. It was not so much the fact that the people she gathered together at Victoria Square were intellectual that alienated Ian (although he was frequently conscious of his lack of formal university training). It was more that they occupied his wife's time, keeping her from him and, more importantly, from making his life comfortable in the way Lisl Popper and others were always telling him a woman should.

That was why Ann minded about Ian's 'Jamaican mistress', who differed from his other girlfriends in that she patently cared about his well-being. Blanche took Ian shopping for Caspar, and looked after and even embellished his house when he was away. Not only was she an attractive Jewish woman of a certain age – a type Ann guarded against because she knew Ian was emotionally susceptible to them – but she also fulfilled a fantasy role in Ian's life. Blanche, with her love of the sea, her unaffected nature and her immersion in Jamaican history and lore, epitomized the romance of the Caribbean, an important feature of Ian's life which Ann had only fleetingly shared.

Jealousy often operates more destructively in such conditions. With her lively imagination, Ann managed to read not only searing criticism of herself but also all manner of sexual couplings into the sheer geographical distance which separated her from Jamaica. While her paramour, Hugh Gaitskell, was flesh and blood – a gentle, overworked politician whom even Ian could not help liking – Blanche was very much the 'other' woman. For this reason, Ann made a point of inviting her rival on to her own soil for another look when Blanche, as was her practice, visited London with her mother during the summer. Asked to lunch at Victoria Square, Blanche found herself in the company of Peter Quennell and Paddy Leigh Fermor, who had come to provide second opinions. "Oh, Mrs Blackwell, I don't think I had the pleasure of meeting you when I was in Jamaica a couple of years ago," piped up Quennell, as if on cue. Before her guest had had time to reply, Ann interrupted, "Blanche is an old girlfriend of Ian's." Seriously discomfited, Blanche could only blurt, "Ann, that is a very unprovoked attack."

But by then the battle-lines had been established, and Ann was fighting back with her own demands. As part of a niggling campaign that Ian took rather too personally, she began, over the summer of 1957, to talk about finding the sort of house that she really wanted. She liked living in Victoria Square, but was tired of her golf-widow existence in a windswept cottage underneath a cliff in Kent. She dreamed of a large country house in what she called a proper English county, such as Wiltshire or Gloucestershire, where she could indulge her love of the countryside. Kent was simply an extension of the stockbroker belt as far as she was concerned. But since Ian was loath to move far from St George's, she agreed a compromise, against her better judgement, and in October the Flemings purchased the Old Palace, a six-bedroomed house, which was grand enough – mainly eighteenth century, with parts dating back to its earliest resident, Thomas Cranmer, Archbishop of Canterbury, a couple of hundred years earlier – but was still in Kent, at Bekesbourne, just outside the cathedral city.

The move hardly improved anything. The Old Palace turned out to be a miserable building. According to Mark Amory, "It was haunted, doors banged, ghostly footsteps were heard. A disused tunnel was said to lead to the Cathedral. Worse, it was too close to the railway." And that was just its physical attributes. As Ann subsequently informed Evelyn Waugh, in one of her amusingly snobbish pieces of social commentary, "Seaweed in the sitting-room and boulders of chalk on the head were the disadvantages of St Margaret's Bay, but here we have to entertain or be entertained by the neighbours. They fall into that category of person which is ever increasing and neither 'landed' nor 'peasantry'. The doctor's wife gave a cocktail party for us in a low raftered room, Ian could not stand upright and was unable to protect himself from the advances of a rapacious old virgin, she was wearing a handpainted skirt, crafty-arty sandals, and used an ebony cigarette holder as a weapon. I was delighted by Ian's misadventures, as it was upon his insistence that for Caspar's sake we were looking for other parents."

Since Ian was considerably more reticent about personal matters than his wife, one has to search for clues as to his state of mind around this time. A series of entries in his notebook dated 16 December 1957 included the resigned observation, "One of the great sadnesses is the failure to make someone happy." It was accompanied by two quotations: one, by Aloysius Horn, expressed his own determination to fight any intimation of his mortality, "Death is like any other untamed creature. He respects a scornful eye", while the other, by St Augustine, seemed to indicate at least one method of achieving this, "Give me chastity but do not give it yet."

Around this time – the exact date is unclear – Ian and Ann decided they should have a discussion, with no holds barred, to clear the air. The upshot was dinner at Scott's, where it was agreed that husband and wife should tell one another exactly how they felt they had been let down. Having won the toss, Ian spoke first in the great debate. But his list of grievances was so long that, by the time he had finished, Ann was completely shattered and unable even to begin the catalogue of woes that she had planned to present.

In the circumstances, the Flemings agreed that they should spend the winter apart. He would go to Jamaica, and she would remain in Bekesbourne with Caspar, ostensibly looking for a suitable pre-prep-school for him. It was the wrong decision because everything Ann hated about the Old Palace was intensified while Ian was away and she had to put up with the thought of his seeing Blanche. "I am alone in an ugly house in the suburbs of Canterbury," she wailed to Max Beaverbrook. "Ian forces me to live here so that on his rare visits to England he can play golf at Sandwich. Alas, how foolish I was to leave Lord Rothermere. Is it too late to marry you?"

In his first letter to Ann, written after a week on the island, Ian tried to humour his wife with an amusing, upbeat account of a bachelor existence –

the kind of letter he had written from Jamaica a decade earlier. The weather
had been filthy – torrential winds and rains. But this had only kept him
glued to his typewriter, hammering away "between bathing in the rain
and sweating round the garden in a mackintosh". He admitted he had
seen Blanche a couple of times, and another neighbour, but otherwise not
a soul. In the absence of other amusements, he turned his satirical focus
on the servants. Violet and Lahoud had not done a stroke of work since
the previous year. Rather, the rat shit on the sofa suggested that they had
used the house as their own in the intervening period. There was paint
peeling off the eaves, chips and cracks all over the floor, and not one
bottle of marmalade or preserves. Ian had had to call in a painter and
other workmen who, he complained, were "still banging away". When he
had voiced his displeasure, Lahoud, his agent, had nodded his head
vigorously and said, "Quite right, Commander."

This breezy style only masked Ian's intense personal torment at the state
of his marriage. Feeling emotionally drained, he had bought some sodium
amytal pills to help him sleep. "My nerves are still jangling like church
bells and I am completely demoralized by the past month," he wrote to
Ann. "I think silence will do us both good and let things heal. Please put
your health before everything else. Try and put a good face on the house
and don't let your hate of it spread to the others or we shall indeed end
up a miserable crew." Things had got so bad, he recalled in another letter,
that he had had to restrain himself from spending his last night in London
at Boodle's "to get away from the blaming and the criticism and the sheer
enmity you were heaping on me and had been heaping for nearly two
months". On another occasion, Ian dropped all pretence of coolness or
rationality, and gave full vent to his emotion. "This atmosphere of constant bad news in which we have lived for years while surrounded by
everything we want – or at any rate as much as a difficult, self-indulgent
couple like us deserves – is really killing me."

Other men might have sought a divorce at this stage. But one of Ian's
many paradoxes was that, for all his licentiousness in print and his
apparent nonchalance about discarding women in the past, he had an
enduring commitment to the state of matrimony, both in general and in
the particular. This was largely for reasons of social etiquette: as a family,
the Flemings simply did not get divorced. In addition, he realized that
Ann provided the companionship and intellectual ballast which enabled
him to write and do virtually what he wanted.

As a result, when he settled into Goldeneye, he was even more unhappy
than his letters suggested. He could not understand how the marriage in
which he had invested so heavily could have deteriorated so badly. When
Blanche Blackwell came to visit him, she was seriously concerned that he
might commit suicide. Initially she tried, against her will, to encourage

him to patch up his relationship with Ann. But when she asked, "Is there anything you can do which will make her love you again?", Ian answered forlornly, "I don't think so." So instead Blanche herself rallied to his side emotionally, and a tropical dalliance developed into a deep love affair. The circumstances were just right for it. Work on her new house had started, and she was on the north coast much more frequently. From Bolt it was just four miles along the coast to Goldeneye and what she considered the best beach in the neighbourhood. But she never pushed herself on Ian, part of her attraction for him being her respect for his routine. She realized from the start that he was a man who kept to a strict timetable. It was no use her turning up at any time in the morning. But around twelve o'clock, he liked to stop working and to swim. She would join him and often stay for lunch. Afterwards she would leave him to rest, returning after he had done another hour's work in the late afternoon.

Outwardly vivacious and amusing, Blanche had a canny Caribbean intuition when it came to the contradictions in Ian's character. She realized that he "was a very private person because he was so many people". Although she admired him as an "intellectual athlete", she did not require him to explain himself. "By the time I met him he'd done his communicating." Instead she encouraged him to relax and enjoy himself. She realized that she could never compete with Ann intellectually, but her strict upbringing coupled with her failed marriage had given her an amusingly detached outlook on life, and she found she could make Ian laugh with tales of life on the estate or encounters with fishes in the sea. Later she described herself as his "safety-valve", but she was rather more than that. Hitherto a friendly, if peripheral presence, she gave Ian the selfless adoration and respect that he needed.

She was helped in her ministrations to Ian's battered psyche by Hugo Pitman, who came to stay at Goldeneye with his wife, Reine, and daughter, Rose, who was pregnant. Ian had been apologetic when he told Blanche that a friend was arriving and he was not sure that she would like him. She put him at his ease by saying, with the blind acceptance that comes from genuine affection, "Of course I'll like him." She showed her tactfulness by taking responsibility for Hugo and his family. Ian was left in peace to write, while she whisked the Pitmans off on long expeditions in the hills. Ian was so grateful that he ill-advisedly reported back to Ann that Blanche was being "an angel" in looking after his guests.

For two weeks he did not hear from Ann. Then two letters, "a left and right hook", arrived together, telling of her visit to the health farm, Enton Hall, where she had tried to get off what Ian called "the tragic switchback of pills" she was using to cope with her own unhappiness. "You've no idea how they change you," he pleaded with her in reply. "First the febrile, almost hysterical gaiety and then those terrible snores that seem to come from the tomb. Darling, forgive me, but it is so and honestly all I get is the fag end of a person at the end of the day or at weekends." Her brother Hugo thought she came out of Enton in improved health, "but still pretty shaky and indirect". At Victoria Square she was soon entertaining in her old style. The guests in February included Somerset Maugham and the Labour politician Roy Jenkins. Maugham wrote to her that he enjoyed meeting Jenkins "and am so glad that you have drawn him – as well as his leader – into your corrupting net. You will soon have the whole Labour party thoroughly softened up." All the while she was reflecting on her future. Eventually, her mind was made up: they would simply have to move again.

Ian took her demands philosophically enough. Bekesbourne had only been a temporary expedient to meet an emergency when she could no longer stand living at St Margaret's Bay. He had hired the best surveyors in Ashford and "really worked like a black to get you out of the Bay and in before Christmas so that you would be warm and safe while I was away". Although he was dismayed that "now you blame me and treat me like an enemy and tell me exactly where I am to live for the rest of my life", he was determined to be as fair and practical as possible. One can sense Blanche's mollifying touch in his willingness to concede that, if Ann was determined to move, then that was obviously what they would have to do. "Anyway living with an unhappy you is impossible." But he had some demands of his own. He wanted a river or stream in the grounds of any future mansion. "I shall simply pine away if we go to live in the middle of a lot of plough with deadly little walks down lanes and dons every weekend." In another letter he expressed a desire to live as far away from London as possible – not somewhere that was just an extension of their London life but "somewhere that will be new – an adventure. Could we go to the Severn? I know nothing about it but there are the birds and wide horizons."

Ignoring, for some reason, the substantial royalties that his books were beginning to earn, Ian expressed unfounded fears that her taste in houses might soon eat away at their joint bank balance. Your pot, he said, referring to her settlement from Lord Rothermere, was "down to about [£]70,000 and two more years at 10,000 a year will reduce it to your iron ration of 50 after which we shall just have to live on income". Since his mother could easily survive for up to twenty years, he noted, that would mean having to live on a combined income of £5,000 a year – enough to support one house, he suggested, but not two.

As he began to recover his equilibrium in the balmy atmosphere of Jamaica, he added, "What we both want is more love and warmth but that is a fire we both need to blow on if it is to burn and for that we need time and self discipline and a determination to keep our marriage alive.

And we must, we simply MUST, stop hacking at each other and grizzling about the way we spend our lives, which is exactly the way we were spending them before we married. We both like to lead vivid lives and that in fact is one of the reasons why we get on."

Their differing lifestyles caused problems, he admitted. Approaching his half-century in May, he needed a calmer, more domesticated existence. "It is unusual for a woman to lead a life like yours unless she is an actress," he chided his wife, "and even actresses have periods without a play. I have always loved broad horizons and new things. But as I get older, I want more and more the home I have never had, and the more of a home I have, the less I shall leave it. That is natural over fifty."

Meanwhile Ian had been making good progress with his new book, *Goldfinger*, which told of a SMERSH-inspired conspiracy to seize all the gold in Fort Knox. As usual, he had done his homework methodically. The research notes he took to Goldeneye included a questionnaire about gold as a precious metal which he had sent to an expert at the livery Goldsmiths' Company in the City of London: has it a smell? (answer: no); what is the value of half a ton? (answer: very approximately £200,000); is it true that the premium on gold smuggled into India was 300 per cent and is now 70 per cent and what dates? (no answer but a question mark).

Having written about other important areas of personal interest, it was inevitable that Ian would some time turn to golf. An important confrontation between Bond and his eponymous villain, Goldfinger, took place during a round of golf at the fictional Royal St Mark's club at Sandwich which, it did not take much imagination to realize, was based on Royal St George's. True to form also, the book reflected the people in Ian's life, including a relative of Blanche Blackwell. Since meeting her, he had become friendly with John Blackwell, a par handicap member at St George's, who was one of her many cousins by marriage. Blackwell, an eccentric, sports-mad bachelor who owned Wellesley House, a superior type of prep school on the Kent coast at Broadstairs, had helped him with some of the golfing details.

Ian was familiar enough with the local colour, of course. When Bond looked around him on the windswept St Mark's course, he could see "the glittering distant sea and that faraway crescent of white cliffs beyond Pegwell Bay", just as at St George's. The names of the golf professional were obviously similar: Albert Whiting at St George's and Alfred Blacking at St Mark's. Before Bond teed off with Goldfinger, Alfred counselled him, "Remember what I told you, sir. I mean about that flat swing of yours. It needs watching – all the time." This was an accurate description of Ian's own game. John Blackwell compared Ian's swing to "a housemaid sweeping the floor. This meant Ian couldn't hit the ball far enough to get into trouble. He was quite good on short play, though; rather cunning on the green. Unless he missed, of course: you'd often see him hitting his chip shots twice." Ian admitted as much himself. In his piece on his round with Peter Thomson the previous summer, he had noted that he only remembered to keep his head down for one shot in three "and that, on occasional shots, 'everything moves except the ball'".

When Ian and John Blackwell teamed up, they made a formidable fourballs pair. Ian's weaknesses were Blackwell's strengths. Ian would only just clear the vast bunker at the par four 466-yard fourth hole at Royal St George's. But this would set up the long-hitting Blackwell to make the green. Ian described the hole faithfully in *Goldfinger*: "The fourth is four hundred and sixty yards. You drive over one of the tallest and deepest bunkers in the United Kingdom and then have a long second shot across an undulating hilly fairway to a plateau green guarded by a final steep slope." At Sandwich, the short, tight sixth is known demurely as "the Maiden"; in Ian's book it became, more salaciously, "The Virgin".

In their fictional game, Goldfinger and Bond sought to outdo one another at gamesmanship. According to John Blackwell, he was responsible for telling Ian about the trick which enabled Goldfinger to beat Bond at the Virgin: "If you are in a bunker and don't like the lie, you pretend you can't see the hole. Then you jump up and down on the sand." Blackwell was less keen to take credit for the controversial interpretation of the regulations which allowed Bond to beat Goldfinger by claiming his opponent had played the wrong ball. He was none too pleased, either, to feature in the book by name as a "pleasant-spoken Import and Export merchant" who, in his efforts to help a beloved sister with an opium habit, became involved in the heroin trade, the subject of Bond's investigation in Central America when he initially met Goldfinger.

But, as the "Boofy" Gore incident the previous year suggested, Ian took innocent pleasure in casting his friends as "hoods". And so, in a roundabout way, it was with Goldfinger himself. Perhaps John Blackwell's greatest contribution to the book was to remind Ian about another relative, Erno Goldfinger, a well-known modern architect who was married to a cousin of his. John did not like the real-life Goldfinger, who was famed for his brutalist high-rise buildings. Ian latched on to the name, which was rather more acceptable than Cyril Connolly's suggested alternative, Goldprick. The two Goldfingers had several similarities. Both Erno and his fictional counterpart Auric were Jews who had come to Britain during the 1930s. Both had overwhelming egos. And, according to journalist Lewis Chester, both had "an almost mono-maniacal attachment to their own vision of the world which had its symbolism in a substance – gold in the case of Auric, reinforced concrete in the case of Erno". However there were also important differences. Auric liked large cigars, while Erno hated smoking. Auric stood "no more than five foot tall", whereas Erno was almost a foot and a half higher. As usual, Ian's villain – like most of his characters – was a composite of many people he had either met or heard about. A closer real-life counterpart was Charles Engelhard, a successful American commodities merchant who banked with Robert Fleming. Part of his substantial wealth came from his ability to circumvent South African restrictions on the export of gold ingots by setting up a local jewellery business, the Precious Metals Development Company, which manufactured expensive baubles for export to Hong Kong, where they were melted down for their inherent gold. As a further example of the connections which counted for so much in Ian's world, Engelhard worked closely with Harry Oppenheimer, chairman of De Beers, while his business protégé Hank Slack, was married to Oppenheimer's daughter, Mary.

By 14 February Ian had completed 70,000 words and was telling Bryce about his author's dilemma: "With only two chapters to go I am in a bad fix as the heroine suddenly got a crush on a divine Lesbian hood who commands a women's gang yclept The Cement Mixers. Miss Pussy Galore, for that is the lizzie's moniker, has got my heroine parting her hair three ways in front of the mirror and I don't see how Bond can possibly get between them with only two chapters to go. The alternative is for him to knock Pussy Galore, a course of action which I favour, but again this involves psychological treatment in depth and the disintegration of Pussy's traumae."

Since Bond did not usually cavort with lesbians, Miss Galore was introduced to prove his masculinity: he could even seduce a man-hating gangstress who had been raped by her uncle at the age of twelve. Possibly, in an imaginative and even confused phase, Ian sublimated his own aggression towards women into an unattainable homosexual figure. Curiously Graham Payn, in his book of reminiscences about Noël Coward published in 1994, recalled that Ian, "tongue firmly in cheek", had based Pussy Galore on Blanche Blackwell. That might have been Noël Coward's little joke, but there was no similarity in reality.

Once Ian had finished his book, Blanche arranged to take him on another short trip. She had committed herself to accompanying a team of scientists from the Jamaica Institute on an expedition to the Pedro Cays, two small islands in the Caribbean forty miles off the south-east coast of Jamaica. The official object of the exercise was to find inshore specimens of birds and beetles. When Blanche hired a yacht belonging to local businessman Sir Anthony Jenkinson, Ian expressed some disquiet since he had known Jenkinson as a charming but unreliable NID agent during the war.

The voyage started inauspiciously since the yacht had no proper charts and the crew little experience. Rather than sail directly to the Pedro Cays, the captain had to rely on Blanche's knowledge of the coastline. That meant tacking along the coast ahead of the wind as far as Negril and then striking south towards the Cays. It turned into a remarkable trip. The sea was so blue that it played tricks with the scientists' senses. They believed wrongly that they had discovered a new species of seagull, so gleaming white did it appear in contrast with the ocean. Once they reached the Cays, the boffins, to Blanche's horror, tipped a quantity of the Indian poison, curare, into the water in an effort to capture a particular specimen. Ian contented himself looking for the West Indian Chank shell which he described to Ann as "white and pink and very beautiful". He added plaintively, "Surely there are some things like that you and I could do in England and Europe." But his suggestion – that, on his return, they should go and stay in Caithness with his crony Duff Dunbar – was hardly designed to endear himself to his estranged wife. It only emphasized the aptness of Ann's comment to Hugo while Ian was away, "I know he's a child, but I love him." Hugo could not help informing his sister Mary Rose and adding, "Child! Crikey, then pass the harness with bells, quick."

There was childish bravado in Ian's gesture when he left Jamaica. Because Blanche's house was under construction down the road, he offered to let her stay in Goldeneye rent-free. He squared this with his conscience by making a determined effort to patch up his relationship with Ann. He promised to take her on a holiday and agreed that, so long as he was able to continue with his literary endeavours, she could look for the kind of country house which suited her (though the Flemings were not to buy Warneford Place, near Swindon in Wiltshire, until the following summer).

Back in London Ian found himself embroiled, for the first time, in real controversy about his books. From the start, there had been an under-current of disapproval about their salaciousness. Several critics had objected, for example, to the uncompromising detail of the scene in *Casino Royale* where Bond was whipped around the genitals with a carpet beater. But, on the whole, their reactions had been muted and polite. Now, as the sixth Bond saga was about to be published on 31 March 1958, Ian was well-known enough to attract some radical revisionism. He was attacked not so much for his books as for his views of the world, which was deemed to be crude and amoral. First into the breach was Professor Bernard Bergonzi who, in the March issue of the magazine *Twentieth Century*, took Ian to task for his conspicuous name-dropping. He contrasted the "vulgarity and display" of the scene in Blade's Club in *Moonraker* with "those subdued images of the perfectly self-assured gentlemanly life that we find in Buchan or even Sapper". In Blade's the waiters talked like advertisements in the *New Yorker*. They came up with statements like, "If I may suggest, sir, the Dom Perignon '46" without any trace of irony. Ian's fantasies of upper-class life could only be a desire to compensate for the rigours of life in a welfare state, Bergonzi shrewdly commented. The Professor also berated Ian for depicting sexual licence (Tiffany in *Diamonds Are Forever*, wanting it "all, James, everything you've ever done to a girl. Now. Quickly") and sado-masochistic voyeurism (the gypsy fight in *From Russia, With Love* which ends with blood dripping from one of the girls' exposed breasts).

The *Manchester Guardian* followed suit with a similarly toned leader entitled "The Exclusive Bond", which pilloried Ian's "advertising agency world" as "symptomatic of a decline in taste". Ian took the trouble to reply to the newspaper, offering "a squeak from the butterfly before any more big wheels roll down upon it". He had chosen the simple name James Bond to get away from an inherent snobbery. True, he had given his creation a few theatrical props like guns, cigarettes and even a cocktail. But he personally abhorred wine and foodmanship, and ate only scrambled eggs. "Perhaps these are superficial excuses. Perhaps Bond's blatant heterosexuality is a subconscious protest against the current fashion for sexual confusion. Perhaps the violence springs from a psychosomatic rejection of Welfare wigs, teeth and spectacles. Who can say? Who can say whether or not Dr Fu Manchu was a traumatic image of Sax Rohmer's father? Who, for the matter of that, cares?"

Five days later, Paul Johnson in the *New Statesman* weighed in with a famous essay, entitled "Sex, Snobbery and Sadism". He took up where Bergonzi had left off, describing *Dr No* as the nastiest book he had ever read. It contained three basic ingredients – "all unhealthy, all thoroughly English – the sadism of a schoolboy bully, the mechanical two-dimensional sex-longings of a frustrated adolescent, and the crude, snob-cravings of a suburban adult". Johnson concluded that "Mr Fleming has no literary skill, the construction of the book is chaotic, and entire incidents and situations are inserted, and then forgotten in a haphazard manner." Its author dished up this recipe "with all the calculated accountancy of a Lyons Corner House". Johnson compared his reaction to *Dr No* with that of George Orwell who, when presented with James Hadley Chase's *No Orchids for Miss Blandish* in 1944, disliked it because it lacked the constraint of conventional upper-class values.

Other critics offered variations on these themes. The anonymous reviewer in *The Times* conceded that the Bond books were "undoubtedly most professional", but their appeal had "its much simpler and much nastier side". Anthony Price in the *Oxford Mail* felt that, as a villain, Dr No was thirty years out of date. Bulldog Drummond had finished off that breed, he argued.

To fight his corner, Ian enlisted the heavy-hitting talents of his mercurial friend Raymond Chandler who had returned to London. Over lunch at Boulestin, Chandler revealed that he was thinking of taking a short holiday in Tangier. From his experience of the previous year Ian advised his friend that it was cold and unpleasant in North Africa at this time of year. Instead he suggested Chandler should go to Capri and, while he was there, he might like to stop in Naples and interview Lucky Luciano, a character who had excited Ian since his days in NID. As an imprisoned Mafia chief in the United States in the early years of the Second World War, Luciano had assisted the FBI in infiltrating dockers' and teamsters' unions and preventing the sabotage of valuable Atlantic convoys – a matter of vital interest to William Stephenson and his BSC agents. Later, Luciano was spirited back to Sicily where he helped the advancing Allied forces make their peace with the local Mafia clans. (This role, underwritten by the Americans, helped establish the alliance between the Mafia and the post-war Christian Democrat political establishment which bedevilled Italian politics for nearly half a century.) Luciano was subsequently paroled and deported to Italy where, during the 1950s, he built up the lucrative and deadly Mafia heroin business.

As a journalist, Ian liked the idea of the famous crime writer meeting the notorious gangster, and suggested it to the *Sunday Times* as a feature. In agreeing to pay Chandler's expenses, the paper did what Ian would have hoped and hired Chandler to review *Dr No*. In his piece, Chandler enthused over three qualities which he argued were "almost unique" in British writers – a willingness to escape from conventional mandarin English, a daring sense of place (though he queried Ian's failure to note that the first thing that happens in a Las Vegas restaurant is the waitress bringing an obligatory glass of iced water), and an "acute sense of pace".

Coming early in the developing debate about Bond's cultural significance, Chandler's review failed to deflect the aggression that was being directed towards Ian. No longer, it was widely argued, were Ian's books slightly risqué: not the sort of thing you would read in front of the servants, but otherwise harmless enough. Now they were identified as inherently malevolent, a symptom and even a cause of Britain's decline. In a world dominated by the United States and the Soviet Union, Bond was portrayed as an impotent figure reduced to cold killing while mechanically going through the motions of the traditional Buchan-type spy-adventurer. On the home front, Bond was a nasty clubland version of the angry young man, an amoral nihilist who found solace in snobbery and violence. In some respects, the critics were right: one of Ian's enduring strengths was his ability, almost in spite of himself, to reflect what was really going on.

But Ian never liked being taken to task and, even though his holiday in the Caribbean had helped him recover some composure, his mental state was still shaky and he was not prepared to protest too much. Two of his next three books (not counting *Goldfinger* which was already in the pipeline) were interesting departures from the traditional Bond genre. And the remainder presented 007 much more firmly as a benign *deus ex machina* helping to save the free world from catastrophe, or, alternatively, as a latter-day St George rescuing damsels from distress and countries from evil.

Ian's *succès de scandale* can be charted in the correspondence between his old friend, Rupert Hart-Davis, and the former Eton schoolmaster George Lyttelton. In answer to Hart-Davis's observation that *Dr No* was "pretty poor", Lyttelton replied, "He has really gone off the rails in the matter of murders and beatings, and tortures, and impossibility, and lust; Bond I thought was becoming a bore in the last book, and must have made it by now. Did you read the analysis of *Dr No* in last week's *New Statesman* by Paul Johnson? I was prepared to mock at P.J. but couldn't help thinking that, if his resumé was accurate, the boot was on the other leg."

Yet only the previous year Lyttelton had been "thrilled" to discover *Moonraker*, so initiating a lively commentary on Ian's output by two self-confessed fans. "I ask weekly at the Library for another Ian Fleming," wrote Lyttelton a couple of months later, "but they are always out." When Hart-Davis lent him Ian's then current book, *From Russia, With Love*, Lyttelton read it into the small hours and reported back, "What an extraordinarily vivid touch [Fleming] has ... One is always holding one's breath or shuddering or agog in some way or another." Hart-Davis noted that a friend had told him that whenever Fleming mentioned any particular food, clothing or cigarettes in his books, he was rewarded with presents in kind. "Ian's are the only modern thrillers with built-in commercials," the friend remarked.

In fact, there is no evidence of Ian seeking to capitalize on his 'product placement'. When a director of Floris sent him some soaps as a thank-you for mentioning his company in *Moonraker*, Ian replied, "My books are spattered with branded products of one sort or another as I think it is stupid to invent bogus names for products which are household words, and you may be interested to know that this is the first time that a name-firm has had the kindly thought of acknowledging the published tribute." Over in North America they take a more aggressively commercial approach. So when *Time* magazine reported the *Dr No* controversy in Britain, Macmillan followed up with an advertisement designed to give Ian a 'bad boy' image when the book was published in the United States.

Ian escaped the furore by setting off on his long-awaited trip to the Seychelles, the latest of his regular springtime safaris on behalf of the *Sunday Times*. Despite official promptings that Ian should travel from East Africa, his colleague Donald McCormick arranged for him to join the *SS*

Karanja leaving Bombay on 11 April, reaching Mahé, the capital of the Seychelles, five days later. This way, his visit would coincide with that of another journalist and they could share facilities round the islands.

Ian's flight to Bombay was interrupted by an unscheduled stop in Beirut because of a de-icing failure on the plane. He was annoyed that he was not able to sleep at all that night at Beirut airport. And flying over Saudi Arabia was not much better. Then, as throughout his life, he showed little enthusiasm for the Arab world, describing it in a letter to Ann from the Taj Mahal Hotel in Bombay as "the most ghastly arid mess I have ever seen". Even Bombay had little to recommend itself: it was like Oracabessa, his home town in Jamaica, "only very much bigger", and he was dismayed that he could not get a drink.

All the time he brooded about the problems of his relationship with Ann. "Your misery travelled all the way and I am devastated with your unhappiness," he wrote from Bombay. "We must straighten ourselves out and get our nerves and healths back. It is ridiculous that you and I have got ourselves into this state." As a conciliatory gesture, Ian suggested they should take their promised holiday in Venice – a "honeymoon" he called it – on his way back. But first, he implored, she must take heed of her physical state. "Husband yourself and save everything for a few weeks or you will have a breakdown."

A member of St George's, Sir Godfrey Ralli, ran one of the largest Anglo-Indian trading companies. On his recommendation, Ian played golf with local executives of the Ralli company – "very ordinary people but kind and nice and a blessing in this bizarre land" – before boarding the *Karanja*. His voyage to the Seychelles hardly whetted his appetite for the place: everyone, including the captain, made it sound like a hell-hole. Ian sweated a lot during the day and sat at the captain's table making polite conversation in the evening. He tried to interest himself in his fellow passengers, who might have come from a Maugham novel: retired tea-planters from Assam with washed-out wives, a "dreadful" American oil man – "a poor man's Hemingway who talks like Humphrey Bogart" – and an Australian surveyor working for the United Nations who had dysentery.

On the Seychelles Ian scurried around the islands with his unlikely journalistic companion, F. C. Cooke, the editor of *World Crops*. He found that treasure was as much a topic of everyday conversation as football in England. Much interest was shown in the fabled riches apparently on board the German raider, the *Koenigsberg*, which had been sunk off the islands in the 1914–18 war. However, little was known, and even less had been done, about the main object of Ian's visit – prospecting for Le Vasseur's hoard.

Ian amused himself meeting the islands' various characters. On Silhouette, three hours by boat from Mahé, he ate jugged bat (he did not like it) with the "king", Henry Dauban, who spun him many tall stories, including one that, on a visit to England in the 1920s, he had seen some athletes practising the javelin. As Dauban had an excellent arm from harpooning, he thought he could improve on their performances. He proved so good that he was chosen to represent Britain in the Olympic Games. Ian did not believe him at the time, but when he returned to London he checked the story and found it was true.

He disliked the "innumerable wave-thin 'Colonels' living on five hundred a year" with their dusky mistresses, calling them the "flotsam and jetsam of our receding empire". But he did enjoy meeting other expatriates, like the Canadian 'Sharkey' Clark who ran a seaside club called Sharkey's Machine. Visiting sailors paid a shilling and could drink till dawn. "Successive Governors have been grateful for this well-oiled safety-valve," remarked Ian, who later entertained Clark at Boodle's, a rather different type of club.

It all made for an amusing series of articles about beachcombers and butterflies for the *Sunday Times*. When Ian eventually met the original treasure-hunter, Reginald Wilkins, he was disappointed but not surprised to discover a dead end. Towards the end of Ian's visit, his movements were restricted by a nasty injury – he had cut his left shin on a piece of coral, and the wound now festered and blew up. Ian developed a bad fever and was taken to hospital in Victoria, where he was pumped full of penicillin and forced to stay for a week. As an added irritation, his type-writer broke.

Already he was thinking restlessly about his forthcoming movements. He cabled Una Trueblood, his secretary at the *Sunday Times*, to arrange the logistical details of his trip to Venice which was timed to coincide with his fiftieth birthday towards the end of May. He intended going from there to Monte Carlo where his Bahamian friend Ship Kelly wanted him to meet Aristotle Onassis, the owner of the casino, to discuss an idea for a film-script. He asked Una to inform Kemsley that his journey was going well and to start chasing up photographs to accompany his Seychelles articles. More mundanely, he wanted the secretary of the Portland Club to know that he could not attend its annual golf meeting. In another letter to Una, he indicated his general lethargy by crossing out the words "Government House Seychelles" on a piece of headed notepaper and inserting "State of Decay". He told her he was longing to "get back to the West where one doesn't pour with sweat all day long and where one isn't constantly being bitten by something". Altogether the reality of the Seychelles had been very different from Jamaica.

When he reached Rome Ian found that Una had been trying to contact him with urgent news of a promising film offer for *Dr No*. When, a couple of months earlier, Jo Stewart, who handled film rights at Curtis Brown, had reported that a small independent producer was prepared to pay $1,000 for an option on the book, against $10,000 if it went into production, Ian had replied that he wanted $3,000 against $30,000. Stewart had now successfully negotiated this sum and her client was "very interested" in proceeding with the project but needed a quick decision.

Ian put this on one side until after his Venetian 'honeymoon'. Ann joined him in Rome, but it was not a happy reunion because his wound had not healed and he still felt unwell. A couple of days later they boarded the midday *Laguna* express for Venice (one assumes Ian did not enjoy the journey from the way he disparagingly described it in his story 'Risico'). Ian had booked the Princess Margaret Suite in the Gritti Palace, the most luxurious hotel in the city. Before long they decided they were spending too much and moved into a double back room which offered more traditional Venetian canal smells. For several days around Ian's birthday they lazed contentedly in the warm summer sun. "May and October are the best months in Venice," he wrote in 'Risico'. "The sun is soft and the nights are cool." Ian sat in cafés, reading newspapers and drinking Campari, while Ann wandered round the galleries. Always interested in literary evocation of place, he gave her a copy of Thomas Mann's *Death in Venice* which helped her understand the city's sad grandeur. Within a short time they had rekindled some of the warmth of their relationship. She complained bitterly when it was time to leave for Nice and Ian's audience with Onassis.

The film about the Monte Carlo casino had been conceived by Bill Paley, the CBS chief, as a way of providing useful employment for his friend Ship Kelly, who would be the executive producer. Onassis was amenable because he too liked Ship. But they needed a bankable writer to develop the idea. Who better than Ian Fleming, who was well-known to both Ship and Paley from various jaunts to the Caribbean, and who was acknowledged as one of the world's best writers on gambling? While Ann stayed with Somerset Maugham at the Villa Mauresque, Ian visited the casino and talked to Onassis. Ship arranged for the two men to meet over a relaxed dinner in nearby Grasse, where he and his second wife Kay-Kay were living at the time, and where Onassis's American girlfriend, Jeanne Rhinelander, also had a house. At the end of it all, Ian had a verbal agreement to proceed.

The project never materialized because of an extraordinary set of circumstances. Independently Hubell Robinson, CBS's head of programmes, had approached Ian the previous year about writing a James Bond television series. When Ian returned to London, he found that Robinson had shown renewed interest in this idea. Ian's response was to dust down the Commander James Gunn synopsis he had developed for Morgenthau a couple of years earlier.

On 12 June he wrote to Naomi Burton telling her he was "on the edge of a vast television deal" which would keep him occupied for the next eighteen months. He asked her to tell her colleague Jo Stewart that he would be out of the television market for the whole of that period. He subsequently informed Stewart that because of his commitment to CBS, he could not proceed with the deal she was negotiating over *Dr No*, since, for the time being at least, he needed to retain all his television rights.

At the end of June he flew to New York to finalize arrangements with CBS. He was clutching a proposal for thirteen episodes (one of which centred on the Monte Carlo casino), together with some suggestions about how James Bond should be played. He counselled Hubell Robinson against introducing "too much stage Englishness. There should, I think, be no monocles, moustaches, bowler hats, bobbies or other 'Limey' gimmicks. There should be no blatant English slang, a minimum of public-school ties and accents, and subsidiary characters should generally speak with a Scots or Irish accent. The Secret Service should be presented as a tough, modern organisation ..." and Bond as a "blunt instrument wielded by a Government Department". Ian's memo for Robinson was interesting for its general comments about how to communicate Bond to an increasingly astute and well-educated audience. He said that in his recent discussions about strip cartoons, he had persuaded the *Daily Express* that "the action can be speeded up far more than is usual in this 'art' form. But, in this speeding up of the action and the leaving of much to the reader's imagination, I suggested that the artist should linger over physical details and perhaps devote as much as four boxes to the details of, for instance, a particular gun." This mannered pictorial style reflected what Ian was trying to do in his books. Indeed, in an interesting commentary on his style, he told Hubell Robinson, "It is the gimmicks in my books, rather than the more or less straightforward plots, that stay in people's minds."

Ian had hoped that Blanche might join him in New York, but she declined his invitation to "snatch what we can", on the grounds that, even at this stage in their relationship, it was not the proper thing to do. So Ian did not enjoy his rushed visit, complaining to Naomi Burton that the city tasted increasingly sour and that even the stone-crabs at his favourite King of the Sea restaurant were frost-blackened and tasteless.

On the business front things went more smoothly, though Ann told Evelyn Waugh glumly that "the prospect of thirty plots and how to save the money from the tax vultures has made [Ian] an unendurable life-companion and a nervous wreck". At the start of June, Curtis Brown had negotiated Ian an attractive $1,000 fee to write a 4,000-word feature on diamonds for *Holiday* magazine by the end of the following month. Ian accepted with alacrity, suggesting he might write a piece about the Diamond Corporation's monthly 'sights'. But when he returned to London on 8 July, he realized he was so tied up with CBS that he warned he might not be able to complete this assignment. A few days later, he wrote again, apologizing that he would have to cancel it altogether.

Although it was unprecedented for Ian to renege on a writing commission, and although this came shortly after the collapse of the *Dr No* project, Jo Stewart persevered with her job of trying to secure Ian his elusive feature film contract. Before long she was in discussions with David Selznick, the Hollywood producer of *Gone With the Wind*. Again Ian was delighted and reminded Jo that, although three of his books were accounted for (*Casino Royale*, *Moonraker* and *The Diamond Smugglers*), the rights to the others were all available. If the CBS television contract was signed, he suggested eagerly, he would be able to command a $100,000 asking price. Noting Jo's exertions on Ian's behalf, Naomi Burton sent her a note: "I hope he's worth all the effort you've expended. If I didn't think one day he'll write a big book I'd love to kick him you know where." She herself continued with her various initiatives on Ian's behalf. By 17 July Naomi was talking with Al Hart about a Bond Omnibus to tie in with the CBS series. She suggested that *Casino Royale*, *Moonraker* and *From Russia, With Love* should be included. How do you like the title *Gilt-Edged Bonds*? she asked Ian.

For all the build-up, the CBS programmes were never produced. When Ship Kelly discovered that Ian was negotiating another television series with CBS through Hubell Robinson, he took umbrage. He imagined Paley was going behind his back to deal with Ian. Although Paley appeared to be unaware of Robinson's initiative, he immediately put a stop to it. According to Ship's wife, Kay-Kay, now remarried as Mrs Douglas Auchincloss, Paley considered his friendship with Ship more important than any television series. In the mutual relationships the casino project was abandoned. Only the omnibus edition of James Bond's adventures survived.

It was all rather anticlimactic when Ian began to edit his Seychelles pieces. A search for photographs took him to the North of England where Lord Richard Percy, brother of the Duke of Northumberland, was professor of zoology at Newcastle University. Percy had visited the Seychelles with his friend Lord Ridley in 1955 and had taken some photographs. (Percy and Ridley had been near contemporaries at Eton, though of a slightly later vintage than Ian.) Ridley wrote to Ian on 18 June suggesting that the Seychelles might provide an interesting backdrop for a James Bond novel. Ian had already thought of that, replying, "I have mentioned your suggestion to James Bond. He was in fact sent there briefly during Makarios's exile. He was sent to fix up the security arrangements and to foil a Greek commando attempt at rescue. While he was there he was involved in a subsidiary adventure featuring a bizarre fish called the Hildebrand

Rarity; and I hope that one day M. will allow me to have access to the relevant files."

Ian was referring to the fact that on his travels he had started to write a series of five short stories which he completed in Jamaica the following spring and which were published as a collection in April 1960. In 'The Hildebrand Rarity' James Bond enjoys the unusual luxury of a week's leave in the Seychelles, where he meets a boorish American millionaire called Milton Krest who is cruising through the islands collecting rare species of animals and fish for his tax-dodge charity, the Krest Foundation. Ian drew on his recent experiences in Jamaica as well as the Seychelles to flesh out the detail. For example, in order to capture the Hildebrand Rarity, an unusual striped fish, Krest is prepared to poison the sea. Reflecting Ian's own love of the ocean, Bond shows an ecological awareness ahead of his time in seeking to halt this unequal struggle between the evil of technology and the beauty of nature. Bond maintains an unconsummated passion for Krest's beautiful ash-blonde wife, Liz. Krest treats her appallingly, beating her with 'the Corrector', a three-foot-long whip made from the tail of a stingray – a typical Fleming touch. Nobody is very surprised when Krest is murdered one night, with his rare fish stuffed down his throat. The evidence points to his wife, but the incident is passed off as a drowning at sea. No one cares and no one is much the wiser.

Although Bond expressed some peripheral professional interest in the incursions of communism into the Indian Ocean, 'The Hildebrand Rarity' was a tale of intrigue and moral ambiguity rather than a typical Secret Service saga. In his desire to write a traditional short story, Ian adopted an even more subdued palate in 'Quantum of Solace', depicting the harsh realities and emotional privations of colonial life in the tropics. Bond plays a purely passive role in this Maughamish tale, acting as the sounding-board for an after-dinner story about a young married couple, a shy diplomat called Philip Masters and his attractive wife, Rhoda, a former air hostess. Bored by married life in Bermuda she has a passionate and very public affair with a local golf professional. Devastated by his humiliation, Masters transfers to Washington for six months to work on a special project. When he returns, Rhoda has finished her affair and is keen to resume normal marital relations. But he refuses to play her game and is determined to make her suffer. For a year they communicate only by note. Then he divorces her and leaves her alone on the island, without money or means of support. Eventually a friend finds her employment in Jamaica where she meets a rich Canadian and remarries. The saga of revenge is given added poignancy when the Governor tells Bond that Rhoda had been among the guests at dinner that evening. Bond had met her as the bubbly Mrs Harvey Miller who made tedious enquiries about "shows" in London.

In various ways, 'Quantum of Solace' was subtly revealing about Ian's private life. First, it was based on a story about a real-life police inspector in Jamaica which Blanche had told him at Goldeneye "in order to take his mind off his troubles". By way of thanks, Ian promised her a "fat present", a surprising way to describe a slim, attractive Cartier wristwatch.

Second, the title contained a coded reference to the problems in Ian's own marriage. The Governor of the Bahamas, who tells the story, defines the Quantum of Solace as a precise numerical notation of the amount of comfort and humanity that is necessary between two people if love is to flourish. When the Quantum of Solace is zero, there can be no love. Bond clearly understands the Governor's prescription, remarking that "when the other person not only makes you feel insecure but actually seems to want to destroy you" – when the Quantum of Solace is at zero – "you've got to get away to save yourself".

Another allusion to Ian's personal circumstances came in Bond's reaction to the Governor's story. He had been in the Bahamas investigating the trafficking of arms to President Castro in Cuba. But hearing about the Masterses "opened for him the book of real violence – of the Comédie Humaine where human passions are raw and real, where Fate plays a more authentic game than any Secret Service conspiracy devised by Governments". Bond concludes that his next scheduled duty – a conference with the US Coastguards and FBI in Miami – will be, by contrast, "edged with boredom and futility", a distinct echo of Ian's own sentiments as he took stock of his life, marriage and career at the start of his sixth decade.

For the Flemings' summer holiday Ann wanted to visit Italy. If Ian had been willing to maintain the spirit of the Venice trip, he might have agreed. But, as his friend Alan Pryce-Jones noted, "Ian was sunk in his own past." Having reached the age of fifty, he wanted to return to his youthful stamping-grounds in Austria where he claimed Caspar "would prefer lake bathing to quattrocento paintings". So the Thunderbird was polished down, the roof (to Ann's dismay) removed and the family embarked for the Villa Pengg in Kitzbühel where the unfortunate Caspar was dressed in lederhosen. The Mittersill Club had extended down the valley and established a summer branch as a golf club in the grounds of Schloss Kaps, the old Lamberg castle. Ian enjoyed himself tremendously, cavorting and playing golf with Central European princes, while Ann sat on her balcony, painting Alpine flowers. When Pryce-Jones joined them for a couple of days, Ian insisted on taking him to his old haunts. "He pointed out the spots where he had gone with various women and it always seemed to be the anniversary of the night he first met X or first slept with Y." They also travelled to Munich, a couple of hours' drive away, where Ian searched the town for a bar which served Flying, a drink he had enjoyed in his twenties – a White Lady, topped up with champagne.

Ann played the game as best she could, but often with disastrous consequences. As part of their summer festivities, the local townspeople waged mock Dionysian confetti battles. Since Ian was again reminded of his youth, he was determined to participate. But he told Ann this was no fun with a wife. So she was bidden to amuse herself elsewhere. One bitterly cold evening, in an effort to keep warm, Ann decided to join the frolicking. Because her shoes were too small and were hurting, she removed them. Taking advantage of this, some local jokers filled them with confetti. When Ian returned from his own revels, "having failed to find romance or enjoy his nostalgia", Ann informed Evelyn Waugh, "the sight of me dancing barefoot while Austrian youths poured confetti from my shoes drove him mad with rage".

Ever skilful in finding himself in the same place as Ann, Hugh Gaitskell also passed through Kitzbühel, on his way to Italy with his wife and family. Ann tried her best to be hospitable. When the Gaitskells wanted to climb to the top of the Kitzbühler Horn, she agreed to accompany them part of the way on the funicular, an experience that was new to them. It was a boiling hot day, and they were sitting close together, swaying across the Alps in a sultry, sweaty cabin, when suddenly Gaitskell's wife Dora saw a wasp on Ann's shirt. "Kill it, Hugh," she shrieked at her husband. Ann had to restrain Gaitskell from assaulting her with his spectacle case and plunging them all to the ground. Dora clearly had a canny idea of what was going on. For when the party took to its feet to climb to the top, she constantly interrupted her husband's efforts to talk to Ann. "Hugh, Cressida wants some milk chocolate," she shouted, or, "Hugh, bring the insect repellent, we've seen a horsefly." When they reached the summit, Gaitskell was gasping for breath, and Ann feared a heart attack. As she later remarked to Peter Quennell, the Gaitskells behaved like lumpen xenophobes out of a Giles cartoon. "Like some good wines Heavenly [her name for Gaitskell] and familly are not exportable," she noted, with careless disregard for spelling.

Despite this interruption, Ian claimed he had enjoyed his holiday. With his remarkable lack of concern about such matters, he informed Blanche that he and Ann had returned "much refreshed and I hope rededicated". By then his articles on the Seychelles had been published, under the general title 'Treasure Hunt in Eden', and Ian had forgotten his discomfort in the islands and written to his friend the Colonial Secretary, Alan Lennox-Boyd, "I am determined to try and help the Seychelles to become the 'Bermuda' of the Indian Ocean and I feel that much could be achieved." (His reference to Bermuda was ironic, given his recent satirization of its stupor in 'Quantum of Solace'.) The first necessity, he felt, was better communications, and that would require the British India Line to double the frequency of its visits to Mahé, though it might be necessary for the government to share in the shipping company's initial losses. Ian proposed that Lennox-Boyd should arrange a small luncheon for Sir William Currie, the line's chairman, and himself. In addition, Ian continued, the islands needed a well-researched guidebook and a decent cold storage.

Ian was not happy at the way his articles were cut – at least that is what he told John Thorp, the islands' Governor, blaming the work of underlings while he was on holiday. But the dramatist Enid Bagnold, wife of his Reuters chief, Sir Roderick Jones, was "so inspired by the poetry of my descriptions" that she wanted to write a play based on something like the search for the Le Vasseur gold. Following in the steps of Rosamond Lehmann, who had been similarly enthused by a trivial series of articles by Ian on caving, Lady Jones saw it as psychological, even moral, fable. Treasure-hunters are fantasists, seeking a short cut to happiness. Once they find their gold, they cock a snook at authority and have everything their own way, she believed.

Ian's personal interest in the development of the Seychelles continued for at least another year. As he told Thorp, he saw it as a fascinating morality tale, with good and evil on both sides. He himself had witnessed the whole touristic cycle in Jamaica, "right down to the Bishop of Montego Bay warning his congregation against the dangers of homosexuality". Thorp humoured him that his articles had proved useful. On 18 October he told Ian he had received one hundred letters as a result of the *Sunday Times* articles, and the British India Line had decided to double its port calls in the Seychelles from twelve to twenty-four in 1959 – a "splendid result of your interest and persuasiveness".

That was not the end of the matter. Later that month, after his friend John Profumo had become the first Foreign Office minister to visit the Seychelles, Ian took up the cudgels with him. Finding a site for an airport was a priority. At Ian's behest, Profumo adopted the case for flattening Cerf Island into a sort of static aircraft carrier. Ian had yet another line to pursue. His brother Richard was a director of Barclays Bank which, as a result of Ian's lobbying, opened a branch in the Seychelles the following year – an essential element in the islands' economy if future generations of tourists were to flock there. Ian's confidence was not misplaced. The Seychelles have developed into one of the world's leading long-haul destinations. If the islands' tourism minister only knew, he might erect a pavilion, or at least a plaque, to Ian Fleming.

12

Film options
1958–1960

Ian was drunk and bad-tempered when he arrived home at Victoria Square one night in November 1958 to find Ann entertaining a particularly rowdy gathering of fuddy-duddies. He had spent the earlier part of the evening in his male preserve of the Portland Club, and, normally adept at avoiding Peter Quennell's cries of "Commander, come and join us", he intended making his way upstairs to his bedroom without disturbing the party. But this time he saw three men – Hugh Gaitskell, John Sparrow, the Warden of All Souls, and Angus Wilson, the novelist – sitting in a row on the sofa, holding hands and reciting Yeats. Although this literary effusiveness epitomized much of what he disliked about his wife's friends, he could not restrain himself from joining in this time. Bursting into the drawing-room, he began lustily declaiming a Cossack nursery song he had learned in Russia thirty-five years earlier. The effect was electrifying. When it came to schoolboy exhibitionism, Ian was showing that he was every bit their equal.

Ian's reaction demonstrated a flicker of his natural combative spirit. But too often, now that he had reached fifty, his bravado was rather more dourly expressed in terms of struggle – struggle at home, struggle to maintain an interest in his Bond books, and struggle with his failing body. Ian might have found it all easier if he had kept his health. But his breathing was poor, and he had recurring problems with his heart, kidneys and back. His most obvious symptom, as far as Ann could tell, was a chronic inability to keep still. Since this only increased the wear and tear on his system, his doctor, Jack Beal, was concerned enough to refer him to another heart specialist Evan Bedford who, while refusing to show alarm, recommended that Ian should cut down drastically on his intake of cigarettes which was still running at around sixty a day. This advice was reinforced by a hypnotist to whom John Godfrey recommended his friend.

Ann had her ailments too. When her general listlessness was diagnosed as having a physical cause, she was admitted to hospital for an operation in November. Although she described it as "a dull, tedious, tiny op. on my womb", she decided she would not be well enough to accompany Ian to Jamaica in January.

In the circumstances, the family had a low-key Christmas at Shane's

Castle. The general festivities were not improved by the lack of preparation by Ann's son, Lord O'Neill, whose cellar and larder were empty save for bottles of vodka for Ian and whisky for Peter Quennell, a perennial presence at this time of year. (Ian insisted now on drinking vodka rather than gin: he believed it was better for his health.)

Ann recovered sufficiently, however, to travel to Chantilly for a "winter holiday" with Diana Cooper in mid-January, a date which neatly coincided with Gaitskell being in Paris. By then, Ian was at Goldeneye where he began to lobby for his wife to join him. Picking up the theme of the previous year, he initially made conciliatory noises about future living plans. He wrote about finding "a nice house where we can really settle". Not wanting to end up "in some huge palace we can't afford to heat or staff or where we have to dress for dinner every weekend", he preferred the idea of "a small box on which we can build low wings", perhaps in Oxfordshire, or, even better, around Petworth in Sussex, which he had recently visited and liked.

More immediately, he made it clear that he hated being alone. But when he berated Ann for equating Jamaica and the whole idea of winter sun with the Bryces, he got it wrong: he should at least have mentioned the Blackwells. Nevertheless he persevered: John Sparrow was due on the island in the near future. Could she not accompany him? Air travel had improved immensely; even for someone like her who hated flying, it would not be too awful an experience. As for his day-to-day existence, he claimed he was being virtuous and smoking nothing but a small cigar after meals. This had the effect of doubling his vitality, but it appeared to do little for his concentration. His output on this visit to Jamaica was just three short stories, two of which were based directly on the plots he had produced for the proposed James Bond television series the previous year. He curtly dismissed one completed story as having "no merit". Almost as an afterthought he mentioned that Blanche had improved the house immensely while living there over the previous year. She had had the place painted in lieu of rent and put Dunlopillo in all the cushions. (Her old admirer Errol Flynn had also stayed, working on his autobiography, a year before he died.) As a parting gift, she had presented Goldeneye with a small wooden coracle which Ian had christened Octopussy. Intending, no doubt, to put Ann's mind at rest, he added that her rival had taken a house in Ocho Rios and they had "exchanged dinners".

The documentary record at this stage is fragmented. It is not clear why Ian was so insistent that Ann should join him or why she succumbed. The answer seems to be a mixture of continuing affection and (in Ann's case) fierce jealousy. Ian's insensitive reference to Blanche's improvements only encouraged Ann to stake out her ground at Goldeneye again.

The failure of her journey and the torment it caused can be gauged from a letter to her from Peter Quennell in mid-February. "No, I never did meet Blanche," he wrote on the blue headed notepaper of *History Today*, clearly forgetting his meeting at Victoria Square two years earlier, "but I remember your description of her, and she does not sound a formidable rival. It's tragic, nevertheless, that she should have cast a shadow over your visit and dimmed the goldenness of Goldeneye! How tiresome of the Commander to let her bother you! And don't I know about the disadvantages of a vivid visual imagination! 'Speak to me somewhat quickly; or my imagination will carry me / To see them in the dreadful act of sin ...' That is what you mean isn't it?"

Astutely Quennell suggested that Ian's "gallant escapades" were only a means of bolstering his own "often badly-battered ego" which, he speculated, was often more severely knocked about by her and her friends "than you have ever quite suspected". As a result the Commander was "in grievous need of the classical 'little woman', whose big eyes reflect only trust and love and admiration". Quennell noted that Blanche was not exactly built like a Bond heroine. "No firm bottom as a boy's? She wouldn't look her best, would she, walking around a Caribbean beach, wearing nothing but a belt and a sheath knife?" Ann was a match for several dozen Blanches, he suggested. She should sweep her rival away "with a single gust of hearty Charteris laughter" and treat her "as a Roman empress would have treated one of the Emperor's more unimportant favourites – and remember that the dreadful act of sin is only as dreadful – or as significant – as one chooses to make it oneself".

The fraught personal circumstances encouraged Ian to stick obdurately to his reduced output of short stories. But he was continually reminded of the problems and obligations of the larger Bond industry he had created. When the architect Erno Goldfinger discovered his name was being used in Ian's forthcoming novel, he threatened to halt its publication. Ian was not happy with Cape's conciliatory response: he wanted his publisher to insert an erratum slip "and change the name throughout to Goldprick and give the reason why". Even while in Jamaica, he was pestered to promote *Goldfinger* at Harrods and Selfridges. For someone so aware of the power of marketing, he was unusually loath to make such appearances. He initially declined (though later relented and accepted) an invitation to be a guest on the television programme *The Bookman*. He also agreed reluctantly to appear on *Right of Reply* where he countered allegations of unnecessary sex and violence in his novels with the argument, "You cannot have thrilling heroes eating rice puddings."

By now the media myth was beginning to run ahead of the man and his books. When *Goldfinger* was published at the end of March 1959, the critics seemed to sense this and were more equivocal than usual. "Who would bother for one moment about James Bond," asked Richard Findlater in the *Sunday Dispatch*, "if he wasn't haloed by the names of his author and publisher?" Anthony Price in the *Oxford Mail* thought the novel started well but became – with the invention of its villain – increasingly unrealistic. "Even Château d'Yquem has poor years," he commented. But the public liked what they heard and read, and his novel raced to the top of the best-seller list, ahead of *Dr Zhivago*, *Angelique* and *The Collected Poems of John Betjeman*.

Back at the *Sunday Times* Ian discovered that the paper was up for sale. After years of failing to make significant headway against the *Observer*, Lord Kemsley had finally thrown in the towel and accepted £5 million for his newspaper interests from a little-known Canadian tycoon, Roy Thomson. This not unexpected move raised long-mooted questions about Ian's future role at the paper. He was closely identified with the outgoing proprietor. On the other hand, he had been in the vanguard of efforts to change its style and his ally, Denis Hamilton, looked the man most likely to succeed the incumbent editor, Harry Hodson.

Ian took an opportunistic approach. He put in for a significant pay-rise and was not too unhappy when his request was turned down. Ann interpreted this as a dispute about money. If that was so, it was quickly sorted out. Thomson was keen to retain Ian's services in one way or another. He arranged for Ian to be paid a retainer of £1000 a year to write occasional pieces for the paper and to attend the regular Tuesday morning editorial meetings. Thomson called Ian a member of the editorial board, a title which Ian liked to use – much to the annoyance of Hodson who insisted that there was no such body. When Ann told Evelyn Waugh that she was annoyed at this development (she wanted inside gossip on the new regime), he quixotically replied that he was sorry Ian was leaving the paper: "as long as his fastidious mind brooded over its pages, I felt that the spirit of Edmund Gosse was still with it."

Although Ian did not formally leave Gray's Inn Road until the end of the year, he now had more time to think about other matters which interested him. One was the decoration of Blanche's new house at Bolt. Several of the women in his life had commented on his flair for design. Lady Jeanne Campbell attributed it to a feminine side to his character, while Ann once admitted that he was much more talented in this area than she. In his communications with Blanche, Ian tended to be demanding, asking her to fix something at Goldeneye or to leave a car for him to pick up at Kingston airport. He had encouraged her to persevere with her house, at one stage saying, in the avuncular manner he often adopted with her, "Irrespective of whether you marry again, or whatever else you do with the rest of your life, it will always be a place to return to and which any sensible husband will be proud of, even if it's only for two or three months a year." Now he counselled her, as if writing for a woman's magazine, "Don't on any account fool around too much with colours. Keep everything white inside and bring the colours in with the curtains and so forth." Having been charged by Blanche to buy her a selection of old paintings and prints of the West Indies for her walls, he spent around £300, including £170 at the Parker Galleries, on what he described as "an extremely fine and large oil painting of about 1800 of Port of Spain, Trinidad, with a really beautiful ship in the foreground and some blackamoors in a rowing boat".

Another interest was the *Book Collector* which, with little direct input from Ian, had recovered from its near demise and had developed into the most authoritative publication in its field in the world. Ian's main job as chairman was to hold regular editorial lunches at Victoria Square, where he served an unpalatable Chianti which he described as "Rhenish" and charged the company £9 each time. More practically, he chased up advertising from friends like Dick Troughton, the managing director of W. H. Smith, and bearded potential writers in the unlikeliest of places. (At the 19th hole at Muirfield, he elicited a promise from the publisher Desmond Flower to contribute something about Churchill's writing techniques.) With his unfailingly populist instincts in publishing, he tried to direct the magazine to become less stuffy. But his aptitude for the daily drudgery of business showed little improvement on twenty years earlier. He suggested that £500 of the guarantors' funds should be invested in Premium Bonds and, when informed that the auditors might balk at the lack of security, he came up with an alternative idea – that the money should go into shares in Anglo-American and Imperial Tobacco instead.

Robert Harling, who helped with the design, has described these lunches as "furious, hilarious affairs with no holds barred. Hayward, pinioned in his bathchair, was as heroic and formidable a cripple as Roosevelt, sparing no man's reputation and trailing his own with every quip and query." On one occasion, Ian attacked a particular issue for being "the most leaden in content we have ever produced". This brought to a head a long-standing difference of opinion about the magazine's future between Ian and Harling, on the one hand and Hayward, who was acting as editorial director, and John Carter, another erudite bibliophile, on the other, with Percy Muir somewhere in the middle. Carter knocked out a forceful memo pleading for the editor to be allowed to edit, adding that, if the magazine had served its purpose as a tax-loss vehicle, it should be sold off to "someone who likes it the way it is".

While agreeing that, without John Hayward, the magazine could not exist, Ian took umbrage at the suggestion that he was milking the company for its tax advantages: "The company was formed at my personal expense to keep the *Book Collector* under the editorship of John alive and for no other purpose whatsoever." When Ian repeated this line – in response to

a suggestion that he might like to pay the company's £42 auditor's fee –
Hayward reminded him sharply, "The *Book Collector* would not have been
'saved from extinction' after you had taken it over from Lord Kemsley,
without the generous financial help of a number of guarantors."

Ian's other extracurricular involvement that summer was a new film
project. Since this one was promoted by Ivar Bryce, it engaged him more
fully than most. Indeed it later came to dominate his life, leading to a law
case which many people think helped curtail his life. So it is important to
understand exactly what happened. At the time, Bryce had just finished
making another film, *The Boy and the Bridge*, with a smooth-talking Irishman called Kevin McClory. Ian, who had laboured for years without
making inroads into the movie business, was duly impressed at the way
Bryce appeared to have succeeded with this, his first film venture.

McClory had been introduced to Bryce in the Bahamas where his fiancée's family, the Sigrists, had a house. He hailed from a theatrical family
(a cousin was the Edwardian music-hall star, Marie Lloyd). After working
at Shepperton Studios, his movie career took off when he was hired to
arrange the foreign location scenes in director Mike Todd's extravagant
film *Around the World in Eighty Days*, one of the cinematic hits of 1957.

Struck by McClory's energy and enthusiasm, Bryce agreed to finance the
Irishman's next project, *The Boy and the Bridge*, which would mark his own
debut in the film business. It had a whimsical and unassuming story-line –
about a young Cockney boy who, after running away from home, finds
solace with an intelligent seagull in his dream castle, the north turret of
Tower Bridge. Bryce and McClory set up a partnership called Xanadu
Productions (after Bryce's Bahamian "pleasure palace") to make the film.
The venture attracted interest and was chosen as the official British entry
for the 1959 Venice Film Festival.

Ian met McClory during the making of *The Boy and the Bridge* and, like
Bryce, was struck by his ability. What is more, lazy old Ivar was talking
and acting like a Hollywood mogul: if he could do it, anyone could. *The
Boy and the Bridge*, more than anything, helped demystify the movie
business for Ian. As for the film itself, he was initially more equivocal:
after seeing it in rushes at the end of 1958, he thought it was far too
sentimental. But he liked McClory and the two men discussed bringing
007 to the screen. Ian pointed McClory towards a couple of his novels,
but the film-maker thought the long-term cinematic potential lay in the
James Bond character rather than the existing books, and recommended
developing a different story-line.

In February 1959, with *The Boy and the Bridge* completed, McClory flew
down to Nassau to see Bryce with a new suggestion. The film had gone
over budget, he admitted, so one way of recouping the costs might be to
set up a film production studio in the Bahamas, which, as a British colony,

could benefit from the Eady Plan, the UK government's protectionist subsidy for home-produced films. Again, the idea of McClory making a Bond film in this new facility was discussed.

Over the next few months, while McClory concentrated on promoting *The Boy and the Bridge*, Bryce explored the studio concept, which excited him greatly. Having asked Ernie Cuneo, his American attorney, to investigate the legal implications, he talked to three potential investors who were each prepared to put $50,000 into the venture. (They were Sir Francis Peek, an Old Etonian baronet who lived in the Bahamas, Charles Wacker III, Ivar's rich friend from Chicago, and Jean de la Bruyère, a young Canadian mining engineer.) Bryce himself was willing to contribute $500,000, which he still hoped he would recoup from *The Boy and the Bridge*. He also wanted Ian to have $50,000-worth of shares in exchange for the rights to a Bond story. With typical panache, he wrote Ian a personal cheque for $50,000 to enable his friend to buy his stake in the studio, which, to everyone's later confusion, was variously described as Xanadu-Bahamas, Xanadu Productions and Xanadu Films. However Ian did not cash the cheque because, as it turned out, the company was never formed.

Towards the end of April, Cuneo travelled to London to represent Bryce's interests in *The Boy and the Bridge* and also to bring his legal mind to bear on future developments. Ian provided Sir William Stephenson with a fond image of their mutual friend "charging around like a bull in a china shop knocking down the Wardour Street and Elstree inmates like ninepins". During his visit Ernie met both Ian and McClory at Moyns, Bryce's house in Essex. Based on their discussions, the idea of filming a Bond story in the studio took a step nearer reality, and Ernie himself knocked out a rough plot. It seemed a natural thing to do. As Ernie later said, he had often helped Ian with his books in the past. His story-line drew on *Around the World in Eighty Days*, allowing "scope for innumerable guest stars" as Bond circled the globe in search of rocket bases.

After returning to Washington, Cuneo wrote Bryce a short lawyer's memorandum summing up the situation. On the commercial side, he confirmed that Xanadu could benefit from the Eady Plan. Indeed, there was an additional advantage in having a Bahamas-based company. Owing to a tax treaty, its film rentals to the United States would not be liable for US taxes. As for the film itself, Cuneo summarized some of the ideas McClory had suggested. For example, to ensure box-office success, the Irishman had recommended that any Xanadu production should be shot in Todd-AO, the camera system developed by his former employer, Mike Todd, and that it should tell an underwater story. As for content matter, Cuneo suggested that if Cecil B. de Mille could use a past best-seller, the Bible, as the basis for a film, Xanadu should surely call upon a current best-seller from the Bond canon.

To his memo, Cuneo added a covering note, dated 28 May, "Enclosed was written at night, mere improvisation hence far from author's pride, possible author's mortification. Haven't even re-read it." Alongside, he put forward what he described as "a basic plot, capable of great flexibility". This was the first-known literary input into the screenplay and novel which became known as *Thunderball* and which later was the subject of much legal wrangling. In Cuneo's draft Bond was informed by M that mysterious radio signals had been picked up from an airplane by a British submarine in the Atlantic. This was odd since the only known aircraft in the area at the time was carrying a troupe of British and American entertainers to perform in a show for Allied troops at a remote Arctic base. Bond subsequently discovered that a baggage sergeant on the plane was a top Russian agent and that one of his trunks contained a short-wave radio. On further enquiry Bond found that the sergeant was planning to explode a series of atomic bombs on an American base. Following up the sergeant's application for a transfer to the Bahamas, Bond's trail led to a mysterious new Soviet front company, which had ordered a fleet of Bahamian fishing vessels, manned by crews of specially trained frogmen, with trapdoor hulls capable of taking atomic bombs on board.

In an infuriatingly undated response, Ian said Cuneo's outline was "first class". With "just the right degree of fantasy", it covered the ground "splendidly" and the suspense was "admirably maintained". Ian could find just two main criticisms: one, that there was no heroine, and, two, that it might be unwise to target the Russians as villains because – curiously from someone of Ian's knowledge and sophistication – he thought that the Cold War might end during the two years it would take to produce the film.

Instead Ian put forward a suggestion that was to prove crucial not just for the film under discussion, but also for the future of the Bond legend. Drawing on his discussions with McClory, he proposed that Bond should confront not the Russians but SPECTRE, an acronym for the Special Executive for Terrorism, Revolution and Espionage (later, in Fleming's novel and in subsequent film-scripts, the Special Executive for Counterintelligence, Terrorism, Revenge and Extortion, which was rather less convincing). SPECTRE would be politically neutral – a small, powerful organization manned by ex-members of SMERSH, the Gestapo, the Mafia and the Black Tong of Peking. Its goal, Ian suggested, would be to place its bombs on NATO bases and later blackmail the Western powers for £100 million.

Later, in June and July, Ian expanded his observations into a 67-page film treatment which he sent to Bryce and McClory. His most important changes were that SPECTRE metamorphosed into the Mafia as the support group for a new villain, Emilio Largo, and there was a new heroine,

Dominique (Domino) Smith. As usual, Ian introduced a few authentic personal touches, such as the appearance of his friend from *Moonraker*, Superintendent Vallance of Scotland Yard. But as Bond historian John Cork has noted, Fleming appears to have been operating quickly and none too seriously.

Meanwhile, during the early summer, Ian had been working on a different tack. He had returned from Goldeneye to find himself swamped with another clutch of film offers. One was from the producer Maurice Winnick, who was linked to the American studio MGM. Winnick was interested in adapting James Bond for television, so it was easy for Ian to dust down another of the unused scripts from his fruitless venture with Henry Morgenthau III a couple of years earlier. Winnick wanted to ensure that Ian had not signed away the entire movie and television rights to the character James Bond by virtue of his 1954 agreement – still awaiting implementation – with Gregory Ratoff to make a film of *Casino Royale*. The solicitor Michael Rubinstein was contacted to confirm this point. Winnick was also keen to ensure the James Bond books did not flout any security regulations. Ian went to the length of obtaining a personal letter from Frederick Hoyer Millar, Permanent Under-Secretary at the Foreign Office, stating that "there are no security objections to any of the books about James Bond which have been published."

At this stage Ian resolved to seek a specialized agent for his film and television rights. Jo Stewart had moved from Curtis Brown in New York, while Cape in London was not geared to the job. "In desperation", so he informed Bryce, Ian approached Laurence Evans, who ran the London office of the Music Corporation of America (MCA), to take on this aspect of his affairs. On 2 July Ian wrote to Naomi Burton informing her of his decision – "after many wonderings and after the pressures of various rival bids and interests have worn me down" – to have MCA handle his film, television and dramatic rights. He begged her to "at least give me credit" for not handing over his literary output. But Burton was in no mood to be placated. "You really stun me," she replied, adding that Ian should have given Jo Stewart's successor a chance and informing him that her experience told her that it would not be long before MCA was asking for his literary rights as well.

During July, *The Boy and the Bridge* opened in London to mixed notices from the critics. But Ian liked the finished product. After seeing the film, he wrote to McClory that "there is no one who I would prefer to produce James Bond for the screen. I think you will have great fun doing it and great success." A few days after the première, Ian invited McClory to lunch at Boodle's, where, with Bryce present, they discussed the progress on their project: Xanadu was indeed going ahead with a Bond film and Ian had embarked on writing a script.

Bryce later recalled his understanding of his relationship with McClory. First, the Irishman had been his partner in a one-off production, *The Boy and the Bridge*, and, second, they had discussed a quite separate business venture, the Bahamian studio operation, with McClory as a sort of promoter. According to Bryce, the two projects were not related, but McClory has argued that both Bryce and Ian arrived at this interpretation of events at a later date and that, at the time, there was never any doubt that Xanadu Productions, his partnership with Bryce, was proceeding, as agreed, with its next project, a film based on the James Bond character. Reconstructing the early developments of a bitter dispute is often difficult, but evidence suggests that McClory was already rather more involved in the James Bond movie than Bryce or Fleming subsequently cared to let on. An article dated 11 June 1959 on the Inside Show Business page of the *Daily Express* stated explicitly that James Bond was going to be brought to the screen with Kevin McClory as the "flamboyant producer". The story even speculated about which actor would play James Bond. McClory had said he wanted Trevor Howard, but Ian was quoted as disagreeing. He thought that, at forty-three, Howard was too old for the part and that someone in his early thirties was required. Ian suggested Peter Finch and, when reminded that Finch was only one year younger than Howard, he replied, "Well, actually, I would be happier if the part could be given to a young unknown actor, with established stars playing the other roles. Otherwise I am keen on the project. The film will not be an adaptation of one of my books. I am writing an original screenplay for it."

Despite the detached tone of their later affidavits, during the summer Ian and Bryce had discussed the merits of McClory as both potential director (though they were less enthusiastic after the lukewarm public response to *The Boy and the Bridge*) and potential producer (though by early August Ian was suggesting – it would have to be put to McClory "very delicately", he told Bryce – that the experienced Anthony Asquith might be hired as co-producer). Although McClory might have sensed a certain cooling from Ian and Bryce, he himself was now able, with *The Boy and the Bridge* safely concluded, to focus seriously on the proposed new film.

At one stage Ian talked of spending August with Ivar in Venice where they could pool their efforts on the screenplay. Since this was not Ann's idea of a summer vacation, she made alternative plans to visit the Leigh Fermors in Greece. Subsequently Ian relented and agreed to take the month off with his family, albeit at another of his old stamping-grounds, the fashionable French Channel resort of Le Touquet. The Flemings stayed at the Hotel de la Mer and, from the start, Ian was determined to enjoy himself, visiting the casino and playing golf with a new friend, General William Mirrlees, whose son Robin was Rouge Dragon in the College of

Arms. Ann, predictably, was bored to tears, calling it a holiday "of a typically sadistic nature".

Ian felt he owed himself a treat because he had given in to her persistent demands and agreed to buy Warneford Place, a large country house in Sevenhampton, near Swindon, in Wiltshire. From her days at Buscot, Ann knew "Mad Boy" Robert Heber-Percy, an eccentric aesthete who lived at Faringdon House on the edge of the same village. When he heard that Lord Banbury, scion of a railway-owning family, was selling Warneford Place, he wanted a sympathetic soul to live there. Knowing that Ann was looking for a house in the vicinity, he suggested that she should make an offer. Warneford Place was certainly impressive, dating from the sixteenth century, with a vast ballroom and forty bedrooms, all set in a small park complete with a large ornamental lake. Before Lord Banbury, it had been owned by the Warneford family, who had been rich wool merchants in the Middle Ages. But the structure had dry-rot and needed almost complete gutting and rebuilding, while the grounds were overgrown and the lake required dredging. The Flemings were to spend four years dealing with builders and architects before they moved in. In the meantime, considering the existing name unnecessarily gloomy, Ann changed it to Sevenhampton Place, though Ian had no such easy solution to what he saw as the main disadvantage: there was no decent golf course for miles.

At Le Touquet he was surrounded by them. Between regular rounds of golf with the General, protracted meals at which Caspar showed an unexpected taste for French cuisine, Ann's periodic fits of bad temper and the inevitable weekend visit from Peter Quennell, Ian tinkered with his screenplay. At some stage McClory arrived for a meeting to discuss his involvement in the film. Fresh from a re-reading of the Bond books, McClory was armed with a set of proposals about the storyline. He thought the idea in Ian's treatment that the atomic bombs were taken from an American base by Largo and his men posing as US officers was "Boy's Own stuff". Instead he suggested that the bomb should be hijacked from an airplane. Thus he later claimed he introduced the idea for one of the first ever cinematic hijacks. "I said I would be able to obtain a Vulcan bomber through Tommy Sopwith's [the yachtsman's] father who worked at Hawker Siddeley. Fleming wouldn't have it. He said it just was not feasible. I said it was much easier than what he had come up with. The bomber could fly in under the radar."

Over three decades later, McClory also recalled that he suggested an international terrorist group as Bond's opponents. The Bond stories were too obsessed with Reds under the bed, he felt, and would work much better if the villains were not agents of any government, but of some more sinister terrorist organization. Ian had apparently anticipated McClory here. His SPECTRE dated from two months earlier, and he had the Mafia as the villains in his more recent screenplay. This became an important issue in the later legal dispute. But McClory remained adamant that SPECTRE was "a cumulative idea", the product of their joint endeavours.

Ian's main priority on returning from holiday was not films but cars. After four years he was tired of his Thunderbird. (Ann probably had some influence on his thinking, following another summer of blustery drives on the Continent.) He wrote once again to Antony Terry in Bonn, saying he was thinking of purchasing a Mercedes 200 SE and asking if his friend could make enquiries with the German manufacturer. Ian wanted a convertible or sports version, rather than a saloon, but was not sure if such a model was made.

When Terry replied almost immediately with the relevant catalogue, Ian travelled to Germany to see him. The visit was also a dry run for a round-the-world journey that had been proposed by Denis Hamilton as a suitable project for Ian's talents. Ian would visit a number of Thrilling Cities (as his articles were later called) to report on their attractions to a man of Fleming's (or James Bond's) exotic tastes and sophistication. Eager to enter the spirit of things, Terry treated Ian to a trip across the border into East Berlin and also took him to the northern city of Hamburg where Ian looked round the docks he had previously only known through wartime aerial photographs. Ian later admitted to William Stephenson that he was happy to hear a guide saying ruefully that the city had raised 3000 wrecks after the war.

Ian sent Stephenson a copy of his article which appeared in the *Spectator* the day after the October general election. Apologizing for his "lack of gravitas", he invited the wartime spy chief to "look at my one excursion into the politics you once tried to get me to take up". In the piece, entitled "If I Were Prime Minister," Ian reversed the line he had taken on American traffic signs six years earlier. This time he adopted a more anarchic approach to government and bureaucracy. His (duly acknowledged) hero was Hugo Pitman's friend, Sir Alan (A. P.) Herbert, who, as Britain's last independent MP, successfully swam against the tide of modern party politics. Ian referred directly back to his previous article when he said his first action as Prime Minister would be to remove the word 'CURVE' from Britain's perfectly self-explanatory road signs. "By this and other small tokens, I would proclaim that the English people are no longer babies and that, after forty years of universal education, I propose to deal with the citizens as if they were in fact universally educated. All my legislation would start with this assumption."

True to form, he wanted to reduce taxes which he argued would cut the widespread practice of fiddling the Inland Revenue. He also proposed that people running company cars should have the name of their business emblazoned on the side of their car. At least shareholders would then know they were paying when Rolls-Royces disgorged mink-clad women outside the theatre. For the working man, he proposed what he called a "scheme of benevolent Stakhanovism" – a minimum wage, supplemented by mounting merit bonuses for any real work that was done.

Ian had a number of practical ideas, such as the introduction of electric cars to counter the harmful effects of the internal combustion engine. (As well as being a Friedmanite, Ian was an ecologist *manqué*.) However, he showed his political naïveté and undermined his anti-bureaucratic case by advocating that the state should provide massive garages on the edges of towns where people could charge up or leave their electric cars. With some personal interest, he also suggested a new government publication called 'Hazard', which would provide up-to-date statistics on the risks inherent in various antisocial activities such as drinking and smoking. Today he would be said to be providing the raw data to allow people to make up their own minds about the dangers associated with their lifestyles. The most radical part of Ian's thesis was his sexual libertarianism. In a passionate assault on puritanism (again in advance of the *Zeitgeist*), he suggested that the Isle of Wight should be turned into a vast pleasure ground, the domestic equivalent of pre-war Paris or Macao, where the casinos and *maisons de tolerance* would be so good that "frustrated citizens of every class could give full rein to those basic instincts for sex and gambling which have been crushed through the ages".

For all Ian's rallying cry for Britons to throw off their sexual chains, he was acting in more traditional, paternalistic mode when, on 1 October, he wrote to his nephews, David, Christopher and Valentine Fleming, sending them each £100 for their twenty-first birthdays. No matter that he had already missed Christopher's and Valentine's anniversaries. He told the boys, "Until now I had not got enough money to give people presents that were really presents, but now I send each of you £100 on one condition – that at least £75 must be spent within a month on one single object, or two or three objects, which you would really like to have." He said that he made this stipulation so that they would not want to fritter away their windfalls on "wine, women or, perhaps, to a lesser extent, song".

Christopher received his cheque while travelling through the Panama Canal on his way back from Australia. With Ian himself about to embark on a similar circumnavigation of the world on behalf of the *Sunday Times*, he had to leave all arrangements for the film in the hands of McClory, who was frankly relieved to see him depart. He found Ian "cynical, a bit of a snob" and, although good company, not easy to work with. With Jack Whittingham, who had been hired as a professional scriptwriter, McClory had now produced further reactions to Ian's draft treatment. Some of their ideas were purely technical. For example, they thought Ian had told too much of the story in dialogue. They also suggested a crucial hook in the plot where, by finding a ring on the bottom of the seabed, Bond was able to show Largo's moll, Sophia (Whittingham did not like the name Domino), that her boss had killed her brother, Jo Petachi, who ostensibly – another Whittingham touch – had stolen the bomb at the centre of the story. Around this time, when various actors' names were mentioned, Whittingham wanted to have Burl Ives, who had recently starred in the successful version *Cat on a Hot Tin Roof*, as the villainous Largo.

Ian was relieved to escape London's early November gloom. With his marriage fraught and his own long-term role at the *Sunday Times* uncertain, he had heard, just before he left, that Naomi Burton, his efficient agent, was leaving Curtis Brown to become a publisher's editor. On the positive side, Ian still had his boyish enthusiasm for travel, and, as Leonard Russell, the paper's features editor, told him (as if he did not realize it already), his journey might provide him with useful background material for his books. So having obtained the necessary visas and inoculations, Ian drew £500 in traveller's cheques as expenses, grabbed his typewriter and made his way thankfully to London airport for BOAC's flight to Hong Kong. For on-board reading he had a proof copy of Eric Ambler's latest novel, *Passage of Arms*, given to him by Ambler's (and Maugham's) opportunistic publisher Alexander Frere of William Heinemann.

Hong Kong was Ian's idea of paradise – a quasi-feudal society, with all mod cons, or as he put it, "modern comfort in a theatrically Oriental setting". It was improved initially by the fact that he was staying in "a sort of luxurious Goldeneye", the house of Hugh and Diana Barton, friends of his brother, Peter. Barton was one of last Taipans of the Orient, perhaps the most powerful wheeler and dealer in the colony as chairman of the great Far Eastern trading house, Jardine Matheson. Ian was particularly impressed that among the seven Chinese servants at his beck and call was a comely masseuse who was able to work on his stiff neck when he complained of the after-effects of his long flight. Then he dressed for breakfast of scrambled eggs and bacon on the veranda overlooking Big Wave Bay.

Hong Kong was all the better because his friend Richard Hughes was there to introduce him to the attractions of the East, and all on company expenses. For his first evening in the colony, they toured the town's bars and experienced some of its night-life. Ian was interested in visiting the most famous whorehouse in town, the Luk Kwok Hotel, which featured in the successful book and film, *The World of Suzie Wong*. From the start Ian was enchanted by the "deft and coltish prettiness" of Oriental girls. But when Hughes suggested a better place on the waterfront, Ian pleaded jet-lag and returned up the hill to the Bartons.

He was in a more adventurous mood the following day when he and Hughes boarded the SS *Takshing* for the three-hour voyage meandering through China's offshore islands to Macao, a seedier Portuguese version of Hong Kong. Ian was interested in visiting the enigmatic Dr P. J. Lobo, whose control of the colony's gold trade made him as near to a real-life Goldfinger as anyone. But first Hughes wanted to take him to the Street of Happiness, with its nine-storey Central Hotel, the "largest house of gambling and self-indulgence in the world". The establishment was designed on a hierarchic principle: the higher the floor, the better the standard of girls, gambling and music. The intrepid *Sunday Times* reporters made straight for the sixth floor where Ian's attentions were initially transfixed by the Chinese gambling pursuit of fan-tan, hitherto only known to him – from his youthful perusal of Doctor Fu Manchu novels – as the "most sinful game on the face of the earth". From there the couple moved to the dance floor where Ian struck up an instant friendship with an ivory-skinned beauty called Garbo – "same like film star". In his account for the newspaper Ian recalled his time with Garbo as an innocent evening of banter and much laughter. Subsequent recriminations from Ann suggested that Ian took the young Chinese girl to bed and, although the effects of drink prevented any consummation of the evening, he thoroughly enjoyed himself. Readers of the *Sunday Times* received the message in code. Oriental ladies have an "almost inexhaustible desire to please": how very different from the West where women, particularly in America (he noted deftly to allay any further criticism from Ann), took "a ferocious delight in cutting the man down to size".

After returning to Hong Kong, the two men flew to Tokyo where they were joined by Hughes's great friend, Torao Saito, known as "Tiger", a journalist with the leading Japanese newspaper group, Asahi Shimbun. Because of overbooking in the international hotels, Ian stayed in a small Japanese inn where, after initial reservations, he came to enjoy his tiny room with no bathroom and a feather mattress on a rush-matted floor. Tiger introduced him to more of the city's sensual pleasures, including a massage by a Japanese girl called Baby who wore nothing but tight white shorts and a white bra, and a visit to the geisha house, which confirmed Ian's favourable ideas about the women of the East.

With only three days in town, Ian had stipulated "there would be no politicians, museums, temples, Imperial palaces or Noh plays, let alone tea ceremonies". He had drawn up a list of things he did want to experience, including visits to a judo academy and to a Japanese soothsayer. For an exhibition of ju-jitsu, the art of self-defence based on the philosophy of judo, he went to the Kodo Kan, a well-known local gymnasium, with his friend Somerset Maugham, who happened to be in Tokyo at the same time. Claiming to have retained a "vague" interest in judo since watching two large sergeant-majors throwing each other about the floor at Eton, Ian was struck not so much by the mock fight between girls which was obligingly staged for him as by the sight of an elderly champion patiently teaching a ten-year-old boy. At first the red belt swept the youngster's legs away every time. But slowly the boy mastered the exercise, and the old man would get to his knees, bow to his vanquisher and start again. Ian was enthralled by the theatricality, ritual and economy of it all.

The fortune-teller impressed him by saying that Ian was a man of very independent spirit who should always walk alone and never go into partnership. But the general standard of his pronouncements varied: Ian took heart from being informed that he was on the verge of a golden period, though he was not quite sure what to make of the observation that he looked more like his mother than his father or that he should stop being so "obstinate" towards his wife. The soothsayer had no special advice when Ian found he was booked to make the long journey across the Pacific to Los Angeles on Friday the thirteenth. It became a double Friday the thirteenth because en route he crossed the International Date Line. But Ian did not mind: as Bond stated in *From Russia, With Love*, "It's always best to travel on the thirteenth. There are practically no passengers and it's more comfortable and you get a better service."

In Los Angeles and, later, Las Vegas he retraced some of the steps he had taken with Ernie Cuneo five years earlier. He even returned to visit Captain James Hamilton, head of intelligence at the Los Angeles Police Department, who informed him that, in the intervening period, the Mafia had become the city's main crime problem. Since at that stage the Mafia were the villains in Ian's proposed film, this was useful information. As usual Ian paid his respects to movie moguls who still prevaricated about filming his James Bond books. The most promising recent approach had been from Twentieth Century-Fox, where Walter Wanger suggested developing a female James Bond as a vehicle for Susan Hayward. Wanger was looking for a story-line about "an intelligent, courageous, well-dressed modern woman as a centre of the Fleming–Hitchcock kind of situation". But Ian was not inspired and the idea soon fell by the wayside.

By the time he reached New York he was fed up with travelling. Although he had enjoyed the Orient, he had been depressed by the lack of British influence there. He complained that, with the exception of the British consul in Hawaii, he had not met one single Briton between Hong Kong and New York. This angered and troubled him, and his acceptance in his early books of Britain's reduced role in the world gave way to more petulant observations about the consequences of "twilight of empire". His sour mood transferred to the city and indeed to the country he had once loved. He felt the American dream was turning bad. The United States was engaged in a mass flight from reality which he blamed – in equal proportions – on television, tranquillizers and the psychoanalyst's couch. His jaundiced view of the world was also influenced by a series of business meetings in New York. His arrival in the city happened to coincide with Naomi Burton's departure from Curtis Brown. Ian had enjoyed a warm relationship with her and, although he was hardly her easiest client, she had responded whole-heartedly. As she had already indicated, she feared Ian would soon be enticed to take on MCA as his literary as well as his film and TV agency. So, to pre-empt his move, she had decided to jump ship herself and move to Doubleday. Perry Knowlton from Scribner's was hired to fill her chair at Curtis Brown. But this only encouraged Ian to do just what Burton had predicted and engage MCA – in the form of the lively Phyllis Jackson – as his literary agents in the United States. To maintain the sense of momentum, he also decided shortly afterwards to change his American publishers. He had long felt that Macmillan did not pay him enough. Other publishers had approached him with inviting offers to move, including Viking, with which he signed a three-book deal in December. He told Al Hart, his editor at Macmillan, that he had made his move after consultation with Graham Greene and Peter Quennell who were both published by Viking. He felt "slightly lost in the huge firm of Macmillan", adding, unconvincingly, that he wanted to try his hand "at a smaller house to whom I would perhaps be more important".

In New York Ian had arranged to meet Bryce to discuss the progress of the film. Kevin McClory was also in town, trying unsuccessfully to sell *The Boy and the Bridge* to the American market. At a meeting in his hotel, Ian learned that Whittingham had now completed a full outline treatment for Xanadu's proposed Bond film and that McClory was predictably bullish about the result: indeed he was talking about a $3-million production. Bryce seemed to share this enthusiasm for, at his behest, Xanadu Productions opened a separate James Bond account at Chase Manhattan Bank in New York, a decision which seemed to indicate that the old partnership was still operating as before.

But even while he made these moves, Bryce began to show signs of wanting to pull out of his agreement with McClory. He later claimed that he feared, on the evidence of *The Boy and the Bridge*, that he was likely to lose money on the film project. Again, according to McClory, this was a retrospective view of events. He has argued that Bryce and Ian by now recognized the potential of his (and Whittingham's) cinematic treatment and began to try to push them out of a deal. The difference in cultures which had long threatened suddenly became abundantly clear. On the one hand were Bryce and Ian, two Old Etonians used to fixing matters on the old boy network; on the other, McClory and Whittingham, experienced film professionals who were determined that their work should not go to waste.

For the time being, McClory managed to convince Bryce that, if money was a problem, one sure way of consolidating his investment was to persevere with the Nassau film studio as a platform for the Bond movie. He and Cuneo flew to Nassau in November to examine possible sites and to discuss setting up a proper Bahamian company. They even had a meeting with the Governor. But by now the other potential investors were also cooling towards the idea. When Cuneo returned to New York, he was much more adamant in his advice to Bryce not to proceed. On 18 December Bryce drafted a letter to McClory informing him that the studio project was not going ahead and terminating his employment on anything to do with *The Boy and the Bridge*. (He gave him two months to close the production's London office.)

But that still left the proposed Bond film-script in a state of gestation. Bryce never denied that he would be happy to see it developed and produced, though now it would be a matter of hawking it round the big studios. Thus the vexed issue of the intellectual property in the treatments, outlines and later script remained unresolved. McClory made it clear that, both as author and as partner in Xanadu Productions, he believed he owned a share of these assets and was unwilling to let it go. Bryce, however, was claiming that he had paid for the work and the finished product was his. In his avuncular way, Cuneo tried to point the way forward by penning a formal assignment of his own rights in the original story idea to Bryce for $1. But McClory was not willing to be badgered into following suit. He still believed the film could be successful and was determined to use the two months' grace Bryce had given him to produce (with Whittingham) a final, convincing screenplay.

When Ian returned to London, he had only a few weeks left at the *Sunday Times*. His priority was to find himself a new office and a new secretary. His friend Rennie Hoare helped out with the first requirement. His family bank, Hoare's, owned a block of offices, Mitre Court, at the back of its main building on Fleet Street. One of the bank's tenants, Dr Hugh Richards, a general practitioner, had a couple of rooms he was willing to rent on the fourth floor. As for a secretary, Ian was put in touch with Beryl Griffie-Williams, an intelligent, sharp-tongued woman who became a pillar of the last few years of his life. 'Griffie', as she was known, came with a pedigree as a writer's personal secretary. She had recently left the employment of Nancy Spain after objecting to having to double as her housekeeper. Prior to that Griffie had had similar jobs as confidential secretary to Edward Hulton, the publisher, Rebecca West, and West's close friend, Walter Thornton-Smith, who owned Fortnum & Mason. For all her Celtic-sounding surname, Griffie had been born Kruger, changing in 1912 when German names were out of fashion.

Towards the end of December 1959 Ian was presented with a silver tea caddy by his colleagues at the *Sunday Times* and departed to make his way for the first time in his life as an independent self-employed man. It is hard to overestimate the importance of this move. Throughout his career, Ian had always enjoyed the security of an office environment. During the war he needed the discipline of Room 39 to flourish as a staff intelligence officer. If he had been an agent working on his own behind enemy lines, his sense of fantasy might have got the better of him, as it threatened to do in the Estoril Casino in May 1941. After returning to civilian life, he chose not to remove himself from the hurly-burly and write books on his own. Instead he took a job in a busy newspaper office. This was another of the Fleming paradoxes: for a man who increasingly flinched from meeting people, he was always too much of a social animal to abandon himself to the solitary life.

In Griffie Ian found exactly the support he needed. She was an adoring, shrewish spinster who quickly sided with her employer against Ann (agreeing with Lisl Popper that Ian needed a more domesticated wife) and who helped him by juggling his social engagements (particularly his girlfriends), guarding him against unpleasant shocks and keeping up the voluminous correspondence which was his buffer against a hostile outside world.

For Christmas Ian had an idea of going to Monte Carlo, where he could play golf in a tolerably warm climate. Instead he was bound, like the previous year, for Shane's Castle, where at least he claimed to be looking forward to a traditional Christmas, "going to church in a long crocodile with the rest of the family". Just in case this was not to his taste, he armed himself with three good thrillers, including the latest Rex Stout. And he found an unimaginative if individual solution to the Christmas present problem: at Fribourg & Treyer he bought everyone the same gift – a dozen snuff handkerchiefs.

Ian saw in the new decade with a typical marital mix-up. On New Year's Day he had an appointment with the poet George MacBeth, who was also a producer at the BBC Third Programme, to record a six-and-a-half minute review of the new Carol Reed film, *Our Man in Havana*, based on Graham Greene's novel. The previous evening he booked two tickets to see the film, one for himself, and one for his wife who he thought might enjoy seeing Noël Coward playing Hawthorne. Somehow, however, Ian had neglected to inform Ann of this, and she had invited Frederick Ashton, William Plomer, Diana Cooper and Cecil Beaton to Victoria Square for a small party to welcome in the 1960s. Thus Ian had to arrange for his wife's guests also to be accommodated at the cinema. But he drew the line at 'Baby' as Diana Cooper was often known, and refused to let her accompany them. She held the same place in his demonology as "Burglar" Bryce in Ann's. He resented having to join in paying court to someone he found

simply "ghastly". And his feelings towards her were not improved because
he saw her as Ann's accomplice in her affair with Hugh Gaitskell. Ann had
to humour Ian and eventually, by subterfuge (Diana was forced to buy
herself a cheaper ticket), they all saw the film which, according to general
consensus, was not very good.

When Ian went into the studio the following day, the film was barely
discussed. He earned his ten guineas' fee by using his review as a platform
from which to deliberate on weightier matters; in this case, the business
of espionage. His line was that the old-fashioned idea of spying, where
the code-book was always purloined by the Embassy valet, was dead.
Today, "and for as long as war is a threat, the spy is a ticking seismograph
on top of the Jungfrau measuring distant atomic explosions on the other
side of the world, or instruments carried in aircraft that measure the
uranium or plutonium contents of the atmosphere". Generally speaking,
today's secret services did not need to know about the numbers of tanks
or the design of bombs. "The big people have the big weapons and the
small people have them not. Details of the weapons are unimportant.
They are known." Therefore, any book or play about the Secret Service
had to be either incredible or farcical, he concluded. He admitted he
himself tended towards the former. "Personally I am sufficiently in love
with the myth to write basically incredible stories with a straight face."
Graham Greene, however, had adopted the latter "more truthful approach
and a more modern one. He takes the splendid myth of centuries and
kicks it hilariously downstairs." Ian felt Greene's SIS agent Wormold, who
managed to satisfy his bosses in London by concocting an imaginary spy-
ring, was "almost too close to those who served in wartime intelligence
to be funny".

The BBC liked what it heard, for two days later Anthony Derville, a
producer at *Woman's Hour*, wrote to ask if Ian would appear as the programme's guest of the week. This was the opportunity for Griffie to wheel
into action for the first time. Mr Fleming was away and not likely to be
back "for several months".

Shortly afterwards the Flemings departed for Jamaica *en famille*. Ian had
prevailed on Ann to travel by plane. She furtively stuffed herself with
tranquillizers while a prim governess called Mona Potterton read to Caspar.
Although the monosyllabic Mona was considerably in awe of Ian, she got
on his nerves. When she spent too long in the bathroom at Goldeneye,
he banged on the door, shouting, "Lights out Miss Potterton," whereupon
the switch was promptly turned off and she crept back to her room in the
dark.

But she was good at her job, keeping young Caspar amused while his
parents attended to more important things. While the Flemings had been
away, Blanche Blackwell, in a spirit of continuing good neighbourliness,

had planted a number of flowers and bushes. Ann's first reaction was to uproot these "ugly shrubs" and throw them into the sea. So hostile was her mood that Ian implored the writer Morris Cargill, Ann's best friend on the island, to tell her that he, not Blanche, had been responsible. This farce would continue year after year: Blanche sowing one season, Ann destroying the next.

Cargill had an important role to play a bit later when Ann's admirer, Hugh Gaitskell, came to the island, ostensibly on a fact-finding tour of the West Indies. By this time the London newspapers had picked up the gossip, widely known in Westminster circles, about Gaitskell's *tendresse* for Ann. The local *Daily Express* stringer seemed particularly determined to make something of it. Cargill was deputy leader of the local Labour Party, a deceptive title because in Jamaican politics his was the right-wing party. Nevertheless, using this superficial similarity as cover to fool enquirers, Ann prevailed on Cargill to act as Gaitskell's occasional chaperone, while for a week she and the Leader of the Opposition played what Ian indulgently called "Charley's Aunt" with the foreign press. On his last day in Jamaica, Ann arranged to take Gaitskell for a picnic in the hills. That morning, however, the *Daily Express* reporter had rung him at his hotel and requested a meeting. Ann was incensed and determined to do something about it. Before departing on their picnic, she promised to cable Max Beaverbrook and ask him to call his hound off. Gaitskell parked his yellow Ford in a side-street in Oracabessa and waited while Ann strode to the post office where she spent four pounds, ten shillings and sixpence on a telegram which read, "EXPRESS PURSING [SIC] HUGH PLEASE DARLING MAX PREVENT GOLDENEYE PUBLICITY URGENT PASSIONATE LOVE AND GRATITUDE ANNIE."

With Ann temporarily absent, the persistent journalist spied Gaitskell sitting in his car. The Leader of the Opposition panicked. Rather than wait for Ann, he put the car in gear and drove off at high speed in the direction of Port Maria where he telephoned Cargill from Johnson's Hardware Store and asked to be collected. When Cargill arrived, Gaitskell, who had been hiding behind a keg of nails, explained the situation as best he could, emphasizing that Ann had left some personal belongings on his front seat and he needed to return them. Cargill offered to secrete him in the back of his station-wagon. Then they would drive over to Goldeneye and put everything right.

Meanwhile Ann had walked the mile or so back to her house. She arrived hot and angry to find Ian lunching with the Pitmans. As she had already absented herself, she had to mouth an implausible excuse about getting the date of her own luncheon appointment wrong. Ian looked on, highly amused. She was just sitting down to her curried goat when Cargill appeared. He asked if he could "borrow Annie" for a moment. Outside, in

the shadow of the veranda, he explained that he had driven Gaitskell to
Goldeneye. They had reached a mile from the house, when the Leader of
the Opposition again became terrified. Ignoring all Cargill's pleas to lie
down, he had demanded to get out. Cargill left him scampering into the
bush, trying to making himself scarce.

Ann found "Heavenly", otherwise known as "Buggins" in her communications with Diana Cooper, cowering "behind a cactus looking like
the spy in L'Attaque". Gaitskell was not amused by Ann's teasing that Ian
intended to challenge him to a duel for leaving her "to be raped by
negroes". He was impervious to any suggestion that he had behaved oddly.
He was certain that Cargill, although the soul of discretion, would spill
the beans. Ann herself later told Clarissa Eden about the incident, adding
the crucial political intelligence that, aside from this charade, the Leader
of the Opposition was "having a horrible time with his beastly party".

When Cargill returned to Goldeneye (Gaitskell had gone with Ann to
his hotel), Ian wanted to know what had happened. Banking on the
probability that Cargill was unaware he had left the *Sunday Times*, Ian
then ordered the Jamaican, who was nominally the newspaper's local
correspondent, to cable the story to London. He even offered the substantial fee of five hundred guineas. Cargill refused on the grounds that it
would make Gaitskell look a fool. And what was wrong with that? asked
Ian, with what must now have been a broad grin. After Cargill had refused
all financial blandishments, Ian invited him in for a brandy.

To boost Ann's spirits after Gaitskell's departure, Peter Quennell came
to stay, hoping for a romantic assignation of his own (which did not
materialize). But by this time Ian had had enough, and took to the hills
in the only available car. Ann was left to survey the emotional debris.
"The gold's out of Goldeneye," she sorrowfully informed Diana Cooper,
adding, "I wish I did not remain in love with [Ian] – isn't it odd?"

As for his own writing schedule, Ian was bereft of ideas. Once again he
considered killing Bond off, but decided to postpone this for one more
year. Writing to William Plomer, he complained he was "terribly stuck
with James Bond. What was easy at 40 is very difficult at 50. I used to
believe – sufficiently – in Bonds & Blonds & Bombs. Now the keys creak
as I type & I fear the zest may have gone. Part of the trouble is having a
wife and child. They knock the ruthlessness out of one. I shall definitely
kill off Bond with my next book – better a poor bang than a rich whimper!"

So, for Bond's last outing, he decided to follow his precedent of the
previous year and turn a recent film outline into a story. This time he took
the idea that he and the others had developed for Xanadu. McClory later
accused him of plagiarism but, as with most things, Ian approached it all

pragmatically. If the film was indeed going ahead, he believed it had already been agreed that an essential part of the "package" was a tie-in book. But if, as seemed possible from the information filtering from Nassau and New York, the film had been aborted, why let a good idea go to waste? What was to prevent him building on its core theme, a theme which he himself had helped create and which was so obviously based on his own fictional hero James Bond?

The news from outside was certainly frenetic. In Nassau Bryce was worried that McClory was about to descend on the Bahamas and involve him in business affairs in the middle of the social season. In New York Cuneo was trying to call down the letter of the law on McClory's head by ordering an audit of his accounts for *The Boy and the Bridge*. A consensus appeared to have emerged that Bryce would take Whittingham's script, which he now insisted to be his property, and would present it to one of the big film producers, with a recommendation that McClory should have a role in its making. Otherwise his dealings with his partner were finished.

But McClory was determined not to be fobbed off. If he and Whittingham could complete the script by the 15 February deadline, he knew he would be in a better position to bargain with Bryce. On 19 January 1960 Whittingham wrote to tell Ivar of the progress he and McClory were making in London. But, he complained, "We are both working in the dark so far as Ian Fleming is concerned – and Bond is very much his personal creation." Thus they needed to get together with Ian to discuss their first draft. "I know that he will be very helpful at this much more detailed stage, and it would encourage us enormously if we felt we were all still pulling at the same rope." Two days later McClory wrote to Ian himself along much the same lines. He and Whittingham were still working hard on the script and expected to be finished by 15 February. Then they would duplicate what they had written and bring it to Bryce in Nassau where McClory hoped Ian would be able to "tear yourself away from your novel round about that time in order to examine the script closely and give us your views on it before Jack writes the final script". Ian later used this letter as evidence that McClory was aware that he had embarked on the book of the film, but McClory denied this.

Ian never hid the fact that he adopted several of Whittingham and McClory's ideas for his book, notably the airborne hijack of the bomb, but he claimed that he added many more of his own. For example, he reintroduced SPECTRE (and not the Mafia) as the main villain, operating in the Bahamas through Emilio Largo, but with a new overall chief called Ernst Blofeld, a surname Ian appropriated from a fellow member of Boodle's, a Norfolk farmer called Tom Blofeld who was chairman of the Country Gentlemen's Association. Ian also devised an ingenious new introductory sequence – at an up-market health farm based on Enton Hall, which he and Ann frequented in real life. When he could not think what to call his fictional establishment, his guest Peter Quennell suggested Shrublands, which was the name of his parents' suburban house. Ian added his usual personal name-checks. The Commissioner of Police in the Bahamas was Harling, the Chief of Immigration Pitman, and the Deputy Governor Roddick (after another of his St George's golfing partners, Bunny Roddick). As a further joke Ian had the Immigration Chief tell Bond that the Nassau hotel, the Emerald Wave, had been full of Moral Rearmament people. Emerald Wave was Mrs Val's house on Cable Beach. In addition, Largo had rented his luxury beachside villa, Palmyra, from an Englishman called Bryce. Its similarity in name and location to the "pleasure palace" Xanadu was unmistakable.

McClory later argued, however, that these details, particularly the health farm sequence, were deliberately introduced by Ian to obfuscate the joint origins of the novel. In an affidavit drawn up by Farrer and Company, the Queen's solicitors, Ian later felt the need to list his personal input into the book, starting with the very first sentence: "It was one of those days when it seemed to James Bond that all life, as someone put it, was nothing but a heap of six to four against." While this may have expressed Ian's personal feelings at the time, it also happened to be an idea which had been put into his head by John Beck, a former captain of the British Walker Cup team, during a recent golf game. Ian's nineteen-point list ran from information about danger levels on a medical traction table, which had been imparted to him by a Mrs Reynolds, physiotherapist at London's Princess Beatrice Hospital, to details of the hydrofoil craft, the *Disco Volante*, which – true to previous meticulous fact-finding form – were obtained from its Italian manufacturer, Messrs. Leopoldo Rodriguez, with the assistance of the *Sunday Times* Rome correspondent, Henry Thody. Although this list was hardly convincing, Ian also claimed that he coined the title Thunderball, which had stuck in his mind ever since he had heard it used to describe an American atomic test in the Pacific. (Prior to that, the draft version of the film-script had had the uninspiring appellation "Longitude 78 West".)

When McClory received no reply to his letter to Ian of 21 January, he determined to visit him in Jamaica – en route to the Bahamas to see Ivar. Ian received a cable on 1 March telling him that Kevin was arriving in Montego Bay that night. The two men had a stormy meeting at Goldeneye, McClory clutching a copy of Whittingham's completed film-script. Ian later said, though this is difficult to verify, that he had completed his book before he even saw this document. Whittingham, for his part, claimed to have discovered eighteen instances where Ian had drawn on this script to "build up the plot". According to Ian, McClory was now fighting for his future as producer of the film. Ian tried to appease him with the emerging "party line" – that he and Ivar would take the script to Jules Stein, the boss of MCA, with a recommendation that the Irishman should be the producer. (Ian's new agent, MCA, was also, through Universal Studios, one of the leading film producers in the United States. In 1963, however, it was forced by anti-trust legislation to split its business and divest itself of its agenting side.) More convinced than ever that he was being sidelined, McClory moved on to Nassau, where he negotiated with Bryce for a further six months to raise the money for what he was convinced was an excellent script.

On his way back to London from Jamaica, Ian had two important meetings on the east coast of America. One, completely unexpected, had the effect of boosting his career and morale at a difficult period of his life. The second was in the agenda and took him back to the stark reality of his faltering film deal.

For a short break, over the weekend of 12 and 13 March, Ian flew down to Washington to take up a long-standing invitation from the local *Sunday Times* correspondent Henry Brandon. There seemed to be only one topic of conversation on people's lips: the forthcoming presidential election and, in particular, the dynamic young Massachusetts Senator, John Kennedy, who was seeking the Democratic nomination. Since the Brandons lived in Georgetown, Ian was able to walk round the corner on Sunday morning and visit 'Oatsie' Leiter for lunch. Oatsie was also an old friend of the Kennedys from her youth in South Carolina. She had introduced John to his first Bond book, *Casino Royale*, when he had been ill in bed in Newport, Rhode Island, five years earlier. Coincidentally she was going to dinner with the Kennedys that very evening. But when she called to ask if she could bring Ian as well, there was no reply. Luckily, driving Ian back along Georgetown's P Street, she saw the Kennedys out walking. The future President was thrilled to meet the mysterious Englishman in Oatsie's white Chrysler and invited him to join them as an extra dinner guest.

Over the meal at the Kennedys' N Street house, Ian kept up an amusing, inconsequential chatter until it was time for coffee and the conversation turned to the Cuban President Fidel Castro whose Marxist revolution had triumphed only the previous year. The question everyone was asking was how to deal with this communist dictator on America's doorstep. Only the previous month Castro had signed an exclusive deal to sell Cuba's sugar crop to the Soviet Union. Ian mentioned that he had just completed a book which dealt tangentially with this very subject. For an important part of the *Thunderball* plot was Blofeld's threat to bomb Miami with his stolen atomic bombs. Feeling an obligation to make some contribution to the proceedings, Ian suggested that the best way to deal with Castro was not to take him too seriously, but rather to make a fool of him. Drawing on one of his own wartime exploits, and with his tongue firmly in his cheek, he came up with the preposterous idea that the Americans should drop leaflets from the air, informing the Cuban people that their beards were a natural receptacle for radioactivity and would lead to their long-term impotence. Ian was unaware that his proposal tallied with similar schemes for the elimination of Castro which were being bandied around within the CIA. Planning for an invasion of Cuba, later known as the Bay of Pigs fiasco, began that very month at the CIA headquarters in Langley. Kennedy was most impressed with Ian and so was another guest, John Bross, a veteran CIA agent, who had served with the OSS in London during the Second World War. Next day Henry Brandon was surprised to receive a call from Allen Dulles, the CIA director, asking to speak to his guest. But Ian had already left the house, en route for the airport and New York, where his second important meeting was scheduled, with Jules Stein, president of MCA.

Having wheeled in his top management to listen to Ian's proposal, Stein did not dismiss the *Thunderball* script out of hand, but thought it was more suitable for the British than the American market. He suggested that Ian should take the matter up with MCA's London office. As a result of "a good deal of rather dispirited, but truthful sounding talk", Ian sub-sequently recommended to Ivar that they should wash their hands of the script. They could sell it to Rank for around £25,000, he estimated. "The important thing I think is that neither you nor I personally should con-tinue to get tangled up as amateurs in this professional problem, which is time-wasting for all of us." But somehow neither Ian nor Ivar was capable of sticking to this sensible-sounding advice.

And so Ian returned to his radically changed working environment in London. He immediately made an appointment to see Laurence Evans and Robert Fenn, who ran MCA's local office. They, not unnaturally, enquired about ownership of the script and wanted to see a copy of Bryce's original contract with McClory. But when Ian asked Bryce for this, he was informed that Ivar had agreed to allow McClory six more months to raise the finance, and a deal with MCA was therefore not possible during that period. What is more, McClory considered Ian's approach to MCA to be hostile because it prejudiced his own efforts to obtain finance for the script from other sources. He was still determined to make *Thunderball* as a Xanadu production.

Ian's personal humour improved in late March when Noël Coward passed through town and Ann held a "gay lunch" (Coward's words) for him and Loelia Westminster. Ann then departed for Chantilly, to bring Diana Cooper up to date about her eventful holiday in Jamaica – "a lovely respite, despite Ian's brown girl friend". Ian used this period to settle into his new office at Mitre Court and begin his new routine as an entirely freelance writer. One important priority, as he contemplated the years ahead, was to secure the services of Dickie Chopping who, since painting the cover of *From Russia, With Love*, published in 1957, had developed his original *trompe l'oeil* style on two more jackets, *Goldfinger* and *For Your Eyes Only*, the book of short stories which was soon to appear. However, the artist was no longer satisfied with his fee of fifty guineas, and wrote to say so. Ian understood the important contribution Chopping was making to his success, and was happy to acknowledge it. Covers were a crucial element in his overall conception of Bond: he had taken trouble to provide his various draughtsmen with ideas and had always made a point of buying and retaining the copyright of the original artwork. He told Chopping that, until then, Cape had paid its standard fee of 25 guineas, and he had topped up the rest. He had done this willingly "since your work is so marvellous and I am left with a picture that both Annie and I love to have". If Chopping felt this was inadequate recompense for his efforts, Ian was willing to offer 100 guineas, and perhaps even more, "but only on condition that you continue to do my jackets every year". Having admitted his debt to Chopping, Ian was in no position to resist the artist's demand for a more market-based fee of 200 guineas for his next painting, the cover of *Thunderball*. In July Ian gave his instructions, which were faithfully adhered to: the picture should "consist of the skeleton of a man's hand with the fingers resting on the Queen of Hearts. Through the back of the hand a dagger is plunged into the table top."

From his new office Ian informed William Plomer that he had just finished a "giant Bond", but having "got thoroughly bored with it after a bit", he had not been able to re-read the manuscript, and it would need "drastic rewriting". When his doubts about the book refused to go away, Cape's Michael Howard felt obliged to write to him, "I suppose it is because you present such an urbane and sturdy front to the world that one tends to forget the quivering sensibilities of the artist which lie behind it. But they must account for those acute pangs of doubt and dissatisfaction about this new James Bond adventure which you have repeatedly expressed to William and me, for which neither of us can see any real justification. Quite the reverse."

By now Ian's mood of weariness and self-doubt was beginning to affect his writing, and the more perceptive critics picked up the signs his hero gave off about this when *For Your Eyes Only* was published in April. As Maurice Richardson noted in *Queen*, Ian's short stories "give you the feeling that Bond's author may be approaching one of those sign-posts in his career and thinking about taking a straighter path".

Ann's brief holiday in France allowed him to catch up with his golf in Kent. After visiting Deal in mid-April for the annual public-school golf tournament, the Halford Hewitt, he wrote his first freelance article for the

Sunday Times, a series of short diary-type vignettes. In the course of a homily about shaving, he managed to incur the displeasure of his editor, Harry Hodson, by recommending Gillette's new Extra-Blue blade. Ian was told to moderate the advertising, though Evelyn Waugh rather enjoyed Ian's arcane knowledge: "I am much in Thunderbird's debt for his telling us it is not necessary to dry our razor," he told Ann.

Waugh was replying to Ann's invitation to a party at Victoria Square to celebrate the wedding of Princess Margaret and Antony Armstrong-Jones at the beginning of May. He himself was unable to attend, but around fifty people did – from the Duchess of Devonshire and Nancy Spain to Sir Harold Nicolson and Hugh Gaitskell. Noël Coward, another guest, was prepared, temporarily, to put aside his antipathy towards Ann and admit that it was "wild and beautifully organized . . . a glorious mix-up".

With Ian starting to plan the second, European, stage of his Thrilling Cities tour, Ann remarked that she was not sure how he made a city "thrilling" because he never stopped to look at anything. Although this sort of comment was usually accurate and made her friends laugh, it was hardly designed to cool the searing temperature of her marriage. Ian was encouraged to hear that Roy Thomson, the *Sunday Times*'s new chairman, had liked his earlier efforts and had even suggested a few more cities – Rio de Janeiro, Buenos Aires, Havana, New Orleans and Montreal – to add to his itinerary. But Harry Hodson was less enthusiastic, reporting a mixed response to his earlier batch of articles. "Those who enjoy light entertaining reading for its own sake have been made very happy," he said. But "more serious readers have tut-tutted a bit about missing the really important things about Hong Kong", such as the colony's million refugees.

Among the various changes in Ian's life was his acquisition of a new car. He decided not to proceed with his enquiries about a Mercedes. Because his two-door Thunderbird had served him so well (50,000 miles in four years without so much as a bulb fusing), he decided to buy a four-door version of the same vehicle. It had a seven-litre engine, capable of 120 miles per hour, and all the extras, such as power steering, which he had disdainfully refused on his earlier T-bird.

His new car had only 1000 miles on the clock when he crossed the Channel at the start of another wind-in-the-hair continental adventure. Driving in Europe remained one of his great pleasures. He delighted in the ritual and sense of achievement of a successful day's motoring – from the eight o'clock start "with some distant luncheon stop as target" to the arrival at some chosen hotel, the walk round the town and the heady smells and sights of "abroad". His journey to Hamburg, his first major destination, took him through Ostend, Antwerp, Haarlem, Wilhelmshaven and Bremen. Nearing the North Sea port of Wilhelmshaven, he was once again reminded of the early days of the

Second World War when, as a recent recruit to NID, he had pored over photographs of the harbour and charts of offshore islands. These unwelcome memories disappeared when he reached Hamburg, where he enthused about the uninhibited sex industry – "how very different from the prudish and hypocritical manner in which we so disgracefully mismanage these things in England!"

Leaving his new vehicle temporarily in Hamburg, he boarded a British European Airways flight to Berlin where Antony and Rachel Terry were waiting to meet him. Terry gave Ian another of his favourite spook's tours of the city – a sortie into communist-held East Berlin, a visit to a cross-border German spy apparently working for the British, a discussion about one of the West's great intelligence failures: the fruitless attempt to listen into Soviet telecommunications traffic by boring a tunnel bristling with communication devices into the Russian sector. Ian does not seem to have known that the initiative had been doomed all along because George Blake, ostensibly a British SIS agent, was secretly working for the KGB. But this did not become general knowledge until Blake's arrest the following year.

Finding Berlin lugubrious, Ian's stay was enlivened by his interest in Rachel Terry, who was estranged from her husband. As a novelist herself, she had carefully studied her husband's boss over the dozen years that she had known him. Like many people, she found him "highly intelligent and accomplished, but his emotional age was pre-puberty". As they drove round Berlin, she noticed that Ian displayed no particular curiosity for history. Ever pragmatic, he wanted facts; he "was only interested in what he could use". To Ian, Antony's world of spying was little more than a fantasy. He preferred the tangible reality of "success, of managing and manipulating the world".

One evening Ian and Rachel went to see the recent Alain Resnais film *Hiroshima, Mon Amour*. Afterwards they returned to Ian's hotel, the solidly comfortable Kempinski. (He would have preferred a pre-war haunt, the Hotel Adlon, but that was now in the eastern sector.) Over dinner, Ian asked Rachel to go to bed with him. In a disengaged, slightly drowsy, manner, he begged her, "It would be wonderful to relax for a moment." It was a typical Fleming approach, emphasizing his need for sex as a form of physical release. Rachel was tempted, finding Ian "tall, good-looking, highly presentable and with the slightly piratical air given him by his broken nose". But she was afraid of what her husband might think and she was annoyed with Ian for taking no trouble to allay her fears. So Ian went to bed alone.

After flying back to Hamburg to pick up his car, he hurtled down the autobahn as far as Salzburg where, departing from the main road as he enjoyed, he drove peacefully to Vienna along country roads on the wrong

side of the Danube. The Austrian capital had never been able to compete
with the Tyrol, in his view. Now he felt it had become even more solidly
bourgeois and boring than before – an impression that audiences with the
Chancellor, Dr Julius Raab, and the Foreign Minister, Dr Bruno Kreisky,
were unable to shift.

After the stupor of Vienna, "clean, tidy, God-fearing" Geneva was hardly
a bracing alternative as a Thrilling City. But Ian had decided that, of the
other possibilities on offer, Paris was too big, Istanbul too Asiatic and
Venice too much a cliché. He had asked an old girlfriend, Ingrid Etler, to
help him collect information about the city he had known so well as a
young man. She was a vivacious German-born journalist who, after escaping to England just before the war, had married a Pole and worked for the
Polish government-in-exile. Now writing for the local English-language
newspaper, Ingrid regaled Ian with details of the latest *crimes passionels*
and financial irregularities taking place behind Geneva's firmly shuttered
doors.

He did not stay long in the city because he was expected at Les Avants,
Noël Coward's mountainside villa near Montreux, where Ann was due to
join him for the rest of his trip. He had enlisted Coward's help for one of
his regular scouting missions on behalf of the *Sunday Times*. The paper's
literary and features editor, Leonard Russell, knew that the comedian
Charlie Chaplin was writing his memoirs and wanted to secure them for
the paper. Since Coward lived close to Chaplin in Switzerland, Ian asked
him to arrange a meeting. This turned out to be dinner at Chaplin's
eighteenth-century house near Vevey, where two actor friends, George
Sanders and Benita Hume, were also present. But Ian failed to make an
impression. Although he wrote gushingly about Chaplin and his young
wife Oona basking "unaffectedly in each other's love", the great comic
failed to reply to Ian's obsequious follow-up letter. But by then the *Sunday
Times* had a contract directly with Chaplin's publisher and the memoirs
were bound for the paper, whatever Ian's role.

Ian and Ann backtracked for one night to stay in one of the few
bedrooms attached to the celebrated star Père Bise restaurant at Talloires,
just across the French border near Annecy. But his stomach was not
prepared for *pâté de foie gras chaud en croute* followed by *gratin de queues
d'écrevisses* and he was sick all night. Ann too suffered a poisonous mos-
quito bite on her eye, which required a penicillin injection the next night
in Turin. Ian found Italy curiously unattractive. Never an enthusiast for
museums (he once said they should provide roller-skates at their front
entrances for visitors), he was forced to stop in Florence to allow Ann to
rush round the Uffizi in two hours flat. The city itself was "a rude shock"
and Rome, in the throes of preparing for the Olympics, even worse.
Although often accused of depravity in his writing, Ian was not psycho-

logically prepared for the sensual decadence of the prototype *dolce vita*. Ann's friend Judy Gendel, the daughter of Herbert Asquith's great love, Venetia Montagu (née Stanley), had recently married an art historian and was living in the Italian capital. After she had arranged a weekend visit to the beach with some dope-smoking Roman aristocrats, Ian was very relieved to "hack" his way through the building site that was Rome's suburbs and join the autostrada south.

Naples was Ann's idea, or so she claimed. "I over-egged it – stories of the rich façade of hotels and murder and dope-peddling in the back streets, and 'Lucky Luciano' organising vice gangs." Ian's interest in Luciano had been further stimulated by the blank drawn by Raymond Chandler a couple of years earlier. Chandler's submission to the *Sunday Times*, entitled 'My Friend Luco', had been so innocuous and unrevealing that the paper was forced to reject it. Ian understood why after inviting Lucky to join him for tea in the comfortable surroundings of Naples' Excelsior Hotel. He was confronted by an unassuming, well-dressed Italian gentleman – "neat, quiet, grey-haired ... with a tired, good-looking face", according to his description; "benign, sedate, distinguished", according to Ann's. (It is interesting to read their different accounts of the same meeting – his describing his fruitless attempts to puncture Luciano's carefully composed exterior, hers full of the humour of this bizarre encounter.) Over China tea and lemon (hardly Ian's tipple, but in keeping with the overall surrealism) Ian tried to draw Lucky on involvement with drugs. But the Mafia chieftain persisted in claiming that he was framed. When Ann, bored with the meeting and keen to continue with her version of sightseeing, asked about a local church where two corpses were preserved by having gold poured into their veins, she was told solemnly, "That sort of thing doesn't happen here, Mrs Fleming." While Ann was objectively a better tourist than Ian, he had a journalist's knack of feeling the pulse of a place. Naples was a "splendidly horrible town", he appended on a postcard from Ann to Evelyn Waugh. It had a "ghastly zest" and "still smells & cheats as badly as one's first visit abroad which is exhilarating for the elderly".

The Flemings broke their long journey home in Monte Carlo, which was destined to become another of Ian's Thrilling Cities. By drawing on his unpublished 1954 piece, 'How to Win at Roulette', he gamely tried to invest his visit to the casino with suitable excitement. Ann left him in Paris where she met up with Caspar and Nanny for a short stay with Diana Cooper at Chantilly. Always preferring the air ferry to the sea crossing, Ian proceeded to Le Touquet, where he enjoyed one last solitary and delicious meal in his favourite airport restaurant, before returning to the reality of his self-employed existence in Britain.

A sour note was soon sounded by his editor. After the publication of the first article from his recent trip (on Hamburg), Hodson contacted Ian to say he had not been happy with the piece. "We have to remember that for a great many of our readers, probably the majority, prostitution is not even a necessary evil, but something immoral and degrading. Again, strip-tease acts may be all right for callow youths and frustrated middle-aged men but are a vulgar and debased sort of entertainment for balanced people." Ian had little time for this censoriousness. He wrote back huffily, "It is clear from your letter that our views on public morals are at variance."

Leonard Russell, his immediate editor, was more positive and more perceptive. "What a curious personality emerges – a mixture of choleric clubman, commonsense aesthete and yellow journalist. Not a bit like Doughty of Arabia, but a highly independent, audacious, and stimulating traveller." Russell asked for a picture of the famous Thunderbird to accompany the articles. But Ian was not able to supply it because on 14 June 1960, on his way back from visiting Summer Fields, a potential prep school for Caspar in Oxford, he ran into a dawdling ice-cream van on a short stretch of bypass close to Nettlebed. The car was a temporary write-off: looking "as if a 50 millimetre shell had hit it", Ian said.

Summer Fields was a minor victory for Ann. The previous summer she and Ian had paid a formal parental visit to Wellesley House, the Kent school owned by his golfing friend, John Blackwell. Ian had made no secret that he wanted his son to go there. But Ann was unimpressed by the cramped dormitories and lack of emphasis on the Classics at what she called "the Blackwell school". Her mind was made up when Blackwell said, "Caspar is just the sort of sturdy little boy I need," and she replied, truculently, "What for?" It was a clash of two English traditions, the intellectual and the sporting. Blackwell later recalled, "Caspar was a nice and intelligent boy. I could have had him going round Sandwich every Sunday with Ian."

Choosing Summer Fields was, of course, a sensible decision since the Flemings were moving to Sevenhampton, only twenty-four miles away. During the summer, work began on dredging the lake which ran the length of the property. In a poetic image, Ann noted that "the traction engines hoot mournfully and the lawn is covered with sludge and dead eels". Drawing inspiration from Robert Harling, who envisaged a fine Palladian-type mansion, she pored enthusiastically over plans for the layout of the main house once it had been gutted and rebuilt.

Ian regained some initiative over the family's shorter-term living arrangements. In August the Flemings sold the Old Palace at Bekesbourne for £10,000 and moved temporarily into an unprepossessing flat in the Whitehall building, looking out over Pegwell Bay, close to the Royal St George's in Sandwich. It was not long before he was thinking of staying there more permanently. Since returning from his search for Thrilling

Cities, his blood pressure had risen (and he toyed with the idea of yoga, after reading an article on the subject by Arthur Koestler in the August edition of *Encounter*). The flat seemed the ideal place to relax, particularly as he was likely to spend more time at St George's after being elected to the club committee in October. Ann was not unreceptive to the arrangement, but was concerned that it might mean that her husband was backtracking on her vision of a grand house in the country at Sevenhampton. The dredging was already encouraging her to think extravagantly of a magnificent park with black swans on the lake. But seeing only interminable weekend parties and prattling dons from Oxford, he now wanted her to build a "rabbit hutch" rather than a mansion – or so she complained to her friends. The Wiltshire–Kent divide, the gap between two entirely different worlds – a mid-twentieth-century version of the Souls and a clubby Saki-ish golfing fraternity – was growing wider, though it had not quite reached the stage where, as Ann told Evelyn Waugh in September, Ian's "only happiness is pink gin, golf clubs and men".

13

Heart problems
1960–1962

Ian's first move when his Air France Caravelle touched down in Beirut at the beginning of November 1960 was to call his friend Nick Elliott, the local SIS station chief. Ian was on his way to Kuwait to fulfil an unlikely assignment, and, as usual when he was doing something specific, he was showing his most cool and efficient public face. The Kuwait Oil Company had approached him to write a book about the Gulf emirate which was due to attain independence the following year. Initially Ian had rejected the idea: the company had demanded too much of a public relations job. But the money was good and, after his problems with *Thunderball*, Ian wanted the satisfaction of another successful non-fiction book.

From a telephone at the airport Ian invited himself to dinner. Although recovering from a stomach bug, Elliott was delighted to see him. Their conversation ranged over a variety of intelligence-related topics, including Kim Philby, a key participant in the Missing Diplomats affair, who had been working in Beirut as a newspaperman since 1956. Ian told Elliott that he had his own minor freelance intelligence assignment to perform: the then NID chief Vice Admiral Sir Norman Denning had asked him for information about the Iraqi port of Basra. Elliott, who had a regional role, offered to help if he could, and Ian later informed Denning that, although the border with Iraq had been closed and he personally had been unable to visit Basra, he had "met one of your good friends in Beirut and told him of your requirements in Basra and he promised to look after it".

In return Elliott requested a more personal favour. He had heard that it had rained in Kuwait. With that country's very occasional precipitation comes one of its rare indigenous gastronomic delights, the large white truffle. Elliott asked Ian to send him a box, but was to remain disappointed. Ian did not delay him and his wife Elizabeth at the dinner table for long. At 10.30 sharp he asked to leave, saying he had a rendezvous with an Armenian in the Place de Canons in the centre of town. Perhaps Ian was meeting Philby, whom he had certainly met during the war. But Elliott had the distinct impression his dinner guest had arranged to see a pornographic film in full colour and sound.

Like Ann in Jamaica in 1948, Ian suffered from instant gloom as soon as he arrived in Kuwait. He found the terrain dry and drab. Having read the available literature, he had an extravagantly romantic picture of the emirate. He imagined an *Arabian Nights* world of pearl divers, exotic bird-life and, of course, desert truffles. He found none. Instead, "his first and most depressing impression" was the number of motor cars and the appalling cacophony of motor horns.

In his book, titled *State of Excitement*, Ian was polite about the oil company which had invited him and about the royal family which ruled the emirate. He really seemed to believe that Kuwaitis were "a traditionally honourable people under a wise leader coping with sudden wealth to the best of human ability". But along the way he could not help being offhandedly dismissive. He told the story (it sounds apocryphal) of an oil company friend who returned to Kuwait after a period away. "Last year there were more donkeys than cars," he remarked to his driver. "Now there are more cars than donkeys." "Yes, sir," replied the driver. "That's because now the donkeys are driving the cars." He poked fun at them for wanting to call the Persian Gulf the Arabian Gulf, or even the Gulf. In France it is not necessary to call the English Channel the French Channel, he argued speciously. Ian spiced his copy with a dubious tale about a Kuwaiti woman who had been so concerned about a foreigner looking at her unveiled face that she gathered her skirts and pulled them over her head, unaware that she was revealing a totally bare bottom. There was also some disparaging stuff about the workings of the Arab boycott which even Ian removed from the manuscript.

The finished copy did little justice to Ian. He tried to inject an element of mystery by devoting a chapter to the story of an RAF plane which crashed off Falaika Island in the Gulf in 1941, carrying a member of the Iraqi royal family, an SIS officer and a cargo of gold. But, as Ian admitted, he knew little of the background, and the saga was no more than an expanded couple of lines of gossip.

When William Plomer began to edit his manuscript, Ian showed scant interest, complaining that he was "so fed up and overstuffed with the subject that the MS had come to nauseate" him. His main concern was therefore to make the book seem as little like a public relations job as possible. He realized that he would "of course get a majestic pasting from the Arabists" who reviewed the book. But, he announced defiantly, "To hell with them! I'm tired of their snobbish coterie and have been for years."

Ian later told Denning that he had enjoyed Kuwait but, as was his official reaction to the Seychelles two years earlier, this was manifestly untrue. There is no mistaking the tone of his letter to Ann from the Kuwait Oil Company rest-house on 6 November: "This is a most ghastly place and thank heaven you didn't come. I really can't describe its horror. There is dirty sea, dirty sand and dirty town. And dirty people, of course. And sand drives in your eyes and there is a smell of oil everywhere. You would have shot me and then you afterwards if you had come. I am desperately depressed. I am on the point of saying I won't go on with the project. We shall see."

Fortunately, perhaps, the matter was taken out of his hands. When he submitted his manuscript to the Kuwait Oil Company, as required in his contract, his patrons chose not to proceed with the project, though interested readers can peruse the only extant copy in the Fleming collection at the Lilly Library in the University of Indiana. Various representations have been made to see if the Kuwait Oil Company, now owned by the Kuwait government, would be prepared to rescind its ban on the work, but without success.

Part of Ian's book was published, however, albeit in a different medium. Before leaving for Kuwait, back in August, Ian had discussed with the BBC a programme about his experiences there. A producer, Eileen Capel, enthusiastically minuted that the author had "no intention of talking about oil and the obvious associations of Kuwait, rather about eagles, deep-sea fishing and, of course, people".

When Ian submitted his script in early December, the BBC was as disappointed as the Kuwait Oil Company. Ian simply sent two chapters of his book (as usual he must have written while he was travelling). On 9 December, four days before the scheduled date for Ian's recording, a crotchety Janet Quigley, assistant head of talks (sound), informed Eileen Capel, "This is not at all what we look for for the Tuesday Talk and I have turned down other scripts, better than this one, because they were simply descriptive narrative. I realise that it is too late in this case to do anything but accept what Ian has written and I expect he will give a good broadcast of a different kind." She added, "No doubt you will go through the script for advertisements. I have marked as many names of cars as I could spot!" As a result the fifteen-minute-long talk went ahead on the evening of 13 December without any references to the Humber Snipe in which Ian went hunting, or the Holland & Holland and Remington twelve-bore rifles used by his party.

During Ian's month-long absence, Ann made significant advances in the overhaul of Sevenhampton. She purported to enjoy the rivers of mud and concrete on the site. But on his return Ian found it all profoundly depressing, a mood that was exacerbated by a visit to a fortune-teller, who informed him, for a fee of five guineas, that the house would cost more than he thought.

For a boost after Christmas or, as his wife put it, to try to recapture some of the excitement of his youth in the Alps, Ian took Ann, Fionn, Caspar and the governess, Mona Potterton, skiing. They stayed at the Grand Hotel Kronenhof-Bellavista in Engadine, outside St Moritz, where they were joined by Ian's friend Duff Dunbar. Like many of Ian's later forays on to the Continent, it was not a successful break. The altitude proved taxing, and Ian had trouble with his breathing. At night he lay panting in his bed, propped up with pillows. One thing that perked him up, Ann remarked, was being fastened into his skis and generally coddled – shades of Kitzbühel in the 1930s – by a strapping fourteen- year-old German girl. Another was traipsing up to the exclusive Corviglia Club at the top of the ski-lift in St Moritz where he and Ann met their friends Whitney Straight, now deputy chairman of Rolls-Royce, and his wife Daphne, Ian's girlfriend from thirty years before. Ian liked the luxury of the club with its warmed lavatory seats. Daphne noted, however, that he found skiing well-nigh impossible. Ian preferred to sit on the sunny terrace, wrapped in a rug, sipping bouillon laced with vodka. He seemed content there.

Ian's basic unhappiness had a habit of resurfacing in fits of rudeness or ill temper. Back in London, he was uncharacteristically curt when someone at the *Sunday Times* asked him for a five-hundred-word review of a new book. Ian fired off a frosty reply, "I do think you ought to have a glance at books before sending them out for review. *Foreign Assignment* is absolute drivel, but it took me an hour of valuable time to be able to say so unequivocally."

Passing through a chilly New York en route to Jamaica in late January, the Flemings stayed one night at the St Regis Hotel, where again Ann happened to run into her lover, Hugh Gaitskell. Partly out of exhaustion, partly as a matter of diplomacy, Ian stayed at the hotel while Ann and Gaitskell went to a showing of a special NBC television programme about the Soviet Union, accompanied by Jeanne Campbell. Ann described it as a boring evening, and when she and the others returned to the hotel they wanted to go out dancing. (Gaitskell had not lost his twinkle toes.) Ian claimed he was still tired and wanted to sleep, but Jeanne insisted, against Ann's wishes, on ringing up to his room and having a chat.

By the time he reached Goldeneye, Ian had developed bronchitis and was running a temperature of 103. Noël Coward went over to see his friend and found him "sweating in a sopping bed and in a hellish temperature". Coward expected him to burst out in spots, like Bunny Colville, the character who develops chickenpox in his only novel *Pomp and Circumstance*. Ann was not in much better form: she looked "exhausted and strained". So Coward was drummed in to act as Ian's nurse, offering – with rather too much alacrity, Ann thought – to change Ian's pyjamas, turn his mattress and bring him iced drinks. Ann joked that this was because Coward had always found her husband "fearfully attractive and jumped at the opportunity to handle him." As she wrote to Evelyn Waugh, "While

Noël fetched ice cubes from the frigidaire, T-B's [Thunderbird's] language was something horrible, he blamed me for exposing him to homosexual advance." Coward drew his own conclusions about his friends: "Their connubial situation is rocky. Annie hates Jamaica and wants him to sell Goldeneye. He loves Jamaica and doesn't want to. My personal opinion is that although he is still fond of Annie, the physical thing of it, in him, has been worn away." He added, "It is extraordinary how many of my friends delight in torturing one another."

Once back on his feet, Ian's first job was to sort out the bad feeling left by the previous occupants of Goldeneye. In his never-ending search for names and publicity to attach to his books, Ian had been wooing Graham Greene to write the introduction to his omnibus, *Gilt-Edged Bonds*, his final book to be published under his old contract with Macmillan in New York. As was clear from his BBC review of *Our Man in Havana*, Ian revered Greene as an original voice in spy fiction. He was also jealous of the esteem in which Greene was held by Ann and her circle. When he learned that Greene and Catherine Walston were visiting the West Indies in the autumn, Ian offered them Goldeneye as a holiday home. Only belatedly did Greene realize that this was part of a barter deal, and that, as a quid pro quo, he was expected to write Ian's introduction. Since he did not want to do this, the episode caused considerable embarrassment, and Ian was forced to turn to Paul Gallico instead.

Although Greene and his mistress did stay at Goldeneye in November 1960, their visit was marred by a serious falling-out with Violet. They accused her of stealing their whisky and overcharging them (by ten pounds a week) for the household provisions. She claimed that they soiled their sheets and, if she needed the odd tot of whisky, it was only to steel herself for the job of washing them. When Greene raised this matter with Ian, he was annoyed that his host's reaction was to appease Violet and say he would deal with her when next in Jamaica. The two men saw little of each other afterwards, and Greene tended to be coolly disparaging about Ian. In an interview in the *New Yorker* in 1979, he told Penelope Gilliatt that he did not like risk-taking and therefore had no time for people like Jack Kennedy who enjoyed the works of Ian Fleming. The emotional traffic was not all one way, however, as Greene wrote to his lover saying that he had had one of his "old jealous dreams" where she had fallen in love with Ian Fleming.

Gallico's introduction to *Gilt-Edged Bonds* turned out to be everything that Ian had hoped for. He skilfully explained how Ian had captured the imagination of a generation with his stories of adventure and intrigue, mixing this exposition with some elementary biography which, since Ian saw it before publication and suggested changes, can be said to bear the subject's imprimatur. Only two things seemed to annoy Ian. He altered Gallico's account (already mentioned) of his beating before a crucial cross-country race. And wishing to scotch the idea of any rivalry with his brother, he crossed out two sentences, "Peter Fleming's books have won distinguished literary acclaim. Ian's have sold, as noted, two million."

Ian's new book *The Spy Who Loved Me* was a significant departure from usual. The narrative was in the first person by a young Canadian woman, Vivienne Michel: Bond only arrived to save her from the unwelcome attentions of a couple of minor hoodlums in the last third of the book. Indicative, perhaps, of Ian's state of mind, it was also his most sleazy and violent story ever. Ian broke new ground personally with his unemotional Spillane-like descriptions of Miss Michel's sexual odyssey through London in the 1950s, including her deflowering to the sounds of the Ink Spots. When she finally succumbed to Bond, Ian gave full rein to his sado-masochism. "All women love semi-rape," he wrote. "They love to be taken. It was his sweet brutality against my bruised body that had made his act of love so piercingly wonderful." Interestingly Ian found writing *The Spy Who Loved Me* the easiest thing he had ever done. He almost apologized when he admitted this in a letter to Michael Howard.

A certain calm was introduced into the proceedings at Goldeneye by the visit in February of Ann's friends Jack and Frances Donaldson. He was later a Labour Minister for the Arts, and she the first serious biographer of Edward VIII. Despite his guests, Ian stuck meticulously to his established writing routine. He told them he never revised what he had typed, claiming, "I couldn't possibly go on if I read what I had written." This was not necessarily true, Frances Donaldson surmised, but it expressed an attitude of mind.

Ian confessed he was happy having the Donaldsons to stay, because, unlike others of Ann's friends, they were not smart, in the social sense of the word. Occasionally, when he was not working, he would take them swimming and sightseeing. They noticed a curious feature about Bond's creator. He liked the idea of danger, but not the real thing. Unlike Ann, he no longer swam out beyond the reef where the sharks and barracudas roamed. When Jack Donaldson ventured further, Ian used a small boat to retrieve him. He did not approve of his guests' amateur efforts at deep- sea diving, either. He believed that if people wanted to dive, they should do it properly and take lessons. Jack Donaldson concluded that, while Ann was naturally dashing, Ian found danger "a bit of an effort".

Like Coward, the Donaldsons immediately picked up on their hosts' incompatibility. As they saw it, Ian and Ann had obviously once loved each other passionately, but their differences were now proving insurmountable. One day, driving back from Port Maria, Ann suddenly remarked, almost flippantly, "On the left is the house that belongs to Ian's Jamaican wife." She was pointing at Bolt. "You may look, but I cannot." Taken in by her friend's throwaway manner, Frances concluded that Ann obviously did not care about Blanche, otherwise she would have shown more emotion. Later she discovered that Ann was devastated by her husband's romance. Ann had seen the Donaldsons as her allies at Golden-eye. She wrote to Frances, "Curiously the most helpful thing you did was to boost my morale by coming to Jamaica."

Typically, Ian used the Donaldsons in the book he was writing. When Vivienne Michel was in London, she worked on a local paper, the *Chelsea Clarion*, where the editor counselled her that, to write a proper news story, she needed to deal with people rather than issues. It was no use putting out a story about the lateness of buses, he said. To make his point, he concocted a fictional story about a bus conductor called Frank Donaldson, who complained he was never home in time to see his family because the buses were always late. "Now you go out and find a Frank Donaldson and make that story of yours come alive," he urged Vivienne. Another of Ian's friends, Robert Harling, put in a cameo appearance. The *Chelsea Clarion* was made up every week by "a man called Harling who was quite a dab hand at getting the most out of the old-fashioned type faces that were all our steam-age jobbing printers in Pimlico had in stock". To the embarrassment of a female north-coast neighbour, Ian borrowed her name, though not her character, for his heroine. Vivienne Stuart was the respectable English wife of Colonel Robin Stuart, a cousin of Ian's friend, John Pringle. Later on, however, there were advantages to this unexpected publicity, for in late 1994, when a market in Fleming memorabilia had developed, she was able to sell her presentation copy of *The Spy Who Loved Me*, with its dedication, "To Vivienne with an X from Ian", at Christie's for £5,000.

During Ian's final few days in Jamaica, Blanche had an unwelcome premonition that he was going to be seriously ill. The last couple of years, particularly the ill-fated *Thunderball* project, had put him under particular strain. She begged him to be careful and to cut his workload. But Ian was not one to take this kind of advice. When he returned to London on 20 March 1961, he discovered some good news and some bad. On the positive side, Ian's dinner with Senator John Kennedy the previous year had paid dividends. The current issue of *Life* magazine featured an article by Hugh Sidey on the newly elected President's top ten favourite books. It was an eclectic list designed to show that Kennedy was both well-read and in tune with popular taste. At number nine, among such great works of literature as Stendhal's *Scarlet and Black*, stood Ian's *From Russia, With Love*. (Annoyingly, the fuddy-duddy Peter Quennell, was placed at number eight with his little-known *Byron in Italy*.) Quite what the White House publicity machine was striving for is unclear: according to some commentators, Kennedy was not a serious reader. Nevertheless JFK's seal of approval was just the fillip that Viking, Ian's new publishers, needed for his books to take off in the United States. Even more delighted was Signet, an imprint of the New American Library, which had acquired Ian's paperback rights in 1957. When Viking became his hardback publisher just over a year earlier, it had demanded a substantial $25,000 advance for his next three paperbacks. (Up till then Ian had been getting $5,000 a book, which had been considered high.) Victor Weybright, the NAL chief, sanctioned the guarantee in the face of internal opposition. Now, after the *Life* magazine article, Signet weighed in with a major advertising campaign, and by the end of the year Ian had become the biggest-selling thriller writer in the United States. His sales were boosted further by the general concern about the Soviet threat to the West following the failure of the Bay of Pigs invasion of Cuba in April 1961. One Signet promotion in the autumn caught the mood. Under the caption 'AN INCREASE IN TENSION', it showed a picture of the White House, with a single upstairs light burning, an arrow pointing to it and the rubric, "You can bet on it he's reading one of these Ian Fleming thrillers".

Ian milked his own White House connections as much as he could. He was thrilled to hear from Henry Brandon the following October that "the entire Kennedy family is crazy about James Bond". The President's sister, Eunice Kennedy Shriver, had read all Ian's books except *The Diamond Smugglers*. Could he please send her an inscribed copy? asked Brandon. Ian obliged with a poem which rhymed her Christian name with "nice". With his generally unfailing charm, he later said that, if he had been informed correctly, it would have been "kiss". He made a point of sending autographed copies of his books to both Jack Kennedy and his brother Bobby, the Attorney-General. When, a couple of years later, Ian arranged for JFK to receive a copy of Cyril Connolly's spoof *Bond Strikes Camp*, he was disconcerted to find that Randolph Churchill had beaten him to it (using the President's wife, Jackie, as the intermediary and adding a note to the effect that the one thing that really concerned him about the White House was the enthusiasm of its inhabitants for James Bond). As soon as the first Bond film, *Dr No*, was released, Jack Kennedy demanded a showing in his private cinema in the White House. On the night before his assassination in November 1963, the President was reported to have been reading a Bond novel, and so, it was said, was his murderer Lee Harvey Oswald.

While his writing career surged ahead, Ian was dismayed to discover, on the negative side, that Kevin McClory, his erstwhile associate in the movies, had obtained an advance copy of his new novel *Thunderball* (which was due to be published in London at the end of March 1961). McClory had concluded that it was based on the filmscripts he, Ian and others had worked on a couple of years earlier. He and fellow scriptwriter Jack Whittingham responded by issuing a writ alleging breach of copyright, and took out an injunction to prevent *Thunderball* being published. Since 130 review copies had already been posted, and some 32,000 books despatched to booksellers in Britain and abroad, a quick hearing on the injunction was required. Within four days Mr Justice Wilberforce ruled in the High Court that, since the publication was already so far advanced, he could not stop it and therefore McClory and Whittingham's application was refused. However, the judge said this was entirely without prejudice to the litigants' pending action for breach of copyright.

Legal action is stressful at the best of times, and it was the last thing Ian needed at this stage. Two weeks later, Blanche's premonition came disturbingly true when he suffered a massive heart attack during the regular weekly Tuesday morning conference at the *Sunday Times*. Suddenly he keeled over and went so white that even the battle-hardened Denis Hamilton was convinced he was dying. When Ian resisted all efforts to remove him from the room, Hamilton adopted his best wartime infantry officer manner: "Come on, Ian," he ordered. "You'll bloody well do as I tell you. We'll go out and I'll get you a doctor." Hamilton summoned a car which took his friend straight to the London Clinic.

Still not quite fifty-three, Ian had had a startlingly clear intimation of his mortality. For several days into his recovery he was not allowed to see anyone. When Somerset Maugham came to visit him one afternoon, he was refused entry. Ian wrote to tell him that "at my age one needed rest after lunch and that he really ought to follow my example and not go traipsing around London at three o'clock in the afternoon". Ian had to remain in the London Clinic for a month, before being sent down to Sussex to convalesce at the comfortable Swiss-owned Dudley Hotel in Hove, just along the sea front from Brighton.

While in hospital, he was comforted by visits from Blanche, who was in London for the summer with her mother, and, as usual, was happy to run errands, like buying smoked salmon, which had been eliminated from his strict diet. Even at this stage, he refused to keep still. A friend, probably Duff Dunbar, gave him a copy of Beatrix Potter's *Squirrel Nutkin* to read and suggested he might use his enforced leisure to write up the exciting children's story he used to tell Caspar at bedtime. This was about an eccentric family who owned a magic flying car. Ian thought this was an excellent idea and began working on drafts of what was to become *Chitty-Chitty-Bang-Bang*. As he wrote in his rueful way to Michael Howard, there was no moment, "even on the edge of the tomb, when I am not slaving for you".

Even this was not enough to occupy him, and his mind was racing with further projects. Not content with the disputed *Thunderball*, which had just been published, with *The Spy Who Loved Me* in the works, or with *State of Excitement* still awaiting the Kuwaitis' final verdict, Ian proposed to Howard on 27 April that he should write a short light-hearted book on golf aimed at the Christmas market. A glance through *The Times Literary Supplement* while he was still at the London Clinic suggested another idea. In the issue of 14 April he read a leading article which put the case for republishing books long out of print. This encouraged him to remind his own publisher that he had several times pushed for a reprint of one of his favourite novels, *All Night at Mr Stanyhurst's* by Hugh Edwards, with an introduction he would write himself. In putting forward such ideas, Ian was thinking about his future. As he told William Plomer, he had again almost killed Bond off in *The Spy Who Loved Me*. He had decided not to, but the appropriate time had now certainly come.

Among the various messages of encouragement, not all were helpful. Noël Coward advised him to be more spiritual. Admiral Godfrey suggested he might like to write the Admiral Godfrey story. Evelyn Waugh prescribed being "sucked off" gently every day. Others tried to be more useful. Knowing Ian would be convalescing on the Sussex coast, John Betjeman wrote to tell him of the fine Gothic revival interiors to be found around Brighton; St Martin's Church in the Lewes Road, from the 1880s, was particularly noteworthy. Beaverbrook thought Ian should give up cigarettes, which were bad for the heart, and rely instead on strong drink which, he claimed, was good. (Ian's doctors had recommended he should stay off both poisons.) Ian replied that the press lord's "inspiring" letter had done him a power of good, particularly as Beaverbrook's paper, the *Evening Standard*, had practically written him off for dead and was already sympathizing with his widow. "Poor Mrs Fleming asks for nothing better than to have me permanently in a bath chair," Ian told Beaverbrook. "At present she is trying to persuade me that going for long walks and looking for birds' nests is the right way to spend the next forty years of my life!" However he promised that although his engine might be "missing a cylinder for a few months", thereafter it would "be purring along as sweetly as ever – if that is the right description".

Another correspondent was the *Sunday Times* proprietor, Roy Thomson, who wrote to Ian on 26 May wishing him a happy birthday and offering the use of his villa at Cap d'Ail in the South of France. Ian thanked him for the kind thought, which he said he would bear in mind, and could not resist the opportunity to refer to something more important – the fate of his cherished *Sunday Times*. "I am frankly worried about the paper," he told Thomson, "and, without knowing how the figures stand, I have definite fears for the future unless we pull our socks up in many departments where there are signs of torpidity and lack of competitive guts compared with our rivals."

Ian took up this theme with his editor who also enquired solicitously after his health. Informing Hodson that his enforced leisure had given him time to read the three Sunday broadsheet papers "with extra concentration", he noted that both the *Observer* and the new *Sunday Telegraph* were "ahead of us in really well planned foreign and home news editing". Ian's old column, Atticus, was becoming stale, lagging behind its rival Albany on the *Sunday Telegraph*, and even star contributors like golf correspondent Henry Longhurst were becoming "a bit torpid" – a favourite Fleming word – and being overhauled by their competitors.

Already by the end of May, little more than a month after his heart attack, Ian had sent his publisher the first two (out of three) manuscript volumes of his children's story, *Chitty-Chitty-Bang-Bang*. He managed to inject some of his fantasy self into Commander Pott, the head of the family, who advised his children, "Never say 'no' to adventures. Always say 'yes', otherwise you'll lead a very dull life." Ian could not resist drawing on real people, even in this book: one of the Pott children was called Jemima, after Hugo Pitman's daughter. Like most of Ian's characters, Chitty was essentially a composite of two cars Ian had known – his own breezy Standard which he had driven in Switzerland in the late 1920s (and had memorably crashed into a train), and a more traditional vintage sports car of the same name, comprising a dark silver Mercedes chassis, an eight-foot-long bonnet and a six-cylinder Maybach aero engine as used on the Zeppelin airships in the First World War. Built by Count Zborowski in Kent, this car had raced in the early 1920s at Brooklands, where Ian had seen it. In his children's tale, Chitty was able to fly, sail and catch crooks. Since it was the kind of book that needed a good illustrator, Ian suggested Trog, the pseudonym of the cartoonist Wally Fawkes who had become a friend after creating a spoof James Bond in his regular Flook strip in the *Daily Mail*.

After his official convalescence Ian still needed time to recuperate. Perhaps unwisely, he and Ann made a cross-Channel sortie at Whitsun to stay with Hilary Bray's friend, Edward Rice, in Normandy, where Ian pottered around the woods using a walking stick. Subsequently he settled down for the summer in his new flat at Sandwich. Playing his favourite sport was not allowed for the time being. But he had the sea, which he loved, and he amused himself with administrative affairs at Royal St George's, where he served on the handicap (and, subsequently, house and finance) subcommittees and took it upon himself to purchase a silver salver for the steward, Mr Hammond, who was retiring.

As quickly and as predictably as Sandwich became a favourite retreat, Ann took seriously against it. In her eyes, the flat was a slum: she hated its dung-coloured wallpaper and curtains. Its situation was execrable; right on the sea front where blaring loudspeaker vans careered up and down, telling the great unwashed British public to beware of jellyfish. She described to Evelyn Waugh a trip with Caspar on the nearby Hythe and Dymchurch miniature railway. So many people were crammed into the small carriages that, while downing a welcome brew of Pimms from a flask, she imagined herself escaping from East Berlin. And Ann loathed what passed for a social life – meeting "very rich people who have houses here and at Sunningdale or Ascot, horrid furniture and pictures, ugly faces and dull minds". At the flat, she told Waugh, the charwoman and Nanny chattered, the children fought. Little wonder that "Thunderbird waits morosely for midday when he joins the golf people and drinks."

Ian's sights were lifted from his impasse with his wife when, at the end of June 1961, the film deal on which he had set so much store finally materialized. Earlier in the year Harry Saltzman, a Canadian producer based in London, had acquired an option to make movies based on James Bond. Saltzman was an unlikely hero of the dogged survival of British film production in the late 1950s. Before the war he had been production manager for touring circuses in Europe, afterwards moving to London where he prospered with what one of his directors called his "bring on the elephants" approach to movie-making. His Woodfall Films, formed in conjunction with director Tony Richardson and playwright John Osborne, was responsible for such gritty movies as *Look Back in Anger* and *Saturday Night and Sunday Morning*. But even he was having difficulty finding the money to finance his Bond project, until his friend, the playwright Wolf Mankowitz, put him in touch with Albert R. Broccoli. Once a Hollywood agent, "Cubby" Broccoli had also crossed the Atlantic, setting up Warwick Pictures which made successful 1950s movies like *The Red Beret*, *Cockleshell Heroes* and *The Trials of Oscar Wilde*, and which variously gave employment to writer Richard Maibaum, director Terence Young and art director Ken Adam, all of whom would work extensively on the later Bond movies. Warwick Pictures collapsed in 1960, and Broccoli was still looking for new ideas when Mankowitz put him in touch with Saltzman. The two men set up a partnership, Eon Productions, to market the Bond project. Initial response was poor: Columbia turned them down. But Broccoli knew people at United Artists. Supported by Bud Ornstein, the UA chief in London, he and Saltzman flew to New York to present their proposal. They had done their homework well. The whole UA board was waiting to meet them and, within an hour, they had signed a historical contract to make six films. Ian was to get $100,000 per film, plus 5 per cent of the carefully defined producers' profit. The first film was to have been *Thunderball*, and Broccoli even hired Richard Maibaum to write the script. But when the complications of the ongoing legal battle with Kevin McClory became apparent, they ditched that plan and started pre-production work on *Dr No*.

This long-awaited film deal almost failed to materialize because, in a fit of romantic largesse, Ian had given away his television rights to a glamorous woman he met over a plate of scrambled eggs and smoked salmon in New York. Passing through Manhattan in March he had lunched in Sardi's with Ann Marlow, an actress turned film producer, who knew Sir William Stephenson in Nassau. Her most successful venture had been a television series, the Somerset Maugham Theatre. Entranced by her, Ian had torn off a piece of the menu, taken out his fountain pen, and written in his distinctive outsize hand: "To MCA – I would like Ann Marlow to be my exclusive television and radio representative – worldwide." At the bottom he signed his name, and added his Victoria Square address on the back.

This was the start of an innocently flirtatious correspondence based on the premise that their written agreement was a quasi-matrimonial engagement. In their letters they joked about their "fiançailles", and when Ann learned he had been in hospital, she playfully admonished him, "If we are to stay 'married' you must take care of your health." But, despite the easy familiarity, their relationship was strictly professional. She immediately set about hawking her potentially lucrative property around various television networks and sponsors. By mid-April, her efforts had come to the attention of a senior executive at MCA, who invited her to his office to explain. Before proceeding, she asked Ian (whom she addressed as "Dear B and B" – for "Blue shirt and Bow tie") for the precise details of his deal with MCA.

On 1 May Ian replied non-committally from his bed in the London Clinic that MCA were his "agents for television, film and radio, and also, in America only, for books and magazine articles etc". When he added that he had been working on a children's book while in hospital, she shot back presciently, "Oh! those poor kids – you'll frighten them to death with James Bond Jr."

However Saltzman and Broccoli's option changed this pleasing scenario. Not unnaturally, they needed to ensure they held all relevant rights, including those for television. The next time Ian wrote to Ann, on 1 June, his tone had altered. He told her he had had a "sharp squawk" from his agent Phyllis Jackson about their unilateral agreement. Exhibiting nimble footwork, he proceeded to interpret "our arrangement" as meaning that Ann would "have a shot at seeing if you can get a James Bond series going in much the same way as you dealt with Willie Maugham. This option will obviously not be in perpetuity and the scribble I gave you over the scrambled eggs was simply to give you freedom of action with sponsors, agents, etc., for a reasonable time to test out the market." But if nothing materialized, "the responsibility will then revert to MCA and you will return the engagement ring". He stated that the purpose of his letter was to ensure that he could "tell MCA with a clear conscience that the James

Bond properties are not in escrow to Marlow in perpetuity", and he asked her to confirm this in writing. Despite its racist undertone, there is no reason to doubt his addendum, "Personally, of course, I am hoping very much that it will be you and not some Mr Finkelstein who becomes commère of James Bond on television."

When he had not heard from her by 7 June, he fired off a brusque-ish telegram: "SORRY BUT IN VIEW PROMISING FILM POSSIBLY REQUIRING FREEDOM OF ACTION PRAY YOU WILL SWIFTLY REPLY ACCOMMODATINGLY TO MY LETTER OF JUNE FIRST STOP THIS DOESN'T NECESSARILY MEAN DIVORCE BUT I NEED A COMPLETELY FREE HAND FOR A FEW WEEKS TO SEE IF THIS NEW HORSE WILL RUN STOP MEANWHILE RELY ON ME TO WATCH YOUR INTERESTS REGARDEST IAN."

Inevitably Ann's reply to his earlier letter crossed with this cable. There was no need for MCA to fret, she said. She understood the arrangement perfectly, and they stood to gain their 10 per cent commission whatever happened. But, she agreed, "If I can't get the property going on a mutually satisfactory basis, I'll return the engagement ring." Delighted at her response, Ian enthused, "You really are an angel." and promised, in return, that he would do his best to get her "a seat on the bandwagon". Ever the lady, Ann Marlow obliged by sending back "the ring", or menu fragment, though, for the first time, she was mildly petulant. She had not been trespassing on any area of MCA's responsibilities, she said. She had found a sponsor and would have finalized a very good deal on Ian's behalf. However she had called a halt: "You see – Ian – I have to feel happy and excited in a working relationship. I have to feel that forces are working with me – and not casting worried furtive glances my way."

Again, on 3 July, Ian told her she was an angel, adding that he was not in the least surprised that she should feel "miffed". "But the point is, as I told you, that there is a considerable film deal pending which greatly depends, of course, on absolute cleanliness of copyright which, according to MCA, could not be achieved while my blank cheque to you was outstanding." As a token of his "esteem and affection", he promised to bring a small memento from Cartier when he came to New York at the end of the month. When the doctors refused to let him travel, he said he would send his present another way. Whatever happened, she could be assured it was coming 'From London with Love'.

Although she replied 'From New York with Love' on 18 July, there was still a certain truculence in her observation that, having learned that Broccoli and Saltzman were going ahead with a James Bond movie, she would have preferred not to read the latter claiming in the *New York Times* that he also had the television rights. "It would have been nice if Mr Saltzman had said TV will be done with Ann Marlow," she told Ian. "But, Ian Fleming has said it, and that's what counts."

Unfortunately for Ian, this letter, which was readdressed from Victoria

Square to Sandwich, found its way into his wife's mail. He later reported how New York Ann's innocently suggestive tone had enraged her namesake who was temporarily ensconced in Kent. "A lot of explaining had to be explained" to prevent imminent divorce proceedings. By that time, Ian's present had arrived. A Cartier ball-point pen was not particularly generous in the circumstances, but Ann Marlow was polite enough to use it to write and thank him profusely.

At the time Ann Fleming was recovering from her daughter Fionn's marriage to an up-and-coming diplomat, John Morgan. Although the ceremony had taken place in St Margaret's, Westminster, in the presence of Princess Alexandra, a former girlfriend of Raymond, Ann complained to Lord Beaverbrook about her daughter's "red-brick wedding" to the son of chapel folk. The newspaper proprietor reminded her that he, as well as the Flemings, hailed from sturdy Scottish peasant stock. Ann took this to heart and repaired to Shane's Castle in Ulster for a short holiday with Caspar in early September, leaving Ian to inaugurate the "Fleming three-day week" – his enviable practice of travelling up to London on Tuesday morning and departing on Thursday evening.

At Mitre Court Ian occupied himself with his usual variety of projects. He wrote a quick introduction for his *Sunday Times* colleague John Pearson's ghosted memoir of Donald Fish, BOAC's top detective, whom Ian had met at several international police conferences, before launching into revising and checking his forthcoming novel, *The Spy Who Loved Me*. To help him, he hired Fritz Leibert, an American librarian, to check some of the American background in the book. Leibert, who later headed the Beinecke Rare Manuscripts section of Yale University Library, had contacted him with an amusing fan letter about the cultural solecisms he, as an American, had found in *Thunderball*. For further fact-checking, Ian still shamelessly called on the services of the worldwide network of *Sunday Times* correspondents such as Antony Terry.

Ian had not lost his enthusiasm for the production side of publishing and was already well advanced with the book's cover. On 22 June he had written to Dickie Chopping that the "jacket season" was upon them. No longer content with Ian's offer of 200 guineas, the artist stuck out for 250 guineas. Ian told him the title of this new novel suggested "a juxtaposition between a dagger or a gun and an emblem representing love, rather on the lines of your gun with the rose" in *From Russia, With Love*. Ian's idea was "one of those frilly heart shaped Valentines with a dagger thrust through it".

Chopping responded with the concept of a carnation pinned to a page of cipher groups. But Ian feared this would look like a flower book, and suggested as a compromise a carnation crossed with a well-polished commando knife belonging to his publisher Michael Howard, The carnation would be pinned to a cipher book with a diamond brooch, from Cartier's or Welby's, from where Guy Welby provided photographs of suitable examples (though Ian was not amused when Glidrose received a bill for £20). Howard wanted Chopping to speed up his work, claiming that subscribing or filling the large order book for a best-selling author such as Ian took considerable time. Chopping replied that he understood these constraints but had made no commitment to Ian about deadlines. Nevertheless, by the end of October he had finished his work which Ian pronounced "superb".

As light relief, Ian was interviewed by the novelist Elizabeth Jane Howard, the future Mrs Kingsley Amis, for a feature on contemporary writers which she was preparing for the centenary issue of *Queen* magazine, one of several briskly metropolitan magazines which flourished in the 1960s. It was a fairly painless exercise: she sent him six questions about his writing habits and ambitions, and he provided the answers. It was also strangely revealing. Despite his repeated protestations that he was "not in the Shakespeare stakes", he spoke of his desire to leave behind one classic thriller – "a mixture of Tolstoy, Simenon, Ambler and Koestler, with a pinch of ground Fleming". A couple of other ideas also intrigued him. He wanted to write "a really stimulating travel guide to the Commonwealth" and also to tackle the book he had proposed to Curtis Brown five years earlier, a biography of Marthe Richard, or, as he put it, the "biography of a contemporary woman, once a professional prostitute and spy, who has changed the face of a certain country".

Looking forward to the next decade he forecast a fusion of Orwell's *1984* and Huxley's *Brave New World*, with life becoming more comfortable but at the same time duller and uglier. Giving an insight into Bond's *raison d'être*, he added, "Boredom with and distaste for this kind of broiler existence may attract an atomic disaster of one kind or another, and then some of us will start again in caves, and life on this Planet will become an adventure again."

Ian was equally direct when asked about the authors he felt would have the most impact on himself and on society. In the first category he placed Graham Greene, who was becoming an obsession ("because each sentence he writes interests me, both as an individual and a writer"), Georges Simenon and William Plomer. As for influences on society, he mentioned Muriel Spark, Bernard Levin and – only slightly flippantly – Trog, the man he wanted to illustrate *Chitty-Chitty-Bang-Bang*.

By September, Ian was well enough to consider a short break in France. He and Ann crammed into the Thunderbird and motored to Provence where they had been invited to stay with the eccentric Australian art critic, Douglas Cooper: "that splendidly robust Don Quixote of the art world", Ian termed him. The artist Graham Sutherland was also staying with his wife Kathleen, and they both became firm friends of Ian's.

Ian refused to play the docile convalescent, however, and his volatile mixture of physical fragility and petulant bravado on the one hand, and Ann's anxiety about his health on the other, made for an unusually tense few days. Matters came to a head in the Massif Central where she complained that he was driving too far and too fast each day and was denying her simple pleasures – gathering autumn crocuses and looking at the magnificent rock churches. He took her to task for incessant carping, and then retreated, wilfully and ominously, into sullenness. When they did stop for meals (Ann was annoyed that the decision was always Ian's), he insisted on disobeying doctor's orders "by stuffing himself with truffles, cream, burgundy followed by smoking hundreds of cigarettes". Ann cried for much of the trip, and her misery and tears continued when they returned to London and squabbled over Ian's business arrangements. Ann was adamant that "he was making a muddle with his myriad of lawyers". But when she tried to use her contacts to straighten matters out, Ian became even more furious at her interference. (Ann probably wanted to introduce Ian to Hugh Gaitskell's solicitor, Arnold Goodman. But despite having met Goodman at the casino in Le Touquet, Ian was unwilling to let him handle his affairs, and Ann was only able to engage the influential lawyer to represent her interests in Ian's estate posthumously.)

Although Ian often gave the impression of tolerating Ann's dalliance with the Leader of the Opposition, Evangeline Bruce had a different impression when she invited the Flemings to dinner that autumn. She was the wife of the new American ambassador David Bruce who, as the former head of the wartime OSS in London, knew Ian well. She placed Ian next to Carmen Esnault-Pelterie, a vivacious Parisian socialite, with whom he seemed to get on famously. However the Ambassador's wife was mortified to overhear part of their conversation. When Mme Esnault-Pelterie asked Ian about the man at the opposite end of the table, he replied, "That's my wife's lover. His name's Hugh Gaitskell."

Evangeline Bruce subsequently became close to Ann, and she never failed to be upset by the brittle state of her relationship with Ian. "It was clear that she was mad about him," she recalled. "But he was irritated to death by her, snarling and saying nasty things. When I first met them, she was in a constant state of nerves about Ian. She knew she wouldn't get him back and he was very cruel to her."

Ann's composure was not improved when, shortly after her return to London, Evelyn Waugh told her that, on a visit to Ireland, his daughter Margaret had heard her host, the Liberal peer Lord Mersey, suddenly announce, apropos of nothing, "Ian Fleming is dying." When the young woman said she had heard he was in increasingly robust health, Mersey bellowed, "Nonsense. I know him well. He's got a very short time to live."

Ian's manner of dealing with reports of his imminent demise was to hurl himself even more wholeheartedly into his work. By the time he returned to London an enthusiastic Trog had completed preliminary drawings for *Chitty-Chitty-Bang- Bang*. But the *Daily Mail*, never a supporter of Ian, refused to allow its leading cartoonist to work for an author whose creations were regularly serialized in the rival *Daily Express*. (After considerable toing and froing the drawings for *Chitty-Chitty-Bang-Bang* were done by John Burningham.) Trog caused a minor rumpus by playfully questioning the veracity of the fudge recipe in the book, so Griffie and the children's book editors at Jonathan Cape spent hours making up, testing and eventually altering Ian's ingredients. Another cartoonist created a different kind of problem. One afternoon Ian, playing an unaccustomed role as the indulgent parent, took his nine-year-old son to the cinema to see the latest Walt Disney film *The Absent-Minded Professor*. One scene in the film – where a flying motor car built by the professor in his back yard circles a church spire – was remarkably similar to Chitty-Chitty-Bang-Bang. "This really is the limit", an aggrieved Ian complained to his publisher.

As for his own film, the *Dr No* project, Ian washed his hands of involvement in the script, and Eon liked it that way. Broccoli told Guy Hamilton, his original choice as director, that he was going to "fix" the book which was "full of nonsense". With input from Mankowitz, he wanted to introduce a variety of fantastic elements such as portraying the reclusive Dr No as a monkey rather than a man. Declining the job this time, Hamilton tried to convince Broccoli that the project's charm lay in Ian's detail.

Ian had his own opinion about who should play Bond. He suggested his friend David Niven and then Roger Moore, who was enjoying some success as The Saint on television. But Broccoli had already set his mind on an almost unknown Scottish actor called Sean Connery. Ian remained equivocal about the choice: he was not sure if a working-class Scotsman had the social graces to play his hero. His mind was swayed by a female opinion. When he invited Connery to lunch at the Savoy, another guest, Ivar Bryce's attractive cousin Janet, who had recently married the Marquess of Milford Haven, pronounced Connery as having 'it', and that was good enough for Ian. His own assistance to the film was limited to helping find location sites in Jamaica, where shooting was scheduled for the following spring. He wrote to his friend Reginald Maudling, the new Colonial Secretary, to ask about the use of Government House. But Maudling replied that, as the Governor was portrayed as a nincompoop and his secretary as a spy, the answer was no. Ian was more successful in securing the Brownlows' Rolling River estate on the north coast of Jamaica.

At the *Sunday Times* Ian kept an eye on the progress of an idea he had floated a few years earlier. At a Tuesday morning meeting he had proposed a series about the Seven Deadly Sins. His idea was now dusted down by Leonard Russell, who commissioned all the authors Ian originally suggested (with the exception of W. H. Auden who replaced Malcolm Muggeridge to write on Anger). After publication in December, Ian arranged for the articles to be collected in book form by Hugo Pitman's son-in-law, Larry Hughes, who was a director of William Morrow in the United States. Ian wrote a pithy introduction which gave some insight into his personal identification with the various sins. If he had not been envious of his older brother, Ian said, "I would not have wished all my life to try and emulate him", and he admitted that in "moments of despair" he had seen the face of sloth, or as he liked to call it in his books, accidie.

Ian had two further writing commitments that autumn. One was his introduction to Hugh Edwards's *All Night at Mr Stanyhurst's*. In August he asked Cape to find out all it could about this author. Gradually various pieces of information emerged. Edwards had broadcast regularly on the BBC Third Programme, where his old producer, E. J. King-Bull, knew him well. The book's first edition, originally published in 1933, had sold around 1500 copies, plus an additional 3000 in a cheaper edition in 1937. The story itself was based on the wreck of the *Grosvenor*. Ian took these various details and moulded them into his introduction to the book, which was interesting for his listing of his own favourite lost books – B. Traven's *The Bridge in the Jungle*, Lynn Brock's "scarifying" *Nightmare* and, from an earlier era, Frank R. Stockton's *Rudder Grange*. Ian showed off a little, demonstrating his familiarity with *The Times Literary Supplement*, which he said would be an essential item in his Desert Island library. He also scored a few points in the book world by referring to several recent books, such as Samuel Beckett's *Murphy* which had dropped into limbo before being revived. He noted that Edwards had served in the Caribbean with the West India Regiment, an experience that had given him the background for his novel. However, the first draft of his introduction, finished in November, quoted too extensively from others, particularly the *TLS* and the drama critic James Agate, causing Plomer to remark, legitimately enough, "Ian seems to be saying, 'You see, although I write thrillers, I read serious literary criticism'. Of course he does; but to say so in this way and place might irritate readers – and reviewers."

Ian's other main writing task was to produce a short story for the first issue of the *Sunday Times* colour magazine, scheduled for early 1962. His behind-the-scenes lobbying for changes at the paper had brought results. Shortly after communicating with Ian the previous May, Harry Hodson had embarked on a long-awaited round-the-world trip with his wife, thus giving Roy Thomson the opportunity to promote Denis Hamilton to the top job. As the new editor – the formal appointment came in October 1961 – Hamilton advanced plans to publish an American-style colour or photogravure section and engaged Ian, still the paper's most bankable asset, to write a major piece for one of the first issues. Initially Ian submitted a Boothroyd-inspired overview of 007's weaponry called 'The Guns of James Bond'. But after Hamilton deemed this too long for a general audience, they agreed that the magazine would publish a new short story, 'The Living Daylights', about Bond visiting Berlin to cover the defection of a British agent who was being hunted by a Russian assassin. On 23 September, following his return from Provence, Ian suggested that the piece should be illustrated with an original Graham Sutherland design – a pink heart with a black arrow through it – which he had commissioned for a "nominal" one hundred guineas.

Ian's file on 'The Living Daylights' – or 'Trigger Finger', in an early draft – revealed the speed with which he went about such a project. He acquired a map of Berlin and an October 1961 catalogue of new records sold by Harrods. He contacted the National Rifle Association for information about the Bisley range where his story opened. By 10 November, Captain E. K. Le Mesurier, secretary of the NRA, had not only fielded Ian's original requests but read and returned corrections to the manuscript. On the first page, for example, Ian had written, "He gave half a turn to a screw on the fixed stand on which his rifle rested. He watched the crossed lines on the Sniperscope move minutely to the right of the bull, to its right-hand bottom corner." Le Mesurier suggested this should read, "He set two clicks more right on the wind gauge and traversed the crossed wires back on to the point of the aim." He explained that, in Ian's description, the sighting arrangements were not right for a sniper's rifle. For really accurate shooting, one needed a sight which could be set off from the line of the barrel to allow for wind.

On 21 October Ian again contacted Antony Terry, to enquire in which sector of Berlin 40A Wilhelmstrasse was situated. He wrote that he hoped his new story would "arouse memories of our stay in Berlin and of the 'friend' we met when there" a reference to the spy to whom Terry had introduced him in Berlin in May 1960. Terry replied that the house was in the American sector, but was barred to civilian traffic, except buses, because it led immediately on to Checkpoint Charlie.

As a twist in his tale, Ian made his Russian assassin not only a woman but also a cello player, code-named Trigger, who bore an uncanny resemblance to his sister Amaryllis. Both girls' hair "shone like molten gold" and both were "vivid with movement and life and, it seemed, with gaiety and happiness". Besides, cello cases were good for carrying concealed weapons. But, Bond reflected, "why in hell did she have to choose the cello? There was something almost indecent in the idea of that bulbous, ungainly instrument splayed between her thighs. Of course Suggia had managed to look elegant, as did that girl Amaryllis somebody. But they should invent a way for women to play the damned thing side-saddle."

A looming problem was that the *Sunday Times* did not like Sutherland's rather crude water-colour. Ian explained to his new friend that "the first reactions, while enthusiastic, are that the green is too gay giving the whole thing rather too much of a pastoral quality". He urged Sutherland to take up his brushes again, adding that, on his way to Sandwich the following week, he might drop in at the artist's house in nearby Trottiscliffe for a lunch of his favourite sausages and mash.

At the end of November, Mark Boxer, the magazine's editor, made up his mind to reject the Sutherland cover, though he softened the blow by telling Ian that the paper could not guarantee the reproduction that the work deserved. Ian did not seem put out, taking the opportunity to try to interest Boxer in taking another look at 'The Guns of James Bond' and, failing that, in publishing the account of the Dieppe raid which he had written for the NID's Weekly Intelligence Report. This was the first thing he had ever published, Ian explained, slightly erroneously, and it still read freshly, he felt.

Ian continued his unsolicited promotion of Sutherland by sending their mutual friend Lord Beaverbrook a Christmas card – a drawing of the Canadian press lord by the artist. Did he have some idea of what would happen next and hope to forestall it? On 9 February 1962 the new *Sunday Times* colour magazine duly appeared with Ian's story, though the overall reception was distinctly cool. The very next day the long-running James Bond cartoon strip in Beaverbrook's *Daily Express* was abruptly curtailed. Less than half the current story, *Thunderball*, had been published. The Friday strip had left a villain aboard a jet airliner muttering, "The Spectre people said that five minutes more would be long enough to kill them all." On Monday the artist and caption writer were told the series was ending. They had one more strip in which to conclude the narrative. They cobbled together the remaining picture frames, adding an abrupt final paragraph: "Giuseppe flies the stolen atom bomber to the Bahamas and the bombs are hidden in the sea. Spectre's ultimatum is sent to the British and US governments – '£100,000,000 in gold or we explode the bombs in your countries'. Every agent, including Bond, searches for the bombs. Bond finds them and the world is saved."

By then the Flemings were both in Jamaica. Passing through New York Ian had dinner with Ernie Cuneo who reported to Ivar Bryce that their friend "looks well and seems to be his old energetic self, but his eyes reveal he has had an ordeal". Only Ian's closest friends could see this clearly. It pained Blanche to realize that he was "fighting like a tiger to live, but everything was against it". Ian's heart attack had marked the beginning of another gradual change in the nature of their relationship as it passed from passionate affair to loving friendship, and her job now was to ease what she was convinced were Ian's last few years. Ian marked this transition in his notebook: "Suddenly you reach the age when it crosses your mind to say no to pleasure. For an instant you think that you have been virtuous. Then you realise the desire was not there. It was dead, and you are sad because sensuality is leaving you."

Ian's mellowing was little comfort to Ann. As soon as the Flemings arrived at Goldeneye, Ann was up in arms because, as she put it, the first thing he wanted to do was to telephone Mrs Blackwell. Ann got her own back with a new ploy – attributing his coolness towards her to his growing literary success. She said this was a general opinion, not just hers. "I fear that since the rise of James Bond you do not care for a personality that in any way can compete with yours, and no doubt there is more adulation to be had at Bolt, and you refuse to see that is an impossible situation for me." Whereas in the past he was usually the one wanting moderation and stability in their lives, Ann now called for less emotionalism. "You need great love, calm and quiet, more than anyone." But, sadly for both parties, she was not the person to provide these emollient qualities.

There were several enjoyable moments in Jamaica, nevertheless. Ian had embarked on his new book, *On Her Majesty's Secret Service*. In it Bond, taking the name of Ian's friend, Hilary Bray, impersonates a researcher from the College of Arms and enlists the help of the Corsican Mafia to infiltrate his old rival Ernst Blofeld's Alpine hideaway and find out about his scientific research into the topical subject of germ warfare. Before leaving London, Ian had hired Robin Mirrlees, son of his Le Touquet friend, to provide him with information about genealogy and heraldry. As Rouge Dragon (later Richmond Herald) at the College of Arms, Mirrlees was ideally placed to investigate the family histories of Bond and Blofeld. He delighted Ian by discovering a coat of arms for the Bond of Peckham family, complete with a motto – "The world is not enough" – that might have been devised for 007.

In his incidental discussion of genealogy and titles, Ian could not resist a light dig at his old boss, Lord Kemsley. In his book he told the story of a certain gentleman who, after being given a peerage "for political and public services" – "ie [he wrote] charities and the party funds" – had wanted to call himself Lord Bentley Royal, after the village in Essex. When this was disallowed because only the reigning family could incorporate the name 'Royal', certain wags suggested he could be called 'Lord Bentley Common'. Exactly the same story had been told of Lord Kemsley when he was living in Farnham.

Ian's story drew on his visit with Ann to Engadine, near St Moritz, the previous year. Its cast of characters in a restaurant at the top of a ski-run was remarkably similar to that in real life fourteen months earlier, with Ian writing about 'Sir George Dunbar' with his enchanting companions,

Mr Whitney and Lady Daphne Straight – "Is she not chic? They are both wonderful skiers." *On Her Majesty's Secret Service* was memorable for its detailed description of M. Ian's characters were always composites of people he knew, but this book aligned M more closely with Ian's old boss Admiral Godfrey than ever before. The door to M's house, for example, had the "clapper of the brass ship's-bell of some former HMS *Repulse*, the last of whose line, a battle-cruiser, had been M's final sea-going appointment". *Repulse* was Godfrey's last command in the Western Mediterranean before he took over as DNI. When Bond visited the crusty M for Christmas he was offered a bottle of Algerian wine, which his boss remembered as the staple drink for the Fleet in the Mediterranean. "Got real guts to it. I remember an old shipmate of mine, McLachlan, my Chief Gunnery officer at the time, betting he could get down six bottles of the stuff." Donald McLachlan, of course, was a colleague of Ian's and Godfrey's in NID. The nautical references reflected the provenance of the title which was suggested by Nicholas Henderson after noticing it on the cover of a nineteenth-century sailing adventure novel displayed on a stall in the Portobello Road.

The fictional ski-slope restaurant had another diner, Ursula Andress, described as "that beautiful girl with long fair hair at the big table". This was a particularly topical reference because, while Ian was in Jamaica, the local scenes for *Dr No* were filmed and the female lead was the relatively unknown Swiss actress, Ursula Andress. Although Ian continued to stay in the background, he recommended Blanche's Old Harrovian son, Chris, to Broccoli and Saltzman as a location manager. This only served to infuriate Ann further, as she accused her husband of taking "every opportunity of patronage and friendship" to the Blackwell family. But Ian was also being astute. As a popular music enthusiast, he was determined to have a good, authentic soundtrack for his first film. He knew 24-year-old Chris Blackwell loved Jamaican music and would provide what he wanted. He could not have chosen better. Chris enjoyed his first job in the entertainment industry so much that he decided to stay in it full-time. Later that year, he founded Island Records, one of the most successful record companies of the next three decades, which he eventually sold to Polygram for £200 million in 1989.

Now more than ever called upon as a pundit on matters of international espionage, Ian was the centre of a rival film circus when CBS sent a production unit from New York to interview him after the pilot of an American U-2 reconnaissance aircraft shot down in the southern Soviet Union two years earlier had been exchanged for a Russian spy. Having had his memory jogged, Ian pumped out an article on the same subject for the *Sunday Times*. Acting like a tougher version of his fictional M, he argued that the Americans should have kept quiet about the incident and thrown the pilot, Gary Powers, "cold-bloodedly to the dogs". That had been the British reaction, Ian wrote, when Commander "Buster" Crabb, an unfit naval frogman had been killed trying to examine the hull of a Russian cruiser in a botched SIS operation in April 1956. But although Ian had been interested in the operation, which was instigated by his friend Nicholas Elliott, he carelessly wrote that the Russian ship had been visiting Portland, rather than Portsmouth.

For her own entertainment, Ann invited Peter Quennell to return to Goldeneye to finish his book on Shakespeare. Also visiting Jamaica was the poet Stephen Spender, who was lecturing on the island for the British Council. One day Ian and Ann took these two literary gents to the set to view the filming of *Dr No* at Roaring River. Director Terence Young was shooting the scene, later famous, where Honey Ryder (as she was known in the film), played by Andress, having emerged from the sea in her bikini, takes refuge with Bond behind a sand ridge while Dr No's desperadoes shoot at them from the sea. Suddenly four people sauntered uninvited on to the set. Young screamed at them to get down. They did so, and the scene was duly shot. Thirty minutes later, Young saw the four visitors still lying spread-eagled on the sand. Ian called the film business a "riot" (in the positive sense of "great fun").

Halfway through her visit, Ann brushed aside any ill-feeling towards Ian and tackled Lord Beaverbrook on his behalf. Ian must have been brooding about his strip's precipitate removal from the *Daily Express*, and Ann was sharp enough to realize that Caspar's, and perhaps even her own, financial interests were threatened. On 19 February, she despatched a frantic cable from Oracabessa to London. "DARLING MAX," she gushed, "WHY HAVE YOU THROWN IAN FROM YOUR HOUSE OF MANY MANSIONS? I HAVE FREQUENTLY HAD TO THROW HIM FROM MINE. I LONG TO KNOW YOUR REASON. PLEASE REPLY. KISSES. ANNIE." The wily Canadian's cabled reply the next day was short and to the point: "IAN HAD TOO LONG A RUN."

Returning home early, as usual, Ann wrote to Ian about her "basic unhappiness" which was only exacerbated by his indifference to it. She excused herself: "I know that misery from far away will not put up your blood pressure, so I would be grateful if you could make an effort to see my point of view by reading this letter carefully." In it she laid out some of her grouses, amongst which the spectre of Mrs Blackwell loomed largely. And the story of his night (apparently unconsummated) with the prostitute in Macao still rankled, for she made the point of wishing that he put half as much effort into his domestic relations.

For some time the painful possibility of Ian selling Goldeneye had been on the agenda, but Ann admitted it was no use asking him to leave his beloved Jamaican home. So now she told him he had "two weeks for adulation at Bolt, and the chank shell on the desk and all the other visible signs of the tenancy of the once loved one and now friend? [Ann's question mark] which is why you wanted me to go". But then she begged him to return home and to devote more of his vitality to keeping their marriage intact. "I can give you all if you give me little," she said touchingly.

Passing through New York for the weekend on his way back to London from Jamaica, Ian subjected himself to an interview which resulted in an adulatory profile in the *New Yorker*'s Talk of the Town column. This was Ian at his most showman-like. Staying at the Pierre, he took his anonymous interlocutor to lunch which he started with a medium-dry Martini of American vermouth and Beefeater gin. He talked about the need for heroes, recalling, of course, how he had been taken up by Jack Kennedy. That morning he had been on a walk in Central Park, he said: "What a wonderful place to meet a spy! A spy with a child. A child is a most wonderful cover for a spy, like a dog for a tart." Turning to his books, he spun his old line that they had no social significance, "except a deleterious one", adding, untruthfully but with a good mind for the plug for his next novel, that he had just finished his latest book, *The Spy Who Loved Me*, in Jamaica. The Miller High Life he drank with his meal must have been getting to him, as he continued, "It's long and tremendously dull ... I think it's an absolute miracle that an elderly person like me can go on turning out these books with such zest. It's a terrible indictment of my own character – they're so adolescent."

Ian was preparing himself for a poor reception for the book when he returned to London. The tone was set by another unnecessary feud, this time with the weekly magazine *Today*. When the *Express* had rejected this very unBondish novel for serialization, Peter Janson-Smith, who was acting more and more as Ian's general agent, offered it to *Today*. But Ian had been unhappy about the way that the magazine had handled its publication of his story "The Hildebrand Rarity" in 1960 and told Janson-Smith to cancel the negotiations.

On publication of *The Spy Who Loved Me*, *Today*'s editor Charles Stainsby wrote a signed article calling it "one of the worst, most boring, badly constructed novels we have read". But this was only the point of entry for a protracted attack on, first, Ian himself, as the perpetrator of "the nastiest and most sadistic writing of our day" and, second, his Establishment friends who promoted and peddled his wares. "It is all part and parcel of the strange nastiness which afflicts many of the Top People in Britain," opined Stainsby. "We stand firmly against all the things represented by Mr Fleming. We find his writings disgusting drivel. We deplore the manner in which they have been puffed. And we deplore even more the fact that a respectable publisher chooses to put his imprint on them."

This outburst led to an invitation to Ian to appear on BBC Television's current affairs programme *Tonight*. There he openly alleged that *Today* had "taken it out" on him because he had refused to allow it to serialize his latest book. This version of events was disputed by Stainsby who claimed he had never wanted to publish any extract from Ian's book in the first place. He called Ian's statement "extremely defamatory" and demanded an apology which Ian, rather ignominiously, had to give.

The unpleasantness had taken further toll of Ian. On 19 April 1962, shortly after the British publication of *The Spy Who Loved Me*, he wrote to Michael Howard expressing dismay at its reception. He lamely tried to attribute this to James Bond's late entry into the book and also, though he said this weighed less heavily, to the "alleged salacity of certain passages". Ian admitted that he had received hostile reviews from critics who had previously "treated the whole of the James Bond saga with a light heart". These hostile notices had disturbed his wife greatly. In a separate note to Plomer, Ian thanked his friend for comforting Ann about the ferocity of the reviews. He admitted he had had "an uncomfortable two or three weeks having to digest a second breakfast every morning of these hommany grits – well deserved though they may be".

To Howard, he tried to explain his objective in writing *The Spy Who Loved Me*. He had become alarmed that his earlier thrillers, designed for an adult audience, were increasingly read in schools (such as Caspar's, he might have added) where young people made a hero out of James Bond. This had not been his intention, he claimed. He did not regard Bond as a heroic figure "but only as an efficient professional in his job". Therefore he had sought to write a "cautionary tale" to put the record straight, particularly for his younger readers. Unable to do this in his usual narrative style, he had invented a heroine "through whom I could examine Bond from the other end of the gun barrel, so to speak". To make her credible, he had to build her up and make her "wordly-wise". Even so, Ian purported that, to lessen any sense of heroism, he had depicted Bond as making a mess of his fight with the gangsters holding Vivienne Michel. And the book had ended with a "long homily" where the chief detective warned her and the readers that Bond was actually no better than the hoodlums he chased.

This was Ian at his most tendentious. In the novel, rather than throwing cool, reflective light on Bond, he had caused Vivienne to gush, "Apart from the excitement of his looks, his authority, his maleness, he had come from nowhere, like the prince in the fairy tales, and he had saved me from the dragon ... And then, when the dragon was dead, he had taken me as his reward." It was the crude manner of this taking that particularly offended the critics. In suggesting that all women love semi-rape, Ian had indulged an enduring personal fantasy that he had explored in his notebooks. In *The Spy Who Loved Me*, Ian had written of the after-effects of such an act – "the coinciding of nerves completely relaxed after the removal of tension of danger, the warmth of gratitude, and a woman's natural feeling for her hero". The underlying problem was that, for all his protestations to Howard, Ian had still not worked out whether Bond was a "blunt instrument", as he often claimed, or a mythical hero. The confusion and ambivalence only added to Bond's interest, it could be argued.

To his publisher Ian admitted that his "experiment" had "obviously gone very much awry". As a result he asked Howard to help him ensure that The Spy Who Loved Me had "as short a life as possible". Calling on Jonathan Cape to accept its share of their inevitable joint financial sacrifice in "as friendly a spirit as you can muster", Ian requested that there should be no reprints and no paperback version of his controversial book. Ann's reaction suggested what a trying partner she could be. Having badgered Ian and made him feel guilty about the book, she wrote to Evelyn Waugh the following day, telling him in confidence of her husband's resolve. But, true to character and conscious of the need to keep the Bond cash cow producing, she could not resist adding flippantly, "I am doing my best to reverse this foolish gesture because of the yellow silk for the drawing-room walls."

14
Kent and Wiltshire
1962–1963

Ian's day-to-day uniform of navy-blue suit, lighter blue shirt and black-and-white spotted bow-tie bore witness to a self-conscious theatricality, particularly when the effect was set off by the tapering ebony cigarette holder, with its smouldering Morland Special. As a young man, Ian had undoubtedly been vain, the 'Glamour Boy' who dazzled Ann and her friends. But, as the years took their toll and he began to lose his mobility, his eyes became more glazed, the veins in his neck stood out and his complexion was puffy and purple. The petulant, sclerotic countenance which had always threatened was now reality.

So it was less from personal vanity than from a desire for posterity that he decided, at the age of fifty-three, to have his portrait painted. The immediate spur was the need for something imposing to hang at Sevenhampton. Surprisingly, given his many artistic connections, he had never sat for a full-scale study before. There was a Spy-like cartoon by Amies Milner from 1925, and a couple of wartime drawings – one by Augustus John and another by his fellow NID officer Robert Bartlett, which was used on the cover of *Casino Royale*. Other representations were a bust by Simone Panchaud de Bottomes, the mother of his one-time fiancée, Monique, and a sketch by the Canadian George Lonn who had worked for the *Sunday Times*.

Now, comfortably off for the first time in his life, Ian felt in a position to commission an old friend, Amherst Villiers, who had turned to painting after a distinguished career as an engineer. Villiers was a characteristically individual choice for such an undertaking. He was best known as the inventor of the supercharger used on the "blown" Bentleys of the mid-1930s, one of which was used by James Bond in the early novels. Having spent much of the previous decade in the United States, working with Wernher von Braun on rocketry and satellites, Villiers had returned to Europe where, after studying in Florence under Pietro Annigoni, he had set up a studio at the back of his house in Kensington.

Looking healthy and tanned in his summer issue of short-sleeved blue Sea Island cotton shirt, Ian spent whole days during May 1962 sitting for his friend. As the two men laughed at memories of youthful escapades, they were often joined by Graham Hill, a young racing driver with whom

Villiers was developing a new engine for the manufacturer, Cosworth. Ian enjoyed talking nuts and bolts with the future world champion and, in his effort to enliven the pages of the *Sunday Times*, recommended him to Denis Hamilton as a potential motoring correspondent. Having heard about Ian's heart attack, Villiers's American wife Nita was worried about what to feed him. Griffie indulgently told her, "Scrambled eggs and sausages, washed down with red wine," even though she knew that, strictly speaking, Ian was not allowed his favourite foods.

Before long Villiers was creating a likeness of Ian's sharp, sad features, but thought the mouth a trifle too severe. Ian and Nita disagreed, persuading him that the expression was correct. "The crankshaft designer is making me look like a mixture between Nehru and Somerset Maugham," Ian told Plomer, but he willingly paid the agreed £500 fee and arranged to use the finished product on the cover of a limited (250 copies) leatherbound edition of his next book, *On Her Majesty's Secret Service*. At the same time he asked Villiers for a design for *Chitty-Chitty-Bang-Bang* – something "really snazzy looking to excite the imagination of children about 7–10". Villiers sketched a low green rakish car, which looked like an SSK Mercedes with a round Delauney Belleville radiator. But too many artists were already involved and Villiers's drawing was not used.

Once the controversy surrounding *The Spy Who Loved Me* had died down, Ian enjoyed a surprisingly relaxed early summer in Sandwich. With the help of his willing researcher Robin Mirrlees, he completed the outstanding heraldic details for *On Her Majesty's Secret Service*. Mirrlees balked slightly to learn that Ian had given someone with his title, Rouge Dragon, an important role in the book. Agreeing to change the reference, Ian invented a new heraldic officer called Sable Basilisk – a play on the facts that Mirrlees had a flat in Basil Street in Knightsbridge and that a basilisk looks like a dragon.

Ian strayed as seldom as possible from the Kent coast. Now, more than ever, St George's was the only place where he could unwind. The reason was not so much the golf as the company. The regular members were an amiable mixture of buffers, amongst whom Ian felt at ease. Ian never had to compete with the retired colonial officers and unassuming stockbrokers in the club-house, as he did with his wife's friends at Victoria Square. Sitting in a leather-backed armchair beside the bar, nursing a pink gin, he could be the centre of attention without having to expend too much of his dwindling energy. Ian recognized as much himself. As he had written in his notebook only the previous June, "After a certain age one must not consort with persons who leave one with a bitter taste in the mind or on the palate. Mefiez-vous du sang âpre. Try and move among people – they may be bores – who are douce. Don't let your face or your mind become stringy with bitterness – or your stomach. Be bland, be relaxed, be kind."

Since the atmosphere at the golf club recalled much of the strange mixture of regimentation and informality of the best English prep school, Ian enjoyed the licence to fool around and act childishly when he went out on the course with one of his regular crowd. In the year since his heart attack, he had lost some of his competitive edge, and his handicap had drifted four shots to thirteen. Nevertheless he still liked some sort of incentive. As a young man he used to play rounds with Hugh Vivian Smith for a 'Smith shilling', or a pound. With Blanche's cousin, John Blackwell, the currency had changed its name and become significantly inflated. When they competed for "the usual five pence", they meant £50. With Bunny Roddick, a former Indian army officer, the prize was usually a material object. Once, after beating Roddick 5&4 to win a pair of pyjamas, Ian, feeling they needed an inducement for the remaining four holes back to the club-house, suggested they play for the monogram. On another occasion, Ian managed to beat Keith Barlow, Sir Godfrey Ralli's brother-in-law, 2&1, by insisting on being awarded any putt that landed within a club's length of a hole.

His relaxed approach to the game was reflected in his decision to contribute a cup to the Old Etonian Golfing Society. This was not the traditional piece of silverware, but a chamber-pot, inscribed with the rubric, 'James Bond All Purpose Grand Challenge Vase'. Several members of the society, including its president, Reginald Turnbull, who had been at Slater's with Ian, considered this in poor taste, but such was Ian's fame that they could do nothing to stop it.

St George's was the focal point for a Kentish way of life which might have been designed to emphasize its difference from Ann's metropolitan lionizing. When not at the club, or when, once or twice, Blanche came to visit, Ian liked to take his lunch at his favourite "pub", the Duck Inn at Pett Bottom, where, with a fine disregard for health, he ate steak and kidney pie or pork sausages. In the evenings he visited John Blackwell's house in the grounds of Wellesley House school at Broadstairs. A more unlikely companion it would be hard to imagine: Blackwell was a bachelor schoolmaster who made no secret of his loathing of women in general, and of Ann in particular. But his fourth-form humour made Ian laugh and, more importantly, he seemed to want nothing in return. At Blackwell's house Ian played bridge in a foursome that included John Brooker, another master, and Hilary Bray, who lived nearby and was no mean golfer himself. Blackwell recalled how the wife of the school gardener used to cook their supper (invariably something from the nursery menu Ian liked). On Sunday afternoons he piled a few pupils into his Volvo estate car and drove to a particular spot by the eighth hole at St George's. While they exercised his dog, he played a rapid eleven holes with Ian. The boys were always excited to meet Ian, and he responded by giving

Blackwell coins and other memorabilia which provided suitable props for Bond-style bedtime stories.

Before long Ian was boasting that the Fleming three-day week had turned into the Fleming two-day week – defined as spending at least four days and five nights in the country. Since Tuesday was the only day on which St George's did not provide lunch, Ian would drive up to London on Tuesday morning (often after having taken morning coffee at the club), sign a few letters under Griffie's watchful eye at Mitre Court, and return to Sandwich in time for lunch on Thursday.

Even the clouds on the horizon seemed innocuous that summer. When the Russians attacked James Bond as a dangerous imperialist creation, Ian tried to incorporate their critique into his publicity. Encouraged by the brouhaha surrounding *Dr No*, an ill-informed article in *Izvestia* on 29 May described Ian as a tool of American propaganda. It mentioned his friendship with Allen Dulles, recycling a line which Ian himself had peddled to a *New York Herald Tribune* reporter earlier in the year – that the CIA director had tried out a couple of his ideas but had found them not to work. (Ian had jokingly called this "a strong indictment of the CIA". Asked later to elaborate on which particular ideas the CIA had tried, Ian mentioned the "Homer" device with which Bond kept track of Goldfinger's movements. He claimed he had read the idea originally in a comic called *How to Be a Detective*.) For *Izvestia*, however, "American propagandists must be in a bad way if they need recourse to the help of an English freebooter – a retired spy turned mediocre writer." Ian wanted to use the article on the jacket of his next book, but later thought better.

Apparently refreshed and ready again for the long-distance matrimonial race, Ian agreed to take Ann to her favourite city of Venice in early June. At the Hotel Bauer Grünwald, she hoped that her husband would continue taking things quietly. But she had not reckoned with his meeting Count Paul Munster, an old White's golfing partner from the 1930s, who introduced him not only to the lush greens of the best local course, the Alberoni, but also to life with the continental jet set which, to Ann's astonishment, he seemed to relish. No longer able to concentrate on her cultural pursuits, she was forced to career around the waterways in a speedboat, a mode of transport she found frightening and boring. Ian quickly wore himself out, and old tensions were already beginning to surface when the Flemings bumped into Denis Hamilton and his wife Olive. Ian did not improve matters when, in response to Ann's complaint about having to discipline Caspar, he noted waspishly that Olive had four sons and coped very well.

The Flemings returned via Chamonix in the French Alps where, in his quest for exotic plants and birds, Ann's father, Guy, was holidaying with his wife Vi. Ian and Ann had only intended to stay one night but remained for four – the result of the unlikely friendship Ian struck up with the Charterises' companion, a fellow naturalist, Cyril Mackworth-Praed. The others were mystified how this happened. Mackworth-Praed, a crack shot and crusty disciplinarian, was known for making his way to bed each night on the dot of 10.30 p.m. But Ian managed to keep him up until the small hours and would only say that his new drinking partner "knew many interesting facts". It transpired that Mackworth-Praed's closest friend was Colonel Richard Meinertzhagen, the soldier, naturalist and spy, whose family had owned Mottisfont Abbey in Hampshire before the Russells. Meinertzhagen had written about his military exploits in *Kenya Diary* and about his great love of birds in a number of books including *Birds of Arabia*. Ian's physical incapacity had increased his admiration for this Bond-type of man of action. Meinertzhagen – described by Malcolm Muggeridge as "a legendary figure without a legend" – became one of Ian's latter-day heroes.

Conceived with the best possible intentions, the holiday crudely highlighted the continuing problems in the Flemings' marriage. Matters came to a head once more over Caspar's behaviour. In a letter to Evelyn Waugh, Ann referred in indulgent tones to her son, now nearly ten, firing his catapult at a party of rich trippers arriving at Sandwich from Goodwood by helicopter. Although equally culpable, Ian blamed his wife for spoiling their son and tolerating his "nauseating" bad manners. "You say that I should impose my authority. I cannot when you abrogate the position of father as well as mother and when Nanny abets you." This not untypical family row masked another cause of friction – Ann's growing concern about Hugh Gaitskell's health. Just at the moment when the Leader of the Opposition looked certain to become Prime Minister at the next general election, the rheumatic pains in his shoulder returned and in June he alarmed his advisers by temporarily blacking out. For Ann, who was already apprehensive about the state of Ian's heart, it was an impossible situation. The two most important men in her life were shadows of their former selves. It is not surprising she was difficult to live with.

Finding the cumulative stress overwhelming, Ian opted at short notice to take an unprecedented mid-July holiday on his own in Jamaica. Uncertain whether Blanche was even on the island, he cabled her that he was coming and invited her to join him on a "honeymoon". En route to New York he composed a sad, stark letter to Ann on BOAC notepaper: "There is so little to be said – or so much. The arguments we have had over the years, our different points of view, are stale – however valid they may be on one side or another. The point lies in only one area. Do we want to go on living together or do we not?" Ian felt they had been hurting each other "to an extent that makes life hardly bearable". More than anything, he needed to "have a rest from it all – and regain some spirit, which, though you haven't noticed it, is slipping out of me through my boots". Staying at the Pierre Hotel in New York, he elaborated in a cable: "AM SO SHATTERED BY YOUR ENDLESS WOUNDING COMPLAINTS THAT I NEED TIME TO REST AND REFLECT ON OUR FUTURE WHICH AT PRESENT LOOKS INTOLERABLE STOP IN MY PRESENT MOOD I WOULD BE NO COMFORT IN YOUR DISTRESS WHICH SOUNDS EQUAL TO MINE STOP." Another short letter from Jamaica only emphasized his impotent suffering: "But for my love for you and Caspar I would welcome the freedom that you threaten me with. It has all been getting worse and worse and I knew this year would be decisive. Either we survive it or we don't. There is no one else in my life. There is a whole cohort in yours. I am lonely, jealous and ill. Leave me my pleasures as I leave you yours. Above all have compassion."

Ian was not being quite truthful. He still had Blanche who, by her own admission, was happy to drop everything whenever, as on this occasion, he called for her. On arriving at Goldeneye, Ian had told her that he had left his wife, and he might have stayed some time in Jamaica had not Ann responded to his melodramatic communication with a crude piece of emotional blackmail. She cabled saying that she was going into hospital for a serious operation. Ian was immediately plunged into consternation. Receiving Ann's message at nine o'clock one evening, he telephoned Blanche and asked her to come over straight away. He was certain Ann was lying, but Blanche convinced him that he should return nevertheless. If it turned out to be true, and something happened to Ann, he would never forgive himself, she said. With its hint of a rejection, Blanche's response, while consistent with her attitude to Ian, indicated that, for all her devotion, she realized that their relationship would never benefit from closer liaison, and certainly not from marriage.

While in Jamaica, Ian began another short story, named after *Octopussy*, the boat Blanche had given to Goldeneye. This was a taut account of a British wartime commando officer, Major Dexter Smythe, first observed living indolently on the north coast of Jamaica where his greatest pleasure is communing with the marine life, particularly his 'pet' octopus, the eponymous Octopussy. His peace is disturbed by the arrival of James Bond with awkward questions about the disappearance of a ski instructor at a time when Smythe worked for the Miscellaneous Objectives Bureau (MOB) in Austria in the latter stages of the Second World War. Bond skilfully prises Smythe's story out of him: that he had forced the ski instructor to take him to the site of a hidden hoard of Nazi gold before killing him. When Bond gives him ten minutes to think over his twenty-year-old war crime Smythe takes his own life in a bizarre manner: he allows himself to be stung by the poisonous scorpion fish which is Octopussy's favourite food. The story had little significance, save that it brought together three of Ian's favourite themes – the mountains around Kitzbühel (he even mentioned Mittersill), the exotic fish of Jamaica, and the hectic activity of commando groups in Austria and southern Germany at the end of the war (MOB – note the acronym – was very similar to Fleming's own 30 AU).

On his return to London, Ian's first social event was a preview of the film *Dr No* at a private cinema in Soho, followed by dinner with Ann at the Travellers' Club at the invitation of the director, Terence Young. But Ian did not enjoy himself, looking sad and distracted as he tried to summon enthusiasm for the carefree, gun-toting character he had created on the screen.

Afterwards Ian felt unable to face the Italian summer holiday Ann had arranged at Auberon Herbert's house in Portofino. While she was away, and he was back among his friends at Sandwich, he took the opportunity to try to settle a matter which had been troubling him and contributing to the clouds over his relationship with Ann. "For a thousand reasons I would like to make peace with you," he wrote fawningly to Lord Beaverbrook, "not the least being that Annie wants this too." Getting to his point, he continued, "I was shocked and distressed when the strong and friendly shoulder of your newspapers, on which I had leaned for so many years, was removed from me and I was completely bewildered as to the reasons why I should suddenly have caused you so much displeasure." Ian rightly concluded that it must have been something to do with 'The Living Daylights' appearing in the inaugural *Sunday Times* magazine in February without being offered to the *Express*. He tried to explain that, as a member of the "editorial board" of the *Sunday Times*, he was constantly urged to write for the paper. He had done "practically nothing" since his "Thrilling Cities" series two years before. He claimed he had never imagined that Beaverbrook might feel that the Express Group had first call on his services, particularly after rejecting *The Spy Who Loved Me* for serialization.

Ian told Beaverbrook that his publishers on both sides of the Atlantic were already describing his latest book, *On Her Majesty's Secret Service*, as his best yet. Would the *Express* like to see it with a view to serialization, the salesman in him could not help asking? But whatever the answer, Ian begged his erstwhile friend to send him "a message of forgiveness for what I assure you was a totally unwitting act of ungraciousness". He again expressed heartfelt apologies for having offended Beaverbrook.

Ian's facility for abasing himself did the trick. Beaverbrook replied that, as far as he was concerned, there had never been any conflict. When 'The Living Daylights' appeared in the *Sunday Times*, he said, the *Daily Express* had 'naturally' taken the view that Ian "had given notice of change of allegiance". But that was all in the past. Beaverbrook called on Ian to forget the matter and, even better, followed this up with a request to send the *Express* his new novel. Having grovelled once, Ian could do it again. "Thank you a thousand times for your enchanting letter which has removed a heavy cloud from my horizon," he replied.

With Ann still in Italy, Ian also wrote an introduction to a biography of his friend Sir William Stephenson which was due to be serialized in the *Sunday Times*. The book had originally been started by an SIS officer, Charles Ellis, who was unable to complete it because he was writing an official history of the Service. The work devolved on Montgomery Hyde, a professional writer who had been a wartime censorship officer attached to BSC, and who, without being able to reveal details of secret Ultra intelligence, was able to make Stephenson's story more interesting and readable. Ian's few hundred words confirmed the greatness of 'The Quiet Canadian', as the book was called in Britain, and, like his Bond books, helped enhance the myth of the invincibility of British Intelligence at a time, shortly after George Blake's arrest and before Kim Philby's defection, when morale was at its lowest. When the proposed serialization did not take place as scheduled in September, Ian informed Stephenson that the delay had occurred because the paper needed to publish the memoirs of the maverick politician Robert Boothby earlier than planned. Equally important, however, was dissent within the SIS about the nature of some of the revelations. Hyde made much of the seduction of Italy's naval attaché to the United States and the subsequent stealing of an Italian naval cipher book by a BSC spy code-named Cynthia. It was not long before the Italian government was complaining, as predicted, that this had been bad form in what was then a neutral country.

The book gave Ian an excuse to fly to New York almost as soon as Ann returned from her Italian holiday – described by him as "sporting herself with a lot of dons and Hugh Gaitskell". Ostensibly he went to liaise directly with Stephenson. But the trip coincided with Blanche Blackwell being in town, albeit on a painful mission, as her much-loved brother Roy had recently collapsed and died there. Ian's way of showing support was to come over without being asked, and to help her arrange for Roy's body to be transported home for his funeral. Otherwise he was undemonstrative: in Blanche's words: "He knew my family is very important to me, so when Roy died, he didn't write but simply flew to New York. Then he telephoned and asked me over to his hotel. He didn't say anything. That was his way of showing he cared." Although she only saw Ian three times on that trip, his simple act of solidarity touched her deeply. Their affectionate friendship seemed to work because of an enduring mutual admiration. An example occurred on this trip when he asked her to find him two hundred Player's cigarettes. Still happy to do anything he demanded, she traipsed all over Manhattan, eventually finding a carton on the Lower East side.

Ian was most impressed when she arrived for lunch, clutching the right package. "How the hell did you do that?" he asked brusquely, but with genuine respect. She in turn was touched that, on this occasion as on all others, he was waiting for her in the restaurant at the appointed time. Whatever his business, wherever they were, she could always rely on him to be somewhere at the exact time he had stated.

Shortly afterwards, Blanche was still in New York when she suddenly felt an urge to telephone Ian, who had returned to London. After the Waldorf Astoria refused to let her call because she was not a resident, she went to Grand Central Station. Standing in a booth, waiting to be connected, she noticed, without paying much attention, a low-slung sports car standing on a dais in the main concourse. When she got through, Ian told her nonchalantly that he was leafing through a brochure for a new car. He explained that, after seven years of trouble-free motoring with Thunderbirds, he felt he needed a change. Since he always appreciated a mixture of American mechanical reliability and European styling, he said that he had ordered "a bomb of a motor", a supercharged black Studebaker Avanti, as designed by Raymond Loewy, the Frenchman who had developed his favourite Studillac. It had black leather upholstery, electrically powered windows and was capable of well over 100 m.p.h. At that moment Blanche looked out of the booth and saw that the car being presented to the world on the dais was the selfsame model, an Avanti.

Splashing out on a car (shortly after his trips to Jamaica and New York) reflected Ian's new-found affluence as the proceeds from his film deal began to accumulate. The purchase also indicated his restlessness as he sensed more strongly, a year or so after his heart attack, that he did not have long to live. He began thinking of other possible adventures, telling Plomer in mid-September. "I am feeling tremendously stuck in an over mink-lined rut and I need to be booted off across the world in old style."

His solution was to return to the Orient which had so impressed him on his visit three years earlier. If he based his next Bond adventure in Japan, he felt he could justify a research trip. Hoping to recreate the camaraderie of his previous visit, he prevailed on Denis Hamilton to allow Dick Hughes a couple of weeks off to accompany him – at Glidrose's expense. Hughes arranged for his journalist friend Tiger Saito to come along as well. Ian then wrote to Hughes outlining his plot and the sights he wanted to visit as his fictional backdrop. He promised his friend a role in his book: "There will be a male foreigner in the old Japanese castle and it will be James Bond's task to bring him to book, with the help of Tiger as the head of the Japanese secret service. You, Dikko, will be Australia's secret service chief in Tokyo." Hughes joked – in a frequently recurring theme – that they were a sort of religious brotherhood, seeking "spiritual inspiration and carnal folklore".

The official premiere of *Dr No* in October delayed Ian slightly. At the first-night party at the Milroy, Ian again seemed a curiously detached, almost superfluous presence on the edges of a noisy gathering where confident movie moguls were being fêted for their professional brilliance. Ian had finally achieved one of his life's ambitions, and audiences thought they were getting the last word in sophisticated entertainment, but his literary responsibility for this celluloid extravaganza was almost forgotten, and, in a curious way, he was rather relieved. So it was with mixed emotions that he left for Tokyo in mid-November, clutching several books that Plomer, an old Japan hand, had pressed upon him to read about the country. Hughes and Saito were waiting to meet him at the airport where he was whisked through customs and immigration as an international celebrity. He played the part, puffing at his Morland cigarettes, carrying an expensive-looking shooting-stick as he now needed to take occasional rests during his sight-seeing, and wearing, of course, his uniform of light-weight blue suit and polka dot bow-tie.

That first night the three musketeers relaxed in a huge bath drinking sake. As a precursor of what was to come, Hughes, knowing Ian's fondness for local espionage lore, took his guest to visit Ketels, the bar where the German-born communist spy Richard Sorge had extricated secrets from a crowd of raucous expatriate Nazis in the 1940s. Only the once lively and sinister *Bierkeller* had been transformed into a dreary up-market restaurant where diners ate to the pervasive sounds of Elvis Presley and Pat Boone. When Ian imperiously ordered the noise to be turned off, it was done immediately, and none of the customers seemed to notice.

As they travelled round the island in every sort of transport from aeroplanes to mulepacks, Hughes noted that Ian had an innate affinity for the minimalism of Japanese culture. He was also impressed by Ian's unending curiosity. The details of the Japanese ON system – the obligation to repay favours – fascinated him. Even while interviewing statesmen or, on one occasion, drinking turtle blood with Japanese secret policemen, Ian would ask the simplest, most disarming questions such as: What happens to all the cherries from the Japanese cherry trees? When, in the interests of research, the trio visited Mikmito's Island, Ian startled one of the young girls diving for pearls by lightly caressing her shoulder. "You must touch to get the precise texture of wet feminine skin," he explained. When Tiger Saito asked about a black girl's skin, Ian admitted he could not say. Each evening, before dinner, he would retire for a couple of hours to his room, where he poured himself a glass of bourbon and wrote up the day's events in his latest notebook.

After his exertion – playing the required part of the acerbic debonair newspaperman to perfection – Ian was so exhausted on his return to London that he needed two weeks' rest at Forest Mere health farm in Hampshire. Ann complained to Aline Berlin that he had been in no condition "to sojourn with the naked Japanese pearl diving girls of the Kyoto islands and share their simple diet". Before Ian left Tokyo, Hughes had had the curious feeling he was seeing his friend for the last time. His sense of foreboding was hardly allayed when he received a postcard from Ian in Jamaica informing him about the book's progress. As well as the usual protestations about the problems he was encountering, this time, in speculating again about the need to kill Bond off, Ian added an unprecedented mawkish note, "Anyway he's had a good run, which is more than most of us can say. Everything seems a lot of trouble these days – too much trouble. Keep alive." Hughes fired back an angry few lines asking what "this ridiculous 'keep alive' business" meant. The Australian cannot have been mollified by Ian's reply, "Dikko, I promise. Don't worry. I'm not worrying any more. Down with death."

Hughes did not know that, in the intervening period, Ian had had three close personal experiences of death. One was his great friend Duff Dunbar, the lazy, erudite Wedgwood collector with whom Ian liked to play draughts and guzzle chocolates in the cinema. He suffered from tinnitus and, when the din in his ears grew unbearable, he committed suicide. In a moving memoir, Ian emphasized his friend's humour, intelligence and love of golf. He did not deny there was a despairing side to his friend's character (Ian even brought up his favourite concept of accidie). But Duff only occasionally showed this in a throwaway phrase to a friend – "a phrase that he would at once cover up with some typical burst of high spirits designed, with an effort no doubt, to close the window quickly on his private feelings." Ian sent his tribute to *The Times*, but the newspaper declined to publish a piece which was interesting not just for its portrayal of an eccentric figure but also for its unusual insight into the personal qualities Ian admired. Duff Dunbar, he wrote, "saw through and out the other side of all people, human circumstances, relationships, his own career and even his hobbies".

Another death was Ian's sister-in-law Mary Rose, whose battle with alcohol finally ended a couple of days before Christmas (which the Flemings, as usual, spent at Shane's Castle in Ireland – with Peter Quennell once more in tow). The third was more complicated. On 18 January 1963 Hugh Gaitskell died at the Middlesex Hospital in London. His death came quickly from lupus erythematosus, a little-known immunological disease in which tissues are attacked by the antibodies circulating in the blood. Partly for ideological reasons and partly because he knew the consultant there, Gaitskell had initially been admitted in November to the trade-union-owned Manor House Hospital in north London. Throughout the cold pre-Christmas season Ann had worn herself out and infuriated Ian by dragging herself up to the other side of Hampstead to visit her admirer. (She was particularly tired because the Crickmeres had peremptorily given notice and she was having to indoctrinate an emotional Spanish couple into the domestic rituals of Victoria Square.) Gaitskell seemed to improve over Christmas which allowed Ann to repair to Shane's. But in the New Year his condition deteriorated and he was transferred to a teaching hospital, the Middlesex. This put Ann in a double quandary. She wanted to see Gaitksell, but felt it was wrong to embarrass his wife, Dora, by appearing publicly at his bedside. And there was also her own husband to think of: before leaving for Jamaica – as usual ahead of her – he had been officially told by his doctor that he had five years at the most to live. Ann clearly felt she had a duty to be at Ian's side.

Eventually she made the heart-breaking decision to follow her husband. But when Gaitskell wrote to say she was the only person he wanted to see, she resolved to visit him the day before she left for the Caribbean. At the hospital, however, Dora was there and Ann decided not to force herself into his room. Even at the last minute she thought of feigning illness to avoid having to travel. But, as she told her brother Hugo, that would have broken Ian and drained for ever what little confidence he still had in human nature.

When she arrived in Jamaica she was disconsolate. Ian told her to pull herself together: he had only married her because she had the heart of a drum majorette. She poured her heart out in a letter to Hugo, who himself was in hospital with gall-bladder problems. "I am totally unhappy and stunned by Hugh G's condition. A cable arrived this minute to say 'dangerously ill and no improvement': for six years he has given me a great bonus of love and support and over this time my love for him has become very considerable indeed: a good man and even more honourable politician than people supposed – in fact totally and rarely honourable. It was an agonising decision to come here with Ian, but I could not see him [Gaitskell], could only leave letters with go-betweens and pray he would recover – it seems only a miracle if this now happens." Even as she wrote, Gaitskell had probably succumbed to his illness. He died two days after Ann had made her last attempt to see him.

So Ann lost a pillar of stability. She never felt that Gaitskell was the love of her life. She was always clear that that position was reserved for Ian: indeed, she told R. A. Butler's wife Mollie exactly this shortly after Gaitskell's death. Her warm friendship with Gaitskell reflected her intelligence and interest in the lighter side of public affairs. According to their mutual friend, Roy Jenkins, choosing his words carefully, "She was flattered by his interest in her and very interested in him; he added an important dimension in her life and she to some extent depended on him."

Ironically Ann discovered that Ian's physical condition had improved considerably during his short period in Jamaica. After the death of a prized Alsatian, he had asked Violet to get him "a good mutt". She had returned with a lively brown bitch called Bimbo, who later gave birth to a black son, Satan, both of whom provided Ian with much amusement. In an interview with Doug Campbell of the local newspaper, the *Daily Gleaner*, Ian sounded almost beatific. He said that, as far as he was concerned, the colour problem did not exist, and as for the Cold War, he predicted that the two superpowers were so evenly matched that "they will finally decide to call the game off and we shall all be able to settle down and not worry about it any more". Ann wondered if she ought not to have stayed in London after all. Ian "only goes mad if he sees my relations and friends", she told Hugo with grim understanding.

Enjoying better health, Ian overcame his low spirits to produce one of his most entertaining books. As he had promised, Hughes metamorphosed into Dikko Henderson, local station chief of the Australian SIS and Saito was Tiger Tanaka, boss of the Japanese intelligence service. ("I'll sue you if you lampoon me," Hughes had told Fleming. "You do that and I'll tell the truth about you," replied Ian with his privileged inside information.) He resurrected Shatterhand, a name he had jotted down in his notebook when he visited Hamburg four years earlier, as an alias for his villain, Ernst Blofeld. The first part of the book drew heavily on the travelogue set pieces which he had accumulated in Japan. While intelligently exploring aspects of Japanese culture, Ian also told an old-fashioned morality tale, with Bond as the force of good fighting Blofeld, the epitome of evil, in his island-bound castle. Once again Bond was portrayed as St George rescuing a maiden (in this case, the pert Kissy Suzuki) from the clutches of the dragon. Ian even managed to develop this as a cross-cultural point of reference, with Tiger Tanaka remarking that the idea of "that foolish dragon dozing all unsuspecting in his castle while St George comes silently riding towards his lair across the waves" would make an entertaining Japanese print.

Towards the end of the novel, Bond went missing, presumed dead. M issued an obituary which filled in several details of 007's early life. (Having been thrown out of Eton for some incident with a girl, he went to the Scottish equivalent, Fettes, for example. With his attention to detail, Ian later asked his former NID colleague, Commander Sandy Glen, an Old Fettesian, to look over the obituary. Glen said it was fine, except he thought Fettes might be described as a British rather than an English public school.) Ian took the opportunity to poke fun at himself in the obituary. Referring to the popular books which had been written round the career of the supposedly dead Bond, the notice added, "If the quality of these books, or their degree of veracity, had been any higher, the author would certainly have been prosecuted under the Official Secrets Act."

By the end of February Ian was sending a breezy "end of term report" to Plomer about his "opus XII". He admitted he was not sure what Arthur Waley, the doyen of Oriental scholars, would have made of it. But he thought even his friend would glean some Japanese esoterica from it. "After all, when was it the last English novel about Japan was written? Just to give you an advance frisson, Bondo-san is about to pleasure Kissy Suzuki after she has stimulated his senses with toad's sweat, a well known Japanese aphrodisiac, as of course you know."

Such rampant heterosexuality was a long way from the mincing world which Cyril Connolly created in his unconvincing parody of Bond, which appeared in the *London Magazine* on Ian's return to England in April 1963. It was ironic that Ian's work should become a literary talking-point in this way. *Bond Strikes Camp* was based on the premise that spying was the preserve of homosexuals, so Bond needed to dress up in drag in order to penetrate a Homintern subculture in search of a traitor who turned out to be M. The sketch was supposed to work on two levels: it lampooned the duplicitous, often sexually ambivalent world of espionage (the saga of the Missing Diplomats had taken a new turn with the disappearance of Kim Philby from Beirut in January), while giving voice to the often quietly held view that, for all his apparent machismo, Bond was actually rather camp.

Friends of Connolly, like Alan Ross, the editor of the *London Magazine*, insist that he wrote his parody as a joke. But this was not the impression of American critic Edmund Wilson when he attended Connolly's sixtieth birthday celebration later in the year. Connolly told him that when the Flemings had come to a reading at his house in Sussex the previous autumn, Ann had laughed, but Ian remained impassive and, at the end, offered him £100 for the manuscript, which Connolly, always strapped for cash, eagerly accepted. Connolly seemed disappointed that Ian had not created a scene. He admitted "he had thought it would expose him [i.e. Ian] to himself – 'his adolescent fantasies' – humiliate him, devastate him". But, instead, Ian had reacted, Wilson noted, "like a whale being nibbled at by a little fish". As Ian (or, strictly speaking, Glidrose) bought the manuscript on 18 October, this enabled him to suggest slight amendments before its publication. The *London Magazine* came out at the same time as the *Sunday Times* let Raymond Mortimer, its principal literary critic, loose on *On Her Majesty's Secret Service*. Mortimer waxed eloquent on Ian's skill and craftsmanship in creating a "culture-hero" – "James Bond is what every man would like to be, and what every woman would like between her sheets. But only in their daydreams." Ian claimed to prefer the Connolly treatment. He cabled his friend, "IT IS AN INTOXICATING PRIVILEGE TO BE PEDESTALLED BY RAYMOND AND PILLORIED BY YOU ON THE SAME WEEKEND STOP

YOUR MINKEN LASHES TINGLE MORE EXQUISITELY THAN THE SPOONFULS OF
TIPTREE LITTLE SCARLET IAN". (Tiptree 'Little Scarlet' was the trade name of
the strawberry jam favoured by Bond, though the telegram could be read
as coming from Little Scarlet Ian.) When Christopher Isherwood read *Bond
Strikes Camp* he told Connolly he was "a second-to-none Fleming fan"
and had read all his books twice. Nevertheless he felt Bond had this
coming to him. "I have several times resented his attitude to the Minority
to which I have the honour to belong. And how exquisitely you do it."
Despite Bond's distaste for homosexuals – "a herd of unhappy sexual
misfits – barren and full of frustrations" – a view very similar to his
author's, some of Ian's best friends, including Noël Coward and William
Plomer, were gay.

He had arranged to lunch with Plomer when he returned to London.
But when the day approached he was unable to keep the appointment
because, as he apologized to his friend, he had "had a squawk from Mama
in Monte Carlo". Mrs Val's aged paramour, the Marquess of Winchester,
had died the previous June at the age of ninety-nine (another in the long
catalogue of mortalities). Now she wanted to visit London and needed her
son to accompany her home. Ian liked the idea of calling on his friend
Graham Sutherland at his house in Menton and he needed to collect some
photographs of Monte Carlo for the forthcoming book version of 'Thrilling
Cities'.

It turned out to be rather more than he bargained for. Mama was living
in a flat in the grounds of the Hotel Metropole in Monte Carlo. Each day
she would stroll down the hill to the main hotel to take her meals. But
she was not allowed by her doctors to walk back. So her ten-year-old Rolls-
Royce would wait to transport her on the 200-yard journey. With old age,
her mind had become rather befuddled, particularly on the thorny old
topic of money: she believed she no longer had any (after paying off some
of the Marquess's debts) and that Ian and his brothers had plenty. After
she hired him a basic room in the basement of the hotel annexe, he felt
unable to move out into something more comfortable because this would
confirm her not wholly mistaken idea that he was very rich and might
even lead her to disinherit him. If this was not exactly a repeat of scenes
which had taken place thirty or more years earlier, it was similar. And
there was an element of *déjà vu*, too, in the journey Mrs Val planned for
herself and her son. As Ian discovered on the morning of their departure,
they were scheduled to share a sleeper and a picnic dinner consisting of a
partridge and half a bottle of vin de pays. Not having the tenacity Rupert
Hart-Davis had shown during his train journey with Eve in 1929, he
arranged the wagons-lits equivalent of an upgrade. But he had to carry
her jewel case and gall-bladder X-rays, while arranging porters for her
fourteen cabin trunks.

With Mama safely ensconced in London, Ian escaped to Istanbul to watch the filming of *From Russia, With Love*. He was present when – to the horror of the film crew – five hundred rats pursuing Bond down a Turkish sewer contrived to break loose. In a nightclub, where the erotic gyrations of a belly-dancer knocked the ash off the end of his cigarette, he remarked that, after a lifetime of observation, he had concluded that buttocks rather than breasts were the most beautiful feature of a woman's anatomy. If Ian was having a good time at the expense of his movie producers, he also had sound financial reasons for being there. For tax reasons the proceeds of his deal with Eon Productions were paid to him under a service contract which allowed that, as long as his services were performed abroad, and he did not bring his 5-per-cent fee into the United Kingdom, he did not have to pay tax on it. Instead he kept it in an account at the Ansbacher Bank in Dublin. Typically, when he returned home to London, he complained about the shortage of caviare in Istanbul.

A week later the so-called Profumo scandal broke, and Ian's friend John Profumo was forced to resign his post as Minister of War after finally admitting that he had shared a young mistress called Christine Keeler with a Russian diplomat and spy. In one way or another, several of Ian's friends were involved on the fringes of the affair, not least Eric Dudley who had wanted to marry Keeler's friend, Mandy Rice-Davis. Profumo's dramatic admission of his guilt provided a topical subject for discussion at Ian's lunch the very same day with Allen Dulles, who had resigned his post as CIA chief in September 1961, after being forced to take the blame for the Bay of Pigs disaster. Dulles had just embarked on a CIA-supported career as an author (his first book, *The Craft of Intelligence*, was shortly to be published) – and wanted to swap tips with Ian. This paid dividends for Ian because, a few days later, Dulles addressed the annual gathering of the American Booksellers' Association. When Victor Weybright reported back to Ian how Dulles had said that the CIA needed half a dozen James Bonds, Ian remarked that he was glad to see that his Agent 008 was doing his stuff.

Further evidence of Ian's celebrity status came in three unrelated events that summer. At Oxford University, some enterprising undergraduates had set up a James Bond Club. Pledging themselves to try live up to the standards of their hero, the founder members of this august institution were Jonathan Aitken, Beaverbrook's great-nephew and later a minister in John Major's government, and Mark Lennox-Boyd, son of the politician who had arranged Ian's visit to the Seychelles, and who would also become a Member of Parliament. The club elected the university's nearest equivalent to a Bond girl. She was Joanna Hare, nineteen-year-old daughter of John Hare, the then Minister of Labour, who had known Ian since the 1930s.

Across the Atlantic at Harvard University, the two editors of the under-graduate monthly, *Harvard Lampoon*, wrote the first full-length spoof Bond novel, called *Alligator*. One of them, Christopher Cerf, had a familiar name, as he was the son of the New York publisher Bennett Cerf who had once shown an interest in publishing *Live and Let Die*. So similar to a Bond novel did *Alligator* look that New American Library, Ian's American pub-lisher, forced the *Lampoon* to limit its edition to 100,000 copies, still a sizeable number.

Finally, in June, Ian was asked to appear on the BBC radio programme *Desert Island Discs*, then as now considered an accolade. A couple of months earlier he had turned down an invitation from the BBC to talk about Jack Kennedy, who it assumed was a close friend. Then Ian had decided against trading on his limited personal knowledge of the United States President. This time, however, he was happy to travel to Broad-casting House to earn twenty-five guineas discussing his favourite records. He arrived an hour before the recording to mull over his selection with the presenter Roy Plomley. If Ian was going through a difficult time, one would not have known it from his music. He put together a superlative selection of popular twentieth-century tunes from 'Does Your Mother Know You're Out, Cecilia' by Whispering Jack Smith, which he described as a great favourite at Eton, to Joe 'Fingers' Carr's more recent 'Darktown Strutters Ball', which he said would be his choice if he were only allowed one record – "this tremendous racket would keep the ghosts away". At the end he thanked Plomley, and added, "I hope it wasn't too light-hearted."

By then the critics had had their say about *On Her Majesty's Secret Service*. There was a perceptible sigh of relief when they discovered that Ian had dropped the "experimentation" of Vivienne Michel's tortured memoir and returned to Bond's winning ways. Ian was only annoyed to discover he had made several silly mistakes. Paddy Leigh Fermor pointed out that Pol Roger was the only champagne not produced in half bottles. In his otherwise friendly review in the *Sunday Times*, Raymond Mortimer noted curtly that Ian Fleming used to be so accurate. "It is really ghastly," Ian told Michael Howard. "I have never made so many mistakes in a book in my life."

This made no difference to the success of the book. Not only did Cape arrange life-size models of James Bond, complete with gun, to be prominently displayed in branches of W. H. Smith, it also promoted a competition to find the best Bond-related bookshop window in Britain. Eon helped with a lavish press briefing during the filming of *From Russia, With Love* at Pinewood Studios. By the time of publication, *On Her Majesty's Secret Service* had received nearly a quarter more subscriptions than any previous Fleming novel (that is, 42,000 advance orders for the hardback edition, compared with 33,000 for *Thunderball*, its nearest rival, and only

28,000 for the previous book, *The Spy Who Loved Me*). With the help of an immediate reprint of 15,000 copies, Cape had published over 60,000 copies by the end of April.

Meanwhile in North America, Ann Marlow, the producer who had tried to kick-start Ian's film career, had recovered after his embarrassed extrication from his deal with her, and was still working hard on his behalf. Having won the backing of Phyllis Jackson, she was soon devising a project with Hollywood producer Norman Felton. In many respects this was a throw-back to seven years earlier when Ian discussed Commander James Gunn with Henry Morgenthau. The idea was that Ian should write a series of Bond-like stories for television, involving a more credibly North American character called Napoleon Solo. By May, they were talking money, which Ian agreed was good. After a lot of thinking, however, he decided not to go ahead. As he told Phyllis Jackson, any plots he might think up he "desperately" needed for James Bond. The series would require long trips to California which his doctors would not like. "But above all, I think it would be almost impossible to avoid a similarity with the Bond character. Although this might not come to a legal issue, the appearance of a Fleming television series before the Bond series would certainly create bad blood between me and Eon Productions, which is the last thing I want to happen. Moreover, I am advised that a Fleming television series would inevitably do harm to the Bond series scheduled for two or three years from now."

Within a month Ian had written to Felton. Understanding rather more now the problems that can arise from misunderstandings about film deals, and taking a leaf out of Ernie Cuneo's book, he penned a formal letter to Felton at MGM Studios in Culver City, California. "This will serve as my assignment to you of all my rights and interest in any material written or contributed by me in connection with an original television series featuring a character named Napoleon Solo. I assign to you all rights of every kind to the use of this character and material ... I hereby acknowledge receipt of the sum of One Pound (£1) in consideration of this assignment."

As he waited patiently in Kent for the inevitable wrench of the move to Sevenhampton, Ian put the finishing touches to *You Only Live Twice*. The signs of a balmy Kentish summer are to be found in Bond's obituary which referred to his youth at a cottage near the "attractive" Duck Inn in "the quaintly named hamlet of Pett Bottom near Canterbury". Hoping to run *The Times's* masthead over the obituary, Ian asked his brother Peter whom he should write to at the newspaper. When Peter said he no longer knew anyone at *The Times*, Ian contacted the company secretary who tried to put him off with the reply that he would have to ask Buckingham Palace, as the Crown only permitted the use of this particular coat of arms on material published by the paper itself.

Peter himself was an additional worry for Ian. In recent years their relationship had improved considerably. No longer were there grounds for rivalry based on professional jealousy. Ian had proved himself a much more successful writer than his brother, and if not quite as deftly ironic, certainly as competent. Indeed one of the ironies of Ian's position was that he was now the fêted professional writer, while Peter had remained a dilettante. Part of the annual ritual of the Bond novels now was the stage when Ian sent his manuscript to "Dr Knittpik", and from Merrimoles Peter would write back with a list of mistakes which had eluded the sharp eyes of Plomer and other readers. From time to time the two brothers would dine at one of their clubs (Peter was a member of the Garrick) and the Fleming family recollection is that, whenever they met, they were usually laughing at some private joke. Even Celia Fleming, never a great fan of Ian's, admitted that, following his heart attack, he became very much nicer.

Towards the end of the previous year, however, Peter had discovered a lump on his neck. When it was removed at a local nursing-home in January 1963, it was diagnosed not only as cancerous but also as a secondary growth. However, a battery of tests could find no further malignancy, so, to everyone's relief, including Ian's, Peter was pronounced free of the disease.

Further revision to *You Only Live Twice* was enlivened by the comments of Ed (E. L.) Doctorow, a new editor at New American Library and later a best-selling novelist. He had mixed opinions: the first half (with all its scene-setting) was too slow and Bond's character was not skilfully developed. "It is as if Bond's sadness and apathy had affected Fleming," wrote Doctorow in a sentence that might have been more insightful if the two names had been inter-changed. On the other hand, he felt "Fleming is constitutionally unable to write a dull sentence" and the book could easily be improved by some changes in construction. He particularly recommended the introduction of Blofeld, the villain, at a much earlier stage. Fleming was interested to read Doctorow's comments, but was not prepared to do the radical rewriting required: 'Apart from detailed corrections, I have never had the stomach to go back to one of my books once I have got it off my chest".

Ian continued to fire off feature ideas to the *Sunday Times*. Texan oil fire-fighters, salvaging the *Titanic* and the first solo climb of the Eiger: they rolled from his typewriter in letters to Denis Hamilton. But his only serious writing was a new story commissioned for Sotheby's yearbook, *The Ivory Hammer*, by a young auctioneer, Michel Strauss, the son of Ann's friend, Aline Berlin. 'The Property of a Lady' was an inconsequential tale about

Bond unmasking the head of the KGB in London by bidding against him
in a Sotheby's auction for an emerald sphere made by the Russian imperial
jeweller Carl Fabergé. Like Bond doing his office paperwork at the start of
the story, Ian found the task boring. He enlisted the help of Fabergé expert
Kenneth Snowman of the jeweller Wartski. But he never became fired up
about the project and eventually wrote to Peter Wilson, the chairman of
Sotheby's, saying he would not accept payment for what was a lacklustre
effort.

Ian's only other commitment was the lavish summer exhibition, 'Printing and the Mind of Man', at Earls Court and Olympia. For several months,
the organizers negotiated with him about using part of his collection of
first editions to illustrate a general theme of the influence of books on
thinking and the material world. Ian's own volumes had to be disinterred
from the vaults of the Pantechnicon in Motcomb Street where, because of
the limited space available in Victoria Square, they continued to be stored.
Eventually forty-four of his books were shown in the exhibition, by far
the largest contribution from a private individual. Ian was invited to serve
on the event's Committee of Honour. Not normally given to honorific
posts, he accepted this one with alacrity. When the exhibition catalogue
was published, with fulsome reference to himself, Ian was even more
thrilled. "A THOUSAND CONGRATULATIONS," he cabled Percy Muir, "ON YOUR
WONDERFUL CATALOGUE AND PARTICULARLY ON HAVING ELEVATED OUR COL-
LECTION TO THESE FANTASTICALLY PROUD HEIGHTS STOP I TRULY BLUSH WITH
EMBARRASSED DELIGHT AND WARM WITH MEMORIES OF THOSE DAYS WHEN YOU
TOOK ME BY THE HAND STOP GRUESS DICH GOTT IAN." When Ian attended the
exhibition's opening, however, Barbara Muir was shocked to notice that
he "looked like death, time-worn and gaunt". But then "Ian always was a
death-wish Charlie", she later reflected.

Halfway through July, after four years of building, waiting and frustration,
the Flemings finally moved into their new house at Sevenhampton. The
first names in the visitors' book were Raymond O'Neill and his wife
Georgina. But even now the work was incomplete. The grounds were full
of workmen who infuriated Ann by retreating into their huts whenever it
rained. She tried to show an example by scurrying into the garden during
cloudbursts and weeding ostentatiously. Ian's spirits were hardly boosted
by news of the death of another close friend, Hugo Pitman, on 25 July. In
a note to Hilary Bray, he adopted unfamiliar shooting parlance: "Friends
dwindle rapidly at our age, and Duff and Hugo were a bad left and right."

Neither Ian nor Ann was too dismayed when it was time for a summer
break. With an assignment from the *Sunday Times* to interview one of his
writing heroes, Georges Simenon, in Switzerland, Ian booked a fortnight

for himself and his family at the expensive Montreux Palace Hotel on Lake Geneva. Having driven ahead in his new Avanti, he was joined by Ann, who travelled by train with Caspar and his cousin Francis Grey who, following the death of his mother, Mary Rose, now became an almost permanent member of the general entourage.

When he finally made his way to Simenon's Château d'Echandens, outside Lausanne, Ian was in defiant holiday mode, dressed in casual slacks, well-worn blue sports shirt and woollen cardigan. He willingly accepted a whisky from a liveried servant and, whatever his doctors might have said, smoked throughout the meeting. His relaxed approach extended to his questioning. He compared Simenon to Balzac, contrasting, as he used to do with Chandler, the master's authentic novels of suspense with his own thrillers which were "a thing of action and no psychology". Ian claimed to have read fifty of Simenon's novels. One can imagine his now jowelly jaw dropping when Simenon admitted he had read none of Ian's. He had given up reading novels in 1928, preferring medical textbooks. One can also sense Ian's disappointment when he asked if Simenon had ever written about Switzerland. In his 'Thrilling Cities' article about Geneva, Ian had mentioned that "Switzerland has a Simenon quality, an atmosphere of still-water-running-deep, which is a great temptation to the writer of thrillers." But Maigret's creator said he never wrote about places he lived in. He needed to get away from them, which Ian obligingly agreed was the reason he liked to write in Jamaica: "I can only write in a vacuum," he said.

At the end of the fortnight Ian packed his family back to England, before embarking on what was apparently a long, leisurely drive home. At this stage he was seized with an intimation that he would never return to Europe. He attempted to visit his old girlfriend Monique who lived close to Lake Geneva, but she refused to see him. He had already made arrangements to be joined in Zurich by Blanche, to whom he was determined to show some of the favourite places of his youth. Driving at breakneck speed, he took her on a whistle-stop tour of Austria and southern Germany before returning to London on the air ferry from Rotterdam. The journey was not without its manic humour: now on regular medication, Ian would terrify his passenger as he careered down the autobahn, one hand on the wheel, the other scooping little white heart pills into his mouth. In southern Bavaria, Ian wanted to show Blanche Hitler's country retreat at Berchtesgaden. But the most poignant moment came when he took her up the Kitzbühler Horn. Although he went up in the funicular, he insisted on making the descent on foot. Halfway down, he stopped, turned to Blanche and said, "That's the last long walk of Ian Fleming."

Back in England, Ann had been scouring art galleries and antique shops for paintings and furniture. Her *pièce de résistance* was a gorilla by the

Australian artist Sidney Nolan, which she bought from Marlborough Fine
Art for £1200. Ann rather enjoyed having "our pornography fund",
meaning Glidrose, to subsidize her purchases. "It's so exhausting spending
Ian's trust money," she told Evelyn Waugh. "I squander a £1000 per
afternoon and envy the poor." After being tipped off by Kenneth Clark,
she bought a handsome unfinished painting of the young Queen Victoria
in top hat and scarlet riding habit by the Scottish genre painter, Sir David
Wilkie. She happily spent £1900 on a Chippendale looking-glass, £1500
for a Louis-Philippe Aubusson carpet, and £950 for a nineteenth-century
chandelier. Rather lower down the list of purchases was a £300 drawing
of Cyril Connolly by Augustus John, which Ian thought would make a
good investment for Caspar.

At Sevenhampton these new acquisitions joined the striking John portrait of Ian's mother and the Lucian Freud of Ann. Mama was hung in the
light, airy drawing-room, with its huge yellow sofas and lots of flowers;
Ann was an imposing presence at the top of the stairs. One entered the
house through a door in a modest façade made from modern Cotswold
stone. The main bedrooms, unusually, were situated to the left on the
ground floor. Climbing a half flight of stairs, one passed through a passage
where Ian's books were kept, and entered the old part of the house, the
Carolean ballroom, which was divided into drawing- and dining-rooms.
Outside the original slightly unkempt aspect was maintained, with enormous trees, overgrown hedges and the water, still stagnant-looking
(despite all its attentions), with its moorhens and ducks – "nothing too
raked and trim," recalled Paddy Leigh Fermor.

Soon Ann's friends were queueing to visit this house so long in the
making. At the end of October she held a house party for Evelyn and Laura
Waugh, Anthony and Clarissa Avon, and Hugo and Virginia Charteris. A
weary and, she herself felt, visibly aged Ann served lashings of beef and
grouse, washed down with Taittinger and Bollinger. Also present was
Waugh's old love, Teresa Cuthbertson (née Jungman) and her pretty
daughter Penelope. Waugh could not help noticing how Ian perked up
and tried to impress the young Miss Cuthbertson. But he was clear that it
was the last gasp of a sick man. As he told Maurice Bowra, "Old Thunderbird ... wishes to end his life and is determined to have his final seizure
on the golf course or at the card table. Ann will be disconsolate."

Having teased Ann rather too much about certain aspects of the con-
version, Waugh was prevailed on by his wife Laura to write a letter of
apology in which he complimented Ann for having fashioned "a house
exactly suited to your own and Ian's needs. If you had bought an old
house it would have imposed its habits on you. You have made something
where there is no predecessor breathing down your neck and you have
insured a happy twenty years in watching it mature and filling it with

treasures." To other correspondents, however, he told a different story, informing Nancy Mitford, "[Ann] has spent as much as the government have on the reconstruction of Downing Street, pulled down a large commodious house and put up a cottage ... The few bedrooms are tiny cubicles with paper thin walls through which every cough and snore is audible."

Having recently returned to the Flemings as housekeeper, Joan Sillick, the old Nanny, marshalled the increasingly headstrong Caspar – a task which gave her a good opportunity to keep up her quietly disapproving campaign against Ian. She was not happy when he gave his young son an air rifle to play with in the Sevenhampton grounds. She thought him unnecessarily cruel to insist that Caspar had his tonsils out on 12 August, his birthday. And she took Ian to task for frightening Caspar with ghost stories. Time and again the boy would creep along to spend the night in Nanny's bed after Ian had terrified him by spinning a baroque tale after his lights were out. Eventually Nanny threatened to put Ian's pyjamas in her room and said she would sleep in his. "Don't be so stupid," Ian replied in his usual fashion when ruffled.

In a letter to Waugh, Ann described her husband's state of "permanent angry misery". When guests arrived, she did her hostess's histrionic best to enliven proceedings with her favourite dictionary game or with what Paddy Leigh Fermor remembered as "passionate" croquet contests. But Ian's underlying mournfulness so took hold of Sevenhampton that Peter Quennell decided to start a Gloom Book, where visitors were invited to write their favourite melancholic quotation. The intention, according to Leigh Fermor, was homeopathic – to ward off the evil spirits. The first entry was Ian's:

Solitude becomes a lover
Loneliness a darling thing.

Having just completed his book about Japan, Ian adopted a Buddhist approach to his personal possessions. He gave Waugh a reclining chair with a variety of retractable arms for books and drinks, while Alastair Forbes and Paddy Leigh Fermor became the proud owners of some expensive clothes. Ian had already tried to present Forbes with a dinner suit, saying he would not be using it again. Forbes initially declined because he thought it would bring bad luck. He did however agree to accept a mohair suit, which he wore happily for years. Leigh Fermor was sitting with Peter Quennell when Ian suddenly appeared, wearing a navy-blue vicuna overcoat and saying, "I can't bear it, it doesn't fit anywhere." At the word, "Quis?", both his guests answered, "Ego", though Leigh Fermor got the prize because he was a better fit. Some years later, during a spate of IRA bombing in London, he was stopped by the police while walking home one evening and asked for identity. When the young constable joked how people liked to claim they were James Bond, Leigh Fermor opened his overcoat to show him the label which read, "Benson, Perry & Whitley, Cork St W1 7.9.1956 Ian Fleming Esq." The policeman was so impressed that he called a car to take Leigh Fermor to his destination in Little Venice.

Ian's largesse even stretched momentarily to his business dealings. Having asked Dickie Chopping earlier in the summer to paint a cover for *You Only Live Twice*, he was delighted with the artist's representation of a toad, dragonfly and pink chrysanthemum and agreed to increase his fee to 300 guineas – enough to allow Chopping to put new central heating into his house. "You and I really are a wonderful team," Ian enthused. And when Chopping told Michael Howard plainly that, contrary to Ian's implied assumption, he wanted to retain the copyright on his Bond book designs, Ian wrote back sweetly saying that "naturally it remains with you". Having won that particular victory, Chopping was emboldened to ask Howard if "we could change the myth about Ian having 'devised' the covers".

The premiere of *From Russia, With Love* in October proved a nightmare for him, even worse than *Dr No*. He did his best to approach the event in the expected Bond-like manner of extravagant nonchalance. He took the whole of the front row of the vast dress circle of the London Pavilion in Piccadilly Circus for himself and his party of friends. But while the other men dressed up in dinner-jackets, Ian insisted on appearing in a suit, and asked his doctor, Jack Beal, who was accompanying him in case he felt ill, to come similarly attired. Afterwards he invited his guests back to Victoria Square. At Ann's suggestion, he had arranged a party themed on the subject of the film. After winning a sizeable sum in the casino at Le Touquet, he had bought a mountain of Beluga caviare from Petrossian in Paris. But once again Ian looked sadly lost on the fringes of the event. He could not cope with the various tensions around him, such as ten-year-old Caspar acting precociously, throwing stones through the open window of the drawing-room to attract attention, and Rupert Hart-Davis beating a hasty retreat from the caviare table when he noticed his former Eton schoolfriend 'Burglar' Bryce looming up to talk. Ian amused himself with the quiet humour of William Plomer to whom he admitted, "I can't bear these Fests. I get claustrophobia and a face that aches with insincere smiles." He told Plomer later that, true to form, Ann and the "Dregs" stayed up till 4.30 a.m. but he crept to bed "beaten to the ground" at around one.

Apart from his health, Ian informed Plomer he was "now winding myself up like a toy soldier for this blasted case with McClory" which had returned firmly to the agenda. Over the previous three years, the unfinished *Thunderball* action had been an intermittent worry at the back of

Ian's mind. The legal process, however, had been grinding away and there was now a date in November for McClory to begin his High Court action against Ian, Bryce and his publishers for breach of copyright.

To her credit, Ann recognized her husband's concerns and also that his "gentle Reader", as he had described Plomer in his dedication to *Goldfinger*, was perhaps the only person she knew in whose company Ian could relax. But Plomer's balm over dinner was only a short-term expedient. Otherwise Ian moped around with little to occupy himself until his court case. He no longer inundated Denis Hamilton with ideas for articles. He declined a request to be interviewed by Brian Johnston for a radio programme, *Living With Success*, telling the producer, "Altogether I am getting far too much involved in this projecting of the image, which is the last thing I desire." However he could not resist a light Fleming touch, adding that there were "plenty of successful people around the place, and though quite a few of them seem to be in the dock at the moment, there are plenty of others whom Scotland Yard haven't caught up with yet".

Uncharacteristically, the one invitation he did accept was to present the awards at the fourth annual dinner of the Romantic Novelists' Association at the very end of October. The main winner was the syrupy Dorothy M. Cray, author of *House Divided*. Before the ceremony, in anticipation of their distinguished guest, the novelists – Denise Robins and Barbara Cartland among them – chatted about the burning issue of their profession: should they cross the threshold of the bedroom? The consensus was that they should not. In a different mood, Ian would have seized this opportunity to make a definitive and witty statement about the Bond genre. But he had not even been up to writing his speech himself. He had asked Evelyn Waugh, his guest at Sevenhampton the previous weekend, to ghost his few words. These turned out to be a lame acknowledgement of the obvious fact that the quickly gratified appetites of James Bond were the antithesis of romanticism. Ann informed a BBC reporter who was present at the event that James Bond had been brought up in the nursery on the works of the well-known sadist Ethel M. Dell.

Once settled at Sevenhampton, Ian established his usual routines. One lasted only as long as Blanche was in the country. Strictly speaking, as a result of an agreement with Ann, he was not supposed to be seeing his "other" woman. Accordingly Ian instructed Blanche to tell all her friends that she had finished her relationship with Ian. But he had no intention of being bound by such strictures. The next day he called Blanche and arranged a meeting as if nothing had happened. Her friends were kept in the dark, however, which caused problems because Noël Coward was so annoyed at Ian for appearing to treat Blanche in this cavalier manner that he refused to see him and, later, when Ian's health deteriorated, she had to beg Noël to visit him. Nevertheless, with the help of the discreet Griffie, Ian set up a pattern: every Thursday morning, after the conclusion of the Fleming two-day week, Blanche would drive him down to Henley where they would have lunch at the Angel Hotel. Then he would continue down to Wiltshire and she would take the train back to London.

Another ritual was his game of golf with the Old Etonian businessman Sir Jock Campbell. Since, following his move to Sevenhampton, he had given up his flat at Sandwich, Ian seldom played at St George's any longer. As an interim compromise, he rediscovered the rough course at Huntercombe, which was close to Campbell's Crocker End House at Nettlebed. A card-carrying Labour Party member and a director of the left-wing *New Statesman*, which had led the attack on Ian's snobbery with violence back in 1958, Campbell was another of Ian's unlikely friends. As owners of the most productive sugar estates in Guyana, his family firm, Booker Brothers, was growing into one of the largest agro-industrial companies in the world. But Campbell himself was a man of simple tastes, a feature which Ian appreciated. He had little time for the champagne socialists who congregated around Ann. Indeed Campbell and Ann disliked each other heartily. He had known her since she was married to Esmond Rothermere, and he had found her intolerable then and intolerable later. He recalled, "She reminded me of Sibyl Colefax, an incredible lion hunter, who is only interested in people's success." Campbell also disliked the way that, by forcing a move to Sevenhampton, Ann had taken Ian away from his two favourite things, Royal St George's and the sea. So there was a conspiratorial aspect to Ian's frequent visits to Crocker End House. After a pink gin, he would eat an early lunch of either toad-in-the-hole or fish cakes with tomato sauce. Then he and Campbell would proceed to the golf course for a round of fourballs, preferably played for money, with two other Old Etonians, Philip Brownrigg and Selby Armitage.

One day that autumn, they were walking down the 13th hole when Ian turned suddenly to his friend and asked, "Jock, would you like to buy me?" When Campbell recovered from his shock and asked what he meant, Ian replied that he was making so much money that all his earnings were disappearing in supertax. He said his accountants had advised him to sell part of his company, thus turning income into capital. Would Booker be interested in buying into Glidrose? Campbell thought for a moment and declined. He told Ian that this kind of transaction was "not our cup of tea". The two friends returned to their game of golf.

Two weeks later, at the same hole, Ian brought the subject up again. The background to his request was more complicated than he had first suggested. British tax legislation made it difficult for small private companies to retain their earnings, which were supposed to be distributed to shareholders, thus attracting income tax at a high rate. The accepted solution to this problem was to become part of a big quoted public company; in this way, only the standard corporation tax needed to be paid. This time, however, Ian only asked Campbell, "What do you think I'm worth?" The businessman did some quick mental arithmetic, built in his own understanding that Ian did not have many years to live, and answered, "About £200,000."

Once more, the topic was dropped and the two friends got on with the serious business of tackling the par-four 14th hole. Approximately a month later, Ian returned to the same subject. He told Campbell that he had tried to sell Glidrose to two merchant banks, including his own family firm, Robert Fleming, but they considered it "too speculative". Anyway, Ian said, he did not want his cottage industry to be part of a bank. He preferred it to belong to a friend. Could Campbell please think again about buying Glidrose?

Campbell reluctantly agreed to put the matter to his next board meeting. Ian's unusual request came at the end under 'Any other business'. Campbell explained the position and later claimed that he was astonished and slightly embarrassed when his directors showed interest in following up Ian's initiative. Negotiators from both sides came together to work out a deal, finally concluded in March 1964, when Booker Brothers paid £100,000 for a 51 per cent stake in Glidrose. Ian was not to know that the reverberations of his successful sale of himself would continue for many years.

Shortly afterwards, he had a card from Ann Marlow in New York. It read, "Heard from Intrepid that you have sold half of yourself. Darling, which half?" And just to be on the safe side, given the earlier rumpus, Marlow added a PS, "If anyone close to you reads this note, be sure to tell her it's just a game we play."

15

Name in lights
1963–1964

Towards the end of 1963, when it became impossible to avoid references to Ian or the James Bond phenomenon, Ann embellished her nickname for her husband into "Thunderbeatle", the fifth Beatle, as rich and as well known as the other four, and as she later put it, "In both cases something undefinable appealed to public fancy, and was immediately fastened on to by those who batten on exploiting original talent." Passing through Piccadilly Circus around this time Lady Mary Clive noticed Ian's name prominently displayed outside the London Pavilion. Amused to see 'Ian Fleming's From Russia With Love' emblazoned on cinema hoardings, she dropped her enigmatic old friend a note, reminding him how, twenty-five years earlier, he had talked about wanting to be famous. "How does it feel to have your name in lights?" she asked. "I hope you're enjoying it."

At the time the film was playing to packed houses in four West End cinemas simultaneously. In Britain, Ian's latest novel *On Her Majesty's Secret Service* had sold 75,000 copies in hardback, while sales of *Dr No* and *From Russia, With Love* in paperback were nudging one million each. Cumulatively Cape had sold 380,000 copies of Ian's books, and Pan, his softback publisher, nearly seven million. In the United States, where the relationship between box-office receipts and book sales was more direct, over ten million Bond paperbacks had been printed. Neither Ann's friends nor his own family could argue with that kind of success.

For public consumption Ian was happy to portray himself as a profitable one-man business. "My contribution to the export drive is simply staggering," he told the *Observer*. "They ought to give me some sort of medal. I suppose it's the equivalent of the earning power of a small boot factory." To Robert Harling, Ian joked that fame was a terrible thing: now, whenever some unknown television producer called, he would fly to the United States for a ten-minute interview (although there is no evidence he ever did so). "Like hashish-taking it has no excuse and no end," he said.

But having achieved worldwide recognition and material reward, Ian was still unsatisfied. Underlying his basic unhappiness was his poor state of health. The inchoate fury which for long had suffused his face, leaving him, a friend once said, with the look of a bloodhound out in the sun, had given way to real anger as he realized how little time he had to live and enjoy his growing wealth. The failure of his marriage still vexed him deeply. But now there was a new version of his childish petulance when reality failed to match his expectations. This was evident in his reply to Lady Mary's breezy note, in which he chided her for being vulgar. She thought he must be joking until she reflected later that he was actually serious. Having striven so long for fame and adulation, he had turned his back on them because he felt he was being fêted for the wrong reasons. As she put it, his success seemed hollow because he was famous, not for being a great man or even a brilliant writer, but for creating a vast money-making machine. Once again "the grown-ups" had cheated him.

Of more immediate concern was his court case with McClory, which began in the Chancery Division of the High Court on 20 November. The opening pleas proceeded at a stately pace, McClory's counsel, William Mars-Jones QC, taking a week and a half to argue that his client's copyright in *Thunderball* had been infringed. James Bond was "a tough, hard-hitting, hard-drinking, hard-living, amoral man who saves the citizens of this country and, indeed, the whole free world, from the most incredible disasters", he helpfully explained to the judge, Mr Justice Ungoed-Thomas.

Each day Ian and Ivar arrived at the nineteenth-century court-house by taxi, accompanied by Ernest Cuneo who had flown from the United States to provide legal advice and moral support. After sitting on hard wooden benches all morning, listening to evidence they often disagreed with, they were happy to repair to a nearby pub, the George, where they had a table booked for lunch at one o'clock.

Among several supporters waiting on the sidelines was Charles Wacker III who, although Bryce's friend, remained in touch with McClory. He had come from Chicago hoping that, as a relatively neutral observer, he might still act as a go-between and help the two main antagonists reach some last-minute agreement. But there seemed little scope for compromise. Three days into the case, on Friday 22 November, when President Kennedy was assassinated in Dallas, McClory informed Wacker that he was prepared to give Bryce one last chance to make a deal. This ultimatum was discussed during the course of the weekend at Moyns and was rejected.

All the more extraordinary, then, was what happened the following Friday afternoon. The opening pleas having been completed, McClory was starting to give evidence when, as Peter Carter-Ruck, his solicitor, has recorded, "The hearing was unexpectedly and somewhat dramatically adjourned after leading counsel on both sides had seen the judge in his private rooms." The proceedings were due to resume three days later on Monday. But, over the weekend, the various lawyers held a series of hurried meetings, leading to a formal conference in the offices of Ian's solicitors, Farrer and Company, on Sunday afternoon.

In an atmosphere of great tension, Ian was accompanied by Ann, Bryce was with Cuneo, while McClory was flanked by his wife Bobo and brother Desmond O'Donovan. Fourteen people, counting the lawyers, were crammed like schoolchildren into a smallish room, with no table, only chairs set in a circle round the edge. In less than ten minutes they had agreed in principle to come to terms, the details of which were thrashed out later. "I do not think James Bond would feel at home in the Chancery Division," Ian wryly remarked to a journalist, while Bryce agreed to pay the costs, and undisclosed damages.

So why, after nearly three years of expensive legal wrangling, did he and Ivar so abruptly throw in the towel? Technically both men decided to settle but, since Ivar was financing the action, it was his opinion that counted. There are several possible explanations. After the hearing, Ivar himself said that he did it because of Ian's health. Carter-Ruck has pointed to the mounting costs after two weeks in the courts. But Bryce was a rich man and, anyway, as soon as Cubby Broccoli and Harry Saltzman heard that Ivar wanted to settle, they offered to underwrite the costs of continuing the case for a further fortnight. As the makers of the Bond films, they had kept a close eye on developments and were understandably loath to see another producer emerging with ownership of Bond film rights.

At the end of the day, however, McClory's case was incontrovertible. If Bryce and Ian had been hoping he would fall down in the witness box, they were mistaken. Showing command of the 540 letters on the case which he had committed to memory, McClory demonstrated that his partnership with Bryce had endured. As a result he was awarded all literary and film rights in the screenplay *Thunderball* and all film rights in the novel of the same name. Ian had to fight to hang on to his novel, but was forced to acknowledge that it was "based on a screen treatment by Kevin McClory, Jack Whittingham and the Author".

Ivar convinced himself that Ian was happy with the outcome. But that was not Blanche's impression. She had been in London during the case, lending Ian valuable background support. Instead of dining, as scheduled, at the French Embassy the evening after the settlement, he invited her out and bitterly denounced his friend's perfidy. Ann took up the cudgels as well. "Dedicated to Ivar Bryce. The man who betrayed Ian in the Thunderball case", she scrawled in her husband's personal copy of *Diamonds Are Forever*. Otherwise Ian kept his counsel. John

Betjeman wrote to commiserate about the outcome of the case. He said he had just been to see the film of *From Russia, With Love* in Bristol and there was never a dull moment. He compared James Bond to an international Sherlock Holmes. "The Bond world is as real and full of fear and mystery as Conan Doyle's Norwood and Surrey and Baker Street. I think the only other person to have invented a world in our time is Wodehouse. This is real art. I look up to you, old boy, rather as I look up to Uncle Tom Eliot and Wodehouse and H. Moore and I suppose Evelyn." He concluded his note, "Write on, fight on." But even at this late stage Ann could not quite bring herself to admit this much. When Ian read her Betjeman's letter, she retorted that "he's the person who has created a world". In telling Betjeman this story, Ian added, "I must warn you I am seriously running out of puff and my inventive streak is very nearly worked out."

Ian's legal wrangling was not quite finished. His own action against the *Daily Sketch* for printing James Bond's obituary in November -- well in advance of the official publication date for *You Only Live Twice* -- was dealt with quickly enough. But then, a week after the *Thunderball* case was over, Ian was served with another writ, this time by the scriptwriter Jack Whittingham, who had been forced to withdraw from McClory's action through lack of funds and who now claimed that he had still not been duly credited for his work on the project. With her lively wit, Ann tried to see the cheerful side of these events. Ian's two weeks at the High Court had been a healthy routine, she told Evelyn Waugh. He had not been able to smoke and had only had "one hour for a simple lunch". But it was obvious she was dissimulating wildly in order to preserve her sanity.

Having been chipper during most of the case, Ian slipped back quickly into his old moroseness. He was in considerable pain and, for the most part, he bore it bravely. Following his heart attack in 1961, he had developed angina and narrowing of the arteries, for which he was prescribed Peritrate and quinidine. But these drugs did not stop the contraction in his chest and the stinging pressure on his heart, which he found particularly unpleasant in the early mornings. To counteract this, he had begun taking nitroglycerine which brought some relief. When his wartime colleague Sydney Cotton mentioned a good heart specialist in West Germany, Ian thought it worth consulting him. Even on his journey to Frankfurt, he could not resist selling the James Bond package. An eagle-eyed journalist spotted him rearranging the display at a London airport bookstall so that the Bond books were on top. In the Hessen town of Bad Nauheim, Dr Ottomar Mechow confirmed much that Ian already knew, adding that he had now physically damaged his heart and was suffering from hypertension. The doctor recommended a moderate life, with long periods of rest and relaxation, and less drinking and smoking. To the existing medical cabinet, he added a phial of digitalis, a poison obtained from the purple foxglove plant which, when used in minute quantities, can bring relief from heart attacks.

Often in dubious health herself, Ann was bedridden with bronchitis over the New Year, which gave her a valid excuse not to accompany Ian when he set out for Jamaica in early January 1964. To Frances Donaldson, however, she hinted that her "ambivalent illness" was a ruse to keep her from having to spend too much time in Jamaica, where Ian had invited Ivar Bryce and Charles Wacker to stay. When Blanche asked him how he could even speak to the man who had recently let him down so badly, Ian answered wearily, "Because I have known him too long." Within weeks, in Jamaica, she was taking his guests off his hands so he could work, a duty she performed so proficiently that Ivar left a believable enough account of an enjoyable week spent with his old friend at Goldeneye. "The weather and the island were at their best, and Ian, although showing signs of deep fatigue to me, seemed to be gaining in strength and tranquillity."

Already Ian had started writing a new novel, The Man With the Golden Gun, an uphill task because, for health reasons, he had been forced to cut his working schedule to an hour and a half each day. At the end of You Only Live Twice Bond had been left on a Japanese island suffering from memory loss. In the new book, it transpired that he had subsequently been brainwashed by the KGB, which sent him back to London, programmed to kill M. Failing to achieve that, he was rehabilitated and "cured" with a course of electro-convulsive therapy (ECT). As an exercise to prove his reliability afterwards, he was sent to Savannah La Mar in the south-west of Jamaica to report on the notorious 'Pistols' Scaramanga, an assassin working for an international gang trying to corner the local sugar crop on behalf of neighbouring Cuba.

As usual, in The Man With the Golden Gun, Ian called on his personal experience to provide names for his characters. His jaundiced view of his schooldays resurfaced as he turned once more to Eton to equip himself with a name for a villain. Like Blofeld, who first appeared in Thunderball, Scaramanga was the surname of a Eton contemporary. In Jamaica the SIS station chief, Commander Ross, was based on Alan Ross, now editor of the London Magazine, who had told Ian about the effects of ECT on his friend, the journalist John Gale, after suffering a nervous breakdown reporting the Algerian civil war. Nick Nicholson, the secretary of Royal St George's, provided the name for the local CIA chief. Having recently written 'The Property of a Lady' for Sotheby's, Ian tried to include topical details of the career of Maria Freudenstein, the double agent exposed in that story. But he called her Maria

Freudenstadt, and none of his proof-readers picked up his error.

Ian soon discovered he was not enjoying the process of writing this saga on his own. Not for the first time, he missed Ann, needing her to worry and cajole him into creativity. Availing himself of a clear, new telephone line, he called his wife in Wiltshire and asked her to join him. With what she called "alarming expansiveness", he told her she was his "solace" and that he needed "some background to banging out Bond". Reluctantly, because she was enjoying the crisp English winter, she agreed to join Ian at the end of January. She told Frances Donaldson truthfully that if she had stayed at Sevenhampton she would have been racked with guilt. Arriving in Jamaica with a copy of *Fanny Hill* she had bought at the renamed Kennedy Airport in New York, she immediately regretted her decision to come. As she told Clarissa Avon, she loathed the tropics and could only think of the glorious early spring "and burgeoning bulbs at Sevenhampton". To make matters worse, a garage had opened at the top of the drive, with a "sound system" blaring out loud calypso music until the early hours of the morning (ironically, often a version of 'Three Blind Mice' which had become a local hit, on Chris Blackwell's Island record label, following its use on the soundtrack of *Dr No*).

For some reason there were more visitors than usual. Ann did not mind Ian's undemonstrative friend Hilary Bray and his sickly wife, Jenny. Of all Ian's friends, he was the one she liked most. But she drew the line at John Blackwell and his brother Tom, a steward of the Jockey Club, who arrived sporting large stomachs and sharkskin shorts. Ian encouraged Ann to take Jenny Bray out to lunch on the day the Blackwells came. But Hilary Bray took this as a slight on his wife and forbade it. Ann commented in disappointed tones to her brother that Hilary had not "grasped the extent of Ian's desire to be his alter ego in this company and Ian's profound disappointment that women are to be present" – in other words, his wish to enjoy a Caribbean equivalent of his male-only golfer's meals at John Blackwell's house in Kent.

The last straw was Professor Northcote Parkinson, the author of the best-selling pseudo-economics book, *Parkinson's Law*, arriving at Goldeneye with his wife Elizabeth. The professor had recently been taken on as a client by Peter Janson-Smith, who recommended him to visit Ian. At lunch it quickly became clear that he was a tiresome pedant. Ian skilfully extricated himself from the proceedings at 2.25 p.m., saying he needed his regular siesta, leaving Ann to entertain his guests until four o'clock when their driver reappeared from a trip down the coast. Ann was just sitting down and expressing her heartfelt thanks that she had seen the back of them when Ian informed her that he had accepted an invitation for them both to join the Parkinsons at their hotel for dinner and a

'Jamaican Beach Barbecue' the following evening. When, over supper, Ann tried telling Ian that this was not quite what she had in mind, he yelled that she was a monumental bore who spoiled everything for him. "Fuck off. Go home at once. Do you expect me to look at your face every evening?"

Ann packed her bags and prepared to leave that night. But it was too late and she had nowhere to go. Eventually, Ian calmed down and Ann agreed to accompany him to the Parkinsons' resort hotel at Frenchman's Cove where they took a room overlooking the sea. She managed to avoid attending the beach barbecue by feigning illness. But her peace was disturbed by the sound of her husband being driven back to his chalet by Mrs Parkinson in a golf buggy. Ian was complaining repetitively in a slurred voice that the cabaret was awful and he could not get a drink. There was little doubt who the bore was on this occasion.

More agreeably, the visit of a film crew from the Canadian Broadcasting Corporation coincided with the surprise appearance of James Bond, the American ornithologist whose name Ian had appropriated for his hero. Bond, who had never met Ian, happened to be passing Goldeneye and decided to call in. Ian took much pleasure in introducing Canadian television viewers to the "real James Bond". But he was not prepared to meet the BBC's Alan Whicker, who requested an interview for a series of profiles whose subjects had previously included the millionaires Paul Getty and Baron Thyssen. Ian declined, adding that he was "not greatly impressed by being equated with any of your previous victims". He suggested Whicker might like to concentrate on Battersea Dogs' Home and forget about him. Whicker later pompously described this letter as the rudest he had ever received.

Ian was also pursued by the British publisher André Deutsch, who wanted him to write a guidebook to Jamaica with his friend Morris Cargill. Over lunch at Cargill's Charlottenburgh estate, Ian grudgingly agreed to cooperate. At one stage, he asked Blanche to read something he had written about the island's fish. But when she tried to discuss it, he told her dismissively that she was illiterate. Later, on his return to England, he was physically unable to complete the project, which caused problems for Deutsch who had pre-sold copies of a title called *Ian Fleming's Jamaica* and needed his input. Ian was forced to cobble together a pedestrian introduction, nominally his last work, which relied heavily on his 1947 article for *Horizon*.

Having completed *The Man With the Golden Gun* by the beginning of March, Ian wrote his usual end-of-term report to William Plomer. Among his playful protestations about running out of steam and suffering under Plomer's lash, Ian commented touchingly that he was proud not to have failed his friend and "gentle Reader". Even at this stage he was thinking up ideas for different types of books. On 3 March he wrote to Michael Howard with a "brilliant notion". As he explained, he was surrounded at Goldeneye by all sorts of reference books – about birds, fish, shells and stars. But he had nothing to satisfy frequent requests from his guests for information about the properties of ganja or marijuana. So Ian suggested an expensive well-illustrated book about the "narcotic flora of the world". Although Cape showed little interest, Ian asked one of his regular researchers to write to the Wellcome Institute for the History of Medicine and the Royal Botanical Gardens at Kew for further information.

Cape was more exercised in exploiting Ian's proven worth as a fiction writer. By the time *You Only Live Twice* was published in mid-March, it had 62,000 advance orders, a 50 per cent increase on *On Her Majesty's Secret Service* the previous year and a record for the publisher. Called upon to represent the "apparatus" in reviewing the book for the *Sunday Times*, Cyril Connolly was surprisingly severe in his criticism that Bond's adventures were becoming far-fetched and called for him to return to "espionage as an exact science".

On reaching Sevenhampton, Ian was determined to be resolute. Taking his cue from the epitaph recorded in Bond's obituary in *You Only Live Twice* – "I shall not waste my days in trying to prolong them. I shall use my time" – he told Ann that he intended to settle down and involve himself in the local community. Since her relative by marriage, Charles Morrison, was standing as a Conservative in a by-election in his Devizes constituency, Ian agreed to put his name to an election address entitled 'To Westminster With Love'. Actually penned by Ann's niece, Sara, who was married to Morrison, and polished up by Ian, a member of the local party, the notice spoke of the candidate's licence to kill despondency in the political world. While Ann canvassed energetically on Morrison's behalf, Ian's only other contribution to the cause was to invite the secretary of a Swindon boys' club to Sevenhampton where he offered him £60 a year and promised to come and talk to his charges. But nothing materialized, for Ian was now steadily losing hope, as the iron crab tightened its hold on his heart and his psyche. As he himself poignantly jotted in his notebook, "I've always had one foot not wanting to leave the cradle, and the other in a hurry to get to the grave. It makes a rather painful splits of one's life."

Roy Jenkins remembered a gloomy, fragile figure walking on his own beside the stagnant lake at Easter-time. Stephen Spender summoned up the same image, but with a glass of whisky in hand. Sara Morrison heard Ian saying he could sniff the Undertaker's Wind. Peter Quennell added a further note. As well as the glass and *de rigueur* cigarette, Ian was asserting that the weeds on the lake were sewage and "that was country life for you". Quennell saw Ian's refusal to give up drinking and smoking as evidence of his fortitude, even a noble foolhardiness. "Words reached: he

listened and replied, but one felt he was listening from a distance ...
Courageous, defiant, aloof, he dismissed all the chance of a recovery that
his doctors offered him. Peace was all he needed, he would say. 'Pace,
Annie, pace!' he would beg if he thought she was planning further 'mis-
chiefs'."

Shortly after Easter Ian caught a cold. Despite running a temperature he
insisted on driving to Huntercombe for a fourball with Jock Campbell and
friends. When Ann protested, he demanded petulantly, "What is there for
me to do at home on a Sunday?" It rained steadily throughout the game,
but Ian dismissed Campbell's suggestion that he should dry off and have
a bath, climbing straight into his Avanti and making for London in soaking
clothes. The next day he was laid low with pleurisy. After two weeks,
during which he complained of agonizing pains in his chest, he reluctantly
agreed to be admitted to Sister Agnes's (the King Edward VII Hospital for
Officers), where he was diagnosed as suffering from pulmonary embolism:
blood clots were forming in his left lung and this accounted for his
secondary symptoms of swollen legs and breathlessness.

Although very weak, he resented returning to hospital, complaining
that the small room gave him claustrophobia and begging Ann to take
him away. With little for him to do except read, Cape tried to interest him
in the proofs of *Funeral in Berlin*, a second novel by a new young signing,
Len Deighton. But Ian found he could not "be bothered with his kitchen
sink writing and all this Nescafé". He had little time for fiction: it lacked
the facts that he craved. And this attitude was beginning to colour what
he felt about Bond. As he told Plomer, mere stories were just not good
enough after books like *Diary of a Black Sheep* by his new hero Colonel
Richard Meinertzhagen, Laurens van der Post's *Heart of the Hunter* and
Francis Chichester's account of his voyage round the world. Once again
he claimed that he would write no more Bond books. Although he had
said this before, there was a certain finality in his statement to Plomer,
who was editing *The Man With the Golden Gun*: "This is, alas, the last Bond
and, again alas, I mean it, for I really have run out of both puff and zest."

One diversion was novelist Kingsley Amis who was fascinated by the
Bond phenomenon. Amis had originally approached Ian to write an
article, but discovering that Ian's output involved "more than simple
cloak-and-dagger stories with a bit of fashionable affluence and sex thrown
in", his project had grown into a full-length book. Ian seized on the
imminent publication of Amis's work as an excuse to delay putting out
The Man With the Golden Gun, which increasingly dissatisfied him. He
hoped he might be able to rework it when he was in Jamaica the following
spring. But Plomer disabused him of that idea, telling him that the novel
was well up to standard.

At the beginning of June Ian was allowed to go home to Victoria

Square with Sister Bridget Forbes, a pleasant and efficient young nurse, in attendance. He no longer was interested in the awards and acclamation which continued to rain down on him, including the nine Golden Pans he was given for selling a million copies of his books. His health was still poor, and only reluctantly did he agree to accompany Sister Forbes for a period of further convalescence at the Dudley Hotel, the stuffy Sussex-coast establishment where he had stayed three years earlier.

Visiting him was a painful experience, as Ann discovered a couple of days later. After lunching at English's, a seafood restaurant in Brighton, Ian refused to take a taxi back to the hotel. He stood in a bus queue in the rain, causing an increase in his pulse rate, and it was no surprise when his doctor refused to allow him to drive to Oxford for Caspar's sports day. On her return to London, Ann drove straight into a taxi in Elizabeth Street, Westminster. Charged with careless driving, she attributed her lapse to the pressure she was feeling as a result of her husband's illness and, finding a lenient magistrate, was let off with a £6 fine.

Ann recognized sadly that her presence only annoyed Ian and raised his blood pressure. For the time being, he found Sister Bridget a much more relaxing companion. He had "deliciously infantile conversations" with her about bingo and walking on the pier – "quite a change from the rich pabulum" he was used to with Annie, he told Plomer.

Most of the time Ian sat on his own on a bench on the sea front, smoking and staring vacantly into the Channel. In the hotel restaurant, he made a point of sitting in the window at table six, where he could continue his meditations on the water. Friends wrote to try to keep his spirits up. Noting that Ian had not "revealed as much about Bond's defecations as of his other bodily functions", Evelyn Waugh sent him as inspiration some sheets of original Bronco lavatory paper – the genuine American product, unavailable in Britain.

Apart from Blanche, Ian was only happy to see William Plomer, Cyril Connolly and Alan Ross. Human contact, as Ann noted, was "profoundly exhausting". In early July Plomer reported to Michael Howard: "I see no reason to be hopeful about his physical condition, but he is up and to some extent about and doesn't expect to be at the Dudley for more than a few days."

Connolly found his friend altogether "sadder, gentler and wiser" than before. Ian reminisced about their first real meeting in Kitzbühel and how, when he first visited Austria in the 1920s, he used to compose horrific sagas about the local grandee, Count Schlick. After Ian had put out a general call for reading matter, Connolly gave him an old copy of his book, *The Unquiet Grave*, with the inscription, "Ian with love from Cyril – see p. 66 for Kitzbühel where our friendship ripened which led to me getting my job on the Sunday Times and so to solvency. Not forgetting St

Margaret's Bay." Connolly added a quotation from an article by Gavin Ewart which had appeared in the *London Magazine* following the publication of *Bond Strikes Camp*. This asserted that "Mr Connolly and Mr Fleming have quite a lot in common", though Cyril did not complete it: "Both are Old Etonians; both are connoisseurs. Mr Connolly of the arts and graces, Mr Fleming (through James Bond) of the Philistine materialist pleasures and status symbols of modern society." Turning to the designated page, Ian would have enjoyed reading Connolly's words: "The body remembers pleasure past and being made aware of it, floods the mind with sweetness. Thus the smell of sun-warmed pine-needles and the bloom on ripe whortle-berries reopen the file marked Kitzbühel and bring back the lake with its muddy water, raft conversation and pink water-lilies; the drive over the white Alpine road through the black fir-wood or the walk over the meadow where runnels of water sing in wooden troughs beside the chalets."

Alan Ross succeeded in dragging Ian to the Sussex county cricket ground at Hove, where they were lucky enough to find Ted Dexter, one of England's most exciting post-war batsmen, making runs in commanding form. Ross was under no illusion that for Ian to survive he needed peace and quiet, and that meant keeping away from his wife. As he put it, "Ann remained constitutionally unable to avoid irritating Ian or to adjust her noisy social life to accommodate his."

Ian was not the only member of the Fleming family suffering from poor health that summer. Since returning to London the previous year, Eve's age had caught up with her and, following a stroke, she moved to the Metropole Hotel in Brighton to recover. She chose this particular spot on medical advice rather than out of any sense of family solidarity or desire to be close to her son. On the evening of 26 July she suffered another stroke, dying the following day with Peter, Richard and Amaryllis at her bedside. Stopping at the Dudley Hotel to inform Ian, Amaryllis was horrified by the aura of death in Ian's room. Gone was the haughty disdain for death he had shown in his notebooks, the certainty that it respects the scornful eye. Afterwards, she told Peter that their brother too was dying. With Fleming phlegm, Peter refused to admit the inevitable. "No, he's not, he can't be," he said.

Tired of his twilight existence, Ian decided, against his doctor's advice, to attend his mother's funeral in Nettlebed and then to proceed to Sevenhampton in time for Caspar's holidays. Alan Ross told his wife that if Ian stayed there for any length of time he would be dead within a fortnight. At the dour Scottish funeral Ian remained silent and lifeless, his face a deep purple, as he gripped Amaryllis's hand tightly throughout the service. On the way back to Wiltshire with Ann, he began talking of the money he would inherit from his mother. "What use is it to me now?" he moaned. When she replied, as soothingly as she could, that they already had everything life could offer, he stated elliptically "That's over and done with. Only the future matters."

At Sevenhampton, his behaviour became unusually quirky and erratic. He developed a fear of the number thirteen and a horror of the colour black. Could he have been reminded of the funereal hue in which his mother had insisted on covering the walls at Arnisdale, the lodge in Scotland, shortly after his father's death? Whatever the reason, Ian made such a fuss that his bedroom carpet had to be changed to red. He seemed anxious whenever Ann drove the car, telling her repeatedly that it was an unlucky time for the Flemings. It was hardly surprising when he admitted that he was an alcoholic. But what scared her more than anything was his obsession about being in the shade. She found this unnatural in someone for whom light and the sun had always been such vital influences.

Nanny Sillick feared for his sanity. On one occasion he told her accusingly that his sweaters were all filthy. She knew they were perfectly clean. But rather than inflame his hasty temper, she appeared to agree to his request to wash them. All she did was hang them out on the most visible clothes-line. Thus satisfied, he later thanked her for a job well done.

Sister Bridget was a constant soothing presence. Once, when she came to give him his medication, she found Ian sitting nursing a glass of whisky. Marching up to him, she said sternly, "I thought I told you not to drink that," handing him instead a glass of water to wash down his pills. Over the early August bank holiday, Ian's doctor, Jack Beal, also came to visit, accompanied by his wife Tina. Still Ian could not resist cocking a snook at anyone who tried to tell him what to do. Sitting in the garden one afternoon, Beal was shocked to see Ian executing a neat dive into his open-air swimming pool. When Beal gently remonstrated, Ian replied, "You said I shouldn't swim. You didn't say I couldn't dive." Another day the Flemings and the Beals motored to the nearby village of Ramsbury for a pub lunch. Tina Beal, who drove Ian, was in no doubt that he was "very depressed, he knew he was for it". He surprised her, however, by insisting on two stops on the way back. One was at a church, where he wanted to say a prayer for the forgiveness of his sins. And the second was at an antique shop, where he bought Ann a painting. Shades of his former self and testament to his abiding if frustrated love for his wife, he became, for just an hour or so, boyishly excited about smuggling it home and putting it on her bed without her noticing.

Feeling his spirits recovering slightly, he was determined to travel down to Sandwich the following week and spend some time at the Guilford Hotel, next to Royal St George's. He told Ann, with a sense of impatience bordering on despair, that he "must get back to life, or else". The previous October he had been elected chairman of the house subcommittee, which dealt with the important things of club life like food and drink, and he wanted to be present at the full committee meeting on 8 August, when he was thrilled at the prospect of being nominated as club captain for the following year.

On his way through London, he visited his specialist, Evan Bedford, who provided a surprisingly positive report on his heart but warned that he had little physical reserve to call on. At lunch with Blanche at Au Père de Nico, he chanced upon Robert Harling. Ian invited him round to Victoria Square the following day where, uncompromisingly, he insisted on having an alcoholic stiffener before lunch. He told his friend that if he continued to drink, as he certainly intended to, he had three more months to live. Even at this stage Ian was arguing with his wife about a painting of a nude which he was convinced was an Old Master. Ann thought differently, so to verify the matter, she prevailed on Harling to accompany her to a dealer in St James's. Most people would have been disappointed to learn that a likely-looking Old Master was a copy. But Harling could not help noticing that Ann displayed a perverse delight in being proved right.

After Ian had called in briefly to attend to business at Mitre Court, Griffie reported to Richard Hughes in relatively upbeat manner, "He certainly looks better and, best of all, he is in much better spirits. He went to Sandwich last Friday and will be staying two weeks, I think, and then proposes to go to Scotland until the end of August." She added that Glidrose was entering the "ghastly world" of merchandizing. Soon, she promised Hughes, "you'll be able to buy James Bond shirts, toilet requisites and possibly even a cook book and most certainly bubble gum".

Ann had few illusions about Ian's progress, however. On Saturday 8 August, when Ian was attending his committee meeting, she wrote to her son-in-law, John Morgan, from Sandwich, telling him, "Ian's life from now on hangs on a thread ... Poor Ian nags at me specially and then Caspar all the time. It ends all fun and is anguish to be with one one loves who is very mentally changed and fearfully unhappy – poor old tiger." Two days later, Ian was in enough pain to consult a local doctor who prescribed an anticoagulant to ease his congestion. Having already discovered that this caused Ian to bleed from the bowel, Dr Beal, who was contacted by telephone, recommended that Ian should be given vitamin K instead.

Any additional effort exhausted Ian now. According to Ann, "He stared from his bedroom window at the sea in total misery." On 11 August he somehow found the energy to stagger to the club for lunch and, in the evening, the Flemings had dinner at the hotel with their friend Michael Astor who lived nearby. But the strain of such an eventful day had proved too much and, shortly after the meal, Ian collapsed and an ambulance was called. As he was being rushed to the Kent and Canterbury Hospital, fifteen miles away, he calmly told ambulanceman James Parker, "I am sorry to trouble you chaps. I don't know how you get along so fast with the traffic on the roads these days."

The ambulance arrived at the hospital at 9.30 p.m. For three hours and forty minutes, doctors and nurses gave Ian oxygen and stimulant injections as they fought to save his life. But it was too late. At eleven o'clock Ann had telephoned Joan Sillick at Victoria Square to tell her that Ian had been taken into hospital. At 1.30 a.m. she phoned again to say he was dead and ask Miss Sillick to come down to Canterbury the next morning to collect Caspar and his cousin Francis, who was also staying. Nanny was met at Canterbury station by Hilary Bray who gave her some money to take the two small boys out to lunch, before escorting them back to London. The horror of Ian's untimely death was given additional poignancy by the fact that it was Caspar's twelfth birthday.

The immediate tributes were, by and large, respectful of Ian and his phenomenal success, while trying rather too hard to match his personality to that of his fictional hero. *The Times* led the way with its sober judgement that he was "one of the most successful and controversial thriller writers in recent years". In the *Daily Mail*, one of his newer acquaintances, Ursula Andress, spoke for many women: "He was not the kind of man you expect to die. He was a fun person." In the same paper Kingsley Amis remarked on the "strong consistent moral framework" in the books. Only his old wartime colleague, Donald McLachlan, had the temerity to note in the *Sunday Telegraph* that Ian was "a deeply complex, unhappy, self-consuming person", though he granted he was "a brilliant staff officer". As for Ian's literary reputation, Michael Baldwin, on the BBC's *The World of Books*, celebrated the invention of the ultimate escapist hero. Ian did not write great books: "His work ignores the more wholesome range of human emotion and rational endeavour. But he was a great writer. The most stupendous set-piece, the sensuous phrase, were always at his fingertips. In the field of escape literature he far outshines Buchan. His peer is the Stevenson of *Treasure Island* and *Kidnapped*, and Fleming alone comes close to offering us something more deeply allegorical than either of those books, something much nearer in importance to *Dr Jekyll and Mr Hyde*."

Three days later twenty family members and friends gathered for Ian's funeral in the parish church of St James's, Sevenhampton. Having walked slowly from her house and paused beside the lake, Ann was slightly late arriving. She found the service had already started, the vicar having mistaken Ian's sister-in-law, Richard's wife Charm, who was sitting in the front row, for the widow and begun his obsequies. Afterward, his brothers Richard and Peter disappeared to Scotland for the annual family retreat. So it was left to Ann to organize his memorial service in the twelfth-

century church of St Bartholomew the Great in Smithfield. From a perch
in the organ loft, Amaryllis played Bach's Sarabande in C minor on her
cello, while, in an inspired address, William Plomer called for Ian to be
remembered "as he was on top of the world, with his foot on the accel-
erator, laughing at absurdities, enjoying discoveries, absorbed by his many
interests and plans, fascinated and amused by places and people and facts
and fantasies, an entertainer of millions, and for us a friend never to be
forgotten". Missing from both ceremonies was Blanche, who suffered the
eternal ostracism of the mistress. Although devastated by Ian's loss, she
comforted herself with her intuitive understanding that Ian would have
hated old age. Peter, strangely, took the same view, writing to Rupert Hart-
Davis, "There was really nothing ahead of him, so I suppose one must feel
that it was, in a repulsive phrase, 'for the best'."

Ian had died at the height of his earning powers, the centre of a large
industry which needed to keep operating smoothly and efficiently. But as
with all such personal posthumous empires, it attracted the interest of the
tax authorities, eager for their share of estate duty. And unravelling its
multi-limbed tentacles was not easy, particularly following Ian's film contract with Eon Productions and his sale of a majority share in Glidrose to
Booker. These deals added layers of decision-making to the complicated
web of trusts which Ian had established to shield his income from the
taxman. Essentially, he had given the publication rights in each of his
books to Glidrose, with immediate members of his family benefiting from
the income from these settlements. The film, serial and, later, television
rights were placed separately in a series of trusts for Caspar, but with
confusingly different trustees. Ian's personal solicitors, who drew up his
will, were the traditional firm Fisher Dowson & Wasbrough. Glidrose used
the Fleming family solicitors, Farrer and Company. (Ian's executors and
trustees were William Fisher, Henry Wasbrough and William Farrer.) Later,
when Ann felt she needed independent advice, she brought in the heavyweight Arnold Goodman, senior partner in Goodman Derrick.

The immediate result, as Peter noted, was that it was all "a bit of a dog's
breakfast, with nobody really in charge of a very complicated situation,
with too few of the answers known, and with too many auxiliary troops
attacking the main objective". Peter took the lead in sorting out matters
in as practical a manner as possible. It seemed diplomatic to give Ann
some status in the affairs of Glidrose. Although, under the contract of the
sale to Booker, Fleming nominees on the company had to be male, the
imaginative solution was to make her Honorary President.

Glidrose's first responsibility, while maintaining its core business of
selling international publishing rights, was preparing *The Man with the*

Golden Gun for publication. Opinion at Cape had changed about the viability of the manuscript, and Kingsley Amis was given a copy to take on holiday to Majorca, with a brief to find out why it was so "feeble". Amis, who was making the final changes to his own *James Bond Dossier*, put his finger on two points – the thinness of Scaramanga as a character and the implausibility of his hiring Bond as a security man when he did not know him or, it transpired, even need him. With a note of triumph Amis believed he had discovered the reason – that Scaramanga was sexually attracted to Bond (there were suggestions in the text that he was sexually "abnormal"), and that at some later stage, "Fleming's own prudence or that of a friend induced him to take out this element, or most of it." Plomer made short shrift of this suggestion: "I can't think that Ian had any qualms about 'prudence' or that he ever had any intention of developing a homosexual pursuit of Bond by Scaramanga." (Having been paid £36 15s for his editorial work on the book, Amis later managed to review it in the *New Statesman*.)

Ian had left three short stories ('Octopussy', 'The Living Daylights' and 'The Property of a Lady') which could be gathered together for publication in 1966. But, after that, how was Glidrose and its multinational parent, Booker Brothers, to keep the Bondwagon rolling? It was not long before the idea was raised of hiring someone to write an 007 sequel. Since Amis was close at hand and knew the Bond opus well, he seemed the ideal candidate. Ann was opposed to the idea in general, and to Amis, whom she considered a left-wing opportunist, in particular. Nevertheless a number of imitation Bond novels were beginning, or threatening, to appear. The established Bulgarian thriller writer Andrei Gulyashki had concocted an East–West battle of wits between Bond and his own master-spy Avakoum Zahov in his latest novel which he had submitted to another London publisher, Cassell. Counsel's unwelcome opinion was that Glidrose could not copyright a character. Authors could write about an agent called James Bond; this was only actionable if they passed him off in any way as the product of Ian Fleming. Eventually Glidrose and the battery of lawyers and trustees behind it decided that the best way of seeing off the plagiarists was to have its own 'Continuation Bond'. To Ann's disgust, a contract for *Colonel Sun* was drawn up with Amis. Peter Fleming suggested that Amis should write under the pseudonym "George Glidrose" but this was deemed unmarketable and the book was attributed to "Robert Markham".

In addition, a second "Continuation Bond" was commissioned after a South African, Geoffrey Jenkins, emerged with a convincing case that Ian had discussed with him details of a new Bond novel about the diamond industry in the Rand. Jenkins had befriended Ian while working in London as the recipient of Lord Kemsley's Imperial Journalistic Scholarship in the late 1940s. The two men kept in touch and, when Jenkins turned his hand to writing thrillers in 1959, Ian reviewed his first novel *A Twist of Sand* generously in the *Sunday Times*. Since Jenkins had secured the support of Harry Saltzman, Glidrose agreed to employ him on the same terms as Amis – £5,000 upfront, and £5,000 on acceptance of the manuscript. In the event it was not happy with the completed work and, under the terms of its contract, was able to reject it.

Following Booker's acquisition of a majority stake in Glidrose, the turnover of Ian's company rose from £102,732 in 1963 to £237,405 in 1964. However the release of *Goldfinger*, the slick and commercially successful third Bond film, in late 1964, together with publicity surrounding its controversial successor, *Thunderball*, led to a superlative performance in 1965 when 27 million copies of Ian's novels were sold in eighteen different languages, producing an income of £350,699, including a fast-increasing contribution from merchandizing, and profits of £206,199. At the time of Ian's death, he had sold 30 million books. In less than two years, his sales had more than doubled and Booker, in what turned out to be a very astute deal, had already earned back its outlay. The Fleming backlist was exploited for all its worth: after the idea of issuing *The Spy Who Loved Me* in paperback arose, Hugh Fisher, one of the title's trustees, was unhappy about appearing to ignore Ian's express wish that it should be assigned to the literary scrapheap. When Peter Janson-Smith, as Ian's agent, produced solid evidence that Ian had not meant what he said, Fisher nevertheless felt duty bound to resign. Though book sales dropped sharply the following year to 'only' 8 million (still more than the Bible), Glidrose's income and profits improved again to their historical zenith, prompting a disgruntled Ann to plead with Peter in March 1967, "Are you sure that Glidrose should not pay a capital sum to the estate for the right to continue Bond? It seems roses all the way for Campbell and taxed income for the family." So concerted became Ann's campaign of vilification towards Campbell that he thought seriously about suing her for defamation. She described his "avarice" to Evelyn Waugh, and when she heard that Campbell was going to appear in a BBC television profile of Ian in late 1969, she wrote telling him that this would make it difficult for her to participate, "unless you are going to tell the truth – how much money you made out of him". Ann did not realize that without the Glidrose deal she might have been paying significantly more in tax. As it was, the American Internal Revenue Service held back $1 million in royalties until it could be certain that Glidrose was genuinely part of Booker.

Although the sales of books were phenomenal, an increasing contribution to Glidrose's earnings now came from peripheral activities linked to the films. Shortly before Ian died, Glidrose had entered an agreement with Eon to share the marketing rights to the 007 trademark. By the end of 1965, 148 licences had been granted to manufacture Bond-related goods from toys and jigsaw puzzles to clothes, shoes and a Colgate-Palmolive range of toiletries (including a Bond deodorant).

New Bond-related ideas poured on to Glidrose's doorstep. Even the Crown Agents sought permission to issue Ian Fleming commemorative stamps in Jamaica. That project never materialized, but one that did was *The Poppy is also a Flower*, a film about the global drugs trade which Ian had originally discussed with Terence Young, the director of *Dr No* and *From Russia, With Love*. Drawing on his proposal for a narcotics handbook, Ian had talked of a story-line which followed the progress of an opium poppy from a flower in an Iranian field to raw heroin in the streets of New York. After Ian's death, Young developed the theme with a writer, Joe Eisinger, who presented it to Glidrose as a possible Fleming film. Ian's executors were unwilling to allow his name to be associated in any promotional capacity, though they were prepared to permit the use of the credit line, "The story is based on an idea by Ian Fleming". The film, known in Britain as *Danger Grows Wild*, was released in 1966 with Terence Stamp as the swarthy secret agent in the lead role and Grace Kelly voicing an admonitory introduction on the dangers of drugs.

The revenues of the Broccoli–Saltzman Bond films did not accrue to Glidrose, but to the various Fleming film trusts, which benefited whenever a new option was taken up. Total returns are difficult to calculate. *Dr No*, which was made for $1 million, went on to gross $16 million theatrically around the world. And from then on, the figures grew almost exponentially. Thirteen years later, Bond films had taken in over $1 billion worldwide, contributing to net profits, so it was claimed in John Parker's 1994 biography of Sean Connery, of over $400 million. Even if the 'producers' profit' on which the trusts' 5 per cent share was calculated was smaller than this, it was still a sizeable sum.

A posthumous backlash was bound to occur. It was initiated by the acid pen of Malcolm Muggeridge, who described Ian as an Etonian Micky Spillane, the creator of a shadowy and unreal character, who was "utterly despicable; obsequious to his superiors, pretentious in his tastes, callous and brutal in his ways, with strong undertones of sadism, and an unspeakable cad in his relations with women, towards whom sexual appetite represents the only approach". Peter Fleming jumped to his brother's defence, pouring scorn on Muggeridge for "vilify[ing], publicly, within a few months of his death, a friend from whom he had received nothing but kindness" and for pontificating on an author by whom he had, by his own admission, read only one novel. Otherwise the most concerted protest against the march of Bond came from east of the Iron Curtain where *Pravda*, smarting from Bond's global success, accused Ian directly of spying when he visited Moscow in 1939, and attacked him for creating "a world where the laws are written with a pistol barrel, and rape and outrages on female honour are considered gallantry". Similar criticisms were reiterated in Communist Party newspapers throughout the Soviet bloc, from *Al Ba'ath* in Syria, which was convinced that the CIA was behind the dissemination of Ian's works, to *Neues Deutschland* in East Germany, which ranted in April 1965, "There is something of Bond in the snipers of the streets of Selma, Alabama. He is flying with the napalm bombers over Vietnam ... The Bond films and books contain all the obvious and ridiculous rubbish of reactionary doctrine. Socialism is synonymous with crime. Unions are fifth columns of the Soviet Union. Slavs are killers and sneaks. Scientists are amoral eggheads. Negroes are superstitious, murderous lackeys. Persons of mixed race are trash."

This line was adopted by David Cornwell, better known as the author John le Carré, when he visited the Soviet Union two decades later. Describing Fleming's novels as "cultural pornography", he said what he disliked most was "the Superman figure who is 'ennobled' by some sort of misty, patriotic ideas and who can commit any crime and break any law in the name of his own society. He's a sort of licensed criminal who, in the name of false patriotism, approves of nasty crimes."

On a personal level, Ann never recovered from the trauma surrounding her husband's death. Having suppressed her unhappiness for so long, she went through a stage of frantic grief, which manifested itself in trembling, nervous exhaustion and smoking too much. She had resented "his refusal to become an easy invalid", and then, feeling "totally unhappy", she was forced to come to terms with the realization that he was "a desperate melancholic". As she told Cyril Connolly, Ian had constantly moaned, "How can I make you happy, when I am so miserable myself?" Connolly tried unconvincingly to reassure her that her marriage had been happy – "the bickering was on the same wave-length". More realistically, he said that James Bond could not have existed without her to "provide the fair weather". She had given Ian "an enormous amount of emotional security which included the freedom to roam and grumble. Imagine his life if he had not been married, a clubman killing time, switching from girl to girl."

Since Ian's estate was largely tied up in trusts, Ann claimed she was "as poor as a church rat" and resented the lawyers who seemed to hold her future in their hands. She had little compunction about asking the trustees for money, however: as she once said, she had supported Ian out of her own capital for long enough to feel perfectly entitled to make demands on his. She put a brave face on family duties, such as going to Tooth's to share out Eve's paintings with her Fleming in-laws, and grudgingly, often tearfully, agreed to assist John Pearson in a *Sunday Times*-approved biography of Ian. But she drew the line at supporting Amis's 'Continuation

Bond'. "No one understands why I am distressed," she complained to Evelyn Waugh; "though I do not admire 'Bond' he was Ian's creation and should not be commercialised to this extent." When *Colonel Sun* was published in 1968, Ann was asked to review it in the *Sunday Telegraph*, but her notice was never printed for fear of libel. Ann lambasted the author and those responsible for commissioning the book. "Since the exploiters hope *Colonel Sun* will be the first of a new and successful series, they may find themselves exploited. Amis will slip 'Lucky Jim' into Bond's clothing, we shall have a petit bourgeois red-brick Bond, he will resent the authority of M, then the discipline of the Secret Service, and end as Philby Bond selling his country to SPECTRE." Amis took Ann's reproaches in good spirit, admitting that he rather enjoyed the money on offer and the chance to twit the beards of erstwhile left-wing colleagues.

By then Caspar was sixteen, and the precocious, intelligent child, whom Ian had doted on but been too old and too busy to relate to, had grown into a fractious, unruly 1960s adolescent. He was plagued with two sides to his character. On the one hand he was a gifted student, with two abiding interests, books and Egyptology. He started a bibliographic club at Eton and invited John Sparrow to address it. Stimulated by a visit to Egypt the year after his father's death, he also assembled a respectable collection of Pharaonic antiquities. On the other hand, he could be rude and bloody-minded, with a hint of cruelty that Evangeline Bruce felt he inherited from his father. Invariably on the receiving end was Ann who ill-advisedly saw him as a genius destined one day to become Prime Minister. According to a friend of the family, Caspar slid seamlessly into Ian's role at the Sevenhampton breakfast table, and the bickering continued as before.

Tragically, Caspar's enthusiasm, verging on mania, for collecting also included firearms. Even as a nine-year-old at Summer Fields, he showed difficulty coming to terms with the James Bond phenomenon – not simply with his father's success but also with the violent adult world Ian portrayed. Before Ian's death, he was taking barbiturates regularly to help him sleep. Inevitably, in the prep-school world of small boys, his connection with 007 gave him great cachet. He traded Ian's autograph and Bond nick-nacks. In a letter of 1 October 1961, he told his parents he had been offered £1 for "Bond's pistol", presumably a toy. At Eton, he became interested in real guns, not imitations. In one letter he told his Uncle Hugo about a "flourishing black market" where one boy was offering to sell him a Luger. Uncle Peter tried to channel the fourteen-year-old Caspar's attentions towards more traditional sporting pursuits, and arranged for the trustees to pay out £115 for a sixteen-bore shotgun until he could handle his father's two twelve-bores, dating from 1912. (Caspar himself wanted a .22 rifle.)

Caspar's fascination with weaponry did not diminish as he grew older. At Sevenhampton he played with daggers, swordsticks and even a lethal crossbow which caused his mother's friends many anxious moments as they amused themselves on the croquet lawn. He was not yet seventeen, preparing for A-levels, when he was found with a loaded revolver in his room at Eton. Since the headmaster Anthony Chenevix-Trench had flu and could not beat Caspar (so Ann reported to Clarissa Avon, in an angry reference to his frequent use of the birch), the police were called. Peter Fleming was present when Caspar was interviewed and seemed to have hushed things up. But the next day Caspar ran away from school and went to stay with a friend who, on being arrested for possession of cannabis, blurted out that Caspar owned other guns. The police returned to interview Peter at Merrimoles, where they found that not only had he locked away four automatic pistols and assorted live ammunition belonging to Caspar, but also he had dropped his nephew's prized Browning automatic down a well. Peter suffered the embarrassment of being hauled before the local magistrates on three charges of illegal possession of firearms and ammunition. He was fined £10 on each count, while Caspar was relieved of £25 when he came before the juvenile court.

Although Ann's staff at Sevenhampton was limited to Nanny Sillick (acting as housekeeper) and a gardener, she usually hired a cook and parlourmaid at weekends, when her *mélange* of Oxford dons, artists, writers and a new clutch of Labour politicians such as Roy Jenkins were every bit as entertaining and interesting as her more formal gatherings at Warwick House and even Victoria Square. Only her closest friends realized that her gaiety, once so natural and vital, was now forced. On the fringes was often found the bulky figure of Arnold Goodman, who became an intimate friend inspiring a typical piece of Caspar's vitriol towards his mother: "he's as ugly as sin, but what do you expect at your age?" Having railed against Jock Campbell for cashing in on Bond, her case was undermined when she sold Ian's library to the University of Indiana in 1968. It was a difficult decision: after Percy Muir had been to Sevenhampton to help her pack the books for transportation to the United States, she told him she had decided not to proceed with the deal, and he quietly had to remind her that she had already signed a contract.

Clearing out the solemn-looking books stamped Ann's aesthetic vision more clearly on Sevenhampton, though it was wrong to think that she was ridding the house of all associations with Ian. She had a panel of two monkeys painted in the Venetian style. The left-hand monkey depicted Ian holding a copy of *Casino Royale*, and the right-hand Ann with a sheaf of lilies of perdition. For Ian's grave she commissioned a four-foot-high obelisk by her friend, the painter and designer Robin Ironside. And she refused to give up her manuscript copy of *Bond Strikes Camp* when it was requested for a benefit sale for the London Library. (She later bequeathed it to Peter's son, Nichol, which was appropriate since it was owned by Glidrose anyway.)

The high tone of her house parties was sometimes rudely shattered by the arrival of Caspar and his friends. After being expelled from Eton, he had worked hard to get himself to New College, Oxford. But he disliked the cloistered atmosphere of the university and left at the end of his second year, hoping to make a career for himself in the antiques business. Although he was seen with a succession of intelligent girlfriends, including Jo Cruickshank and Rachel Toynbee, his inner life was tormented and he became increasingly reclusive.

Once he was twenty-one in August 1973, Caspar was able to lay his hands on his trust money, which only served to finance his growing drug habit. With his coming of age, he also inherited his father's property in Jamaica. Under Blanche Blackwell's watchful eye, Goldeneye had been rented out to Ian's old friends, Alan and Nancy Miller, who finally put in a reliable hot-water system. In August 1974 Caspar visited the house for the first time since his father's death. He was amazed to learn about a side to Ian's life which had been written out of the historical record by his mother. In a fit of depression he took an overdose and swam out to sea in a bid to commit suicide. He was only saved by the prompt action of friends who summoned a helicopter and rushed him to hospital in Kingston. By now Ann, who had always looked indulgently on her son, simply did not know how to deal with him. When Nanny bravely responded to Caspar's striking his mother to the ground by hitting him as hard as a 64-year-old woman could, Ann's reaction was to dismiss her after nearly fifty years' service with her family. Now acknowledged to be a severe depressive, Caspar was given psychiatric treatment, including electric-shock therapy. But he was obsessively determined to end his life and, on 2 October 1975, he succeeded with another drugs overdose, leaving a pathetic note that "if it is not this time it will be the next".

Although Ian was mercifully no longer alive to witness his son's sad end, Ann was plunged into a new round of grief which she tried, unconvincingly, to mask with alcohol. Her own death from cancer in July 1981 opened a new chapter in the history of the Ian Fleming estate. While she, Caspar and Peter Fleming were alive, Ian's line of succession was clear; now, under the terms of Ian's will, the trust which controlled the most lucrative part of his legacy, the film revenues, was bequeathed to Peter's children, Nichol, Kate and Lucy. A distinguished trio of new executors, Lords Goodman, Charteris and O'Neill, was appointed by Ann to oversee this. The succession was initially slow, largely because of continuing reverberations from the *Thunderball* case. When McClory won his action in 1963, he retained the film rights to the *Thunderball* material. In order not to confuse the public with a rival James Bond on the screen, Eon Productions came to an agreement with McClory to co-produce the film version of *Thunderball* in 1965. As a result, McClory waived his rights to make another movie based on his *Thunderball* material for ten years. When that date passed and McClory began making noises about a new film, Eon and the Fleming estate tried to prevent him. (Broccoli and Saltzman had now parted company. Saltzman, always the showman, sold his share of Eon to United Artists, the Bond films' distributors, and splashed his profits on often ill-conceived business ventures.)

Although again confronted by a formidable legal team, McClory established his right to make a 'continuation' *Thunderball*. And, to cock an additional snook, he hired Sean Connery as his 007. After a series of confrontations with Eon, Connery had by then not only given way to Roger Moore as Bond but was also preparing to sue Broccoli and United Artists for allegedly not paying him what he thought he was owed. (The case was settled out of court.) McClory obtained the backing of Jack Schwartzman, an influential Hollywood producer, and in 1983 made *Never Say Never Again*, which enjoyed average success.

McClory's insistence on his legal rights in the Bond franchise contributed to a six-year hiatus in the making of official 007 films in the early 1990s. (Another factor was corporate turbulence at United Artists.) In 1995 Eon took up production again, releasing the hugely successful *Goldeneye*, which starred a new James Bond in Irish actor Pierce Brosnan, and further films have followed. This did not stop McClory continuing to press his legal suit. At one stage he won the backing of Sony to make what was touted as an alternative series of 007 films. But his legal success ran out in 2001 when his claim for compensation over alleged rights in the Bond films was thrown out by a Los Angeles court.

By then the situation with the Fleming Estate had changed. After the death of Ian's nephew Nichol Fleming in 1995, his nieces, Kate and Lucy, began taking a more active role in their Bond interests. They acquired full control of Glidrose (from Booker) and by 2001 Ian's old company was being run out of a plush Mayfair office where the Fleming family financial interests had decamped following the sale of the Robert Fleming bank to Chase Manhattan for a figure reportedly in excess of $7 billion. One of the new Glidrose's first initiatives was to strike a deal with Penguin to re-release the complete novels of Ian Fleming – an event which took place to a fanfare of considerable publicity in April 2002.

Fifty years after *Casino Royale* was written, there were signs that the focus of attention was beginning to swing back from the cult of 007 to its author and his literary works. After the blandness of international affairs in the wake of the Cold War, the role of Al Qaeda in the atrocities in New York on 11 September 2001 might have been plotted by Ian, with its spectacular act of terrorism and its clear delineation of right and wrong.

Without denying the stupor and moral ambiguity of the mid-twentieth century, Ian managed, almost without thinking, to convey a sense that it was possible to live positively and excitingly. Anthony Burgess, one of the more perceptive critics in recent years, said Ian had a sort of "Renaissance gusto", a controlled *joie de vivre* "which contradicted the socialist austerity of the fifties and yet did not endorse the permissiveness of the sixties."

Ian achieved this partly because of the contradictions in his character – the puritan and the libertine, "in proportion about nine days' desert to three days' fleshpots," said Cyril Connolly; the traditionalist and the rebel – and partly because he was so plainly a man of his age. He would not have enjoyed living thirty years after his death when the patriotic clubland values he cared about had all but disappeared and his literary offerings would have been pilloried for their lack of political correctness.

From a later vantage point it is too easy to criticize Ian for his selfishness, cruelty, and superciliousness (a *Sunday Times* colleague once coined a wonderful phrase for Ian's afternoons: *l'apres-midi d'un phony*). But he was in so many ways an agreeable man – good company, surprisingly thoughtful (when he could be bothered), and, despite his tendencies to moroseness, with a remarkable capacity for friendship. Someone who numbered Noël Coward, William Plomer, Cyril Connolly, Hugo Pitman and Ernie Cuneo among his close circle cannot be all bad. And, while only Ann really knew him and bore the brunt of his character with all its complications, every woman who loved him spoke fondly and positively.

Ian Fleming encapsulates both the tragedy and the triumph of his time. Despite his personal advantages, he ended his short life in misery. He failed in that he did not have quite the strength of character to choose one or other of the two main women in his life. However, if he had abandoned his wife for Blanche it would not have changed his destiny.

For Ian's triumph could only have happened in the world in which he grew up. He managed to loose himself from the rigid straitjacket in which his mother sought to confine him. As an intelligent *arriviste* from the City, he held his own in the landed establishment represented by the extended Charteris family. And some time, in the early years of his fifth decade, he was able to overcome his natural tendency to escapism and channel his fantasy and energy into producing a fine creative work that is as gripping today as it ever was.

Acknowledgements

I would like to acknowledge permission from the following individuals, companies and institutions to quote from various copyright material:

The Countess of Avon (for her letters), Clare Blanshard (for her letters), Virginia Charteris (for her husband Hugo Charteris's letters and for his unpublished novel *The Explorers*), Jonathan Cuneo (for his father Ernie Cuneo's papers), the Duchess of Devonshire (for Nancy Mitford's letters), Lord Dudley (for his father's letter), Kate Grimond and Lucy Williams (on behalf of the Ian Fleming Estate for the papers and letters of their uncle Ian Fleming and their father Peter Fleming), Sir Rupert Hart-Davis (for William Plomer material), Deirdre Levi (for the papers of Cyril Connolly), Candida Lycett Green (for John Betjeman's letter), Dr Stephen E. Malawista (for his mother's letters), Leonard Miall (for his diary entry), Fionn Morgan (for papers and letters from her mother Ann Fleming's estate), Barbara Muir (for her husband's letters), John Pearson (for material he collected for his book *The Life of Ian Fleming*), Lady Quennell (for her husband's letter), Jim Sanger (for his father Gerald Sanger's diaries) and Auberon Waugh (for his father's letters).

BBC Written Archives Centre, Jonathan Cape (for archive material), Chatto & Windus (for archive material), Francis Sitwell (for Dame Edith Sitwell's letters), Glidrose Publications (for Ian Fleming's Bond-related writings © Glidrose Productions and for archive material), Methuen (for Noël Coward's published verse), Michael Imison (on behalf of the Nöel Coward Estate for Noël Coward's unpublished material) and Reuters (for archive material).

The following institutions have kindly provided access to their collections, and granted permission where necessary:

Churchill Archive Centre, Churchill College, Cambridge; Lilly Library, Indiana University, Bloomington; Franklin Delano Roosevelt Library, Hyde Park; Georgetown University, Washington; Henry Ransom Humanities Research Center, The University of Texas at Austin; Department of Special Collections, McFarlin Library, University of Tulsa; Rare Book and Manuscript Library, Columbia University, New York; University of Reading; College Library, Eton College; Guildhall Library; House of Lords Record Office; and News International.

*In addition the following people have helped with interviews, letters and other
material:*

The Countess of
  Airlie
Rupert Allason
Rachel Ames
The Marquess of
  Anglesey
Eric Ambler
Mark Amory
Joan Astley
John Atkins
Mrs Douglas Auchincloss

Oliver Baring
Major Keith Barlow
Margaret Bax
Dr Jack Beal
Lady Berlin
Antony Beevor
Alan Bell
Blanche Blackwell
Christopher Blackwell
John Blackwell
Hetti von Bohlen und
  Halbach
Geoffrey Boothroyd
Joanne B. Bross
Philip Brownrigg
Evangeline Bruce
Naomi Burton
Lady Butler of Saffron
  Walden

Lady Jeanne Campbell
Professor Donald
  Cameron Watt
the late Lord Campbell of
  Eskan
Tim Card
'Oatsie' Charles
Lord Charteris of
  Amisfield
the late Violet Charteris
Lewis Chester
Dr Anthony Clayton
Lady Mary Clive

Mrs Gerald Coke
John Collard
Bill Corney
Keith Cousins
Lori Curtis

Lord Dacre of Glanton
Lieut. Commander
  Patrick Dalzel-Job
Lady D'Avidgor-
  Goldsmid
Felix Delmer
The Duke of Devonshire
Lord and the late Lady
  Donaldson of
  Kingsbridge
Captain Charles Drake
Julian Drinkall
Gay Dyer

the late Nicholas Elliott
Captain Jeremy Elwes

Douglas Fairbanks Jr
Patrick Leigh Fermor
Clive Fisher
Lady Foley
Alastair Forbes
Christina Foyle
Amaryllis Fleming
Christopher Fleming
Fergus Fleming
the late Nichol Fleming
Robin Fleming
G. H. Forster

Grace Garner
Martha Gellhorn
Frank Giles
Lord Gladwyn
Sir Alexander Glen
the late Lord Goodman
Francis Grey
John Guest

Lord Hailsham
Guy Hamilton
Lady Olive Hamilton
Robert Harling
Al Hart
Duff Hart-Davis
Christopher Hawtree
Richard Helms
Sir Nicholas Henderson
the late Hon David
  Herbert
Didy Hill
Tristram Hillgarth
H. V. (Harry) Hodson
the late Princess 'Honey'
  Hohenlohe
Patrick Howarth
Larry and Rose Hughes
Joan Hurst

Deirdre Inman
Molly Izzard

Peter Janson-Smith
Lord Jenkins of Hillhead

James Kirkup
Perry Knowlton

James Lees-Milne
Anthony Lejeune
Marie-Louise Leschallas
Judith Lenart
Deirdre Levi
Bernard Levin
the late Brian Lewis
Jeremy Lewis
Mary Lowell

Bill Macdonald
Larry Macdonald
Romana McEwen
Kitty McLachlan
Sir Fitzroy Maclean of
  Dunconnel Bt
Paddy McNally

Ella Maillart
Wolf Mankowitz
David Mason
Alexie Mayor
Michael Meredith
the late Monique de
    Mestral
Charlotte Mosley
Leonard Miall
Janet, Marchioness of
    Milford Haven
Nancy Miller
Robin de la Lanne
    Mirlees
Sheridan Morley
The Hon Sara Morrison
Lord Ivar and Lady Penny
    Mountbatten
Henry Morgenthau III
Andrew Mouravieff-
    Apostol
Peter Munster

Nigel Nicolson
Lord Norwich
Columbus O'Donnell
Lord and Lady O'Neill

Stokes von Pantz
John Parkinson
Frances Partridge
Graham Payn
Nuala Pell
Sir Edward Pickering
Jemima Pitman
the late Dilys Powell
John Pringle
Liz Pringle
Alan Pryce-Jones

the late Sir Peter
    Quennell

Elizabeth Ray
Doug Redenius
Geoff Richard
Barrington Roper
Alan Ross
Martin Russell
the late 'Nin' Ryan
Graham Rye

Alan Schneider
Moira Shearer
John H. Shephardson
Lord Sherfield

Joan Sillick
Brad Smith
Godfrey Smith
Lady Helen Smith
Sir Peter Smithers
the late Sir Stephen
    Spender
Dr David Stafford
William Stevenson
Peggy Strachey
Colonel John Stephens
Lady Daphne Straight
Michael Strauss
John Taylor
Letitia Thomson
Mac Tulley

Michael Van Blaricum
Hugo Vickers

Charles Wacker III
Kenneth Wagg
Lord Weidenfeld
Charles Wheeler
Grace Wherry
Rev. David Wild

Gavin Young

While every effort has been made to trace copyright holders, if any have inadvertently been overlooked, the publishers will be pleased to acknowledge them in any future editions of this work.

This book could not have been possible without the efforts of Andrew Lownie, my literary agent. It has been a delight to work with Ion Trewin, my publisher and editor, with Cassia Joll, his assistant, and with Elizabeth Blumer. With the minimum of fuss, Jane Birkett copy-edited the script and Douglas Matthews produced a comprehensive index in double quick time.

I would like to thank Colin and Mary Ellen Davies for hospitality and friendship in Washington, and John Cork, Nigel Cross, Caroline Dakers, Jane Dunn and Michael Holmsten who all read my manuscript and provided useful suggestions. I would especially like to pay tribute to John

Cork's encyclopaedic knowledge of Ian Fleming's works. Closer to home, Sue Greenhill has been wonderfully supportive and enthusiastic throughout the long haul. My love and thanks to her.

Bibliography

Ian Fleming's published works
(all published by Jonathan Cape in London)

fiction:

Casino Royale, 1953
Live and Let Die, 1954
Moonraker, 1955
Diamonds are Forever, 1956
From Russia, With Love, 1957
Dr No, 1958
Goldfinger, 1959
For Your Eyes Only, 1960
Thunderball (based on a screen treatment with Kevin McClory and Jack Whittingham), 1961
The Spy Who Loved Me, 1962
On Her Majesty's Secret Service, 1963
You Only Live Twice, 1964
(*Chitty-Chitty-Bang-Bang*, 1964)
The Man with the Golden Gun, 1965
Octopussy, 1966

non-fiction:

The Diamond Smugglers, 1957
Thrilling Cities, 1963

Peter F. Alexander, *William Plomer*, Oxford University Press, 1989
Christopher Andrew, *Secret Service*, William Heinemann, 1985
Kingsley Amis, *The James Bond Dossier*, Jonathan Cape, 1965
Mark Amory (ed.), *The Letters of Ann Fleming*, Collins Harvill, 1985
Mark Amory (ed.), *The Letters of Evelyn Waugh*, Weidenfeld & Nicolson, 1980
Joan Bright Astley, *The Inner Circle*, Hutchinson, 1971

John Atkins, *The British Spy Novel*, John Calder, 1984

Enid Bagnold, *Autobiography*, William Heinemann, 1969

Cecil Beaton, *The Years Between Diaries 1939–44*, Weidenfeld & Nicolson, 1965

Cecil Beaton, *The Strenuous Years Diaries 1948–53*, Weidenfeld & Nicolson, 1973

Nicola Beauman, *Cynthia Asquith*, Hamish Hamilton, 1987

Patrick Beesly, *Very Special Admiral*, Hamish Hamilton, 1980

Ralph Bennett, *Behind the Battle*, Sinclair-Stevenson, 1994

Raymond Benson, *James Bond Bedside Companion*, Boxtree, 1988

Georgiana Blakiston (ed.), *Letters of Conrad Russell 1897–1947*, John Murray, 1987

Phyllis Bottome, *The Goal*, Vanguard Press, 1962

Richard Bourne, *Lords of Fleet Street*, Unwin Hyman, 1990

Ann S. Boyd, *The Devil with James Bond*, John Knox Press, 1967

Susan Braudy, *This Crazy Thing Called Love*, Knopf, 1992

Anthony Cave Brown, *Secret Servant*, Michael Joseph, 1988

Ivar Bryce, *You Only Live Once*, Weidenfeld & Nicolson, 1975 and 1984

Thomas L. Bonn, *Heavy Traffic and High Culture*, Meridian, 1990

Shelagh Campbell, *Resident Alien*, Robert Hale, 1990

Morris Cargill, *Ian Fleming Introduces Jamaica*, André Deutsch, 1965

Morris Cargill, *Jamaica Farewell*, Cinnamon Books, 1979

Anne Chisholm and Michael Davie, *Beaverbrook*, Hutchinson, 1992

Kenneth Clark, *Another Part of the Wood*, John Murray, 1974

Cyril Connolly (Palinurus), *The Unquiet Grave*, Horizon, 1944

Artemis Cooper (ed.), *Mr Wu and Mrs Stitch: The Letters of Evelyn Waugh and Diana Cooper*, Hodder and Stoughton, 1991

Noël Coward, *Collected Verse*, Methuen, 1984

Noël Coward, *The Noël Coward Diaries*, ed. Graham Payn and Sheridan Morley, Weidenfeld & Nicolson, 1982

Geoffrey Cox, *Countdown to War: A Personal Memoir of Europe 1938–40*, William Kimber, 1988

Caroline Dakers, *Clouds*, Yale University Press, 1994

Sefton Delmer, *Black Boomerang*, Secker and Warburg, 1962

Frances Donaldson, *A Twentieth Century Life*, Weidenfeld & Nicolson, 1992

Sybil and David Eccles, *By Safe Hand: Letters 1939–42*, Bodley Head, 1983

Hugh Edwards, *All Night at Mr Stanyhurst's*, Jonathan Cape, 1933

Patrick Leigh Fermor, *The Traveller's Tree*, John Murray, 1950

Iain Finlayson, *Tangier City of the Dream*, HarperCollins, 1992

Clive Fisher, *Cyril Connolly: A Nostalgic Life*, Macmillan, 1995

Fergus Fleming, *Amaryllis Fleming*, Sinclair-Stevenson, 1993

Kate Fleming, *Celia Johnson*, Weidenfeld & Nicolson, 1992

Joyce Grenfell, *Darling Ma: Letters to her Mother*, Hodder and Stoughton, 1988

Denis Hamilton, *Editor in Chief*, Hamish Hamilton, 1989

Cecil Hampshire, *The Secret Navies*, William Kimber, 1978

Duff Hart-Davis, *Peter Fleming*, Jonathan Cape, 1974

Rupert Hart-Davis, *The Arms of Time*, Hamish Hamilton, 1979

Rupert Hart-Davis, *The Power of Chance*, Sinclair-Stevenson, 1991

Harold Hobson, Phillip Knightley, Leonard Russell, *The Pearl of Days: An Intimate Memoir of the Sunday Times 1822–1972*, Hamish Hamilton, 1972

Geoffrey Household, *The Third Hour*, Chatto & Windus, 1937

H. Montgomery Hyde, *The Quiet Canadian*, paperback edition with introduction by Ian Fleming, Mayflower Dell, 1964

Laurence Irving, *The Precarious Crust*, Chatto & Windus, 1971

Alaric Jacob, *Scenes from a Bourgeois Life*, Secker and Warburg, 1949

David Kahn, *Seizing the Enigma*, Souvenir Press, 1991

Barbara Kaye, *The Company We Kept*, Werner Shaw, 1986

Ludovic Kennedy, *On My Way to the Club*, Collins, 1989

James Kirkup, *I, of All People*, Weidenfeld & Nicolson, 1988

Judith Lenart, *Yours Ever Ian Fleming*, published privately, 1994

Cole Leslie, *The Life of Noël Coward*, Jonathan Cape, 1976

Norman Lewis, *A View of the World*, Eland, 1986

Donald McCormick, *17F: The Life of Ian Fleming*, Peter Owen, 1993

Donald McLachlan, *Room 39: Naval Intelligence in Action 1939–45*, Weidenfeld & Nicolson, 1968

Frank McLynn, *Fitzroy Maclean*, John Murray, 1992

Frank MacShane, *The Life of Raymond Chandler*, Jonathan Cape, 1976

Norman MacSwan, *The Man who Read the East Wind*, Kangaroo Press, 1982

Laura, Duchess of Marlborough, *Laughter from a Cloud*, Weidenfeld & Nicolson, 1980

Ted Morgan, *Somerset Maugham*, Jonathan Cape, 1980

Charlotte Mosley (ed.), *The Letters of Nancy Mitford*, Hodder and Stoughton, 1993

Conrad O'Brien-ffrench, *Delicate Mission*, Skilton & Shaw, 1979

Harold Nicolson, *Public Faces*, Constable, 1932

John Parker, *Sean Connery*, Victor Gollancz, 1993

Graham Payn (with Barry Day), *My Life With Noël Coward*, Applause, 1994

John Pearson, *The Life of Ian Fleming*, Jonathan Cape, 1966

Thomas Pellatt, *Boys in the Making*, Methuen, 1936

Anthony Powell, *Journals 1982–1986*, Heinemann, 1995

Alan Pryce-Jones, *The Bonus of Laughter*, Hamish Hamilton, 1987

David Pryce-Jones (ed.), *Evelyn Waugh and his World*, Weidenfeld & Nicolson, 1973

David Porter, *The Man who was "Q"*, Paternoster Press, 1989

Peter Quennell, *The Wanton Chase*, William Collins, 1980

Donald Read, *The Power of News*, Oxford University Press, 1992

Bruce A. Rosenberg and Ann Harleman Stewart, *Ian Fleming*, Twayne, 1989

Alan Ross, *Coastwise Lights*, Collins Harvill, 1988

Michael Shelden, *Friends of Promise*, Hamish Hamilton, 1989

Michael Shelden, *Graham Greene: The Man Within*, William Heinemann, 1994

Barbara Skelton, *Tears Before Bedtime*, Hamish Hamilton, 1987

Barbara Skelton, *Weep No More*, Hamish Hamilton, 1989

Denis Smyth, *Diplomacy and Strategy of Survival*, Cambridge University Press, 1986

David Stafford, *Camp X*, Viking, 1987

Richard Usborne, *Clubland Heroes*, Constable, 1953

Hugo Vickers, *Cecil Beaton*, Weidenfeld & Nicolson, 1985

Hugo Vickers (ed.), *Cocktails and Laughter: The Albums of Loelia Lindsay*, Hamish Hamilton, 1983

Baron Hubert von Pantz, *No Risk No Fun!*, Vantage Press, 1986

George Weidenfeld, *Remembering My Good Friends*, HarperCollins, 1995

Nigel West, *MI6*, Weidenfeld & Nicolson, 1983

Nigel West (ed.), *The Faber Book of Espionage*, Faber, 1993

Edmund Wilson, *The Sixties*, Farrar Straus Giroux, 1993

Philip Ziegler, *Diana Cooper*, Hamish Hamilton, 1981

Index

Works by Ian Fleming are listed directly under title; works by others appear under authors' names

Absent-Minded Professor, The (film) 393
Acquart, Reginald 165, 280
Adam, Ken 387
Adler, Dr Alfred 32–3, 40, 77–8
Admiralty *see* Naval Intelligence Division
Agate, James 394
Ailwyn, Major Ronald Townshend Fellowes, 2nd Baron 25, 27
Aitken, Janet 26, 68, 296
Aitken, Jonathan 418
Aitken, William 260
Alexander, Albert Victor (*later* Viscount) 116–17
Alexandra, Princess 390
Alphabet and Image (magazine) 204
Alpine motor trials (1932) 52–3
Ambler, Eric 195, 224, 277–8; *The Mask of Dimitrios* 278, 273; *The Night Comes* 278; *Passage of Arms* 356
Amis, (Sir) Kingsley 438, 443, 445; *Colonel Sun* ('continuation Bond', by 'Robert Markham') 449, 445; *James Bond Dossier* 445
Amory, Mark 164, 322
Andress, Ursula 398, 443
Anglo-American Corporation 258
Anglo-Persian Oil Company (*now* British Petroleum) 2, 54–5
Annigoni, Pietro 403
Antibes 241–2
Antonio (Jamaican storekeeper) 305
Arethusa, HMS 116
Argyll, Margaret, Duchess of (*née* Whigham; *then* Sweeny) 65
Arlen, Michael: *The Green Hat* 18
Armitage, Selby 428
Armour, Tommy: *How to Play Your Best Golf All the Time* 315
Arnisdale (estate), Argyllshire 13, 23, 441
Arnold, Ralph 34
Arnold-Forster, Commander Christopher 145
Around the World in Eighty Days (film) 349
Ashcombe, Roland Cubitt, 3rd Baron 187

Ashcroft, (Dame) Peggy 41
Ashton, (Sir) Frederick 179, 228, 361
Ashton, Winifred *see* Dane, Clemence
Asquith, Anthony 352
Asquith, Cynthia (Herbert's wife) 93
Asquith, Herbert Henry, 1st Earl of Oxford and Asquith 70, 94
Asquith, Herbert (son) 94
Asquith, Margot, Countess of Oxford and Asquith (*née* Tennant) 77, 93
Astor, John Jacob 281
Astor, Michael 442
Astor, Vincent 128
Astor, Mrs Vincent (Brooke) 194
Athenaeum Court, Piccadilly 135–6
Atticus (*Sunday Times* column): IF writes 251–3, 269, 292, 317
Auchincloss, Kay-Kay (*formerly* Kelly) 336, 338
Auden, W.H. 394
Augustine, St 323
Australia: IF visits 156
Austria 92–3, 340–1
Avon, 1st Earl of *see* Eden, Sir Anthony
Avon, Countess of *see* Eden, Clarissa, Lady
Ayub Khan 25
Azores 117–18

Bacon, Francis 248, 296
Bad Neuheim, Germany 433
Bagnold, Enid (Lady Jones) 46, 342
Bahamas: Eve settles in 210; IF on flamingo count in 287–8, 294; Bryces' house in 294; IF gambles in 294; in *Thunderball* 366
Bailiff's Court, Sussex 178
Baillie-Hamilton, Charles 67
Baillie-Hamilton, Wanda (*née* Holden) 39, 67
Bainbridge, Emerson 92
Bainbridge, Peggy (*née* Barnard) 25–8, 30, 92
Baldwin, Michael 443
Balfour, Arthur James, 1st Earl 93

Ball, Sir Joseph 90, 95
Banbury, Charles William, 2nd Baron 353
Barber, Noel 260
Barbezat family 45
Bariffe, Felix (Goldeneye gardener) 281, 303
Baring, Olive (née Hugh Smith) 70
Barlow, Keith 405
Barnard, Peggy see Bainbridge, Peggy
Barnes, Susan 280
Barnsley, Dr Alan 262
Barrie, Sir James Matthew 93
Barry, Bill 7
Barry, Mabel 7
Barton, Hugh and Diana 356
Basra 376
Battle of Britain (1940) 118
Baxter, Edward 1
Bay of Pigs see Cuba
Beal, Dr Jack 81, 176, 197, 290, 343, 426, 441
Beal, Tina 441
Beaton, (Sir) Cecil: on Dorchester in war 122; at Ann's parties 136, 248, 261, 361; and IF-Ann betrothal 215; stands godfather to Caspar Fleming 229–30
Beatty, Chester 60, 316
Beaumont-Nesbitt, Major General Frederick George ('Paddy') 113
Beaverbrook, William Maxwell Aitken, 1st Baron: and José Collins 17; IF's relations with 71, 292; wartime activities 122; success with Daily Express 161, 167; in Jamaica 167, 211; Ann writes on 191; relations with Coward 194; on Ivar Bryce 208; sends wine as wedding present to IF and Ann 226; supports IF's writings 233, 243, 255, 269; IF writes profile of 269; and Ann's dislike of Bryce 271; Ann's friendship with 275, 295–6; and IF's reluctance to have Caspar in Jamaica 281; IF praises bridge-playing 292; Ann complains of isolation to 323; Ann solicits to call off journalists 363; and IF's convalescence from heart attack 385; Ann complains of Fionn's wedding 390; IF sends Sutherland drawing to 396; Ann pleads to restore Bond strip 399; IF writes for reconciliation with 409–10
Beck, John 366
Beckett, Samuel: Murphy 394
Bedford, Dr Evan 343, 442
Bedford, Sybille: Jigsaw 75
Beesley, Patrick 115
Beirut 377
Beit, Sir Alfred 77, 282
Beit, Clementine, Lady 282
Beit, Lillian, Lady 77

Beit, Sir Otto 77
Bekesbourne, Kent 322–3, 326, 374
Bellevue (house), Jamaica 144, 164
Bendern, Count John de 192
Bendern, Countess Patricia de 192
Benson, Sir Rex 166, 240
Bentley, Nicolas: The Tongue-Tied Canary 232
Bergonzi, Bernard 330–1
Berkeley, HMS 116
Berlin: Reuters post IF to 62; IF visits for Thrilling Cities article 371; in IF short story 395
Berlin, Aline, Lady 413, 421
Berlin, Sir Isaiah 130
Bermuda 128, 286
Berners, Gerald Hugh Tyrwhitt-Wilson, 14th Baron 92
Bernhard, Prince of the Netherlands 119, 123
Berry, Anthony 255
Berry, Dennis 170
Berry, Lionel 273
Berry, Lady Pamela 106, 170, 174
Berry, Rodney 187
Berthoud, Georges 68–9
Betjeman, (Sir) John 243, 279, 385, 433
Bevan, Aneurin 81
Biarritz 247–8
Bicester, Vivian Hugh Smith, 1st Baron 70, 147
Biggs-Davison, John 269
Birch, Frank 122
Birley, Commander G.H. 131
Bishirgian, Garabed 66, 69
Bismarck (German battleship) 128–9, 134
Black Daffodil, The (IF; poems) 39
Black Hole Hollow Farm, Vermont 208–10, 258, 272, 316
Black Sun Press 43
Blackwell, Blanche (née Lindo): background 279–80; relations with IF 280–1, 285, 301, 303, 308–9, 321–5, 329, 337, 339, 396–7, 407–8, 427–8, 434, 453; and Edens' visit to Jamaica 304; Lahoud resents 306; alluded to in Dr No 308; Ann's attitude to 308, 322, 344, 362, 382, 397, 399, 427; supposed representation as Pussy Galore 329; on trip to Pedro Cays 329–30; stays at Goldeneye 330, 344; IF buys watch for 340; and decoration of house (Bolt) 346–7; plants shrubs at Goldeneye 362–3; premonition of IF's illness 382, 384; visits IF in hospital in England 384; and IF's condition after heart attack 396; IF meets in New York 410–11; joins IF in Germany and Austria 423; and IF's settlement with McClory 432; IF accuses

of illiteracy 436; IF meets in last months 442; absent from IF's memorial service 444; looks after Goldeneye 451

Blackwell, Christopher 280, 398

Blackwell, David 280

Blackwell, Gordon 280

Blackwell, John 280, 327–8, 374, 405–6, 435

Blackwell, Joseph 280

Blackwell, Tom 435

Blairman, David 236

Blake, George 371, 410

Blake, Robert, Baron 90

Blanshard, Clare: meets IF in Ceylon 154–5; travels to Australia 155–7; sends cake to IF 157; IF recommends to Harling 168; in New York 225, 236–7, 245; works for Welby 290; Catholicism 298; visits IF in hospital 298

Blanshard, Paul 155

Bletchley Park (Government Communications Headquarters; *earlier* Government Code and Cypher School) 102, 104, 114, 119, 121

Blitz (London) 122–3, 135–6, 147

Blunt, Anthony 230

Blyth, Jimmy 114

Bodker, Victor 62

Boissevain, Sarah 209

Bond, James (fictional character): origins 112, 216; name 158, 180, 223; character 220–3, 238, 284, 313, 337; IF's doubts over 255, 268, 364, 438; parodied 271, 383, 416, 419; Chandler on 289; uncertainty of fate in *From Russia, With Love* 293, 314; guns 299–301; as cartoon strip 316, 337, 396, 399; criticized for vulgarity and nihilism 330–3, 401–2; film casting of 352, 393; criticized by Russians and Communists 406, 447–8; obituary 415, 420, 433; posthumous ('continuation') stories 445, 448–9

Bond, James (naturalist) 436; *Field Guide to Birds of the West Indies* 180, 223

Bonham Carter, Mark (*later* Baron) 244

Boodle's Club, London 175–6, 200, 261

Book Collector (formerly *Book Handbook*) 202, 227, 273–4, 347–8

Book Handbook see *Book Collector*

Booker Brothers (company) 428–9, 444–6

Bookman, The (TV programme) 345

Boothby, Robert, Baron 295–6, 410

Boothroyd, Geoffrey 298–301, 320, 395

Bordeaux: 1940 evacuation from 115–17

Bormann, Martin 157

Bottome, Phyllis (Mrs Forbes Dennis) 24, 32–5, 77–8; *The Goal* 77

Boucher, Anthony 275, 301

Bowater (paper company) 257

Bowes-Lyon, David 105

Bowes-Lyon, John ('Jock') 71

Bowra, (Sir) Maurice 189, 261, 424

Boxer, Mark 396

Boy and the Bridge, The (film) 348–9, 351–2, 359–60, 365

Boyd of Merton, 1st Viscount see Lennox-Boyd, Alan

Brandon, Henry 169, 367–8, 383

Braun, Werner von 403

Bray, Hilary 177, 196, 386, 397, 405, 422, 435, 443

Bray, Jenny 435

Braziers Park, Ipsden, Oxfordshire 5, 13

Bridgeman, Maurice 54

Briggs, Joyce 276

Bright, Joan 135–6, 148–50, 167, 252, 257

British-American-Canadian Corporation (*later* World Commerce Corporation) 166

British Broadcasting Corporation: IF broadcasts for 361–2, 378

British Fashion Council 178

British Movietone News 161

British Purchasing Mission (USA) 128

British Security Coordination (BSC) 127–8, 143, 194

Broccoli, Albert R. ('Cubby') 387–9, 393, 398, 432, 447, 452

Brooker, John 405

Bross, John 368

Brownlow, Peregrine Francis Adelbert Cust, 6th Baron 240, 305

Brownrigg, Philip 200–1, 258, 316, 428

Bruce, David 392

Bruce, Evangeline 392, 449

Bruna, A.W. (Dutch publisher) 278

Bruyère, Jean de la 349

Bryce, Ivar: first meets IF 8; at Eton with IF 16–20; in Paris 39; and IF's gambling 67; in Capri 87–8; joins Ian for trip to Austria 91–2; wartime mission in Jamaica 144; home in Jamaica 165; visits IF at Goldeneye 173–4, 180, 210, 434; friendship with IF 176, 261, 293–5; and Ann's attitude to IF's affairs 178; Ann dislikes 180, 271; marriage difficulties 182; Austrian house (Schloss Mittersill) 194–5; lives in USA 208–10, 271, 316; third marriage (to Marie-Josephine) 208–9; IF advises on writing 216; meets IF and Ann after wedding 218; alluded to in Bond novels 222, 238; helps buy typewriter for IF 225; and US publication of *Casino Royale* 233; in New York 236–7, 281; IF writes up in Atticus column 252; buys control of NANA 260–1; IF travels across Atlantic with 262; IF dedicates *Diamonds Are Forever*

Bryce, Ivar—*cont*
to 272; on bird-watching expedition to
Bahamas 287; at Moyns 293–4; and
proposed collaboration with IF on TV
series 297; and Edens' visit to
Goldeneye 305; sybaritism 321; film
making 348–52, 359–60, 364–7; and IF's
condition after heart attack 396; Hart-
Davis avoids 426; in McClory court case
431–2

Bryce, Marie-Josephine (*née* Hartford;
Ivar's third wife; 'Jo') 208, 210, 218,
252, 281, 294

Bryce, Sheila (Ivar's second wife) 144, 180,
182

Burgess, Anthony 452

Burgess, Guy 213, 221, 230, 275, 283

Burmester, Captain Rudolph 104

Burningham, John 393

Burton, Naomi: criticizes IF's erotic scenes
249; and US publication of IF's works
255, 275; and film/TV rights 276, 337,
351; and IF's religious practice 298; on
Jo Stewart 338; leaves Curtis Brown 356,
359

Buscot, Oxfordshire 122

Butler of Saffron Walden, Mollie, Lady
(*formerly* Courtauld) 98, 414

Byron, George Gordon, 6th Baron 178

Cabritta Island, Jamaica 238

Cadogan, Sir Alexander 81

Cairo: Sextant Conference (1943) 149–50

Calypso (research ship) 242

Camp X, Oshawa, near Toronto 149

Campbell, Douglas 415

Campbell, Lady Jeanne 208, 296, 346, 379

Campbell, Sir Jock (later Lord Campbell of
Eskan) 428–9, 438, 446, 450

Campbell, Olivia 61

Campbell, Rodney 231

Campbell-Grey, Ian 80

Camrose, William Ewert Berry, 1st
Viscount 160, 192

Cannes 273

Cape, Jonathan: accepts *Casino Royale*
226, 233; IF negotiates with 231–2,
277–8

Cape, Jonathan (publishers): Hart-Davies
joins 42; publish IF 201, 226, 244–5,
255, 257, 292, 313, 317, 345, 402, 420,
430, 437, 444; and film rights 250, 275–
6; and jacket illustrations 369

Capel, Eileen 378

Capote, Truman 281–2; *Answered Prayer*
272

Capri 87–8

Card, Tim 14

Carey, Joyce 196

Cargill, Barbara 287

Cargill, Morris 174, 287, 363–4, 436

Caribbean Cement Company 166

Carlyle Mansions, Chelsea 207, 223–4,
236

Caronia (liner) 307

Carr, Anne 309

Carter, John 347

Carter-Ruck, Peter 431–2

Cartland, (Dame) Barbara 427

Carton de Wiart, General Sir Adrian 113

Casino Royale (IF): gambling scene in 128;
writing 216–17, 230; Bond character
introduced in 220–3; plot, names and
content 221–3, 237; publication 241;
reception 243; film rights 249–50, 255,
264, 268, 338, 351; modified for US publication 249, 255; first TV film version
264–5, 297; US paperback version (as
You Asked For It) 275; sadism in 330

Castellane, 'Boni', Marquis of 49

Casteret, Norbert 247

Castro, Fidel 320, 340, 367–8

Cavendish, Anthony: *Inside Intelligence*
169

Cavendish, Henry 106

Cavendish-Bentinck, Lord William (*later*
7th Duke of Portland) 104–5

CBS (corporation) 264–5, 336–8, 398

Central Intelligence Agency 131

'Cercle, Le' 81–2, 196

Cerf, Bennett 74, 249, 255

Cerf, Christopher: collaborates on
Alligator 419

Ceylon (Sri Lanka) 154–5

Chamberlain, Neville 90, 106

Chamonix 406–7

Chancellor, Christopher 50, 62, 72

Chandler, Raymond: IF meets 270–1;
reviews *Diamonds Are Forever* 289, 292;
and Luciano 332, 373; reviews *Dr No*
332

Chandos, Oliver Lyttelton, 1st Viscount
318

Chaplin, Charlie 372

Chaplin, Oona (*née* O'Neill) 372

Charteris family 61

Charteris, Frances (*née* Tennant; Ann's
mother) 93, 239

Charteris, Guy (Ann's father) 93, 239–40,
406

Charteris, Hugo (Ann's brother): and
Alaric Jacob 51; born 93; and Ann's
marriage to Rothermere 158; at Warwick
House 176; and Ann's attachment to IF
187, 199, 330; works on *Daily Mail* 199;
dislikes IF 205–6; supports IF and Ann
on decision to marry 215; on *Casino
Royale* 244; quarrel with IF over

diamond smuggling story 314–15; and Ann's dilemma over dying Gaitskell 414; *Picnic at Porokorro* 415, 314; visits Sevenhampton 424; and Caspar's interest in guns 449; *The Explorers* 205–7; *The Tide is Right* 314

Charteris, Laura (Ann's sister) *see* Dudley, Countess of

Charteris, Martin (*later* Baron Charteris of Amisfield) 205, 451

Charteris, Mary Rose (Ann's sister) *see* Grey, Mary Rose

Charteris, Violet (Ann's stepmother) 239–40, 406

Charteris, Virginia (*née* Forbes Adam) 176, 179, 186, 188, 200, 215, 424

Chase, James Hadley 270; *No Orchids for Miss Blandish* 331

Chatham, William Pitt, 1st Earl of 5–6

Chatto & Windus (publishers) 74, 85

Chenevix-Trench, Anthony 450

Chester, Lewis 328

Chewning, Mary 317

Chiang Kai-shek 150

Chicago 263

Chichester, Sir Francis 438

Chitty-Chitty-Bang-Bang (IF) 384, 386, 393, 404

Cholerton, A.T. 57, 98

Chopping, Richard: designs IF's book covers 300, 369, 390–1, 426

Churchill, John (Sir Winston's brother) 9, 12

Churchill, Pamela (*later* Harriman) 136, 247

Churchill, Randolph 295, 383

Churchill, Robert 119

Churchill, (Sir) Winston: and Valentine Fleming 7, 9, 11–12; introduced to Augustus John 20; education 21–2; friendship with IF 60; anti-Nazi activities 77; Eve recommends sons to 95; and Naval Intelligence Division 103; apathy over clandestine operations 108; praises Hillgarth 109; and March's ship-buying plan 110; and fall of France 115; and US support 120; Mediterranean strategy 137; meetings with Roosevelt 148–9; returns from Fulton speech in USA 167; and 1951 election 213

Claparaide, Mme 43

Clark, Kenneth, Baron 24, 424

Clark, 'Sharkey' (of Seychelles) 335

Clarke, Arthur C. 257

Clayton, Rear Admiral John W. ('Jock') 121

Clifford, Alexander 50–1, 188

Clifford, Jenny 188

Clive, Lady Mary (*née* Pakenham) 82–8, 98, 225, 230, 430–1

Cobra, Operation 154

Coke, Gerald 55, 81

Colefax, Sibyl, Lady 50, 92, 94

Collard, John 310–13, 315–16

Collier, Lawrence 98

Collins, José (Lady Innes-Ker) 17

Colville, (Sir) John ('Jock') 106

Colvin, Ian 169

Connery, Sean 393, 447, 452

Connolly, Cyril: on Peggy Barnard 26; in Kitzbühel 92; IF proposes starting magazine with 94; IF praises 164; edits *Horizon* 174; friendship with Ann 196; and Burgess and Maclean 213, 230; in Kent 224, 233–5, 252; marriage to Barbara Skelton 224; IF invites to write for Queen Anne Press 228; and IF's view of *Punch* 236; 50th birthday party 248–9; tutors Charles D'Costa 279; *Bond Strikes Camp* 416–17, 440, 450, 383; Ann buys John drawing of 424; criticizes *You Only Live Twice* 437; IF's friendship with 439–40, 453; and Ann's reaction to IF's death 448; on IF's contradictions 452; *The Unquiet Grave* 439

Conrad, Augustus 60

Cooke, F.C. 334

Cooke, Sidney Russell 71

Cooper, Alfred Duff (*later* 1st Viscount Norwich): career 30; friendship with IF 60, 89; friendship with Ann 124, 146, 179; in Algiers 152; visits Ann in St Margaret's Bay 225, 234; *Translations and Verses* 201

Cooper, Lady Diana (*née* Manners): marriage 30; cottage at Aldwick 41; friendship with IF 60, 89; acting career 92; friendship with Ann 124, 146, 179, 296, 361, 368; in Paris 178; and Ann's account of yachting mishap in Jamaica 211; and Waugh's reaction to IF–Ann marriage 224; visits Ann in Kent 234, 272; winter holiday with Ann 344; IF's antipathy to 361; and Ann's attachment to Gaitskell 364; Ann meets in Chantilly 373

Cooper, Douglas 391

Cork, John 351

Corkran, Major-General C.E. 28

Corney, Bill 72–3

Cornhill Magazine 227

Cornwell, David *see* le Carré, John

Corsica 41–2

Cotton, Sydney 106–8, 433

Courtauld, August 98

Cousins, Aubyn 183

Cousins, Christie ('Busha') 165, 297

Cousteau, Commander Jacques 241–2, 246, 252, 264

Coward, Noël: IF's relations with 71; in Jamaica 173, 193–4, 239; rents Goldeneye 183–4; St Margaret's Bay house 192, 195–6, 235; relations with Beaverbrook 194; on Ann and *Daily Mail* 199; and Pells' yachting mishap 211; rescues IF from Rosamond Lehmann 211; and Burgess and Maclean disappearance 213; on IF–Ann betrothal 215–16; and writing of *Casino Royale* 217; at IF–Ann wedding 217–18; stands godfather to Caspar Fleming 229; on IF's marriage relations 234, 288, 380; praises *Moonraker* 257, 269; friendship with Ambler 277; friendship with Blanche Blackwell 280, 285; builds and settles in Jamaica villa (Firefly) 281, 285; IF introduces Truman Capote to 282; friendship with IF 286, 453; Ann offends 303–4; and Edens' visit to Jamaica 303, 305–6; on Blanche Blackwell 329; plays in *Our Man in Havana* 361; Ann entertains in London 368, 370; IF visits in Montreux 372; nurses sick IF 379–80; and IF's heart attack 385; homosexuality 417; objects to IF's treatment of Blanche 427; *Pomp and Circumstance* (novel) 379; *Tonight at Eight-Thirty* 304; *Volcano* 308–9

Cowles, Virginia *see* Crawley, Virginia

Cox, (Sir) Geoffrey: *Countdown to War* 115

Crabb, Commander Lionel ('Buster') 292, 399

Crawley, Aidan 233

Crawley, Virginia (*née* Cowles) 181, 233

Cray, Dorothy M. 427

Creake Abbey, Norfolk 247

Crickmere, Edgar and Mary 241, 414

Crosby, Caresse 43

Crosby, Harry 43

Crosland, Anthony 296

Cross, Odo 239

Cruickshank, Jo 451

Cuba 320, 340, 367–8, 383, 418

Cull, Anders 60

Cull and Company 60, 64–6, 147

Cummings, Violet 173, 179, 239–40, 304, 324, 380, 415

Cunard, Maud Alice (Emerald), Lady 181, 188

Cunard, Nancy 39

Cuneo, Ernie: IF meets 143–4, 168; IF visits in USA 209–10, 237, 258; marriage and son 229; and IF's interest in NANA 260–1, 275; US train and air tour with IF 262–6, 358–9; on IF's romantic remoteness 263–4; alluded to in

Diamonds Are Forever 267–8; IF dedicates *Diamonds Are Forever* to 272; and Bryce's film enterprises 349–50, 359–60, 420; on IF's appearance after heart attack 396; attends McClory court case 431–2; friendship with IF 453

Cuneo, Margaret (*née* Watson) 229

Cunningham, Admiral Sir Andrew 124, 137, 153

Currie, Sir William 241

Curtis, Lieutenant Dunstan 145, 152–3

Curtis Brown (literary agency) 245–6, 249–50, 264–5, 275–7, 298, 335, 337, 359

Curzon, Mary, Marchioness (*née* Leiter) 167

Cuthbertson, Penelope 424

Cuthbertson, Teresa (*née* Jungman) 424

D'Abernon, Edgar Vincent, Viscount 20, 38, 48, 64, 99

Dahl, Roald: 'Lamb to the Slaughter' 193

Daily Express: success of 161; IF criticizes to Beaverbrook 167; James Bond strip in 316, 337; Bond strip terminated 396, 399–400; IF offers *On Her Majesty's Secret Service* for serialization 409–10

Daily Gleaner (Jamaican newspaper) 193–4, 415

Daily Graphic 160, 231

Daily Mail 161–2, 173, 199, 393

Daily Sketch: IF brings action against 433

Daily Telegraph: Camrose acquires 160

Dane, Clemence (i.e. Winifred Ashton) 196

Danger Grows Wild (film) 447

Dansey, Claude 90, 169

Danube, River: wartime plan to block 110–12

Darlan, Admiral Jean François 115–17, 146

Darwin, Robin 274, 292

Dauban, Henry 335

Davenport, Nicholas 70

Davidson, Major General Francis 132

Davies, Marion 143

Dawson, Geoffrey 113

Day, Philip 255

Day-Lewis, Cecil 211

D'Costa, Sir Alfred 279

D'Costa, Charles 175, 222, 279

D'Costa, Mildred 279

Deane, Kathleen (*née* Rose; Eve's sister) 4, 68

Deauville 67

De Beers (diamond corporation) 258, 267, 310–11, 316

Deighton, Len: *Funeral in Berlin* 438

Delhi 155

Dell, Ethel M. 427
Delmer, Isabel 123
Delmer, Sefton: on Trade Mission trip to Moscow 96–7; on Room 39 102; organises wartime black propaganda 108, 132–4; bombed in war 123; meets Loelia Westminster 135; at war's end 158
Denning, Vice Admiral Sir Norman 376–7
Dennis, Nigel 34
Derville, Anthony 362
Desert Island Discs (BBC radio programme) 419
Deutsch, André 436
Devas, Nicolette 72
Devonshire, Deborah, Duchess of 370
Dexter, Ted 440
Diamond Corporation 316, 337
Diamond Smugglers, The (IF) 205, 317, 338, 383
Diamonds Are Forever (IF): gadgets in 119, 259; Maugham praises 242, 288; writing and research 257–9, 267–8, 310; plot 268; IF's embarrassment over 270; dedication 272; film rights 275; US publication 275, 297, 301; 'Boofy' Gore objects to name in 289; Chandler reviews 289, 292; reception 289; IF's satisfaction with 292; criticized for sexual licence 331
Dickens, Kenneth 53
Dieppe raid (1942) 139–41, 396
Dr No (IF): Inagua (Bahamas) depicted in 287–8; Patricia Wilder (Hohenlohe) alluded to in 295; plot 307–8; publication 315–17; Paul Johnson attacks 331, 333; Chandler reviews 332; film offer 335–6, 337; filmed 383, 387, 393, 398–9, 409, 412; sales 430
Doctorow, E.L. (Ed) 421
Donaldson, Frances, (Lady) 381–2, 434–5
Donaldson, John (Lord Donaldson of Kingsbridge) 381–2
Dönitz, Admiral Karl 118, 156–7
Donovan, General William J. ('Big Bill'): wartime intelligence activities 120, 124–6, 129–31, 137, 143–4; sets up World Commerce Corporation 166
Dorchester Hotel, London: in war 122–4, 135, 150
Doubleday (US publishers) 233
Douglas-Home, Henry 15
Drake, Captain Charles 105–7, 139, 142
Drew, Dr (of Jamaica) 286
Driberg, Tom (*later* Baron Bradwell) 204
Dropmore Press 43, 201–2, 227
Dudley, Eric Ward, 3rd Earl of 146, 152, 172, 176, 418

Dudley, Laura, Countess of (*née* Charteris; *then* Viscountess Long; Ann's sister) 93–4, 101, 146, 176, 178, 289
Duff-Sutherland-Dunbar, Sir George *see* Dunbar, Sir George Duff-Sutherland-
Dulau (London bookshop) 43, 75
Dulles, Allen 368, 406, 418; *The Craft of Intelligence* 418
Dunbar, Sir George Duff-Sutherland- 81, 176, 229, 254, 280, 330, 379, 384; suicide 413, 422
Duncan, Sir Andrew 110
Dundee 1–2
Dunderdale, Commander Wilfred ('Biffy') 112, 114–15, 118, 147, 223
Dunkirk evacuation (1940) 113
Dunne, Dominick: *The Two Mrs Grenvilles* 272
Duranty, Walter 57
Durnford school, Dorset 9–10, 13, 34
Dykes, Colonel Vivian 124

Easton, Jack 213
Ebury Street, London: IF's property in 79–81
Eccles, David (*later* 1st Viscount) 129–30, 141
Eden, Sir Anthony (*later* 1st Earl of Avon): and Vansittart 77; and 1951 election 213; IF and Ann visit 274–5; stays at Goldeneye 302–7; buys property in Barbados 307; visits Sevenhampton 424
Eden, Clarissa, Lady (*née* Churchill; *later* Countess of Avon): stands godmother to Caspar 229; IF and Ann visit 275; and Foreign Office defectors 275; stays at Goldeneye 302, 304–7; meets Blanche Blackwell 308; and Gaitskell's visit to Jamaica 364; visits Sevenhampton 424; and Ann's dislike of tropics 435; Ann complains of Eton beatings to 450
Edwards, Hugh: *All Night at Mr Stanyhurst's* 385, 394
Eisinger, Joe 447
Eliot, T.S. 189, 207
Elizabeth II, Queen (*earlier* Princess) 205
Elkin Mathews (booksellers) 76, 85
Elliott, Nicholas 169, 212–13, 376, 399
Ellis, Charles 410
Ellis, Patricia 311–12, 376
Ellis, Toby 131, 311
Engadine 379, 397
Engelhard, Charles 329
Engelhard, Henry ('Hank') and Mary (*née* Oppenheimer) 329
Enigma (German encoding machine) 114, 121, 133, 137, 142
Enton Hall, Surrey (hydro) 281, 290, 325, 366

Entratta, Jack 266

Eon Productions (company) 387, 393, 418, 420, 444, 446, 452

Ernst, Lily 174

Escoffier (chef) 99

Esnault-Pelterie, Carmen 392

Etler, Ingrid 372

Eton College: IF's father at 3; IF and Peter attend 14–21; IF leaves 21–2; Caspar at 449–50

Evans, Laurence 351, 368

Ewart, Gavin 440

Fabergé, Carl 422

Farrer and Company (solicitors) 432, 444

Farrer, William 444

Faulks, Neville 319

Fawkes, Wally ('Trog') 386, 391, 393

Felton, Norman 420

Fenn, Robert 368

Ferguson, Major Ronald and Susan (née Wright) 83

Fermor, Joan Leigh (formerly Rayner) 181, 234, 261

Fermor, Patrick Leigh: visits Goldeneye 181, 184; visits Ann in Kent 234; A Time to Keep Silence 235, 1.227; The Traveller's Tree 238, 2.181; Ann visits in Greece 261; and Fionn 309; and Blanche Blackwell 322; corrects IF mistake over champagne 419; on Sevenhampton 424–5; IF gives clothes to 425–6

Fettes school, Edinburgh 415

Finch, Peter 352

Finch-Hatton, Lady Daphne see Straight, Daphne

Findlater, Richard 346

Firefly (house), Jamaica 281–2, 286

Fish, Donald 390

Fisher Dowson & Wasbrough (solicitors) 444

Fisher, Hugh 446

Fisher, William 444

Fitzgerald, F. Scott 74; The Crack-Up 291

Fleming, Amaryllis: birth 20; childhood 30, 79; cello playing 79, 180; Muriel Wright befriends 141; on IF's au pairs 175; visits Jamaica 180; dislikes Ann 214; alluded to in 'The Living Daylights' 395; with dying Eve 440; plays at IF's memorial service 444

Fleming, Ann (née Charteris; then O'Neill; then Rothermere): IF meets 61; in Austria 92–3; background 93–4; first marriage (to O'Neill) 94; relations with Esmond Rothermere 94, 124, 126, 135, 146, 154; early relations with IF 95–6; and IF's entry into Navy 101; sees IF in wartime 105, 135–7, 152; stays at

Dorchester 122–4, 135, 150; wartime move to Buscot (Oxfordshire) 122; and IF's wartime activities 123; holds wartime parties 136; Christmas present from IF 150; instructs US servicemen 150–1; and death of O'Neill 154; marriage to Rothermere 158; election night parties 161, 214; interest in and influence on Daily Mail 161–2, 199; as hostess 162, 171, 187, 248–9, 261, 270–1, 321, 325–6, 345, 368, 370, 424, 450; relationship with IF after marriage to Rothermere 162–5, 172, 175, 176–9, 188, 192, 193–5; selection of letters published 164; alters spelling of first name 172; masochistic practices with IF 172, 179, 181–2, 198, 217, 243; visits to USA 172–3, 181–2; in Montagu Square 175; and IF's girl friends and affairs 177–8, 182, 188, 199; as director of British Fashion Council 178; visits Goldeneye 179–81; suggests marriage to IF 182; loses child by IF 186–8, 196; writings 190–1; return to Jamaica 192–5; at St Margaret's Bay 195–6; on IF's ageing 199; and Pells' boating mishap in Jamaica 210–11; divorce and settlement from Rothermere 214, 326; son by IF (Caspar) 214, 217, 228–30; marriage to IF 215, 217–18; domestic life with IF 224–5, 262; as director/secretary of Glidrose 232; marriage relations with IF 234, 261–2, 281–2, 288, 307, 309, 317, 321, 323–4, 330, 340, 364, 380–2, 397, 399, 407–8, 453; Barbara Skelton criticizes appearance 236; Victoria Square house 236, 241, 248–9; in Antibes 241; Freud portrait of 241, 424; mocks Rosamond Lehmann 248; holidays in Greece 261; attitude to Jamaica 267, 281–2; fear of flying 267, 362; dislikes IF's Thunderbird 269, 354; and Queen Anne Press 273–4; health treatment 281, 325; takes barbiturates 281, 325; at Paris fancy-dress party 282–3; Coward turns against 286, 303–4; word-consciousness 288–9; holiday in Vienna 290–1; illnesses 292, 295, 343; and IF's married infidelities 295; relations with Gaitskell 295–6, 322, 343–4, 361, 363, 379, 392, 407, 410; accompanies Caspar to Jamaica 301, 307; and Edens' visit to Jamaica 303; attitude to Blanche Blackwell 308–9, 322–3, 344, 362–3, 381–2, 397, 399, 427; and brother Hugo's quarrel with IF 314–15; and Ian's mother's court case 320; buys Old Palace, Bekesbourne 322; holiday in Venice with IF 335–6, 406;

Austrian holiday with IF 340–1; holiday in Le Touquet with IF 352–3; moves to Sevenhampton (Warneford) Place 353, 374–5, 378, 422, 428; and Diana Cooper 361; sees film *Our Man in Havana* 361–2; returns to Jamaica 362; joins IF on Thrilling Cities trip 372–3; meets Luciano 373; and Caspar's schooling 374; skiing holiday at Engadine 378–9; dislikes Kent life 386–7; and Fionn's wedding 390; Provence holiday with convalescent IF 390–1; and hostile reviews of *The Spy Who Loved Me* 401–2; cables IF in Jamaica about serious operation 409; in Italy 409–10; and Gaitskell's illness and death 414; on holiday visit to Simenon 422–3; buys pictures and antiques for Sevenhampton 423–4; and IF's appearance at Romantic Novelists' Association 427; hostility to Sir Jock Campbell 428; and *Thunderball* court case 432–3; on Betjeman 433; bronchitis 434; joins IF in Jamaica for *The Man With the Golden Gun* 435–6; and Ian's health decline 437–8; and IF's release from hospital 438–9; fined for driving accident 439; dispute with IF over painting 442; and IF's death and funeral 443, 448; and IF estate 444, 446, 448; sells IF's library 450; and Caspar's behaviour and suicide 451; death 451

Fleming, Caspar Robert (IF and Ann's son): born 214, 217, 228; name 229; childhood 233, 239–40; IF's relations with as child 240–1, 262, 281, 308, 425; IF's unwillingness to have in Jamaica 262, 281; frightened by Waugh 272; IF sets up trust for 276–7, 444; visits Goldeneye 285, 301, 307–8, 362; Austrian holiday 340; on Le Touquet holiday 353; in France with Ann 373; schooling 374; skiing holiday at Engadine 378–9; IF takes to cinema 393; behaviour 407, 426, 449, 451; in Switzerland 423; at Sevenhampton 425; and IF's death 443; adolescent interests 448–9; relations with Ann 449; suicide 451

Fleming, Celia (Peter's wife) *see* Johnson, Celia

Fleming, Charm (Richard's wife) 443

Fleming, Christopher (IF's nephew) 355

Fleming, David (IF's nephew) 355

Fleming, Evelyn Beatrice Ste Croix (*née* Rose; IF's mother; Eve): character 4; marriage 4–5; musical interests and playing 4, 24, 27; birth of children 5; London social life 7; and IF's education

9, 21, 25; and husband's death and will 12–13, 65; moves to Chelsea 19; relations with Augustus John 19–20, 135; and birth of Amaryllis 20; and IF's resignation from Sandhurst 28, 29; IF's relations with 29, 31, 40, 48, 51, 68, 78–9; and IF's candidature for diplomatic career 37–8, 46; in Munich 40; Corsica holiday 41–2; and IF's appointment with Reuters 46–8; intervenes over Monique Panchaud 48, 59; considers remarriage 64–5; and IF's move to Cull & Co. 64, 66; and Robert Fleming's death and will 64, 68; objects to Peter's marrying Celia 68, 78–9; buys and sells Greys Court 78–9; and IF's entry into Naval Intelligence 101; and Peter's reported death in Norway 113; moves to Sutton Courtenay 141; financial help for IF 207; lives in Cannes 207; attachment to Marquess of Winchester 210, 319; settles in Bahamas 210, 366; court case over Marquess of Winchester 319–20; IF accompanies back from Monte Carlo 417; John portrait of 424; death 440

Fleming, Ian Lancaster:
Activities and interests early reading, 10, 20–1, 34; golf 11, 13, 44, 67, 69–70, 82, 186, 196, 197, 293, 312–13, 315, 327–8, 369–70, 405, 428; athletics 14–15, 22; dislike of animals and riding 14; languages 20, 24–5, 34, 40; Hawaiian guitar-playing 24, 358; shooting and hunting 24, 208; book collecting 34, 43, 46, 75–6, 422; motor cars and driving 39, 44, 69, 82, 242, 259, 262, 268, 354, 370, 411, 423; climbing 44–5, 92; skiing 44, 55, 83, 378–9; gambling 67, 127, 248, 265–6, 294, 373; bridge-playing 81–2, 105–6, 293, 405; pornography 85–6; diving (underwater) 174, 197–8, 242, 246, 285, 287; shark and barracuda hunting 183, 198; caving 246–7; treasure-hunting 246–7; bird-watching 287–8, 317; interior decorating 346–7

Career: schooling, 9–11, 14–21; leaves Eton 21–2; at Sandhurst 24–5, 27; resigns from Sandhurst 28; studies in Kitzbühel 29, 32–7; as candidate for Diplomatic Service 37–8, 45–6; at Munich University 39–41; in Geneva 43–5; works with Reuters 46–56, 62; reports Alpine motor trials 52–4; covers Metro-Vick trials in Moscow 57–9; resigns from Reuters 63; joins Cull and Co. 64–6; with Rowe and

Career—*cont*
  Pitman (stockbrokers) 69–75;
  directorship in Elkin Mathews 76;
  interest in intelligence work 90; in
  Moscow for *Times* 96–8; with Naval
  Intelligence Division 99–111, 118;
  called 'Chocolate Sailor' 103;
  promoted Commander 103; in France
  during 1940 fall and evacuation 114–
  17; wartime missions to Portugal and
  Spain 117–18, 124–5; plans and
  forms intelligence-gathering
  commando unit 121–3, 145–6, 152–3;
  in USA on missions with Godfrey
  127–31, 142–3; denied posting to
  Moscow 132; broadcasts to Germany
  133; interrogates German officers
  134–5; accompanies Dieppe force
  139–41; attends 1943 Churchill-
  Roosevelt conferences 148–50; in Far
  East 154–6; and defeated German
  naval archives 157; as Foreign
  Manager for Kemsley Newspapers
  159–60, 168–70, 200–4, 241, 245–6;
  and Kemsley's publishing houses
  201–2; runs competitions 204–5;
  peacetime training with RNVR 208;
  resigns RNVR commission 212;
  elected to Council of Royal College of
  Art 274; remains on *Sunday Times*
  under Thomson 346; leaves *Sunday
  Times* 360–1
Characteristics: moodiness and
  melancholy, 19, 179–80, 425, 433,
  453; conformism 38, 215; self-
  centredness 45, 87–8; complexity
  and contradictions 68, 86, 225, 452–
  3; deference to older men 71, 104,
  242; superciliousness 75, 132, 230;
  attitude to women 82, 84–6, 91–2,
  98, 151; self-consciousness 84–5;
  enthusiasm 86–7; puritanism 88;
  dominating personality 126;
  aloofness 200; coldness 203–4;
  pernicketiness 240; remoteness from
  life around 263–4; xenophobia 282;
  rudeness 379, 436; caution 381;
  generosity 425–6
Health: broken nose and repair plate,
  15, 59, 143; gonorrhoea 28, 82;
  hypochondria 59; tape worm 59;
  appendicitis 87; chest and neck pains
  172, 187, 197; heart disease 197;
  kidney stones 197, 291, 297; sciatica
  290, 297; poisoned shin wound 335;
  general disorder 343; bronchitis 379;
  suffers heart attack 384–5; post-heart
  attack condition 396–7; angina 433;
  pulmonary embolism 438; decline

  440–4
Literary life: juvenile writings, 18, 23,
  35, 37; poetry 31, 36–7, 38–9;
  knowledge of European literature 51;
  history of Rowe and Pitman rejected
  73; aims to write thriller 85–6, 154,
  158, 193; proposes magazine to
  Connolly 94; articles on Jamaica 174–
  5; writing routine 216, 256; stylistic
  ambition 221; as editorial director of
  Queen Anne Press 227, 235;
  journalism and occasional writings
  231, 247–8, 317–18; royalties and
  rights 231–2, 245, 276–8; book
  promotion 244; film and TV deals
  and rights 249–50, 255, 264–5, 268,
  275–6, 297, 317, 335–8, 348–55, 358–
  60, 387, 418, 420, 447; writes 'Atticus'
  column in *Sunday Times* 251–3, 269,
  292, 317; self-parody 255; parodies
  and pastiches of 271, 383, 416, 419;
  acquires *Book Collector* 273–4, 347;
  foreign sales and rights 278, 313;
  Chandler suggests greater seriousness
  in 289–90; pilot TV project (*James
  Gunn*) 297–8, 336; articles published
  in book form 317; books attacked for
  vulgarity and crude view of world
  330–2, 400; travels for *Sunday Times*
  articles 354–7, 370–4; favourite lost
  books 394; introduction to Edwards's
  All Night at Mr Stanyhurst's 394;
  attends Romantic Novelists'
  Association dinner 427; posthumous
  sales 446
Personal life: family background 1–4;
  born 5; early rivalry with Peter 7;
  affairs and romances 11, 17, 26–8, 30–
  1, 36, 45–6, 48, 53, 55, 59–62, 67–9,
  82–4, 88–9, 98, 136, 154–5, 177, 279;
  and father's death 13; London social
  life 26–7, 66–7, 81–2; relations with
  mother 29, 31, 40, 48, 51, 68, 78–9;
  appearance and dress 31, 136, 143,
  155, 200, 235–6, 252, 403, 412, 430;
  clubs 51, 66, 106, 123, 175–6, 200,
  293, 307, 335; fined for driving
  unlicensed car 59, 62; first meets Ann
  61; custom-made cigarettes 75, 136;
  defends Peter's marriage 78; acquires
  and decorates Ebury Street property
  79–81; early relations with Ann 96,
  126; in London blitz 123–4, 135,
  147; moves to Athenaeum Court 135;
  first visit to Jamaica 144–5;
  hesitations over commitment to Ann
  158, 159; earnings 159–60, 188, 418;
  relationship with Ann after marriage
  to Rothermere 162–5, 172, 176–9,

188, 192–5; buys and develops property in Jamaica 164–7, 173–4; drinking and smoking 172; sado-masochistic practices and ideas 172, 179, 181–2, 198, 217, 243, 317, 381; circles ('octagons') of friends 176–8; fathers Ann's lost child 186; consciousness of ageing 191, 396–7; view of marriage 195; spectacles 197; depicted in Hugo Charteris's *The Explorers* 206–7; moves to Caryle Mansions 207–8; political views 213–14, 246, 354–5; and birth of son Caspar 214, 217, 228–9; decision to marry Ann 214–15; wedding 217–18; married domestic life 224–5, 262; marriage relations 234, 261–2, 281–2, 288, 307, 309, 317, 321, 323–4, 330, 340, 364, 380, 397, 399, 407–8, 431, 453; religious views 235, 238, 298; moves to Victoria Square house 236; and Caspar's upbringing 240–1, 262, 308; travelling routine 247; interest in NANA 259–60; relations with Blanche Blackwell 279–81, 285, 301, 308–9, 321–5, 397, 407–8, 427–8, 434, 453; infidelities as married man 295; and mother's court case 319; resists idea of divorce 324; longing for domestic stability 326–7; visit to Seychelles 333–5; buys Sevenhampton (Warneford) Place 353, 422; convalescent holiday to Provence with Ann 391–2; profiled in *New Yorker* 400; portrait 403–4; told of short life expectancy 414, 430–1; good later relations with Peter 421; sells Glidrose to Booker Brothers 428–9; celebrity 430–1; at mother's funeral 440; death and tributes 443–4; estate 444–8, 452

Fleming, John (IF's great-grandfather) 1

Fleming, Sir John (IF's great-uncle) 1

Fleming, Kate (*née* Hindmarsh; IF's grandmother) 2–3, 13, 21, 31, 64, 68, 83; dies intestate 95

Fleming, Kate (Peter's daughter) *see* Grimond, Kate

Fleming, Lucy (Peter's daughter) *see* Williams, Lucy

Fleming, Michael (IF's brother): born 5; appearance 31; career 65; death in war 124

Fleming, Nichol (Peter's son) 451, 452

Fleming, Peter (IF's brother): born 5; childhood ill-health 7, 13; early rivalry with IF 7; schooling 10, 14, 20–1; and father's death 12; edits *Eton College Chronicle* 18; on Amaryllis as baby 20;

in Kitzbühel 29, 32; at Oxford 29; appearance 31; Corsica family holiday 41–2; marriage to Celia Johnson 41, 68, 78; and grandfather Robert's death and will 65; travels and travel-writing 65; *Brazilian Adventure* 65, 1.42; Nettlebed house (Merrimoles) 80, 95, 105; IF's envy of 84; in Military Intelligence 96, 108, 113; in Norway campaign 112–13; in India as Wavell's adviser on deception 134; and Joan Bright 135; at 1943 Washington Conference 143; IF meets in wartime Delhi 155; IF's closeness to 159, 421; journalistic earnings 160; recommends Maclean's *Eastern Approaches* 201; visits Barbados 210; stands godfather to Caspar Fleming 229; writes as 'Strix' in *Spectator* 252; and mother's court case 319; and IF's decline 440; with mother at death 440; and IF's death 443–4; and IF estate 446; defends IF against Muggeridge 447; and Caspar's obsession with guns 450; *The Flying Visit* 113; *One's Company* 65; *The Sett* (unfinished novel) 222; *The Sixth Column* 217

Fleming, Philip (IF's uncle) 3, 7, 64, 80, 95, 208

Fleming, Richard (IF's brother): born 5; appearance 31; career 65; gives furniture to IF 207–8; and mother's court case 319; with dying mother 440; at IF's funeral 443

Fleming, Robert (IF's grandfather): career 1–4, 6; holidays in Scotland 23–4; death and estate 64, 95

Fleming, Robert and Company (merchant bank) 2, 6, 54, 63, 72, 452

Fleming, Valentine (IF's father): born 3; education 3; marriage 3–5; political life 6–9; war service 8–9, 11–12; killed in action 12; will 13, 65; effect on IF 101; as model for Bond 223

Fleming, Valentine (IF's nephew) 355

Florida 237–8

Floris (perfumiers) 333

Flower, Desmond 347

Flynn, Errol 280, 344

Fonda, Henry 181

Fonteyn, (Dame) Margot 179

Foot, Florence, Lady 303–4

Foot, Sir Hugh 303–4, 306

For Your Eyes Only (IF; collection) 209, 369; jacket illustration 369

Forbes, Alastair 150, 165, 192, 214, 425

Forbes, Sister Bridget 439, 441

Forbes Adam family 314

Forbes Adam, Virginia *see* Charteris, Virginia

Forbes Dennis, Ernan 24, 29, 31–40, 43–6, 66, 77, 87, 90
Foreign Office: meets IF over Russian report 98
Forest Mere health farm, Hampshire 413
Forster, C.H. 158, 223
Foster, Jimmy 92
Fowler, John 92
Fox, Sir John 20
Fox-Strangways, John 81, 86, 173
France: 1940 defeat and collapse 114–18
Franco, General Francisco 109, 130
Frankau, Gilbert: *The City of Fear* 20
Fraser-Smith, Charles 119
Frere, Alexander 356
Freud, Lucian: at Ann's party 172; visits Ann in Jamaica 215, 239–40; friendship with Ann 234, 248, 296, 309; portrait of Ann 241, 424
Fritsche, Hans 135
From Russia, With Love (IF): on Alps 44; on making love in railway carriage 98; Red Grant alluded to in 267, 273; Kalkavan depicted in 273; completion 276; writing 281, 290–2, 297; plot 284, 293; Bond's uncertain fate in 293, 314; guns in 299–300; jacket illustration 300, 369, 390; Al Hart enthuses over 301; publication and reception 313–14; IF's fondness for 315–16; on travelling 358; Kennedy chooses as a favourite book 382; film 418, 419, 426, 430, 433; sales 430
Fuchs, Klaus 312
Furse, Commander Paul 138

Gaitskell, Dora, (Baroness) 295, 341, 414
Gaitskell, Hugh: relations with Ann 295–6, 322, 344, 361, 363–4, 379, 392, 410; in Kitzbühel 341; at Ann's parties 343, 370; visits Jamaica 363–4; in New York 379; ill-health 407; death 413–14
Gale, John 434
Gallico, Paul: on IF's beating at Eton 15–16; introduction to *Gilt-Edged Bonds* 15, 380–1; praises *Casino Royale* 232; writes for Mercury service 260
Gandy-Deering, J.P. 79
Garbo, Greta 230
Gargoyle Club, London 153
Gathorne-Hardy, Eddie and Robert 76
Gaunt, John of, Duke of Lancaster 5, 86
Gellhorn, Martha 181
Gendel, Judy (*née* Montagu) 194, 373
General Strike (1926) 22
Geneva 43–6, 68, 372, 423
George, Daniel 226, 271, 292, 315
Gerlach, Baron Rudolfo von 91
German Navy Warfare Science

Department 157
Gibraltar: in war 109, 117, 125, 131, 138, 145, 150
Giles, Frank 168–9
Gilliatt, Penelope 380
Gilt-Edged Bonds (IF; compendium) 15, 338, 380–1
Gladisch, Kontradmiral 157
Gladstone, Robert 19
Glanville, Lieutenant T.J. 157
Glen, Commander Alexander ('Sandy') 112, 147, 415
Glenconner, Christopher Tennant, 2nd Baron 77, 89
Gleneagles, Scotland 67, 186
Gliddon, John 232
Glidrose Productions Ltd 232, 277, 424, 428–9, 444–7, 452
Glyn, Elinor: *Three Weeks* 85–6
Gneisenau (German heavy cruiser) 137
Godfrey, Admiral John Henry: IF's relations with 71, 103–4, 132; as Director of Naval Intelligence 98–9, 102, 105, 108; meets IF 98; and press liaison 106; and purchase of German ships in Spain 110; and fall of France 114–15, 118; and SOE 118; Donovan meets 120; and IF's plans to capture Enigma codes 122; and cooperation with US intelligence 124; missions to USA 127–9, 131, 142; and Delmer's black propaganda 133; IF praises 136; develops NID resource base 138; and IF's plan to capture enemy documents 138; dismissed and posted to Bombay 142; post-war reunions 168–9; as model for 'M' in Bond novels 222, 398; recommends hypnotist to IF 343; suggests IF as biographer 385
Goebbels, Joseph 62, 112
Gogarty, Oliver St John 17
Goldeneye (film) 452
Goldeneye, Jamaica: IF's life at 165–6, 173–4, 179–81, 183, 210–11, 239–40, 267, 281–2; let to visitors 183–4; Coward's poem on 184–5; Edens stay at 302–7; IF visits without Ann 323–5; proposed sale of 400; Caspar inherits 451
Golden Eye, Operation 125, 131, 145
Goldfinger, Erno 328, 345
Goldfinger (IF): on Geneva 45; writing 327; characters and plot 328–9; promotion 345; reception 345–6; jacket illustration 369; dedication to Plomer 426; film 446
Gollancz, (Sir) Victor 76
Goodman, Arnold, Baron 392, 444, 450, 451
Gordon-Canning, Bobbie 82, 196

Gore, Arthur (*later* 8th Earl of Arran; 'Boofy'): at Plâs Newydd 68; supports RCA charity dance 274; objects to IF's use of name in *Diamonds Are Forever* 289, 328
Gosse, Philip: *The Aquarium* 198
Government Communications Headquarters (Government Code and Cypher School) *see* Bletchley Park
Graham, Katharine 130
Graham, Virginia 41
Grant, Red 267, 273
Graupe, Paul 75
Greene, Graham: in *Night and Day* libel suit 74; IF proposes as contributor to magazine 94; in Jamaica 240, 380; published by Viking 359; declines to write introduction to *Gilt-Edged Bonds* 380; *Our Man in Havana* 380, 361–2; IF admires 391
Greenleaves, H.L. 125, 131
Grenfell, Joyce (*née* Phipps) 41
Grepe, Mary 145
Grey, Francis (Mary Rose's son) 423, 443
Grey, Mary Rose (*née* Charteris; Ann's sister) 93, 244, 314–15; death 413, 423
Greys Court, Oxfordshire 78–9
Griffie-Williams, Beryl (*née* Kruger) 360–1, 393, 404, 406, 428, 442
Grimond, Kate (*née* Fleming; Peter's daughter) 451, 452
Grivolin, Jeanne Aurélie: *Breviary of Love* 89
Groedel, Dr Franz 197
Guest, Ivor 26, 68
Guest, John 195
Guinness, Tanis (*later* Phillips) 253
Gulbenkian, Calouste 60
Gulyashki, Andrei 445
'Guns of James Bond, The' (IF; article) 395–6
Gunzberg, Niki de 218

Hadley, W.W. 160
Haggard, Edith 277
Hailsham, Quintin McGarel Hogg, Baron 20
Hall, Admiral Reginald ('Blinker') 71, 99, 108, 112
Hambro, Olaf 166
Hamburg 354, 370–1, 374
Hamilton, (Sir) Denis: succeeds IF at *Sunday Times* 200; supports *Sunday Times* magazine section 256; IF advises to slow down 272–3; suggests diamond trade as subject for IF 310; edits *Sunday Times* 346, 394; proposes 'Thrilling Cities' trip to IF 354; present at IF's heart attack 384; IF recommends Graham Hill to 404; in Venice 406; and IF's trip to Far East 411; IF's feature suggestions to 421, 427
Hamilton, Guy 393
Hamilton, Hamish 241
Hamilton, Police Captain James 266, 358
Hamilton, Olive, Lady 406
Hammond (Royal St George's steward) 386
Hampshire, Cecil: *The Secret Navies* 157
Hannay, Kathleen (*née* Fleming; IF's aunt) 3, 64, 95
Harcourt Brace (US publishers) 233
Hare, Joanna 418
Hare, John 418
Hare, Nancy 96
Harley, Dido 7, 30
Harley, Primrose 7, 30–1
Harling, Amanda 229
Harling, Phoebe 229
Harling, Robert: and IF's first lovemaking 17; on IF at Naval Intelligence 104; works with McLachlan at NID 134; meets Wolfson 147; Pamela Tiarks speaks of IF to 153; in Normandy 154; works on *Sunday Times* 160–1; IF recommends Clare Blanshard to 168; and IF's friendships 176, 204; travels to Jamaica with IF and Ann 193; and IF's role at *Sunday Times* 200; gives coat of arms to IF 207; and *Book Collector* 227, 347; child's name 229; and IF's marriage relations 234, 261; designs NANA logo 260; alluded to in *The Spy Who Loved Me* 382; and IF's success and celebrity 430; meets IF in last months 442
Harmsworth, Esmond Cecil *see* Rothermere, 2nd Viscount
Harriman, Pamela *see* Churchill, Pamela
Harris, Air Marshal Sir Arthur ('Bomber') 146
Hart, Al 249, 268, 278, 282, 301, 307, 338, 359
Hart, Nancy 282
Hart-Davis, Deirdre 30–1, 36–9, 41
Hart-Davis, (Sir) Rupert: and Amaryllis Fleming 20; and Peter's stay in Austria 29; in Ireland with Flemings 30–1; Corsica holiday 41–2, 417; marriage to Peggy Ashcroft 41; publishing career 42, 201, 270; at Ann's party 270; on *Dr No* 333; at IF's film premiere party 426; and IF's death 444; *The Arms of Time* 19
Hart-Davis, Sybil (*née* Cooper) 30, 38
Hartley, L.P. 93
Harvard Lampoon (magazine) 419
Hastings, Captain Eddie 137
Hauser, Gaylord 201

Hays Mews, London 175, 197
Hayward, John 202, 207, 227, 274, 347–8
Hayward, Leland 181
Hayward, Susan 358
Healey, Donald 52–3
Heber-Percy, Robert ('Mad Boy') 353
Hedervary, Margit, Countess 88
Helms, Richard 307
Hemingway, Ernest 260, 294, 320; *The Old Man and the Sea* 230
Henderson, Ian 292
Henderson, Nicholas (Sir) 251, 398
Hepburn, Katharine 240
Herbert, Auberon 409
Herbert, David 22, 119, 311
Herbert, Sir Alan P. 354
Hess, Rudolph 113
Heuvel, Count Frederick ('Fanny') vanden 169
Heveningham Hall, Suffolk 60
'Hildebrand Rarity, The' (IF; story) 339, 358, 400
Hill, Diana ('Didy') 68–9, 85, 88
Hill, Martin 45, 68–9
Hillgarth, Captain Alan: as naval attaché in Madrid 109, 131; and fall of France 117–18; and Operation Golden Eye 125; and Italian human torpedoes 145; post in Ceylon 154; travels to Australia 155–6; IF praises in London 158; and proposed purchase of *Tangier Gazette* 170
Hilton, Conrad 177
Hiroshima: bombed 156
Hiroshima, Mon Amour (film) 371
Hitler, Adolf: rise to power 41, 55, 62; Kemsley interviews 106, 160; declares war on USA 133
Hoare, Major C.E. 49
Hoare, Rennie 360
Hoare, Sir Samuel 106, 117, 125
Hodson, H. V. (Harry): edits *Sunday Times* 160, 386; on IF's editorial suggestions 168; declines IF articles 231, 248, 374; and IF's absences from *Sunday Times* 245; IF circumvents 251; favours magazine section for *Sunday Times* 256; and Thomson purchase of *Sunday Times* 346; and IF's 'Thrilling Cities' articles 370, 374; round-the-world trip 394
Hogarth Press 20
Hohenlohe, Prince Alex 295
Hohenlohe, Princess 'Honey' (*formerly* Patricia Wilder) 295, 308
Holden, Wanda *see* Baillie-Hamilton, Wanda
Holiday (magazine) 337
Holland: publication of Bond books in 278
Holland, Captain Cedric ('Hooky') 115

Hollis, Christopher 193
Hollis, Sir Roger 307
Holmes, Archdeacon E.E. 38
Hong Kong 356–7
Honolulu 358
Hood, HMS 128
Hoover, J. Edgar 128–9, 246, 251
Hopkinson, Henry 105
Horizon (magazine) 174–5, 193–4
Horn, Aloysius 323
Horniblow, Stanley 162
Horrox, Reginald 202
Household, Geoffrey: *The Third Hour* 85
'How To Win at Roulette' ('Roulette Without Tears'; IF; unpublished article) 248, 373
Howard, Elizabeth Jane 391
Howard, G.Wren 257, 275, 284, 320
Howard, Michael: IF complains to of unavailability of book 244; and IF's relations with Janson-Smith 278; and Boothroyd's gun expertise 300; and *Dr No* 315, 317; and IF's reservations about Bond 369; and *The Spy Who Loved Me* 381, 401; and IF's writing during convalescence 384; IF proposes book on golf to 385; and Chopping illustrations 391; and *On Her Majesty's Secret Service* 419; IF suggests book on narcotic flora to 437; and IF's ill-health 439
Howard, Trevor 352
Howe, Ellic 134; *The London Bookbinders 1780–1806* 201
Howe, Sir Ronald 273, 313
Hudson, Robert 96–7
Huggins, Diana 194
Huggins, Sir John 183
Huggins, Molly, Lady 180, 183
Hugh Smith family *see* Smith
Hughes, Larry 394
Hughes, Richard 212, 252, 283, 356–7, 411–13, 415, 442
Hugill, Tony 153
Hulton, Sir Edward 360
Hume, Benita 372
Huntercombe Golf Club 13, 293, 428
Hutchinson, St John 77
Huysmans, Martha 123
Hyde, Harford Montgomery: *The Man Called Intrepid* 410

Ian Fleming's Jamaica (guidebook; with IF introduction) 436
Iddon, Don 163
Ideal Home Exhibition 197
'If I Were Prime Minister' (IF; article) 354
Ilchester, Giles Stephen Holland Fox-Strangways,6th Earl of 86
Inagua, Bahamas 287–8

Indiana, University of: buys IF's library 450

Ingrams, Leonard and Victoria 123

Interpol: IF attends conferences 273

Investment Trust Corporation 2

Ironside, Robin 274, 450

Irving, Laurence 10–11

Isherwood, Christopher 417

Ismay, General Hastings (*later* Baron) 135

Istanbul 273, 278, 418

Ivory Hammer, The (Sotheby's yearbook) 421

Izvestia (Soviet newspaper) 406

Izzard, Ralph 128, 156

Jackson, Phyllis 359, 388, 420

Jacob, Alaric: friendship with IF 50–1, 66; and Metro-Vick trial 55; IF visits in Washington 75; meets IF in Cairo 154; *Scenes from a Bourgeois Life* 51–2

Jacob, General Sir Ian 168

Jacobs, Dr Lenworth 306

Jacobson, Dan 317

Jamaica: IF first visits in war 144; IF settles in 164–6, 173–4; IF writes article on 174–5; IF and Ann return to 236–8; voodoo ceremony in 239–40; IF attacks high hotel prices in 252; Ann's coolness towards 267, 434–5; *Dr No* filmed in 393; *see also* Goldeneye

James Gunn – Secret Agent (IF; pilot TV script) 298

James, Montague Rhodes 16

James and Shakespeare (company) 66

Jamieson, Archie 177

Janson-Smith, Peter 278, 400, 435, 446

Japan 411–12, 416; *see also* Tokyo

Jellicoe, Geoffrey 89

Jenkins, Geoffrey 445–6

Jenkins, Roy (*later* Lord Jenkins of Hillhead) 326, 414, 437, 450

Jenkinson, Sir Anthony 329

Jesse, Tennyson 257

John, Augustus: draws for IF's *Wyvern* 17; relations with and portraits of Eve 19, 68, 80, 99, 135, 424; draws Sybil Hart-Davis 30; and Hugo Pitman 72; and Churchill 95; drawing of IF 136, 403; Ann buys drawing of Connolly 424

John, Admiral Sir Caspar 229

Johnson, Celia (Mrs Peter Fleming): and Hart-Davis 41; and death of Peter's grandfather 65; Eve opposes marriage to Peter 68, 78; marries Peter 78, 90; and Peter's reported death in Norway 113; view of IF 141, 421; and IF's reaction to Muriel Wright's death 152

Johnson, Paul: 'Sex, Snobbery and Sadism' 331, 333

Johnston, Brian 427

Johnstone, Harcourt 77

Joint Intelligence Committee (JIC) 104–5, 139, 292

Joint Intelligence Staff 105

Jokl, Lisl *see* Popper, Lisl

Jones, Sir Roderick 46–7, 50, 54–5, 59, 62–3, 72

Joyce Grove (house), Oxfordshire 3, 13, 95

Jung, Dr Carl Gustav 44, 189, 206

Justice, James Robertson 50

Kahn, Otto 92

Kalkavan, Nazim 273

Keeler, Christine 418

Kelly, Grace 447

Kelly, John Sims ('Shipwreck'; 'Ship') 294, 335–6, 338

Kemsley, Edith, Viscountess 106, 159–60, 200

Kemsley, James Gomer Berry, 1st Viscount: runs publishing houses 43, 201–2, 227; house (Dropmore) 51; IF's relations with 71, 106, 200, 260, 273; interviews Hitler 106, 160; and Peter's reported death in Norway 113; IF works as Foreign Manager for 159–60, 168, 192; Ann writes on 191; and Royal Commission on the Press 191; IF and Ann entertain 227; IF submits article to 231; campaign against Mailer's *Naked and the Dead* 233; supports IF's novels 233; and 'Atticus' column 251; considers magazine section for *Sunday Times* 256; offers Queen Anne Press and *Book Collector* to IF 273–4; rewards Richard Hughes 283; title 397

Kemsley Empire Journalists' Scheme 202

Kemsley Manual of Journalism 171

Kemsley Newspapers: IF works as Foreign Manager for 159–60, 168–70, 200–1, 202–4; employs former intelligence officers 169, 212; *see also Sunday Times*

Kennedy, Ailsa 228

Kennedy, John F. 367–8, 380, 382–3, 400, 431

Kennedy, Joseph 120

Kennedy, Ludovic 228

Kent, Prince George, Duke of 26

Kidd, J.B.: *Views in the Island of Jamaica* (prints) 166

King, Admiral Ernest 143

King George V, HMS 150

King George V Stamp Book 202, 227

King-Bull, E.J. 394

Kingston, Jamaica 175

Kinkead, Robin 57

Kirkpatrick, Sir Ivone 203
Kirkup, James 147–8
Kitzbühel, Austria 24, 29, 31–7, 75, 83, 90, 92, 341, 409, 439–40
Knickerbocker, Cholly 182
Knowlton, Perry 359
Knox, Frank 120
Koenigsberg (wrecked German warship) 334
Koestler, Arthur 307, 375
Korda, Sir Alexander 250, 253, 255
Krebs (Swiss book collector) 46
Kreisky, Bruno 372
Kuwait 376–8, 385

Lahoud, Anthony 302–3, 306, 324
Lamberg, Max, Graf von 35
Lamberg, Paula von (Max's sister) 35
Lambton, Antony, Viscount 289
Lancaster, Sir Osbert 292
Lang, Iain 203
Lansdowne Club, London 123
Larsonnier (French teacher) 20
Las Vegas 262, 265–6, 267–8, 332, 358
Lausanne, Switzerland 7
Lawrence, T.E. 202
League of Nations 45, 54
Lean, David 250
Leathers, Frederick James, 1st Viscount 149
le Carré, John (David Cornwell) 448
Left Book Club 176–7
Lehmann, Rosamond: in Jamaica 183, 211–12; at Edith Sitwell lunch 189–90; congratulates IF on caving article 248, 342
Leibert, Fritz 390
Leigh Fermor, Patrick *see* Fermor, Patrick Leigh
Leiter, Marguerite Hyde (Daisy) *see* Suffolk, Countess of
Leiter, Marion ('Oatsie') 167, 210, 229, 367
Leiter, Tommy: in Jamaica 167, 210; depicted in Bond novels 222
Le Mesurier, Captain E.K. 395
Lend-Lease (wartime) 120
Lennox-Boyd, Alan (*later* 1st Viscount Boyd of Merton) 302, 318–19, 341–2
Lennox-Boyd, Mark 418
Lesley, Cole 193, 195–6, 217–18, 286–7
Le Touquet 67, 69, 82, 352–3, 373, 392
Le Vasseur, Olivier 318, 334, 342
Levin, Bernard 391
Lewis, Norman 320–1; *The Volcanoes Above Us* 320
Life magazine 382
Lindo (astrologer) 201
Lindo family 279
Lindo, Roy 280, 285, 410

Linklater, Eric: *Juan in America* 164
Lion and Unicorn Press 292
Lisbon 118, 127–8, 131
Litvinov, Maxim 59
Live and Let Die (IF): Fox-Strangways in 81; swim to tanker episode 149; writing 237–8, 245; plot and themes 238, 253; film rights 250, 265; banned in Ireland 255; reception 255, 261; US publication 268; Chandler praises 270
'Living Daylights, The' (IF; story) 395, 409, 445
Lloyd George, David 5
Lobo, Dr P.J. 357
Lockhart, Sir Robert Bruce 118, 132, 251
Lodge, (Horace) Vallance 232, 274, 277
Loehnis, Clive 114
Loewy, Raymond 411
London, HMS 150
London Library, The 451
London Magazine 290, 416
Londonderry, Edith, Marchioness of 26
Long, David, 2nd Viscount 192
Longford, Francis Aungier Pakenham, 7th Earl of 82, 136, 226
Longhurst, Henry 386
Lonn, George 403
Loraine, Lorn 195
Lorre, Peter 265
Los Angeles 264–5, 358
Lovat, Simon Fraser, 17th Baron 139
Lowther, Tommy 183
Luce, Clare Booth 194
Luce, Henry 130, 194
Luciano, Salvatore ('Lucky') 332, 373
Lyttelton, George 333

Macao 357, 399
Macaulay, Dame Rose 309
MacBeth, George 361
McCarthy, Senator Joseph 246, 251
McClory, Bobo 432
McClory, Kevin: makes film *The Boy and the Bridge* with Bryce 348–9, 351–2, 359–60; proposes Bond film 349–50, 352–3, 355, 359; prepares script of *Thunderball* 350; attitude to IF 355; in dispute over *Thunderball* script 364–8, 383–4, 387; wins court case against IF 426–7, 431–2, 451
McCormick, Donald 169–70, 202, 319, 333
MacDonnell, Angus 99
McDougall, Jock 74, 85
MacKenna, Stephen 51
Mackworth-Praed, Cyril 407
McLachlan, Donald: on Room 39 102; on IF at NID 104, 129, 138; and wartime propaganda 133–4; alluded to in *On Her*

Majesty's Service 398; obituary of IF 443

McLaren, Anna 123

Maclean, Donald 213, 221, 230, 275, 283

Maclean, Fitzroy 97, 118; *Eastern Approaches* 201, 244

Macmillan (US publisher) 245, 249, 255, 268, 276, 297, 301, 333, 359

McWhirter, William 162

Maibaum, Richard 387

Mailer, Norman: *The Naked and the Dead* 233

Maillart, Ella 90

Makins, Roger (*later* Baron Sherfield) 130

Man With the Golden Gun, The (IF): writing 434–5, 436; posthumous publication 444–5

Manchester Guardian 331

Mankowitz, Wolf 387, 393

Manley, Norman 305

Mann, Klaus: *Anja and Esther* 34, 44, 47

Mann, Thomas: *Death in Venice* 336; *The Magic Mountain* 51

March, Don Juan 109–10

Margaret, Princess 370

Marie-Louise, Princess 21

Markham, Robert 445

Markham, Robert *see* Amis, (Sir) Kingsley

Markwert (German agent) 91

Marlow, Ann 388–90, 420, 429

Marris, Denny 130

Mars-Jones, William 431

Marx, Hermann 60, 147

Mary, Queen 21

Mason, Michael 110–12, 223

Mason-Macfarlane, Major General Noel 91, 132

Maudling, Reginald 393

Maugham, W. Somerset: IF's relations with 71, 242, 307; and Ann's marriage to IF 224; Ann visits in France 241–3, 336; praises *Diamonds Are Forever* 242, 288; writes on ten best novels for *Sunday Times* 256; IF's admiration for 264; Ann entertains 326; IF meets in Tokyo 357; and IF's heart attack 384; Ann Marlow produces TV series of 388

Maxwell, Elsa 183, 255, 271, 294

Maxwell, Robert 274

May, Cecil Fleetwood 47, 49, 73

Mayor, Alexie 61

Mayor, Sybil 7, 29

MCA *see* Music Corporation of America

Mechow, Dr Ottomar 433

Medhurst, Air Marshal (Sir) Charles Edward Hastings 145

Medley (unpublished magazine) 22

Meiklejohn, Sir Roderick S. 38

Meinertzhagen, Colonel Richard 407, 438

Mellon, Paul 274

Menzies, Sir Stewart 99, 138, 213

Mercury (Kemsley Imperial and Foreign Service) 169–70, 202–3, 246, 260, 275

Merrimoles (house), Nettlebed 80, 95, 105

Mers-el-Kebir 117

Mersey, Edward Clive Bigham, 3rd Viscount 392

Metropolitan-Vickers (Metro-Vick): Moscow trials 55–8

Meyer, Stanley 265

Miall, Leonard 133, 142

Micklem, Hugh 60

Milford Haven, David Mountbatten, 3rd Marquess of 295

Milford Haven, Janet, Marchioness of 295, 393

Millar, Sir Frederick Hoyer 351

Miller, Alan and Nancy 177, 451

Miller, Gilbert and Kitty 183

Milner, Alfred, Viscount 47

Milner, Amies 403

Ministry of Economic Warfare 110, 118, 130

Minshall, Merlin 110–12

Minton, John 274

MI(R): Peter works for 108

Mirbach family 39–40

Mirrlees, General William 352

Mirrlees, Robin 352–3, 397, 404

Mitford, Nancy 170, 288, 424

Mittersill, Schloss, Austria 294–5, 409

Monkhouse, Allan 56

Montagu, Commander Ewen 147

Montagu Place, London 175

Montagu, Venetia *see* Stanley, Venetia

Monte Carlo 178, 336–7, 373

Montgomery, Field Marshal Bernard Law, 1st Viscount 27

Montgomery, Sir Hubert 38

Moonraker (IF): use of benzedrine in 85; plot and themes 253; writing and research 254–5, 257; film rights 265, 276, 297, 317, 338; reception 269; attacked for vulgarity 330; characters 351

Moore, Roger 393, 452

Moorehead, Alan 188

Morgan family 163

Morgan, Fionn (*née* O'Neill; Ann's daughter): at Buscot 122; teases IF 152; and father's death 154; on Peter Quennell 193; devotion to IF 214; studies 224; on Caspar's first tooth 238–9; at Victoria Square 241; laughs at Rosamond Lehmann 248; holiday in Greece 261; and 'Boofy' Gore's complaints 289; 21st birthday party 308–9; skiing holiday at Engadine 378; marriage 390

Morgan, Harry 143
Morgan, John (Fionn's husband) 390, 442
Morgan, John Pierpont: friendship with
  Robert Fleming 2
Morgan, John Pierpont, Jr. 43, 65, 120;
  and Lancelot Hugh Smith 71; Neil
  Primrose stays with 142
Morgan, Commander Junius 141–2
Morgan Grenfell (company) 147
Morgenthau, Henry III 296–8, 336, 351,
  420
Morrell, Lady Ottoline 6, 76
Morrell, Philip 6
Morrison, Charles 437
Morrison, Herbert 136
Morrison, Sara 437
Morrison-Bell, Shelagh 130
Mortimer, Raymond 416, 419
Moscow: IF reports Metro-Vick trials in
  55–9; IF reports British Trade Mission
  to 96–7, 447; IF denied wartime posting
  to 132; *Sunday Times* appoints
  correspondent in 203
Mosley, Diana, Lady (*née* Mitford) 79
Mosley, Nicholas 314
Mosley, Sir Oswald 50, 79
Mottisfont Abbey, Hampshire 60–1, 77,
  89–90, 407
Mountbatten, Admiral Lord Louis (*later*
  1st Earl) 139, 145
Mouravieff, Andrew 152, 177
Moyns (house), Essex 293–4
Muggeridge, Kitty 236
Muggeridge, Malcolm 57, 236, 309, 394,
  407, 447
Muir, Barbara 422
Muir, Percy: advises IF on book-collecting
  43, 46, 75–6; and IF's boredom 59; and
  Fleming family concern for money 60;
  anti-Nazi activities 75, 77, 80; in
  Germany 75; on Eve's treatment of IF
  79; and outbreak of war 100; writes for
  Book Handbook 202; as director of Queen
  Anne Press 227, 235; underwrites *Book
  Collector* 274; and editing of *Book
  Collector* 347; prepares catalogue for
  'Printing and the Mind of Man' 422;
  and sale of IF's library 450
Muir, Toni (*née* Silverman) 75
Muirhead, David 131
Munich: IF studies at University 38–41; IF
  reports Alpine motor trials from 52–3;
  IF holidays in 92
Munster, Count Paul 92, 406
Munster, Countess Peggy 92
Murphy, Robert 287–8
Music Corporation of America (MCA) 351,
  359, 367–8, 388–9
Musset, Alfred de 204–5

Mussolini, Benito: IF acquires passport 46,
  80; British attitude to 95

NANA *see* North American Newspaper
  Alliance
Napier, Diana (Mrs Richard Tauber) 98
Naples 373
Naval Intelligence Division (Admiralty):
  IF works in (Section 17) 99, 101–9;
  interrogates U-boat crews 133; Unit 17Z
  133; post-war organisation 138; BP
  Committee 152
Nazi-Soviet Pact (1939) 97
Nelke, Paul 60
Nelson, Admiral Horatio, 1st Viscount 144
Nettlebed, Oxfordshire: Robert Fleming
  buys estate in 3
Never Say Never Again (film) 452
New American Library (US publishers)
  383, 419, 421
New York: IF visits 74, 127–9, 142–3, 163,
  172–3, 245–6, 281, 359, 400, 408, 410–
  11; Ann in 172–3, 181–2; IF and Ann
  visit after marriage 219, 236–7
New Yorker (magazine): profile of IF in 400
Niarchos, Stavros 271
Nichol, David 81
Nichols, Philip 98
Nicholson, (Sir) Harold 20, 40, 214, 370;
  Public Faces 50
Nicholson, Nicholas 434
Nicholson, William 30
Night and Day (magazine) 74, 94
'Nightmare Among the Mighty' (IF;
  article) 315
Niven, David 393
Noailles, Mme de 282
Nolan, Sidney 423
Norfolk House, St James's Square, London
  151
Norman, Sir Montagu 99, 101
Normandy: invasion and campaign
  (1944) 152–4
North Africa: wartime campaign in 117;
  1942 landings ('Torch') 139, 141, 144–
  6
North American Newspaper Alliance
  (NANA) 259–61, 275, 281
Norway: 1940 campaign 112–13
Norwich, John Julius Cooper, 2nd
  Viscount 146, 200
Nugent, Tim 105
Number 33 Section (special unit) 146
Number 36 Troop (special unit) 145–6

O'Brien-ffrench, Conrad 90–1
O'Brien-ffrench, Maud 90
'Octopussy' (IF; story) 37, 408, 445
O'Donovan, Desmond 432

Office of Strategic Services (OSS; *earlier* Office of Co-ordinator of Information) 129, 141–2
Old Etonian Golfing Society 405
Old Palace, Bekesbourne *see* Bekesbourne
Olterra (Italian tanker) 145
On Her Majesty's Secret Service (IF): Salcombe described in 8; Alpine research station in 295; writing 398, 404; IF offers to Beaverbrook for serialization 409; reception 416, 419; factual errors in 419; success and sales 419–20, 430
Onassis, Aristotle 294, 335–6
O'Neill, Ann, Lady *see* Fleming, Ann
O'Neill, Fionn (Ann's daughter) *see* Morgan, Fionn
O'Neill, Georgina, Lady (Raymond's wife) 422
O'Neill, Raymond, 4th Baron (Ann's son): at Buscot 122; and death of father 154; owns pictures by Coward and IF 212; and Ann's divorce from Rothermere 214; and domestic life with IF 224; buys Rolls-Royce station-wagon 239; visits Jamaica 307; entertains family (Christmas 1958) 345; visits Sevenhampton 422; as executor to Fleming estate 451
O'Neill, Shane, 3rd Baron (Ann's first husband) 61, 94, 101, 124; killed in action 154
Operational Intelligence Centre (OIC; Admiralty) 102
Oppenheimer, Ernest 258
Oppenheimer, Harry 316, 329
'Ordeal of Caryl St George, The' (IF; juvenile story) 18
Ornstein, Bud 387
Orwell, George 331
Osborne, John 387
Oswald, Lee Harvey 383
Our Man in Havana (film) 361
Overlord, Operation 152
Ovey, Sir Esmond 56
Owen, Frank 162, 195
Oxford University: Peter attends (Christ Church) 29; James Bond Club 418
Ozanne, Marie 38–9

Paget, Lady Caroline 68
Pakenham, Frank *see* Longford, 7th Earl of
Pakenham, Lady Mary *see* Clive, Lady Mary
Paley, Grace ('Babe') 194
Paley, William S. ('Bill') 194, 336, 338
Pan (publishing house) 430
Panchaud de Bottones, Monique 45–6, 48, 53, 55, 59, 68, 423

Panchaud de Bottones, Simone 403
Pantz, Baron Hubert von 295
Paracelsus 44, 189
Paris 200
Parker, James 443
Parker, John 447
Parkinson, Cyril Northcote, and Elizabeth 435–6
Parkinson, Sir John 197
Patcevitch, Iva 233, 308
Patton, General George S. 153
Payn, Graham 194, 196, 286–7, 329
Payne, John 275–6
Peacock, Sir Edward 99, 110
Pearl Harbor 133
Pearson, John 390, 448
Pedro Cays (islands) 329–30
Peek, Sir Francis 349
Pell, Claiborne 210–11
Pell, Nuala 210–11, 317
Pellatt, Biddy 25–6
Pellatt, Elinor (Nell) 10–11, 34
Pellatt, Hester 11
Pellatt, Tom 9–11
Percy, Lord Richard 338
Pétain, Marshal Philippe 115–16
Peters, A.D. (literary agent) 170
Petrov, Vladimir 252
Pevsner, Sir Nikolaus 3
Philby, Kim 50, 275, 376, 410, 416
Phillips, Teddy 253
Phipps, Paul 95
Pickering, (Sir) Edward 316
Pimlico Literary Institute 79
Pinewood Studios 275
Pitman, Fred 72
Pitman, Hugo: IF works with 72, 74; qualities 72, 177; in New York with IF 74, 120; pays IF's salary during absence on war service 147, 159; friendship with IF 177, 453; helps find flat for IF 207; and IF's decision to marry 214; stays at Goldeneye 325; death 422
Pitman, Jemima 142, 177
Pitman, Reine 72, 325
Pitman, Rose 142, 177.325
Pitt House, Hampstead 5–6, 13, 19
Plâs Newydd, Anglesey 68
Playboy (magazine) 358
Pleydell-Bouverie, Captain Edmund 115
Plomer, William: friendship with IF 42, 426–7, 439, 453; *Turbott Wolfe* 42, 20–1; in Naval Intelligence Division 119; and Edith Sitwell 189–90; and IF's writing of *Casino Royale* 226; recommends *Live and Let Die* 245; on *Moonraker* 257; works with Daniel George 271; praises *From Russia, With Love* 292; and Bond as cartoon strip 316;

Plomer, William—*cont*
and IF's attitude to Bond 364; and
Thunderball 369; edits IF's *State of
Excitement* 377; and *The Spy Who Loved
Me* 385; IF praises 391; criticizes IF's
literary pretensions 394; and hostile
reviews of Bond novels 401; IF
complains of restlessness to 411; and
IF's visit to Japan 412; and IF's *You Only
Live Twice* 416; homosexuality 417; at
IF's film premiere party 426; and *The
Man With the Golden Gun* 436, 438, 445;
and IF's decline 438; and IF's relations
with Ann 439; gives IF's memorial
address 444
Plomley, Roy 419
Plunkett-Ernle-Erle-Drax, Admiral Sir
Reginald 254
Polignac, Princess Charlotte de 49
Polignac, Prince Pierre de 49
Polignac, Winnaretta, Princess de 49
Political Warfare Executive 104, 118, 132–
3
'Poor Man Escapes, A' (IF; story) 35
Pope-Hennessy, James 261
Popov, Dusko 128
Popper, Lisl (née Jokl) 36, 75, 80, 177–8,
207, 321, 361
Poppy is also a Flower, The (film) 447
Porter, Cole 65
Portland, 7th Duke of *see* Cavendish-
Bentinck, Lord William
Portland Club, London 293, 307, 335,
343
Portofino 188–90
Portugal: IF's wartime missions to 117–18
Pott, Rear Admiral Herbert ('Bertie') 129
Potter, Stephen: *Gamesmanship* 201
Potterton, Mona 362, 379
Pound, Admiral Sir Dudley 107–8
Powell, Anthony: *Journals* 243
Powell, Dilys 200
Powers, Gary 399
Pravda (Soviet newspaper) 447
Price, Anthony 331, 346
Primrose, Neil 142
Prince of Wales, HMS 133
Pringle, Carmen 174, 194, 287
Pringle, John 174, 382
Printing and the Mind of Man (exhibition,
London, 1963) 422
Profumo, John 342, 418
Profumo, Richard 342
'Property of a Lady, The' (IF; story 421,
434, 445
Pryce-Jones, Alan 248, 340
Punch (magazine) 236
Purdy, Ken 28
Pym, Christopher (pseud.) *see* Ray, Cyril

Pyrenees 247

Quain, Sir Richard (Eve's grandfather) 4
'Quantum of Solace' (IF; story) 294, 339–
41
Quebec: Quadrant Conference (1943)
148–9
Queen (magazine) 391
Queen Anne Press 43, 227, 234, 273–4
Queen Elizabeth, RMS 172, 245, 263
Queen Mary, RMS 182
Quennell, (Sir) Peter: on Olivia Campbell
61; on IF's character 87; on IF in war
123; in Ann's wartime circle 150; as
book critic on *Daily Mail* 162; IF praises
164; on Ann's parties 171–2, 343; and
IF's relations with Ann 173; friendship
with IF 192–3; Fionn objects to 193; on
Coward's treatment of IF 211–12; visits
Ann in Kent 234–5, 252; reviews *Casino
Royale* 243; on IF's remoteness 263, 296;
stays in Goldeneye 267, 364, 399; and
Blanche Blackwell 322, 345; hears of
Gaitskells in Austria 341; at Shane's
Castle 344, 413; visits Ann at Le
Touquet 353; published by Viking 359;
suggests name for health establishment
366; starts 'Gloom Book' at
Sevenhampton 425; on IF in later life
437; *Byron in Italy* 382
Quigley, Janet 378
Quill, Colonel Humphrey 156

Raab, Julius 372
Ralli, Sir George 335
Ramsay, Admiral Sir Bertram 156
Random House (US publishers) 255
Rank Organisation 276, 317
Ratoff, Gregory 264, 268, 297, 351
Raven, Simon 243
Ray, Cyril ('Christopher Pym') 203, 243
Ray, Elizabeth 203
Ray, Man 80
Reed, Carol 250, 361
Reiss, Rosie 80
Renshaw, Micky 282–3
Repulse, HMS 133, 398
Resnais, Alain 371
Reuters: IF works with 46–56, 62; IF resigns
from 63; IF proposes transatlantic cable
service to 72–3
Reynaud, Paul 115
Reynolds, Mrs (physiotherapist) 366
Rhinelander, Jeanne 336
Rhodes James, Robert (Sir) 302
Rhys, Jean 71
Rice, Edward 386
Rice-Davis, Mandy 418
Richard, Marthe 277, 391

Richards, Dr Hugh 360
Richardson, Maurice 243, 269, 369
Richardson, Stanley 58
Richardson, Tony 387
Rickatson-Hatt, Bernard 47–9, 52–5, 57, 63, 99
Ridley, Matthew, 3rd Viscount 338
Right of Reply (TV programme) 345
'Risico' (IF; story) 336
Ritz, César 99
Robins, Denise 427
Robinson, Hubell 336–8
Roche Fleuri, Villa, Monte Carlo 178
Rodd, Peter 170
Roddick, Bunny 405
Rodriguez, Messrs Leopoldo 366
Rogers, Millicent Huddleston 164, 167, 172, 182
Romantic Novelists' Association 427
Rome 372–3
Room 39 (Admiralty) 101–2, 104–5, 118, 138, 146
Room 40 (Admiralty) 71
Roosevelt, Eleanor 129
Roosevelt, Franklin D. 75, 120, 129, 137, 148–9
Roper, Barrington 285, 297, 307
Rose, George (Eve's father) 4
Rose, Harcourt (Eve's brother) 4, 68
Rose, Ivor (Eve's brother) 4, 68
Rose, Kathleen (Eve's sister) *see* Dean, Kathleen
Rose, Norman 232
Rose, Sir Philip (IF's maternal grandfather) 4
Rosebery, Albert Edward Archibald Primrose, 6th Earl of 258
Ross, Alan: reviews *Casino Royale* 243; and Connolly's parody Bond story 416; alluded to in *The Man With the Golden Gun* 434; friendship with IF 439–40; *Something of the Sea* 261
Rothermere, Esmond Cecil Harmsworth, 2nd Viscount: Ann's relations with 94, 122, 124, 126, 135, 146, 154; marriage to Ann 158; and control of *Daily Mail* 161–2; friendship with IF 176; Monte Carlo house 178; in USA 181, 186; and Ann's lost child 186–8; Gleneagles golfing holiday with IF 186; and Ann's relations with IF 188, 192, 193, 195; Ann writes on 191; infidelities 193; divorce from Ann and settlement 214, 326; election night parties 214; coolness towards IF's books 233
Rothermere, Harold Sidney Harmsworth, 1st Viscount 7, 94; death 124
Rottingdean, Sussex 50
'Roulette Without Tears' (IF) *see* 'How To

Win at Roulette'
Rowe and Pitman (stockbrokers) 69–75, 90, 96, 147, 258
Royal College of Art 274
Royal Geographical Society 98, 176
Royal St George's golf club 196, 292–3, 374–5, 386, 404–6, 428, 441; depicted in *Goldfinger* 327–8
Rubinstein, Michael 351
Rushbrooke, Rear Admiral Edmund: succeeds Godfrey as DNI 146; in Normandy 153–4; in Colombo 158
Russell, Conrad 89
Russell, Gilbert 60–1, 64, 66, 69
Russell, John 242, 271
Russell, Leonard 201, 289, 356, 372, 374, 394
Russell, Maud (*née* Nelke): IF's relations with 60–1, 64, 66, 89–90, 98, 136, 177–8; anti-Nazi activities 77, 89–90; and Ann 94; in Naval Intelligence Division 119; and IF's wartime mission to Gibraltar 125
Russia *see* USSR
Ruthless, Operation 122–3
Ryan, Cornelius 131
Ryan, Nin 92–3, 172
Ryder, Commander Robert ('Red'), VC 145

Sackville, Lionel Sackville-West, 2nd Baron 40
Sackville, Victoria, Lady (Vita's mother) 40
Sackville-West, Vita (Lady Nicolson) 17, 40
St Aubyn, Cora 303, 306
St George's *see* Royal St George's golf club
St Ives, Cornwall 8
St James's Club, London 51, 54, 66, 123, 228–9, 292
St Margaret's Bay, Kent 192, 195–6, 224, 233–6, 257, 262, 266, 321, 322–3; *see also* Sandwich
St Moritz 379
St Phalle (stockbrokers) 49
Saito, Torao ('Tiger') 357, 411–12, 415
Salcombe, Devon 7–8
Salter, Cedric 169
Saltzman, Harry: makes Bond films 387–9, 398, 432, 446–7; parts from Broccoli 452
Sampson, Anthony 317
Sanders, George 372
Sandhurst: Royal Military College 22–5, 27–8
Sandwich, Kent 386, 404, 441; *see also* Royal St George's golf club
Sanger, Gerald 161–3, 195

Saratoga Springs, New York State 258, 267, 271
Sargent, John Singer 93
Saunders, Joan 257
Scharnhorst (German heavy cruiser) 137
Schiaparelli, Elsa 127
Schiff, Jacob 2
Schlick, Count 35, 439
Schneider, Lieutenant Alan 151
Schwartzman, Jack 452
Scotland: Fleming family holidays in 23–4, 208–9, 441
Scott, Edward 320
Searle, Alan 243, 256
Secret Intelligence Service (SIS) 102, 104, 114–15, 169, 292
Section 17 (Admiralty) *see* Naval Intelligence Division
Seif, Dr Leonard 40
Selection Trust(company) 60
Selznick, David 338
Serocold, Claud 71, 99
Sevenhampton Place (*formerly* Warneford Place), Wiltshire 330, 353, 374–5, 378, 422, 424–5, 428, 437.440–1
Sextant Conference *see* Cairo
Seychelles: treasure 318–19, 334; IF visits 333–4; proposed as setting for Bond film 338; IF's articles on 341–2; tourist development 342
Shand, James 134
Shane's Castle, Co. Antrim 179, 210, 343–4, 361, 413–14
Shaw, Paymaster Captain 107
Shearer, Moira (Mrs Ludovic Kennedy) 228–9
Sheepshanks, Robin 50
Shelley, Commodore Tully 151
Shepbridge, John 264
Shephardson, Colonel Whitney H. 141
Shetland bus (clandestine wartime service to Norway) 119
Short, Sylvia 260
Shriver, Eunice Kennedy 383
Sidey, Hugh 382
Sidgwick & Jackson (publishers) 273
Sierra Leone: diamond trade 311, 313–14
Sierra Leone Selection Trust 311, 316
Signet (US publisher) 383
Sillick, Joan (nanny) 152, 233, 240–1, 262, 307, 425, 441, 443, 450, 451
Sillitoe, Sir Percy 258, 310, 312, 316
Simenon, Georges 391, 422–3
Simplon-Orient Express 273
Sinclair, Sir Archibald 77
Sinclair, Admiral Sir Hugh F.P. ('Quex'; 'C') 98, 102
Sinclair, Sir John ('Sinbad') 213
Singapore: falls to Japanese 137

Sitwell, (Dame) Edith 188–90
Sitwell, Sir Osbert 188
Sitwell, (Sir) Sacheverell 251
Skelton, Barbara: marriage to Connolly 224, 233–5; criticizes IF's Atticus 252
Slater, E.V. (Sam) 14
Slocum, Captain Frank 119
Smith, Arthur 127
Smith, Rear-Admiral Aubrey Hugh 70–1, 99
Smith, Hugh Colin 70
Smith, Vice-Admiral Humphrey Hugh 70
Smith, John Hugh 70
Smith, Lancelot Hugh ('Lancy') 69–73, 90
Smith, Mildred Hugh 70
Smith, Owen Hugh 70
Smith, W.H. and Sons 233
Smith, 'Whispering' Jack 24, 419
Smithers, Peter (Sir): on IF's relations with Godfrey 104; with SIS in France 114–17; on IF's fascination with firearms 119; and IF's plan to capture Enigma machine 122; and IF's secret trip to Spain 125; in USA 125, 130, 136–7, 148; and IF's aborted trip to Moscow 132; and IF's black propaganda broadcasts 133; posted to Mexico 144; IF informs of work at NID 146–7; as model for Bond 223
Snapdragon (Eton ephemeral magazine) 16–18
Snowdon, Antony Armstrong-Jones, 1st Earl of 370
Snowman, Kenneth 422
Sorge, Richard 252, 284, 313, 412
Sotheby's (fine art auction house) 421–2, 434
Souls, the (group) 61, 93
South Wraxhall Manor, Wiltshire 178, 192
Southend: rumoured German attack on 113–14
Spain: wartime position 109–10, 117–18, 125, 131, 138, 145
Spain, Nancy 360, 370
Spark, Muriel 391
Sparrow, John 345–4, 449
Special Engineering Unit 145
Special Operations Executive (SOE) 102, 118, 132, 138
Spectator (journal): Peter writes as 'Strix' in 252; IF writes in 268, 354
SPECTRE (fictional organization) 350, 354, 365
Spender, Natasha, Lady (Natasha Litvin) 270
Spender, (Sir) Stephen 211, 248, 270, 399, 437
Spock, Benjamin: *Baby and Child Care* 240
Spy Who Loved Me, The (IF): accounts of

Windsor area in 17, 26; on Green Mountains (USA) 209; plot and themes 381–2, 385; writing 385, 390, 400; jacket illustration 390–1; reception 400–2, 404; IF restricts printings 402, 446; sales 420

Stafford, David 149

Stainsby, Charles 400–1

Stalin, Josef V.: and Metro-Vick trials 56–7, 59; at Teheran Conference 149

Stamp, Terence 447

Stanley, Ed (Lord Stanley of Alderley) 101, 158, 164

Stanley, Lady Maureen 96, 105, 124, 178

Stanley, Oliver 77, 96, 105, 124

Stanley, Venetia (later Montagu) 194, 373

Stanway, Gloucestershire 60–1, 93–4

Stark, Freya 261

State of Excitement (IF; unpublished) 377–8, 385

Stein, Jules 367–8

Stephens, John 27

Stephenson, (Sir) William S. ('Little Bill'): liaison with US intelligence 120, 124, 127–9, 137, 143; settles in Jamaica 166–7, 194; and Dansey 169; and Loelia Westminster 183; IF maintains relations with 213; and IF in New York 237; and Saratoga Springs 258; and Luciano 332; IF sends Spectator article to 354; IF writes introduction to biography of 410

Stewart, Jo 298, 335–8, 351

Stoltenberg, Gisela 45

Storm (bubble dancer) 61–2

Strachey, Lytton 76

Straight, Lady Daphne (née Finch-Hatton) 67–8, 230, 379, 398

Straight, Michael 230

Straight, Whitney 230, 379, 398

Strangman, Laurence 82

Strauss, Dr E.B. 254

Strauss, Michel 421

Stresemann, Gustav 20

Stuart, Sir Campbell 71

Stuart, Colonel Robin 382

Stuart, Vivienne 382

Suez war (1956) 302

Suffolk, Charles Henry George Howard, 20th Earl of 119

Suffolk, Marguerite Hyde, Countess of (née Leiter; 'Daisy') 119

Sulzberger, Arthur Hays 129

Summer Fields (school) 374

Sunday Chronicle 227

Sunday Graphic 201

Sunday Times: Kemsley acquires and runs 160–1, 273; IF works at 168–71, 202–3, 241, 245–6, 321; Denis Hamilton with 200, 346, 394, 421, 427; appoints

Moscow correspondent 203; and IF's treasure hunt 247; magazine section 256–7; serializes Maugham book 256; IF's pessimism over 273, 283, 385–6; prints Hughes's interview with Burgess and Maclean 283; proposes adventure articles from IF 318; Thomson buys 346; IF's travel articles for 354–6, 374; IF leaves 360–1; IF's free-lance articles in 370; series on Seven Deadly Sins 393–4; colour magazine 394, 396; IF suggests features to 421; see also Atticus

Sutherland, Graham 391, 396

Sutherland, Kathleen 392

Sutton Courtenay, Berkshire 141

Swanson, H.N. ('Swanee') 233, 265, 275

Sweeny, Charles 65, 67

Switzerland: IF holidays in 24–5

Symons, Arthur 30

Symons, Julian 243

Sysonby, Victoria Lily, Lady 241

Tangier 118, 131, 170, 310–13

Tauber, Richard 98, 124

Teheran Conference (1943) 149–50

Temple, Shirley 74

Tennant, Christopher see Glenconner, 2nd Baron

Tennerhof, Villa see Kitzbühel

Terry, Antony 169, 171, 203, 254, 354, 371, 390, 395

Terry, Rachel (née Stainer) 169, 203, 291, 371

'The Man Who Never Was' (wartime deception) 147

Thirkell, Angela 93

30 Assault Unit 152–4, 156–7, 409

36 Club 168–9

Thody, Henry 366

Thomson, George Malcolm 255, 289

Thomson, Peter 315, 328

Thomson, Roy (1st Baron Thomson of Fleet) 346, 370, 385, 394

Thornton, Leslie 56

Thornton-Smith, Walter 360

Thorp, John 319, 342

Thrilling Cities (IF): on Forbes Dennis 34; on Geneva 44, 423; on gambling 248; IF travels for 354, 370–5

Thunderball (IF): submarine base in 145; health establishment in 290, 365–6; plot 350, 367; dispute over film script 354–5, 364–8, 383–4, 387, 426, 431–3, 451–2; names in 366; jacket illustration 369; sales 419; film 446, 452

Tiarks, Henry 41

Tiarks, Pamela (née Silvertop) 89, 119, 136, 153, 158

Tiarks, Peter 89

Times Literary Supplement: reviews *Casino Royale* 243–4; IF quotes 394
Times, The: IF reports on Moscow Trade Mission for 96–7; reviews IF's novels 255, 269, 313, 331; IF seeks to use masthead for Bond obituary 420; IF's obituary in 443
Tito, Josip Broz 112
Today (magazine) 400
Todd, Mike 348–9
Todd, William 169
Tokyo 357, 412
Tonight (TV programme) 400
Torch, Operation *see* North Africa: 1942 landings
Toynbee, Rachel 451
Transition (magazine) 43
'Treasure Hunt in Eden' (IF; articles) 341–2
Trefusis, Violet 40
Trevor, Colonel William 22, 27
Trident Conference (1943) *see* Washington, DC
Trog *see* Fawkes, Wally
Troughton, (Sir) Charles ('Dick') 347
Trueblood, Una 335
Tunney, Gene 128
Turing, Alan 122
Turnbull, Reginald 19, 405
Turner, J.W.M. 19
Twentieth Century (magazine) 330
Twentieth Century-Fox (film corporation) 358

U-2 incident 398
U-boats: wartime activities 121, 137–8, 142; and British propaganda 133–4
Ultra intelligence 114, 160
Ungoed-Thomas, Sir Lynn (Mr Justice) 431
United Artists (film corporation) 387, 452
United Fruit Company 279
United States of America: intelligence cooperation with Britain 120, 124–6, 127–30, 142–4; neutrality 120; enters war 133; IF's attitude to 163–4, 262–3, 282, 359; publication of IF's books in 245–6, 249, 255–6, 268, 275, 297, 301, 338, 359, 383, 421, 430; anti-Communism in 246, 251; IF's train and air tour in 262–6
USSR (Soviet Russia): Metro-Vick trials in 55–8; British 1939 Trade Mission to 96–7; British arctic convoys to 143; *see also* Moscow

Van der Post, Laurence: *Heart of the Hunter* 438
Vansittart, Sir Robert 77, 90
Venice 38–9, 335–6, 406
Venlo, Holland 102
Vermont *see* Black Hole Hollow Farm

Vernay, Arthur 287
Vesuvius, Mount 88
Victoria Square, London 236, 240–1, 248–9, 261, 321
Vienna 290–1, 371–2
Viking (US publishers) 359, 383
Villiers, Amherst: portrait of IF 403–4
Villiers, Nita 404
Vivian Smith, Lady Helen 69–70
Vivian Smith, Hugh (*later* 2nd Baron Bicester) 69–70, 142–3, 258, 405
Votier, Baron Beycha 45

Wacker, Charles III 349, 431, 434
Wagg, Albert 69
Wagg, Kenneth 67
Waley, Arthur 90, 416
Walston, Catherine 240, 380
Walton, Bill 317
Wanger, Walter 358
Warburg family 2
Ward, Edward 22
Ward, George 22
Warneford Place, Wiltshire *see* Sevenhampton Place
Warner Brothers (film company) 265, 268
Warwick House, Green Park, London 171, 175–6, 214
Warwick Pictures (company) 387
Wasbrough, Henry 444
Washington, DC: British Joint Staff Mission to 137; 1943 Trident Conference 148–9
Waterfield, Gordon 170
Waterfield, Lina 170
Watson, Arthur 53
Waugh, Auberon 164
Waugh, Evelyn: seeks post in Naval Intelligence 106; and Nancy Mitford 170; seeks title for autobiography 205; accepts Ann's marriage to IF 224; visits Ann in Kent 234, 272; *The Holy Places* 228, 234; religious conversations 235, 238; on IF's writing 256; encounter with Quennell in Jamaica 267; on writing love scenes 268; Ann writes to 269, 323, 402, 407, 424, 425, 446, 448; frightens Caspar 272; Ann invites to write for Queen Anne Press 274; and Ann's breach with Coward 304; and Hugo Charteris's quarrel with IF 315; and Eve Fleming in Winchester court case 320; and Ann's marriage relations 337, 341, 375; and IF remaining on *Sunday Times* 346; and IF's tips on shaving 370; suggestions for IF's convalescence 385; Ann recounts miniature railway ride to 387; and IF's heart attack 392; and Ann's spending 424; visits Sevenhampton

424; IF gives chair to 425; writes IF's speech to Romantic Novelists's Association 427; sends lavatory paper to IF 439
Waugh, Laura 424
Waugh, Margaret 392
Wavell, General Archibald (*later* Field Marshal Earl) 134
Wedlake Saint (solicitors) 277
Welby, Guy 290, 391
Wells, Linton 58
Wemyss, Hugo Charteris, 11th Earl of (*earlier* Viscount Elcho; Ann's grandfather) 93
Wemyss, Mary, Countess of (*née* Wyndham; *earlier* Viscountess Elcho) 93
Wertheimer, Milt 265–6
West, Dame Rebecca 360
Westminster, Hugh Richard Arthur Grosvenor, 2nd Duke of ('Bendor') 135, 186
Westminster, Loelia, Duchess of: friendship with Ann 124, 135, 163, 176, 368; marriage breakdown 135; at Send House 150, 163; returns from USA 167; accompanies Ann to Goldeneye 179–82; and Ann's entertaining after losing child 187; visits Ann in Kent 235; alluded to in *Moonraker* 254
Weybright, Victor 383, 418
Wheatley, Dennis 134
Wheeler, Charles 153
Whicker, Alan 436
Whigham, Charles 65
Whigham, George 60, 65
Whigham, Gilbert 65
Whigham, Walter 6, 65–6
Whistler, Rex 89
White Cliffs, St Margaret's Bay, Kent 192, 195
White, Sir Dick 292
White's club, London 106, 176
Whiting, Albert 327
Whitney, Bill 137
Whittingham, Jack 356, 359–60, 365–6, 384, 432, 433
Wilberforce, Richard (Mr Justice; *later* Baron) 384
Wilder, Patricia *see* Hohenlohe, Princess Patricia
Wilkins, Reginald 318, 335
Williams, Lucy (*née* Fleming; Peter's daughter) 451, 452
Williams, Mona Harrison 88
Williams-Ellis, (Sir) Clough 79
Wilson, (Sir) Angus (novelist) 242, 343
Wilson, Angus (orchid enthusiast) 239
Wilson, Edmund 416

Wilson, Group Captain H.J. 122
Wilson, Peter 422
Winchell, Walter 143, 246
Winchester, Bapsy, Marchioness of (*formerly* Pavry) 319–20
Winchester, Henry William Montagu Paulet, 16th Marquess of: Eve's relations with 210, 319–20; death 417
Winchilsea, Guy Finch-Hatton, 14th Earl, and Margaretta, Countess of 67
Windsor, Edward, Duke, and Wallis, Duchess of 181, 294
Winn, Rodger 119
Winn, Sepand Anthony 101
Winnick, Maurice 351
Winterbotham, Squadron Leader Frederick 107
Wiseman, Sir William 129
Wohl, Louis de 134
Wolff, Emma 291
Wolfson, Captain Vladimir 147, 212
Woodfall Films 387
Woodward, Ann 259–60, 272
Woodward, William, Jr 259–60, 272
Worthington, Greville 76
Wraxhall Manor *see* South Wraxhall Manor
Wray, J. and Nephew (company) 279
Wright, Fitzherbert 84
Wright, Henry 83
Wright, Muriel: relations with IF 82–5, 95, 136, 141; as Air Raid Warden 105; as wartime despatch rider 119, 136; killed 151–2
Wright (Rothermeres' butler) 172
Writers' and Speakers' Research 257
Wyfold, Dorothy (*née* Fleming; IF's aunt) 3, 64, 95
Wyndham, Dick 170–1, 179
Wyndham, Joan 170
Wynne-Morgan, David 303
Wyvern, The (Eton ephemeral magazine) 17–19, 22

Xanadu Productions (film company) 348–9, 351, 352, 359, 368

York, Sarah, Duchess of (*née* Ferguson) 83
You Asked For It see Casino Royale
You Only Live Twice (IF): on death of Bond's parents 44–6; writing 416, 420–1; jacket illustration 426; Bond's fate in 434; reception 437
Young, Gavin 312
Young, Terence 387, 399, 409, 447
Yugoslavia 112

Z Organization 90, 169
Zographos, Nicholas 67